Politics and Economics of External Debt Crisis

The Latin American Experience

edited by Miguel S. Wionczek

in collaboration with
Luciano Tomassini

Westview Press / Boulder and London

Westview Special Studies on Latin America and the Caribbean

Copyright © 1985 by Westview Press, Inc.

Published in 1985 in the United States of America by Westview Press, Inc.,
5500 Central Avenue, Boulder, Colorado 80301; Frederick A. Praeger,
Publisher

Library of Congress Cataloging in Publication Data
Politics and economics of external debt crisis.
    (Westview special studies on Latin America and the Caribbean)
    Includes index.
    1. Debts, External--Latin America--Addresses, essays,
lectures. 2. Latin America--Economic policy--Addresses,
essays, lectures. I. Wionczek, Miguel S. II. Series.
HJ8514.5.P65 1985   336.3'435'098   84-15377
ISBN 0-86531-797-6

46,104

Printed and bound in the United States of America
Composition for this book was provided by the editor

10 9 8 7 6 5 4 3 2 1

Contents

iii

iv

Tables and Figures

Figures

viii

Preface

The immediate origin of this volume can be traced
to a small informal meeting of a group of Latin
American economists and political scientists held in
Mexico City in late August 1983 under the auspices of
the Tepoztlan Club. After having discussed the most
recent information on crisis and debt in Latin America
and the external debt management experiences in Argentina,
Brazil, Chile, Mexico, Venezuela, and Central America,
the participants came to the following conclusions:

1. Although the current international economic
crisis presents many of the characteristics of a
particularly severe and prolonged recessive phase of the
economic cycle, it also contains structural factors
that distinguish it from the crisis of the 1930s.
2. The current crisis has spread to all parts of
the world, including socialist economies, via multiple
and complex channels, due to the evolution of an interdependent world with a highly integrated economy.
3. The causes of the acute external and internal
economic imbalances in Latin America go back to the
1960s. The actual depressive and almost desperate
economic situation in the 1980s, however, reflects a
new crisis within a crisis due in part to external
factors and in part to the inadequacies or extravagance
of most Latin American domestic economic policies. When
one looks at the policies followed in the past ten
years by individual countries, particularly in fiscal,
monetary, and trade matters, one has to recognize the
lack of coherence, forethought, and realism that predominated in successive stages of policy implementation
in the region.
4. Recently and with prodding and the blessing
of international financial organizations, many Latin
American countries, facing external and domestic crises
of a magnitude never registered before, took the road
of adjustment of the external sector by means of
recessive policy, which compromises long-term productive

capacity and growth potential and puts to the test the
political and social tolerance of the highly indebted
countries. Little, if anything, has been done in the
framework of the extremely negative international
developments to set in motion selective changes in
development, investment, consumption, and importing
patterns that would permit the achievement in the medium
term of some sort of balance in the external sector
without compromising the economy's growth potential.

5. The probability of Latin American countries
overcoming the present economic crisis will depend on
their capacity to undergo a process of internal
structural adjustment and on the reactivation of the
world economy. The current world scene is characterized
by uncertainty as regards the possible evolution of the
world economy and perplexity as to how the crisis must
be faced in the industrial countries themselves.

6. Despite the overall gloomy circumstances of
the world and the Latin American economic scene, a
number of emergency measures could be taken to alleviate
the crisis and, in particular, the financial difficulties of the region born from its unusually high external
indebtedness. All these measures might bring some
positive results providing the political will were present
in industrial countries, international official financial
and development agencies, and the international financial
system. Presently, little evidence of such political
will is available.

7. Such emergency measures were identified as the
reprogramming of debt payments and, as far as possible,
the refinancing of the accumulated interests on the
debt; the strengthening and improvement of the role of
international financial organizations; the undertaking
of additional action designed to increase the credit
available from all possible sources--public and
private--in order to lighten the burden of indebted
Latin American countries; and an increase in the overall
international liquidity.

8. Such emergency measures should be complemented
by others of medium- and long-term nature, including
the design of a more stable medium-term financing; the
increase in the participation of international financial
organizations in external development-oriented financing;
the issuing of bonds and similar documents, negotiable
in secondary capital markets, by a number of industrial
countries; and the creation, within the International
Monetary Fund (IMF), of special terms with the aim of
financing that part of the balance-of-payments deficits
of the debtor countries attributable to the increase in
interest rates over and above traditional levels.

9. Additional measures that are strongly advisable
are the reversion of protectionist tendencies in the
industrial countries, the selective increment of direct
foreign investments in Latin America, and the

strengthening of regional and subregional economic integration schemes in Latin America, which go through the disintegration stage because of both extraregional and intraregional difficulties.

The substantive discussions of the Mexico City meeting, whose major analytical points and proposals for remedial actions appear above, also made it clear to all its participants that whereas the subject of Latin American crisis and indebtedness is presently very fashionable in the industrial countries, most of the growing literature on these matters originates in them and reflects their concern. Very often the question is phrased in the form of the possible costs to industrial countries, and especially to the international banking community, of the present Latin American misfortunes. Moreover, many otherwise competent experts from the northern latitudes look exclusively at the economic and financial aspects of the crisis, raising only marginally the key issue of how long Latin American societies can live with the austerity resulting from the painful external IMF-tailored adjustment programs. Very little if anything is written by these industrial countries' experts about both the political and social consequences of all these merciless exercises for the Latin American region itself. Moreover, the Latin American writings on the subject are hardly accessible to those on both sides of the North Atlantic because of the language barrier, among others.

Thus, the purpose of this book is to diminish to some degree this dangerous asymmetry of views available in the North that distorts greatly the real picture in which the major factors are not only the international banking community's interests and international financial agencies' viewpoints but Latin American interests and viewpoints as well. After all, the recycling of privately held funds of the order of some US$250 billion lent to Latin America in the 1970s was not a charity or rescue exercise but a big business operation that resulted in very sizable profits for lenders--whether of discriminate or indiscriminate type--year after year. What kinds of benefits and profits ensued from all this, not to direct official and private Latin American borrowers but to Latin American societies, still remains to be established. Since the literature on these aspects of Latin American crisis and indebtedness is, to say the least, very scant in the lender countries and even within independent academic circles, the asymmetry of views is much greater than it would appear.

All but three contributors to this volume are Latin Americans. Moreover, not only are practically all these Latin American writers technically competent observers of the regional economic and financial scene, but many

have participated either directly or indirectly in the
most recent attempts to renegotiate the crushing burden
of external debt at national level. I have also been
exposed for some time to all these issues as suggested
by two books, LDC External Debt and the World Economy
and International Indebtedness and World Economic
Stagnation, published in English under my editorship
in Mexico City and Oxford in 1978 and 1979, respectively.
They appeared at the time when the Latin American crisis
and debt were still considered by both the lenders and
the borrowers as a minor and passing issue. What might
seem almost amusing, but is in fact tragic, is that
the contents of these volumes--which stressed that
the structure of the LDC external debt was not sound
(in the late 1970s), nor was the volume of borrowing
in international private financial markets and the
conditions attached to it sustainable for the borrowers
in longer terms--were dismissed by some distinguished
reviewers in prestigious economic and financial
journals of the industrial countries as the expressions
of the "undue pessimism of a group of like-minded
people."

The first part of this book presents eight
chapters on the Latin American crisis and indebtedness
within the framework of the worldwide economic crisis
from which the long-heralded recovery is still not yet
in sight. Most of these contributions concentrate not
only on economic and financial issues but on political
and social aspects as well. All contain a number of
prescriptions as to what could or might be done to free
both the world economy and Latin America from the
present complex predicament comparable only, albeit
partially, with the Great Depression of the 1930s.
It is particularly satisfying to me that Part 1 starts
with a contribution by Dragoslav Avramović. During his
long intellectual and professional career that took
him subsequently through the World Bank, the Secretariat
of the Brandt Commission, and the UN Conference on
Trade and Development (UNCTAD), he dedicated most of
his time and attention to the international indebtedness
problems, as witnessed by his two seminal studies Debt
Servicing Capacity and Postwar Growth in International
Indebtedness (1958) and Economic Growth and External
Debt (1964).

Part 2 contains seven case studies of the process
of external debt accumulation and the rarely successful
attempts at renegotiation in 1982 and 1983. The
chapters in this part deal respectively with Argentina,
Brazil, Mexico, Venezuela, Chile, Peru, and Central
America (discussed as a subregion). As readers will
find out for themselves, the authors do not necessarily
form a "like-minded group" from either the theoretical
or the ideological viewpoint. Some of them are more
neoclassical and some more structuralist. But, since

all are knowledgeable, intellectually independent, and clear minded in their respective analytical approaches and, in addition, know their "stories" from first-hand experience, some sort of composite picture emerges from their findings that is not necessarily complimentary of each of the major actors in the "indebtedness game."

The fact that most authors of the seven case studies dedicate considerable attention to domestic political aspects of the indebtedness and its re-negotiations adds additional dimension to this second part of the book. One learns from it that, contrary to the established wisdom, neither the international financial agencies, the international banking community, government officials of the borrowing countries, nor even the private borrowers are dispassionate angels. All have their ideologies, political and economic objectives, and bureaucratic interests, among others, which more often than not are in conflict with those of the other actors, independent of whether the actual transactions are of a multilateral or bilateral nature. Under these conditions, crisis gestation, indebtedness accumulation, and external adjustment processes cannot be reduced to models, equations, targets, and statistical series manipulations. The international financial relations have always been, are now, and shall be exercises in power and politics. This is perhaps the most important message of this book.

This volume could not have been produced without the most efficient cooperation of a group of contributors dispersed in the triangular area limited by such distant points as Santiago, Chile; San Francisco, California; and Geneva, Switzerland. The manuscript was prepared within a record time of four months thanks to the generous logistic facilities of El Colegio de México in Mexico City with the no less generous help of the Program for Joint Studies on Latin American International Relations (RIAL) at Santiago. Both institutions deserve sincere thanks for their most sympathetic and helpful attitude toward the project.

Miguel S. Wionczek
Mexico City

Introduction

Miguel S. Wionczek
Luciano Tomassini

A majority of experts agree that the world economy
is passing through its worst crisis since the depression
of the 1930s. Less consensus exists, however, about the
nature and causes of the crisis and therefore about
whether at a global level a sustained economic recovery
is now underway. The fact that the recession in the
industrialized countries has been superimposed upon profound structural transformations makes the situation all
the more complex and provokes a general climate of
intellectual confusion.

This confusion is even greater in the case of Latin
America. In effect, the international crisis has struck
the region with singular force because of the high
decree of integration that Latin America has achieved
with the world economy and because the development
strategies pursued by many countries in recent years
were highly dependent on foreign borrowing. Among the
principal manifestations of the crisis in the region, the
one that stands out is the explosive growth of the Latin
American external debt service and the high social cost
of the adjustment that Latin American countries have been
making in order to pay their external obligations under
conditions of domestic and external crisis. Although
under present circumstances it would be unrealistic to
expect the countries "to adjust without pain," it is no
less certain that the costs of adjustment should be
better distributed among all the parties concerned--
debtor nations, lending banks, industrialized countries,
and international financial organizations--if sacrifices
that could exceed the limits of political tolerance in
Latin American societies are to be avoided.

It is because of all this that both debt and adjustment not only constitute two very closely linked themes
but also have economic and political content. One of the
factors that has complicated the understanding and the
management of the crisis has been the reserve with which
the majority of Latin American countries have treated
these links between the politics and the economics of the

1

external indebtedness. The debt problem used to be considered as the almost exclusive responsibility of the monetary authorities and private banks of the debtor countries, on the one hand, and the foreign creditor banks and the IMF, on the other.

Observing the long-lasting lack of acknowledgment of the close links between the economic and the political nature of the debt problem, reflected in the extremely limited scope of the groups that have to date managed the crisis, one comes to the conclusion that little progress on the external debt will be achieved in the region as long as the entire issue is not put in the broad political context. Since the worsening of the crisis in late 1982 the first important step in this direction was made at the Quito economic conference held in January 1984, the conference called in response to an initiative of the president of Ecuador, Osvaldo Hurtado. At the Quito conference for the first time formal consideration was given to the debt problem at the political level. The regional consensus reached there was that the external debt service policies, as well as the modes and intensity of adjustment, must keep in mind proposals formulated by the Latin American countries themselves, because the whole exercise would fail in the longer run if the need to assure economic growth and acceptable living conditions for the Latin American societies of the region were for-gotten during the adjustment process. Specifically, the Quito conference proposed that debt service not exceed a reasonable proportion of the debtor countries' export earnings.

This small progress toward more equitable treatment of the Latin American debt servicing and the adjustment process was in part the consequence of a wide and diverse discussion of the whole indebtedness problem that took place in Latin America in 1982 and 1983, lifting the curtain of secrecy that had surrounded that issue traditionally. The UN Economic Commission for Latin America (ECLA) and the Latin American Economic System (SELA) contributed to this debate but so too did a number of academic independent research organizations qualified to promote a frank debate on the subject. In effect, these academic institutions paved the way to a more open dialogue among governmental and nongovernmental sectors affected by the indebtedness crisis.

In this regard, two institutions joined forces to organize the conference of which this book is an indirect result. The Program for Joint Studies on Latin American International Relations (RIAL) with headquarters in Santiago, Chile, an association of Latin American social research centers, promoted during 1983 a series of meet-ings in various parts of the region about the external debt problems of Latin America. The other organization was the Tepoztlan Centre, a small Mexican think tank dedicated to reflection and debate about fundamental

questions concerning contemporary developing societies in
Latin America and elsewhere. Joint efforts of these
two institutions translated themselves into a conference
that took place in the Tepoztlan Centre, Morelos, Mexico,
in July 1983. This book represents in a way a follow-up
of that gathering. The authors of several of the
chapters included in this volume participated in the
above-mentioned encounter, the major conclusions of which
are reported in the Preface.

Part 1

Global and Regional Issues

1
External Debt of Developing Countries in Late 1983

Dragoslav Avramovič

In the fall of 1983, forty to fifty developing countries engaged in debt-rescheduling negotiations. These countries included twelve of the twenty largest debtors, accounting for more than half of the total debt of developing countries. No immediate prospects for relief were in sight. Interest rates in real terms were almost as high as at the peak of the international credit crunch of mid-1982, which was the immediate cause of the debt crisis, and no improvement had taken place in the average maturity of the debt. Export commodity prices of developing countries had improved from the low point of November 1982, but new pressures on sensitive commodity markets had appeared since the summer of 1983. Capital market lending to developing countries had not recovered from the near collapse of August 1982. The debt-rescheduling and emergency-financing operations arranged at great effort during late 1982 and early 1983 would be running out in most cases during 1984, and new arrangements had to be made, frequently under more difficult circumstances than the first round. Deflationary pressures on the major developing debtor countries had already taken their toll in reduced real incomes and increased unemployment. Social and political tensions were on the increase in large parts of the developing world as 1983 drew to a close.

In an earlier study of the debt problem of developing countries I argued that over the long run the risk of debt failure was small, provided the present crisis was successfully handled.[1] Most of the heavily indebted countries have proved that they can absorb modern technology, organize efficient production, penetrate the international market at extraordinary speed, and give priority to meeting their external financial obligations under most circumstances. This argument still stands. I also emphasized that over the short and medium term the risk of transfer difficulties and interruptions in payments was acute in many cases because of the adverse movements in the terms of trade, a large overhang of

6

short-term debt, excessive interest rates on the part of
the debt, uncertainties concerning future capital market
lending, insufficient access to product markets, and
lapses in domestic financial policies. This risk has now
materialized. I also stated that the extent and duration
of the transfer problem would depend in part on the
willingness of the international community to cope with
the present liquidity crisis and in part on the willingness of debtor countries to improve on their performance
in several critical areas, and it was concluded that a
failure to resolve the short-term problem quickly and
decisively might affect adversely the long-run future.

The need for a comprehensive program has now become
even more urgent. Failure to adopt it will lead to a
further sharpening of the internal difficulties in some
major debtor countries because of the pressure of debt-
service payments on an already weakened structure; it
will prolong the present chaos in external financial
flows of many developing countries and raise further the
uncertainties concerning stability of major parts of the
international financial system; and it could harm the
future capacity to pay of a number of developing countries, as a continuing low level of investment would
adversely affect their competitive capacity in the
international market.

AMOUNTS AND PROPORTIONS

The aggregate external disbursed public and private
debt of all maturities owed by developing countries was
of the order of US$750-800 billion at the end of 1982.
The long- and medium-term portion was estimated at about
US$600 billion.[2] The short-term debt, of a maturity
under one year, was estimated at US$150-160 billion.[3]
This latter amount may well be an understatement: In
most recent liquidity crises the actual amounts of short-
term debts turned out to be higher than the estimates.

About 70 percent of the aggregate debt and an even
higher proportion of debt service are accounted for by
twenty countries. The individual country figures are
set forth in Table 1.1.

The largest debtors in absolute amounts--Brazil,
Mexico, Argentina, South Korea, and Venezuela, together
accounting for US$290 billion or almost two-fifths of
developing-country total debt--do not invariably carry
the largest debt per capita or as a proportion of gross
national product (GNP). Debt per capita is highest in
Israel (US$5,437), followed at a considerable distance by
Venezuela (US$2,139), Chile (US$1,594), and Portugal
(US$1,424). Argentina, Mexico, and South Korea are
farther down. Brazil is in the middle of the list
(US$771), and Indonesia, Pakistan, and India are at the
end, with the latter at US$29 per capita. As a proportion

Table 1.1 Largest Debtor Countries (debt in billions of U.S.
           dollars)

| | Aggregate Disbursed Debt (long-, medium-, and short-term) | | Long- and Medium-Term Debt | |
| | | | Disbursed Debt End | Debt Service Paid in |
	Mid-1983	End 1981	1981	1982
Brazil	93.0	70.0	65.6	18.5
Mexico	85.0	72.0	54.4	15.2
Argentina	40.0	35.7	20.0	4.9
South Korea	39.0	32.8	20.8	4.8
Venezuela	33.0	18.9	14.9	7.8
Israel	21.5	18.0	--	--
India	20.0	--	19.4	1.7
Indonesia	20.0	--	18.2	3.4
Philippines	20.0	15.8	9.5	2.1
Yugoslavia	20.0	20.0	16.8	4.7
Algeria	18.0	17.8	17.0	4.8
Chile	18.0	15.0	12.3	3.3
Turkey	16.2	15.5	14.1	1.9
Egypt	16.0	15.0	14.0	2.4
Portugal	14.0	10.0	--	--
Nigeria	13.0	--	6.0	1.9
Peru	11.6	9.7	7.3	1.9
Morocco	11.0	--	8.0	1.9
Colombia	10.0	--	6.0	1.1
Pakistan	9.0	8.8	8.8	--

Source: Organization for Economic Cooperation and Development,
External Debt of Developing Countries: General Survey 1982 (Paris,
December 1982); press reports.

of GNP, debt is again largest in Israel (105.0 percent),
followed by Chile (62.3 percent) and Morocco (61.2 percent). South Korea, Peru, Egypt, and Portugal follow.
The median value is slightly above 50 percent, with
Mexico marginally above (53.1) and Brazil (34.7),
Yugoslavia (31.8), and particularly India (11.3)
substantially down. Tables 1.2 and 1.3 in the chapter
appendix provide details. Changes from the earlier
study are marginal.[4]
    The newly industrializing countries carry most of
the debt, but they are not the only debtors. The low-
income countries (under US$600 capita) owe US$110 billion
or 18 percent of the total developing-country medium- and
long-term debt (at the end of 1982). The proportion of
their exports absorbed by service on this debt (debt-
service ratio) amounted to 23 percent in 1982, barely
lower than for the newly industrializing countries and
higher than the 19 percent average for the developing
countries, including the Organization of Petroleum
Exporting Countries (OPEC), as a group (see Table 1.4 in
chapter appendix). In addition, it is in the low-income

countries where most of the payments arrears are encountered: Twenty of the thirty-three countries specifically identified as having arrears at the end of 1982 were at or below US$600 per capita income.[5]

The rise in debt and debt service reflected in part the great inflation of the last decade. It was accompanied by a sharp increase in the nominal and real value of output and exports in most cases. Debt and debt service rose even faster, however. As a result, the debt-service ratio rose by some 50 percent between the early 1970s and the early 1980s (Tables 1.4 and 1.5 in the chapter appendix). Its average level in 1981-82 of 20-25 percent on medium- and long-term debt was not out of line with the ratios recorded for Canada, Australia, Argentina, and the Union of South Africa--the traditional successful borrowers--in the early 1900s and the 1920s.[6] The ratios were much higher, however, when the repayments of short-term debt are included: In five cases, aggregate debt service exceeded the total value of debtor-country exports in 1982.[7] The continuing rollover of short-term debt and long-term capital inflow without interruption are crucial for the maintenance of debt service in such a situation: The breakdown in these and the collapse of world trade led to massive defaults in the 1930s, at an even lower level of debt-service ratios than at present (Table 1.6 in chapter appendix).[8]

DEBT-SERVICING TERMS

It is not the absolute amounts of the debt, but the unfavorable terms of servicing for maturity and interest that now pose the most formidable problems in most cases. First, periods of repayment are too short. At the amortization (repayment) rate of 1982, the aggregate medium- and long-term debt of developing countries would be retired in seven and a half years.[9] This is shorter than the life of most development projects. During the last few years, according to competent observers, there occurred a remarkable shortening of debt maturities in a number of countries, resulting apparently from the replacement of maturing medium-term bank credit by shorter-term loans.[10] Furthermore, short-term credit was withdrawn in a number of cases. Prior to 1981, short-term debt was almost automatically rolled over, as it financed mostly current trade. In the debt crisis of 1981-82 this practice stopped, and a number of developing countries experienced a sudden need to repay massive amounts out of dwindling or nonexistent exchange reserves. Particularly affected were interbank credit lines, but ordinary trade credits were not spared.[11] What was happening in recent years may be called debt reorganization in reverse: Longer-term debts were partly converted into short-term, and some of the short-term debts were cashed in.

Second, real interest rates are at a level that an average debtor will find hard to sustain. More than US$300 billion of the debt of developing countries is now owed to banks.[12] Most of it is contracted at floating interest rates and is denominated in U.S. dollars. These rates, consisting of the base rate (mostly London Inter-Bank Offer Rate--LIBOR--and sometimes U.S. prime) and the margin to reflect "country risk," were running at 12 percent on the average in October 1983. The U.S. prices are now increasing at 3-4 percent per year, giving a real rate of interest of 8-9 percent. The real rate facing the developing-country borrowers is even higher, as their export commodity prices have stopped increasing on the average and their prices of export manufactures are probably falling. For these countries the nominal interest rate of 12 percent can be considered at least equal to the real rate.[13] At this rate the debt burden will be rising with almost mathematical certainty for most debtor countries. They will be compelled to borrow at 12 percent interest just to pay interest; and debt will increase faster than real output, resulting in a rising proportion of national income being absorbed by debt service abroad. The hopes of late 1982 and early 1983 that interest rates would fall toward their long-run real level of 2 percent did not materialize.

In 1982, service on aggregate medium- and long-term debt of developing countries (amortization and interest) amounted to US$125 billion or 21 percent of this class of debt principal (US$600 billion). Service on short-term debt is not known, but it must have been substantial. For 1983, service on all debt of the twelve largest debtors was estimated at the staggering sum of US$190 billion, or 44 percent of their aggregate debt principal.[14] Seven of these twelve debtors, including four of the top five, requested postponement of payments on a part of the debt or emergency financing.

PRODUCTIVITY OF LOANS

A view has been expressed by the GATT (General Agreement on Tariffs and Trade) Secretariat that current debt-servicing difficulties reflect unproductive use of funds rather than unfavorable external events and diffi-cult debt-servicing terms: "A difficulty for the financial system is posed by the fact that a significant, though not precisely determinable, proportion of the additional indebtedness incurred in the 1970s represents what is best called 'deadweight debt'--that is debt to which there correspond no additional production facili-ties from which to service it."[15]

The World Bank has disagreed with this diagnosis and argued that on the whole the developing countries used

borrowed funds productively.[16] Essentially the same
argument has been made by the Bank of England.[17] William
Cline of the Washington-based Institute for International
Economics in a recent study found that "it would be in-
accurate to conclude that the bulk of the debt contracted
has failed to go into productive investments; the
evidence tends to indicate that most borrowing was
productively used."[18]

In the earlier study I argued that the economic
results achieved by the newly industrializing countries--
the major debtors--have in most cases met the long-run
debt-servicing-capacity requirements. The latter have
been defined as a continuing growth in per capita production and the underlying process of rapid accumulation
of productive capital, so that the incidence of debt
service falls on a part of the increment in per capita
income and allows the domestic consumption and investment
to rise pari passu with the growth of debt service.
Specifically, I argued that over the preceding two
decades:

1. The rates of growth of gross product, in the
   aggregate and per capita, had been impressive
   and sustained; the aggregate had surpassed the
   growth rates recorded in the industrialized
   countries by a substantial margin, and the per
   capita income growth, after a moderate lag in
   the 1960s, had exceeded that of the industrialized countries in the 1970s. An important
   exception had been the low per capita growth rate
   in the industrializing countries of South Asia
   and particularly in Africa south of the Sahara.
   For developing countries as a whole, the
   aggregate growth rate in the 1960-1980 period
   averaged 5.8 percent and the per capita rate
   3.5 percent per annum.
2. The growth achievement had been a result of the
   capacity to absorb modern technology and to
   organize efficiently low-cost production, after
   an initial period of infancy. The share of
   manufacturing in gross domestic product (GDP)
   in Latin America, southern Europe, southern
   Asia, the Middle East, and northern Africa
   averaged some 23 percent in the late 1970s
   compared to 19 percent in 1960; it was
   approaching the share that obtained in the
   developed countries (27 percent). A number of
   developing countries had ceased to be the
   periphery of the world economy and had become
   industrial centers in their own right.
3. Accelerated industrialization led to diversification of the export structure of the newly
   industrializing countries. Manufactures in 1983
   accounted for slightly more than one-half of the

total exports of eastern and southern Asia and
southern Europe, compared to less than 30 percent twenty years before. The Latin American
progress had been less rapid until a few years
ago, but there had been a major upsurge in the
late 1970s, led by Brazilian automotive exports.
The developing countries' overall exports of
manufactures had continued to grow in the 1970s,
as they had in the 1960s, at an average annual
rate of 12 percent (in constant 1978 prices),
compared to 8.5 percent for total world trade in
manufactures in the 1970s. It must be added,
however, that vast areas of developing countries,
including the newly industrializing ones, remain
major commodity suppliers to the world markets
and continue to be exposed to vicissitudes of
demand and prices. This is particularly the
case with Latin America, the Association of
Southeast Asian Nations (ASEAN), and parts of
the Indian subcontinent.

4.   Investment had been increasing faster than
aggregate production, indicating a rising share
of the plowback into future capacity to produce.
As a result, the rate of investment as a proportion of GDP in developing countries had showed
an upward leap from 19 percent to 26 percent
between 1960 and 1980; it was above the level in
the industrializing countries by the late 1970s,
in the reckoning of the World Bank.

5.   National savings rates had risen on the average
by a third. Within this, an enormous upward
shift had occurred in eastern Asia, from under
10 percent of income in 1960 to almost 24 percent in 1977. A remarkable increase had also
occurred in southern Asia, from 12.5 percent to
17.6 percent of income. In Latin America and
southern Europe, national savings had only kept
pace with income, at levels averaging about 20
percent.

6.   For a successful outcome of a growth process
financed partly by foreign borrowing, it is
crucial that the gap between investment and
savings, initially large, starts closing as
growth proceeds, to be ultimately replaced by a
surplus that will be used to retire the debt if
necessary. If the gap starts falling as a
proportion of income, the debt will cease to
grow at a certain point, and the entire borrowing process will be self-liquidating. The
available data suggested that despite the rise
in the price of imported oil, the gap in the
current account as a proportion of GDP had
fallen in both eastern and southern Asia between
1970 and 1977. It had increased moderately in

Latin America and more sharply in southern
Europe. For developing countries as a whole,
it had declined.[19]

Despite the above evidence, the GATT Secretariat has
a point concerning wasteful use of foreign loans. For
one thing, a part of capital inflow was offset by capital
exports in some countries; it was used for purchases of
military supplies in others; and there was inappropriate
use of public funds for private benefit in an unknown
number of cases. Private capital outflow from Mexico
has been variously estimated at US$17-39 billion,
Venezuela US$6-18 billion, Argentina US$8-11 billion,
and Brazil US$12 billion (1982 alone).[20] Military
purchases and fees in Argentina have been quoted at
US$10 billion.[21] Second, free-trade policies, coupled
with frozen exchange rates, led to a massive increase in
imports financed by foreign borrowing, without a
corresponding increase in domestic capital formation.
Instead of resulting in improved resource allocation
claimed for them, such policies led to excessive foreign
competitive pressure on domestic production, increased
unemployment, and large external debt. This happened in
Chile.
    Major commercial banks have not been anxious to sell
their loans to major developing debtor countries. There
is a limited secondary New York market in syndicated loans
to Latin American governments. The sellers are small
U.S. regional banks and the European banks. In early
1983 the discounted paper included Brazilian and
Venezuelan loans, and the discounts ranged between 5 percent and 12.5 percent of face value. It was stated that
the bigger banks are reluctant to sell because they do
not want to take write-offs.[22] Another explanation,
offered to me by a prominent London investment bank, was
that large commercial banks wanted to stay in major
developing debtor countries in view of their favorable
long-run growth prospects even though the banks were
reluctant to increase their current exposure. The
Japanese banks, required by the government to set aside
a special reserve against losses on their doubtful
foreign loans, made only nominal provisions with respect
to their major borrowers. It was unofficially reported
that the banks set aside funds equal to around 50 percent
of the maximum allowed in the cases of loans to Poland,
Vietnam, Cuba, and Zaire; 25 percent in the cases of
Bolivia, Honduras, Costa Rica, Romania, Senegal, and
Sudan; 10 percent in the cases of Yugoslavia and Liberia;
and only 5 percent in the case of loans to Mexico,
Argentina, Brazil, and Venezuela.[23]

EXTERNAL FORCES 1981-1982

During 1981 and 1982 the developing countries were
exposed to three shocks of major proportions and in rapid
succession. They were the main cause of debt-servicing
troubles in most major debtor countries. First, commodity
prices fell sharply as the world recession became deeper
and more widespread and as the upswing in interest rates
forced sales from commodity inventories, the cost of
carrying them having become increasingly prohibitive.
Export commodity prices other than oil in 1982 were on the
average 30 percent down from the average of 1980. The
president of the World Bank estimated that between 1980
and 1982 the annual export revenue of developing countries dropped US$40 billion, as a result of falling
prices of nonfuel commodities and stagnation of other
categories of developing-country exports.[24]

Second, the upward shift in the international rate
of interest not only meant a sharply increased cost of
new borrowing but also led to a revaluation of charges on
the existing debt contracted at floating interest rates
(see the section on "Debt-Servicing Terms"). From 1978
to 1981, LIBOR doubled, and according to the managing
director of the International Monetary Fund (IMF),
interest payments by the nonoil developing countries on
their long-term foreign debt alone rose by some US$23
billion. Furthermore, the average maturity shortened.
The president of the World Bank estimated that the annual
debt service for medium- and long-term debt went up
US$37 billion between 1980 and 1982.[25] According to
the Organization for Economic Cooperation and Development (OECD), the increase amounted to US$33 billion for
non-OPEC countries and US$11 billion for OPEC, or a total
of US$44 billion between 1980 and 1982.[26] A continuing
appreciation of the U.S. dollar has been an additional
element hardening the terms of debt servicing.

Third, in August 1982 international capital market
lending to developing countries, mostly syndicated bank
lending, nearly collapsed. In the period September-
December 1982, this lending was running at US$19 billion
annually, compared to US$51 billion in 1981, a shortfall
of US$32 billion. For oil-importing countries alone,
this shortfall amounted to US$30 billion.[27]

The aggregate adverse swing for non-OPEC developing
countries, resulting from falling export revenue, rising
debt-servicing costs, and the fall in capital market
borrowing, amounted to about US$170 billion over the two
years 1981 and 1982.[28] The situation in 1979 and 1980
was already quite difficult for those countries, as they
had just sustained the second oil-price increase.

Although the oil-importing countries were carrying
the brunt of the adversity, the oil-exporting countries
did not escape it. The volume fell sharply following the
1979 price increase, the recession, and the chaotic

marketing conditions, leading to a large reduction of export and fiscal revenue. The exports of OPEC countries in 1982 amounted to US$213 billion, compared to US$295 billion in 1980, a decline of US$82 billion or 28 percent. The cumulative decline over the two-year period 1981-1982 amounted to US$105 billion.[29] The few surplus-oil countries recouped a part of their revenue decline through higher earnings of interest on their foreign bank deposits and similar assets abroad. For the majority of oil-exporting countries there was no such remedy, and they went through a deflationary experience similar to that of many oil-importing developing countries.

EXTERNAL FORCES 1983

Export commodity prices of nonoil developing countries improved during 1983 as economic activity picked up in the United States, with the associated increase in the U.S. demand for inventories. The price of oil stabilized, after much effort, through a collective action of OPEC and non-OPEC exporters, commonly concerned about the potentially disastrous financial effect of a continuing slide in the oil commodity market.[30] The commodity situation remained uncertain, however. In September 1983 the dollar price index of export commodities of developing countries other than oil was 16 percent higher than its bottom level of November 1982, but still 22 percent lower than the precrisis average of 1980. Prices of metals, which had led the price recovery in early 1983, started weakening again after the summer of 1983, perhaps presaging a new slowdown in the industrialized countries.[31] Nominal interest rates were lower than their peaks recorded from time to time in 1980-1982, but they remained high in real terms. Net bank lending to nonoil developing countries in the first half of 1983 was reported at US$5.8 billion, that is, at an annual rate half of that in 1982 and one-quarter of the precrisis level of 1981.[32] In summary, the international situation at the end of 1983 was somewhat easier than in 1982, mainly due to a partial recovery in commodity prices; but in the meantime the internal situation in a number of debtor countries had become worse as deflationary programs took their toll.

EMERGENCY ACTION IN 1982 AND 1983

A series of international measures was undertaken, swift under the circumstances, to cope with the most critical country situations. These measures, usually initiated by the U.S. government and orchestrated by the IMF, included assistance by central banks of some key creditor countries and some of their official agencies,

"involuntary" lending by creditor commercial banks,
bridging assistance of the Basel-based Bank for International Settlements (BIS), and drawings on the IMF.
The arrangements were short term, and the amounts provided were tight. The situation was shored up in
different degrees for the time being, but further actions
are virtually inevitable. The bankers' views on the
continuing gravity of the problem leave little room for
doubt:

> The international debt situation is far more
> serious than anticipated a year ago. Solutions
> were found for the major debtor countries, but
> they are strictly short-term. If we are lucky,
> the packages that were put together for 1983 will
> actually hold until the end of the year, but . . .
> this is not certain. Moreover, the arrangements
> that will have to be agreed on for 1984 for many
> debtor countries will be difficult to arrive at.
> . . . It is going to be extremely difficult to
> make the additional net funds available which
> will be necessary every year to keep the develop-
> ing countries going.[33]

Although only two of the recent restructuring
agreements for lesser developed country debt have
actually been signed, it is already clear that a
second round of negotiations is inevitable. There
are several lessons to be learned from these
recent efforts before determining what to do next.
First, debt problems will take much longer to work
out than was thought originally. Second, fear is
now mounting that a growing number of countries
will be unable to cope with their post-rescheduling
obligations. Some countries are already having
trouble keeping their interest payments current,
and are unlikely to meet their payment schedules
once the grace period has elapsed. Third, present
rescheduling mechanisms are inefficient. Creditors
and key LDC policymakers have been so tied up in
marathon sessions to patch up current reschedulings
that they have been unable to address any of the
long-term issues. Fourth, it has become clear that
the debt problem cannot be solved in isolation
from other problems. Any solution must address
a much wider range of economic and monetary issues
than is currently being considered, and packages
must be paced to an actual increase in world trade,
rather than simply based on the assumption that an
increase will occur.

The "rescue packages" hastily put together by
Western governments, international organizations
and commercial banks in the first months of 1983,

cannot ultimately reduce the vulnerability of the international financial system so long as new money is used merely to pay interest. In order for growth to be resumed and for confidence in international banking to recover, ad hoc bail-outs must give way to long-term policies geared to a sustained recovery.[34]

The flaw in the current strategy is that there is not enough _direct_ emphasis on LDC growth. We are all talking about growth, but there is too much risk that current policies won't be sufficient. Without faster growth, we are buying not only economic and financial chaos, in my view, but _de facto_ defaults on the order not yet seen.[35]

Carlos Alzamora and Enrique Iglesias have stressed that the "rescue schemes" have offered few prospects for economic growth as the additional resources committed by the banks, the IMF, and others have not been sufficient for payment of interest. Coupled with other unfavorable factors, primarily export crisis, this has led to domestic difficulties that have aptly been called "internationalization" of the world recession. Domestic interest rates in the debtor countries have skyrocketed to levels in real terms that do not seem credible: in some cases 30-40 percent per year. The domestic financial crisis is now increasingly seen as a more intractable problem than the inability to pay foreign creditors.[36] In fact, both are interrelated as resource drain to pay debt service is accompanied by domestic recession that leads to underutilization of capacity and unemployment of labor: The deflationary policy compounds their effect. Serious weakening of the finances and ability to grow of many enterprises in developing countries has occurred: High cost of borrowing, declines in sales due to both the domestic and the international recessions, and devaluations that have raised enormously the cost of debt servicing have caused corporate distress on a wide geographical basis--Argentina, Brazil, Chile, Ecuador, Korea, Mexico, Philippines, Turkey. Lag in new investment and replacement leads to obsolescence that will affect the capacity to compete in the international market: "Brazilian businessmen believe that, if the squeeze goes on much longer, the best of the country's industry will collapse."[37]
Uncertainty as to where the deflationary pressure on the developing debtor countries will ultimately lead has recently been expressed by the governor of the Central Bank of the Federal Republic of Germany, an institution not known for financial laxity:

With remarkable flexibility and in a striking act of international cooperation a number of central

banks, the IMF and the large commercial banks
averted the worst in August last year. Since
then we have been in a period of permanent crisis
management. I am not by any means using this
term in a derogatory sense. We need crisis
management in order to gain time to correct faulty
developments on a durable basis; but we should not
succumb to the illusion that crisis management
itself is the solution.

An outstanding role in the process of crisis management is played by the International Monetary Fund.
It has imposed tough conditions on the countries
concerned. Their political and social consequences
are not completely foreseeable, at least not for
me. I can also understand that the question is
increasingly being asked whether the IMF's
philosophy is at all applicable to the problems
of the countries with which we are now concerned.
As we all know, the philosophy of the IMF was
developed in 1944 in Bretton Woods for quite
different cases, namely for overcoming temporary
balance-of-payments disequilibria on the part of
developed countries, whereas today's acute cases
involve mainly long-term structural problems of
developing countries. Current-account deficits
are, of course, completely normal for rapidly
developing countries such as Brazil or Argentina.
It is only by this means that they are able to
import real resources. This is why it is an unsatisfactory state of affairs that in the train of
the adjustment process imports of capital goods,
and hence the future growth potential of these
economies, also have to be restricted. The
exceptionally heavy debt-service burden, which in
many cases is higher than export receipts, leads
to the undesirable result that a transfer of
real resources takes place in the opposite
direction to the one that is necessary.[38]

INTERDEPENDENCE

The depression in major debtor countries has had
adverse trade effects on the outside world and may have
adverse effects on the international financial system.
Cancellation and postponement of a number of major
investment projects in Brazil, Mexico, Indonesia, Nigeria,
Philippines, Venezuela, Yugoslavia, and Egypt, as well
as in other countries of the Middle East, have affected
the suppliers in both the more advanced developing
countries and the developed countries. As capital-goods
exports dominate the European sales, the latter have
suffered: Exports to Mexico from the Federal Republic of

Germany in the first eight months of 1983 fell by 57
percent, to Venezuela by 48 percent, and to Brazil by
27 percent, compared to the first eight months of 1982.[39]
British exports to Argentina in the same period fell by
91 percent, to Mexico by 51 percent, to Venezuela by 47
percent, and to Chile by 22 percent.[40] In the case of
the United States, a wide range of manufactured and
agricultural exports was affected. Total exports to non-
OPEC countries fell by 46 percent between the first half
of 1981 and the first half of 1983, and exports to Mexico
by 52 percent. "The depression in the non-OPEC developing countries has had a much greater adverse effect on
our [U.S.] exports than the appreciation of the dollar."[41]
     Another victim of the debtors' depression has been
the trade among developing countries: The import
capacity of those affected by the crisis has fallen
sharply while the capacity of developing-country exporters
to provide export credit has been drastically curtailed
in light of their own acute shortage of convertible foreign
exchange. Brazil's exports to the rest of Latin America
dropped from US$5.5 billion in 1981 to an estimated
US$1.7 billion in 1983, and a Yugoslav oil exploration
enterprise had to withdraw from projects in four countries.[42] The reduction in the intratrade and investment
of developing countries came at a time when it was most
needed to offset in part the consequences of slow growth
in the rest of the world economy and to contribute to its
recovery.
     Loans to developing countries are a small proportion
of total bank loans, but they are a large proportion of
bank capital. In periods of payments difficulty, the
attention inevitably shifts to the latter: It is bank
capital that ultimately serves to meet depositors' claims
if the loans the bank has extended fail. At the end of
1981, the U.S. banks had outstanding loans in developing
and East European countries of about US$100 billion;
this compared with total capital of the thirty largest
U.S. banks of US$40 billion. The hundred largest non-
U.S. banks had an estimated total of outstanding loans in
the two areas of US$200 billion; against this they had
total capital of US$120 billion.[43] The exposure of banks
on the average was 200 percent of capital. Most of the
U.S. banks' exposure is in developing countries; most of
the East European debt is owed to non-U.S. banks.[44]
     Loans to Mexico in mid-1982 amounted to US$64.4
billion, of which US$24.4 billion was owed to U.S. banks.
As a proportion of capital the loans ranged, for ten
major U.S. banks, from 40.0 percent to 66.7 percent.[45]
It was with respect to one of these that "about noon on
19 August 1982 rumours swept through Wall Street that a
major U.S. bank was going to fail. Bank stocks plunged.
According to the rumours Mexico was about to default on
its foreign debt, and this would undermine the unnamed
bank. Could this be the beginning of a panic and

chain-reaction collapse?"[46]   Rumors about Mexican
exposure were enough to make Manufacturers Hanover, the
fifth-largest U.S. bank in terms of capital, support the
prices of its own bond issues on Friday, August 20, 1982.[47]
By that time action was already well under way by the
U.S. Treasury to inject funds into Mexico.[48]

In the case of Brazil, which owes to U.S. banks about
US$22 billion, exposure to capital for major banks ranges
from 43.9 to 77.7 percent.[49]   Share prices of a number of
these fell sharply in New York on October 21, 1983,
apparently as a result of renewed apprehension that
continuing difficulties in Brazil-IMF negotiations,
sharpened by the conflict over the IMF insistence on a
reduction of Brazilian wages, would make it impossible to
reach agreement on a new "package" of financial and policy
measures by a scheduled date in November.[50]   A week later
it was reported that commercial banks were exerting heavy
pressure on the IMF to be more understanding of the
political difficulties facing the Brazilian government in
the implementation of its wage policy, and it was felt
that Brazil should be given more credit for the austerity
measures it had already undertaken.[51]

Cline has examined the possible effect on the U.S.
financial system of serious debt difficulties and possible
action by the debtors:

> For Western banks, repudiation of a substantial
> portion of loans to developing countries and
> Eastern Europe would be crippling. Even wide-
> spread moratoria could have a severe impact on
> the banks. . . . As a hypothetical illustration,
> consider what would happen if Argentina, Mexico,
> and Brazil were to miss one year's payment on
> principal and interest, and were to do so in a
> sufficiently aggressive way that it seemed
> appropriate to write off fully the payments missed.
> The complete loss of one year's payments due from
> these three countries would cause losses equal
> to 28 percent of the capital of the nine largest
> U.S. banks even after taking into account of
> offsetting profits on other loans. . . . These
> three countries owe US$31.3 billion to the nine
> largest banks, whose capital broadly defined is
> only US$29 billion. For 1983, debt service due
> (before recent restructurings) on this amount
> was US$13.7 billion. Profits of these banks in
> 1982 amounted to US$5.5 billion before taxes.
> Thus a loss of US$13.7 billion would cause total
> losses of US$8.2 billion or 28 percent of capital,
> and without offsetting items generating taxes,
> these losses would have to be fully absorbed out
> of capital. Although the resulting cut in capital
> would not cause insolvency, it would mean that
> the banks would have to begin to reduce their

total loans sharply in order to reestablish the
5 percent ratio of capital to loans required by
regulators. The Wall Street Journal, June 10 and
20, 1983, pointed out that although the capital
requirement for large banks has not been rigid,
it is becoming more so as regulators respond to
increasing congressional pressure. A new formal
requirement of 5 percent capital backing for large
banks was adopted in mid-1983. There would thus
be a multiple reduction in loans. Potentially
the nine largest banks would have to cut their
loans outstanding by approximately US$160 billion
as a result of a loss of US$8 billion of their
capital from one year's loss of principal and
interest from Argentina, Brazil, and Mexico under
conditions where these losses had to be written
off. Both because of loan cutbacks and because
of the sharp increase in risk premium, the
interest rate could be expected to rise, causing
recessionary pressure. Even if the Federal Reserve
loosened the capital backing of loans temporarily,
the potential would exist for economic shock waves
through reduced credit availability to American
business and consumers and, as a result, increased
unemployment. To a considerable extent, the
sequence of events that would follow major bank
losses because of country losses remains un-
charted waters. . . . To the extent that central
banks made loans to the affected private banks in
an attempt to replace at least partially the
repayments that otherwise would have been received
from countries failing to make payments, there
could be inflationary consequences. . . . Despite
the fact that the Federal Reserve could respond
in a crisis, there would be enormous economic
risks from a large-scale banking crisis. If a
wider front of country defaults were to occur,
many major banks could become insolvent. For the
nine largest banks this result would occur if
just Brazil, Mexico and Argentina repudiated
their debt, or if all developing and East European
countries experienced sufficient difficulty that
one-third of their debt had to be written off.
Normally bank insolvencies are dealt with by
merger, with a larger, sound bank absorbing the
bankrupt concern. But in the situation just
described, merger would be highly unlikely. There
would be no banks larger than the failing banks
to absorb them. In the past merger has tended to
guarantee the deposits of all depositors. In a
bankruptcy of the major banks, however, it is likely
that only deposits covered by the Federal Depositors' Insurance Corporation would be guaranteed
[in the United States], a maximum of $100,000 per

account. For the U.S. banking system, deposit
insurance covers only 73 percent of total deposit
value. . . . A truly massive failure of external
debt could bring down many major banks. Regardless of the emergency public measures that might
be mounted in response, the potential economic
consequences could be devastating.[52]

Another element that raises the risk of chain reaction among financial institutions is substantial
interdependence of banks. Interbank deposits account for
almost 40 percent of total Euromarket deposits; in the
Asian dollar market, the proportion is 55 percent.
Domino-style effects under these circumstances are almost
inevitable.

The risks inherent in the situation are reflected in
low prices of bank shares despite high bank profits, in
some cases very high. As a multiple of profits, the
share prices of major U.S. banks with a heavy foreign
exposure amounted to 5:1 in late October 1983. By
comparison, the average price-earnings ratio for all
companies listed on the New York Stock Exchange was 14:1.[53]
Almost all major bank shares, it was reported, were trading substantially below book value, in some cases at
around half.[54] What bank shareholders were getting
in dividends they were partly losing in market valuation
of capital: An unsatisfactory situation reflecting
market disbelief in the durability of profits derived not
from prosperous borrowers but from a squeeze on their
stagnating or falling incomes.

THE FUTURE

Three sets of proposals have been made to deal with
the debt problem. The first suggests a continuation of
present practices. The second calls for readjustment of
debt terms through a takeover by a public agency of debts
at a discount. The third proposal calls for an extended
moratorium.

Continuation of present practices is the current
official doctrine of most creditor countries. Their
implications, with some modifications, were worked out by
Cline in what he called "a containment strategy."[55]
The strategy was based on the assumption that OECD growth
would recover to 3 percent per year, that the debtor
countries would have a lower growth rate than in the past
(2.5 percent in 1983, 3.5 percent in 1984, and 4.5 percent in 1985 and 1986), and that the base real interest
rate (London Inter-Bank Offer Rate--LIBOR) would fall
from 11 percent in 1982 to 5 percent in 1983, 4 percent
in 1984, and 3 percent in 1985 and 1986. Behind these
assumptions was a belief that the reduction in the
developing countries' current account deficit that has

already taken place due to shortage of finance and that
has mainly affected imports can be sustained without major
political upheavals and that the existing "rescue packages" are functioning well.[56] Cline proposed expansion of
World Bank lending, expanded export credits, and the
approval of the IMF quota increase; the latter is crucial
for success of the strategy. Private banks should continue new lending at modest rates to countries in adjustment. In extreme cases new approaches may be needed such
as the rescheduling of interest and the use of zero-
coupon bonds (bonds issued at a deep discount on which no
service is paid until maturity). Cline's model shows the
current account deficit and particularly the debt-burden
indicators falling over time; but for oil-importing
countries the model implies a net resource outflow on a
rising scale, with interest payments exceeding capital
inflow and the debt still rising. The analysis has the
merit of showing realistically the present position. It
caused sharp reactions: that its main concern is the well-
being of banks, that it will stretch to the breaking point
the political and social fabric of debtor countries, and
that it is based on too many things going right at the
same time instead of providing for a lender of last
resort.[57]

Many proposals have been made for a takeover of the
existing debts by a new agency on terms that would involve a reduction of the principal or interest or both.[58]
None of them seems to have been thoroughly considered by
creditor-country governments, for three reasons: They
would involve the establishment of a new agency calling
for budgetary resources; they would involve losses for
the banks; and debtor countries' bargaining power has not
been behind them.

Throughout the debt crisis, debtor countries have
been careful to preserve their good relations with the
banks. A major, probably decisive, reason has been the
need to preserve access to bank credit. It has been
more expensive, but it had proven, until the debt crisis,
more easily available and more freely usable than credit
extended by governments or international lending
agencies.[59]

A solution to the debt problem would have to be
found that achieves the objective of facilitating substantially the debt-servicing burden and yet stays within
two constraints. These are that it preserves access to
bank credit and that it involves little, if any, budgetary
outlays of developed countries.

One of the bases for the solution will need to be an
understanding between the debtor countries and the banks
that it is in their mutual interest to postpone amortization payments for several years, say three to five, while
preserving intact the debt principal. Such a postponement would not affect the profit position of the banks
or the value of their assets. On the other hand, if the

breathing space provided by the postponement of
amortization is properly used for expansion and modernization of the production structure of the borrowers, their
debt-servicing capacity will improve, and this ultimately
represents the best guaranty of debt repayment.[60] Two
corollaries follow. First, the banks need to be satisfied that productive investment will take place. Second,
payment of debt-rescheduling fees and extra interest
charges ceases to be justified: They are intended to
compensate the creditor for increased risk, and the risk
will have fallen.[61] For a rescheduling proposal to be
seriously considered it would be necessary to identify the
affected countries, creditors, amounts, classes of debt,
the effects on the debtors and the creditors, the need
for public support to banks suffering from illiquidity,
and the role of international financial institutions.[62]
Some organization of developing countries needs to do
this work; a New York banker has suggested that the
central banks of developing countries may establish a
suitable body that would, among other things, organize
and manage debt-rescheduling exercises.[63] Such a body
could be a counterpart of the Institute of International
Finance, recently established by major creditor banks.
One of the aims of the institute is the provision of "a
convenient forum through which individual country borrowers can present to lenders information concerning their
borrowing needs." There is no reason why the borrowers
could not do this collectively and why borrowing needs
could not include postponement of amortization. An
understanding would also need to be reached concerning
modalities of revision of the arrangement and conditions
under which amortization payments would be resumed before
the expiration of the postponement.

Scaling down the rate of interest is crucial not
only for the countries in debt-servicing difficulties,
but for all developing countries that borrow abroad:
Not only will their future debt-servicing burden be very
large at present rates, but the range of investment
projects that can be undertaken has narrowed down, thus
dampening the rate of investment, growth, and the
associated debt-servicing capacity. Furthermore, the
issue of interest rates is critical for the developed
countries as well: As long as the present rates last it
is difficult to expect a revival of private investment,
and government budgets operating under an enormous burden
of interest payments (and armament spending) are not in a
position to accommodate a satisfactory level of public
investment.[64] Individual country actions to reduce the
rate of interest are constrained under present conditions
of international financial integration, as speculative
capital movements would tend to defeat such individual
efforts. An international solution to the problem must
be sought. Both the theoretical basis and the practical
modalities of any such international arrangement would

have to be worked out, but it is difficult to see how
without such an effort the present unsatisfactory situation
can be resolved. For the countries experiencing debt-
servicing difficulties, an internationally arranged
general reduction of interest rates would relieve the
burden while simultaneously preserving their access to
international credit. As stated in the 1983 annual
report of the U.S. Council of Economic Advisers:

> The problems of the developing countries are not
> insoluble. If growth in the world economy re-
> sumes and real interest rates fall to historical
> levels, the debt burden of even the most heavily
> indebted countries will become much more
> manageable. Mexico and Brazil, among the most
> heavily indebted countries, both have debts
> well below half their GNPs. At a historically
> typical real interest rate of 2 percent, the
> real burden of debt service would fall to less
> than 1 percent of GNP--a fully manageable level
> in a growing economy.[65]

The trouble is that the present rates are over five times
the historical rate.
    As an interim solution, while debt rescheduling and
international interest-rate policies are worked out, I
have been proposing, since before the Cancun meeting in
1981, a large injection of Special Drawing Rights (SDRs)
through a special issue, confined to developing countries.

> The effect of the special issue would be to gain
> time in which the existing debts and other
> obligations can be reorganized and suitable
> domestic policies of adjustment adopted, without
> going first through a massive deflation which is
> otherwise in prospect. . . . SDR allocation is
> normally without conditions. In this case, in
> view of the needed size [US$55 billion], it is
> suggested that the country allocation of the
> special issue be accompanied by conditionality
> and monitoring in which the developing countries
> would play a major role. Only the developing
> countries among themselves can successfully
> grapple with central issues of performance, such
> as capital flight, inappropriate use of public
> funds and unproductive expenditures. A procedure
> which would give them a great deal of authority
> would contribute to improvement in North-South
> relations in which conditionality and its
> administration have proven to be among the most
> difficult issues; and it would provide an
> experience in participatory management which,
> if successful, could offer valuable lessons for

future reform of international institutions.

The effects on the international monetary system
of a large issue of SDRs may be of major importance. It would raise their share in aggregate
reserve assets to a respectable level at which,
with suitable modifications at a later stage to
widen their marketability, their larger supply
would in a sense create the demand for them.
The national reserve currency standard has proven
to have had an inflationary bias. It has con-
ferred doubtful advantages on reserve currency
countries, first the U.K. and then the U.S.,
as the short-run payments gains have been followed
by long-run losses in competitive strength and
ultimately deflationary pressures. Exchange
rate instability in the world is increasing, and
the world system now operates without a fixed
point of reference. A growing role of international currency under appropriate international
control is a necessary condition for economic
growth with stability. It would also facilitate
international monetary cooperation badly needed
to stop the downward slide on which we now find
ourselves.

Spotty and frequent rescheduling efforts now under
way in many cases are not an alternative to decisive action: they will essentially only continue the agony, in addition to being very costly
in terms of effort, charges and fees, and inability to plan beyond the next month.[66]

A continued absence of international action will
inevitably raise the prospect of unilateral moratoria
for an extended period. A "sovereign moratorium" has
been proposed by the opposition party in Brazil. Speaking about the need for a moratorium lasting at least
three years and covering both amortization and interest,
Celso Furtado, former minister of planning of Brazil,
stated that Brazil cannot continue to pay with the hunger
of its citizens.[67]

APPENDIX

Table 1.2 External Debt Per Capita (in U.S. dollars)

	Aggregate Disbursed Debt Mid-1983 (billions)	Population Mid-1981 (thousands)	Per Capita Debt
Israel	21.5	3,954	5,437
Venezuela	33.0	15,423	2,139
Chile	18.0	11,292	1,594
Portugal	14.0	9,826	1,424
Argentina	40.0	28,174	1,419
Mexico	85.0	71,215	1,193
South Korea	39.0	38,880	1,003
Algeria	18.0	19,602	918
Yugoslavia	20.0	22,516	888
Brazil	93.0	120,507	771
Peru	11.6	17,031	681
Morocco	11.0	20,891	526
Philippines	20.0	49,558	403
Colombia	10.0	26,425	378
Egypt	16.0	43,290	369
Turkey	16.2	45,529	355
Nigeria	13.0	87,603	148
Indonesia	20.0	149,451	133
Pakistan	9.0	84,501	107
India	20.0	690,183	29

Note: The per capita debt figures are slightly overstated, as the aggregate debt data refer to mid-1983 and the population data to mid-1981. The overstatement is small, especially as in many cases debt data are incomplete.

Source: External debt totals used in the computation are from Table 1.1. Population data are from 1983 World Bank Atlas: Gross National Product, Population, and Growth Rates, Washington, D.C.

Table 1.3 External Debt as Proportion of Gross National Product

	Aggregate Disbursed Debt Mid-1983 as % of GNP 1981	GNP (U.S. dollars) (billions)	GNP (U.S. dollars) (per capita)
Israel	105.0	20.42	5,160
Chile	62.3	28.89	2,560
Morocco	61.2	17.96	860
South Korea	59.1	66.09	1,700
Peru	58.1	19.98	1,170
Egypt	56.8	28.16	650
Portugal	56.5	24.75	2,520
Argentina	55.4	72.12	2,560
Mexico	53.1	160.23	2,250
Philippines	51.2	39.01	790
Venezuela	50.7	65.08	4,220
Algeria	42.8	42.01	2,140
Brazil	34.7	267.73	2,220
Yugoslavia	31.8	62.93	2,790
Pakistan	30.2	29.80	350
Colombia	27.5	36.39	1,380
Indonesia	25.4	78.75	530
Turkey	23.1	70.21	1,540
Nigeria	17.1	76.17	870
India	11.3	176.66	260

Note: The GNP proportion figures are slightly overstated, as the aggregate debt data refer to mid-1983 and the GNP data to 1981. The overstatement is small, especially as in many cases debt data are incomplete, and GNP has been stagnating since 1981.

Source: Aggregate disbursed debt from Table 1.2. GNP data are from 1983 World Bank Atlas: Gross National Product, Population, and Growth Rates, Washington, D.C.

Table 1.4 Country Group Debt-Service Ratios: Total Debt Service (DS) and Interest (INT) as Percentage of Exports[a]

Income Group		1970/71	1973	1974	1975	1977	1979	1980	1981[b]	1982[b]
Low-income	DS	12	14	13	16	14	14	17	19	23[c]
countries	INT	4	4	4	2	4	6	6	7	9[d]
Middle-	DS	16	12	10	10	12	14	12	14	16
income countries	INT	5	3	3	3	3	4	6	7	8
Newly	DS	15	13	12	15	18	21	18	21	24
indus- trializing countries	INT	5	5	5	6	6	8	9	11	13
Total	DS	15	13	12	15	18	21	18	21	24
non-OPEC	INT	5	5	5	6	6	8	9	11	13
OPEC	DS	6	8	4	4	7	8	7	10	14
countries	INT	2	2	1	2	2	3	2	3	4
Total	DS	13	11	8	10	12	14	12	15	19
developing countries	INT	4	3	3	4	4	5	5	7	9

[a]Service on medium- and long-term debt, public, publicly guaranteed, and private; service on short-term debt is not included. Exports include goods and services and net private transfers.

[b]Preliminary estimates

[c]Also 23 percent for the least developed countries

[d]8 percent for the least developed countries

Source: Organization for Economic Cooperation and Development, External Debt of Developing Countries: General Survey 1982 (Paris, December 1982), table 13.

Table 1.5 Country Debt-Service Ratios: Interest and Amortization
as Percentage of Exports[a]

Country	1971/72[b]	1975	1976	1977	1978	1979	1980[c]	1981[c]
Mexico	34	37	50	63	59	68	41	60
Brazil	51	37	43	47	55	60	57	58
Chile	20	34	32	31	45	32	34	45
Peru	23	28	27	32	32	26	36	42
Ivory Coast	10	9	9	11	17	23	36	39
Venezuela	6	5	5	11	15	17	26	37
Algeria	9	17	20	21	29	31	30	36
Morocco	10	7	10	13	22	26	28	35
Argentina	26	30	30	20	28	18	25	27
Philippines	9	12	16	13	23	20	18	24
Egypt	31	22	19	24	22	19	20	20
Yugoslavia	20	16	15	17	15	18	16	20
Greece	12	15	15	15	13	14	16	18
Turkey	12	10	12	12	16	18	14	17
Thailand	11	9	8	13	15	15	14	17
Korea (South)	19	12	10	10	11	15	14	16
Portugal	6	6	8	9	8	10	13	15
Indonesia	10	10	11	13	15	15	11	12
Pakistan	19	18	17	17	14	12	11	10
India	22	14	12	11	11	10	9	10
China (Taiwan)	5	5	5	5	6	5	6	6
Nigeria	3	3	4	4	6	4	4	4

[a]Service on medium- and long-term debt, public, publicly guaranteed,
and private; service on short-term debt is not included. Exports
include goods and services and net private transfers, including
reported workers remittances.

[b]Average

[c]Preliminary estimates

Source: Organization for Economic Cooperation and Development,
External Debt of Developing Countries (Paris, October 1981),
table 11.

Table 1.6   Ratios of Total Debt Service to Merchandise Exports for
Selected Developing Countries in the 1920s and the 1930s (Percentages)

	Argentina	Bolivia	Brazil	Chile	Colombia	Cuba	Peru	Uruguay
1926	10.0	7.3	13.2	5.5	2.7	3.1	2.6	7.6
1927	7.9	6.1	14.4	8.7	4.4	2.7	3.2	9.2
1928	8.9	8.5	14.6	9.5	8.1	3.3	6.0	8.5
1929	10.4	7.8	16.5	9.2	11.9	3.6	7.4	9.5
1930	18.2	13.5	23.5	18.0[a]	14.0	6.1	9.5[a]	9.7
1931[b]	22.5	24.5	28.4	32.9	15.6	13.4	16.3	22.4
1932[b]	27.6	50.0	41.0	102.6	21.8	18.1	21.4	36.3
1933[b]	30.2	38.5	45.1	81.9	29.6	22.4	21.7	31.3

[a] Probably underestimated

[b] Scheduled debt service as a proportion of exports. Bolivia, Peru,
Chile, Brazil, and Uruguay stopped payments during 1931; Colombia
during 1932; Argentina and Cuba partially in 1933.

Source: Dragoslav Avramovič, Debt Servicing Capacity and Postwar
Growth in International Indebtedness (Baltimore: Johns Hopkins
University Press, 1958), pp. 193-194.

32

NOTES

1. Dragoslav Avramovič, "The Debt Problem of Developing Countries at End-1982," Aussenwirtschaft, Schweizerische Zeitschrift für Internationale Wirtschaftsbeziehungen, St. Gallen, March 1983.

2. Organization for Economic Cooperation and Development (OECD), External Debt of Developing Countries: General Survey 1982, Paris, December 1982.

3. Estimates by the Federal Reserve Bank of New York as reported in the Wall Street Journal, November 5, 1982, and Journal de Genève, November 6, 1982; and by the World Bank in World Development Report 1983, p. 16.

4. Avramovič, "The Debt Problem of Developing Countries," p. 67.

5. International Monetary Fund (IMF), Exchange Arrangements and Restrictions, Annual Report 1983, p. 37.

6. David Finch, "Investment Service of the Underdeveloped Countries," International Monetary Fund Staff Papers, September 1951.

7. Argentina 179 percent of exports, Mexico 129 percent, Ecuador 122 percent, Brazil 122 percent, and Chile 116 percent (Morgan Guaranty Trust Company of New York, World Financial Markets, New York, October 1982).

8. Peterheinz Werhahn, Kapitalexport und Schuldentransfer im Konjunktur-Verlauf, Jena, 1937.

9. Amortization in 1982 amounted to US$70 million, and the debt outstanding at the end of 1981 amounted to US$530 million (OECD, External Debt of Developing Countries).

10. Azizali F. Mohammed, "Latin American Debt--A World Crisis?" North-South Roundtable, April 1983; Pedro-Pablo Kuszynski, "Latin American Debt," Foreign Affairs, vol. 61, no. 2 (Winter 1982-1983). Their findings refer to the Latin American countries, but they also apply to some other developing countries and to Eastern Europe.

11. Carlos Alzamora Traverso and Enrique V. Iglesias, "Bases for a Latin American Response to the International Economic Crisis," United Nations, Economic and Social Council, Doc. E/CEPAL/G.1246, May 16, 1983, pp. 31-32.

12. According to Paul A. Volcker, chairman of the Federal Reserve Board, the debt to banks of non-OPEC countries amounts to US$285 billion (BIS [Bank for International Settlements] Press Review, October 28, 1983). The debt to banks of OPEC countries probably exceeds US$50 billion.

13. No index of prices of export manufactures of developing countries is available. However, export prices of South Korea fell sharply through mid-1983, and they probably reflect the general trend.

14. Georges Corm, "Ménaces sur le Système Financier International," Le Monde Diplomatique, March 1983.

15. General Agreement on Tariffs and Trade (GATT), *International Trade 1981/82*, Geneva, 1982, p. 19.

16. World Bank, *World Debt Tables 1982-83 Edition*, February 1983, p. ix.

17. Statement by Lord Richardson, governor of the Bank of England, of April 12, 1983 (*BIS Press Review*, April 21, 1983).

18. William R. Cline, "International Debt and the Stability of the World Economy," *Policy Analyses in International Economics*, no. 4, September 1983, p. 29.

19. These findings are mainly based on: World Bank, *World Tables, The Second Edition*, 1980; World Bank, *Annual Report 1982*; and United Nations Conference on Trade and Development (UNCTAD), *Trade and Development Report 1982*.

20. *Financial Times*, January 12, 1983; *Inter-Press Service*, October 15, 1982, quoting an IMF estimate; *The Economist*, April 30, 1983; Cline, "International Debt," p. 27; Pedro-Pablo Kuczynski as reported in *International Herald Tribune*, November 5, 1983.

21. *Financial Times*, October 28, 1983.

22. Statement by Martin Schubert, chairman of Eurinam International, New York (*Financial Times*, May 13, 1983).

23. *Wall Street Journal*, June 8, 1983. The required set-aside reserve is equivalent to between 1 percent and 5 percent of the outstanding loans to "problem" debtor nations, held by the banks.

24. Statement at the GATT ministerial meeting in Geneva on November 24, 1982.

25. Statement at the École supérieure in Cergy-Pontoise, France, on November 26, 1982.

26. OECD, *External Debt of Developing Countries*. A part of the increase should be attributed to a normal rise in debt, but the latter was distorted due to capitalization of interest at rising rates.

27. For 1982 as a whole, bank lending to nonoil developing countries amounted to US$25 billion, compared to US$51 billion in 1981 (Richard Williams, Peter Keller, John Lipsky, and Donald Mathieson, *International Capital Markets: Development and Prospects, 1983*, IMF Occasional Paper 23, July 1983, p. 46).

28. Cline, "International Debt," estimates the swing at US$140 billion, exclusive of shortfall in bank lending (p. 25). His estimates and mine are thus almost identical.

29. IMF, *International Financial Statistics*, October 1983.

30. The interactions between the financial and commodity markets have recently attracted attention. See Carlos F. Diaz-Alejandro, *International Financial and Goods Markets in 1982-83 and Beyond*, March 1983 (manuscript).

31. UNCTAD, *Monthly Commodity Price Bulletin*, October 1983.

32. BIS report as quoted in Financial Times,
October 19, 1983, and International Herald Tribune,
October 19, 1983.
33. A prominent Swiss banker, in a private
communication of July 20, 1983.
34. Christine B. Bindert, "Talks Point to Troubles
down the Road," International Banker, July 27, 1983, and
"Debt: Beyond the Quick Fix," Third World Quarterly,
vol. 5, no. 4 (October 1983), p. 828. Bindert is a
vice president of an investment banking firm in New York.
35. Jeffrey E. Garten, "Sovereign Debt: Next Steps,"
International Monetary Conference, Brussels, May 18, 1983.
Garten is from Lehman Brothers Kuhn Loeb Inc., New York.
36. "Debtors' Depression," The Economist, August 6,
1983.
37. Ibid.
38. Address by Karl Otto Pöhl of October 19, 1983,
BIS Press Review of October 31, 1983.
39. Ibid.
40. Financial Times, November 2, 1983.
41. Edward L. Bernstein, Brookings Institution,
as reported in International Herald Tribune, November 5,
1983.
42. Financial Times, November 2, 1983.
43. Data on outstanding loans are from Common Crisis
North South: The Brandt Commission 1983, p. 48; data
on bank capital, Financial Times, October 15, 1982.
44. At the end of 1981, East European debts to U.S.
banks amounted to US$7.3 billion and to non-U.S. banks
US$53.1 billion (Common Crisis).
45. Cline, "International Debt." A wider range,
from 38.7 to 77.6 percent, is shown for the end of
September 1982 in Financial Times, December 9, 1982.
46. John Odell, "The IMF Meeting: Banking for Rich
and Poor," International Herald Tribune, October 16, 1982.
47. Financial Times, August 23, 1982.
48. "Stanley Wilson, America's LDC Troubleshooter,"
Institutional Investor, March 1983.
49. Cline, "International Debt."
50. Journal de Genève, October 22, 1983; International Herald Tribune, October 22, 1983.
51. Financial Times, October 28, 1983.
52. Cline, "International Debt," pp. 36-40.
53. Leonard Silk, "Banks Face Public-Relations
Problem in Seeking Support for Their Rescue," International Herald Tribune, October 22, 1983.
54. Financial Times, November 1, 1983.
55. William Cline, "A Containment Strategy That
Should Work," Financial Times, October 12, 1983. The
details are given in Cline, "International Debt."
56. Cline, "International Debt," p. 43.
57. Letters to Financial Times by Stephany Griffith-
Jones and Michael Lipton, October 18, 1983, and by Stephen
McClelland, October 20, 1983.

58. Reviews of the proposals are contained in Bindert, "Debt: Beyond the Quick Fix," and Cline, "International Debt."

59. The Brandt Commission Papers, chapter on Debt, Geneva, 1981, p. 122.

60. I am grateful to Professor Ivo Fabinc, University of Ljubljana, Yugoslavia, for this point.

61. The refinancing terms of Brazil's latest debt rescheduling, agreed in principle in October 1983, have provided for reduction of fees and interest charges in recognition of this principle, and the same is expected for the next Mexican refinancing (Financial Times, November 4, 1983).

62. It is reported that the World Bank is studying the possibility of establishing a new affiliate with a paid-up capital of US$0.51-1.0 billion and the gearing ratio of 10:1 (compared to the commercial banks' 20:1), which would thus be able to mobilize up to US$10 billion. The paid-up capital would come from the bank's ample cash reserves, and loans could be made to the countries in debt difficulties (Journal de Genève, October 14, 1983; Tribune de Genève, October 17, 1983; Financial Times, September 30, 1983).

63. George J. Vojta, "Appropriate Intermediate Objectives for the International Financial System," North-South Roundtable, Istanbul, August 1983. Vojta is from Solomon Brothers, New York.

64. In the United States, interest on the national debt amounted to US$129 billion in the fiscal year 1983. This was 66 percent of the budget deficit of the federal government of US$195 billion.

65. The annual report of the Council of Economic Advisers, February 2, 1983.

66. Avramovič, "The Debt Problem of Developing Countries," pp. 77, 79, 80, 81.

67. Le Monde, November 2, 1983.

2

The World Crisis and
the Outlook for Latin America

Víctor L. Urquidi

It is common knowledge that during the 1970s, which were considerably dynamic years, Latin America's GDP rose at an annual rate of 5 to 6 percent, following the trend of previous years. However, during this same period a number of changes began to take place that have not been taken fully into account in much of the current discussion. First, import substitution was broadened and intensified: It encompassed heavy industry on a scale larger than before, and gaps in the industrial structure began to be filled with extensive production of intermediate goods. Import substitution in Latin America has been both accidental and deliberate and therefore has never been adequately planned. It was introduced through a number of governmental initiatives aimed at modifying industrial structure, as in the case of Brazil, Mexico, and, to a lesser extent, Venezuela. It was also generated spontaneously as a consequence of protectionism and reinforced by devaluation, tariffs, import and exchange controls, and other measures designed to create a protected market for the manufacture of consumer goods (household durables and motor vehicles) and later on other products. However, a number of areas remained unaccounted for, particularly that of chemicals and other intermediate products. These areas were partially covered during the 1970s.

At the same time the industrial structure began to change in order to supply international markets. The increase in manufactured exports undertaken by several Latin American countries, including a number of the smaller nations, was outstanding. This was due partly to the diversity of international demand, to competitive advantages, and to a determined effort on the part of countries with export capability.

An earlier version of this paper was given at a conference in Avilés, Oviedo, Spain, organized in August 1983 by the Ibero-American Cooperation Institute of that country.

The fact that many Latin American countries were obliged to import petroleum products at the higher 1970s prices obviously obliged them to intensify their efforts to export manufactures. This meant that a transition became necessary from a highly protected manufacturing industry of doubtful productivity and competitiveness to one competitive in the international market in order to sell to the industrialized countries and to compete with the latter in other Latin American and Third World countries. This required either substantial technological innovation and adaptation or considerable efforts to promote trade as well as to negotiate at the international agencies in order to take advantage of modest changes occurring in the trade policies of the industrialized countries, such as the general preference schemes.

In the early 1970s a substantial improvement in the terms of trade took place, particularly--though not exclusively--on account of oil. Oil is usually considered separately from other commodities, but its price did rise for the oil-exporting Latin American countries. For example, the impact on Mexico of this improvement in the terms of trade was really extraordinary. There were good periods for other commodities, although toward the end of the decade they began to decline. It should be recalled, on the other hand, that for oil-importing Latin American countries the overall favorable change in the terms of trade was less obvious and that toward the end of the decade it was actually negative.

The oil shock of 1973-74 and particularly that of 1979-80 had both positive and negative effects on Latin America. The major adverse effect was felt by Brazil, because for a long time the Brazilian economy had been completely adapted to the use of relatively cheap imported oil and because manufactured exports were on the rise. Brazil was forced to absorb the oil shock as if it were a rich country with a high level of technology and great industrial capacity within the OECD, and this explains largely why the Brazilian miracle came to an end and why this economy could not continue to grow at the same rate as before, particularly in the industrial sector. Brazil had to adopt a policy incorporating the real international oil prices into its economy. The smaller countries in Central America, some Caribbean islands, and a number of other countries were obliged to do the same, although under different circumstances and in different ways. All were affected adversely. In the case of Costa Rica, for example, the situation was acute despite the narrow economic structure and industrial capacity. In the case of Brazil, a simulation study that I am familiar with shows that the need to import expensive oil is one of the main determining factors that will prevent Brazil's future growth at the past rate, unless new oil is discovered or unless one of the possible alternatives suggested in Brazil--which do not appear to have matured yet--comes true.[1]

As to the positive aspects of the two oil shocks, there were five net oil-exporting countries: Mexico, Venezuela, Ecuador, Trinidad, and Bolivia. With the rise in export prices, these countries obtained unexpected and huge additional foreign-exchange receipts. This was the basis for a vast expansion of the public sector, of public and private industry, and of the oil industry itself. The effect on the economy was widespread in Mexico and Venezuela, where the state-owned oil industries provided fiscal resources that otherwise would not have been available. By a "positive" effect is meant that exerted on the real economy and on the prospects for exports in general. Undoubtedly, however, in the case of Mexico the negative aspects of the sudden great inflow of foreign currency and of the spending psychology generated by the oil (or any other boom experienced in Mexico's history) should also be considered; in the 1950s, for instance, Mexico had begun a dynamic spending process with revenue from cotton exports, as it had done in the distant past with revenue from mining and so forth.

It should be mentioned, when dealing with the effects of the oil shock, that several countries that were able to supply their own needs to a great extent (such as Argentina, Colombia, and Peru) found themselves in an intermediate position without an acute problem of foreign payments but not without the need to incorporate much higher real prices into their economy or to subsidize these while they adapted to the new economic situation. (Mexico in fact--and Venezuela to an even greater degree-- maintained excessive subsidies on domestic oil prices, with the result that the financial position of the state oil companies was weakened and all notion of conservation and economic use of fuel was disregarded.)

The crisis in Latin America's agricultural sector, which arose as a result of many different factors, was another important aspect of the transition of the 1970s. Several of the contributing factors were agrarian, that is, related to the system of land tenure. Others arose from domestic policy relating to relative prices, by which agriculture was "punished" in favor of industrial development. However, the feedback from this policy affected agricultural output adversely because farmers were obliged to purchase equipment (such as tractors) and other inputs from protected industries--a consequence of import substitution--at very high prices. Generally speaking, the need to create adequate incentives to stimulate agricultural output was neglected (of course, this is not the case in every country nor in certain favored zones).

Food-deficit countries (there were several in Latin America before the 1970s, to which a large country, Mexico, was added) found themselves in the very difficult position of having to import foodstuffs at the time of

the food-price "shock" of 1974. At this time the international price of cereals rose, as a consequence of
massive buying of U.S. output by the Soviet Union and
subsequent policies designed to keep the price of farm
products high. There were a few factors to be considered in this process, one of which was that the
importation of foodstuffs did not replace rural income,
even though it did supply a country with these products.
On the other hand, the effect on the balance of payments
for some countries was severe. The food deficit can be
interpreted as the result of the lack of policies designed to encourage agriculture, combined with changes in
consumption patterns, organizational problems, and the
urban-rural income differential. Furthermore, the effect
in urban centers of modernization in food systems must
be taken into account: Processed foods, advertising,
and a highly elastic market for high-quality foodstuffs
all created the need to import inputs that had previously not been imported, in order to produce animal
protein foods increasingly in demand by the urban
population.

During the 1970s, on the other hand, "Latin American
economic disintegration" began to occur. In the last
few years we have not only witnessed the crisis but the
virtual collapse of the whole structure of common and
integrated markets. We have seen the passing away and
the discreet burial of the Latin American Free Trade
Association (LAFTA), which has now been replaced by the
Latin American Integration Association (LAIA), which may
be labeled "a feeble-trade association." Profound crises
have also arisen in the Andean Pact, which at one time
was offered as a very advanced and intensive integration
scheme. The Central American Common Market eventually
collapsed not only because of the political unrest in the
area but also as a result of a series of other previously
existing circumstances. Moreover, the Caribbean Common
Market is weak and has almost ceased to function. Very
little remains for two fundamental reasons: first,
because the economically stronger countries never took
regional and subregional integration very seriously
(even Mexico, which had been very enthusiastic to start
with, ended up by losing interest); second, because the
manufactures of several of the larger countries were
absorbed by the international market. Having established
this relationship, it was much easier to export outside
Latin America than it was to make the tremendous effort of
trading with the rest of Latin America, a process that,
apart from much red tape, meant passing through the Lima
clearinghouse and being faced with tension and internal
resistence. This is not the right place to go into an
analysis of the integration problems of Latin America,
but it is important to point out that there has been
disintegration and a neglect of cooperation possibilities
among the Latin American countries, although the formal

schemes were maintained.

Another significant aspect of the 1970s was that very conflicting short-term policies were introduced in response to the inflationary process. On one hand, the dimensions of the problem grew. It was not the same to cope with a rate of inflation of 10 percent as with one of 50 percent or more, or with an even higher rate compared to one of, say, 30 percent in previous years. This situation was aggravated by special or difficult external circumstances in many countries. For example, in the case of Mexico and Venezuela, the relationship of increased real expenditure (both investment and consumption) to the inflationary process was not fully realized. Several of the elementary aspects of Keynesian economic analysis were forgotten. The heterogeneous nature of each nation's economy, that is to say, scarcities, lack of productive capacity in many areas, excess capacity in others, and segmented labor markets, was not recognized either. Added to this, governments were incapable of controlling public-sector deficits and of undertaking appropriate tax policies for the implementation of an antiinflationary policy. In some countries where the rate of inflation was particularly high (Brazil, Argentina, and Chile), an acute crisis in short-term policy arose, although the attempted solutions to the problem were different. Brazil decided upon indexation, which was doomed to failure and collapse in the medium term, even with the minidevaluations introduced in order to aid exports. In Argentina and Chile, monetarist policies and exceedingly open economies, with overvaluation of national currency in relation to the dollar and European currencies, ended in failure, as they tended to repress the real economy and make revival of growth impossible.

Mexico and Venezuela, under excessive growth rates of real expenditure (in investment as well as in consumption), also made the mistake of maintaining overvalued currencies, which led to such gigantic current account balance-of-payments deficits that they had to resort to indiscriminate external financing, much of it short term. In the light of the well-known fact of Argentina's stagnant economy, as well as that of Chile (even though for a short period it showed a certain amount of growth), it is obvious that the appropriate balance between short-term and development policies was not achieved.

Yet another extraordinary phenomenon of the 1970s is worth noting: the sudden easy access to international bank loans, particularly from countries of the North, bypassing the multilateral financial agencies. At first there was a considerable flow of medium-term credit, with appropriate periods of grace and reasonable interest rates, for specific industrial projects and for creating infrastructure. Toward 1979 and 1980, a rise in international real interest rates occurred that coincided with further balance-of-payments problems of domestic origin. At the same time access to short-term foreign bank credit, considered by many to have been rendered too easy, was taken advantage of injudiciously and was actually encouraged by foreign banks on the basis of their ample liquidity. This led to a situation that by 1982 had become supercritical, as the banks would not or could not renew the greater part of the shorter-term maturities.

To the critical financial factors must be added the continued political instability of many Latin American countries, or at least the existence of a considerable number of cases of repression in which the probability of change taking place sooner or later was high. The least that could result under these circumstances was restraint in domestic private investment, irrespective of what the public sector did to promote growth. The obvious contrast is Mexico with its political stability and regular six-year changes in government. There were in fact times when the private sector was inhibited, but with the oil boom and the euphoria that ensued in 1977-1981, the private sector also participated to excess in the expansion of the economy and, like the government, did not assess the overall economic prospects sufficiently. The private sector in Mexico also had access to foreign credit as never before and committed the very same mistakes as regards the indiscriminate use of short-term credit.[2]

Within this whole panorama there is a wide range of situations. It is hardly necessary to emphasize the special characteristics (which go a long way back) of Brazil, Mexico, Venezuela, and other countries. The cases of Argentina, Chile, and Peru and the pathetic cases of the Central American region each have distinctive features. Studies undertaken by the UN Economic Commission for Latin America (ECLA) tend to overgeneralize. For example, in recent studies (those that were used as the background for important meetings in 1983) and in the report signed by the executive secretaries of ECLA and of the Latin American Economic System (SELA) at the request of the president of Ecuador,[3] this excessive generalization is evident. For reasons that may be easily explained, the position of each country--or at least each major country--is seldom examined individually or is examined very superficially. The tendency to treat Latin America globally results in overlooking some of the most important events that are occurring in the region. In the statistics supplied by ECLA on "Latin America," at times one is not sure of the coverage of figures because occasionally two or three countries are omitted or some country or other may have been omitted for the purpose of the analysis. Of course, it may be assumed that the position of six or seven of the major countries, because of their combined GDP, is indicative of the overall picture, but there are significant differences among them also.

DEVELOPMENT STRATEGIES FOR LATIN AMERICA

Let us now consider some of the strategic elements in the prospects for Latin America.

The first is related to the nature of industrialization in Latin America, which has not been analyzed or evaluated adequately. This applies to the most important country cases, as well as to the general characteristics and implications of industrialization undertaken within the context of an import-substitution policy, indiscriminate protectionist measures, and absence or insufficiency of planning. At the same time, the domestic market was left open to transnational corporations, which brought with them new technology and which produced goods that were important for the countries, such as tractors and electric motors, but also saturated the local market with a vast range of consumer goods--durables and others-- for which the technology used has at times been excessive in relation to the basic needs of Latin America. A good example of this is the fourteen-speed blender made available to the middle-class housewife, when there are low-income families still using the traditional methods of grinding and mixing whose needs would be satisfied with a single-speed blender of the kind available twenty years ago. This kind of excessive "technification" of consumption designed for highly developed societies and introduced into Latin America has been a waste of resources, encouraged by commercial advertising and television. The diversion of resources to these areas reduces the amounts available to fulfill basic needs.

For the most economically important Latin American countries at least, overprotected industrialization gives rise to the problem of how to achieve the capacity necessary to compete on the international market, assuming the aim of exporting manufactures to the highly industrialized countries and to other parts of the world. Due to the employment created, this would be a valuable supplement to the export of basic products. This is a problem that should be analyzed further, as its solution will be essential to development strategy from now on.

A second aspect of industrialization is the real cost of energy. In countries endowed with abundant natural resources of this kind, the pace of industrialization has been maintained partly through subsidies for energy consumption by industry in several different ways: for example, by offering natural gas and diesel almost without cost (Mexico), applying subsidies to the cost of electricity (several countries), and creating very favorable transport conditions by subsidizing gasoline. These factors have been beneficial to industry, trade, and services. Nevertheless, these subsidies can no longer be financed. The oil and electricity industries, and governments themselves, have had to back down and eliminate a large proportion of the subsidies. Even so, in Mexico in mid-1983, for example, the real price of oil products was barely one-fifth of the international price. This situation cannot continue for any length of time because it encourages neither the economic use of energy nor the introduction of changes in industrial equipment to substitute for that based on the use of cheap energy. Sooner or later even those countries with abundant hydrocarbon reserves will have to incorporate the real (opportunity) cost of energy into their development process.

Industrialization in Latin America has also been based on easily obtainable foreign technology, at least as far as the major modern industrial branches are concerned. This technology has been introduced and incorporated in the investment of transnational corporations or has been acquired through licensing agreements and contracts for the use of foreign industrial technology. A certain amount of control does in fact exist, and evaluations have been made of the cost of contracts. Restrictions have been established in some instances and a certain amount of leeway has been achieved in the restrictions imposed by the contracts themselves. However, technology substitution has been only slight because sufficient overall efforts have not been made to develop or adapt technology locally through public-sector research institutes and laboratories or by means of innovative research within enterprises themselves. Needless to say, there are exceptions in Latin America, and any one of us could mention some specific case of elaboration of technology or of adaptation of foreign technology for local use. Several Latin American countries also export technology. However, the technological foundations of Latin America itself are still very weak. What happens is that foreign technology is simply brought into the countries irrespective of its cost and of the harmful effect that this may eventually have on local scientific and technical development.

Latin American industrialization is also characterized by the lack of attention paid to medium and small industry. The greater part of industrial development has concentrated on the large industrial complexes, both private and public. Perhaps with the exception of Argentina, subcontracting to small business, as is done particularly in Japan and Europe, hardly exists in Latin America. Small industry is badly neglected from the point of view of technology, organization, financing, and the training of labor. This sector is also poorly organized as a whole. However, it could become a good source of employment, partly counteracting the labor-saving trends of big industry with its imported technology.

In considering development strategy, we must return to the agricultural sector and to the relationship of the rural to the urban industrial economy. There are, of course, cases of very prosperous farming and of very refined traditional agriculture, like the growing of coffee in Central America and Colombia. However, as stated earlier, there is no assurance of incentives for the farming sector as a whole. This does not mean necessarily advocating support for private farming as opposed to systems of communal land tenure and agrarian reform. It simply means that there must be incentives to encourage improved farming, the production of necessary foodstuffs, and the generation of adequate marketing, credit, and so on, for there is plenty of idle land and there are also outstanding examples of increased output and yields. In the majority of Latin American countries, however, farming performs badly. Perhaps Brazil has the possibility of exporting farm products and together with Argentina might help to solve the problem of Latin America's food deficit, although until now there has been insufficient evidence to support this idea.

The third factor in the development strategy that I would like to underline, which is related to the other two, is the problem of income distribution and the pattern of public expenditure in the face of social pressure that has had considerable influence on both. No matter how the distribution of income is measured, in almost all Latin American countries it is extremely uneven. Consequently, this situation does not ensure the creation of the large domestic market that has been the basis of industrial development in the major advanced countries. Inequality has its origin in the unequal distribution of property, differences in productivity and education, and many other factors, be they social, political, or whatever. As long as inequality exists, there cannot be an adequate domestic market. Moreover, the structure of public expenditure is unfortunately not making the creation of a large rural market any easier. Why? Because public expenditure in Latin America is organized on the basis of pressure from certain groups or vested interests, which is as far from any sort of planning as anyone could imagine. Large amounts are spent on education because this has to be done, for children must be sent to school and the system of education must be established and developed. But at the same time the quality of education at all levels has declined. Much is spent on creating infrastructure, sometimes with success, but more often with mediocre results and low productivity. Health budgets are large but most of the money is spent on enormous hospitals and very little on improving basic health, on preventive medicine, or on providing rural health care, which would help increase productivity and create future sources of income for the rural sector. And so on.

Quite apart from the vast and inefficient bureau-
cracies, public expenditure does very little to improve
the distribution of income; in fact it may even make it
worse. Military expenditures of many Latin American
countries have a negative effect both domestically and
on external accounts. There are studies that attempt to
show that provision of education, health, and other
services free of charge to low-income people partly
compensates for their relative poverty. Nevertheless,
this has not been proven; among other things, the tax
systems, in the form of indirect taxes, fall more heavily
on the income of poor families. The social-security
systems, which are as expensive as in wealthy countries,
are deficient in that sense and barely able to sustain
themselves financially.

Among the strategic factors is also to be found the
relative lack of good fiscal policies in the broader
sense of including not only taxation but also the pattern
of expenditure and the ways of financing budgets. Even
during the booms, adequate fiscal reform ensuring a broad
tax base, independently of the tax schedules established,
has not been achieved. If introduced, it would at least
cover the financing of current public expenditure.
During the boom in Mexico during 1977-1981, the tax
system became inelastic, for it was left almost untouched; indeed, on the contrary, enormous fiscal and
other kinds of subsidies were granted.

Let us move on to what may be termed "slow-acting
factors" that, taken together, become important to the
whole prospect. We are used to thinking of any rate of
3 percent as being insignificant but, if this rate is
applied to population, it means a doubling over a period
of only twenty-three years. The birthrate in Latin
America has in fact declined, as a consequence of socioeconomic and organizational factors and of deliberate
family-planning policies. Birthrates are still high,
however. In Mexico, for example, the number of births
per thousand has fallen from forty-five, ten years ago,
to thirty-one at the present moment. If mortality is
calculated at seven per thousand, population growth
is still 2.4 percent per annum. The fall in Latin
American population growth has been achieved through the
joint contribution of socioeconomic factors and policies
established for this effect. However, this rate is
higher than the average for Third World countries and has
had, and will continue to have, repercussions as new
cohorts stream into the labor market. In actual fact,
Mexico's problem, which can be extended to Venezuela,
Colombia, Brazil, and the Central American countries,
is that despite economic growth, and assuming adequate
patterns of expenditure, it is not absorbing into employment (nor is it capable of absorbing) the increase in the
labor force. If we add to this the fact that women are
increasing their participation in the work force--a

cultural and social factor--and that in many cases they
are preferred for certain types of work, we see that a
situation of permanent oversupply of labor is being
created, reinforced by many other factors related to the
rural economy, the continual introduction of labor-saving
technology, and so on. Mortality will continue to fall,
which is often forgotten. There are countries in Latin
America where the infant mortality rate is very high,
particularly in the vast rural areas. As the mortality
rate falls, the real probability of achieving the same
population growth as Europe becomes more and more remote.
     Because of the nature of the educational system and
other factors, including the rural origins of the labor
force, the oversupply of labor will be mainly unskilled.
This situation partly explains, in Mexico, the intense
international migration of the labor force toward the
north. A main attraction in this case is also the wage
differential offered by the United States together with
the demand for workers for certain specific occupations.
Massive migration can also be expected from Central
America toward Mexico and the United States, although
economic incentives are obviously not the only cause.
These are all long-term factors; we must not be influenced by what happened yesterday or last year but must
take note of the trends. Concurrently, there has been
very heavy internal migration, as in Brazil toward São
Paulo, which will continue well into the future. In
Mexico internal migration was effective while Mexico City
and other industrial cities were able to absorb part of
it. However, this process could become inefficient and
even contribute to social instability in the future.
     A new slow-acting, long-term factor is the environ-
ment. Eleven years ago in the United Nations Conference
on the Human Environment, in Stockholm, a Brazilian
delegate publicly declared that Brazil wanted pollution
because it meant industrialization. The Brazilians
obviously must now regret having made this statement and,
in fact, have changed their policy. The impact of
industrialization, urban concentration, and modern farming on the environment has begun to make itself felt, and
solutions are bound to be costly. This is another real
cost incurred as a result of development that the
economy will have to absorb. There is no local solution
to this problem, for the science and technology required
to counteract the negative effects on the environment are
not locally available, but must be brought in from abroad.
There is no use stating that solar energy will replace
hydrocarbons, for Latin America is far from being able to
introduce solar energy on a large scale.
     Another slow-acting factor that has both positive
and negative aspects is the evolution of the educational
systems. During a meeting of experts at the Inter-
American Development Bank some years ago, an Argentine
economist argued that by 1990 all school-age children in

Latin America would be actually enrolled in primary education.[4] However, the dropout rate is still very high in most countries. But he added that the sequel to this social evolution and population growth would be an eventual "university explosion." Unfortunately, this would be an explosion from the point of view of numbers and not of knowledge. Furthermore, it is doubtful whether there is a single case in Latin America where it could be stated that, in the last fifteen years, the standard of university education has not declined, despite modernization and the linking of teaching and research in some departments and postgraduate schools or institutes. Moreover, the overall level of research is very low. There are literate people, more educated people, more who have had technical education, and more people going through university. But there is something desperately wrong with the aims of the educational systems and with the quality of education and teaching, the libraries, the laboratories, and so forth. Apart from this, there are almost no scholarships, nor books, nor services.

Behind all this is the theory of human capital from which it is inferred, not always logically, that all investment in education is worthwhile. But one must also consider the real outcome of such investment, and this is a serious problem that cannot be solved in the short run, especially not in countries with the dynamic population growth that, as pointed out earlier, is characteristic of the majority of Latin American countries.

The lack of scientific and technological research constitutes yet another slow-acting factor, but one that is cumulative in the negative sense. We have been discussing this problem now for ten to fifteen years. We have at our disposal all the literature on the subject, all the national science and technology councils, and the influence of the UN Educational, Scientific, and Cultural Organization (UNESCO), the OECD, and other international agencies. However, the work done in science and technology in Latin America, particularly research, except for a few remarkable exceptions, is very poor. No country has ever reached a high level of development without concentrated efforts being made in research in basic science and applied technology. In Latin America we are still not doing this, even though there are a number of instances where considerable effort is being made.

Among the slow-acting factors there is also health. One needs merely to quote the figures for nutrition in Latin America: Roughly a third of the population--120 million people--is undernourished; in certain areas and certain countries the proportion is even higher. The incidence of undernourishment on disease; the lack of drinking water, waste-disposal services, and even elementary hygiene; overcrowding in urban dwellings and marginal urban areas; and contamination, all of which are important elements in many large cities, contrast with the modern system of hospitals and the emphasis placed on curative as opposed to the expansion of preventive medicine. Although there has been an improvement and mortality has declined, the consequences of these problems are very important, especially the economic ones.

There are both positive and negative aspects in all the preceding questions. It must be emphasized that these are slow-acting factors. The 3 percent rate, sometimes considered to be insignificant, over a period of twenty years can become enormous and is capable of creating inflexibility in the systems and of altering parameters.

LATIN AMERICAN INTERDEPENDENCE

We in Latin America are faced with a problem of enormous complexity. We are not in the same situation as in the 1930s, exporting a few primary products, importing all kinds of manufactures, and having very few problems involving financial interaction with the exterior. Today Latin America is intertwined in a whole series of international and domestic complications, and a lack of data sometimes makes it very difficult to evaluate the situation. The fact is that we have become deeply involved in a system of interdependence (whatever the value judgment about this term). This is at least true for the major Latin American countries. Unfortunately we have never taken advantage of the real international context of this interdependence that could be used to our favor externally. On the other hand, we have utilized it to excess in the negative sense in, for example, external financing and the ease with which we have imported the necessary and the superfluous with these funds, even technology, while we have neglected long-term development strategy and technological substitution.

We are interdependent and vulnerable in this crisis of the last few years, in a completely different way than in the past. If we do not continue to act within this interdependence, we shall be unable to continue growing. This deserves more study and consideration.

THE PROSPECTS FOR LATIN AMERICA

Several remarks may be ventured in relation to the prospects. The deterioration of the external sector lends itself to a more interesting analysis by individual countries than for the region as a whole, due to the wide variety of conditions. There are countries like Mexico, Brazil, Argentina, Venezuela, and Chile, for example, that have a larger debt but a greater capacity to negotiate and come to terms with international agencies

and with creditors. Others, whose foreign debt per
capita is large but whose aggregate figures are relatively small, are faced in any event with serious problems
of liquidity and have a very reduced capacity to service
the debt: Costa Rica is an example.

In this respect, to treat Latin America as a whole
would appear to be particularly difficult, because it
would probably lead us to adopt a very pessimistic
attitude regarding the region's overall capacity to face
the financial and external debt. However, if the problem
is examined country by country, the external aspect is
practically solved. Renegotiation, rescheduling of the
debt, renewed confidence, and improvement in domestic
policy have been achieved in order to face the problem.
Mexico is an outstanding example. In the case of Brazil,
there are still disagreements to be ironed out with the
International Monetary Fund. Chile and Argentina are
working toward a solution. A number of difficulties still
persist in Venezuela. However, these aspects of the
situation can be expected to sort themselves out,
especially if economic recovery in the industrialized
countries becomes steady. Undoubtedly, there will be
very difficult problems for some of the smaller Latin
American countries, but the outlook for the major countries should not inspire pessimism.

Unfortunately, I see no short-term prospects of
reaffirming Latin American integration policies from the
point of view of schemes for common markets, free-trade
areas, and so on. Other aspects of Latin America
cooperation that have been developed mainly through the
SELA are still too weak. Some efforts have arisen as a
result of the emergency situation but have not met with
much confidence on the part of the major countries. However, bilateral or trilateral action could be undertaken
among Latin American countries (in some cases this has
been done), which may turn out to be important. Perhaps
this is the course the major Latin American countries
should take in the next few years in order to avoid the
treaties, the agreements, and the rhetoric and to turn to
real reciprocally advantageous action. (In the case of
Central America this would depend on many other factors.)

In the medium term, what we should be worried about
is Latin America's capacity to redefine its objectives as
regards development, not necessarily for the region as a
whole but more in terms of individual countries or groups
of countries. These objectives would have to be long-
range but would have to be expressed in medium-term
programs, which in turn would have to be reconciled with
short-term stabilization and adjustment policies currently
being defined and being put into practice. Obviously,
such policies have their difficult and even dangerous
points, for all adjustments of the present type imply
repressed expenditure, particularly in investment, which
slows down economic growth, generates a high level of

unemployment, and forces large sectors of the economy to accept lower real incomes.

In my opinion, the most important problem facing us is how to reconcile the implementation of short-term programs, social agreements, and adjustments, with the resumption of former trends, or the 5 to 6 percent growth rate that Latin American countries were accustomed to, and at the same time to redefine the objectives related to development so as to avoid getting caught again in the same situation. Unfortunately, in most of Latin America this is not being tackled in a clearly defined way.

Let us assume that in the longer run, say over the next ten years, the economy of the industrialized countries picks up. The question is, at what rate? At present the rate of recovery is being exaggerated because it is being calculated from a very low base and from previous declines. If the medium-term GDP forecast for the OECD countries is 2 to 3 percent per annum, it is doubtful that this would have much effect on Latin America or other parts of the Third World, except perhaps to steady somewhat the prices of some basic commodities. It must not be overlooked that the industrialized countries themselves compete in the international market for basic commodities and that they are not overly concerned about protecting the interests of developing countries. The oil market would also not appear to indicate a future real price increase exceeding about 1 percent per annum over a period of several years. Therefore, the effects of the recovery of the developed countries on the trade of the developing countries--Latin America in particular-- would probably not be very noticeable.

The consequences for the North-South relationship would be that Latin America would have to find a pragmatic course in order to take advantage of all the openings provided by the lowering of tariff and non-tariff barriers, the GATT, general preferences, and so on and to obtain special agreements with the European Economic Community (EEC), Japan, and others. It will be necessary to try and penetrate the barrier of protectionist restrictions and discrimination established by the northern countries. This would be an important aspect, not for global negotiations or for those on the New International Economic Order that have been the subject of so much rhetoric at the United Nations and in the Third World, but simply as part of the strategy of each individual country or group of countries. I do not feel that a "concerted Latin American effort" would work under current external conditions.

Second, we should explore even further the possibility of establishing links with the rest of the Third World, which is something that has been sorely neglected. There have been many cases of exports to African and Asian countries, of exchange programs and technical cooperation. But this potential has only just begun to

be explored and could be very profitable for the
development of Third World countries. There is a tendency
in Latin America, and even in ECLA, to act as if the rest
of the Third World did not exist. We tend to forget that
there is India, that China is important, that two or three
of the African countries have great industrial potential,
that Southeast Asia is fast growing, and that the Arab
countries also show promise. It would be of considerable
significance if specific posibilities for cooperation and
interchange and for interrelation in trade, technology,
financing, and other areas were to be found other than by
the formal signing of treaties and agreements. The
interrelation between countries of the Third World would
place the latter within a strategy of self-reliance,
but at present it has not gone beyond wishful thinking
and rhetoric; that is to say, it has not materialized
in the form of specific action. In the meetings of the
nonaligned countries, in the Group of Seventy-Seven at
UNCTAD, one fails to discover what is meant in practice
by collective self-reliance or real cooperation among
Third World countries. Similarly, what is said in certain
regions, such as Africa, amounts to little more than
declarations, signing of agreements, and so on, with very
little application--as in Latin America today. Nevertheless, Latin America--at least those countries that are
willing and capable of doing so--must make an effort to
open up to the rest of the Third World, to selected
countries in those areas, in order to benefit from the
useful effects of interaction.

The framework for such relationships may seem
pessimistic, but, at bottom, I do not feel that the South
can expect very much from the North. The northern
countries have their own structural problems and conflicts
among themselves, massive unemployment, policies of
recovery that may fail, and disillusionment over the
cooperation with the South, despite the first and second
Brandt reports (which do not appear to have had much
impact). The industrialized countries are looking inward.
We in Latin America, along with Africa and Asia, will
have to do the same, for there is no alternative. We
shall have to continue industrialization with import
substitution, while paying closer attention to international competitiveness. We shall have to continue to
protect ourselves in the presence of the GATT and the
idea of economic openness coming from the North. We
shall have to make a much greater internal effort,
evaluate our problems more deeply, and stop expecting the
solutions to our problems to come from outside. In this
context, Latin America (one speaks in general terms but
thinks, of course, of a few countries with larger
capability) possesses the elements necessary for positive
action, as is the case with many countries in Africa and
Asia.

Lastly, there is the relationship between Latin America and the European socialist economies whose trade with Latin America has followed essentially the old colonial model of importing raw materials and exporting equipment (and very little else). Financing has been more in keeping with the interests of these countries and not with the needs of Latin America or the Third World in general. However, if these countries are able to limit their expenditure on defense and make their civil economy more efficient, they will also have the potential to participate in the selective interchange and relationship that Latin America could establish pragmatically, without the need for general agreements. It is a well-known fact that the socialist countries are also faced with structural problems in industry and other basic activities, as are the Western market economies. These are problems that they will have to solve among themselves and with the West, and they are more important than the problems they may have with the South, at least in the field of economic relations.

NOTES

1. See Víctor L. Urquidi, "América Latina y el Orden Económico Internacional: Población, Alimentos, Energéticos," Demografía y Economía, vol. 13, no. 4 (40) (El Colegio de México, 1979), pp. 393-404.
2. For data on the Mexican boom and its background, see Víctor L. Urquidi, "Perspectivas de la Economia Mexicana ante el Auge Petrolero," Revista de Occidente, no. 14 (Madrid, June-July 1982), pp. 45-64; also Víctor L. Urquidi, "Not by Oil Alone: The Outlook for Mexico," Current History, vol. 1, no. 472 (February 1982), pp. 78-81, 90.
3. Carlos Alzamora Traverso, for SELA, and Enrique V. Iglesias, for CEPAL (Comisión Económica Para América Latina), Bases para una Respuesta de América Latina a la Crisis Económica Internacional, United Nations, Economic and Social Council, Doc. E/CEPAL/G.1246, May 16, 1983.
4. José Dagnino Pastore, "Nivel y Estructura de los Costos y del Financiamiento,Educativo en Latinoamérica," in Mario Brodersohn and Maria Ester Sanjurjo, Financia-miento de la Educación en América Latina, México, 1978, pp. 144-197.

3
The International Scene and the Latin American External Debt

Luciano Tomassini

The force with which the current international crisis has hit Latin America and the region's high external debt are, fundamentally, consequences of the changes that have taken place in the international system over the last fifteen years and of the transformation of the Latin American economies and societies, including the changes in the ways in which they both participate in the world economy. The situation is also undoubtedly a consequence of the domestic policies followed by these countries in recent years; however, these policies represent a response--right or wrong--to the new conditions prevailing during this period on both the regional and the international scenes. The external indebtedness of these countries may be viewed as a variable that depends on other, more far-reaching factors. This means that the causes of the phenomenon may be interpreted in a variety of ways and, moreover, that more comprehensive, longer-term solutions may be sought than when only financial considerations are taken into account.

Since the late 1960s the rigidly hierarchical world that emerged from World War II, where international relations revolved around the concept of security, has begun to be eroded by a strong trend toward a fragmentation of world power and a vigorous process of transnationalization. As a result, the interests of the various national societies now overlap each other in an increasing variety of ways, thus promoting the flow of international relations. The international economic crisis, the first symptoms of which go back to the late 1960s, altered the evolution of productivity and the traditional distribution of specializations in the industrialized countries, putting an end to the cycle of unprecedented expansion of the previous twenty years and paving the way for the producer countries to raise the price of oil; this in turn led to a large surplus of liquidity and created a climate of extraordinary international financial permissiveness. In the meantime, some of the developing countries, including the larger countries of

Latin America, progressed more rapidly than others, achieving an intermediate stage of development and becoming more closely involved in the international economy. This made it possible--and even inevitable--for them to take advantage of the opportunities and assume the risks posed to them by the international environment much more intensely than in the past. This explains why the current international economic crisis has had such an unusually strong impact on the Latin American countries, far greater than the impact of the crisis of the 1930s, at which time these countries were in a much better position to disconnect themselves from the external cycle.

This chapter includes an analysis of the changes that have occurred in the international system, the characteristics of the current world economic crisis, and how the Latin American countries have been exposed to these factors as a result of the transformations they have undergone during the past few decades. In the last section, some conclusions are drawn with regard to the causes and characteristics of the external indebtedness of Latin America, and finally, some extremely tentative suggestions are made regarding possible responses to that problem in the light of the aforementioned analysis.

THE TRANSFORMATION OF THE INTERNATIONAL SYSTEM

The international system that emerged from World War II and lasted until the late 1960s has since then undergone a complete transformation.

During the immediate postwar period, the structure of world power was rigidly hierarchical and bipolar and was strongly influenced by the cold war. That structure began to change significantly as a result of (1) the relative decline of U.S. power; (2) the appearance of tensions within the trilateral system and, in particular, the Atlantic alliance; (3) the internal difficulties experienced by the Soviet bloc and the exhaustion of the model it represented; and (4) the increasing development and external projection of certain Third World countries and the trend toward fragmentation of the international system, a phenomenon that makes it necessary to seek formulas for collegiate management of the system.

According to the "new orthodox" school of thought,[1] the power of the United States in the world declined sharply during the 1970s, particularly vis-à-vis the Soviet Union and the Middle East; this may explain the concern revealed by the fact that in 1980 "a 42% plurality of Americans named foreign policy as the 'most important problem facing the country today'--ahead of the economy and substantially ahead of energy concerns."[2]

Paradoxically, the decline of U.S. power has gone hand in hand with the appearance of a profound malaise in the socialist camp. Although Soviet military power has

increased at a rapid pace so that it is at least
comparable with that of the United States, looked upon
from a longer-term structural point of view, this increase may be a sign not of strength but rather of weak-
ness. The instability of the Soviet presence in the Third
World, the invasion of Afghanistan (considered a defensive
measure that the Soviet empire had to take on its own
border), and the strong challenge that Poland represents
for the survival of the political and social system on
which the entire Soviet bloc is built are matters that
raise very serious questions that have not yet been
adequately weighed.[3] To these are added the difficulties
that the Soviet economy has consistently had to face, both
as regards its food base and as regards the production and
distribution of consumer durables and the urgent need to
acquire Western technology.[4] The Soviet model as an
alternative for the construction of other societies,
particularly in the Third World, would appear to be
vanishing amid the frustration of the populations of the
socialist countries and the growing militarization of
those regimes.

The tensions that have arisen within the trilateral
system constitute another factor of change. The most
recent indication of this may be seen in the conflicts
that have arisen within the Atlantic alliance. The fact
that the United States has unilaterally substituted a new
version of power politics for détente has alienated its
European allies. It should be remembered that détente
has produced positive results, in both economic and
political terms, for the Europeans, but not so much for
the United States. Moreover, the globalism of U.S.
foreign policy is incompatible with the European approach,
according to which détente can be "divided," depending
on which questions and regions are at stake. The conflict
generated by the Soviet gas pipeline issue reflected this
tension.[5]

The emergence of the Third World on the global
scene, around the middle of the postwar period, constitutes a new factor of instability and change. Today
this group is represented by over one hundred countries,
half of which became independent during this period.
Many of them have reached intermediate stages of development and have promoted accelerated industrialization
processes, thus becoming more closely integrated in the
international system. The movement of nonaligned countries, the Group of Seventy-Seven, and OPEC have come
into being, and the newly industrializing countries
(NICs) are now an essential part of the world economic
and financial picture. The viewpoints of the various
regions of the developing world must now be taken into
account in the management of international relations
while conflicts of regional origin are increasingly
affecting the stability of the world in general. This
latter circumstance is aggravated by the repeated attempts

of the two superpowers to view these situations within
the context of the East-West conflict.[6]

All these factors have brought about a phenomenon of
"diffusion of power," giving rise to a more interdependent
but also more fragmented world. This new structure of
world power presents the developing countries--and
especially the Latin American countries--with a complex
balance of limitations and opportunities.

These trends have led us to the point where we are
moving from a world dominated by strategic security
considerations and by confrontation between the two
superpowers to a world characterized by a certain degree
of détente and by an atmosphere that is more propitious
to the pursuit of other interests--economic, technological,
social, ecological, and cultural--in relations between
nations. To the fragmentation of world economic and
political power are added the increasing complexity and
dispersion of strategic conflicts. This process has also
been stimulated by the appearance of global problems--
such as energy, the environment, stagflation, or external
indebtedness--on the solution of which depends the welfare
of ever-larger sectors of the national societies.

These societies in turn are also undergoing transformations. The prolonged period of economic growth,
social development, and democratic strengthening
experienced by the industrial societies during the postwar period has steadily raised the standard of living and
promoted the strengthening and diversification of the
civil societies of these countries. Under pressure from
their societies, the national states have committed themselves to a wider and wider range of objectives that
include, in addition to national security, economic
development, the raising of incomes, the maintenance of
employment, the preservation of the environment, and the
protection of the cultural identity and quality of life
of the society concerned. These objectives have become
a decisive force in the external relations among states.
At the same time, as the civil society has grown and
become articulated into many different interest groups,
the latter have aspired to take into their hands an increasing proportion of the issues that concern the
community. As responsibilities have been transferred
from the state to the civil society and nongovernmental
groups have therefore proliferated, in a world in which
the performance of such responsibilities depends more and
more on international factors, these groups have often
had to seek the satisfaction of their interests at the
external level.[7]

These new trends, which may be seen at both the
worldwide and the national levels, reveal the fact that a
transition is underway from the international system
dominated by the concepts of "power" and "security" that
generally prevailed during the immediate postwar period
to one based on "interdependence" and aimed at maximizing

the domestic welfare of national societies.[8]

The "realistic" approach to international relations that prevailed earlier during the postwar period was based on several assumptions. The first was that international politics were centered on the interests of the superpowers and that the smaller states should align themselves with one or the other of them; this gave rise to the formation of blocs or spheres of influence within which the hegemonic power settled conflicts and imposed a certain order. Relations between the blocs consisted of a precarious coexistence governed by certain rules. The second assumption was that national societies were relatively simple units from the standpoint of their external projection, with their actions depending on a limited number of objectives, which were usually subordinated to the need to maintain peace and security. The third assumption, one that followed from the first two, was that the agenda of international affairs was limited to a small number of items and that these were ranked according to a rigid order of priorities, with the question of security indisputably holding the first place. The fourth assumption was that the agents acting in international life were basically homogeneous and that they were represented by national states that did not recognize the legitimacy of any other agents having the capacity to act between or within states. It is not surprising that the fifth assumption was equally limited in that it held that the repertory of ways in which a state could use power to influence another state was limited mainly to political and military matters and that the arenas in which such power could be deployed were also limited, well defined, and well known.

All these assumptions were called to question as a result of the newly emerging trends. At this point one might venture to propose the hypothesis that, contrary to the case in the past, (1) international relations are currently run by a growing number of centers of power; (2) the external action of these centers of power is aimed at meeting a much broader range of objectives than in the past; (3) the agenda of international affairs is more diversified, more complex, and less hierarchical; (4) international matters are managed by many new state and private agents; and (5) these agents can use power resources in a large variety of nontraditional ways and in a much wider range of arenas that are more likely to change and to be interrelated than before.

These trends have given rise to a new type of transnational system in which one may reconstruct the structure and operation of many "spheres," "games," or "circuits" that operate on the basis of the hypothesis just described, using the agents and power resources contained in it and that link in many new and diverse ways the different national societies in the pursuit of a wide range of specific interests. From this perspective, one might postulate that transnationalized circuits have arisen in the fields of energy, food, industry, technology, finance, strategy, science, ideology, culture, and religion. Each of these circuits has certain very specific features. The conditions under which the different countries have access to each of them and a country's relative position within a circuit do not depend exclusively on its position within the international hierarchy (whether in the context of the East-West conflict or of North-South relations) but rather on its relative position with respect to the interests at stake in the circuits and to the division of labor established within each circuit to attain these interests.[9] The international structure is becoming more fluid and interdependent, but paradoxically it is also becoming more fragmented and unsettled. The crisis with respect to the development style prevailing in the industrialized countries, discussed next, tends to accentuate this trend. Within this scenario, the developing, and especially the Latin American, countries that are more integrated in the international system have become more vulnerable to external influences even though at the same time their maneuvering room has expanded, so that they must juggle a complex set of risks and opportunities.

THE CRISIS IN THE WORLD ECONOMY

The prevailing postwar style of development, which was based on the ideology of modernization and growth and on the global projection of such a model through the demonstration effect brought about by the transnational corporations and their supportive institutional apparatus, was made possible by the international structure that prevailed during the early postwar period. The main features of this structure were the hegemony of the United States and the predominance of considerations centered on the maintenance of that nation's strategic security, as well as that of the other countries with which it had defense commitments within the context of the cold war. This international structure made possible the extension of a development style that both expressed and promoted the interests of the United States and, as time went on, of its main allies. As the structure of the international system broke down, so did the attempt to expand and disseminate the development style developed by its central power.

Hence, since the late 1960s the world economy has entered into a state of profound crisis. There can no longer be any question that the crisis is structural--rather than merely cyclical--in nature. It has dealt a serious blow to the developing world, particularly to the Latin American countries that had become more integrated in the international economy. The first manifestation of

this crisis took place in the ecological foundation of the
economic growth process; it later became evident that the
crux of the problem was the industrial transformation of
the advanced societies; finally, and over the shorter
term, the virulence of the crisis was fully manifested in
the financial disequilibria that occurred at the world
level and that have had a particularly strong impact on
the developing countries, especially in Latin America.

Although according to this hypothesis the breakdown
of the prevailing postwar development style stemmed from
the industrial transformation of the advanced countries,
it must be stressed again that the first signs of the
problem were to be found in the disequilibria that
affected the ecological base. These disequilibria were
caused, among other things, by the recent trends in
population growth, the various factors limiting efforts to
increase foodstuffs' production, the uncertainty and increased costs involved in the supply of energy and industrial raw materials, the problems posed by the
excessive concentration of industrial growth in a few
geographic areas, and the threat of environmental
pollution, generated fundamentally by the high density of
urban population and economic activity.

The first report on these issues, published under
the sponsorship of the Club of Rome, started a debate
that gave rise to a number of reactions at the theoretical
level. The decisions adopted by OPEC in 1973 in respect
to international oil trade sounded the alarm at the level
of reality.[10]

Thus, it began to be recognized that the rate and
concentration of growth in the large industrial centers
had taken place at the expense of the environment, the
natural resources base of economic development in general,
and the countries' ecological capacity to sustain productive activity. An awareness arose of the physical
limits to economic growth.

In the final analysis, the awareness that such
limits did exist was one of the signs that the advanced
societies were reaching the frontiers of their postwar
industrial development. "The crisis of the world economy
is above all an industrial crisis," begins one of the most
recent reports on the world economy's prospects, written
from a European viewpoint.[11] One might argue as to
whether the weakening of the momentum of industrial growth
that has been evident in recent years in most of the
developed countries is leading to a postindustrial society
or to the industrialization of services, in which this
tertiary sector will become the moving force behind
economic growth and ensure the dissemination of the
technological transformations on which the progress of
these societies is to be based. One may also argue as to
whether the world economy has entered a prolonged stage
of slow growth or whether the rapid adoption of
technological changes already underway will lead it to

recover its past dynamism. One may attach a great deal
of importance to the limitations imposed by the supply
of energy and natural resources or may take an optimistic
view of the potential of recent technological developments in connection with energy and the production of new
materials. Whatever the predictions may be with regard to
these questions, the fact remains that world industry is
going through a profound transformation, that recent
technological advances are very important, and that human-
kind is on the threshold of an industrial revolution the
like of which has not been seen since the late eighteenth
century.

The extraordinary growth of international trade
during the early postwar period was fundamentally the
result of the increased demand for those consumer durables
that made it possible to adopt the "American way of life"
--and to spread it all over the world, a demand met by
increasing specialization among the industrialized
countries in accordance with Ricardian principles. Thus,
each country attained a predominant position on the
market in certain industrial sectors, and this situation
led to constant price increases. These, along with the
reconstruction of Europe and the emergence of Japan as a
great industrial power, stimulated competition and
transformed the range of specializations already achieved
by the different countries. At the same time, the growth
of the demand for durables that had been the basis for
the development of the more dynamic industries during the
immediate postwar period began to weaken toward the end
of the 1960s and was followed by a substantial contraction, while the composition of the demand changed as
the markets for durables became saturated.

A factor contributing to this was the change in the
preferences of the public in a growing number of social
sectors as a result of the profound sociocultural
transformations that have been changing life-styles in
the industrial societies that have led to the spreading
of attitudes attaching less importance to having more of
the same and more oriented toward values relating to the
quality of life. These trends have been associated with
the decline of productivity in the industrialized
countries, the fall of investments and the reduction of
the profitability of enterprises, the appearance of idle
capacity in a growing number of industries, the slowdown
in the rate of technological innovation, the increased
operating costs of systems of production and of societies
themselves resulting from increases in wages and in
public expenditures, and, in general, the loss of
competitiveness in an ever-greater number of productive
activities.

The aforementioned process of transnationalization,
which allowed for the extension of the prevailing postwar
development style, also allowed for the subsequent changes
in the market structure, in the pattern of technological

innovation, and in the form of organization that world production began to adopt in order to adjust to those changes. Here there tends to be a new international division of labor; although its future shape cannot yet be clearly perceived, it is already causing conflicts among developed countries and could alter the ways in which the developing countries have traditionally participated in the world economy.

The developed countries had to make major adjustments in order to cope with these changes. The adjustments were even more painful in the case of the developing countries that had become more integrated in the world economy. They had dependent and precarious economic structures and lacked resources to palliate the negative effects of the crisis on their economic growth or to finance the trans- formations the crisis made necessary. Both types of countries tried in different ways to make these adjust- ments as smooth as possible by making massive use of external financial resources. This was possible because of the extraordinary liquidity of the world economy from the beginning of the 1970s, when after almost half a century a rebirth of the private financial markets began as a result of the weakening of the dollar and of the accumulation of surpluses by OPEC countries.

THE TRANSFORMATION OF THE DEVELOPING COUNTRIES

The remarkable growth rates of an increasing number of developing countries throughout the last twenty-five years and their gradual integration into the inter- national economy have given rise to profound changes in their economic, political, and social systems, as well as in their relations with the industrialized countries. As has already been noted, in the early 1950s no one had much hope that the development of the countries of the periphery might be brought about by stimuli from the external markets and go hand in hand with their gradual integration into the world economy. Instead, it was argued that they should promote industrialization policies based on import substitution together with mechanisms aimed at regulating the international markets for raw materials.

During the early stages of industrialization, many developing countries tried to replace imports of manu- facturers by domestic production, particularly in the case of Latin America. Import substitution was aimed at in- creasing the proportion of national consumption that was satisfied by local production. One of the immediate reasons for adopting this strategy was that the developing countries were experiencing chronic balance-of-payments crises because of the structural situation of external strangulation in which they found themselves. This strategy was also in line with the long-term political objectives of the national governments. On the one hand, it was hoped that import substitution would make it possible to reduce outlays in foreign currency and increase the autonomy of those countries. On the other, the governing elites found that the demands of certain social sectors whose bargaining power was increasing as a result of the development process itself could be satisfied by applying a policy designed to encourage simultaneously growth, income distribution, and employment. To the extent that domestic demand allowed for the creation of new industries that might some day--and this consideration has now become a very important one--be able to compete with the external producers displaced, it was possible to justify the levels of protection applied with the arguments that had been put forth in favor of infant industry in the past. Naturally, to the extent that this condition was not met, the import-substitution strategy was bound to come up against serious limitations. In other words, industry had either to begin to generate the foreign exchange required for its subsequent development or to adjust its growth rate to the availability of foreign exchange generated by primary production, which in certain cases had been given second priority in the context of these economic strategies. In practice, what usually happened was that imports of consumer goods were replaced by imports of capital goods and inputs required for the operation and expansion of the new industrial parks.

In time, many countries acknowledged that the tendency to use foreign exchange without generating it was not inherent to manufacturing, and one after another they reached the conclusion that they should place less emphasis on protection and more on efficiency, competitiveness, and export promotion. Since the mid-1970s (and even earlier in the case of island states or entrepôt city states that had no alternative) many countries have begun to try out, at different rates and in different ways--some of them clearly exaggerated, as in the case of some Latin American countries--new strategies based on the liberalization of the domestic market and the opening up of their economies to the exterior.

Although this transition has often been portrayed as a struggle between rival schools, the perspective of time has now enabled us to realize that these stages should not in fact be considered as alternatives, but rather as complementary processes. For many Third World countries, the import-substitution strategy was the only option available at a given historical moment, in light of the stage of development at which they found themselves and the existence of an adverse external situation. In many cases, import substitution provided a basis not only for industrialization but also for the consolidation of a country's national identity. Moreover, not only did they not see at the time any essential conflict between

producing for domestic and external markets, but their
domestic markets often served as a springboard for reaching the international markets. Although it is true that
the growth strategies and forms of external relationship
of the developing countries did subsequently undergo
changes, it is no less true, as the Brandt Commission's
report pointed out a few years ago, that these changes
did not take place overnight:

> They cannot accomplish these changes suddenly;
> but since the 1960s many developing countries
> have moved towards strategies to promote exports
> and to offset disadvantages due to the insulation
> of their domestic markets. . . .
> A number of countries which have introduced
> export-oriented policies have been able to exploit
> their comparative advantage in world markets.
> They include some Latin American countries with
> a fairly long history of national independence,
> and some island and city state economies which
> were from the outset obliged to rely on export
> demand. Once industrialization has taken root,
> it is not only in labour-intensive industries
> like clothing or leather products, but also in
> moderately capital-intensive industries like
> electronics, steel and shipbuilding, that they
> can become highly competitive in world markets.[12]

As a result of the implementation of the strategies,
as the same report mentions, all in all manufactures
are looming much larger in the total exports of developing countries. In 1955 they made up only 10 percent of
their nonfuel exports; ten years later they were 20 percent; and in 1975 they passed 40 percent.
This growth of exports evidently reflects more
complex transformations in the economies that have
reached intermediate stages of development, although it
is true that this growth was concentrated in a limited
number of countries. In view of the above, I must
comment, even though in general terms, on the increasing
differentiation that has occurred in recent years among
the countries of the periphery and on the situation of
the developing countries that are at an intermediate
stage.
The literature on the subject has proliferated in
recent years. The first report on the evolution of the
international economy, prepared by the World Bank in 1978,
provides a useful, although controversial, point of
departure for a discussion of the question:

> The developing countries have grown impressively
> over the past twenty-five years: income per
> person has increased by almost 3 percent a year,
> with the annual growth rate accelerating from

about 2 percent in the 1950s to 3.4 percent in
the 1960s. Contrasted with what little can be
gleaned of the experience of these countries
before 1950, this is a substantial improvement
over the historical record. Moreover, it
compares extremely favorably with the growth
rates achieved by the now developed countries
over the period of their industrialization.[13]

The report went on to note, however, that there had been
marked differences in the performance of individual
developing countries in this period: "Growth rates have
generally been lower in the low income countries of Africa
and Asia, where the majority of the world's poor live.
In countries accounting for half the population of the
developing world, income per person has risen by less
than 2 percent a year."

It must be borne in mind, therefore, that the
developing countries differ greatly as regards the size
of their economies, their income levels, their resources,
their economic structures, their organizational forms,
their technical capabilities, and their links with the
world economy. Thus, a legitimate distinction may be
drawn, at least, between: (1) the oil-exporting countries, (2) countries that are at intermediate stages of
development, and (3) the less developed countries, or low-
income countries, that make up the so-called Fourth
World. There are also great differences among the low-
income countries: In this regard, the World Bank has
established a distinction between mining economies and
predominantly agricultural economies.

The World Bank report used per capita income as the
fundamental indicator for distinguishing between the
latter two categories of countries. Other analyses take
into account, in addition to per capita income, the share
of manufactures in total exports, the per capita value of
industrial exports, and the share of "complex products"
in such exports. "Simple" industrial products usually
include textiles, clothing and footwear, and chemicals
that are obtained mainly from the elementary processing
of other primary products; all other industrial goods
are considered "complex."

The fact is that in recent years some Latin American,
Asian, and southern and eastern European countries have
rapidly emerged as producers of manufactures that are very
competitive on the international market. This phenomenon,
sometimes described as "the emergence of two or three
Japans" in the field of trade, is becoming increasingly
important. In Anglo-Saxon literature, these countries
are referred to as newly industrializing countries (NICs).
OECD includes in this category Hong Kong, South Korea,
Singapore, Taiwan, Brazil, Mexico, Portugal, Turkey,
and Yugoslavia. A United Kingdom Foreign and Commonwealth
Office report entitled The Newly Industrialising Countries

and the Adjustment Problem, published in London in 1979,
also lists the Philippines, India, Iran, Malaysia,
Pakistan, Thailand, Argentina, Spain, Greece, Israel,
Malta, Hungary, Poland, and Romania.

A feature common to all these countries is that they
all have a substantially higher growth potential than the
less developed countries and consequently have more
opportunities for raising the living standard of the poor;
these opportunities are not exclusively concentrated in
the rural sector. Another feature of these countries is
the high growth rate of their industrial exports over the
last fifteen years and their increasing access to international credit in the most recent period. This means
that their development is much more dependent upon international trade and the world capital markets than that
of the poorer countries and that their economies are much
more sensitive to trends in the industrialized countries.

It is not surprising that in order to maintain their
economic growth or to palliate the impact of the international crisis on this process, some of these countries
should have required substantial external financing,
on the one hand, or that they should have obtained access,
to an unprecedented degree, to the international capital
markets, on the other. At the same time, it must also be
noted that because of the defects in their accumulation
processes and the social inequalities inherent in their
political systems, the public and private sectors of many
of these countries used this external credit inefficiently
and inequitably and considerably aggravated the consequences of their external indebtedness.

THE EXTERNAL INDEBTEDNESS OF LATIN AMERICA

The above-described changes in the international
system provided the necessary, although not sufficient,
conditions for the Latin American countries to reach such
a high level of external indebtedness.[14]

Indeed, throughout the last ten years, the external
debt of the Latin American countries rose more than ten-
fold, reaching a total of around US$300 billion, a figure
that represents almost half the external debt of the
developing countries as a whole. From another point of
view, one might say that whereas in 1970 the external
debt of the Latin American countries represented a little
under 12 percent of the gross domestic product of these
countries, toward the end of 1982 it represented 30 percent of that product. At the same time, as a result of
the combined effect of the increase in the level of the
debt and the increase in interest rates, the service of
the debt, which in 1970 represented around 7 percent of
the value of exports, represented almost 40 percent of
the value of exports at the end of 1982. Moreover, since
most of the new credits obtained by the Latin American

countries came from private sources, the repayment terms were much shorter than ten years earlier, so that the short-term external debt became dangerously higher than the amount that might reasonably be expected to be incurred in connection with the financing of trade. It should be remembered that, whereas in the early 1970s around 80 percent of Latin America's external financing came from public sources, at the beginning of the 1980s exactly the same proportion came from private sources. It should also be borne in mind that since most of these debts are subject to fluctuating interest rates, it has been impossible to make any forecasts at the time of signing the loan agreement about the future service costs that in the late 1970s have shot up abruptly. At more or less the same time as the flows of direct foreign investment to Latin America have fallen, Latin American countries found themselves in the sudden financial squeeze.

The level and characteristics of Latin America's external indebtedness may be explained by both international and domestic factors, the relative weight of which is very difficult to assess as yet. On the one hand, the fact that this external indebtedness has affected countries that have followed very different economic policies would seem to underline the importance of external factors in explaining the phenomenon. On the other, the circumstances that the external sector of Latin America seems to have been affected more than other developing regions that had achieved a considerable degree of integration in the world economy, such as Southeast Asia, would seem to indicate that domestic policies had a great deal to do with what happened in Latin America. Still it must be kept in mind that the Latin American countries have very distinct economic, social, and political structures and hence are very different as regards their capacity to adjust to the external cycle.

It is worthwhile noting three of the factors that led to such an abundance of external resources during the past decade. The first has to do with the impact of the two large oil-price increases and the resulting accumulation of financial surpluses in the hands of the OPEC countries, which had to be recycled by the private banks. The second is related to the fall in the rate of investment and the application of anti-inflationary monetary policies by the main industrial countries, in the context of a protracted period of recession, which meant that these countries could not absorb surpluses as dynamically as they had been able to do in the past. The third has to do with the fact that the strengthening of the role of the private banks and the increasing use of mechanisms such as syndicated loans obtained on the Eurocurrency market (which accounted for over 90 percent of capital flows to the developing countries during the last decade) led to a lowering of standards for creditworthiness.

This is because these markets operate on a global scale and feel that, at that level, they do not need to analyze specific operations very carefully; it was therefore possible to increase operations dramatically, lowering costs in exchange for risks that are now coming to light in very complex ways. The fact is that during the 1970s the banks competed for customers to whom they could loan their surpluses and that previously ineligible clients, including the relatively more advanced developing countries, became eligible for loans.

At the same time, the demand for international credit in the Latin American countries rose abruptly as a result of the aforementioned trends. Many of these countries had to undertake considerable changes in order to adjust to the shifting conditions of the international economy--whether to meet the higher cost of oil or to penetrate the markets more efficiently--while at the same time they had to press on in their struggle against inflation. That is why many Latin American countries tried during this period to transform their economies, revising the incentives offered, their tariff policies, and their financial, tax, and social-security systems, among others. In the process, enterprises had to seek credit, either to stay in the market if they had been unfavorably affected by the changes or to expand if their competitive position had improved. This generated pressures that raised domestic interest rates and created a strong incentive to obtain credit abroad, where interest rates were more favorable. The demand for external credit rose to unprecedented levels as a result of the increased public expenditure that some Latin American countries undertook in order to finance expansion plans based on projects that were either subject to a long period of maturity or very large in scale, particularly in the case of the oil-exporting countries. In other cases the excessive expenditure of the private sector, a process that was accompanied by a strong preference for consumption and a deterioration of the investment process, brought the demand for external credit to formerly unknown levels.

The development strategy based on external indebtedness that was followed by the Latin American countries during that period seemed reasonable at the time because the loans were granted on very flexible terms and at negative or very low real interest rates and long maturities. In fact, this strategy made it possible to palliate for some time the impact of the international recession on the Latin American countries and for most of the past decade enabled them to grow at a considerably higher rate than the industrialized countries. However, the advocates of these careless policies of external indebtedness underestimated the risk that fluctuating interest rates and short maturities might raise the cost of servicing the debt above and beyond the short-term

repayment capacity of the countries concerned, reversing
the trend toward permissiveness of the international banks
and beginning a period of expensive and restricted credit.
    The risks implicit in such situations were aggravated
by the surprising lack of regulation of the international
financial markets during this entire period. As has been
mentioned, the international private banks played a major
role in recycling the financial surpluses accumulated
during those years, whereas the role of the international
financial institutions was drastically curtailed. For
example, International Monetary Fund financing, which in
the 1960s was equivalent to 16 percent of the value of
world trade, in the late 1970s only represented 3 percent.
Likewise, in the case of Latin America, loans authorized
by the Inter-American Development Bank, which had amounted
to the equivalent of 25 percent of the deficit on current
account of those countries during the period 1965-1970,
dropped to 11 percent during 1975-1980, and the World
Bank's share dropped from 21 percent to 12 percent between
those two periods. The deterioration of the role of
public agencies in providing external financing for Latin
America had very serious implications, inasmuch as, when
faced with the crisis, the international private banks
proved to be very unreliable and to lack vision: They
cut down on credit and, taking advantage of the fact that
the debtor countries were forced to renegotiate, shortened
maturities and increased the cost of loans (i.e., raised
interest rates and commissions) precisely at a time when
the debtors were experiencing difficulties and despite
the fact that the renegotiations reduced the banks' risks.
    This leads to a final observation--one that is
directly related to the purpose of this chapter--concern-
ing the links that exist between the external indebtedness
of Latin America and the general trends of the world
economy and of world politics. I am referring to the
responsibility that the international community should
assume with regard to the debt problem. So far, the
search for ways of dealing with the crisis has been left
almost entirely to the creditors, while national monetary
authorities and international financial institutions have
played a very limited role and other sectors, either
economic or political, have been virtually excluded. In
referring to the interests involved in the crisis, U.S.
Secretary of the Treasury Donald Regan pointed out the
following:

> It is right for American citizens to ask why
> they and their government need be concerned about
> the international debt problem. Why should we
> worry if some foreign borrowers get cut off from
> bank loans? and why should we worry if banks
> lose money? Nobody forced them to lend, and they
> should live with the consequences of their own
> decisions like any other business. . . .

If all the U.S. government had in mind was
throwing money at the borrowers and their lenders,
it would be difficult to justify using U.S. funds
on any efforts to resolve the debt crisis,
especially at a time of domestic spending
adjustments. . . . But of course, there is more
to the problem, and to the solution. First,
a further abrupt and large-scale contraction of
LDC [less developed country] imports would do
major damage to the U.S. economy. Second, if
the situation were handled badly, the difficulties facing LDC borrowers might come to appear
so hopeless that they would be tempted to take
desperate steps to try to escape.[15]

It must be recognized that the current situation is
a consequence not only of the policies applied by the
debtor countries but also of the inconsistent behavior
of private sources of financing that was aggravated by
the lack of regulation of the international financial
markets. Hence, it must also be acknowledged that the
entire international community is responsible for dealing
with the crisis.

In the first place, in the future the servicing of
the debt will have to be scheduled in accordance with the
requirements of the development processes of the debtor
countries and the exigencies of world economic recovery;
to this end, the renegotiation of existing loans or the
granting of new international loans must be carried out
with these objectives in mind. In the second place,
the disposition of private bankers to operate with
borrowers in the developing countries must not be subject
to sudden changes; to this end, the banks should work in
closer contact with the debtors themselves, with the
monetary authorities of their own countries, and with the
international financial institutions. Finally, measures
must be taken to enable these agencies to work effectively
to ensure the necessary compatibility between international financing and the reasonably smooth behavior of
the world economy, without neglecting the role of the
developing countries in it.

In this regard, it is essential to strengthen the
link between financing and trade, which has been seriously
weakened by the deterioration in recent years of the
terms of trade for most Latin American export commodities,
by the strong protectionist measures adopted by the
developed countries, and by the general breakdown of the
rules that governed the system of international trade.
Helmut Schmidt, former chancellor of the Federal Republic
of Germany, had this to say on the subject: "Credit
creates trade, trade secures credit. Major developing
countries balance-of-payments problems cannot be cured if
we shut our markets to them. In many respects the
developing countries are now in a position similar to

that of the German Reich in the 1920s: Germany could not
meet its 'reparation' payments because the allies were
not prepared to tolerate German trade surpluses. So
Germany could not meet its debt repayments and lost its
credit-worthiness."[16]

It is to be hoped that, given the present circumstances, the international community will be more far-
sighted about Latin America and the rest of the developing world than it was about Germany after World War I and
that it will thus be able to prevent the social dis-
orders that would inevitably break out, albeit under new
forms, if greater pressure were to be put on the debtor
countries.

NOTES

1. So called by Stanley Hoffmann in the New York
Review of Books, April 16, 1981. In this regard, see
also Robert W. Tucker, "The Purposes of American Power,"
Foreign Affairs, vol. 59, no. 2 (Winter 1980) and his
"America in Decline: The Foreign Policy of 'Maturity,'"
Foreign Affairs: America and the World 1979, vol. 58,
no. 3 (1980). See also: International Institute of
Strategic Studies (IISS), Strategic Survey 1980,
London, 1981.

2. D. Yankelovich and L. Kaagan, "Assertive
America," Foreign Affairs: America and the World 1980,
vol. 59, no. 3 (1981).

3. See S. Bialer, "Poland and the Soviet Imperium,"
Foreign Affairs, vol. 59, no. 3 (1981); and S. Bialer
and J. Afferica, "Reagan and Russia," Foreign Affairs,
vol. 61, no. 2 (Winter 1982). See also W. G. Hyland,
"Clash with the Soviet Union," Foreign Policy, no. 49
(1982-1983).

4. See Marshall Goldman, USSR in Crisis: The
Failure of an Economic System, New York, 1982.

5. See Josef Joffe, "The Enduring Crisis,"
Foreign Affairs, vol. 59, no. 4 (Spring 1981); and
Eliot A. Cohen, "The Long-Term Crisis of the Alliance,"
Foreign Affairs, vol. 61, no. 2 (Winter 1982). See also
David A. Andelman, "Struggle over Western Europe,"
Foreign Policy, no. 59 (1982-1983).

6. See Christopher Bertram, "Introduction," in
Third World Conflict and International Security, Adelphi
Papers no. 166, London. See also, on Latin America,
Estudios Internacionlales, America Latina Después de las
Malvinas (entire issue), no. 66 (Santiago, October-
December 1982).

7. See Organization for Economic Cooperation and
Development (OECD), The Welfare State in Crisis, 1981;
and L. Thurow, The Zero-Sum Society: Distribution and the
Possibilities for Economic Change, New York, 1980.
For a Latin American viewpoint, see F. H. Cardoso, Las

Políticas Sociales en la Década del 80: Nuevas Opciones, Santiago, 1982, as well as the articles published in Crítica y Utopía, no. 6, under the heading Sociedad Civil y Autoritarismo, especially A. Flisfisch, "Notas Acerca del Reforzamiento de la Sociedad Civil."

8. Some of the earliest studies of this phenomenon, in the field of economics, are Richard N. Cooper, "The Economics of Interdependence and Foreign Policy in the Seventies," World Politics, vol. 24, no. 2 (January 1972). Fundamental books, from the standpoint of international relations, are Power and Interdependence: World Politics in Transition by Robert O. Keohane and Joseph S. Nye, Boston, 1977; and the earlier work by the same authors entitled Transnational Relations and World Politics, Cambridge, Mass., 1972. For other literature on the subject, see R. Rosencrance and A. Stein, "Interdependence: Myth or Reality?" World Politics, vol. 28, no. 1 (1976); and the many papers on the subject published by International Organization, such as H. Alker, "A Methodology for Design Research on Interdependence Alternatives," vol. 31, no. 1 (1977); R. Rosencrance, "Whither Interdependence?" vol. 31, no. 3 (1977); and K. J. Holstie, "A New International Politics? Diplomacy in Complex Interdependence," vol. 32, no. 2 (1977). Some of these papers, as well as others, are collected in R. Maghrori and B. Ramberg, Globalism Versus Realism: International Relations' Third Debate, Boulder, Colo., 1982. Finally, see also J. N. Rosenau, The Study of Global Interdependence: Essays on the Transnationalization of World Affairs, New York, 1980.

9. This concept has been studied by a working group on interdependence and national development of the Program for Joint Studies on Latin American International Relations (RIAL). I have published a paper entitled "Interdependencia y Desarrollo Nacional," El Trimestre Económico, no. 200 (October-December 1982); see also K. R. Mirow and H. Maurer, Webs of Power: International Cartels and the World Economy, Boston, 1981 (which includes an interesting reference to Brazil).

10. D. H. Meadows, et al., The Limits to Growth, Washington, D.C., 1972. See also E. J. Mishan, The Economic Growth Debate, London, 1977; K. D. Wilson, Prospects for Growth: Changing Expectations for the Future, New York, 1977; W. Leontieff, "The Future of the World Economy," Études et Expansion, no. 273 (New York, July-August-September 1977); and C. Freeman and M. Jahoda, World Futures: The Great Debate, London, 1978.

11. CEPII, Économie Mondiale: La Montée des Tensions, Paris, 1983.

12. Independent Commission on International Development Issues, North-South: A Programme for Survival, London, 1980.

13. International Bank for Reconstruction and Development, World Development Report, 1978.

14. For a Latin American perspective on this problem, see the document prepared by ECLA for the Bogotá high-level meeting held in May 1983, entitled "La Crisis Económica Internacional y la Capacidad de Respuesta de América Latina." See also Enrique V. Iglesias, "Reflexiones sobre en economio latinamericana en 1982," CEPAL Review, no. 19 (April 1983); and the articles collected under the heading Crisis y Deuda en América Latina, Estudios Internacionales, (Santiago, no. 64 October-December 1983).

15. Donald Regan, Statement to the United States Congress, 7 April 1983, Washington, D.C., 1983.

16. Helmut Schmidt, "The World Economy at Stake: The Inevitable Need for American Leadership," The Economist, February 26, 1983.

4
External Debt Problems of Latin America

Enrique V. Iglesias

By the end of 1983 the total external debt of Latin America amounted to approximately US$310 billion (Table 4.1). It is estimated to have grown by 7 percent during the year, a rate that was much lower than the 12 percent of 1982 and far below the growth rate of around 23 percent, which was the average between 1979 and 1981. The net flow of external capital to Latin America fell from a peak of US$38.0 billion in 1981 to US$16.6 billion in 1982 and US$4.5 billion in 1983 (Table 4.2).

This sharp drop in the growth rate of the debt was mainly the result of the restrictive policy adopted by the international commercial banks with respect to Latin America. In 1983, these banks granted virtually no new autonomous loans to the region, channeling their credit through the renegotiations of the external debt initiated by several Latin American countries. Under such circumstances, a substantial part of the increase in the debt was accounted for by the fact that the banks capitalized interest payments. This was partly a result of pressure brought to bear by the International Monetary Fund to induce the banks to refinance part (usually around 50 percent) of the interest earned, as a contribution to the adjustment program sponsored by the Fund.

The need to refinance a considerable portion of the interest payments becomes obvious when one takes into account the tremendous burden that they represent for most of the countries of the region. Indeed, despite the fact that in 1983 interest payments fell, mainly as a result of the slight decline in the prevailing rates on the main international financial markets, they still amounted to the equivalent of 35 percent of the value of exports of goods and services for the region as a whole (Table 4.3).

The share of the banks in the region's external indebtedness has of course increased notably. In the 1960s it was relatively insignificant, whereas in the 1980s it was over 50 percent and in some countries (Argentina, Brazil, Chile, Mexico, Venezuela) amounted to

73

Table 4.1   Latin America: Total External Debt
(end-of-year balance in billions of U.S. dollars)

Country	1981	1982	1983[a]
Latin America	257.890	289.437	309.800
Oil-exporting countries	116.777	128.948	134.500
Bolivia[b]	2.450	2.373	2.700
Ecuador[c]	5.756	5.788	6.200
Mexico[d]	72.007	81.350	85.000
Peru[c]	8.227	9.503	10.600
Venezuela[c]	28.377	29.934	30.000
Non-oil-exporting countries	141.113	160.489	175.300
Argentina[d]	35.671	38.907	42.000
Brazil[c]	65.000	75.000	83.000
Colombia[d]	8.160	9.506	10.300
Costa Rica[b]	2.345	2.603	3.050
Chile[d]	15.542	17.153	17.600
El Salvador[c]	980	917	1.200
Guatemala[d]	765	858	1.000
Guyana[c]	687	689	800
Haiti[c]	326	765	800
Honduras[b]	1.055	1.198	1.500
Nicaragua[b]	2.163	2.789	3.400
Panama[b]	2.333	2.733	3.100
Paraguay[c]	1.120	1.195	1.300
Dominican Republic[d]	1.837	1.921	2.000
Uruguay[d]	3.129	4.255	4.250

[a]Preliminary estimates subject to revision

[b]Public debt

[c]Includes officially guaranteed public and private external debt,
plus nonguaranteed long- and short-term debt with financial
institutions reporting to the Bank for International Settlements

[d]Total public and private external debt

Source: Economic Commission for Latin America, on the basis of
official figures and publications of international financial agencies.

more than two-thirds of the total debt. Obviously,
debts with private banks reached these proportions because of the willingness of the banks in question to
finance most of the region's deficit on current account
from 1974 on. In actual fact, bank loans have been
available in abundance, except during a short recession
in the mid-1970s. Recently, however, the banks have
become much more cautious about making new commitments
in general and particularly in respect to granting loans
to the developing countries.

Table 4.2 Latin America: Net Financing Available After Payment of Profits and Interest (billions of U.S. dollars)

Year	Net Inflow of Capital (1)	Net Payments for Profits and Interest (2)	Net Available Financing (3) = (1)−(2) (3)	Net Real Available Financing[a] (4)	Exports of Goods and Services (5)	Net Available Financing/ Exports of Goods and Services[b] (6) = (3)/(5) (6)
1973	8.1	4.4	3.7	8.3	30.3	12.2
1974	11.6	5.3	6.3	11.9	46.0	13.7
1975	14.5	5.8	8.7	15.0	43.7	19.9
1976	18.3	7.0	11.3	18.7	49.9	22.6
1977	17.3	8.6	8.7	13.5	58.7	14.8
1978	26.4	10.5	15.9	22.9	64.5	24.7
1979	29.0	14.2	14.8	19.0	85.8	17.2
1980	29.9	19.0	10.9	12.3	110.9	9.8
1981	38.0	29.1	8.9	9.2	119.6	7.4
1982	16.6	36.8	−20.2	−20.4	109.0	−18.5
1983[c]	4.5	34.0	−29.5	−29.5	107.6	−27.4

[a] Obtained by deflating column 3 by the U.S. wholesale price index, base 1983 = 100

[b] In percentages

[c] Preliminary estimates subject to revision

Source: International Monetary Fund, Balance of Payments Yearbook (several issues); Economic Commission for Latin America estimates on the basis of official figures.

Table 4.3 Latin America: Ratio of Total Interest Payments to Exports of Goods and Services (percentages)

Country	1977	1978	1979	1980	1981	1982	1983[a]
Latin America	12.4	15.5	17.4	19.9	26.4	38.3	35.0
Oil-exporting countries	13.0	16.0	15.7	16.5	22.3	31.1	31.0
Bolivia	9.9	13.7	18.1	24.5	35.5	43.5	35.5
Ecuador	4.8	10.3	13.6	18.2	24.3	29.3	25.5
Mexico	25.4	24.0	24.8	23.1	28.7	37.6	38.0
Peru	17.9	21.2	14.7	16.0	21.8	24.7	31.5
Venezuela	4.0	7.2	6.9	8.1	12.7	21.4	19.0
Non-oil-exporting countries	11.9	15.1	18.8	23.3	31.3	46.2	39.0
Argentina	7.6	9.6	12.8	22.0	31.7	54.6	51.0
Brazil	18.9	24.5	31.5	34.1	40.4	57.0	43.5
Colombia	7.4	7.7	10.1	13.3	21.6	22.7	21.5
Costa Rica	7.1	9.9	12.8	18.0	25.5	33.4	43.5
Chile	13.7	17.0	16.5	19.3	34.6	47.2	37.5
El Salvador	2.9	5.1	5.3	6.5	7.5	11.1	10.5
Guatemala	2.4	3.6	3.1	5.3	7.5	7.6	7.5
Haiti	2.3	2.8	3.3	2.0	3.2	2.3	3.5
Honduras	7.2	8.2	8.6	10.6	14.5	22.5	16.0
Nicaragua	7.0	9.3	9.7	15.7	15.5	31.7	36.0
Paraguay	6.7	8.5	10.7	14.3	15.9	14.9	15.5
Dominican Republic	8.8	14.0	14.4	14.7	10.5	22.6	25.0
Uruguay	9.8	10.4	9.0	11.0	13.1	22.4	32.5

Note: Interest includes interest payment on short-term debt.

[a] Preliminary estimates subject to revision

Source: 1977-1982: International Monetary Fund, Balance of Payments Yearbook; 1983: Economic Commission for Latin America on the basis of official information.

Many factors are responsible for this tighter
attitude on the part of the commercial external credit
institutions. In the first place, the cyclical decline
in the industrial economies has weakened the bank markets
in their countries of origin, causing national clients to
meet with payments difficulties or to go bankrupt while
at the same time increasing the demand for credit; moreover, many of the banks' clients in developing countries
have experienced payments problems. Other factors
accounting for the banks' lack of interest in granting
loans to developing countries include a more generalized
attitude of circumspection concerning the diversification
of their portfolios and disequilibria in the relation
between their capital and their assets.

The payments problems of the developing countries
with regard to the private banks have been especially
apparent in Latin America. In 1982 there were serious
payments crises in Mexico and Argentina, which were
among the leading bank debtors, and also in Bolivia,
Ecuador, and Costa Rica. In addition, other countries,
such as Cuba and Venezuela, announced that they were to
reschedule their next payments.

THE ORIGINS OF THE PROBLEM

The International Recession

More than at any other time since World War II,
after 1982 the growth of the periphery in general and of
Latin America in particular was heavily conditioned by
constraints deriving from the poor economic evolution of
the center. It is true that causes of internal origin--
such as those linked to the unsatisfactory management of
fiscal and exchange policies and to problems of an extra-
economic character--account for most of the big decreases in the product in the countries of the Southern
Cone, for decline of GNP in several Central American
economies, or for the stagnation of economic activity in
countries such as Mexico. Nevertheless, the major
external constraints stemming from the recession in the
industrialized economies constituted a brake that had a
generalized handicapping effect on the economic growth
of the entire region.

Thus, the main origin of the problem is to be found
in the international recession, which has been unusually
drawn out. In practice, the recession in the industrial
countries has reduced the aggregate demand of the central
countries and consequently has brought down the price of
Latin American exports; to make matters worse, the
developing countries have sought to offset the drop in
prices by exporting larger volumes, a move that produces
an even greater glut on the market and lowers prices in
its turn. Here again, the countries as a whole must step

up their efforts simply to remain in status quo. In any case, the recession has an eroding effect on what looks like a means of paying off the debt (i.e., exports) and affects the banks' opinion of the solvency of countries, to the detriment of the real source of payment (i.e., loans granted on reasonable terms).

Although the recession in the industrialized economies in 1974 and 1975 was more critical than its counterpart today (the gross domestic product of the OECD countries fell by 1 percent in that period), it lasted only two years. Instead, 1982 was preceded by a period of meager growth in the center, in which real interest rates fluctuated around 6 percent, and in which OECD's volume of imports decreased or only marginally expanded. Continuing this trend, 1983 was also a year in which the prices of the primary commodities produced by the periphery fell again and the sixth consecutive year in which the terms of trade deteriorated for the non-petroleum-exporting developing countries.

To this set of unfavorable circumstances was added yet another of particular significance: the above-mentioned reduction in absolute terms of the net flow of capital into the periphery. This decline was especially severe in the case of the non-petroleum-exporting countries of Latin America.

This situation was linked, in turn, to the un-expected duration of the recession in the center. Its prolongation, and the repeated postponement of the first signs of recovery beyond the anticipated date, brought about a liquidity crisis in the industrialized economies that made itself felt in an upsurge of demand for credit, which was no longer due to the prevalence of inflationary expectations--since, as already shown, the rate of in-flation had decreased--but stemmed from the need to supplement the low cash flows caused by the continuous and unexpected reduction of sales. As this heavy demand for credit coincided with stabilization policies center-ing on monetary restrictions, it generated unprecedented real interest rates and led to declines in production, particularly in the sectors most sensitive to the rate of interest (such as those producing capital goods and durable consumer goods) and to reductions in inventories.

Unfortunately, primary commodities, which constitute the periphery's staple exports, are among the goods for which adjustment to a contraction in demand is made mainly through a fall in prices. In other instances they constitute inputs for industries that are particularly hard hit by a recession in the center (for example, metal products for the motor vehicle and construction in-dustries), or again their inventories are liable to be drastically reduced when the rate of interest rises.

Viewed from this angle, the persistence of de-flationary policies in the center has especially affected the periphery's export prices but only partly hit domestic prices in the center itself. Consequently, downward price rigidity as regards the goods produced in the industrialized countries has aggravated the deterioration of the periphery's terms of trade.

Of course, there is nothing new about the fact that stabilization policies applied in the central economies are more prone to bring down the periphery's terms of trade than to reduce inflation in the center. What is new is that because of the unexpected prolongation of the recession a liquidity crisis occurred that kept real interest rates exceptionally high--in contrast with what happened in 1974 and 1975, when the real interest rate was negative--and that also made for restriction of the net flow of capital into the periphery, a circumstance that likewise implied a significant difference from what had occurred during the 1974-1978 crisis and again in 1980.

As was already said, this decline was partly due to the high levels of indebtedness reached by the developing countries and to the slower expansion of bank capital and partly to the reluctance of the international banking system to increase its loan to the periphery at a time when the value of the latter's exports was diminishing. The perverse nature of this change lies in the fact that the reduction in the value of the periphery's exports was due not to a contraction in their volume (in fact it expanded) but to the very marked fall in export prices. Thus, since the banking system took as the index of the periphery's capacity of payment the current value of its exports--and not their future value, which would incorporate more normal terms of trade, capital movements tended to aggravate rather than to alleviate the external crisis.

The High Cost of Credit

All the indicators suggest that the terms on which Latin America contracts its debts have reached a point where new loans barely provide minimum relief from the burden of indebtedness. Thus Figure 4.1 shows that interest rates have become very positive in real terms in the past years, after having been negative, also in real terms, ever since the mid-1970s.

However, from the point of view of the debtor countries, the high interest rates must primarily be considered in relation to the prices of the region's exports. It can then be seen that the real cost of credit for Latin America increased spectacularly between 1981 and 1982, since the LIBOR rate rose unusually high while at the same time there was a sharp drop in export prices (Figure 4.1). This clearly shows the extent of the deterioration in the region's external debt-servicing capacity due to exogenous factors.

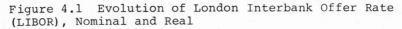

Figure 4.1 Evolution of London Interbank Offer Rate (LIBOR), Nominal and Real

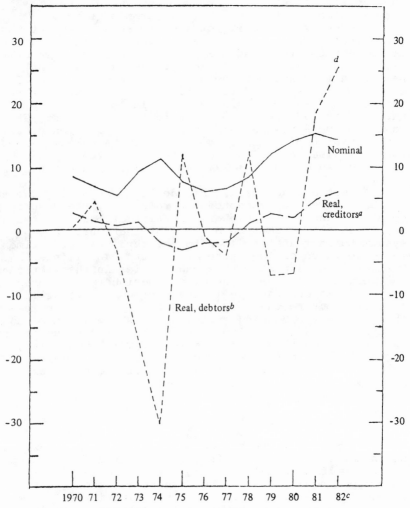

[a]Nominal LIBOR for 6 months, deflated by industrialized countries' consumer prices
[b]Nominal LIBOR for 6 months, deflated by the unit value of Latin America's exports
[c]Up to September
[d]Provisional estimates

Source: LIBOR: Morgan Guaranty Trust Co., World Financial Markets (several issues); consumer prices: IMF, International Financial Statistics, Yearbook, 1981 and December 1982; unit value of exports: ECLA, on the basis of official data.

The available data also show that the effect of the high basic interest rates since 1981 has been even further aggravated by the rise in the variable component of interest on loans in Eurocurrencies to developing countries, which, in turn, reflects the greater risk run by the banks in lending money to the countries in question. The negative effect of the high basic interest rates is, moreover, twofold in that they increase not only the cost of new loans but also that of loans previously contracted at variable interest, which have increased notably in Latin America since the beginning of the 1970s.

The recent interest-rate trends have thus given rise to a new phenomenon, that of interest rates being a debt burden in themselves. Thus, it is estimated that in 1983 interest payments amounted to the equivalent of 35 percent of export earnings of Latin American countries and almost to 4 percent of these earnings in the case of the non-oil-exporting countries of the region.

The second cause of the increase in the cost of indebtedness has to do with the evolution of the average time in which the loans mature. Even in the absence of complete data on debt repayment periods for 1982, it seems likely, to judge by trends in the preceding year, that they were shorter, thus accelerating debt-servicing payments and putting pressure on the countries' capacity to pay.

It is interesting to observe that Brazil has opted for longer payment periods at the cost of accepting much bigger margins of interest. Because of this, its interest payments have increased to such an extent that they have given rise to balance-of-payments problems. Mexico, on the other hand, has accepted shorter payment periods but smaller margins of interest in recent years; consequently, the main feature of its indebtedness crisis has been the maturing of a large number of loans within very short spaces of time. Thus, both Brazil and Mexico have experienced severe debt-servicing difficulties, although the pressure point has been different in each case.

Contracting short-term debts is usually symptomatic of payments difficulties: Debtors need new loans in order to serve their debt, but the entities granting the credits, in consideration of the greater risks involved, are unwilling to grant long-term loans. This increases short-term lending and means that there is a greater accumulation of debts that have fallen due. Even though it is still difficult to obtain accurate data concerning short-term indebtedness, provisional data suggest that it amounted to 30 percent of Latin America's total debt in 1981, a figure that probably rose in 1982.

The increase in short-term indebtedness, combined with the shorter maturities of medium-term instruments, means that it is necessary to refinance progressively larger proportions of the debt each year. However, as has already been stated, the burden in terms of interest

payments has already reached serious proportions. In
addition, the traditional rescheduling of amortization
payments would scarcely relieve the country in these
circumstances. Moreover, the greater the share of the
debt to be paid to the banks, the greater their risk,
which makes it even more difficult to obtain new loans
on reasonable terms.

Development Strategy Based on Indebtedness

During the 1970s, Latin America opted for a development strategy based on indebtedness. For a number of
years the result was positive. Although after 1974 the
expansion of the world economy was feeble, the economic
growth of Latin America was relatively brisk and considerably greater than that of the OECD economies. In
addition, this strategy seemed eminently reasonable
since indebtedness was "cheap," with very low or negative
real interest rates, lengthy payment periods, and servicing payable in dollars, whose real value was being eroded.
However, those who argued in favor of rapid entry
into international capital markets and the concomitant
strategy of growth based on indebtedness may have underestimated the real cost of credit; during the period
nominal costs did not reflect the implicit risks of debt-
servicing problems should a conflict arise between the
increase in liabilities with commercial banks and the
limits set by those institutions in respect to their
commitments. These implicit risks obviously became
greater owing to the fact that the structural problems of
the OECD countries caused their economic growth rates to
fall during the 1970s (by comparison with those recorded
in the preceding decade), which meant that Latin America
had to contract even more debts in order to maintain its
high growth rates at a time when general economic conditions were not propitious for creating the capacity to
cope with the accumulation of the bank debt.
From another point of view, the inflation unleashed
in the mid-1970s was unexpected, so that the low real
cost of loans was a temporary and artificial phenomenon;
once the creditors' expectations became more realistic,
the cost of credit more than recovered. Another factor
related to the strategy of growth based on indebtedness
was that some countries obviously obtained more credit
than they could use productively: External loans took
the place of domestic saving and facilitated an increase
in consumption, speculation, and the purchase of weapons.
Although much of this state of affairs may be
attributed to erroneous indebtedness strategies, there can
be no doubt that the structure of the international banking market also helped to create the problem. In the
initial phase of the loan cycle, the banks granted a
large number of loans, with the aim of rapidly investing

their surplus on account of competition and excess liquidity. However, there was often some asymmetry between what the banks were able to loan and the capacity of the countries to absorb the funds obtained efficiently. Thus, the combination of low interest rates, the prestige gained by attracting international credit, and the ease of obtaining bank loans when a large dollar reserve existed persuaded some countries to borrow more than their possibilities for investment warranted and to post-pone making of internal adjustments.

The Weaknesses of the International Financial System

In 1974 the international banking system became, de facto, a kind of central bank for the world economy. However, it was not in a position to perform this function and, at best, was able to assume it only for a very short time. Its operation was relatively satisfactory during 1974 and 1975, when its net initial commitments with the developing countries were still very low; today, on the other hand, in view of the high level of its commitments in the Third World, considerations attaching to loan risks and the need for banks to obtain profits stand in the way of efficient recirculation of liquidity.

Moreover, in practice the banks do much to accentuate the cyclical movements of economic activities at both the national and the international level. Although in the 1970s those cycles were not closely synchronized in the Third World, they are now. This synchronization is due not only to the prolonged OECD recession but also, and largely, to the lack of interest shown by the banks in granting new loans, the factor that at one time, as has been seen, was decisive in stimulating the economic growth of the region.

THE ADJUSTMENT EFFORT

In 1983, Latin America made a tremendous effort to reduce the disequilibria that had been accumulating in the external sector since the late 1970s. Thus, to the higher exchange rates adopted by numerous countries of the region in 1982 were added, in 1983, new devaluations, various other measures aimed at controlling imports and encouraging exports, and strict fiscal, monetary, and wage policies aimed at reducing domestic expenditure.

As a result of these adjustment policies, and despite the unfavorable trends in world trade and external financing, in 1983 the region achieved a large surplus in its merchandise trade, notably reduced its current account deficit, and also considerably reduced the negative balance on the balance of payments.

External Trade and the Terms of Trade

As already mentioned, however, the 1983 surplus of over US$31 million was only achieved through a drastic reduction of imports, which fell by almost 30 percent, after having fallen by 20 percent in 1982. Since the unit value of imports did not vary in 1983 and since it had fallen slightly in 1982, the decline of the volume of imports was just as drastic as the decline of the total value of imports.

In particular, in countries such as Venezuela, Uruguay, Mexico, Peru, Argentina, and Chile, the contraction of the volume of imports was so spectacular as to reveal clearly the enormous magnitude of the adjustment effort that had been made. Thus, the quantum of imports fell by 60 percent in Venezuela; declined by 39 percent in Uruguay and by 36 percent in Mexico, after having already dropped by 30 percent and 41 percent, respectively, in 1982; fell by 27 percent in Peru; and declined by 17 percent in both Argentina and Chile, in both of which imports had already fallen by around 40 percent in 1982.

In contrast to the unusual reduction in the volume of imports, the volume of exports rose by 7 percent in the region as a whole and by 9 percent in the non-oil-exporting countries. As was the case with respect to the real decline of imports, the increases in the volume of exports mainly reflected the adjustment effort made by the Latin American economies through measures aimed at modifying the relative prices of tradable and non-tradable goods and reducing domestic expenditure.

Nevertheless, the unfavorable evolution, for the fourth year in a row, of world trade and the considerable drop in the international prices of oil and other commodities prevented this relatively satisfactory increase in the volume of exports from bringing about a similar increase in their value. In fact, the value of exports fell slightly in the region as a whole and by almost 6 percent in the group of oil-exporting countries. Indeed, although the drop in the international price of oil had a lot to do with the drop in the unit value of exports in 1983, it also resulted from the decline of the international prices of the region's major export commodities, such as coffee and sugar, and of a good number of minerals.

Since the unit value of exports fell much more than that of imports, Latin America's terms of trade declined by slightly over 7 percent, after having fallen by 5 percent in 1982 and by 7 percent in 1981. During the last two years, the decline of the terms of trade was more pronounced in the oil-exporting countries than in the other economies of the region. Among the oil-exporting countries, the deterioration in the terms of trade during 1981 and 1982 did not offset the remarkable advance that had been made during 1979 and 1980. On the contrary,

since the terms of trade of the latter biennium had
already deteriorated sharply over the previous five years,
not only was the relevant index around 30 percent lower
in 1983 than in 1978, but it reached the lowest level of
the last half century. Indeed, during the period 1980-
1983, it was much lower, on average, than it had been
during 1931-1933, the most critical period of the Great
Depression.

The Balance of Payments

     Because the value of imports fell much more than that
of exports, the merchandise trade balance underwent
another significant change in 1983. After the radical
turnabout of 1982, when the US$1.6 billion deficit of 1981
had been replaced by a surplus of over US$9.7 billion,
1983 brought an extraordinary growth in the trade surplus
to more than US$31 billion, over three times that of the
previous year. This was, in particular, the result of
the enormous increases in the trade surpluses of
Venezuela, Brazil, and Mexico and of the considerable
changes in the merchandise trade of Argentina, Chile,
Peru, Ecuador, and Uruguay. The drastic contraction of
imports was also the main cause of the new increase in
the trade surplus achieved by Argentina, the increased
surplus obtained by Ecuador, and the substitution by
Peru of a small surplus for its deficit of the previous
year.
     By contrast with what happened in 1982, when the
impact of the change in the trade balance on the current
account was neutralized to a large extent by the sharp
increase in payments for interest and profits, in 1983
the part played by the increased trade surplus in reducing
the disequilibrium on the current account was reinforced
by a decline in foreign remittances. Such payments,
which had more than quadrupled over the previous five
years, rising from US$8.6 billion in 1977 to almost
US$36.8 billion in 1982, fell a little to under US$34
billion in 1983. This was a result of the limitation on
the payment of profits caused by the sharp contraction of
domestic economic activity and the slight decline of
interest payments brought about by reduction of nominal
interest rates on the international financial market.
     Under these circumstances, the deficit on current
account--which in 1982 had already dropped by 10 percent,
after having reached a record high of US$40 billion in
1981--fell spectacularly to under US$8.5 billion in 1983.
Nevertheless, in 1983 the net inflow of capital was also
lower than the deficit on current account, a situation
that had already occurred in both 1981 and 1982. Consequently, the global balance of payments closed with
a deficit for the third year in a row.

The External Financing and the Real Transfer of Resources

As has been noted, the abrupt adjustment of the balance-of-payments current account that took place in 1983 was forced, to a very large extent, by the no less violent contraction of the net inflow of capital. Indeed, in 1983, the total inflow of capital was barely one-fourth that received in 1982 (which had already been very low) and only 15 percent of the average inflow of capital during the four-year period 1978-1981.

The negative impact of this sharp drop in the net inflow of capital becomes even more obvious when one compares the amount of capital received with the amount represented by net payments for interest and profits, which in 1983 exceeded, for the second year in a row, that of net loans and investments received. Consequently, as in 1982, instead of receiving a net transfer of real resources _from_ abroad, Latin America made a net transfer of resources _to_ the rest of the world. Thus, a situation was provoked that, considering the relative development of the region, may be described as perverse.

The amounts involved in this transfer, moreover, were very high: US$20 billion in 1982 and almost US$30 billion in 1983, magnitudes equivalent to 19 percent and 27 percent of the value of exports of goods and services and between 2.5 percent and 4 percent of the gross domestic product. Considered from another angle, the reversal in the direction of net financial payments that took place between 1981 and 1983 was equivalent to a deterioration of one-third in the terms of trade.

Thus, the spectacular change in the direction of net financial flows played a decisive role in the widespread contraction of economic activity in Latin America and in the difficulties that some countries experienced in servicing their external debt. As may be clearly seen from the data in Table 4.2, up to 1981 the gross amount of capital received by the region was well in excess of its amortization payments, investments abroad, and payments for interest and profits. Indeed, during the period 1973-1981, this transfer of resources was equivalent, on average, to 16 percent of the value of exports that, in turn, increased during that period at an annual rate of around 20 percent. Under such circumstances, Latin America was able to make amortization and interest payments on its external debt and on profits earned by foreign capital through the new loans and investments it received each year.

Nevertheless, the magnitude of this net transfer of resources began to fall in 1979, when the increases in the net inflow of capital were more than offset by the even larger increases in payments for interest and profits. This trend reached a peak in 1982 and 1983, when the net inflow of capital dropped sharply and the region had to meet the bulk of its payments for interest

and profits from resources originating in the trade
surplus or from the international reserves it had previously accumulated. As has already been explained, however, because of the unfavorable external situation, the
trade surplus was produced not by an increase in exports
but rather by an extremely severe contraction of imports,
and this in turn had a negative effect on economic
activity. Because of this chain reaction, the drastic
reduction in the net inflow of capital had a definite
effect on the levels of production and employment. At
the same time, the fundamental cause of the decline in
net loans and investments that took place during 1981 and
1982 was the procyclic reaction of the international
commercial banks--Latin America'a main creditors--vis-à-
vis the unfavorable external situation with which the
region was faced.

This attitude on the part of the banks was clearly
evident for the first time in 1982 and persisted in 1983.
Thus, according to figures provided by the Bank for
International Settlements, new loans granted by private
banks to Latin America (excluding Venezuela and Ecuador)
fell from US$21 billion during the second half of 1981
to US$12 billion during the first half of 1982 and barely
US$300 million during the second half of 1982. During
the first half of 1983, the banks granted loans amounting
to US$3.7 billion. Nevertheless, this improvement was
not the result of a "spontaneous" response on the part of
the banks but rather was accounted for by the banks
being pressured by the International Monetary Fund to
contribute to the "rescue packages" designed by that
institution to facilitate the adjustment process in a
number of Latin American economies.

PROBLEMS AND PROSPECTS

The Unique Profile of the Latin American Economic Crisis

The figures given so far show the unusual scope and
depth of the recessive crisis that almost every Latin
American country is experiencing and leave no doubt that,
for the region as a whole, 1983 was the worst year in
the last half century. For most of the countries, the
reduction of income during the period 1982-1983 has
meant going back to the standard of living of several
years ago.

It was already said that in many cases the crisis
was partly the result of domestic factors related to ill-
advised economic strategies or policies, the prolonged
application of which was facilitated by the accelerated
growth of external indebtedness and by the national
financial permissiveness that prevailed during the 1970s.
It is no less true, however, that the serious balance-of-
payments crisis with which Latin America has been faced

in recent years may be attributed, to a large extent, to external causes that by their very nature were beyond the control of the countries of the region. Such was the case of the spectacular drop in the terms of trade, the high nominal and real interest rates, and the severe contraction of the net inflow of private capital. Even more unpredictable were the intensity and the duration of this phenomenon, a situation clearly atypical by comparison with what has happened in the large central countries during previous recessions.

In any event, it is obvious that at this stage of the game the solution to some of the most serious problems facing the region will depend mainly on external factors over which the region has little or no control. That is why the domestic economic policy options open to the countries are so complex and fraught with difficulties and also why the prevailing atmosphere is one of uncertainty and perplexity.

In order to deal with the balance-of-payments crisis, beginning in 1982 many Latin American countries implemented drastic and painful adjustment measures with which imports were reduced dramatically, to the point that in many cases the volume of imports fell by over 50 percent during the last two years. In addition, the sharp devaluations made by many countries in order to balance their external accounts contributed to the reinforcement of inflationary pressures that, after some time, led to the application of stabilization policies. Thus, the recessive effect normally produced by such policies over the short term was added to that produced by the sharp drop in imports.

The combination of these factors had another serious consequence: Investment fell very sharply, and in some countries a significant proportion of installed capital deteriorated or was destroyed, as many enterprises went out of business. The social consequences of the current situation have been no less serious. Indeed, in many countries, employment and real wages have reached the lowest levels since the Great Depression and in some cases have nearly reached the critical limits of social tolerance. In some countries the situation has been further aggravated by unusually severe natural disasters, which have accentuated the loss of income and the slowdown of the economy caused by the general crisis.

Nevertheless, not everything was negative during the last years. Some countries that had already followed cautious policies with respect to foreign debt were able to cope with the negative aspects of the international situation. Many other countries of the region have implemented programs aimed at adjusting their balance of payments and in this effort have received some cooperation from the international financial community; this has prevented the immediate effect of the crisis from worsening. Moreover, a relatively calm atmosphere has been restored

on the immediate financial scene; this, of course, does
not mean that the problems have been solved or that the
risk of serious financial crisis has been eliminated.

These and other aspects of the situation discussed
in this chapter show that the Latin American recession has
a profile of its own. The situation of Latin America is
different from that in other regions of the Third World
and, as a matter of fact, from any similar situation that
has arisen during the entire postwar period.

The Questions of the Moment

Latin America has undoubtedly shown an extraordinary
sense of responsibility in the way that it has responded
to the challenges posed by the current external crisis.
Suffice it to recall that in the last few years many of
the countries implemented sharp real devaluations with
a view to promoting their exports, replacing essential
imports, and eliminating nonessential imports. To reduce
excessive domestic expenditure and fiscal deficits, they
also have substantially raised the prices of many public
utilities and reduced a number of subsidies. Nevertheless, these measures—which, in fact, are not easy to
implement, politically speaking, and which were oriented
toward reallocating resources to the production of
tradable goods—were taken on the assumption that a
reactivation of the international economy would facilitate
exports and restore the terms of trade and bring interest
rates back to levels closer to those that had historically
prevailed.

Unfortunately, this was not the case. Although 1983
saw the beginning of a recovery in the main central
economy—the United States—this has not benefited Latin
America through any of the above-mentioned mechanisms.
Moreover, over the last few years, and especially in
1983, the region has been affected by yet another unfavorable change on the external scene: the drastic
reduction of the inflow of capital, the effect of which
has been equivalent to a deterioration of one-third in
the terms of trade.

That is why domestic adjustment had to be recessive
in nature and why it was based on an unprecedented
reduction of imports—even essential ones—and not on an
increase in exports. Thus, precisely at the worst time—
during an international recession—the region was
obliged to generate a substantial trade surplus, to
become a net exporter of resources to the central countries, and to accept additional and exceedingly burdensome costs in order to be able to refinance part of the
external debt it had accumulated.

It therefore seemed only natural at the end of 1983
to ask ourselves the following questions: What can Latin
America expect, over the short term, of the current

reactivation of the international economy? How long
can the indispensable domestic reactivation be postponed
if the present situation of the international economy
continues to prevail? After the profound traumas of the
last few years, will moderate rates of economic recovery
be adequate to deal with the serious social problems that
have arisen as a result of the recession of the last
three years?

In the first place, how steady are current indicators
of international economic recovery? International public
opinion views the economic recovery of the United States
with satisfaction, but also points to the contradictions
and puzzles posed by the phenomena that accompany it. On
the one hand, the so-called locomotive theory, according
to which the U.S. economy would be dynamic enough to pull
along the other industrial centers, shows no sign of
having been confirmed at this point. On the other hand,
there are still three elements that are vital if the
international recovery is to have any significant effect
on the countries of the periphery and, in particular, on
the Latin American economies.

First, in the field of trade, the terms of trade of
Latin America continued to deteriorate--with some
exceptions--during 1983 and no substantial increase in
commodity prices seems to be in sight in the near future.
Moreover, as a result of certain well-known phenomena,
some of which have to do with the high level of real
interest rates, protectionist trends in the central countries have persisted and even increased; this detracts
from the transparency and dynamism of international trade
and particularly hinders the growth of new exports.

Second, in the financial field, real interest rates
continue to be very high, as a result of many factors:
the fact that the governments of some industrial countries
have used the financial system to cover their substantial
fiscal deficits; the nature of the anti-inflationary
policies applied in the large central economies; the
disappearance of the liquid surpluses of the oil-exporting
countries; the pressure to attract savings in order to
deal with new capital-intensive investment; and others.
Thus, hardly anyone thinks that in 1984 there will be any
substantial reduction of real interest rates, a
phenomenon of fundamental importance to the management
of the external debt of the developing countries.

Third, in the field of capital transfers, there has
been a drastic reduction in the net inflow of capital,
which, after reaching an unprecedented level of
US$38 billion in 1981, fell to barely US$4.5 billion
in 1983; this drop would have been greater had not the
International Monetary Fund prevailed on the commercial
banks to increase somewhat their loans to Latin America.

The behavior of these variables in the reactivation
process is fundamental to the viability of the current
adjustment processes. It should be remembered that if

the terms of trade had been similar in 1983 to what they
were in 1980 (25 percent higher) and if at the same time
real interest rates had been similar to those prevailing
when the bulk of the debt was contracted (on average,
four points lower than at present), the region would have
had US$25 billion more during 1983; with this amount it
could easily have met its commitments without having to
reduce its imports so drastically and without having to
resort to new external indebtedness. In other words, if
normal conditions were restored in the area of trade and
finance, Latin America would be able to meet its external
commitments without having to sacrifice its potential
for growth.

On the other hand, Latin America cannot continue to
contract its economy. It must be made quite clear that
the region cannot continue applying the current adjustment mechanisms for much longer under the existing
external conditions. This could lead, at least in some
countries, to situations that would be difficult to
control, both economically and socially, and could give
rise to tensions that would jeopardize the very capacity
of the economies to recover and hence to service their
accumulated debt on time. It is advisable, therefore, to
ask what the main limitations of the current adjustment
processes are.

We should distinguish, first, among adjustment and
overadjustment. In recent years, the region has had to
carry out what essentially amounts to a twofold adjustment. The first and better known one is the adjustment
to the extremely unfavorable trend in the terms of trade
and in real interest rates. The second one has been the
adjustment aimed at dealing with a more recent but no
less serious development, the massive contraction of the
net inflow of private capital. Thus, because the
sluggishness of international trade and the "financial
depression" have occurred simultaneously, the region has
not only had to adjust but has had, in actual fact, to
overadjust.

Second, we have to realize that there is a perverse
process of transfer of resources. Because the net inflow
of capital fell so sharply and payments for profits and
interest were so high, Latin America--first in 1982 and
again and to a greater extent in 1983--made net transfers
of resources to the exterior that amounted to US$20
billion and US$29 billion respectively. This situation,
which contrasts sharply with what had historically been
the case in the developing countries, has become a key
element in the profound depression of Latin America and
one that will also be a decisive factor in the establishment of any economic recovery policy to be pursued in the
future.

We should consider, third, the asymmetry of the cost
of adjustment. There are other elements that have
contributed to the aggravation of the balance-of-payments

problems. Among these, special mention should be made of
the high costs and the bank surcharges that are involved
in the renegotiation process, which have been added to
the negative effects of the high interest rates. This
increase in the financial costs, which contrasts with
past experiences and with the crisis measures that banks
normally apply to any enterprise, has aggravated external
imbalances and has meant that virtually all the cost of
adjustment has been transferred to the debtor countries.
Indeed, this procedure is tantamount to an abdication,
on the part of the international commercial banks, of
their share of the responsibility for triggering the payments crisis with which the region is now faced.

Thus, Latin America cannot prolong the current
process of recessive adjustment; instead, what it needs
is to carry out a growth-oriented adjustment. Insofar as
it must for some time generate a trade surplus, it will
have to achieve this by increasing exports--by resorting
to a factor that helps raise the rate of economic growth--
rather than by again reducing imports, which would only
make the recession worse.

The Inevitable Recovery

One of the most puzzling questions of the moment is
the prevailing uncertainty about the possible modalities
of and the prospects for international recovery. However,
if the current situation with respect to prices of raw
materials, real interest rates, and transfers of private
capital continues, two different courses are open to the
economies of the region during 1984. Some countries whose
external situation is better and whose domestic adjustment programs have been relatively successful may see a
modest recovery in their economic growth rate. However,
because the service of their external debt represents
such a heavy burden, they have little room for the
recovery of domestic expenditure and hence of employment
levels. Other countries that face more serious external
situations and in addition have to deal with heavy inflationary pressures may see a persistence of recessive
trends, and this will aggravate the critical economic
and social situation that has prevailed in recent years.

In actual fact, neither of these two options is
acceptable. Indeed, what Latin America needs is a firm
and vigorous recovery policy. There is no question,
however, that any recovery process aimed at strengthening
the deteriorated regional economy will be conditioned by
both external and internal factors.

Among the former, rescheduling of the external debt
is the most important and the one that in the last
analysis determines, over the short run, the maneuvering
room that most of the Latin American governments will have
for implementing their economic recovery. Over the

medium term, on the other hand, the key element for enabling Latin America to achieve rapid and persistent economic growth is the expansion of its external trade, both within the region and with the rest of the world.

Two of the internal factors that condition the effort to put more dynamism into the economy seem to be dominant: (1) recovery programs must be made compatible with the abatement of inflationary pressures, both traditional and recent; and (2) the patterns of growth must be restructured over the medium term in order to make it possible to achieve, among other objectives, a substantial increase in the exporting capacity of the region. The latter is, moreover, a prerequisite for enabling the region to pay the service of its accumulated debt on time.

External Factors: A New Mechanism for Rescheduling the External Debt

It is important to stress that not all the Latin American countries are in the same situation as regards the servicing of the debt under the current adjustment mechanisms; moreover, the unfavorable international situation does not affect all of them in the same way. That is why it would be very difficult to arrange for a joint rescheduling of the external debt of Latin America. Nevertheless, because of the absolute necessity of conditioning the service of the debt to the requirements of domestic recovery and economic development, the time seems to have come, for many countries, to make global proposals for changes in the existing rescheduling mechanisms. To this end, in accordance with the proposals made by the Group of Twenty-Four, joint action should be undertaken in international forums such as the International Monetary Fund and the World Bank to promote measures to improve the existing international financial mechanisms and to improve the international environment in which the adjustment processes are carried out.

It is also important to consider the possibility of the countries of the region jointly proposing to the international financial community certain minimum conditions that must be met in the immediate future in connection with the adjustment processes, until such time as the conditions on the international financial commercial markets improve. These conditions should include, among others, the following:

1. In no case should a country devote to the service of its external debt resources amounting to more than a prudent percentage of its export income, guided by the need to maintain the minimum level of imports required for its economic recovery and development.
2. The cost of making adjustments should be distributed more evenly by drastically reducing the

current financial costs that are added to the high
interest rates. Consideration should also be given to
the possibility of using provisional mechanisms such as
the interest-rate subsidies that were studied during the
1960s, especially for international loans from public
sources, which would considerably alleviate the financial
burdens, so vital to the current adjustment process.

3. Amortization periods should be extended considerably in order to avoid in future the persistence of
a perverse transfer abroad of resources.

4. Firm commitments should be made to obtain
additional resources in order to provide for the refinancing of a higher proportion of interest payments, to
facilitate the expansion of trade in the countries of the
region, and to ensure the financing of satisfactory levels
of domestic investment. In this regard, renewed support
for the efforts of the World Bank, the Inter-American
Development Bank, and other regional financing agencies
will be fundamental.

In recent times, long-term global solutions have
been proposed that have not yet been given proper attention by the large financial centers of the world. Nevertheless, if the current international situation continues
for much longer, the force of circumstances might make
some of these alternatives viable. In particular, it
would be worthwhile to consider the possibility of con-
verting a substantial part of the accumulated debt into
long-term bonds, with real interest rates being brought
back near to historical levels and with grace periods
being granted for their servicing. This would enable
the countries to gain time for undertaking the necessary
domestic adjustments and for ascertaining the effect of
the measures aimed at increasing their export capacity
and substituting imports.

In any event, the management of the debt under
existing international circumstances presents the region
with a difficult dilemma. On the one hand, in order to
eliminate the perverse transfers of resources abroad so
as to sustain domestic recovery programs, it would be
necessary to obtain new net credits that would raise the
already high level of the existing external debt. On the
other hand, in order to meet part of the service of the
debt with resources generated through a trade surplus, it
would be necessary, in the absence of a significant
increase in exports, to again reduce the already low
volume of imports, and this would work against any effort
to reactivate the economy. That is why, over the short
term, any effort that is made in this regard must provide
for both an inflow of new resources and a substantial
abatement of financial costs.

Internal Factors

The Recovery of International Trade. The current preoccupation with the problems pertaining to the management of the external debt has led the countries to overlook the close linkage that exists between their debt and their trade problems. As is well known, in the last analysis the final solution to existing and future balance-of-payments problems can only be found by expanding trade and increasing export income.

To achieve this, it will of course be necessary to increase the countries' exporting capacity; however, it will also be necessary to create an international environment in which the markets for Latin American exports can be expanded and the prices of these exports can be improved.

The protectionist practices that have increasingly been applied in the central countries certainly do not make it easy for these conditions to be met.

The Protection and Expansion of Regional Trade. Concomitant with the contraction of Latin America's trade with the rest of the world, there has been a sharp deterioration of regional trade and a recrudescence, in by no means a few Latin American countries, of defensive measures of protectionist nature arising from the difficult balance-of-payments situation faced by almost all these countries.

This situation must not continue. In order to reverse it, it would be necessary, in the first place, to put a stop to the imposition of new measures that hinder intraregional trade and, in the second place, to adopt various measures of a preferential type, such as ad hoc agreements of limited scope or the utilization of the purchasing power of state governments to promote trade. To this end, it will also be essential to expand the existing regional financial mechanisms and promote a more imaginative role for Latin American financial institutions, some of which are already implementing programs to support the expansion of intraregional trade.

These and other joint policies that might be adopted by the region under the present circumstances, both in order to promote collectively the adoption of measures at the international level and to accelerate and give greater depth to the regional cooperation processes, were studied in January 1984 in Quito during a meeting (proposed by the president of Ecuador) of heads of state and their personal representatives at the ministerial level.

Domestic Factors That Condition Recovery. I shall not discuss this matter in detail here. I did so at the session of the Economic Commission for Latin America (ECLA) held in April 1984; on that occasion, the ECLA Secretariat presented its views on this matter. Nevertheless, I cannot neglect now to mention that in the very

near future the region will have to deal with a series of
factors that will force it to take a serious look at the
development policies and strategies that have been
applied up to now. This is essential if a degree of
economic dynamism is to be achieved that will enable the
region to respond to its serious social problems, which,
as was mentioned above, have been aggravated by the
current recession.

The rather difficult changes that may have to be
made in international finance and trade; the burden of
the accumulated debt--which is, in a way, a mortgage on
Latin America's future development; the continuation and,
in some cases, aggravation of old structural rigidities;
and inflationary pressures, the solution to which is only
with difficulty compatible with schemes for development
and social justice, are some of the elements that will
require revision of some ideas and the seeking and
formulation of new policies. In this regard, as has been
illustrated by recent experience, it is important to
remember the risks involved in development strategies
that are indiscriminately linked to international finance
and trade. These risks are now obvious, considering the
violent, prolonged, and unpredictable changes that have
occurred in the international parameters in which we have
been trusting.

Nevertheless, it is also of crucial importance to
make it quite clear that the current crisis is one of
liquidity and not one of solvency and that the region has
the capacity to respond and the means to deal in future
with its main problems.

It is to be hoped that the international financial
community, recognizing the unique profile of the Latin
American crisis, will cooperate intelligently, bearing
in mind the existing circumstances, and will help the
region overcome these problems of liquidity so as to
prevent a real crisis of solvency from developing.

5
Coping with the
Creeping Crisis of Debt

Albert Fishlow

INTRODUCTION

The total debt of developing countries, short and
long term, stood at more than US$800 billion at the end
of 1983, according to one recent estimate. The non-OPEC,
non-OECD developing countries most affected by the instability of the international economy in the past decade
account for some 80 percent of the total. More than 30
percent of their gross national product is owed abroad,
and in 1982, before reschedulings became the order of the
day, probably close to 50 percent of their export earnings was earmarked to meet debt service and rollover of
short-term credits. Such aggregates, and the thirty or
so countries forced to reschedule their debt payments
since 1981, make clear that the debt problem penetrates
deeply and broadly.[1] Indeed, the anxiety of creditors
now extends--as well it might--to such OPEC members as
Nigeria and Venezuela, whose oil resources had earlier
been an assurance of creditworthiness.

After all, it was the dramatic inability of oil-
rich Mexico to meet its obligations in August 1982 that
first moved dry statistics relating to external debt from
the obscurity of financial pages to the headlines.
Mexico was the second-largest developing country debtor
at US$80 billion and with proven oil reserves of seeming-
ly unlimited value. If it could not service its debt,
what of other countries less favored? With abrupt
suddenness, the degree of exposure of the banking systems
of the industrialized countries became a matter of grave
concern. Although a relatively small proportion of
total assets--little more than 10 percent--loans to
developing countries far exceeded the capital bases of
the largest money center banks. Interruption in debt
service threatened to provoke systemic financial instability. Beyond that loomed potential adverse real
repercussions on the economies of the United States and
of the other industrialized countries through loss of
developing-country markets. Interdependence was

97

transformed from a rhetorical slogan to a practical imperative.

It was no wonder that the Federal Reserve Bank, the other central banks largely working through the Bank for International Settlements, and the International Monetary Fund responded with a sense of urgency to the Mexican crisis. Fortunately, they also responded with imagination. Emergency credits were made available while an adjustment package was readied. The IMF boldly conditioned its own finance on commitments of new money from the commercial banks and designed its policy recommendations on the basis of assured total capital inflows rather than projected private-sector participation. Instead of counseling the Mexican government to adopt policies that might succeed in attracting new loans from the private sector, the IMF required the banks to put up new money as an integral part of a feasible adjustment package. Conditionality now was imposed on the banks as well as the countries.

These unprecedented arrangements soon became the order of the day through repetition in the cases of Argentina and Brazil as the fall of 1982 unfolded. There was no alternative, given the importance private creditors had assumed. In little more than a matter of months, but not without elaborate negotiations involving hundreds of banks, more than US$50 billion of debt had been rescheduled, about half as much short-term debt rolled over, and more than US$20 billion in involuntary new loans contracted for these three countries. Overall, probably US$100 billion in reschedulings have occurred. By far the most difficult problem was Brazil. Renegotiation of unrealistic targets originally agreed upon with the Fund and the banks earlier in the year extended until November 1983, when the government accepted additional austerity measures.

In the same month, a recalcitrant U.S. Congress, after a considerable delay, finally approved a US$8.4 billion appropriation to fund an enlarged IMF quota and expansion of the General Agreement to Borrow. It came with little time to spare, as the Fund was running out of resources to meet potential new needs of developing countries. The initial lag of the Reagan administration in recognizing the seriousness of the Mexican problem, and the failure to use the September 1982 IMF meeting as an occasion to mobilize support for the Fund, almost proved very costly. Scant weeks later, as Brazil tottered, Secretary of the Treasury Donald Regan became a convert to the cause of a more active role for the Fund. Conservatives in the Congress, more in tune with the earlier lack of enthusiasm of the administration for multilateral institutions, proved more difficult to persuade. It required almost a year, and liberal support, to obtain passage of the measure.

The relief occasioned by approval of the quota increase and resolution of Brazil's long-pending renegotiation with the Fund, in conjunction with signs of economic
recovery in the United States and the other industrialized
countries, has given rise to a certain optimism. The
first significant shock to the spontaneous system of
international lending that evolved in the 1970s has been
weathered, and modest repairs to the institutional framework are in process. Talk of more elaborate reforms is
less fashionable, and everyone seems to want to hope for
the best.

But the crisis may linger on--if not for the
financial system, then for the developing countries that
are bearing the brunt of the adjustment. As the Wall
Street Journal succinctly put it, "Despite the recent
rescue efforts, debt-ridden developing countries face
some bleak prospects for the years ahead: anemic export
earnings, sluggish investment and crushing interest
costs. The total foreign debt of developing countries
that don't produce oil, now estimated at $664 billion,
is expected to double by 1990."[2] That reality introduces
new elements of medium-term political, as well as
economic, viability into the debt picture. Will countries accept the burden, particularly if the magic of
economic recovery is less powerful than has been claimed?

Moreover, the future of the financial system is far
from certain. The very success of the short-term crisis
response ironically also signals the end of the market
system of Euromarket financial intermediation that had
flourished for more than a decade. Only by vigorous
official intervention have private banking arrangements
been salvaged. More than a new relationship between the
IMF and the commercial banks is involved. Within the
United States, the Federal Reserve Board has been called
upon to persuade recalcitrant regional banks of the
necessity to continue to lend to developing countries
when their desire is to reduce their exposure. Few
anticipate, even with improved economic circumstances,
a return to the buoyant capital markets of the 1970s
that served so well to recycle the petrodollar surpluses.
Can, or should, the quasi socialization of international
lending we have seen under the auspices of the IMF
replace it?

Questions, and the debt problem, thus persist. In
this chapter, I focus on four of its aspects. First, I
examine the origin of the problem in the disequilibrium
of the international economy in the 1970s and in the
responsive domestic policies of the developing countries.
From that basis I consider the possibility of industrialized-country recovery as a solution. Third, I take
up the appropriateness of the IMF adjustment packages
now in place in many countries, with regard to both their
economic and political viability. Finally, I evaluate
the adequacy of the existing institutional framework for

coping with the debt problem, and the financial needs of
the developing countries, in the medium term.

THE ORIGIN OF THE DEBT PROBLEM

From Debt-Led Growth to Growth-Led Debt

The expansion of the Eurocurrency market in the
1960s was, on the whole, of little significance to
developing countries. European central banks and transnational corporations were the principal transactors.
Only as the decade was drawing to a close, largely under
the impulse of a recession-induced declining conventional
demand for loans, did money center banks begin to search
out new prospects. They found a hitherto untapped
clientele among the rapidly growing countries of the
developing world that later would be christened the
"newly industrializing countries": Brazil, Mexico, and
Korea, among others. Capital began to flow to finance
the increased imports required by accelerating economic
expansion. Such loans, and not merely export promotion,
were the basis of a more elastic supply of foreign
exchange facing these countries and permitted a more
aggressive and accelerating growth strategy. Brazil's
economic miracle in particular was characterized by such
debt-led growth.

The sudden injection of petrodollars into world
financial markets in 1974 altered both the pace and the
purpose of borrowing. OPEC exporters realized a current
account surplus in that year of almost $70 billion as a
result of the quadrupling of oil prices and placed much
of it in short-term deposits with commercial banks.
Those dollars were loaned for a longer term to countries
that were importers of oil in order to finance their much
larger balance-of-payments deficits. Amid predictions of
impending doom and disaster, private financial markets
found a way not only to keep the global economy afloat,
but within short order, to fuel renewed expansion. That
way was unprecedented increase of external debt,
especially on the part of the developing countries.

Countries did not have to borrow at that time. They
could have reduced their purchases of oil, or failing
that possibility, have restricted other imports. But
such responses would have implied passing along the oil
tax in the form not only of lower real incomes but also
of diminished output and employment. That was an unpopular choice for most governments, especially when
they were taking credit for improving economic performance.
The other option was to accelerate the growth of exports
to offset the increased cost of imports; although no
less a reduction of real income, such a strategy at least
promised to be less contractionary than policies aimed
primarily at import reduction. That choice again seemed

dubious when recession in the industrialized countries was slowing aggregate trade growth in 1974 and 1975.

More gradual, debt-financed adjustment was therefore attractive to many countries, an option rendered the more alluring by its cheap cost. Not all countries were eligible. Those that had the luxury of borrowing were predominantly the ones that had already established prior links to the market: They turned from debt-led growth to growth-led debt. In the earlier period they could count on an elastic supply of foreign capital and could, and did, set ambitious growth targets independent of a foreign-exchange constraint. In the later period, they operated under greater restriction. Although they borrowed more, countries were not facing unlimited supplies of credit: Their growth rates had to be set more modestly, with larger debt financing the larger needed import requirements.

Not all eligible countries chose such a path. Taiwan and Singapore, for example, accepted a more immediate adjustment and realignment of real wages to remain competitive in exports. The more dependent economies were upon their exports, the more inclined they were to favor aggressive efforts to expand market shares rather than to accept continuing debt-financed balance-of-payments deficits. In such small open economies, import substitution was not a prominent part of medium-term adaptation, and export competitiveness was best accomplished by short-term flexibility.

Enough countries opted for deficit finance to permit financial markets to sustain world demand. By making money cheap the banks induced borrowers to maintain and expand their imports to offset the export surplus of the oil producers. In this fashion, a classic potential oversavings, non-full-employment solution to the surplus problem was averted, and global recovery could build upon the continuing growth of the middle-income developing countries. Increased indebtedness thus had positive externalities.

From a national perspective, this sort of strategy also produced favorable results. The select group of countries that were able to borrow experienced better economic performance. The poorest countries, on the other hand, had to adjust immediately and painfully, despite larger official lending mobilized in their behalf. As a consequence, a wider gulf opened between the middle-income and the low-income countries in the 1970s, even as it narrowed between semiindustrialized and industrialized countries. Per capita income grew between 1970 and 1980 at an annual rate of 3.2 percent in the middle-income countries, 2.4 percent in the industrialized countries, and not at all in the low-income countries other than India and China.[3]

Table 5.1 confirms this dominant role of the NICs in credit markets in the immediate aftermath of the oil-price

Table 5.1 Developing-Country Debt[a] (in billions of U.S. dollars)

	1973	1974	1975	1976	1977	1978	1979	1980	1981	1982	1983
Non oil exporters	130.1	160.8	190.8	228.0	280.3	334.3 / 300.7[b]	354.5[b]	421.4[b]	492.6[b]	551.3[b]	585.6[b]
NICS[c]	51.3	66.2	82.3	101.5	122.7	149.5 / 115.9[b]	135.0[b]	160.9[b]	185.4[b]	211.9[b]	217.7[b]
Brazil	13.8	18.9	23.3	28.6	35.2	48.4	57.4	66.1	75.7	88.2	97.0
Mexico	8.6	12.8	16.9	21.8	27.1	33.6					
Korea	4.6	6.0	7.3	8.9	11.2	14.8	20.5	26.4	31.2	35.8	42.0
Southern Cone	10.1	12.4	12.7	13.0	14.9	19.2	27.5	38.3	51.3	55.2	60.0
Argentina	6.4	8.0	7.9	8.3	9.7	12.5	19.0	27.2	35.7	38.0	42.0
Chile	3.7	4.4	4.8	4.7	6.2	6.7	8.5	11.1	15.6	17.2	18.0
Low income	26.4	30.9	34.6	40.1	48.6	54.8	62.7	71.4	75.2	81.8	88.0
Selected oil exporters	15.4	17.9	21.2	27.3	35.3	47.1	58.2[b]	65.2[b]	70.5[b]	78.3[b]	90.0[b]
Algeria	2.9	3.3	4.5	5.8	8.3	12.7	14.9	15.1	15.3	14.8	17.0
Indonesia	5.7	7.1	8.9	11.0	12.8	14.5	14.9	17.0	18.0	21.0	23.0
Mexico							40.8	53.8	67.0	82.0	83.0
Nigeria	2.2	2.2	2.1	1.8	1.9	3.6	4.7	5.6	7.9	11.2	17.0
Venezuela	4.6	5.3	5.7	8.7	12.3	16.3	23.7	27.5	29.3	31.3	33.0
Total	145.5	178.7	212.0	255.3	315.6	381.4	453.5	540.4	630.1	711.6	758.6
All developing countries					329.3	398.2	472.0	559.9	646.5	724.8	767.7

Sources of Change (percentages of total)

	1973-1976	1976-1978	1978-1980	1980-1982	1983
NICS	45.7	38.1	28.3	29.8	12.3
Southern Cone	2.6	4.9	12.0	9.9	12.3
Low income	13.4	11.7	10.4	6.1	13.2
Oil exporters	10.8	15.7	24.1	24.1	27.0
			(11.4)[b]	(7.6)[b]	(24.9)[b]

Table 5.1 (cont.)

[a]Developing countries include IMF definition of nonoil developing countries plus Algeria, Indonesia, Nigeria, and Venezuela; includes Mediterranean European countries. Debt includes short- and long-term debt, including nonguaranteed. Excludes loans from IMF.

[b]Excludes Mexico

[c]Major exporters on manufactures, less Argentina, but including Mexico

Sources: Nonoil countries, 1973-1976: International Monetary Fund (IMF), World Economic Outlook, 1983; NICs, 1973-1976: IMF, World Economic Outlook, 1983, plus short-term debt estimated as .45 times total nonoil short-term debt; low income 1973-1976: IMF, World Economic Outlook, 1983, plus short-term debt estimated as .05 times nonoil short-term debt; all developing countries, NICs, low income, nonoil countries, 1977-1983: IMF, World Economic Outlook, 1984; Brazil, Mexico, Korea, Argentina, Indonesia, and Venezuela, 1973-1982: W. Cline, International Debt and the Stability of the World Economy (Washington, D.C., 1983); Nigeria and Algeria, 1973-1982: World Bank, World Debt Tables and World Financial Markets, June 1983; Chile, 1973-1982: R. Zahler, "Recent Southern Cone Liberalization Reforms and Stabilization Policies: The Chilean Case (1974-82)," Journal of Interamerican Studies and World Affairs, November 1983, and World Financial Markets, June 1983; Brazil, Mexico, Korea, and Argentina, 1983: Organization for Economic Cooperation and Development, External Debt of Developing Countries, 1983 Survey; Chile and Venezuela, 1983: Euromoney, March 1984; Algeria, 1983: Economist, Quarterly Economic Review, no. 1, 1984; Indonesia, 1983: Economist, Quarterly Economic Review, no. 1, 1984 (estimate of incremental loans); Nigeria, 1983: Wall Street Journal, February 21, 1984.

shock. They accounted for over two-fifths of the increase in all developing-country debt between 1973 and
1976. Mexico and Brazil, together, accounted for about a
quarter. All low-income countries could manage little
more than 10 percent, almost exclusively from official
sources. Five of the nonsurplus-oil exporters virtually
matched that participation.

For some of the borrowers, the new credits became
habit forming, even after real prices of oil began to be
eroded and industrial-country growth recovered after
1975. Balance-of-payment deficits declined only
gradually, as bank willingness to continue to lend opened
up new possibilities for public spending. The data in
Table 5.1 reveal a continued high level of participation
of the NICs in total borrowing and expansion of the role
of the oil-exporting countries. Although borrowing had
its origins in the oil crisis, it took on a life of its
own, one influenced by the higher price not merely of oil
but also of manufactured imports.

Since banks preferred official guarantees, and these
could more readily be given on public loans and indirect
borrowing of state enterprises, private international
credit markets imparted a significant bias toward public-
sector expansion. This, too, favored those middle-income
countries with a more pervasive network of state enterprises and interventionist tradition. Countries found
the speed and less exigent requirements of the private
banks a welcome contrast to the rigidities of official
loans.

Banks, on their side, found their new customers an
important source of profits. Banks made their money on
the higher up-front commission fees and spreads for loans
to developing countries, and low real interest rates, or
even negative rates, were no worry. Indeed, they were
welcome in minimizing the debt-servicing problems of the
developing-country borrowers. As long as bank depositors
were willing to accept negligible returns, and surplus-
oil producers had such a preference for liquidity that
they were, the arrangement was quite satisfactory.

As a result, developing-country debt grew at a rate
of about 20 percent a year from 1973 to 1978, increasingly weighted by the floating-rate loans of banks.
Lenders bore the risk of a mismatch between overnight
deposits and six- or eight-year loans; borrowers bore the
risk of changing interest rates and had their costs pegged
to the London Inter-Bank Offer Rate (LIBOR). In addition,
countries were exposed to the high rates of loan turnover
implicit in the short-maturity structure of commercial
loans. This translated into debt-service ratios that
far exceeded previously conventional standards, without
providing comparable access to increased real resources.

A relatively small number of countries thus embarked
on a strategy of growth-led debt in the 1970s subject to
special vulnerabilities. They were financing medium- and

long-term capital formation on the basis of short-term
credits with an uncertain and variable price. Inherent
in any debt strategy was an inability to know its real
return because the future prices of exports were an
important determinant of the potential benefits.
Compounding it in this case were an uncertain cost of debt
and a dependence upon future conditions of supply of
credit required to roll over existing loans.

Yet up to the second oil-price shock, the gamble was
worth taking. Export growth was sustained in world
markets at favorable prices despite worries about
protectionism. As a consequence, the ratio of debt outstanding to export proceeds was more favorable for nonoil developing countries in 1979 than in 1970-1972
(although assisted by rising oil revenues for some new
exporters in the group). Debt service, even if claiming
a larger share of exports than earlier (as grace periods
expired and interest rates crept upward), was still a
modest 19 percent for the group as a whole. Short-term
loans were not yet much in evidence and posed no cash-
flow problem. The ratio of reserves to debt outstanding
at the end of 1979 was a third more satisfactory than the
level in 1970-1972.[4]

In the meantime, as noted earlier, those developing
countries with access to the financial market succeeded
in sustaining their rates of growth far more effectively
than those forced to do without. They did so because
they utilized increased foreign savings to finance higher
levels of investment. Evidence on the consumption behavior of a number of the major debtor countries is
reported in Table 5.2.[5] It confirms the productive
application of the much larger foreign capital inflows in
the period after 1973.

In the first place, despite the acceleration in
borrowing, the propensity to consume out of net foreign
proceeds in 1965-1978 was not statistically significantly
greater than in the prior period. If foreign resources
were not all applied to investment, neither were they
diverted to consumption in proportions different than
they had been. Second, the share allocated to savings
from foreign borrowing in 1965-1978 was significantly
greater than the allocation from gross national product
for Korea; for both Brazil and Mexico, the deviations
are in the right direction although falling short of
statistical significance. Indeed, for these three largest
debtors, the savings coefficients from net capital inflow are high enough so that the hypothesis that all
borrowing was saved cannot be rejected. At the margin,
for these countries, debt translated more than pro-
portionally into investment. Third, even after the
second oil shock in 1979-80 provoked further uncertainties and reduced growth and investment, there was no
systematic tendency toward greater consumption out of
borrowing. Some countries did show a rise, Brazil most

Table 5.2   Consumption Behavior of Debtor Nations

	Marginal Propensity to Consume from National Product 1965-1981	Marginal Propensity to Consume from Foreign Capital 1965-1978	1979-1981
Argentina	.76 (21.39)[a]	.82 (2.49)	1.02 (1.20)
Brazil	.79 (48.24)	-.02 (.04)	.90 (1.91)
Chile	.86 (33.92)	.95 (2.84)	.51 (1.62)
Colombia	.73 (35.68)	.69 (2.67)	.20 (.50)
Indonesia	.67 (37.80)	1.00 (6.84)	.76 (4.63)
Korea	.68 (34.87)	.20 (1.82)	.48 (1.97)
Mexico	.76 (36.26)	.43 (1.30)	-.51 (1.54)
Venezuela	.46 (1.16)	.54 (7.40)	.38 (1.72)

[a] t-values in parentheses

Source: Data on national accounts from International Monetary Fund, International Financial Statistics, various issues.

prominently, but the only statistically significant change was Mexico's in the direction of greater saving. Finally, the pattern of expenditures in a nondebtor country like Colombia is not much different from that in the largest debtors.

This conclusion of no gross displacement of domestic saving is corroborated by IMF studies comparing changes in average ratios of saving to GNP with relative changes in the current account between the late 1960s and the 1970s. Taking into account as well simultaneous investment increases, the "increases in external deficits can in most cases be accounted for by expansion of investment (relative to total output) rather than by growth of consumption."[6] The cross-sectional methodology leads to the stronger result that debt had its principal application in investment, not true in my sample for such borrowers as Argentina, Chile, and Indonesia. What seems clear is that countries did not borrow in order to increase their consumption ratios, although their absolute consumption may have risen.

Although some countries encountered difficulties and were forced to reschedule and although some analysts remained skeptical of the magic of the market, the consensus judgment about developing-country debt until the second oil shock was a positive one. Rapidly growing debt was a solution rather than a problem. Even in 1980 it could be stated in an IMF Occasional Paper:

In sum, the overall debt situation during the 1970s adapted itself to the sizable strains introduced in the payments system and, in broad terms, maintained its relative position vis-à-vis other relevant economic variables. Though some countries experienced difficulties, a generalized debt management problem was avoided, and in the aggregate the outlook for the immediate future does not give cause for alarm.[7]

A Changed International Environment

Even as those lines were being written, the bases for optimism were being eroded by a deteriorating global economy. In the first instance oil prices soared again under the impulse of uncertain supplies as war broke out in the fall of 1979 between Iran and Iraq. After considerable volatility in the spot market, the new average 1980 oil price settled at a level almost two and a half times greater than its 1978 value of US$12.83 a barrel. The immediate impact, reminiscent of the first oil-price shock, was a large OPEC surplus offset by a large nonoil developing-country deficit.

Once again there was a recession in the industrialized countries, as contradictory policies sought to contain inflation, but this time more seriously. The impact on developing-country exports and terms of trade was to prove longer lived. Finally, there was a new element in the formula: Real interest rates began an upward ascent. Where before the capital market facilitated deficit finance, it now penalized not only the flow but also the stock of past debt contracted on a floating basis to boot.

Table 5.3 quantifies the approximate contribution of each of these three adverse factors to the current account deficit realized by the group of nonoil developing countries as a whole. The role of the oil-price shock, even allowing for the favorable impact on such countries as Mexico, Peru, Egypt, and a few others, is shown as paramount in timing and magnitude. In second place is the recession-induced reduction in export earnings, the result of both slower growth in volume and deterioration in price. This negative influence is most pronounced in 1982. By that time the severity and length of the slowdown in the industrialized countries produced a volume decline as well as an increasing cumulative price effect. It is not surprising that by 1982 countries found themselves in more and more balance-of-payments difficulty.

Higher interest rates, despite the attention they have received, are of lesser, but accelerating, importance

Table 5.3 Sources of Deterioration in the Current Account of
Nonoil Developing Countries, 1979-1982 (billions of U.S. dollars)

	1978	1979	1980	1981	1982	Cumulative 1979-1982
Actual trade balance	-36.6	-51.3	-74.3	-79.6	-52.2	
Adjusted trade balance		-46.3	-57.3	-47.8	8.8	
Oil effect		5.0	17.0	18.6	14.8	55.4
Recession effect				13.2	46.2	59.4
Export volume					23.2	23.2
Terms of trade				13.2	21.3	34.5
Debt service (gross)	-19.4	-28.0	-40.4	-55.1	-59.2	
Interest Rate effect (gross)		-1.1	.5	11.4	23.0	33.8
Interest rate effect (net)		-.5	.2	6.5	14.0	20.2
Current account	-41.3	-61.0	-89.0	-107.7	-86.8	
Adjusted current account	-41.3	-56.5	-71.8	-69.4	-11.8	

Source: Actual trade balance and current account based on
International Monetary Fund, World Economic Outlook, 1983;
adjusted trade balance: actual minus sum of oil and recession
effects; oil effect: actual cost of net imports of oil (using oil
import price of industrialized countries) minus estimated cost using
oil price that varies after 1978 with export prices of oil-importing
countries; recession effect: composite of terms of trade and
volume effects (does not add because of interaction); export volume:
nonoil export value times cumulative negative percentage deviation
between actual export volume of oil-importing countries and volume
predicted by 3.2 percent OECD growth in 1980-1982; terms of trade:
cumulative negative percentage deviation between actual nonoil
terms of trade (export prices of nonoil, oil-importing countries,
import prices of oil-exporting countries in 1973-1974, 1979-1980,
nonoil countries in others) and terms of trade predicted by 3.2
percent OECD growth and deceleration of industrialized country
inflation at one percentage point per year; debt service (gross):
based on International Monetary Fund, International Financial
Statistics; interest-rate effect: based on a 1975-1978 average
real prime rate (measured using the December to December price
index) of .75 applied to short-term loans, and for effect net of
earning assets, to short-term net liabilities. Interest on long-
term and medium-term loans was calculated by using the real prime
rate with a weight of one-third and the OECD long-term fixed interest
rate with a weight of two-thirds, corresponding to portfolio weights
reported in Organization for Economic, Cooperation and Development,
External Debt of Developing Countries (Paris, 1982). Rates were
applied to average annual debt, obtained by using average of year-end
debts. This method approximates well actual gross and net interest
payments reported in International Monetary Fund, World Economics
Outlook. Adjusted current account: actual minus sum of oil effect,
recession effect, and net interest effect.

in explaining the deterioration in the current account.
One reason for their limited power is the offsetting
effect of developing-country assets on which earnings
would have been lower had real rates not increased
abruptly in 1981 and 1982. This is reflected in the
smaller net improvement for current account for 1982
compared to the adjusted current account, as shown in
Table 5.3.

But this does not capture the full significance of
the rise in the interest rate. The increase not only
contributed to the current account deficit but also had
immediate adverse effects on the debt-service ratio. Between 1978 and 1981 interest payments on the debt rose
from $19 billion to $55 billion for all nonoil developing
countries, and the ratio to exports increased from 7.3
to 11.9 percent. The change for Latin American borrowers
was much greater, as the ratio of interest service to
exports climbed from 14.9 to 25.4 percent. Only declining amortization kept the overall debt-service ratio within bounds. Potential lenders were concerned. That the
higher nominal rates at first were partially equivalent
to shorter maturities, because they were compensating for
inflation rather than signaling a deterioration in the
capacity to pay, did not always register.

Such higher rates thus exacerbated the crisis and
were a crucial factor in making developing-country
adjustment more difficult just when export demand was
falling off. Recession in the industrialized countries
in the past had at least been partially offset by more
abundant and cheaper loanable funds. Higher rates had a
further effect: They determined the inertial growth of
the debt, an inertial growth that would have to be offset
by export surpluses that reversed the real resource flow
to developing countries. I explore this consequence in
the next section.

The new real-interest-rate regime was largely the
consequence of conscious policy in the industrialized
countries. Tighter money became the principal instrument
to reduce inflation. Reaganomics carried the process a
further step by marrying lax fiscal policy and an insistence on lower inflation; the predictable consequence was
higher deficits, interest rates, and unemployment.
Restrictive policy also produced other consequences that
reinforced the tendency for interest rates to rise.
Reduced surpluses were realized by oil producers facing a
softer and more competitive market, so that former source
of savings to finance the deficits of the oil importers
was no longer available.

International capital markets magnified the shock.
Banks, concerned about their exposure, raised premiums
to oil-importer borrowers; more importantly, they became
more reluctant to lend. They began to prefer shorter
loans--ostensibly trade credits, but in reality, like all
lending, balance-of-payments finance. Estimated debt of

less than a year doubled between 1977 and 1982 while medium- and long-term finance increased by about 50 percent.

As the data in Table 5.3 suggest, the cumulative effects of the external shocks experienced after 1979 were sufficient to convert the large 1982 deficit of $87 billion to one of $12 billion. In the absence of these cumulative effects, the sometimes drastic efforts on the part of countries to curtail their imports would have led to significant improvement in their payments situation rather than the severe difficulty actually experienced.

All together, the total value of imports was cut back by some $40 billion in 1982. That was the inevitable consequence of confronting mounting debt-service ratios with first claim on foreign-exchange receipts. For the largest debtors--Argentina, Brazil, and Mexico--debt service in 1982, excluding rollover of short-term debt, averaged about 80 percent of export earnings.

But the data in Table 5.3 also make it clear that the sharp initial rise in the deficit from its 1978 level must be explained on other grounds. By 1980, even leaving aside the oil-price shock and the price of exports, the current account deficit had risen by a third. It is a mistake to blame the oil-price and recession shocks alone for what was also an inadequacy of the functioning of capital markets.

For one thing, as the data in Table 5.1 showed, there was much increased borrowing by Chile and Argentina as they pursued more open capital markets as an integral part of their new international monetarist stabilization experiments. Between 1978 and 1981 their previously moderate debt almost trebled, as they alone accounted for some 12 percent of increased developing-country indebtedness. High domestic interest rates in conjunction with preannounced and--in the case of Chile--fixed exchange rates encouraged rapid capital inflows that were translated into larger imports, but without the same proportion saved as was true of the earlier NIC borrowing in the aftermath of the 1973 oil shock.

For another, oil exporters, and in particular Mexico, relied heavily on external finance to sustain high rates of growth of product and, disproportionately, of imports. The very initial shock of higher oil prices worked to their advantage. They borrowed not to accommodate to adverse external circumstances, but rather to exploit their new riches. Needless to say, they were attractive clients for banks again flush with Eurodeposits in search of application.

Finally, some oil-importing countries, prominently Brazil, became habituated to debt-financed adjustment, understated the different and more persistent international recession, and took few precautionary measures. Brazil chose for internal political reasons to expand in 1980 at the expense of a deteriorating payments position.

It was checked early on by an increasingly inelastic supply of credit. As a consequence its debt expanded relatively less than that of its Latin American neighbors. Between 1978 and 1981, the principal debtors in Latin America were responsible for more than 40 percent of the increased debt tabulated in Table 5.1, compared to an initial participation of 30 percent. Almost all of the new debt was accumulated on a floating-rate basis, and progressively the cheap interest rates became unavailable. For many, prudent import policies might have averted some of the later grief. A prominent exception was Brazil, whose large outstanding debt absorbed virtually all of the foreign exchange borrowed and whose real imports remained compressed. Brazil was also exempt from the capital flight that complicated debt management in Argentina, Mexico, and Venezuela. The excess of debt change over the current account deficit and reserve accumulation amounted to some $45 billion between 1979 and 1982. Public-sector obligations financed accumulation of private assets abroad in these cases.[8]

This country variability is lost in the aggregation of Table 5.3. The countries with relatively large reserves that gained from higher interest rates are not those most affected by payments problems because of lagging exports. Nor did prices for all products move uniformly. The terms of trade of Asian oil-importing countries fell by 5.5 percent between 1980 and 1982; those of the Latin American countries by 13.6 percent.[9] However much external events impinged, nevertheless (as they impressively did), domestic policies and international negligence were also components of the seriously deteriorating situation that finally became patent in 1982.

Global equilibrium in response to the second oil shock was achieved at lower levels of real income. Instead of buffering the impact as before, developing-country debt now transmitted it. Only so long as growth-led debt was compatible with developed-country aversion to recession and with OPEC willingness to hold Euro-currency deposits yielding low or negative real rates could the strategy be effective. It made little difference that current account deficits in the early 1980s would have been in line with the trend of modest improvement had the external environment remained stable. What counted was that the strategy chosen was no longer viable, but also not easily reversible. Once in debt, it was more difficult to maneuver.

A LIQUIDITY CRISIS?

By the fall of 1982 there was widespread agreement that there was a debt problem. Time magazine, perhaps with an overeagerness to sell copies, made the situation a cover story and christened it a "debt bomb." Others

more sober and analytically inclined differentiated between a liquidity crisis and a solvency problem: a short-
term interruption of cash flow versus a long-term ability
to repay debt. The majority view, including that of
bankers, government officials, and independent observers,
inclined to the former. The World Bank, in its 1983
report on external debt, stated it as follows:

> There is no generalized debt crisis: rather,
> the mutual difficulties of developing countries
> in servicing foreign borrowing and of commercial
> banks in obtaining service payments on foreign
> lending are an outgrowth of the broader economic
> problems that grip all of the world's economies.
> The resolution of these difficulties lies in a
> restoration of economic health to the global
> economy and a resumption of strong growth in
> international trade.[10]

There is basis for such a characterization in the
magnitude of the effects set in motion by the oil-price
shock in late 1979 and the policy response to it, as
Table 5.3 has already brought out. There is also
persuasive evidence from casting the perspective forward
rather than backward. As the IMF's medium-term scenarios
show, as Morgan Guaranty's balance-of-payments model
confirms, and as William Cline's more recent projections
for nineteen of the largest debtors reemphasizes, "If
this growth rate [3 percent annually for industrialized
countries] can be achieved, the debt problems of the
developing countries should be manageable and should show
considerable improvement. . . . The central result of
this analysis is that the debt problem can be managed,
and that it is essentially a problem of illiquidity, not
insolvency."[11]
I am partial to this assessment. Yet at the same
time it requires qualification in two important respects.
For one, the analogy of countries to firms is not entirely
adequate. Solvency for a firm is defined by an excess of
assets over liabilities; otherwise it is bankrupt, and
its creditors may benefit from the dissolution. On the
other hand, countries do not cease to exist, nor can
their assets, at least any more, be seized for distribution. Second, the technical requirement for solvency
at a country level--a zero cumulative balance of payments
over a very long time horizon, in order to guarantee
repayment of accumulated intervening debt--is of limited
practical significance. Since policies are variable,
such a condition in principle could always be met over a
suitably long period. So can the additional requirement
that the real return on borrowing repay its cost, since
capital in the developing countries remains relatively
scarce.

A more relevant solvency criterion is therefore not
the eventual capacity to pay, but the medium-term prospect
for decelerating the increase in debt relative to exports.
Such a criterion incorporates availability of foreign
exchange rather than saving as the determining constraint
in meeting external obligations.[12] It also substitutes
the existence of a limiting debt-export ratio, with
continuous growing debt, for the condition of debt full
repayment.

For the debt-export ratio to converge to a maximum,
with developing countries still recipients of a net
resource transfer from the industrialized, requires that
export growth exceed the interest rate.[13] If it does not,
the further borrowing necessary to cover both interest
payments and import purchases will exceed the increase
in exports and force the debt-export ratio to continuously higher levels. With imports and exports
exactly equal, the rate of growth of the debt is simply
equal to the uncovered interest costs that must be
borrowed. If exports do not grow at the interest rate,
the debt-export ratio rises.

Only by running a merchandise surplus (i.e.,
transferring real resources to creditor countries) can
debtors prevent the debt-export ratio rising when interest
rates exceed export growth. That, of course, is what
many such countries have been forced to do since 1982,
but that does not make them solvent. Rather, it amounts
to their acceptance of the present disequilibrium as a
permanent state and their refusal to see beyond the
temporary favorable balance of payments to the longer-
term implications. Estimates suggest that such a
transfer of real resources from the Latin American countries amounted to US$20 billion in 1982 and US$30 billion
in 1983, representing 19 and 27 percent respectively of
the value of exports of goods and services. "Thus was
prolonged a situation that, taking into account the
relative degree of development of the region, can only
be qualified as perverse."[14] More generally, for all the
countries in the World Bank reporting system, the positive net transfer of $16 billion in 1981 was converted
to a negative US$7 billion in 1982 and a larger negative
$21 billion in 1983.[15]

Favorable medium-term projections of the balance
of payments, without regard to the necessary transfer of
resources to the developing countries, are thus no ipso
facto guarantee of solvency. Nor are even demonstrations of declining debt-export ratios, if they are
achieved through premature graduation to export of real
resources. Such exercises ignore the magnitude of the
sacrifice entailed for the developing countries. They
assume that ability to pay is equivalent to willingness
to pay regardless of the costs.

But I have an additional objection to the prevalent
characterization of the debt problem as a simple

liquidity crisis. My concern is that the balance-of-
payments projections underlying such a diagnosis are
overly optimistic. They place an undue emphasis upon
economic recovery in the industrialized countries as a
solution to the debt problem of the developing nations.
    Careful attention to the quantitative estimates put
forward is therefore in order. Because of both their care
and their influence, I focus upon William Cline's recent
detailed projections.[16] He started with a statistically
estimated relationship of total OECD imports to industrialized-country income growth. He made this applicable
to all nonoil-developing-country exports by adding a
1 percent higher trend rate of growth. That translated
a 3 percent annual growth in OECD income into a 6 percent
real increase in developing-country nonoil exports. It
also implied a higher elasticity of three between percentage changes in industrialized country income and
exports. Volume effects were only half of the story.
Favorable terms-of-trade effects, higher prices from
dollar devaluation, and enhanced developing-country
competitiveness owing to aggressive real devaluation made
up the difference. The terms-of-trade estimates were
country specific where possible, unlike the volume
estimates.
    It was necessary also to estimate import requirements.
For all countries, an import elasticity of unity was
assumed for nonoil imports, with a cyclical adjustment
for increasing growth. To these nonoil trade balances
were added imports and exports of oil, both of which were
held constant in volume terms. Finally, the service
balance, including interest obligations, was added to
arrive at the current account deficit. With additional
assumptions about reserve accumulation and foreign investment, one arrives at net borrowing needs.
    In accordance with the earlier discussion, special
attention should be directed to the estimates of export
growth. I have reestimated export volume for non-oil-
importing countries as a whole as well as for some sub-
groupings directly as a function of industrialized income growth. I have done the same for real export prices,
introducing the real interest rate, the change in the
rate of inflation, and variation in the value of the
dollar as additional relevant variables. The latter two
are especially significant. Table 5.4 presents the
responsiveness of export volume and the terms of trade
with respect to the growth, and changes in the growth,
of the industrialized countries. Underlying estimating
equations are presented in the Appendix to this chapter.
    The data in Table 5.4 suggest in the first instance
that Cline's estimates, and others constructed similarly,
overstated the sensitivity of real growth of developing-
country exports to conditions in the industrialized
countries. Whether for nonoil countries as a whole or
for subgroups, for the longer period or for the shorter

since the first oil shock, these directly estimated elasticities are smaller than three. The sole exception is the country-specific estimate for Korea, whose much higher export growth produces a higher value. As a result, industrialized-country recovery has a much less dramatic impact on export performance. Whereas Cline implied a doubling of nonoil export growth from 3 to 6 percent if industrialized countries moved from a 2 to 3 percent rate of expansion, the comparable effect for non-oil countries as a group is a much more limited rise from 4.7 to 5.7 percent; for oil-importing countries in the period after 1973, the estimate is a difference between 5.0 and 6.7 percent.

What these more modest responses reflect is the strength of developing-country exports in recent years even in the face of international recession. As output growth in the industrialized countries slowed continuously from 4.1 percent in 1978 to -.3 percent in 1982, exports of the oil-importing countries continued to increase at high rates well in excess of world trade generally. In 1980 they grew at 9.2 percent; in 1981, at 5.3 percent; declining finally by 1.1 percent in 1982. That is shown in the small weight attributed to export volume short-falls in Table 5.3. By Cline's formula, growth rates should have stood at .9, .6, and -3.9 percent respectively.

Developing-country exports were able to hold up better because of increasing competitiveness in indus-trialized-country markets that made sales more independent of total demand. They also could because developing-country demand was better sustained, at least through 1980. Something between 20 and 25 percent of all nonoil exports were sold to other developing countries. The sharp falloff in trade in 1982 reflected the closure of such markets as income decreased.

Recovery in the industrialized countries will there-fore make a difference to the performance of the developing countries, but perhaps less centrally than has been maintained. In particular, it is far from obvious that the more rapid expansion now anticipated for 1984 will have the further beneficent effects presumed, especially since developing-country growth will continue to lag. My quarrel is with exaggeration of the sensi-tivity rather than with the order of magnitude of export growth if recovery should proceed at 3 percent. Some-thing like 6 percent is a reasonable level consistent with my estimating equations.

Reduced export volume is not, as we have seen, the most important factor responsible for softer developing-country earnings. Rather, despite rather successful efforts to export, the prices of their products have fallen dramatically in recent years. During 1981 and 1982 prices of primary commodities exported declined by more than 25 percent. Even developing-country exporters of manufactured products encountered diminishing prices

Table 5.4 Elasticities for Developing-Country Export Volume and
Terms of Trade with Respect to OECD Income Growth and Changes
in Income Growth

Export Volume	
	Industrialized Country Growth
Nonoil developing countries, 1963-1982	1.08
Brazil, excl. coffee	1.83
Brazil, incl. coffee[a]	
Korea (1964-1982)	4.30
Nonoil, oil-importing countries, 1973-1982	1.73
Exporters of manufactures	2.46
Low income[a]	
Asia	2.29
Western Hemisphere	1.51

Terms of Trade[b]	
	Changes in Industrialized Country Growth[c]
Nonoil developing countries, 1964-1982	1.37
Brazil, excl. coffee	1.46
Korea (1965-1982)	.77
Nonoil, oil-importing countries, 1974-1982	1.27
Exporters of manufactures	1.18
Low income	1.86
Asia	1.29
Western Hemisphere	2.50

[a] Standard errors greater than coefficient

[b] Terms of trade measured by percentage change in developing-country
export unit prices minus percentage change in developed-country
export prices

[c] Average of current and lagged responses to changes in growth
rates; terms of trade improvement realized over only a two-year
period

Source: For data 1963-1982: International Monetary Fund (IMF),
International Financial Statistics, Handbook, 1983; 1973-1982:
IMF, World Economic Outlook, 1983; for underlying regressions,
see Appendix to Chapter 5.

and deteriorating terms of trade.
Projections of exports must therefore take into
account the evolution of prices as well as quantity.
Cline's estimates of considerably improved terms of trade
were on shaky ground. The relatively high elasticity
of three that he obtained with respect to a one-percentage-
point increase in industrialized country growth is not
corroborated in Table 5.4. There, most elasticities with
respect to changes in industrialized-country growth are
smaller, especially for the categories of high-volume
growth. This response is cyclical, leading to improvement
in the terms of trade as a result of accelerating income
growth without continuing gains in spite of stable, higher
levels. I have presented the average impact on the terms
of trade, realized over a two-year period since both
current and lagged changes in income growth enter, of a
one-percentage-point acceleration in growth. One of
the reasons for Cline's higher responsiveness is
semantic: He apparently summed the two-year effect.
Another is that one of his few statistically significant
estimates was for Brazil, which showed a large impact,
and that the average was then applied to countries without information. The group results are more reliable.[17]

These terms-of-trade estimates are an intermediate
stage in the forecast of developing-country export and
import values. Cline proceeded to such absolutes by
first projecting the export prices of the industrialized
countries as the sum of general price inflation and
dollar depreciation. This gave import prices. Then he
added the estimated improvement in the terms of trade to
get export prices. All told, these factors add about 20
percent to the value of exports and are thus the most
important source of improvement in foreign-exchange
earnings in 1984.

The implicit assumption is that depreciation of the
dollar will affect exports and imports fully and therefore neutrally. But the joint rise in prices of traded
goods will act to ameliorate the burden of a debt
denominated in dollars. The real interest rate denominated
in export prices will be forced down to lower levels as
will the outstanding principal. Some of the consequences
of disinflation are thus reversed.

Such neutrality is not confirmed by the experience
with a variable dollar during the 1970s. Although
developing-country import prices almost reflected
fully the combined effects of inflation and changing
valuation, export prices did not. Indeed, the statistical
measurement of the effects shows a perverse tendency.
There is a positive, rather than neutral, relationship
between the annual terms of trade and dollar appreciation,
other relevant factors held constant.

More concretely, in the last case of significant
dollar depreciation in 1978, when industrial-country
income growth was at a rate of 4.1 percent, export prices

of primary commodities fell considerably. Export unit
value of major developing-country exporters of manufactures failed to rise as rapidly as the value of manufactured exports of the industrial countries. As a
consequence, the aggregate terms of trade of oil-importing
countries declined by 3.4 percent.

The response to dollar appreciation depends upon the
underlying demand and supply conditions of developing-
country imports and exports. Only if non-U.S. supply is
perfectly elastic over the relevant range will the dollar
price change of imports exactly reflect dollar appreciation or depreciation. The same is true for developing-
country exports, for which an additional determinant is
the share of non-U.S. demand in world demand in the
absence of such a perfect elasticity. In short, there is
no theoretical reason to impose neutrality in the face
of opposing empirical evidence.[18]

Beyond the material already presented, I have also
examined the quarterly changes in prices of Latin American
export commodities since 1973, because annual changes
obscure the within-year movements. These regressions--
various forms were tried--do not replicate the more than
unitary elasticity of prices with respect to the dollar
exchange rate found by IMF studies.[19] The coefficient is
much smaller and insignificant, although of correct sign.

The implications of dampening the price increase for
Cline's estimates, and those of Morgan Guaranty that
assume a 25 percent increase in prices of nonoil commodities between 1982 and 1985 (and now more concentrated
because of the failure of significant recovery in 1983),
are quite important. Table 5.5 maintains the assumptions
of a 10 percent depreciation of the dollar and a 5 percent inflation and adjusts import prices by slightly less
than their sum in accord with past responsiveness.[20] It
merely substitutes an assumption of no terms-of-trade
increase over the 1984-1986 period, a generous reading of
the recent experience, in which dollar depreciation would
more than offset the initial cyclical effects of higher
growth in 1983 and 1984 and some modest increase in
inflation with recovery. Further, it makes no allowance
for the potential additional effects of country devaluations on the export volume of the aggregate. Part of the
supply effect will be offset by compensating removal of
internal subsidies, as well as on the demand side by
substitution among developing-country suppliers as they
compete with each other. There is a fallacy of composition in simply aggregating individual country responses
without regard for the policies of others. Moreover,
the projection is intended to bring out the tendencies
inherent in the external environment, rather than possibilities of changed domestic policies.

The data in Table 5.5 reveal how sensitive Cline's
optimism was, not with respect to international recovery,
but to the valuation of exports. Elimination of the

Table 5.5 Alternate Balance-of-Payments Projections for Large
Oil-Importer Debtors (in billions of current U.S. dollars)

	1983	1984	1985	1986
Exports	125.2	149.5	166.4	185.2
Imports	135.4	157.2	172.1	192.0
Interest	29.3	30.1	30.7	32.6
Fishlow				
Current account	-30.9	-28.3	-26.7	-28.6
Debt	327.6	354.3	377.6	403.0
Net debt/exports	1.88	1.86	1.78	1.71
Cline				
Current account	-30.9	-20.2	-12.6	-12.6
Debt	327.6	346.6	355.8	365.5
Net debt/exports	1.88	1.55	1.40	1.28

Source: Exports: 1983 base year times real growth of 6 percent
times price increase of 12.6 percent in 1984 and 5 percent subsequently; imports: 1983 base year for nonoil imports times
Cline's real growth times price increase of 12.6 percent in 1984
and 5 percent subsequently (oil imports from Cline); interest: based
on debt at end of previous year, with rate weighted at two-thirds
of LIBOR plus premium, one-third at fixed rate, less income on
reserves (Cline's methodology); current account: incorporates
services calculated using Cline's methods and his estimates of
transfers and merchandise balance and interest as above; debt:
current account less Cline's direct investment and reserve
acquisition of .2 times change in imports (Cline's methodology).

surge in exports he projected in 1984 with more rapid
growth, large dollar depreciation *and* significant
improvement in the terms of trade means that debt would
have to grow almost twice as rapidly as originally
indicated. Debt-export ratios fall, but much more
slowly, making obvious the continuing precariousness of
the situation if the scenario is even marginally less
favorable. Export price increases serve as the medium
for recreating the inflationary environment of the 1970s
and lessening the burden of the debt.
    Cline's emphasis upon the virtues of developed-
country recovery, even at the expense of high interest
rates, was therefore equally overstated. At the lower
elasticities estimated in Table 5.4, the immediate impact
on value of exports of a one-percentage-point increase
in industrial country growth is much closer to 3 percent
than to 6. Hence the margin of superiority over the
foreign-exchange savings of a single-percentage-point
reduction in interest rates is halved to 2.5 rather than
the 5 claimed.[21] Moreover, the proportional decline of
a single percentage point in interest rates is much
smaller than a similar one-percentage-point increase in
growth rates and much easier directly to negotiate.

Because the effect of industrialized-country growth on exports is cumulative, continuing expansion at reasonable rates implies much larger levels of future foreign-exchange earnings and hence capacity to service debt. The policy issue, however, is not a tradeoff between recovery and high interest rates; rather, it is the concern that the ballooning U.S. public deficits, despite a positive effect on demand, will stifle expansion by raising rates. Nor should it be forgotten that the continuing high real rates are equivalent to a deterioration in the terms of trade: Offsetting that deterioration by volume increases still means lower income for the developing countries.

And interest rates enter critically, as pointed out earlier, in preventing debt from accumulating inertially. Cline's projections satisfied the condition of a higher export growth than interest rate both by a low real rate by vigorous export response by oil importers. Indeed, the debt-export ratio converges to zero as larger and and larger merchandise surpluses would be obtained. The amended results in Table 5.5 do likewise, although at a much slower rate. Yet it is essential to emphasize that neither meets an amended solvency requirement that allows for a continuing transfer of resources, on commercial terms, from the rich to the poor countries. That would call for debt to expand at higher rates, or interest payments to proceed at a lower. Under conditions of a resource transfer equivalent to 1 percent of nonoil-developing-country income, and a gross interest rate of 10 percent, debt would have to expand initially at an annual rate of almost 13 percent. With export growth at 12 percent, the debt-export ratio would initially climb, converging to a value of 2 from its 1982 level of 1.4. For countries with lower than average export-income ratios, the level would be even higher. Rapid expansion of exports, however necessary as a component of solvency, should not be made into a mechanism for premature capital export.[22]

The consequences of the modest restatement of the rate of nominal export growth in Table 5.5 should introduce equal caution about other optimistic scenarios. I am not alone. The Data Resources, Inc. (DRI), and Wharton projections of developing country exports have been less buoyant than those of Cline or Morgan Guaranty. So, too, have been the expectations of the IMF.[23] That such a difference is possible through very limited alteration of export projections reveals the inherent vulnerability of the debtor countries and the precariousness of the present situation.

There is basis for concern on grounds other than careful examination of recent experience. Extrapolation of past trends, if anything, may be too optimistic. We may not return to such favorable relationships in the future.

In the first place, it is by no means assured, with the higher unemployment rates now prevalent in the industrialized countries, that recovery will be as trade intensive as it was after 1975. Protectionist tendencies are much stronger as a consequence and are additionally fed by an asymmetric pattern of growth among the industrial countries. A lagging and increasingly less competitive Europe is a source of special concern. But so is a United States in which election-year politics strengthen the hands of special interests. Within a single week in January 1984, four escape-clause actions were filed, not alleging unfair trade, but merely injury; during the preceding three years only five such cases had been brought. Note as well that developing countries competitive in heavy industries (they tend to be the NIC debtors) are a special target. Under the formula proposed for carbon-steel imports, for example, the share for Japan and the European Economic Community would hardly be affected, while that for developing countries would decline from a current market share of about 10 percent to a mere 3 percent.

In the second instance, the present commitment to restrain inflation reduces the likelihood of replicating the commodity booms of the last decade. Demands for stocks are unlikely to expand as rapidly with real recovery. Increasing prices will also encounter resistance from purchasers who will see them as changes in relative prices, rather than as accompanying general inflation. High real interest rates will have the same effect of moderating demand.

In the third place, an exclusive focus on recovery in the industrialized countries ignores the consequences of debt-imposed depression in the developing countries upon their trade growth. Currently, intra-developing-country trade is responsible for about a fourth of developing-country exports. This market is most rapidly growing for the manufactured products many of the largest debtors are especially able to supply. Finally, there are even some who question the likelihood of continuing recovery, especially if U.S. budget deficits persist beyond 1984.

These concerns are more than theoretical. It is relevant to note that the initial stages of the industrialized-country recovery in 1983, more vigorous at 2.5 percent than had been predicted and therefore a larger change in income growth than projected for 1984, had little positive effect on the value of developing-country exports. Preliminary results for the most indebted Latin American countries showed continuing deterioration in the terms of trade, along with absolute declines in export prices.[24] To be sure the dollar continued to appreciate, but many analysts, because of prospective high interest rates, were less inclined to predict significant depreciation in 1984. That will have

its repercussions upon export prices and further erode
the benefits of OECD recovery.

Despite lack of buoyant export demand in 1983,
the balance of payments of the principal debtors did not
deteriorate. On the contrary, the current accounts
improved, especially those of oil exporters like Mexico
and Venezuela. These countries had little alternative
but to compress their imports dramatically to adapt to
the lack of credit. They did so at the expense of income
growth. For the oil exporters, it meant learning the
necessity and possibility of import substitution practiced
earlier by the oil importers.

The reason for this detailed treatment of Cline's
projections is not to substitute another set, nor even to
question the manageability of the crisis with developed-
country recovery *and* developing-country adjustment.
Rather it is to emphasize that the responsibility for
adapting to the overhanging debt seems likely to fall
disproportionately upon the debtors, with only partial
amelioration from the magic of industrialized-country
growth. The IMF says as much:

> . . . the results of Scenario A are less
> favorable as far as growth is concerned, and
> imply stronger adjustment efforts, than those
> presented last year. In part because of a
> lower flow of bank lending, the new Scenario A
> envisages . . . a lower deficit . . . despite
> conditions that would be less favorable for
> exports. The result is that the aggregate
> real GDP of non-oil developing countries in
> 1986 is now expected to be about 5½ percent
> less than previously estimated. The volume
> of their imports is projected to be nearly
> 13 percent less.[25]

Optimism about international recovery has the luxury of
ignoring the implications for the willingness of
developing countries to pay under adverse conditions.
Realism requires a closer look.

THE IMF ADJUSTMENT PACKAGES

The Economics of Stabilization

Whatever the future may hold, the recent past has
been unambiguous in forcing adjustment programs upon many
debtor countries, as well as on others adversely
affected by the downturn of the world economy. Such
adjustment has been under the aegis of the IMF in both
instances, but with a crucial difference. For the
debtors, these arrangements have included a crucial
component of continuing, if reduced, bank lending. The

IMF has thus taken on an enhanced role, quite apart from the impressive quantitative expansion of its commitments.

The emphasis on developing-country adjustment in arriving at such agreements speaks to a structural component of the debt crisis that adherents to a sheer liquidity view tend to ignore. If the issue were one of mere temporary balance-of-payments difficulties of the debtor countries, owing to unanticipated external circumstances, the Fund's own criteria would call for compensatory finance rather than the conditionality imposed in fact.

That conditionality is based on the premise that many debtor countries have adjusted incompletely and imperfectly to a new and harsher external environment. For the IMF, the failure arises from excess aggregate demand as well as from an allocation of expenditure that is biased against exports. Whatever the variability in the specifics of particular programs, these elements are the central ones.

First, identification of balance-of-payments problems with excess demand entails a need for restrictive policies to restrain domestic expenditure. In particular, the public sector is typically singled out for deficits that contribute not only to demand but also to domestic credit creation. Elimination of subsidies, increased taxes and prices of public services and of products produced by state enterprises, and reduced outlays are typically recommended. The emphasis on fiscal policy is augmented by insistence upon controls over expansion of domestic credit. Before it gained wider academic fashionability, the Fund pioneered in the monetary theory of the balance of payments that relates changes in net international reserves to internal monetary policy. Starting from that premise means that financial balance is as important as control over expenditures. In practical terms, it means advocacy of high real interest rates to eliminate financial repression and encourage domestic saving.

Second, a further consequence of the Fund outlook is to link domestic inflation directly to balance-of-payments performance. Although it is possible significantly to attenuate that link by a flexible exchange rate that does not become overvalued, as the Fund itself has conceded by backing away from the fixed-rate regimes it insisted upon in the 1950s and 1960s, attainment of price stability is a principal objective. Inflation is not regarded as neutral, because its acceptance reduces discipline of the public sector as well as inevitably leading to inefficiencies in resource allocation. A direct implication is containment of nominal wage increases and rejection of indexing arrangements that carry forward past inflation.

The exchange rate is the third key price that must be set right. Real devaluation, in which the Fund still believes, if not the neoorthodox international monetarists, has two effects. In the first instance, it reduces real income by increasing the price of tradable goods and thereby contributes to the objective of decreasing expenditure. In the second place, the relative price change makes exports and import substitutes more profitable and imports more expensive. Realignment of production improves the trade balance, which--given the restrictions on supply of external capital and continuing high interest rates--is the only source of improvement of the foreign accounts.

The package is a formidable undertaking, particularly when combined with other efforts to dismantle controls and to rely more fully on market incentives. For all the emphasis upon aggregate demand in devising adjustment programs, there is an implicit, if simple, theory of supply: Supply responds elastically to market signals. For efficiency's sake the signals must be the right ones. The programs may thus be exigent, but nothing less will work. The Fund goes farther in their defense, suggesting that the adverse effects of conditionality--criticized since the 1950s by Latin American structuralists--should not be exaggerated.

> It is sometimes contended that the restrained demand management policies--which are always central to Fund programs--are inimical to growth. . . . However, an analysis of 26 recently approved stand-by and extended arrangements reveals that, in a great majority of the cases, real growth rates are projected to improve even during the first program year by comparison with the two years prior to the program; only in 7 of the 26 cases is growth expected to decline.[26]

Since such programs typically are adopted in the midst of decline, such a statistic does not preclude a legitimate concern for the output consequences of demand restraint under conditions now prevailing in many of the debtor developing countries. In principle, were the diagnosis of generalized excess demand correct and demand for exports very elastic, the IMF policies would lead to reduced real income, but not at the expense of unemployment or excess capacity. Growth could and would resume, led by production of exports and of import substitutes, even as the balance of payments improved and inflation diminished. In 1982 and 1983 there was scant evidence for such a conclusion, as the countries most afflicted by the debt crisis and following policies of restraint experienced significant declines in growth, accompanied in some cases by accelerating inflation.

The reasons are related to structural characteristics of many of these developing countries. Instead of the stable and responsive aggregate supply function presumed by Fund orthodoxy, and therefore ignored, supply conditions are a critical factor influencing the effectiveness of stabilization attempts.[27]

In the first instance, adjustment lags between expenditure reduction and output reallocation are important. Reduced fiscal deficits, even accompanied by devaluation, do not necessarily translate quickly, and in the right proportions, into private decisions to employ labor and capital to produce exports. Nor is such labor and capital fully mobile. Export supply is not perfectly elastic. The direct adverse output results of expenditure contraction are felt immediately whereas the indirect beneficial effects take longer to work themselves out.

In the second place, the contraction in domestic credit and rise in interest rates will create shortages of working capital and lead to curtailment of output--not merely demand. Firms will find it more profitable to speculate financially than to produce. Adding to this impulse is the effect of reduced imports. Because inputs are not perfectly substitutable, imports are an important determinant of potential supply. Balance-of-payments improvement obtained by cutting back on essential imports soon has ramifications that extend throughout the productive system.

In similar fashion, drastic retrenchment of the public sector can be costly. The most flexible components of public budgets, of central and local governments as well as of state enterprises, are investment expenditures. Capital formation, frequently complementary to private production, is sacrificed for immediate economies, with implications for subsequent productive capacity.

Aggregate supply is therefore not continuously forthcoming at the point of full employment as demand is reduced, with the effects of restraint falling solely on the rate of inflation. In fact, inflation is fed by the reforms introduced. Corrections of distorted public-sector prices, removal of subsidies, increases in taxes, and so on all lead to a once for all increase in prices. So do the increase in real interest rates and the rise in import prices following from devaluation. These cost components of inflation may be extended in two ways. Wages may be indexed to the inflation rate, and so also rise. Increased interest rates, and devaluation, will also force up government payments on internal and external debt respectively. These, of course, place additional demands upon domestic credit and further pressure on interest rates.

Disinflation, in other words, is much more complicated than simply reducing demand and carries with it the risk of exacerbating output declines. The very instruments of structural reform through relative price change make it more difficult to accomplish. Concentrating on inflation, at the expense of real balance-of-payments and production targets, may be counterproductive.

Eliminating index links and influencing expectations more favorably make the task of dampening inflation easier. The former is easier and more reliably done for wages than the interest rate or the exchange rate, with adverse consequences for the distribution of income. Convincing the public of declining inflation, in the midst of contrary inertial tendencies and historical evidence, may also lead to serious distortion of the exchange rate, with eventual adverse consequences for the balance of payments. That is certainly one lesson of the Southern Cone experience, in which preannouncing (and, in Chile, fixing) the exchange rate became the centerpiece of neoorthodox policy. Preoccupation with the wrong target proved costly, not least in contributing to the accumulation of excessive debt.

The Fund's approach to inflation makes it too central a goal, while at the same time giving inadequate attention to the potential short-term inconsistencies between adjustment and disinflation. In establishing its inflation targets, and hence credit limits, it errs, apparently deliberately by the testimony of one of its staff, on the side of unrealism: "In general, corrective policy programs should aim at reductions in the rate of inflation that are perceived as significant--even if they do not appear particularly realistic--in order to influence expectations in the right direction."[28] But such a strategy contributes to inadequate, excessively stringent monetary policy and to expectations that cannot long be maintained. It is surprising to see the Fund rely upon irrational expectations to make its policies work.

On the positive side, the Fund program is designed to encourage and, now, to require continued capital inflow to lessen the costs of adjustment. But equity investment, now being emphasized as a substitute for borrowing, is actively discouraged by the declines in income and makes no contribution. Nor is new money in the form of loans flocking to countries in the midst of wrenching internal contraction.

This discussion of the orthodox adjustment programs now being undertaken by the largest debtor countries makes clear two essential points. One is that they may be costly in their output consequences over some time, although attaining their balance-of-payments and inflation targets. Of these, a favorable trade account is much more certain, if only because the constraint of limited external finance makes it a necessity. Moreover, the very decline in national production reduces import demand and becomes the basis for the trade improvement registered. Even in failure, the interests of the creditors are guaranteed priority.

In the second instance, granted fully successful adjustment, there will still be a devaluation-induced loss in real national income. Changed relative prices

for labor and capital as wages are restrained and
interest rates raised may also provoke a possible
deterioration in its distribution. In addition, the
public sector's role will have diminished. Direct
expenditures will have been reduced, and state enterprises curbed. In short, the impact of adjustment will
have significant and differential effects upon important
interests and therefore necessarily a significant
political content.

The Politics of Adjustment

It should come as no surprise after this discussion
that stabilization policies encounter significant popular
resistance. More than a decade ago, Richard Cooper
calculated that currency devaluation approximately
triples the chance that the responsible finance minister
will be gone within the following year and doubles the
probability that the government will fall.[29] If contemporary statistics are perhaps more favorable, it does
not reflect a change in popular reaction, but rather
speaks to the durability of authoritarian regimes whose
claim to power partially rests on the willingness to
impose the unpopular.
     Austerity programs understandably encounter resis-
tance because they affect established interests and claims
on income. Workers resist erosion of wages and mounting
unemployment. Employers complain about higher taxes and
interest rates and about reduced subsidies. It is not
difficult to construct a coalition of opposition to
policies that seem to guarantee certain present losses,
while only holding out the probability of eventual
benefits. To a beleaguered citizenry, stabilization
appears a negative-sum game, even in comparison with the
deteriorating economic conditions that provoked it in the
first instance.
     But to frame the matter in terms of perceived self-
interest is to characterize the opposition too narrowly
and materialistically. If it were not for past experience,
more replete with stop-go cycles than successful stabilization, and a respectable literature skeptical of the
excessive costs of orthodox policies, dissent would not
run as deep.
     What has been added to these traditional responses
this time is the further conviction that the origins
of the problem are external. This is a crisis manufactured in the boardrooms of New York banks, requiring
payments due despite an industrialized-country recession
and high interest rates. For even the oil importers,
the effects of the oil shocks recede in favor of these
factors that have weighed more heavily in 1981 and 1982.
There is also a conviction that the burden is being
shared unequally, without regard to the cost imposed on

poorer countries ill equipped to bear it.

A recent letter to the Economist from Brazil made the point more eloquently than the rhetoric of formal statements:

> Citizens of the "first world" refuse to under-
> stand that recession, for us, means more starva-
> tion, more children abandoned by miserable
> parents and a sharp increase in infant mortality
> and illiteracy. . . . Yesterday I helped a man
> who had an epileptic fit. He had told his doctor
> he was taking only half of the prescribed quantity
> of medicines in order to make them last longer.
> . . . If this illiterate Brazilian finds out that
> the loss of his job was caused by a recession
> provoked by the obligation to pay back the money
> which first-world bankers enticed us to borrow,
> plus interest, he will certainly become a sort
> of Sandinist, or worse.[30]

Under mounting social consequences of adjustment, and in conjunction with external interest payments that exceed new borrowing, default--or at the least uni-lateral renegotiation--becomes an ever more attractive option. Both Mexico in 1982 and Argentina after the election of President Alfonsin have essentially imposed a moratorium without repudiating their obligations. The precedent has been lost on others, although it has not diminished the zeal of the IMF in its conditionality or the preference of the banks for case-by-case treatment.

Rigid stabilization programs and seeming bank intransigence do not fit well with the new political effervescence in Latin America. A civilian president rules in Argentina with a majority mandate. In Brazil, the military is beating a retreat to the barracks in disarray. In Chile and Uruguay, pressures for greater popular participation are mounting. The present crisis does not have its roots in populist excesses or democratic failures: It is the product of a now in-creasingly repudiated technocracy that deemed economic management above and beyond political control. It does no good to insist upon the technical quality of the adjustment package and to ignore these new realities nor to flaunt external intervention at a time when restora-tion of national pride is a central source of legitimacy for the new civilian politicians.

These new political realities in some of the largest debtors, and not alone in Latin America as the Philippines exemplify, cannot help to influence responses to the debt crisis. Up to a point, austerity can improve the prospects for meeting obligations by generating trade surpluses and hence the ability to pay. But applied too long and too painfully, austerity can provoke a hostile rejection of international claims in favor of domestic pressures. Seemingly rational calculations that demonstrate the futility of default because of the penalties of interrupted potential future capital flows and interference with current merchandise transactions carry less weight in the face of social disruption. An uncertain future may seem less adverse than the known depression, against which conventional reactions seem futile.

Even were the prospects for trade to improve, more popular governments cannot fully ignore the magnitude of the transfers they are being asked to make out of national income. As the external debt mounts to more than half of total product in Argentina, Mexico, Peru, Korea, the Philippines, and Chile--in the latter to 90 percent--high real interest rates impose a palpable effect on the standard of living. At a 7 percent rate, in the Chilean case in 1984, the interest payments amount to more than the equivalent of the income of the poorest fifth of the population. If the impact is less dramatic for others with lower debt-income ratios, the reduction in national income still remains significant and sensitive to reigning interest rates set abroad.

I raise the issue of the potential diminished willingness to pay contractual debt service without concluding, as some erroneously may, that a return or continuation of authoritarianism can avert the problem. It can assure only illusory stability. Effective medium-term economic adjustment requires a flexibility in the face of changing conditions that military regimes have rarely, rather than commonly, shown. The capacity to engage in continuing income transfers of large magnitude ultimately depends upon informed consent rather than force. Even in the short term, discredited authoritarian governments have shown little capacity to manage stabilization programs.

Moreover, the new political forces have learned from the errors of the past. Few political leaders in the large debtors believe in easy populist solutions. There is broad recognition that although most countries erred by excessive and asymmetrical integration into world capital markets in the 1970s, export promotion and expansion are an indispensable commitment in the 1980s to reduce dependence. In the second place, there is no illusion that foreign resources will be available in the future in the proportions of the recent past; internal saving will be required. Third, there is widespread appreciation that sheer expansion of the public sector does not constitute an acceptable development strategy any more than full reliance upon market signals. Finally, there is little faith in the possibility of massive income redistribution in the short term.

These are important bridges to a more consensual stabilization strategy whose prospects for minimizing the real income decline turn critically upon the capacity to distribute the losses equitably. The apparent success in the Mexican stabilization program stems from the ability not merely to enforce lower real wages but to limit the effects of inflation on the prices of certain essential products for the mass of the population. Another element, of course, was the immediate and substantial debt-service relief by restructuring short-term debt and putting off amortization until 1985.

Such a consensual strategy, ironically, may involve measures more drastic than the conventional ones imposed by the Fund. In a depression of this magnitude for Brazil and Argentina, and with inflation well in excess of three digits, more dramatic efforts may well be necessary to deal with an internal debt whose interest payments alone are the principal pressure on public-sector borrowing requirements; to reduce real interest rates that have sharply curtailed private investment; to halt the unleashed spiral of rising prices and costs. These are not easy tasks, and it would be wrong to minimize their difficulty or to ignore the potential problem of reconciling austerity and legitimate popular claims. Only if there are degrees of freedom for domestic policymakers to act can adjustment be achieved. If the balance of payments and debt service take absolute priority, internal disequilibrium will persist and will be a constant provocation for unilateral default that could well be inimical to restoring global recovery in the 1980s.

THE INSTITUTIONAL FRAMEWORK

The Policy Matrix

At the beginning of 1984, the elements in place to deal with the debt problem were little changed from what they were in August 1982. What had been added was additional resources from the quota increase of the IMF and the considerable experience gained by the repetitive tasks of renegotiating debt and of hammering out country adjustment packages on a case-by-case basis. That there was so little change derived less from satisfaction with the policy matrix than from lack of consensus on the appropriate more far-reaching reforms. Financial circles were far from tranquil. World Financial Markets, in its June 1983 assessment, found wanting the "relatively optimistic, laissez-faire school that assumes the current debt situation is a fairly short-term liquidity issue" to be solved primarily through LDC (less developed country) adjustment along with some OECD recovery. "By ignoring long-term structural elements of the international debt problem or overstating the prospects for global recovery, this approach risks forcing excessive deflationary costs on borrowers. It is also overly optimistic about market forces providing ample new borrowing."[31]

The present situation derives its stability from the
tenuous mutual interests of creditor banks and debtor
countries in this moment of crisis. Banks are committed
to extending additional credits to countries currently in
difficulty only because they perceive such a policy to be
in their self-interest. They are not development institutions. Banks are lending involuntarily in order to
avert defaults that would expose the precariousness of
their balance sheets and with some hope of ultimate repayment under better future conditions. Their "lending
trap" is the counterpart of the "debt trap" ensnaring
countries that must borrow to meet their interest payments, increasing their debt without counterpart resources
for adequate imports to underwrite recovery or even export
expansion. Countries continue to pay because they fear
the immediate losses from trade potentially interrupted
as a result of default and hope for resumption of needed
capital flows in the future.

Such a situation serves each party badly. It has
led banks to short-sighted efforts to obtain larger
profits to compensate for their perceived greater risk.
This has taken the form of increased margins in the form
of one-time fees and of ongoing premiums over the deposit
rate. For the reschedulings completed for Latin America,
amounting to some US$44 billion for seven countries, banks
have obtained commissions of between 1 and 1.25 percentage
points, as well as revised spreads that have usually added
about a full percentage point to previous ones. These
earnings might have added between US$70 million and
US$130 million to profits of the largest nine U.S. banks,
depending on the relevant marginal tax rates. They
translate into an increased return on loans to those
seven countries of about 25 percent in comparison with
previous terms, quite independently of higher spreads
being charged on new loans.[32]

Ironically, the absolute effect on total profits is
relatively small, as is the effect on the borrowers. The
cost of the higher premium over LIBOR to Mexico is less
than 1 percent of foreign-exchange earnings, for example,
since what is relevant to the country is the total interest
rate and not the margin. But the ill will is considerable of arbitrarily imposing increased costs of servicing on an already burdensome debt. Such charges are
not market determined because the lending is involuntary;
pressed by Mexico, Argentina, and Brazil, the banks in
fact subsequently agreed to reduce their spreads somewhat. The countries were joined in their protests by
Paul Volcker, motivated by concerns of system stability
rather than immediate profits.

At the same time, of course, the large money-market
banks are themselves not pleased by the demands on them.
Citibank, in particular, seems to have reacted against
Volcker's intervention, although all these banks are being

forced to set aside larger loan loss reserves to satisfy
bank examiners and a Congress concerned with excessive
bank exposure. Large U.S. banks must also cope with
second-tier banks who have much less to gain from a continued lending relationship with developing countries and
do not want to renew outstanding loans, even at higher
spreads. Michigan National Bank has even taken Citicorp
to court over the involuntary extension of a US$5 million
participation in a Petróleos Mexicanos (PEMEX) loan. For
new money, the money-market banks can no longer count on
tapping their regional colleagues.

On their side, as we have seen, the countries have
fared badly. For all of Keynes's oft-quoted dictum
about the advantage of large rather than small debts in
dealing with creditors, the countries have been able to
extract only modest additional resources from financial
markets and that at the expense of austerity programs.
They have been forced to give priority to merchandise
surpluses and in the dominance of a single policy
objective have failed to design as yet more adequate and
longer-term responses to their situation.

The Fund has performed three essential functions in
making this delicate arrangement work. For one thing,
it has offset individual bank prudence that would call
for a reduced commitment and shorter maturity by imposing
proportional lending targets. This new conditionality
imposed on the banks defeats the free-rider problem
inherent in a pure market relationship. Each bank would
hope the others would participate, making it better off;
such behavior, because none would, would make them all
worse off. For another thing, the Fund has devised
adjustment programs that assure the lenders of developing-
country efforts to meet their obligations and thereby
avoid the moral hazard of countries simply borrowing more
without an intention to repay. Finally, the IMF, in
conjunction with the BIS, central banks, and industrial-
country governments, has made available public resources
to satisfy immediate liquidity requirements and to
supplement the private market.

Central authority has thus been indispensable to a
continuing bank-country relationship. The principal
virtue of this implicit tripartite debt regime has been
its capacity to blunt serious repercussions to the
financial system of the debt shocks that have occurred.
Strains have been evident. Countries have reacted
against the discipline imposed by the Fund, and in the
case of Venezuela, no agreement has yet been possible.
Banks have, in the case of Brazil, found the Fund so
preoccupied with the integrity of its own stabilization
package that their loans were in danger of being declared
nonperforming. Until the program was approved, they
could not lend Brazil the money needed to cover the overdue interest payments. Still, because both banks and the
countries need the Fund, this case-by-case framework has

survived.
As successful as this ad hoc arrangement has been
thus far in responding to crisis, it has two serious
deficiencies. For one, it has contributed to a continuing
short-term mentality. The banks still see their advantage
in a minimum amount of additional lending or renegotiation
they are prepared to undertake. They, and even the Fund,
prefer to see the country on a short leash and constantly
accountable. Although the arrangement may eliminate the
moral hazard problem, it does so at the risk of mis-
calculating the provocation to default. And, of course,
it is precisely that uncertainty that reinforces the
preference for dealing not only with one country at a time,
but also one year at a time. The structure is thus
potentially unstable.
In the second place, current policies fail to
address the adequacy of the long-term supply of capital.
Quasi socialization of the international banking system
by the Fund in an emergency is one thing; continuing
imposition of broader systemic goals is quite another.
There is no reason to believe that the private profit
calculus will produce the right amount of capital for the
right developing countries in the future. One of the
causes of the present crisis is precisely such market
failure.
Voluntary lending will not recuperate quickly,
according to all present signs and past historical
reaction to external debt problems. Present U.S. economic
policy makes the prospects even bleaker. A recent
quarterly report of the Bank for International Settlements
called attention to the evolution of a segmented financial
market. "On the one hand, Western banks have now virtually stopped all voluntary lending to the third world
and Eastern Europe, because of concern about repayment.
But business transactions among the industrial nations
appear to be picking up briskly as American banks
accelerate their borrowing from other Western countries
to finance America's payments deficit."[33]
Dealing exclusively to avert the worst is not
necessarily equivalent to the good, let alone the best.
The present policy context is fraught with dangers.
Recovery may not continue at its present pace, placing
more demands upon a potentially unstable bank-country
relationship. Social costs in some of the developing
countries may lead to failure to live up to stabilization
targets. The continuing pattern of adjustment via trade
surpluses may evoke even more pronounced tendencies
toward protectionism, with significant consequences for
the structure of the trading system. Reaction against
rapidly rising imports from the NICs can spill over to
imports from industrial-country competitors. These
possibilities, and with them slowed industrial-country
growth, are real. That reality contributes to a pervasive
uncertainty, itself a constraint on recuperation of the

global economy in the 1980s.

More Radical Alternatives

In the aftermath of the Mexican shock, when prospects seemed much dimmer for muddling through and the perils more immediate, a variety of more radical reforms were suggested.[34] Despite differences among them, many shared common characteristics. One was reduction of current debt service to developing countries in a decisive fashion, thereby alleviating the foreign-exchange constraint that forced sharp reduction in economic growth. Another was reduction of the total debt burden faced by the countries through a transfer of resources from creditor banks and/or industrial countries, either in the form of writing down the debt or rescheduling on favorable terms. A third was an enhanced role for a public presence in financial markets to monitor and influence lending and borrowing as well as country adjustment.

The most common means offered for achieving these objectives was purchase of bank developing-country loans by an existing, or new, international agency. Banks would sell their loans at a discount in exchange for the securities of the agency, thus substituting a known but limited loss for their present uncertain exposure. The agency in turn would recontract the debt of the countries at longer maturities and lower prices, passing along the bank write-down and possibly additional concessions from special governmental appropriations. The new arrangements would thus improve the quality of bank portfolios, shift the debt to an international development institution whose concerns would be broader, and distribute the costs of excessive debt accumulation more equitably among banks, industrial countries (through forgone taxes on potential bank profits and capital contributions to the agency), and developing countries.

Another approach, analogous to corporate reorganization, would substitute for present bank loans fixed shares in country export earnings, thus a virtual equity participation. Countries would pay only a ceiling percentage of export receipts for debt service, and creditors would share in the benefits of recovery by larger absolute repayments.

These plans have been criticized for their short-comings.[35] Most salient has been the failure explicitly to provide for flows of new capital once past debts have been reorganized. Another is the volume of public resources required to fund purchase of the bank loans, even if capital is only fractionally paid in. Although the agency would issue its own securities, as the World Bank does, and no actual expenditure would need to occur, an appropriation for capital would be necessary and subject to the resistance recently encountered in the

expansion of IMF quotas. A third criticism is that
their generality encourages even sound debtor countries
to relax their adjustment efforts in favor of unneeded
debt relief.

These observations, although they have merit,
exaggerate the deficiencies inherent in the plans. The
failure to assure new lending in the needed amounts is,
after all, one of the indictments of the present situation. In this respect, the plans share the optimism of
those who believe that in the long term capital markets
can be trusted to provide the necessary resources. It
would not be difficult to assure continuing involuntary
lending of banks since their entire portfolio would not
be eliminated, nor would the requirements be as great
with reduced debt service. Interestingly enough, other
proposals that do emphasize guarantees to underwrite
capital flows have fared no better.[36]

Nor is the issue impossible levels of public
expenditure. Had an appropriation of the magnitude extended to the Fund been applied to purchasing debt, it
could have made possible, with paid-in capital of 10 percent, a transfer of almost US$300 billion in loans,
close to the entirety of bank exposure.

Finally, the potential excess alleviation of the
burden on developing countries by substituting debt
relief for adjustment is easily managed. Characteristic
of these reforms is an expanded, rather than reduced,
public presence in developing countries. Indeed, by
redistributing the portfolio of debt ex post, it compensates for the excessive reliance on private institutions
to resolve a development problem.

The real issue is not the technical adequacy of one
proposal versus another. Designs can be perfected, and
additional features added. Nor is it even the specific
distribution of costs to be shared among banks, developing countries, and industrialized countries. These will
determine the preference for one or another approach and
are a matter for negotiation. Indeed, we have already
seen how the banks have lowered their spreads in response
to pressures on them; other concessions, like a cap on
interest payments that converts costs above a specified
rate into automatic--and cheaper--rescheduling, may also
emerge.

But neither these changes, nor more far-reaching
reforms that would involve larger transfers of resources,
are encouraged by the present debt regime. Banks are
unwilling to opt for modifications even if both they,
and the system, could be made better off. To admit the
need for change is to confirm the inadequacy of present
arrangements and to risk testing them. All along the
banks have been saying that the problem is minimal, even
while agreeing to reschedule some $100 billion in debt.
To call for help that did not come would be counterproductive; at best therefore, banks are reactive and

limited to short-term palliatives under their control.
Developing countries are not much better situated.
The leading debtors must proclaim their commitment to
the present system and the unfailing integrity of their
obligations if they are to have access to the assistance
they need. For all the talk of a "debtor's OPEC,"
incentives for individual compliance are much stronger
than group repudiation. Differing individual circumstances and prospective lack of a united front make any
other policy a risky one. Foreign ministers may jointly
advocate general resolutions, but individual central
bankers continue to pay periodic visits to New York to
deal with the problem.

In the last analysis, lack of leadership by the
industrialized countries, and especially the United
States, rather than the inability to devise a better
framework for dealing with the debt problem, explains the
present inaction. The Reagan administration is self-
confessedly skeptical of the multilateral Bretton Woods
system and even of extensive cooperation among the
industrialized countries. In the election year of 1984,
as the crisis atmosphere of 1982 receded, case-by-case
emergency care rather than systemic analysis gained in
allure. Making the debt issue a narrow liquidity problem
conformed to such a mind-set. Absent a financial collapse,
the costs remain implicit rather than budgetary: Taxpayers pay through slower growth and increasing aliena-
tion of the developing world rather than by appropriations.

It is not a unique predicament. Keynes, in the midst
of the Great Depression, wrote a less cited passage
appropriate to present circumstances:

It is as though two motor-drivers, meeting in
the middle of a highway, were unable to pass
one another because neither knows the rule of
the road. Their own muscles are no use; a
motor engineer cannot help them; a better road
would not serve. Nothing is required and
nothing will avail, except a little clear
thinking. So, too, our problem is not a human
problem of muscles and endurance. . . . On the
contrary, it is, in the strictest sense, an
economic problem or, to express it better, as
suggesting a blend of economic theory with the
art of statesmanship, a problem of political
economy. I call attention to the nature of the
problem, because it points us to the nature of
the remedy. It is appropriate to the case that
the remedy should be found in something which
can fairly be called a device. Yet, there are
many who are suspicious of devices, and in-
stinctively doubt their efficacy. . . . But the
lorries of these people will never, I fear,

get by.[37]

It required the Great Depression of the 1930s for Keynesian counsel finally to be adopted, and then imperfectly. Billions of dollars of potential output were irrevocably lost. The developing countries are confronting no less an economic tragedy in the 1980s. So far it has not much influenced official perceptions in the industrialized countries. "Clear thinking" remains sporadic and limited to short-term crises like the response to the Mexican situation in August 1982, a by-product of which was easing of U.S. monetary policy. Ideological insistence upon the magic of the market dominates pragmatic adaptation to its failures. The debt problem we confront is testimony to limitations of market forces. An active participant in lending concedes as much by affirming, "while the international debt situation is manageable, it will not manage itself."[38]

We have failed once. Three years ago, I wrote of the then looming crisis:

The principal danger is not the wholesale default by developing countries and the possibility that it may bring the world financial system crashing down. The principal danger is that available international finance will be inadequate to maintain a reasonable level of world economic growth in the 1980s. If the supply of funds proves inadequate, it will be the largest debtors--many of them Latin American countries--who will be most in danger. They will have to bear the brunt of the adjustment burden themselves. . . . The developed countries may not react to strengthen the system in time to avoid slowing of growth of their exports to the developing countries. The burden will fall primarily on the developing countries. Interdependence is still asymmetric.[39]

That prognosis unfortunately has proven accurate.

The apparent limited impact upon the U.S. recovery, and that of other industrialized countries now showing signs of more rapid growth, is the wrong lesson to draw from this experience. The right one is that there is still time to act to deal with the problem before the economic and political consequences become irreversible. There is no shortage of practical proposals, or "devices." Even in the absence of U.S. leadership and larger resources for official lending or transferring some of the debt, the World Bank and the International Monetary Fund can help break the impasse by extending the horizon of developing-country adjustment and bank participation beyond the current preoccupation with the immediate term. More flexibility in the design of adjustment programs, undertaken in closer collaboration with the commercial banks, and more political sensitivity would make a significant difference.

The largest banks, in their own self-interest, could take more initiative in proposing changes in current lending practice, such as accepting more of the risk of interest-rate variability, making renegotiations more automatic in the event of adverse external shocks, renegotiating larger sums for longer periods, and so forth. Continuing passiveness is a formula for developing-country discontent and ongoing uncertainty in financial markets. The banks' stake need not be left to others to defend.

In the last analysis, the debt problem is a development problem, not one of liquidity or solvency or even of the vulnerability of the financial system. As such, it is not exclusive to the performance of the developing countries alone, but has ramifications, increasingly if still unequally, for the developed as well. Nor is the issue a technocratic one, devoid of political content. Until this realization becomes more pervasive, we shall continue to cope with the creeping crisis of debt rather than confronting and resolving it.

APPENDIX

Table 5.6 Estimating Equations for Export Volume Elasticity in Table 5.4

Percentage Change in Export Volume of:	Constant	Percentage Growth of Industrialized-Country Product	D-W	Adjusted R^2
Nonoil developing countries, 1963–1982	2.5 (2.4)[b]	1.08 (.52)	1.61[a]	.10[a]
Brazil, excl. coffee	6.0 (5.8)	1.83 (1.40)	2.25	.04
Brazil, incl. coffee		-.03[c]		
Korea, 1964–1982	10.2 (6.5)	4.30 (1.59)	1.42	.26
Nonoil, oil-importing countries, 1973–1982	1.5 (1.4)	1.73 (.41)	1.50	.64
Exporters of manufactures	2.1 (1.7)	2.46 (.51)	1.71	.71
Low income		-.10[c]		
Asia	3.9	2.29 (2.5)	1.95 (.74)	.49
Western Hemisphere	1.1 (3.8)	1.51 (.73)	1.78[a]	.31[a]

[a] One observation omitted to adjust for autocorrelation of the residuals

[b] Standard errors in parentheses

[c] t-value less than one

Source: Nonoil developing countries: International Monetary Fund (IMF), International Financial Statistics, Yearbook, 1983; nonoil, oil-importing countries: IMF, World Economic Outlook, 1983.

140

Table 5.7 Estimating Equations for Terms of Trade[a] in Table 5.4

	Constant	D73,74	Change in Industrialized-Country Growth Rate	Change Lagged	Inflation Rate	Interest Rate	Dollar Appreciation	D-W	Adjusted R^2
Nonoil developing countries, 1964-1982	.4 (.9)[b]	8.0 (2.1)	1.21 (.29)	1.53 (.25)	1.63 (.45)	-.30 (.27)	.73 (.17)	2.21	.89
Brazil, excl. coffee	-.2 (3.2)	13.9 (7.8)	.87 (1.08)	2.05 (.91)	.22 (1.64)	-.23 (.99)	.70 (.61)	2.49	.28
Korea, 1965-1982	4.0 (3.2)	-5.7 (7.9)	1.85 (1.11)	-.32 (.92)	3.30 (1.67)	1.56 (1.01)	.22 (.62)	1.20	.07
Nonoil developing countries, 1981-1982	1.5 (1.3)		1.58 (.49)	1.45 (.37)	2.51 (.59)	-.52 (.42)	.73 (.21)	1.70	.86
Brazil, excl. coffee	.4 (4.5)		1.96 (1.69)	2.04 (1.29)	2.47 (2.04)	.001 (1.46)	.57 (.74)	2.30	.15
Korea	3.30 (1.99)		2.07 (.74)	-.59 (.56)	2.81 (.89)	1.40 (.64)	.23 (.32)	1.84	.54
Nonoil oil-importing countries, 1974-1982	-.3 (1.3)		1.16 (.22)	1.38 (.20)	1.75 (.30)		.86 (.11)	2.81[c]	.95[c]
Exporters of manufactures	.8 (.7)		1.26 (.31)	1.10 (.23)	1.85 (.37)		.76 (.13)	2.61	.91
Low income	-1.9 (2.9)		.95 (.30)	2.78 (.27)	.62 (.42)		1.06 (.16)	2.02[c]	.95[c]
Asia	.8 (1.81)		1.24 (.88)	1.33 (.64)	2.24 (1.01)		.86 (.36)	2.69	.58
Western Hemisphere	1.1 (10.1)		2.17 (.58)	1.83 (.54)	4.18 (.84)		1.36 (.30)	2.17[c]	.86[c]

[a] Percentage change in export unit values of industrialized countries

[b] Standard error in parentheses

[c] Corrected for autocorrelation

Source: Nonoil developing countries: International Monetary Fund (IMF), International Financial Yearbook, 1983; nonoil oil-importing countries: IMF, World Economic Outlook, 1983.

NOTES

1. See Table 5.1 and sources indicated there, as well as Organization for Economic Cooperation and Development (OECD), External Debt of Developing Countries: General Survey 1982, Paris, 1982, for debt estimates at the end of 1982. The US$800 billion estimate is from A. W. Clausen, president of the World Bank, as cited in the New York Times, January 26, 1983, p. 45. Such a total presumably incorporates a broader developing-country definition than the other sources cited, in view of their estimate of approximately US$700 billion outstanding to developing countries at the end of 1982 and of a slowing flow of additional private loans in 1983.
2. Wall Street Journal, November 25, 1983, p. 1.
3. World Bank, World Development Report 1982, p. 21.
4. International Monetary Fund (IMF), World Economic Outlook, Washington, D.C., 1983, p. 200.
5. These data cover the period 1965-1981. During that interval the combination of export opportunities and access to credit gives reason to suppose that simple least squares captures a savings function unconstrained by foreign-exchange shortage. To avoid problems of appropriate deflators, the functions are estimated in ratio form:

$$S/Y = a + b1/Y_r + c_1 CA + c_2 CA$$

where S is gross national savings, Y is gross national product, Y_r is real gross domestic product, and CA is the current account deficit. The coefficient 1-a is the estimated marginal propensity to consume out of gross national product, and c_1 and c_2 are the period-specific propensities to consume out of the deficit for 1965-1978 and 1979-1981.
6. IMF, World Economic Outlook, p. 143.
7. IMF, External Indebtedness of Developing Countries, Occasional Paper no. 3, Washington, D.C., May 1981, p. 11.
8. See my "Causes and Consequences of the Latin American Depression of 1979," MS, October 1983, for a detailed discussion of the impact of external and internal conditions upon the expansion of the debt of the region and of principal debtor countries.
9. IMF, World Economic Outlook, table 14, pp. 183-184.
10. World Bank, World Debt Tables, 1982-83, Washington, D.C., 1984, p. vii.
11. William R. Cline, International Debt and the Stability of the World Economy, Washington, D.C., September 1983, p. 71.
12. That is, it takes as the appropriate constraint for developing-country repayment the capacity to generate foreign-exchange earnings rather than domestic saving.

142

For an example of the latter, see OECD, External
Indebtedness of Developing Countries, app. 3.
    13. Specifying the following equations:

$$x_t = x_0 e^{gt}$$
$$M_t = (1+a)X_t$$

$$dD = M_t - X_t + iD_t$$

we can solve for debt, D_t, $= a/(g-i)X_0(e^{gt} - e^{it})$. Then
the limiting debt-export ratio, $D(t)/X(t) = a/(g-i)$.
    14. Economic Commission for Latin America, Balance
Preliminar de la Economia Latinoamericana Durante 1983,
Santiago, December 1983, p. 29.
    15. World Bank estimates reported in the New York
Times, January 26, 1984, p. 45.
    16. Cline, International Debt, pp. 46-71.
    17. See Arthicus R. Cline, "Developing Country Debt
Under Alternative Global Conditions: 1983-86," in
International Debt: Systemic Risk and Policy Responses,
Washington, D.C., 1983, where he reports in table A-1
very low unadjusted R^2 for his country estimating
equations. The largest is for Brazil: .31. The
regressions in the Appendix do consistently better and
are a better basis for assessing the evolution of trade
for developing countries taken together.
    18. The analysis of the effect of changes of the
value of the dollar on the prices of developing-country
exports has to start from the demand and supply curves
for industrialized-country imports expressed in dollars.
A changing value shifts the non-U.S. demand, because
prices are different, and supply originally is expressed
in non-U.S. currency in similar fashion. Only if
developing-country supply is all expressed in non-U.S.
dollar terms, and perfectly elastic, will appreciation
and depreciation be fully reflected in dollar prices.
But a large proportion of supply is contracted in dollar
terms and is not necessarily elastic in the short term.
    19. IMF, World Economic Outlook, app. A.9,
pp. 154ff. The commodity price index in question can be
found in Inter-American Development Bank, Economic and
Social Progress in Latin America, Washington, D.C., 1983.
Petroleum was excluded.
    20. For determining the price of developing-
country imports in the presence of both dollar depreciation and general price increase, I have used the
estimating equation:

OECDP = 4.9 + 1.18DCP - .79DI + 1.03CP R^2 = .94
       (2.63) (.41)   (.12)   (.09)   D-W = 2.07

where the constant is for 1973-1974 only, CP is inflation
in the industrialized countries measured by the consumer
price index, DCP is change in inflation, and DI is change
in a dollar index against other currencies in accord with

the IMF weights. Standard errors are in parentheses.

21. Cline found an elasticity as great as seven based on the aggregation of country estimates, and a value of five derived from the elasticity estimates of his projection model. See International Debt and the Stability of the World Economy, p. 65. The actual simulations show a wider divergence because the sharp decline in the debt-export ratio reduces the relative importance of interest payments.

22. One percent of developing-country GDP is approximately equal, on average, to 4 percent of exports. Using the 1982 export-debt ratio and the current interest rate yields the result in the text.

23. See the Wharton World Economic Outlook, October 1983, and the DRI results for the Latin American principal debtors, both quoted in Thomas O. Enders and Richard P. Mattione, Latin America: The Crisis of Debt and Growth, Brookings Discussion Papers in International Economics, no. 9, Washington, D.C., December 1983.

24. Economic Commission for Latin America, Balance Preliminar, table 11.

25. IMF, World Economic Outlook, 1983, p. 20.

26. Ibid., p. 16.

27. For a recent review of stabilization policies, see R. Dornbusch, "Stabilization Policies in Developing Countries: What Have We Learned," and R. C. Porter and S. I. Ranney, "An Eclectic Model of Recent LDC Macroeconomic Policy Analyses," both in World Development, vol. 10, no. 9 (Oxford), 1982.

28. Manuel Guitian, in T. Killick, ed., Adjustment and Financing in the Developing World, p. 95.

29. Richard N. Cooper, Currency Devaluation in Developing Countries, Essays in International Finance, no. 86, Princeton, N.J., June 1971.

30. The Economist, October 15-21, 1983, p. 4.

31. World Financial Markets, June 1983, pp. 11, 12.

32. These estimates start from the terms and sums rescheduled as reported in Latin American Weekly Report, May 20, 1983, plus subsequent news accounts. On average, spreads were 1 percent higher than during the period when the loans were initially contracted in the late 1970s, allowing for intervening grace periods. Commissions for rescheduling ranged between 1.25 and 1.5 percent, of which 1 percent was regarded as profit (taking into account the World Bank typical commission payment of .25 percent).

Commissions are presumed to be paid initially, even if not accounted in bank earnings in that fashion, and to yield a return of 10 percent a year. The average annual value, spread over the life of the loan, is therefore greater than the simple average (approximately twice as large).

To the before-tax annual earnings obtained by summing incremental spreads and the average annual value of commissions, alternative marginal tax rates are applied to arrive at after-tax profits. These are then compared to the approximate share of loans to these countries in total bank assets to assess the increased returns on their holdings.

Equivalently, one can approximate the result, excluding commissions, by noting that the spread on rescheduled loans has doubled. Since such rescheduled loans are about one-fourth of the total extended by banks to these countries, the effect is about a 25 percent rise in after-tax earnings.

The calculations are reported in the Wall Street Journal, December 5, 1983.

33. New York Times, January 26, 1984.

34. Among the authors of various swap proposals are Peter Kenen, Felix Rohatyn, and Richard Weinert. I myself advanced a similar proposal much earlier that the World Bank absorb some of the commercial bank portfolio of developing-country loans in exchange for World Bank bonds. See Albert Fishlow et al., Rich and Poor Nations in the World Economy, New York, 1978, pp. 67-68. The exchange of debt for export participation shares has been advocated by Norman A. Bailey. Many of these plans are cited in Cline, International Debt and the Stability of the World Economy, pp. 114-115.

35. These criticisms and others are summarized in Cline, International Debt and the Stability of the World Economy, pp. 117-119.

36. Among those advocating such policies are Harold Lever, William Bolin, Jorge del Canto, and financier Minos Zombanakis. For detailed references see ibid., p. 117.

37. J. M. Keynes, Essays in Persuasion, vol. 11, Collected Writings of J. M. Keynes, London, 1972, pp. 335-336.

38. World Financial Markets, June 1983, p. 15.

39. The Political Economy of the Western Hermisphere: Selected Issues for U.S. Policy, Joint Economic Committee, 97th Congress, 1st Session, September 18, 1981, p. 163.

6
Latin American Debt: Act Two

Pedro-Pablo Kuczynski

INTRODUCTION

Although events have not changed my earlier two assessments,[1] it is appropriate to consider whether fundamental changes have occurred in recent months, as of the end of 1983.

First, it is clear that the economic recovery in the United States has not so far been accompanied by an equivalent recovery elsewhere in the industrialized world. As a result, the recovery in the growth of world trade is still slow, and the growth of the industrialized world is still below what was envisaged by a number of observers as one of the key ingredients for major debtors to be able to meet the interest on their external debts.[2] Furthermore, although some commodity prices have rebounded from the depths of 1982, others--particularly minerals--are still extremely depressed, so that the terms of trade of a number of developing countries are well below the peak levels of two or three years ago.

These two discouraging trends, which are related, may well change for the better. But a number of factors lead one to question whether such an improvement would be a sustained one: the continuing high level of real interest rates; the lag of investment, particularly as a result of sick heavy industries in North America and Europe; and therefore the possibility that the world faces a long cycle of slow economic growth, with the Latin American countries left with a large debt incurred in a past inflationary and high-growth era.

The third important feature of the last months has been the extent of belt-tightening and austerity in a number of countries. Mexico has been the most visibly successful, and its efforts have been aided by the close links of Mexican trade and services to the United States and have therefore benefited from the economic recovery there. The adjustment effort in other countries has been very large also. In part, of course, it has been the unavoidable result of the lack of international loans and

145

the shortage of foreign currency. The current account
deficit of Latin America has fallen from US$38 billion in
1981 to my estimate of US$18 billion in 1983, largely
as a result of the squeeze in imports. At the same time
income per person has declined sharply, by as much as 10
percent in the three-year period 1981 through 1983. The
size and suddenness of the adjustment give rise to
questions about whether it is sustainable for very long
from a political point of view, particularly if it is
considered that the bulk of the adjustment probably falls
on urban lower-income groups. The fact that, given the
lack of resources, there is no alternative to belt-
tightening does not mean that it will necessarily be
accepted or that the economic managers who are implementing it will be kept on.

The additional factor to weigh in the outlook is
that new capital flows are very difficult to mobilize.
Although the external financing needs of Latin America
have for now shrunk sharply, the availability of external
finance has fallen even more. In the analysis that
follows, I estimate that net commercial bank loans--after
repayment or refinancing of amortization to Latin American
countries for 1983--would be on the order of US$8 billion,
compared to about US$25 billion annually in the period
1979-1981, an admittedly unsustainable rate. But now it
appears that the net new lending in 1983 will only be
about US$6 billion or less because disbursements on
major loans accompanying restructurings, especially in the
cases of Argentina and Brazil, were delayed for several
months when those countries were unable to meet various
targets in the stabilization programs agreed with the
International Monetary Fund. In fact, periodic renegotiations of programs and targets have in several
cases cast doubt on their viability and implementation.
Of the larger countries, only Mexico met the agreed
program and lowered its public-sector deficit from 17
percent of GNP in 1982 to about 8-9 percent in 1983,
a giant step accompanied by a 5 percent decline in per
capita income. Major program renegotiations have taken
place in Argentina, Brazil, Chile, and Peru, and further
renegotiations may well be necessary.

No large-scale expansion of net lending from
official sources has yet taken place to offset the
shortage of funds, although there are beginnings both at
the multilateral agencies and at national export credit
agencies, while private investment capital flows obviously
remain at very low levels. As a result, some countries
have had to "finance" the gap by delaying payments, and
large arrears of interest and trade payments have built
up.

Despite this somewhat unsatisfactory picture, both
lenders and borrowers have shown that they can overcome
major obstacles successfully, in the sense of averting an
international financial crisis. "Muddling through"

appears to have worked, at least so far. However, the potential political and social cost to debtor countries has been high. There has not been enough emphasis on this cost; much discussion in the mass media of the industrialized countries has focused on such questions as whether the debt can be "paid back" (not the real issue for capital-importing countries--the key issue being the payment of interest) or whether the international banking system is severely endangered (unlikely, although some banks face potential earnings problems). Although everyone recognizes that major adjustment is necessary, focusing on ways to ease the cost of adjustment in the debtor countries might help to create the climate in which mechanisms could be established to prevent the eventualities that lenders fear most. Among them would be a prolonged suspension of interest payments by a major debtor country, which would force lenders to place such loans on a nonaccruing basis and would be particularly painful for the banks that have not so far made enough reserve provisions for such loans, particularly in North America.

A more centralized approach to the study of such mechanisms should be contemplated, with a larger role for the governments of lenders and borrowers rather than exclusive reliance on the present market arrangements. Among areas of priority are acceleration of disbursements and new lending from official sources and ways to diminish the interest burden, given the fact that at present general interest levels, including the cost of refinancings, Latin America is spending close to 45 percent of its export income to meet interest payments.

It is difficult to judge the likelihood of a breakdown in the present system in the case of major debtor countries. Even though it obviously should be avoided-- it would be harmful to both borrowers and lenders--and there are economic signs that it could be avoided, it is to a considerable extent a matter of people and politics. Politics lags behind economic trends. So far, there has been little political backlash to economic problems in major debtor countries. But trends argue for an attitude of readiness rather than mere hope: sharp income declines; rapid inflation and growing unemployment; increasing malnutrition; and last, but not least, a perceived loss of sovereignty. It is to be hoped that the so-called debt problem will in time disappear as other crises have, but a more deliberate approach would be a useful way of making such a hope come true.

LATIN AMERICAN DEBT: ACT TWO*

There is a distinct rumble. Is it the noise of an
impending second crisis of Latin American and other
developing-country debtors, or is it the start-up of world
economic recovery, which will gradually pull away lenders
and borrowers alike from the edge of a financial abyss?

In this chapter, I will update what has happened
since the fall of 1982, when the financial world awoke
to the possible consequences of the inability of Mexico
to meet the principal repayments on its external public
and private debt. I will then look at the present status
of the refinancings and of the debtor economies, and what
the prospects for the future appear to be.

The debt problem of developing countries is largely
a Latin American one.[3] The relative size of the debt of
the region is much larger than in the case of other
developing areas; its composition--two-thirds from
commercial banks--gives it short maturities and commercial
interest rates; and export earnings with which to service
the debt are modest in relation to the burden of debt
service. These features mean that the grave economic
problems that have been facing most Latin American countries in the last year or so are unlikely to spread, at
least with the same force, to other developing areas.
On the other hand, the regional concentration of the
problem means that virtually all countries in Latin
America and the Caribbean are viewed as one by commercial
bank lenders, an attitude that has drastically cut capital
inflows to the region, regardless of country differences,
and thus makes the task of recovery much more difficult.
The fact that the external debt has been built up over
the last decade, but especially in the last four years,
shows that the problem is not only a cyclical one but a
longer-term one. As in a natural catastrophy, the first
step is emergency action, followed later by reconstruction
and recovery.

The high interest rates of 1981-82, together with
the unexpected depth and duration of the international
recession, which led to a sharp deterioration of the
terms of trade of developing countries, were the critical
factors that sparked the debt crisis of 1982-83. In the
wake of Argentina and Mexico, international commercial
bank lending ground to a halt, forcing, as foreseen, the
renegotiation of part of the external commercial bank
debt of Brazil, Chile, and Venezuela, as well as Ecuador,
Peru, and Uruguay.

---

*"Latin American Debt: Act Two" is the title of my
article in the Fall 1983 issue of Foreign Affairs, as
well as the title of this chapter.

DIMENSIONS OF THE DEBT PROBLEM

In 1983 the interest payments on the external debt of the Latin American and Caribbean countries are expected to be close to US$40 billion, as long as international short-term interest rates do not increase above their level at midyear. This number has to be set against projected merchandise exports of about US$96 billion, compared to US$110 billion in 1981. Even with a significant immediate recovery of export earnings as a result of renewed economic growth in the industrialized countries, the interest burden would still be very heavy, likely to continue into 1984 and 1985, unless there is a major offsetting inflow of capital. The problem for the major Latin American debtor countries is therefore simple and stark: major outflows without comparable inflows.

Even though developing countries, regardless of their levels of income, suffered heavily from the international consequences of the 1981-82 recession, the debt aspect of the problem is basically concentrated in Latin America. Other developing areas have major balance-of-payment problems, of course. For example, much of sub-Saharan Africa has been engulfed in a chronic balance-of-payments problem since the oil-price increases of the early 1970s. Today some important oil-exporting countries, such as Indonesia and Nigeria, are caught in a financial and economic squeeze as a result of the drop in oil prices and the cuts in exportable volumes. Others, such as Korea, the Philippines, and Yugoslavia, have been hard hit by the international recession. However, the major problem brought on by the international recession and the high interest rates of 1981-1982 is concentrated in Latin America. Only the Philippines, among the countries shown in Table 6.1, has levels of debt that are comparable to those of the major Latin American borrowers.

The question is not only a statistical one. The fact that most international banks have cut back very sharply on new loans to Latin America almost regardless of country differences--other than operations that are tied to reschedulings and to stabilization programs supported by the International Monetary Fund--has tended to precipitate payments problems. Even countries with low debt burdens, such as Colombia and Trinidad and Tobago, are not finding it easy to obtain new loans. Fortunately, these attitudes of lenders, who have gone from optimism to pessimism, have not extended to the economies of Asia, so that at present there is little risk of a generalized debt crisis.

The fact that the debt problem is largely, although not exclusively, a Latin American one is illustrated by repeating two simple comparisons, which are illustrated in the table:

Table 6.1 Estimated Debt Burden of Some Major Developing Countries (in billions of U.S. dollars)

	(1) Total External Debt, Including Undisbursed, at End 1982	(2) Short-Term[a] Debt as % of (1)	(3) Estimated 1983 F.O.B. Merchandise Exports	(4) Ratio of (1) to (3) Debt to Exports	(5) Estimated Interest Due 1983 as % of Exports (3)
Argentina	39	25	9	3.9	50
Brazil	86	20	22	3.9	46
Chile	17	19	4	4.5	50
Mexico	86	30	22	3.9	46
Venezuela	33	45	14	2.3	29
Total Latin America[b]	330	25	96	3.4	42
Algeria	15	5	12	1.3	14
Indonesia	22	13	19	1.2	21
Korea	37	28	24	1.5	18
Philippines	21	38	5	4.2	48
Nigeria	11	27[c]	12	0.9	11
Total other LDCs[d]	350	--	330	1.1	12

Note: These are estimates, subject to error, and should be used with care.

[a] Original short-term debt; excludes refinanced amounts in 1983 and also excludes portions of longer-term debt falling due within one year

[b] Including Caribbean and other countries not listed

[c] Excluding trade payment errors

[d] All other developing countries except centrally planned economies and Middle East OPEC countries

Source: Derived by the author from Bank for International Settlements, Maturity Distribution of International Bank Lending (July 1983); Morgan Guaranty Trust Co., World Financial Markets (June 1983); International Monetary Fund, International Financial Statistics, various issues; and World Bank, various Annual Reports.

- The ratio of the stock of outstanding debt to the flow of merchandise export earnings, which provide the foreign exchange to service the debt--admittedly an oversimplified measure of the weight of debt[4]--is more than three to one in the case of Latin America compared to about one to one for the rest of the developing world.

- As a result, in 1983 Latin American and Caribbean countries as a group will need to devote, at present interest rates, about 42 percent of their merchandise export earnings to pay interest on their external debt, compared to 12 percent on average for other developing countries. The ratio approaches 50 percent for the large debtors such as Argentina, Brazil, and Mexico. It is as if a homeowner had to devote half his monthly income to interest payments on his home mortgage. These numbers assume that world interest rates do not rise for the second half of 1983, and that export earnings are on target. While the latter is nevertheless a good possibility in view of the improved competitiveness of Latin American exports as a result of the large devaluations of the last year, the outlook for interest rates is uncertain. Obviously, repayments of principal are not counted in these numbers. On the medium- and long-term debt, principal repayments represent approximately another 20 percent of export earnings for Latin America as a whole, after the refinancings committed or under discussion so far in 1983.

TRENDS IN THE DEBT PROBLEM

Since Mexico announced in August 1982 that it was unable to meet the repayment of principal on the external debt of its public and private sectors, a number of major events and trends have unfolded. At the risk of over-simplification, these trends can be grouped into negative and positive, although the interrelationships are quite complex.

Perhaps the most striking on the negative side has been the virtual interruption of new commercial bank lending to almost all Latin American countries. According to the last annual report of the Bank for International Settlements, the net flow--after repayments--from commercial banks to Latin America in the second half of 1982 was only about US$5 billion, mostly because of the disbursement of earlier commitments to Brazil, compared to an annual rate of about US$25 billion starting in 1979 and up to the first half of 1982.[5] Net flows have fallen further in 1983, and are likely to be much above US$8 billion, mostly as a result of net lending associated with debt rescheduling. The music has indeed stopped. Net flows, in the other developing countries, mostly in Asia, have also declined but at a slower pace.

Since commercial banks provided more than two-thirds of the capital inflow into Latin America, not just for the last three years but for the last decade, the interruption creates major adjustment problems. The interruption of net new lending adds to the inability of Brazil to meet its principal repayments after December 1982 and to the subsequent similar problems of Venezuela, Chile, Ecuador, Peru, and Uruguay, in addition to the existing problems in Argentina and Mexico. It is equally true that lending was proceeding at an unsustainable pace, much faster than the growth of the capital of the lending banks, and that large fiscal deficits in most borrowing countries were a major cause of excessive borrowing.[6]

A second and related development has been the cutback in trade financing. Lenders, particularly the smaller banks, have naturally enough reduced their lines of credit for export and import financing and in some cases eliminated them altogether. Official export agencies, which play a key role in medium-term equipment financing, have also cut back. Although clear statistics are not available, the dearth of new financing, combined with the drastic economic recession in virtually all Latin American and Caribbean countries, has led to a sharp drop in the exports from the industrialized countries to Latin America, and also in the exports between Latin American countries and between them and other developing countries. In the case of Brazil, for example, one-third of exports in 1981 went to the rest of Latin America and to other developing countries, primarily in Africa and the Middle East, all of them depressed markets at present.

Exports from the industrialized countries to Latin America, which accounted for one-third of their exports to non-OPEC developing countries, fell by 21 percent in 1982 and were still falling in 1983. U.S. exports in Latin America, which were in 1981 equivalent to two-thirds the value of U.S. exports to Western Europe and double those to Japan, also fell by the same proportion in 1982. This fall in export sales from US$42 billion in 1981 to US$34 billion in 1982 had a cost of between 100,000 and 130,000 direct jobs lost in the United States, and is continuing in 1983.[7] Even though Latin America absorbs only about 7 percent of the exports of the industrialized countries, the sharpness of the drop in exports, which affects in particular already depressed industries such as equipment and machinery, is undoubtedly a drag on world economic recovery. For some European countries, the fall in sales to developing countries could, in 1983, make the difference between a mild economic recovery and no growth at all.

A third related point is the extent of the economic depression in Latin America. For a time in 1981, some economies, particularly Mexico, shielded themselves from the world recession by massive external borrowing to finance public investment and consumption. As the lending stopped and long-delayed adjustment measures, such as devaluation and public spending cuts, had to be taken, the recession hit with double force. Devaluations had to be much larger than if they had been taken in time, giving a tremendous impetus to inflation, which is running well above 100 percent annually in the three largest economies of Latin America. For example, Mexico has had a devaluation of about 400 percent (in terms of pesos per dollar) in the last eighteen months. Comparable devaluations have taken place over the same period in Argentina, Chile, Brazil, and Venezuela.

The effect on the industrial private sector, which in all these cases had been encouraged by the policies of the authorities to borrow abroad, has been devastating: Domestic sales in some cases have fallen by 30 to 40 percent in real terms as incomes have lagged behind inflation. This has sharply cut the ability of enterprises to generate cash flow, while the amount needed in local currency to service external debt has increased three or four times in the last year. It is not an exaggeration to say that a major portion of private large-scale industry in Latin America--not to mention chronically sick state enterprises--is today in effect bankrupt. The worldwide intensification of trade barriers, a direct result of the international recession, aggravates the problem.

The policy of stimulating economies through public spending reached its peak in 1982, when the public-sector deficits of several countries reached records. In Argentina, Brazil, and Mexico, the public-sector deficits as a proportion of the Gross National Product peaked at 14, 12, and almost 17 percent respectively. Deficits of this magnitude, leading to large subsequent exchange-rate devaluations, have pulled up annual rates of inflation so far in 1983 to perhaps 300 percent in Argentina, about 130 percent in Brazil, and over 100 percent (although declining) in Mexico. Such stratospheric numbers eventually lead to major social and political strains. Inevitably, the process of strengthening public finances creates for a while even more inflation and discontent, as public enterprise prices and taxes are raised.

No one can deny the urgent need for major financial surgery, particularly on exchange rates and public finances. However, the suddenness and size of the measures required, together with the fact that they have not been backed up by a significant external capital inflow to help the adjustment, are creating a potentially explosive mixture of failing incomes, rising unemployment, and galloping inflation. For example, for Latin America as a whole 1983 will be the third successive year of declining real income per person. I estimate that over the period 1981-1983 real income per head will have fallen by about 10 percent, and by larger percentages in the lower middle-income groups, such as government workers and nonunionized service workers. Unemployment rates, which are admittedly very difficult to measure in Latin America, are probably hovering close to 20 percent in major industrial centers such as Buenos Aires, Mexico City, São Paulo, and Santiago de Chile, without counting the indirect unemployment of people working part time or selling lottery tickets and knickknacks on street corners.[8] With the gradual weakening of the system of extended families helping their kin, and without any unemployment insurance, such numbers are not sustainable for very long.

Why has there been no social explosion so far? There is no easy general answer. In the case of Mexico, for example, the rapid income growth until 1981 has provided some cushion, as has temporary or permanent migration to the United States. A well-disciplined political organization and tradition, with close control over the major trade unions, has enabled the government to keep wage adjustments behind price increases, a key element in the fight against inflation. In other cases, the lack of apparent reaction may come from the suddenness of the change, which has left populations stunned, so to speak. Another element has been the increasing discussion of economic issues in the press which, as a result of growing literacy in urban areas, has created an awareness of the magnitude of the economic problems being faced. The new Peruvian finance minister, for example, got an unexpectedly sympathetic public response earlier in 1983 to his program to cut public spending to the bone. In general, however, if there is no bread on the table, these positive developments can over time be offset by great social strains. The combination of inflation, unemployment, and declining real incomes provides a breeding ground for such tensions. Explosions are usually not announced.

On the positive side of the ledger, the most important development in the last year has been the unquestioned desire of most governments to put their financial house in order. Brazil took that decision as early as December 1980, but it takes time and a hospitable international environment to succeed. All the governments of the major economies of the region have taken significant and, in some cases, drastic economic steps in the last six to nine months. Undoubtedly, the interruption of significant new lending by commercial banks has been the major stimulus for such measures. But that interruption is also the biggest question mark on whether the stabilization programs can succeed in a

reasonable period of time. We will look at that crucial
question later.

The other positive but also qualified development is
the decline in world interest rates since mid-1982. The
London interbank rate for six-month deposits, which has
been the base rate for most international bank loans, has
fallen from a peak of 16 percent in June 1982 to about
10 percent in the last quarter of 1982, the level which
it had in July 1983, at the time of writing. Two points
qualify this progress: the significant increase in bank
charges above this base rate, and the uncertainty surrounding future interest rates.

The increase in bank charges is particularly important in the case of Mexico, which was paying very low
margins over the interbank rate. On the basis of the new
charges, Mexico is paying about 13 percent as of mid-1983
on its refinanced debt (a total of about US$40 billion
out of US$60 billion in variable rate debt). This level
results from three changes: The base rate is now (at the
option of the lenders) the prime U.S. lending rate,
which is generally higher than the interbank rate (which
is a deposit rate); the spread above that base rate has
been substantially raised; and various additional fees
have been attached to the refinancings and the new loans
associated with them. Similar charges are included in
the refinancings negotiated for Argentina, Brazil, Chile,
Ecuador, Peru, and Uruguay.

Most of these countries were already paying higher
costs than Mexico, so that the effect on them of the
changes is smaller. Furthermore, there are reasons for
the changes; management fees for new loans are normal
(although the new charges are on the high side), and the
shift to a U.S. prime rate base option was important in
order to convince smaller regional banks in the United
States to remain in the loans. On the other hand, the
argument that higher charges are justified because debtors
had become riskier is more debatable. For one thing,
the risk becomes difficult to measure when a debtor cannot service his debt; no premium can compensate that risk.
In fact, in the case of major U.S. and Canadian corporations which have undergone debt restructurings in recent
years, the interest rate charged by banks during the
reorganization period has often been below market rates.
These corporations have been represented by financial
advisers independent of the banks: So far most major
Latin American debtors have not wanted to antagonize
lenders by hiring independent financial advisers, although
the history of the refinancings so far shows that there
might have been merit in an outside opinion on realistic
debt-servicing possibilities.

The other uncertainty concerns the trend of U.S.
short-term interest rates, which are the preponderant
influence on rates in the Eurocurrency market. Already
in the second quarter of 1982, the interbank Eurodollar

rate was up by about 1 percent, adding on an annual basis US$2.2 billion to Latin American interest payments abroad. If short-term U.S. rates were to go up another point or so in the second half, as some economists predict, because of the effects of the U.S. budget deficit, the total increase in debt-servicing cost for Latin America since the spring of 1983 would have been close to US$5 billion on an annual basis, a very significant sum at a time of sharply reduced capital inflows.

A third positive development, which flows from the decline in imports and in interest payments, is the sharp reduction in the current account deficit of the region, namely the requirement for external finance that remains after current inflows, principally exports of goods and services, have been used to pay for current outflows, mainly imports and interest. The very nature of developing economies, which need to import capital in order to supplement their inadequate domestic savings, means that they have a current account deficit and thus a need to borrow abroad and attract investment capital. However, Latin America and the Caribbean, largely as a result of the drop in incomes and the sharp decline in imports of the last year, has greatly reduced its need for external finance. The current account deficit of the region has fallen from US$38 billion in 1981 to US$33 billion in 1982, and is expected to fall to about US$18 to 20 billion in 1983, as long as international interest rates remain at midyear levels. If interest rates were to rise again, the financing gap would begin to rise again. A return to the interest rates prevailing in mid-1982, for example--even though it is highly improbable--would entirely wipe out the improvement in the current account deficit of the last year.

The uncertainties about how Latin American and Caribbean countries will finance themselves over the next couple of years are undoubtedly a crucial concern of both lenders and debtors. Even though the financing gap has been sharply cut, the availability of external resources has declined even more. The future trend of commercial bank lending is uncertain and a part of the new loans that have accompanied recent reschedulings of commercial bank debt is being used to finance the higher charges above the base interest rate. Foreign direct investment, which until recently covered about one-fifth to one-quarter of the current account deficit, has slumped in the wake of the recession both in the industrialized countries and now in Latin America. The return of flight capital that left a number of major Latin American economies in recent years could be important, but will take time. Finally, as we will discuss later, the multilateral development institutions --such as the World Bank and the InterAmerican Development Bank--face resource constraints. Identifying sources of net capital inflows--including about US$8 billion of

commercial bank lending, approximately US$2 billion of
net disbursement from the Multilateral Development Bank,
and an equivalent amount of supplier credits previously
negotiated--leaves a significant financing gap, larger
than what can be covered from private investment. Thus,
even though the overall financing gap has declined, the
problem of covering it has become far more acute.

Is it reasonable to expect countries to work their
way out of their present economic and financial predicament? In recent months various projections[9] have been
constructed to show how and whether major debtors can
work their way out of their present problems. Most of
these projections show that if the industrialized
economies grow at a reasonable rate (say 3 percent per
year), if interest rates do not increase beyond mid-1983
levels (10 percent for the six-month Eurodollar interbank rate), and, most especially, if a modicum of capital
inflows can continue, then most of the major debtors
could resume economic growth and service their external
debt more or less comfortably by about 1986. But there
are many uncertainties. Most projections highlight the
very limited room to maneuver in the next two or three
years.

The relationship between lenders and debtors has
created an unusual degree of interdependence. This is
particularly the case with commercial banks, which have
provided the bulk of external capital to Latin America in
the last decade. The relationship is a little like that
of two people on a see-saw: If one jumps off suddenly,
both are likely to get hurt. Very large losses could
affect major international commercial banks if countries
are unable to work their way out of trouble. The problem
does not only concern U.S. banks, but also banks in
Europe, Canada, and Japan as well as part of the debt to
suppliers. However, given the large share of the Latin
American debts held by U.S. banks (about 45 percent of
the debt to commercial banks), it is likely that leadership on the issue will have to come from the U.S. side.
Sizable reductions in net income could affect some large
banks if significant loan loss reserves had to be set
aside for major Latin American debts, in the event that
interest payments lagged substantially behind schedule.
Banks have already set up such reserves for some of the
debts owed by the Latin American private sector.

For problems to be worked out, there is a clear need
to change the perception of hopelessness that permeates
the international climate at present, particularly as
seen by debtor countries. This pessimism could encourage
some debtors to leave the hard road of financial
discipline and adjustment and be tempted by apparently
easier solutions such as a "cartel" of debtors. Export
more? Import quotas on yarn, orange juice, specialty
steels, which are just three recent examples, are con-
veying the wrong message. More official funds? The

quota increase for the IMF is having an uphill battle in the U.S. Congress. Economic recovery in the industrialized world? High and rising real interest rates could slow down the recovery. As lenders and borrowers look for solutions, they find closed doors and blocked paths.

Another important need is to maintain an atmosphere of calm. Each new confrontation creates an air of crisis that makes it difficult to maintain a flow of lending from banks less involved internationally. Smaller and so-called regional banks, which account for about 15 percent of the international commercial bank debt outstanding of Latin America, undoubtedly want to get out of these loans, a trend that would put great pressure on the larger banks to increase their exposure even more than planned. So far a confrontation has been avoided, but any rumors of an impending crisis in a particular country obviously make the task more difficult.

The sensitivity of individual countries' problems is illustrated by the case of Brazil, which faces a fairly drastic adjustment program with the IMF. As of this writing, it appears that the IMF has restored the ability of Brazil to draw under the facility agreed earlier in the year, after Brazil implemented a new, tough set of anti-inflationary measures mainly to keep wage adjustments below inflation. This has avoided, for the time being, a major problem for Brazil's lenders, whose disbursements on a US$4.4 billion loan are tied to disbursements on the IMF facility. However, the dearth of additional capital inflows continues to make it difficult for Brazil to service interest on time. As problems are aired publicly, including the initial well-publicized requirement by the Bank for International Settlements that Brazil had to repay an earlier emergency loan on time, the task of avoiding confrontations and possible crises becomes more difficult.

STIPULATIONS FOR DEBTORS AND LENDERS

Until now, market mechanisms have handled the problems of debtor countries as they arose. But it is not clear whether such mechanisms can continue to be effective by themselves, without leadership by the governments of the major industrialized countries. For the lending banks, a serious dilemma arises: On the one hand, it is quite clear that they cannot continue lending at anything like the breakneck pace of 1979-1981; on the other hand, if net lending does not expand moderately and lending does not continue, it will be very difficult for lenders to collect interest on past loans. For debtor governments, most of which clearly recognize the need for tough belt-tightening measures, the problem is that austerity may be too costly in social and political terms and that a gradual approach may not be feasible because

of the lack of external finance and the delay in the
recovery of export earnings.

Rather than discussing whether we are or are not in
a crisis, or whether it is an issue of insolvency (that
the borrowers can "never" pay) or illiquidity (that
they cannot pay now), which are questions of degree and
definition, it is more useful to outline the preconditions
for both the debtors and the lenders to work their way
out of the problem.

First, it is useful to distinguish between the
immediate future and the longer term. The coming year is
probably the critical one, since export income of the
debtors will still lag for a time until an international
recovery is in full swing, while large interest payments
will continue at a time of very limited capital inflows.
This is not to say that there is not a longer-term
problem, as the refinancings being arranged now start
becoming due in three or four years. Moreover, there are
historic reasons, summarized later, which suggest that
the pattern of development of Latin America cannot easily
be changed. Nevertheless, from the practical point of
view of dealing with the most urgent problems first, it
is important to analyze possible action in terms of what
is politically feasible now, not a year or two from now.
Anyone familiar with the mood of parliaments in major
industrialized countries, especially the U.S. Congress,
has to recognize that there is no room for quick big-
scheme solutions where taxpayers would directly or indirectly have to put up substantial new funds.

Second, no single party can carry the whole load of
adjustment. Any arrangements must involve some effort on
the part of both the lenders and the borrowers. This has
been the case so far, although the degree of effort by
each side--namely continuing some positive net flow of
lending by the banks, and financial discipline and
austerity on the part of the debtors--is viewed
suspiciously by the other. It is doubtful if serious
problems can be avoided in the future without some intervention by the governments of the main lenders to help
stimulate a larger capital inflow.

Third, any way out thus has to emphasize the
restoration of capital inflows. To be sure, these flows
cannot over time rely only on commercial bank funds. A
better balance than in the last decade has to be found
between investment capital and loans. Obviously direct
and portfolio investment will take some time to revive.

Finally, it is essential to remove the obstacles to
the revival of export growth. The extent to which the
growth of protectionism in recent years has affected
Latin American economies is not clear. Countries in
South and East Asia have been affected as much, if not
more. But it is clear that special interests in North
America, Europe, and Japan, for what are locally very
understandable reasons, but which affect only a relatively

small percentage of labor forces and of commerce, are gaining strength as the effect of the recession gets translated, after a lag, into political processes. Governments are applying remedies that may no longer be needed by the time they are implemented but which could have proportionately significant effects in the ability of debtors to sell abroad and earn foreign exchange.

In looking at the immediate future, the most urgent measures are to keep up an inflow of capital, to reduce the burden of interest payments, and to stop the rise of protectionism. The role of the governments in the major industrialized countries is crucial in all three actions, although the extent to which governments are politically able to commit themselves, hopefully in a concerted approach, is quite limited.

PROPOSED SOLUTIONS

The ability of the international financial fire brigade, the International Monetary Fund, to function is crucial. It is essential to put in place as soon as possible the increase in the resources (paid-in quotas of countries) of the IMF. Several points should be made. First, available IMF resources are nearly depleted. If any large industrialized country were to need special assistance from the Fund now, a distinct possibility, the resources of the Fund would be exhausted. Second, even the quota increase contemplated, of about 50 percent, simply catches up with past world inflation and would not contribute significant new real resources. Third, the Fund is not as some politicians appear to think a give-away to developing countries. It is a currency pool, which makes foreign exchange available to all member countries--the United States has been a borrower in the past--under rather strict conditions, in order to replenish the foreign-exchange reserves of countries facing balance-of-payments problems. It is not a pro-vider of long-term capital. Finally, since the quota increase will probably take at least until mid-1984 to be put into place, there is still a need for a temporary special facility, financed by the existing General Agreement to Borrow or some other form of cooperation among capital surplus countries.[10]

If the quota increase of the IMF cannot be approved as proposed, even if the approval takes many months, such a negative would be a clear signal, both to debtors and to lenders, that the major countries of the world do not consider the present problems important enough. Some debtors would be tempted to default, and lenders would then wind up knocking at the doors of their central banks for what could then amount to a costly bail-out. It is unfortunate that the increase in the resources of the IMF, which was needed anyway, has coincided in time with a political debate, especially in the United States, on whether the debt problem should be laid at the door of the lenders or the debtors, both of which are seen as villains.

A second avenue that should be explored quickly is how to stimulate more lending by the World Bank and the InterAmerican Development Bank. Unfortunately, the net resource transfer--disbursements less payments of principal and interest--of the World Bank to Latin America in the fiscal year ended in June was only about US$500 million, a relatively modest sum, and has stayed at approximately that level since 1980. Even though disbursements rose in fiscal 1983 to US$2.3 million, because of a larger proportion of sector support loans, amortization and interest absorbed the whole of the increase. The InterAmerican Development Bank, which has a lower cost mix of funds because of the concessional Fund for Special Operations supported mainly by the United States, has been able to raise the net transfer moderately from about US$600 million to US$800 million over the same period. In order to increase World Bank lending, which is tied to projects, many of which have either been suspended or been sharply slowed down in the last two years, there is a need for greater resources and for more flexible lending policies. The United States has basically opposed such policies, which would emphasize sector-support or "structural adjustment" loans, although it has recently toned down its opposition somewhat.

The entry of China into the Bank, and the uncertainty of future contributions of industrialized countries, particularly the United States, to its concessional window--the International Development Association--has drawn Bank funds away from possible loans to Latin American borrowers. Latin American countries are thus giving special support to the InterAmerican Development Bank. With its recently approved increase in capital, the regional bank can now significantly expand its activities, although some redirection of lending policies may be needed for the difficult two or three years ahead.

In both the case of the World Bank and the Inter-American Development Bank, a quick-fix solution to future funding has been promoted by those who recommend a doubling of the so-called gearing ratio, which is the ratio of capital contributions by the major credit-worthy members of the institution (basically the OECD countries) to the outstanding borrowings. The solution envisaged is thus simply to borrow more without providing more guarantee capital. This is not a worthwhile course. The fact that deposit-taking commercial banks have a ratio of paid-in capital to assets in the United States of about 5 to 6 percent is not relevant to a long-term development institution that has to borrow the bulk of its resources in the capital markets. Bondholders, who rightly view the obligations of both institutions (and

the Asian Development Bank as well) as guaranteed by the
United States, Japan, Germany, etc., would now begin to
look instead at their loans to developing countries. The
resulting downgrading of the bonded debt of the World
Bank and the regional multilateral development banks
would be costly to borrowers and would end up being an
irreversible step.

It is easier to increase as soon as possible the
capital of the World Bank--and restore funds to the Fund
for Special Operations of the Inter-American Development
Bank--particularly since the capital increases require
little cash. The recent InterAmerican Development Bank
capital increase involved only 4.5 percent in cash. In
essence, the development banks are thus already like
insurance or guarantee schemes organized to pass through
relatively low-cost funds to their borrowers. It is
probably easier to increase their callable capital, or
"guarantee" capability, than to establish a whole new
guarantee scheme, although that idea should not be dis-
carded if it becomes absolutely necessary to stimulate a
net flow of commercial lending.

New lending by the multilateral agencies, as long as
it can be targeted at the real problems faced by countries, is preferable to more emphasis on cofinancing with
commercial banks. In the present market cofinancing with
commercial banks will not work simply on the basis of
cross-default clauses, such as the World Bank and Inter-
American Development Bank have provided between their
loans and the related commercial bank loans. The whole
of international bank lending is cross-defaulted; namely a default on one loan can trigger a legal default
on all the debt and guarantees of a particular borrower,
yet that has not prevented payment delays and de facto
defaults. In the present market, only a guarantee will
work, but in that case both the international institutions
and the countries are better off with straight lending
at the less-than-commercial rates that the multilateral
development banks can provide.

Third, it is urgent to reduce the interest burden,
but the problem is complex. Much depends of course on
the course of international interest rates themselves,
which are closely linked with U.S. rates and difficult
to predict. But even if basic rates remain at their mid-
1983 level, it is clear that the interest burden is very
heavy indeed. This has stimulated a number of proposals[11] to refund the debt of some (or all) developing-
country debtors into long-term obligations at less than
market interest rates. Unfortunately, most of the
schemes are unlikely to be feasible politically and would
probably also have negative side effects, principally
in drastically reducing new commercial bank lending for a
long time.

It is quite unlikely that any of the schemes so far
advanced to reduce the load of debt could be implemented

in the next year, since they all require, in varying
degrees, the multilateral approval of governments.
Opinion in creditor countries is generally not sympathetic
to such schemes. Progressives look upon these ideas as
a bail-out of imprudent lenders, and conservatives as a
bail-out of irresponsible debtor governments. Notwithstanding the need to study and define possible general
arrangements for the medium term, remedies and palliatives
are needed now rather than later since the coming year is
probably the most critical one.

The schemes, in the improbable event that they were
economically and politically feasible, also run into the
problem that they would probably stop further bank lending for a very long time. The charge against bank earnings would be too large because the loans could not be
recycled except at very large discounts. Moreover, the
idea that official institutions, such as the IMF, which
are having a hard time raising additional resources for
their established operations, should bear this additional
burden seems impractical.[12] Yet the recycling schemes do
make the important point that the debt-service burden is
too high.

Perhaps it is possible to combine, in a contingency
plan that would be activated in an emergency, a temporary
reduction of the interest burden without damaging the
prospects for continued lending on a moderate scale.
For the banks, many of which would obviously resist such
a move strongly, it would at least have the advantage of
reducing the increase in their lending, since at present,
before Latin American export growth revives and new
sources of capital inflows can be developed, an additional dollar of interest service by the borrowers is
financed (in simplified terms) by an additional dollar
of bank lending and exposure. It may be better, at
least during the immediate recovery period, for lenders
to sacrifice about fifty to sixty cents of net after-tax
earnings which a dollar of added interest income provides, in exchange for not having to put up an extra
dollar of lending.

It is worth considering whether the banks might not
be better off working out a temporary arrangement on
interest charges than having to come up with last-minute
financing packages in the midst of a crisis. I stress
that such an arrangement would have to be temporary and
could not be done below the market costs of funds, if
the central objective of keeping some flow of lending is
to be maintained. Under several of the refunding schemes
proposed so far, the interest reduction would be below
the cost of funds to the commercial bank lenders. Let us,
for the purpose of argument, assume that the new rate
under these schemes were set at 9 percent. The savings
to the Latin America debtors in interest per year, at
today's cost of money, would be about US$7 billion. That
saving, however, would greatly if not irreparably damage

the chances of financing the remainder of the current
account deficit of Latin America. A more modest proposal
to reduce interest charges, for example, to no more than
1 percent over the London interbank rate, including all
other charges, for a period of about two years--until
world recovery begins to pull up Latin America foreign-
exchange earnings--would still save debtors at present
rates about US$4.5 billion annually without damaging to
the same extent the chances for new lending.

It is unlikely that bank lenders would by themselves
accept such a scheme, even if it were proposed on a
contingent basis. There would no doubt have to be some
government persuasion. Given the time constraints, direct
persuasion, as has occurred in the recent refinancings,
may be better than a large international conference, which
requires much preparation. If interest rates look at all
as if they are again on the rise, consideration of some
sort of scheme to reduce the interest burden at least
temporarily will become urgent. Otherwise, as export
earnings failed to recover in the wake of the negative
effects of higher interest rates on recovery in the
industrialized countries, lenders would find themselves
facing the dilemma of having to lend more in order to get
paid the higher interest due.

A related point is whether a quid pro quo for the
reduction in interest charges might be necessary, such as
some form of medium-term international or government
guarantee for net new lending. Even if this were
politically feasible, however, it would take time to put
such an arrangement in place. Perhaps the understanding
that a guarantee would, as a last result, be given
serious consideration by governments would be enough
stimulus to arrange a contingent scheme to reduce interest
costs in the immediate future. That and the continuation
of net capital inflows are the only avenues of action
open for the short term, together with the continuation
of difficult austerity measures in the borrowing countries.

Medium-Term Solutions

For the medium term, the proper emphasis should be
to continue to find ways to stimulate new capital flows,
especially in the immediate years ahead. To do that
within the short time available is extremely difficult.
No one scheme or source of flows will do. Complicated
new arrangements are unlikely to be feasible. Nor can
new flows simply be blank checks to underwrite a revival
of state enterprise deficit spending in borrowing countries.

Long-Term Solutions

It is clear that the policies that could yield results soon are difficult to enact. Moreover, something is needed on each front, especially on replenishing the resources of the IMF and on lowering the interest burden without jeopardizing new flows, a most difficult task. In order to put all the pieces of the package together, some form of concerted action by the governments of the major money and capital markets of the world is needed. Of course, each month that passes without a major crisis reinforces the feeling in some quarters that the worst is over and that eventually the problems will evaporate in the wake of world recovery. Such a view gives an uneasy comfort but is not consistent with the problems as seen from the debtor countries, which face enormous problems.

So far, the temptation to stray from the path of IMF-supported austerity has been avoided by the governments of Latin America. But the present equilibrium is a tenuous one. It is quite conceivable that the government economic teams that have followed such policies could be jettisoned in the face of strong political opposition. The refinancings linked to the IMF credit facilities would then be called into question and a period of confusion could well follow. At that point some governments may be tempted to talk and think of a debtors' cartel, in the sense of a coordinated suspension of debt service. The idea is at present viewed by financial policymakers in most countries as a product of the lunatic fringe. But if these officials and their policies do not receive enough external support now, there is the risk that the lenders might face a very different cast of characters. That is why it is important to focus in a more concerted fashion on possible solutions while the problem appears to be in remission.

Besides the areas already mentioned, there are others that could be of great importance to economic recovery, although not immediately. The longer horizon does not mean that the necessary policies should not be put in place now. Two important areas are private investment and credit insurance. Private investment is not a promising source for the next year or two, but could be of great importance once economies revive. In the early 1960s, private direct investment provided about 40 percent of the net capital inflows into Latin America, particularly into Brazil and Mexico. In recent years, the proportion has fallen to 20 to 25 percent. In 1981-82, net flows were about US$6 to 7 billion annually, a sum that has fallen in 1983. It is essential to establish the preconditions now for an investment recovery later. Mexico has already begun to take measures, for example by reducing in practice the requirements for domestic ownership. Peru is breaking away from the Andean Group's ill-conceived restrictions on foreign

direct industrial investment. Multilateral investment
guarantee schemes, which have been under study for many
years at the World Bank and elsewhere, deserve another
look. Of equal or even greater importance is private
domestic investment, since its revival would pull back
into Latin American countries part of the large sums
which have fled in 1981-1983. For example, perhaps
US$20 to 25 billion is estimated to have left Mexico
and Venezuela, the two most notable cases, in that period.
While some of what has gone out will stay out, more
realistic exchange rates, political stability, and a
revival of domestic markets would, in time, begin to
attract some of the flight capital. Unrecorded flows of
this type could make a big difference once the beginnings
of improvement are visible.

Since it is important to keep some bank lending
going, albeit on a more controlled scale, several schemes
have been advanced under which a multilateral credit
insurance facility could be established, to be run on an
agency basis by the World Bank or the IMF, or a combination of the two. The facility would cover additional
lending. Setting up a multilateral arrangement is
probably desirable but politically difficult and time-
consuming. In the meantime, individual export credit
agencies, working with the World Bank and the Inter-
American Development Bank, could more quickly get themselves organized.[13] The resources are there: For
example, as of May 1983, the U.S. Export-Import Bank had
barely committed one-tenth of its authorized lending for
fiscal 1983, largely because of the cutbacks in development projects around the world. Commitments for the
full fiscal year are wholly to be well below authorizations. Of course, changes in legislation would in some
cases be required, but they would probably be easier to
obtain than for a multilateral scheme and could be set in
motion while a multilateral arrangement is designed and
evaluated. On the multilateral front, the idea of an
Export Development Fund[14] has much appeal, especially if
it could be expanded from lending to developing countries for capital goods imports to helping to finance the
exports of these countries, which represent, in general,
transactions that are liquid, usually secure, and
suitable for commercial finance.

By definition, the most urgent task is to confront
the more immediate problems. There is, however, only
limited time to put into effect policies which would
produce results by 1986-87, when the first big repayments
on the recent refinancings are due. The struggle into
recovery will not be easy, since the economic problem in
the case of the major Latin American countries is not
simply a cyclical one but arises in part from their
historical stage of development. For countries such as
Argentina, Brazil, Mexico, and Venezuela, with relatively
large internal markets in comparison with the export-

oriented East Asian economies, the thrust of development has been industrialization for domestic consumption and the building of infrastructure for a rapidly growing population. In that sense, the pattern of development has some similarities with that of the United States a century ago, which also emphasized infrastrueture and industry for a growing internal market. The difference is that real interest rates were then at the historic norm of about 3 percent in real terms, whereas today, for Latin American borrowers, the real rate on their commercial debt is closer to 9 percent in real terms. Moreover, three-quarters of this external commercial debt is owed by the public sector. The railroad and steel barons of a hundred years ago have been replaced as borrowers by inefficient state enterprises, and the widows and orphans of the British Empire as lenders by large and powerful banks. The balance of negotiating power has therefore significantly changed.

Another important feature has been that the major Latin American economies have not in the last three decades been able to provide enough jobs, particularly for the growing lower middle class, which wields increasing political power. Political pressures have thus built up to provide jobs through the government and state enterprises. Similar pressures act to maintain overvalued exchange rates and interest-rate subsidies--which help middle-class consumption--all of which tends to build up budget deficits, stimulate borrowing, and hold back the growth of export earnings. This set of policies also tends to hold back employment, particularly in manufacturing, where advanced social legislation for a minority of the labor force tends to push up wage costs to levels that are uncompetitive internationally.

Such policies underlie, with periodic changes in emphasis, much of Latin America's rapid economic growth in the postwar period and will not change quickly. There is therefore a long-term aspect to the debt problem beyond the admittedly more pressing cyclical problem.

CONCLUSIONS

A clean and simple, conceptually satisfying scheme to "solve" the debt problem obviously has intellectual appeal, while the present muddling through is fraught with danger. For the time being, however, political realities, especially in the United States, make it very difficult to envisage an all-encompassing scheme. There is far more political concern within the United States on Central America than on the debt question, although the long-term effects of the latter could turn out to be very serious. As long as nothing explodes, there will be little interest in setting up contingency mechanisms. Only a real crisis, which hopefully will not occur but

is unfortunately a distinct possibility, will powerfully
concentrate the minds of policymakers other than the
central bankers and Treasury officials who have already
been involved. In the meantime, everyone would be better
off if lenders, authorities in the lenders' countries,
and major borrowers work together in setting up a concerted program to help existing official institutions to
do more and to establish contingency plans to lower the
interest burden of commercial debt, if necessary, in the
event that the debt burden cannot be managed.

Both lenders and debtors face a critical period.
While there are indeed some chances that the problem will
gradually be overcome by world economic recovery, the
risk of major crises ahead are high indeed. It is therefore vital to anticipate these problems in a concerted
fashion, well ahead of time, rather than run the risk of
facing them at the very last minute.

NOTES

1. The article that appears in this chapter was in
the Fall 1983 issue of Foreign Affairs. It is reprinted
by permission of Foreign Affairs, Fall 1983. Copyright
1983 by the Council on Foreign Relations, Inc. The
article was written some months earlier, following a
first article on the same subject published in the same
journal in the Winter 1982-1983 issue. Foreign Affairs
has given permission for the reproduction of the paper
here. I am indebted to Elizabeth K. Rabitsch of First
Boston for help with background for the article. The
views expressed are personal.
2. See, for example, William Cline, International
Debt and the Stability of the World Economy, Washington,
D.C., September 1983.
3. "Latin American Debt," my article in Foreign
Affairs, Winter 1982-1983.
4. Comparing stocks to flows can be misleading.
However, since interest is a proportion of the debt outstanding, the comparison is of some use. Also, it could
be argued that all exports, including services (such
as tourism), should be taken into account. Since Latin
America as a whole has a negative balance on services,
the concept of export of goods and services seems an
inappropriate measure.
5. Bank for International Settlements, Fifty-Third
Annual Report, Basle, June 1983, p. 116, showed only
US$100 million. However, a later estimate of July 1983
showed US$5 billion of net flows for the second half of
1982, largely for the reason noted. The first quarter
of 1983 showed no net loan flows to Latin America other
than those associated with the Mexico and Brazil
refinancings.

6. See "Latin American Debt," pp. 354-357, 359.
7. My estimate, based on a ratio of about twelve thousand to fifteen thousand jobs per US$1 billion in sales.
8. Official statistics, which are sometimes based on narrow statistical amounts in Argentina, Brazil, and Mexico, show lower numbers, however.
9. For example, among others, Morgan Guaranty Trust, World Financial Markets, June 1983; William R. Cline, Developing Country Debt Under Alternative Global Conditions, 1983-86, Washington, D.C., 1983. The largest international banks have their own projections, as has the Federal Reserve Bank of New York.
10. See "Latin American Debt," pp. 362-363.
11. For example, Felix Rohatyn of Lazard Freres (in Business Week, February 28, 1983) suggested that a major portion of credits be turned into long-term low-interest bonds, under the aegis of the IMF. Peter Kenen of Princeton University (New York Times, March 6, 1983) proposed that a special agency buy the loans from the commercial banks at a discount with the proceeds of long-term bonds. A proposal along similar lines, but using the World Bank, has been made by Richard Weinert in Foreign Policy (Spring 1983). Minos Zombanakis has proposed a Loan Guarantee Fund in the IMF (The Economist, April 30, 1983). There are a number of other interesting proposals.
12. For a discussion, see Yves Laulan, "A New Approach To International Indebtedness," the Banker, July 1983.
13. See, for example, Harold Lever, "The Lever Plan," The Economist, July 9-15, 1983.
14. See William H. Bolin and Jorge del Canto, "LDC Debt: Beyond Crisis Management," Foreign Affairs, vol. 61, no. 5 (Summer 1983).

7
Capital Market Financing to Developing Countries

Ariel Buira

The world economy has faced serious difficulties in recent years. These have been related essentially to the external debt problems that have arisen in an important number of developing countries, which have threatened the stability of the international monetary system. Thus far, the system has been able to adjust to these problems in such a way as to avoid its breakdown. Nevertheless, there is an urgent need to adapt it to the new circumstances prevailing in the world economy, if the emergence of recurrent crisis is to be avoided. In this context, the search for new mechanisms for recyling financial resources from surplus to deficit nations to ensure the appropriate supply of funds for balance of payments and development finance has been of particular concern. The purpose of this chapter is to put in perspective the origins of the present difficulties and their implications with regard to future financing for LDCs, and possible solutions.

ORIGINS OF THE CRISIS

Until recently, the number of developing countries with access to the international capital markets was limited and the amounts they received did not represent a substantial proportion of the markets concerned. The rapid expansion of international lending to LDCs can be associated with the growth of the Eurodollar markets in the 1970s.
As late as 1970-1972, external financing to the developing countries was still largely provided through non-debt-creating flows from official sources and long-term capital investment from private sources. However, in the years following the quadrupling of world oil prices at the end of 1973, the international capital markets experienced an explosive growth--by some estimates growing from US$200 billion in 1973 to US$2,000 billion in 1982--becoming the single most important channel for

the transfer of savings from surplus to deficit countries.
A large part of the resources for this expansion
was provided by short-term bank deposits of the governments of oil-exporting countries, and the largest part
of the markets' assets were private bank credits to the
governments and official entities of deficit countries.
The flexibility of the Euromarkets and the relative ease
with which they were able to transform short-term deposits
into medium-term loans determined their strong growth.
    The increase in the demand for credit generated by
the sharp rise in oil prices was more than matched by an
inflow of funds into the market, and until mid-1979 spreads
were generally falling, interest rates were barely positive, and credit conditions in the international capital
markets tended to favor borrowers. As a result of these
factors, the share of financing provided by official
creditors--both government and multilateral development
finance institutions--to nonoil LDCs diminished in
relative terms from some 67 percent in the period
1967-1970 to about 35 percent by 1982; likewise, private
markets supplied approximately half of the capital needed
by these countries to finance their current account
deficits in 1981-82.
    Borrowing by the developing countries tended to be
heavily concentrated in some individual nations; although
some forty to forty-five countries gained access to the
markets, the two largest borrowers, Mexico and Brazil,
accounted for about 40 percent of all the funds raised
in 1978-1981, and the five largest averaged 67 percent
in the same period. In 1982, Brazil and Mexico together
accounted for 26 percent of the total LDC debt service,
and the share of the five largest debtors amounted to
40 percent.
    The role played by the international financial
markets has to be underscored. In bridging the large
current deficits, the private markets made it possible
for industrial countries to meet the higher world oil
prices without a deeper and longer recession than they
suffered. The more advanced nonoil developing countries
were able to borrow heavily to maintain their levels of
investment; thus, their economic growth was sustained at
about the average trend rate of 5 percent. In so doing,
this group of countries helped sustain international
trade and activity in the world economy.
    However, since commercial bank loans are character-
ized by higher interest rates and shorter maturities
than credits provided by official sources of development
finance, this change in the structure of finance was to
give rise to a more than proportional increase in the
debt-service burden of borrowers. This, coupled with the
sharp increase in lending to LDCs, was bound to give rise
to questions regarding the long-term viability of this
pattern of finance and of the creditworthiness of the
developing countries. Nevertheless, the conditions in

the international capital markets, along with the expanding world trade, allowed the postponement of the problem. These favorable trends were reversed in 1979. The sustained increase in world energy demand, together with the existence of negative real interest rates in the international capital markets--which made it more profitable to keep oil in the ground, set the conditions for a second oil crisis. This led to a sharp deterioration in the balance-of-payments position--and thus the credit-worthiness--of the oil-importing countries, especially those among the developing group.

Furthermore, as a response to the inflationary pressures generated by the oil-price increase, most of the major industrial countries adopted restrictive monetary policies after late 1979. Thus, the cost of borrowing, as indicated by LIBOR plus average spread, which had fluctuated between 6.5 and 7.75 percent in the period 1975-1977, averaged 13 percent in 1979, nearly 18 percent in 1981, and around 15 percent in 1982. These historically high rates of interest, in both nominal and real terms, were to result in a sharp increase in the burden of debt-service payments of the developing countries.

Since 1980, the tightening of credit conditions has also been reflected in a widening of spreads and a greater risk differentiation among borrowers. Maturities on new borrowing, particularly for the major borrowers, were shortened. Thus, the ratio of short-term to total debt for the group of nonoil developing countries rose from 15 percent in 1978 to 18 percent in 1982; for the four largest debtors, such ratio increased from 16 percent in 1978 to more than 25 percent by 1982.

The restrictive stance of the monetary policy adopted by the United States and other major industrial countries was to have other significant effects on the level of international economic activity and the external environment. The volume of world trade, which had grown at annual rates of 9-10 percent in the 1960s and 6 percent in the 1970s, has remained stagnant since 1979. In addition, the deep and protracted recession in the industrial countries was to result in a sharp fall in commodity prices, which in some cases fell to their lowest levels in real terms since records exist. On average, commodity prices fell by more than 30 percent between December 1979 and November 1982; since then, they have followed a moderate upward trend, increasing by some 15 percent in the ten months to September 1983.

As a result of falling commodity prices and continued inflation, the terms of trade of nonoil developing countries deteriorated sharply.[1] Moreover, the recession and resulting unemployment in industrial countries have given rise to strong protectionist trends, which have been particularly apparent in a number of sectors in which developing countries have a comparative advantage.

In an effort to sustain economic growth under such
extremely adverse external conditions, nonoil LDCs
increased sharply their external indebtedness. Total
outstanding debt of these countries is estimated to have
increased from US$130 billion in 1973 to US$390 billion
in 1979 and to more than US$600 billion in 1982 (see
Table 7.1). In relation to the group's output and exports,
external indebtedness rose to record levels and for an
unprecedented number of countries the debt-servicing
burden reached critical proportions, as reflected in
the record number of debt rescheduling (see Table 7.2)
and the sharp rise in external payment arrear.

By the middle of 1982, intense concern arose in the
international community regarding the ability of some of
the larger borrowers to meet their external financial
commitments; thus, a growing reluctance of banks to
extend new credits was apparent. Another factor that
contributed to the tightening of market conditions was
the sharp decline and virtual disappearance of OPEC
surpluses in 1981 and 1982. Furthermore, some estimates
show that even if the price of oil does not fall below
US$29 a barrel--the benchmark price agreed upon in
March 1983--the OPEC countries will experience a deficit
of between US$25 and US$35 billion for 1983 and of some
US$10 to US$20 billion in 1984.

One effect of the reduction of OPEC surpluses has
been a decline in the amount of resources available to
the international financial markets. Although OPEC
surpluses have been replaced by a greater volume of
deposits by firms and corporations of industrial countries,
banks tend to regard these deposits as less permanent
and more volatile than those of surplus-oil-exporting
countries and therefore tend to manage these funds more
cautiously.

As a result of these factors, it is estimated that
net bank lending, which had increased from US$26 billion
in 1978 to more than US$50 billion in 1981, was cut back
to some US$25 billion in 1982, and a further drop has
been registered in 1983. According to the BIS, new
credit to Latin American countries fell from US$11.7
billion in the first semester of 1982 to only US$300
million in the second. Statistics show an increase in
new credit to Latin America of US$3.7 billion in the first
semester of 1983; however, such loans were mostly supplied
in association with financial programs supported by the
IMF.

After a long period of rapid growth, the abrupt
slowing of credit commitments by the private banking
system generated the concern that the inability of a few
major borrowers to refinance maturing loans could give
rise to a liquidity crisis in these countries. Given the
high exposure of the private banking in these nations,
serious fears arose with respect to a possible collapse
of the international financial system.

Table 7.1 External Debt of Nonoil Developing Countries

	1978	1979	1980	1981	1982	1983[a]
Total outstanding debt (billions of U.S. dollars)						
All nonoil developing countries	336.3	391.1	467.6	550.8	614.2	659.1
Major borrowers[b]	233.4	276.0	330.5	400.0	445.3	474.6
Latin American countries[c]	119.1	143.5	176.6	218.0	231.1	254.5
Ratio of external debt to exports of goods and services						
All nonoil developing countries	130.2	117.2	111.0	123.8	143.6	145.1
Major borrowers[b]	175.5	162.8	156.1	172.9	199.4	200.5
Latin American countries[c]	186.7	168.6	164.9	190.7	224.4	230.0
Ratio of external debt to GDP						
All nonoil developing countries	27.9	26.8	26.9	30.4	35.8	37.8
Major borrowers[b]	30.7	29.0	29.5	34.3	41.1	43.8
Latin American countries[c]	28.6	27.8	27.9	32.1	38.6	40.0
Debt service ratio						
All nonoil developing countries	19.0	19.0	17.6	20.1	23.4	19.3
Major borrowers[b]	28.9	30.6	28.0	32.7	38.4	30.1
Latin American countries[c]	38.3	37.2	32.9	38.4	48.8	42.0

[a] Estimated

[b] The twenty major borrowers among the nonoil developing countries are Brazil, Mexico, Argentina, Korea, Chile, Yugoslavia, Philippines, Greece, Portugal, Malaysia, Israel, Thailand, Hungary, Peru, Turkey, Egypt, Romania, Colombia, Ecuador, and Morocco.

[c] Includes the Caribbean countries; external public debt.

Source: International Monetary Fund (IMF), World Economic Outlook; IMF, International Financial Statistics; IMF, Recent Economic Developments; Merrill Lynch Economics Inc., Latin American Quarterly.

Table 7.2 Multilateral Debt Renegotiations, 1974-1983

	1974	1975	1976	1977	1978	1979	1980	1981	1982	1983
Argentina			C							C
Bolivia									C	C
Brazil										C
Central African Republic							P			
Chile	P	P								C
Costa Rica										P,C
Cuba										C
Ecuador										C
Gabon					P					
Ghana	P									
Guyana						C			C	
India	A	A	A	A		C				
Jamaica						C				
Liberia							P	C	C	C
Madagascar								P	P	
Malawi									P,C	C
Mexico							C	C	C	
Nicaragua							C	A		
Pakistan	A									
Peru			C		P,C		C	A	C	
Poland									P,C	P
Romania								P	P,C	C
Senegal										
Sierra Leone				P			P	C	P	P
Sudan						P	C	P		P,C
Togo						P	A	P		
Turkey					A	A,C	A	P	C	
Uganda								P	P	
Yugoslavia							C			C
Zaire	P		P	P		P	C	P		P
Zambia										
Total number of renegotiations	4	2	4	3	4	7	8	13	14	17

(continued)

176

Table 7.2 (cont.)

Note: This table does not include some cases for which sufficient information was not available.

A: Aid consortia renegotiations
C: Commercial bank agreements
P: Paris Club agreements

Source: World Bank Debtor Reporting System.

The responsibility for the current difficulties is widespread. Part of the current debt problems can be traced to bank lending practices. Underpinned by the confidence that a country could not go bankrupt or disappear, bank analyses of countries' debt-servicing capacity and prospects were often perfunctory and the traditional yardsticks of credit appraisal were not applied.[2] Nevertheless, credit expansion was stimulated by the higher average profitability of international lending operations, the good record of foreign borrowers, and the fierce competition among banks.

It is equally clear that a number of important country borrowers did not undertake sufficiently large and timely adjustment efforts, believing that the recession would be short-lived and that demand for their exports would soon recover. Moreover, they did not expect real interest rates to remain at very high levels for such a lengthy period. In fact, they would not have, had major industrial countries adopted a more balanced fiscal and monetary policy stance.

The current liquidity problems in the developing countries may be attributed more to the sharp rise in interest payments than to the increase in external debt outstanding. While interest payments on the external debt of nonoil LDCs increased almost ninefold between 1973 and 1982, amortization payments only increased approximately fourfold. Indeed, at more normal levels of interest rates of, say, around 3 percent in real terms, and with annual rates of economic growth of 4 percent, those nations maintaining a constant external debt-to-GDP ratio would be able to finance significant current account deficits and to cover their interest payments without difficulty.

Corrective policy measures are already under way in many countries, and the external current account deficit of the nonoil LDCs appears to be moving into a more viable range. However, the scale of the dependence on external financing for many nations is such that the situation cannot be turned around overnight without the risk of severe internal disruption for the countries concerned, as well as worrisome implications for the world economy. There is a danger that the cutback in capital flows to developing countries may be so sharp that it may not only prevent orderly positive adjustment, but may prove destabilizing, initially to the countries but soon after to the banks, who would suffer losses that would impair their capital base.

The strains that have recently become apparent in the financial system--namely the high exposure of the private banking system to the largest LDCs, the difficult current situation and prospects faced by most developing countries, the increased nervousness of the market, and the recent shift in banker's attention toward a greater political analysis of potential borrowers--suggest that

in the future commercial banks will not continue per-
forming the role of major financial intermediaries in
the recycling of funds from surplus to deficit nations
that they have played in the recent past. At the same
time, the elements of instability that such a pattern of
recycling has introduced to the international monetary
system have generated doubts about the desirability of
its continuation.

Consequently, a need arises for designing new
financial mechanisms for recycling. The issue is twofold: (1) in the short run, to ensure that financial
flows to countries with serious debt or liquidity problems
continue at an appropriate rate, so as to avoid a world
liquidity crisis; and (2) given that present problems
arise to a considerable extent from an absence of adequate
sources of development finance that has forced LDCs to
resort to short- and medium-term financing, a second
issue still remains for the medium and long terms, that
of appropriate development financing.

THE PROVISION OF ADEQUATE SHORT-RUN
FINANCIAL ASSISTANCE

Notwithstanding all the difficulties and uncertainties still inherent in the current situation, the threat
of a liquidity crisis in the world economy appears to
have been considerably diminished in recent months. The
fears of an interruption or even reversal of private
capital flows to LDCs seem to have been averted by
collective lending agreements, involving the authorities
of the affected countries, the private banks, and international institutions--mainly the IMF and the BIS.[3]
Nevertheless, a strengthening of the international
financial system's ability to cope with such a potential
liquidity crisis would be the best way to avoid its
occurrence, since it would increase substantially the
confidence in the system.

Indeed, the International Monetary Fund has an
important role to play in this overall process. However,
Fund resources--presently around 2-3 percent of the value
of international trade--are clearly insufficient to allow
it to play this role to the extent required. The need to
increase the size of the Fund has been widely recognized.
In practice, however, this process has been considerably
hindered by a lack of cooperation on the part of the
industrial nations. The decisions taken regarding the
Eighth General Review of Quotas, which will serve the
international community through much of the present
decade, are a clear example of such situation.

Notwithstanding the technical studies supporting
the need for an increase in quotas of 100 to 125 percent
and the demands of the developing nations, agreement
could not be reached for an increase of more than 48

percent. It is evident that such an increase will be insufficient to allow the IMF to meet the financial requirements of member countries during the coming years. As a result, the Fund has been forced to supplement its resources by borrowing from member countries.

It is important to note that the Group of 10 decided in early 1983 to increase their aggregate commitments under the General Agreement to Borrow (GAB) from SDR6.4 billion to SDR17 billion. They also agreed that, in the future, GAB's resources would be available for purchases by those members--including non-GAB participants--whose payments difficulties might endanger the international monetary system. Obviously, this may be considered as a mechanism that alleviates the possibility of payments difficulties by one or two major debtor countries giving rise to a world banking crisis. However, the enlargement of the GAB does not benefit all LDCs, since only the largest among them may endanger the international monetary system. It is also important to note that the widening of GAB raises some questions regarding the decision-making process of the Fund, since the Group of Ten has a veto on the approval of loans under such agreements. Thus, it is obvious that the increase of resources under the GAB can under no circumstances be considered as a substitute for an increase in quotas.

The recent experience of countries that have faced a liquidity crisis and resorted to the BIS shows that when rapid financial support is needed the Fund cannot provide it under existing policies. However, since BIS support is often conditional on a Fund-supported adjustment program, the question comes to mind whether the Fund should not itself provide such support. There is no certainty that the BIS will in the future assist non-BIS countries; thus, an increased capacity of the Fund to deal with emergency situations at short notice would appear necessary.

In addition to increasing its resources, therefore, the Fund would have to modify its policies to make drawings available in a matter of days rather than months. The need to establish a new facility, which had been informally considered in the past in connection with problems caused by capital fight, should be recognized in the light of current problems. Access to this facility would be limited to those countries facing a liquidity crisis as a result of capital outflows or of a very sharp decline in access to external credit. In such cases, if the Fund were not satisfied that the stance of the country's current economic policies was in broad terms appropriate, it would require a policy statement by the authorities similar to that required at present for upper credit tranche drawings.

Obviously, the commercial banks must continue to play an important role. The resources of multilateral institutions should be seen as complementary and supportive of financial flows on commercial terms rather than competitive with them. Equally important is the adoption of cooperative and responsible attitudes on the part of the private banking community and the authorities of creditor countries leading to rescheduling of debt-service payments and to refinancing important amounts of short-term debt at longer maturities. This would contribute importantly to avoiding a potential liquidity crisis.

MEDIUM- AND LONG-TERM FINANCIAL NEEDS OF LDCs

The present debt crisis has resulted to a considerable extent from an excessive dependence of LDCs on short- and medium-term external financing, a situation that has been determined by the absence of adequate sources of development finance. It is apparent that the continued usage of medium- and short-term financing is bound to give rise to liquidity problems in the medium term for countries that rely heavily upon it, even if the financing is all destined to sound investment projects.
The situation is even more serious presently, since the structural nature of the economic adjustment requirements faced by LDCs calls for larger amounts of longer-term financing. Furthermore, payments on a large proportion of the external debt of LDCs will be falling due in the medium term; therefore, if no additional measures are taken, recent debt-rescheduling agreements could, through the bunching of maturities, compound the external debt problems in the coming years.

The Current Economic Adjustment Problems

Profound economic adjustments have become necessary in developing countries in recent years, partly as a result of the important changes in technology and in the structure of markets, but mainly because of the changes that have taken place in relative prices--in the fields of energy, raw materials, and manufactures--and the unprecedented levels reached by interest rates. It is evident that adjustments are much more difficult to achieve in a world suffering from stagnation than in an expanding economy.
This is the problem that must be addressed by adjustment programs today. To do so, it is not sufficient to restore or maintain a certain balance between aggregate supply and aggregate demand. It is also necessary to restructure the economy in such a manner that it will permit an increased production in certain strategic sectors and the diversification of exports, so as to restore economic growth.[4] This process must be accompanied by an increase in the rates of savings and investment.

External debt service requires the generation of substantial trade surpluses in the debtor countries. However, it is essential to distinguish between: (1) the strengthening of the balance of payments that results from a reduction in growth and economic activity (i.e., from a deflationary policy), and (2) attaining a solution to balance-of-payments problems compatible with acceptable rates of growth and viable over the medium term.

That is to say, it is necessary to distinguish between a temporary improvement in the balance of payments that results from a depressed cyclical position and a more lasting structural adjustment compatible with higher levels of activity and employment. This distinction suggests that adjustment programs require, besides a prudent management of demand, an increase of investment and production in certain key sectors of the economy that play a strategic role in its restructuring. Evidently, this type of adjustment needs substantial financial resources.

There exists a number of LDCs where economic disequilibria have been generated predominantly by growing public-sector deficits. In fact, a great deal of the foreign borrowing by such countries resulted from pronounced increases of their fiscal deficits, creating a strong link between debt service and fiscal policy. If the governments of these nations are to pay the service on their external public debt, they must either extract an excessive share of resources from the private sector or reduce expenditures. Thus, the service of the external debt in these cases requires a sharp reduction of fiscal deficits. Nevertheless, substantial amounts of longer-term external financing must be directed to these countries if their growth prospects are not be seriously impaired. These financing flows will also help to reduce the risk of a possible default on external payments.

Furthermore, the recovery of world trade may be hindered if the adoption of excessively deflationary adjustment programs in LDCs generates a substantial decrease in these countries' imports. It is essential, therefore, that the developing countries implement policies leading to the required structural adjustment of their economies, consistent with the maintenance of international trade flows. Consequently, the financial requirements of the group must be placed within the framework of the international adjustment process and recognized as a problem of the international community.

The Role of External Debt Rescheduling

In general, external debt rescheduling may provide benefits of two kinds. In the first place, as has already been described, it may contribute substantially

to the solution of short-run liquidity problems. Second,
by spreading external payments over longer periods, it
may alleviate the pressures on the external sector of
LDCs and faciliate the adoption of an orderly program of
economic adjustment; indeed, the final purpose of rescheduling should be the restoration of the debtor
country's creditworthiness. The benefits of the first
kind have already been evident in the present crisis.
However, it seems less certain that the reschedulings
recently agreed will allow a substantial improvement in
the capacity of LDCs to service the external debt.

So far, a substantial amount of the external payments
falling due in the short term has been renegotiated by
the major borrowers. The terms in which the operations
have been settled comprise, in general, an interest rate
of LIBOR plus two points or more and amortization periods
of around six to eight years, with grace periods between
two and four years. This suggests that many LDCs will
face a very heavy concentration of amortization payments
in the near future. In order for these countries to be
able to cover the repayments falling due, their balance
of payments and economic conditions would have to
experience major improvements over a relatively short
period of time.

However, in a number of cases external as well as
internal factors may prevent those countries from reaching such an improvement within the time span allowed by
current rescheduling agreements. On the one hand, the
moderate economic recovery of the developed countries
and the persistence of protectionism are likely to undermine the developing countries' ability to sustain a
large export expansion. On the other hand, the structural
nature of the economic imbalances faced by most developing countries requires, besides large amounts of development finance, periods of adjustment longer than those
involved in many of the rescheduling agreements that
have been agreed.

Obviously, if the length of the adjustment period is
not enough to permit the structural changes required,
the creditworthiness of these countries will not be fully
restored, and therefore the main condition of a successful rescheduling will not be reached. In such an event,
the rescheduling operation would merely represent a postponement of the problem for the near future.

Although commercial banks seem to earn record
profits out of the debt-rescheduling exercise, for the
debtor countries successive debt-restructuring exercises
imply a high cost. They are often seen as a new failure
to meet international obligations and create an atmosphere
of uncertainty, if not of recurring crisis, that hinders
the recovery of confidence, gives rise to capital flight,
discourages investment, and disrupts economic life.

Moreover, unless debtor countries can greatly expand
their exports, the fulfillment of debt payment obligations

may turn them into substantial capital exporters.
Interest payments at prevailing rates of interest alone
on a total external debt of the order of US$300 million
would require Latin America to generate a trade surplus
of some US$35 billion a year. In that event, and after
several years of costly economic adjustment, it is
possible that LDCs governments would face growing
political pressures to direct export surpluses to offset
some of the negative social effects of the adjustment
programs instead of using them to pay their international
creditors; that is, the willingness to pay of some LDCs
might decrease.

Assets that are within a debtor's jurisdiction are
not liable to claim by the banks. Thus, debtor's willingness to pay is the factor that ultimately determines
the reimbursement of credit sources. Willingness to pay
has not been a major issue in the process of international
lending, because the net transfer of resources--which has
a negative relation with interest rates--was positive
until 1982. Since then, it has been negative; nevertheless, the rescue packages have kept net exports of
capital from LDCs at low levels. It would appear that
the reduction in net flows resulting from the elimination of these packages together with the high spreads
charged by commercial banks on the restructuring of debt
and the new money lent and the persistance of adverse
external developments--related essentially with the
evolution of world economic recovery, interest rates, and
protectionism in the industrial countries--could bring
the willingness-to-pay issue to the forefront of the
lending process.

POSSIBLE OPTIONS FOR THE FUTURE

Although the financial difficulties of LDCs generally
reflect a liquidity rather than a solvency crisis, it is
evident that the avoidance of recurrent liquidity problems in this group of nations requires the adoption of
measures oriented toward a structural adjustment of their
economies and an improved functioning of the international
monetary system. The debt problem, therefore, cannot be
separated from the issue of development finance. Indeed,
the solution of these problems seems to be one of the
major challenges facing the world economy in the 1980s.

Obviously, the best long-run solution to the debt
crisis would be for the countries concerned to "grow out
of debt." This would require, besides the continuation
of the serious adjustment efforts already under way in
many LDCs, a sustained recovery in the world economy,
a decrease in international interest rates, and the
reversal of the protectionist tendencies in the industrial
countries. A continued expansion of LDCs' exports would
make the external debt situation of these nations much

more manageable and, at the same time, would provide them
with the foreign exchange they require for their development.

Nevertheless, whether the LDCs will face such a
favorable external environment in the next years is still
uncertain. As a result of a combination of factors, the
pace of expansion in the world economy over the medium
term is likely to remain slower than during earlier
periods. Likewise, the prospects of large fiscal deficits
in certain industrial nations generate serious concerns
regarding the future evolution of interest rates. Such a
scenario does not suggest the rapid elimination of
protectionist barriers in the developed world.

It would appear, therefore, that the solution to
present debt difficulties requires securing sufficient
financial flows to LDCs on longer maturities. As has
been stated, at present it seems unlikely that the
capital markets will satisfy such needs spontaneously.
Furthermore, the possibility that collective lending
agreements--involving the commercial banks, international
institutions, and the authorities of the affected coun-
tries--would become a permanent arrangement is almost
nil, since this would imply long periods of outside
supervision of the debtor country's economic policies,
and because it is doubtful that it will be possible to
secure the continued participation of hundreds of small
banks in such an exercise over a number of years. The
political strains that such a situation could create
are enormous.

In this context, the need to design alternative
mechanisms for providing LDCs with adequate flows of
financing seems evident. The increase of foreign direct
investment has been frequently mentioned as one possible
option.[5] In fact, risk capital provided a large share
of the finance required for the development of LDCs
during the nineteenth and early twentieth centuries.
The commercial banking system has assumed this role in
recent years. Given the current problems, it would seem
desirable, from a financial point of view, for equity to
play a much larger part in development finance today.
The potential threats to the stability of the world's
financial system would decrease if risks were shared by
thousands of investors, whose capital or equity could
become nonperforming without the risk of spreading to
others.

However, the balance-of-payments and financial
problems that developing countries face have substantially
decreased their attraction to foreign investors in view
of their reduced capacity to transfer profits and other
payments on foreign direct investment. This, coupled
with the fact that the developed countries account for a
growing share of total direct investment--LDCs' share in
foreign investment fell from 31 percent in 1970 to 27
percent in 1980--makes it very unlikely that the rates of

growth reached by such investment during the 1970s may be sustained in the coming years. Therefore, it would seem necessary to develop policies that encourage a greater inflow of external direct investment, including the development of regulatory frameworks satisfactory to the foreign investor and the host country.

It seems clear that meeting LDCs' financial needs in the medium and long run requires a substantial increase in credit flows to these nations on much longer maturities and at lower spreads.[6] The difficulties seem to be particularly serious for the Latin American countries, given the larger magnitude of their external debt.

Covering the public sector's financial needs could be achieved by greatly enlarging the resources of instituions such as the World Bank and the regional development banks to permit them to recover the relative position they held in the 1960s. Evidently, this solution calls for the cooperation of industrial countries in the form of higher contributions to the capital base of these institutions and of strong leadership to overcome the political difficulties it faces in major countries.

Another approach that has been suggested is the creation of a multilateral government-guaranteed fund that would operate on commercial lines, obtaining long-term credits in domestic and international markets. The fund would grant, say, fifteen-year financing for public investment projects and for the purchase of capital goods, permitting the achievement of higher levels of investment and growth in developing countries, as well as improving their profile and therefore their ability to pay and their creditworthiness. For industrial countries faced with a recession, this could mean higher levels of exports and economic activity, making it easier to overcome political resistance to increased development assistance as well as the protectionist trends apparent in the world today. Such a scheme would also contribute to the growth and stability of international capital markets.

Other schemes, some of which have been in existence on a small scale, might be used as supporting mechanisms to deal with the external financing needs of the public sectors of LDCs over the medium and long terms. It has been suggested that the role of export credit guarantee agencies may be extended, so as to ensure against risk not only the trade flows to the developing world but also the lending required to cover its resulting current account deficits.[7] With this purpose, individual agencies in the creditor nations would insure bank lending for balance-of-payments financing, relying both on their own analysis and on the advice of the IMF. With insured credit available, each debtor country would be in a better position to meet both the trading deficit and the interest payments on existing debt.[8]

It has been suggested that such a mechanism might be further reinforced by public or private companies offering political risk insurance on loans to developing countries. This suggestion may be applicable to some regions. Nevertheless, it does not seem to appeal to the Latin American countries since such guarantees have never been provided, not even by the largest borrowers in the area. Political guarantees could give rise to both political and legal problems in these nations since they are contrary to the Calvo doctrine incorporated in the constitutions of several countries.

The recycling of adequate financial flows to the private sector of LDCs could be considerably eased through the creation of official guarantee programs. Evidently, the authorities of debtor countries should stand ready to assume the risks related with currency convertibility and transferability of external payments, but not those linked to purely commercial risks that by their very nature must be assumed by the private entities involved. This distinction must be clearly made if the private sector is to continue to develop as such.

Likewise, private credit to LDCs' private sectors could be directed toward the financing of specific projects. This would have the advantage of ensuring the productive usage of credits and might allow, by diminishing the risks involved in such operations, a decrease in spreads. At the same time, to the extent that insurance mechanisms in lending to LDCs--such as those already suggested--are established, private banks might be able to keep their asset levels below the limits set by regulatory authorities, while increasing the amount of credit potentially available to LDCs by selling off part of their loans. For instance, a combination of transfer guarantees and private risk insurance could convert a syndicated loan into a marketable security that could be sold to pension funds, regional banks, and so on.

Cofinancing with multilateral development institutions could, if procedures were made more agile, contribute substantially to the expansion of capital flows to the developing countries. Similarly, a new form of cofinancing between governments and commercial banks could be considered as a means of stretching maturities and reducing costs to borrowers while preserving an important role for the financial markets.

The magnitude of the problems related to the provision of adequate financial flows to the developing countries in the medium and long run may be roughly quantified. Let us consider first the demand side. During the last few years, imports of capital by LDCs rose to levels between 4.5 percent and 6 percent of GDP. Although these nations must be considered structural capital importers, such figures seem to be high by historical standards. Assuming that the current account deficit as a percentage of GDP falls to more normal levels--of, say, 3 percent of GDP--and using the basis of World Bank projections for the future evolution of economic growth in the developing world and world inflation--around 5.5 percent in real terms and 5 percent respectively--one could reasonably expect the current account deficit of the nonoil LDCs to be of about US$125 billion by 1990. To this, one should add a moderate increase in international reserves to reach an equivalent of three months' imports. This would mean an additional reserve accumulation of some US$40 billion in 1990. Thus, total financing requirements of the nonoil developing countries would be of the order of US$165 billion in 1990.

Let us now consider the supply of financial resources. Assume that commercial banks are willing to expand significantly their loans, so that net bank lending to LDCs increases at 3.5 percent per year in real terms between 1982 and 1990. On the basis of the above assumption for inflation, such net flows would amount to about US$40 billion in 1990. This is in fact a very optimistic assumption. It must be recalled that as a result of the debt-restructuring agreements, maturities of about US$80 to US$100 billion have been shifted to the second half of the 1980s in Latin America alone. Therefore, the exercise assumes that a large part of these maturities plus those originally falling due in the second half of the 1980s will be refinanced.

This would imply such very high levels of gross bank lending to the developing countries, particularly those in Latin America, that it is doubtful that they may be attained without the active support or participation of the authorities of industrial countries through some type of official cofinancing arrangements. However, at present there does not appear to be a sufficient awareness of this problem. In fact, some of the bank regulatory agencies of financial centers are moving in the opposite direction, that of tightening supervision and limiting bank exposure to developing countries.

If the rates of growth of private direct investment and official transfers maintain the trend registered during the last ten years, these annual flows to nonoil LDCs would amount to some US$40 billion by the end of this decade. Credit from official sources--namely the World Bank and the regional development banks--may contribute importantly to meet the financial requirements of these countries; nevertheless, the reluctance of the industrial countries to increase substantially the capital base of these institutions might limit--by simply maintaining its trend rate of growth--net new flows of credit to LDCs from these sources to some US$35 billion in 1990.

Therefore, under such optimistic assumptions, there would still remain an external gap of approximately US$50 billion by the end of the 1980s even without taking into account the possibility of capital outflows. More

realistically, on current trends, the gap is likely to be
several times larger. If there is a failure of leadership in the major industrial countries and the mechanisms
necessary to finance such a gap are not created, the
developing countries will be forced to reduce even
further their current account deficits and to limit
significantly their rates of economic growth.

An alternative method, and perhaps a simpler one,
for securing the necessary net flows would involve a
major restructuring of amortization payments on external
debt owed to commercial banks so as to produce a positive balance on capital account that would supplement
domestic savings and permit these economies to attain
acceptable rates of growth and effect a positive adjustment. For instance, assume a country faces over the
second part of the decade debt-service payments, including amortization, equivalent to 60-70 percent of export
revenues, a result of adding the amortization of the
recently restructured debt to the existing amortization
schedule. Such a situation would be difficult to sustain
since it would seriously limit the country's growth
possibilities. Suppose on the other hand, that after an
initial period of adjustment, a new debt restructuring
takes place that extends the grace period through the
rest of the decade and distributes amortization payments
over ten to fifteen years starting in 1990. Debt-service
payment for the rest of the 1980s would be reduced to
interest payments alone, the equivalent of, say, 25 to
30 percent of export earnings.

This is clearly a much more manageable prospect,
since it will contribute to the restoration of confidence
both external and internal and will permit the attainment of satisfactory rates of growth, placing the economy
in a better position to face the 1990s. Over the next
ten to fifteen years the restructured maturities of the
1980s would represent a signficantly smaller proportion
of export revenues, both because of their distribution
over a longer period and because the debtor would have
a larger export base. Thus, the restructured maturities
should prove much easier to refinance through the market.

In a sense, a new and longer-term restructuring
could be seen as complementing short-term measures
adopted in 1982 and 1983 under the pressure of events,
completing the required process for putting major Latin
American debtors back on a sustainable growth plan.
At the same time and by so doing it would dispel uncertainties and risks that still hang over the international financial system.

CONCLUSIONS

The strains that have recently arisen in the international monetary system, and the prospects for the

coming years, suggest that most of the debtor countries
will not receive adequate financial flows unless a new
pattern of financing is developed. In the short run,
the main objective is to ensure adequate financial flows
to the more indebted countries, so as to avoid repeated
financial crisis. Although this possibility has been
considerably alleviated so far by collective lending
agreements, it is still necessary to strengthen the
system's ability to cope with the likely recurrence of
such crisis. This requires, among other measures, a
substantial increase in IMF resources, a modification of
its policies on drawings to allow a rapid financial
support to those countries in serious liquidity problems,
and the cooperation of the private banking community to
reschedule important amounts of external debt at longer
maturities.

However, even if the short-run problems related
with potential liquidity crisis are appropriately dealt
with, there still remains the issue of securing sufficient
financial flows for development financing purposes. In
fact, it may be stated that present problems have resulted
to a great extent from the lack of adequate sources of
development finance. The difficulties are more serious
presently, given the structural nature of the economic
problems faced by most LDCs and the possibility that
recent debt-rescheduling agreements give rise to new
liquidity crisis when the grace periods come to an end.
The external indebtedness problem thus is closely linked
to the issue of development finance.

The best possible solution to these problems would
be one of "growing out of debt." In addition to the
adoption of serious adjustment efforts in the developing
countries, "growing out of debt" would require a strong
and sustained recovery in the world economy, a significant
decline in interest rates, and at least the attenuation
of protectionist trends in the industrial world. In
this context, it is evident that developments outside
the control of LDCs are playing and will play a decisive
role in the success of the adjustment efforts of debtor
countries.

Today, most developing nations are fully aware of
the need to adjust their economies in order to find a
solution to their current problems. Taking into account
the common interest in overcoming the debt crisis and in
restoring the growth of the world economy, it seems
reasonable to demand that industrial nations support
these efforts by adopting measures that contribute to
these ends.

Nevertheless, since it is doubtful that the external
environment will take a very favorable turn in the near
future, adequate financial flows to LDCs must be secured
with longer-term maturities, if a solution to the debt
difficulties is to be found. These flows would contribute
importantly to the expansion of international trade and

190

the growth of the world economy.
At a time when capital markets will not be able to
play the leading role of the past decade, multilateral
financial institutions--such as the World Bank and the
regional development banks--and government agencies should
play a much larger role in the recycling process. These
mechanisms could be reinforced by schemes to ensure
balance-of-payments lending to LDCs and by stimulating
the increase of foreign direct investment. These
measures, as well as sustained efforts of adjustment and
cooperation, can allow us to find a way out of the present
problems.
Alternatively, and perhaps more simply, the required
improvement in the capital account could be secured by a
major restructuring exercise that would significantly
reduce or eliminate amortization payments to the banks
over the rest of the decade, distributing them over a
period of ten to fifteen years starting in 1990. This
would allow Latin American economies to effect a positive
adjustment, diversify their exports, and recover reasonable rates of growth, thus placing them in a better
position to face the future.
Although the external debt problem will be with us
at least for the rest of the decade, it is in the interest
of debtor and creditor countries that it not be allowed
to sharply reduce the development prospects of LDCs.
The social and political consequences of failing to
secure acceptable rates of growth in the developing
world during a protracted period would be very grave
indeed.

NOTES

The ideas expressed in this paper are strictly
personal. The author wishes to acknowledge the invaluable
assistance of Javier Guzmán C. in the preparation of
this paper.
1. According to estimates of the IMF, of the
US$67 billion increase in the aggregate current account
deficit of the nonoil LDCs from 1978 to 1981, more than
90 percent may be explained by the combined effect of
the rise in net interest payments, the deterioration of
the group's nonoil terms of trade, and the adverse
change in the group's oil trade balance.
2. For instance, the 20 percent debt-service ratio
suggested as external indebtedness limit by the World
Bank was exceeded by many countries.
3. The rescue packages that have emerged from such
agreements have generally included the rescheduling of
debt-service payments, the provision of financial
assistance both by banks and by official institutions,
and the adoption of stabilization programs by the
debtor countries.

4. The case of energy is a good instance of a
structural adjustment. Adjustment to the higher cost of
imported energy will certainly require increasing the
price to consumers and reducing somewhat the rate of
growth of GDP. However, any attempt of the country to
achieve higher rates of growth would result in unsustainable balance-of-payments deficits, unless the
structure of the economy is adapted to the new prices
through the development of domestic energy sources and a
more efficient use of energy.

5. According to some estimates, although the flows
of direct investment to LDCs increased from US$2 billion
in 1970 to about US$15 billion in 1982, they remained
small compared to the volume of borrowing in the international financial markets.

6. Obviously, in the case of many low-income
countries, substantial amounts of financial resources on
concessional terms are required.

7. This is, with minor modifications, the Lever
plan. Lord Lever suggests the creation of a central
agency that would advise each agency on the provision of
financing to LDCs, relying largely on the recommendations of the IMF.

8. In fact, most of the main countries have set up
export credit agencies. Each agency, acting independently,
has supported its exporters' trade with insurance
facilities, placing limits on the amounts of credit
insured.

BIBLIOGRAPHY

Azar, S. A. The Involvement of the Oil Surplus Countries
   in the International Financial and Trading System.
   Study on the International Financial and Trading
   System, Commonwealth Secretariat. London, March
   1983.
Buira, Ariel. The Role of the IMF in the 1980's:
   Report to the Group of Twenty-Four. UNDP/UNCTAD-
   Project INT/81/046. January 1983.
____. "Prospects for Private International Financing to
   Developing Countries." Address delivered to the
   Institute on International Finance at the Southern
   Methodist University, Dallas, Tex., November 1982.
Cline, W. R. International Debt and the Stability of
   the World Economy. Washington, D.C., 1983.
Frank, C. R. Future Financing of the Capital Needs of
   Developing Countries. Study on the International
   Financial and Trading System, Commonwealth
   Secretariat. London, March 1983.
International Monetary Fund. World Economic Outlook:
   A Survey by the Staff of the International Monetary
   Fund. Washington, D.C., 1983.

192

Krul, Nicolas. The Debt Problem: A Search for a New
    Financial Balance. Geneva, April 1983.
Morgan Guaranty Trust Company of New York. "Global Debt:
    Assessment and Long-Term Strategy." World
    Financial Market, June 1983.
O'Brien, Richard. The Role of Commercial Banks in the
    International Financial System: A Summary Report.
    Study on the International Financial and Trading
    System, Commonwealth Secretariat. London, April
    1983.
Organization for Economic Cooperation and Development.
    World Economic Outlook, July 1983.
Pealtry, Michael G. The Policies of International
    Monetary Authorities with Respect to the Inter-
    national Debt Credit. Geneva, April 1983.
Segré, Claudio. The External Causes of the Crisis.
    Geneva, April 1983.
Sjaastad, Larry A. "The International Debt Quagmire:
    To Whom Do We Owe It?" Prepared for the Leeds
    Castle Meeting, July 14-16, 1983.
Soros, George. The International Debt Problem:
    Diagnosis and Prognosis. New York, July 1983.
Streeten, Paul. Direct Private Foreign Investment,
    Transnational Corporations and Development. Study
    on the International Financial and Trading System,
    Commonwealth Secretariat. London, March 1983.
Suratgar, David. Oil Exporters and World Financial
    Markets. Study on the International Financial and
    Trading System, Commonwealth Secretariat. London,
    April 1983.
World Bank. World Development Report 1983. Washington,
    D.C., 1984.

8

The World Monetary System, the International Business Cycle, and the External Debt Crisis

José Luis Feito

The international financial system can be seen as a set of devices for correcting any eventual malfunctions of the world economy, particularly those rooted in the monetary side. The rationale for international monetary agencies is to ensure that automatic and other built-in mechanisms operating within the financial system will respond adequately to phases of strain. In the presence of pressures and difficulties that threaten the system, international agencies and arrangements are supposed to generate appropriate signals and carry out actions in order to make the system react along desired lines. Over the recent past the international financial system has been put to the test. The aim of this chapter is to analyze the stimulus-response pattern of the international financial system over the recent years in order to shed light on the adequacy of present international monetary arrangements to cope with widespread economic disturbances like the external debt crisis and recession currently plaguing the world economy.

The overwhelming presence of overindebtedness and depression should be seen as a manifestation of business cycle phenomena. The main thesis of this chapter is that the external debt crisis is a result of fundamental changes in the nature of the international monetary mechanism, mainly brought about by the emergence of world financial intermediation and rapid integration of major capital markets in the late 1960s and early 1970s. These changes, together with the cyclic instability of the U.S. economy, expose the world economy to the sort of credit-induced business cycle some national economies experienced during the nineteenth century and the inter-war period. These ideas are developed in the first section, in which the relationships between the international business cycle and the external debt crisis are analyzed and some inferences to be drawn from this analysis are put forward.

One of the conclusions of that section is that international monetary policy should aim not only at

facilitating the smooth transition of the world economy
to an equilibrium position but also at ensuring the
stability of the world financial system so that the
probabilities of another occurrence of worldwide economic
depression and overindebtedness are minimized. The
armory of international monetary policy is not well
equipped to achieve these ends. Ideally, actions should
be taken simultaneously in those two fronts. Reforms of
the international financial system should be initiated by
allowing international financial institutions to play a
more active role in the conduct of international monetary
policy in current circumstances.

By now it is clear, however, that discussion on
reform of the international monetary system is a very
slow process going through a kind of stop-and-go cycle.
Therefore, it may be convenient to separate the analysis
of the scope for short-run actions within the boundary
of current international arrangements (covered in the
second section), the shortcomings and limitations of
present international monetary institutions to cope with
the current crisis (the third section), and the needed
reforms of the world monetary mechanism from a longer
perspective (the fourth section). Finally, the last
section provides a summary of the arguments and views
expressed in the chapter.

THE INTERNATIONAL BUSINESS CYCLE
AND THE EXTERNAL DEBT CRISIS: AN INTERPRETATION

Should there be any doubt, the current world
economic recession has officially been certified by the
National Bureau of Economic Research as the eighth of
the postwar period, more serious than the 1973-1975
recession, second in severity only to the slump of the
1930s. All these postwar worldwide economic depressions
have had in common that they have originated in the
United States because of the heavy weight this economy
has on world trade and, more importantly, on world
financial conditions. In some instances, as in 1973-
1975, these depressions may have been induced by disturbances outside the United States, but they have been
reinforced and made worldwide by the response of the
United States and other large industrial countries to
these disturbances. By the same token, it is obvious
that phases of worldwide growth have been set in motion
by the functioning at near full capacity of the U.S.
economic machine.

The intensity and pervasiveness of the current world
depression are frequently seen as the result of the mix
of economic policies implemented in the United States to
check the drift toward greater inflation and lower growth
that has characterized the performance of this economy
over the last decade.   Table 8.1 provides some

Table 8.1 The International Business Cycle and Nonoil Developing Countries

	1976	1977	1978	1979	1980	1981	1982
Sources of cyclical disturbances							
Percentage changes in U.S. nominal stock of money (M_1)	6.2	8.2	8.3	7.4	7.3	5.0	8.5
Percentage changes in U.S. real stock of money (M_1)[a]	1.5	2.0	-0.2	-0.7	-2.6	-3.5	3.9
Channels of transmission							
U.S. nominal short-term interest rates	5.0	5.3	7.2	10.1	11.4	14.0	10.6
U.S. real short-term interest rates[a]	-0.2	-0.5	-0.2	1.3	1.9	4.2	4.4
U.S. real GNP rate of growth	5.4	5.5	5.0	2.8	-0.4	1.9	-1.7
Percentage changes in U.S. volume of imports	22.8	13.3	6.6	2.7	-7.5	0.5	-4.4
Impact on nonoil LDCs							
Total flows of external lending in the BIS reporting area (in billions of U.S. dollars)	70	68	90	125	160	165	95
Of which: external lending to nonoil LDSs	21	15	25	40	49	51	25
Debt-service ratio[b]	15.3	15.4	19.0	19.0	17.6	20.4	23.9
Percentage changes in export volumes	11.3	4.9	8.7	9.6	9.0	6.3	0.8
Percentage changes in prices of nonoil primary commodities	13.3	20.7	-4.7	16.5	9.0	-14.8	-12.1
Terms-of-trade changes from preceding year	5.9	5.9	-3.7	-0.3	-6.2	-3.9	-2.7
Real GDP rate of growth[c]	6.0	5.2	5.4	4.6	4.3	2.4	0.9

[a] Nominal rates adjusted by changes in GNP deflator
[b] Interest payments and amortization as percentage of exports of goods and services
[c] Weighted average of nonoil LDCs, excluding China

Source: International Monetary Fund, World Economic Outlook, Annual Report, and Occasional Paper no. 23, (1983).

quantitative indicators of the major domestic effects of
these policies as well as the channels through which they
have been transmitted to the rest of the world and their
impact on nonoil developing countries.

The table is intended to illustrate the following
process. The policy of monetary restraint that has been
implemented in the United States since 1978, coupled with
a growing fiscal imbalance, has led to a marked upsurge
of nominal and real interest rates (to which other countries have had to adjust) and gradually declining rates
of GNP growth.   As can be seen from the data in
Table 8.1, the rate of change of M_1 in real terms was
negative for four years in a row, considerably shrinking
the real stock of money (M_1) and leading to real interest
rates that were extremely high by historical standards.
The time profile of the shift from negative to positive
real interest rates may well have been somewhat different
from that suggested by figures in Table 8.1, which
depicts real rates simply by subtracting the GDP deflator
from nominal rates. Expected rates of inflation tend to
be greater than recorded price increases in the initial
stages of an inflationary process, whereas the opposite
is true for a deflationary process like the one initiated
in 1980. In any event, the high real interest rates
brought about by such a liquidity squeeze have given rise
to a strong differential favorable to assets denominated
in U.S. dollars, which have imposed corresponding
financial tightening and increases in interest rates in
other countries to prevent excessive capital outflows
from taking place. Thus, the excess demand for money
and corresponding excess supply of goods and services,
particularly those whose demand is highly sensitive to
changes in interest rates, caused by policies of monetary
restraint in the United States have been immediately
paralleled in other major industrial countries and
ultimately in the rest of the world.

Additionally, the falling rates of real GDP growth
in the United States have reduced its volume of imports,
thereby channeling deflationary impulses to the rest of
the world through a reduced external demand. These
effects have been compounded by the cyclic behavior of
the U.S. income elasticity to import. Due to speculative
inventory cycles and protectionist pressures, import
volumes tend to grow faster than output when real GDP is
accelerating and to decrease faster when it is decelerating. Moreover, the inflow of capital associated with
the differential favorable to assets denominated in U.S.
dollars has given rise to a sharp appreciation of the
dollar. The beneficial effects for the rest of the
world that should spring from the appreciation of the
U.S. currency have been offset by the cyclic behavior of
imports just mentioned. Indeed, the appreciation of the
dollar has been very harmful to countries that have
external debt and that import intermediate goods and raw

materials (mostly denominated in U.S. dollars), by
sizably raising the local currency value of their foreign
liabilities and of their most inelastic items in the
import basket.

The impact on nonoil developing countries has been
particularly severe, as can be inferred from Table 8.1.
The rate of growth of their export proceeds has fallen
sharply as a result of lower unit prices and volume of
exports. They have undergone a marked deterioration of
their terms of trade and have experienced capital outflows that have been attracted by the jump in the rate of
return of financial assets denominated in U.S. dollars
and a substantial acceleration of the speed with which
the debt charges pile up. Those developing countries
with a heavy external debt have undergone not only a
sizable augmentation of the debt burden but also the
effects of decreased international flows of credit
stemming from the growing propensity of the banks to
reduce their ratio of aggregate external assets to
capital in general and their ratio of aggregate external
assets to capital in debt-ridden economies in particular.

The main aim of this sketch of recent developments
of the evolving world economic scene is to identify the
major deflationary forces in the international economy
and the channels through which they have been operating.
In essence, these forces are the liquidity squeeze and
accompanying high real interest rates induced by U.S.
financial policies, channeled to the rest of the world
through capital markets and the fall in income and demand
for foreign goods transmitted through the markets for
goods and services. The appreciation of the U.S. dollar,
the standard of value of the international monetary
system, has transmitted deflationary impulses through
both channels.

The preceding account is a rather standard analysis--
though placing perhaps too heavy emphasis on the
direction of causality running from the monetary forces
to the real side of the economy--of the current world
economic crisis. One of the limitations of this
approach, useful as it is in other respects, is its
concentration on explaining the recent downward movement
of the international business cycle, implicitly assuming
that the world economy was in a stable state of near
equilibrium at the beginning of the downswing in, say,
1978. The setting in motion of deflationary forces and
their propagation through the world economy is frequently
described as an exercise in comparative statics by which
the current position of the world economy is seen as the
result of changes in certain causal variables, such as
the rate of real growth of net private assets in the
United States, or any other monetary aggregate starting
from a stable equilibrium situation.

This analysis carries with it its own policy
recommendations. Since the initial position was one of

acceptable equilibrium, and current conditions point to
the existence of excessive underemployment equilibrium
and financial strains all over the world, the adequate
course of policy is to reverse the causal variables to
their original values: to reduce the U.S. federal deficit
and increase credit to the private sector, thereby
attaining a new equilibrium comparable to the initial
one in the United States as well as in the rest of the
world. The usefulness and elements of truth in this mode
of analysis and policy recommendations should not be
denied. Nevertheless, there is a need for supplementary
explanations of the weaknesses currently plaguing the
world economy and fundamental questions of international
monetary policy that cannot be answered by using this
analytical frame. The answers to questions relating to
the relative stability of the new equilibrium achieved
by pursuing the policy actions based on the foregoing
analysis and to the conditions that should be met to
prevent another phase of world recession and severe
financial strains require some knowledge of the dynamic
properties of the world economic system. An attempt to
furnish some elements out of which tentative answers to
these questions could be given is made in the following
paragraphs.

A Business Cycle View of Current Strains in the International Financial System

The dynamic properties of the world economy can be
ascertained by using the same business cycle analytical
apparatus applied to the study of national economies.
Specifically, the sort of cyclic oscillations to which
the world economy is now subject are best analyzed by
reference to the sort of processes studied by the so-
called monetary explanations of the business cycle.[1]
Before proceeding, there is one question worthy of some
detailed consideration regarding the extent of interdependence needed among national economies, for the
different countries of the world are following essentially
the same cyclic path. It should be pointed out that,
for the validity of the views and corollaries drawn from
seeing the different economies of the world moving around
a common business cycle, it is not a necessary condition
that goods and capital markets are fully integrated and
ruled by perfect arbitrage relationships. For the
validity of those considerations, it is sufficient that
the degree and nature of interdependence among national
economies be such that disintegrating devices like
capital controls, flexible exchange rates, or protectionism either have a very narrow insulating capacity or
none at all, their insulation effects being rapidly
offset and short lived. A brief account of the main
features of this interdependence will suffice to show

that this is certainly the case with the current structure of the world economy.

The Nature and Degree of World Economic Interdependence

The nature and intensity of the international links binding the economic life of each country to that of every other prevent national macroeconomic policies, with the exception of those in the United States, from exerting any systematic influence on the internationally imposed cyclic path. As is well known, until recently international trade in goods and services has been growing faster than national output, thereby increasing the overall exposure of national markets for goods and services to events and policies in other countries. Over that period, convertibility among the main currencies-- and through them among the other, hanging, currencies, the gradual lifting of capital controls, and the emergence of a powerful system of world financial intermediation have considerably increased the international mobility of capital as well as the share of tradable financial assets in national stocks of capital. The efficiency of remaining, or newly imposed, capital controls has been eroded considerably in the course of time, making it very difficult to control international movements of capital to any significant degree.

Many of the devices currently in place to control capital movements were conceived and implemented when the stock of capital was rather small relative to normal conditions. On the whole, current capital-control mechanisms were designed during the interwar depression and the period immediately following World War II. It was relatively easier to control capital movements during the 1950s, in a world economy impoverished by the war, than in successive periods where the normal stock-flow ratio between capital and income was restored. The accumulation of capital all over the world resulting from the high rates of growth during the 1960s, together with the integration of major capital markets, has made it increasingly difficult for remaining, or newly established controls, to prevent capital from moving into the financial centers offering better prospects through the many leakages left open by technological advances in communications and transport systems, financial innovations, and more integrated markets for goods and services.

In relation to the nature of this growing international interdependence, the relevant data are the increasing weight of the United States in world production of internationally traded goods and in internationally traded assets. Over the past decade, the propensity of the U.S. economy to import goods and nonfactor services has more than doubled, arising from oscillations around a trend of about 4 percent to about 10 percent, the

export propensity having followed a corresponding behavior. More importantly, the role played by U.S.
dollar-denominated financial assets and liabilities in
world finance, which had increased continuously since the
inception of the Bretton Woods system, has been dramatically strengthened with the recycling processes of oil
surpluses and development of international banking and
Eurocurrency markets.

The main implication of this is that as a producer
of traded goods the United States is comparable in size
to other major economies, whereas its position as a price
setter in world financial market is, for all practical
purposes, that of a monopolist. Thus, for example, the
implementation of a policy of monetary restraint in the
United States leads to higher interest rates that attract
capital inflows from the rest of the world. The size of
the U.S. capital market is such that those inflows of
foreign savings are not likely to have any significant
effect on U.S. domestic interest rates. Consequently,
the behavior of interest rates in the United States,
and on other assets denominated in U.S. dollars linked to
U.S. domestic assets, are the result of essentially U.S.
economic policies.[2] This is a major departure from the
British-led world economy of the nineteenth century and
first decades of the twentieth, when financial conditions
in Lombard Street were highly sensitive to external
capital flows. It is also a situation that violates
crucial conclusions of conventional balance-of-payments
theory based on such a world.

Perhaps the major implication is the inability of a
system of flexible exchange rates to provide the non-U.S.
world with protection against foreign disturbances. A
policy of financial restraint in the United States will
communicate its effects to the rest of the world through
the rapidly clearing capital markets. The impact of
monetary contraction and the fall in external demand on
the production levels of tradable and nontradable goods
in those countries will be immediate, and there is not
much that exchange rates can do to improve that situation.
They can certainly induce the process pointed out in
Note 1, but the importance of these effects is relatively
negligible. Flexible exchange rates, however, can have
important insulating effects for individual nations if
the responses of different countries to U.S. policies
differ significantly. It is not probable, however, that
there can be more than a few countries that manage to
escape from the U.S.-induced deflationary impulses at the
expense of others, and in conditions of worldwide
recessions, it is doubtful that they can do so at all
for any significant period of time.[3]

The Monetary Mechanism of the Expansion and Contraction Processes

The main aim of these paragraphs is to apply the monetary theories of business cycles, phenomena developed by pre-Keynesian economists, to the analysis of the world economy. There is a need to return to this theoretical approach because, contrary to standard static analysis, it links the expansion and ensuing contraction phases of an economy evolving over time, and the relationships between real and monetary disequilibria are not as easily forgotten.

Although there are significant differences among the various theories of business cycles that place heavy emphasis on monetary factors, and it is certainly difficult to put forward a presentation doing justice to them all, it is possible to synthesize some common features and give a simplified account of a business cycle induced by monetary forces.[4] This is done in the following lines trying to single out the main elements behind the upswing and the downturn of a cyclic movement. In what follows, references to a money, capital, or credit market should be understood as an analogue for the set of all deposit-taking and lending banking activities that are made in dollars and other international reserve assets. Additionally, no breakdown of the term structure of interest rates is done. Therefore, references to the long-term rate of interest should be seen as referring to the natural or equilibrium rate. This rate, in turn, would be the one that, under given conditions, keeps the rate of growth of money income in pace with that of real output and noninflationary expectations.

The Expansion Process

A typical monetary cycle is set in motion by a growing discrepancy between flows of voluntary hoarding and rates of credit creation. If unchecked, this discrepancy, whether it is originally caused by over-extension of·credit or is the result of maintaining rates of credit while voluntary savings fall, will generate tendencies leading to overinvestment and over-indebtedness situations. Assuming that previous rates of growth of credit and flows of monetary savings were consistent with full employment growth of output and noninflationary expectations, disequilibrium in the money market will cause nominal income to grow faster than output volumes. Money rates of interest will usually fall or, in any event, real rates of interest will decline in relation to the natural long-run rate, creating a premium for borrowers that further increases their demand for credit. During these initial stages of a process of monetary overexpansion, the total supply of

credit by banks is highly elastic and can accommodate the
increasing demand of borrowers without significantly
eroding the differential between the going real interest
rate and the long-term one. This process has also a
counterpart on the real side of the economy since the
rate of interest not only regulates monetary phenomena
but also influences the allocation of productive factors
to different branches of economic activity.

As long as monetary disequilibrium persists, sectors
where the capital constraint is more binding will tend
to expand faster, relative to trends, than others. They
will absorb a greater share of the excess supply of bank
credits that have no counterpart in voluntary hoarding
but rather are backed by artificial savings coming out of
the very monetary overexpansion. These sectors, in
greater need of capital and more benefited by the lowering of real interest rates and availability of credit,
will be prone to achieving faster rates of growth relative
to other sectors than would be the case in conditions of
monetary equilibrium. Thus, many investment projects are
launched, financed out of bank credit creation in excess
of voluntary savings, whose viability depends on the
persistence of disequilibrium conditions in the money
market. Many investments, not viable at equilibrium
real rates of interest, are undertaken on the expectations that current relationships between financing
conditions and inflation will persist long enough to
make them profitable. Overinvestment and malinvestment
phenomena, investment projects whose maturity and
profitability are not compatible with equilibrium conditions in the money market, are thus emerging.

Standard monetary theory of national economies
usually neglects the analysis of the effects on the
relative structure of sectors of the distribution of an
excessive stream of money creation, by considering them
transient effects. According to that theory, although
the first impact of monetary disequilibrium may be un-
evenly distributed, in time it will be proportionately
shared by all sectors of the economy; relative prices
are thus determined only by real factors, monetary
disturbances being able only to produce transient altera-
tions of the price structure. In the case of the world
economy, however, excessive international money creation
may lead to the structure of relative prices or relative
rates of growth of countries, which can be approximated
by the simile of sectors in the preceding lines, being
distorted for prolonged periods.

It should not be difficult to identify a cumulative
process of monetary disequilibrium in the world economy
in the late 1960s and early 1970s and, again, in the
mid-1970s in broad conformity with that theoretical
pattern. The impact of monetary overexpansion in the
United States during the late 1960s and early 1970s
was largely channeled to developing countries and was

perpetuated by the accelerated development of Euro-
financing. This development was itself accelerated by
the persistence of negative real rates of interest.
Although Eurocurrency markets offered greater nominal
rates of interest than other capital markets, those rates
were not keeping pace with inflationary expectations.
The degree to which monetary disequilibrium continued to
persist during the first oil shock is difficult to assess.
With the benefit of hindsight, however, it could be said
that credit creation was allowed to finance greater
current account deficits of nonoil countries, and greater
increases in the price of oil, than would have been
desirable from a long-term perspective.

The incentive to overlend to developing countries was
reinforced by the tendency of their export prices and
export proceeds to incfease faster than the prices of
other tradable goods and international trade, respectively.
There also was an incentive to overborrow on the part of
producers of nontraded goods in some of these countries.
In those countries where domestic policies were such that
prices of nontradable goods were expected to rise faster
than the exchange rate plus the international rate of
interest, there was a premium for producers of nontraded
goods to resort to external indebtedness--all the more so,
if they were facing domestic credit or external resources
constraints. These factors had a bearing on enlarging
the already high differential between home and international real interest rates and induced commercial
bank and public-sector entities in some developing countries to overborrow.

These differential effects of a monetary disequilibrium on different sectors help to explain the
distribution of the debt problem among developing countries as well as sectorial aspects within a given country.
For a given international nominal rate of interest there
will be different real rates of interest for different
borrowers, according to the relative pace at which their
earnings are expected to rise, whereby domestic factors
may influence the degree of world monetary disequilibrium
absorbed by the country. As shown by the data in
Table 8.2, the resort to indebtedness with the international credit system has been much greater by developing countries in the Western Hemisphere than in Asia.
This has been due partly to different structural characteristics and partly to different domestic policy
responses between the two regions. For instance,
economies in Asia have usually a more developed long-
term financial segment in their capital markets.
Additionally, their public sectors have achieved a more
balanced financial performance, whereby the degree of
credit rationing of the private sector was lower than for
countries in the Western Hemisphere. Real interest rates,
therefore, were generally higher for developing countries
in Asia than in the Western Hemisphere during the

Table 8.2 Aspects of the External Debt Cycle in Selected Groups of Developing Countries

	Average Rate of Growth 1968-1973	1974	1975	1976	1977	1978	1979	1980	1981	1982
Ratio of external debt to exports of goods and services[a]										
LDCs in Western Hemisphere		163.4	195.8	204.1	194.1	211.5	192.9	178.4	207.4	245.6
LDCs in Asia		81.0	91.6	84.4	83.3	77.7	70.2	68.2	72.5	80.9
Debt-service ratio[b]										
LDCs in Western Hemisphere		27.9	32.2	35.4	31.2	41.7	40.9	35.6	41.7	54.0
LDCs in Asia		7.8	8.5	7.7	7.6	9.6	8.7	8.2	9.2	9.8
Real GDP annual changes[c]										
LDCs in Western Hemisphere	7.6	8.4	6.9	3.1	5.5	5.0	4.5	6.0	-0.1	-1.5
LDCs in Asia (excluding China)	4.2	3.8	4.9	7.5	6.6	7.9	3.3	3.4	5.8	3.7
Changes in consumer prices[d]										
LDCs in Western Hemisphere	18.5	37.5	52.0	66.1	51.2	42.4	49.6	58.2	65.4	76.0
LDCs in Asia (excluding China)	8.3	30.1	13.2	0.5	7.3	5.6	9.8	15.9	14.8	9.9

[a] Ratio of year-end debt to exports for indicated year
[b] Interest and utilization payments as percentages of exports of goods and services
[c] Arithmetic averages of country growth rates weighted by the average U.S. dollar value of GDPs over the previous years
[d] Geometric weighted averages of country indices

Source: International Monetary Fund, World Economic Outlook, 1983.

inflationary expansion process.
Although domestic factors are, of course, important
in determining the distributional impact of world monetary
disequilibrium, it should not be inferred from this that
adequate domestic policies could have avoided, to any
significant degree, the current external debt crisis in
the Western Hemisphere. For one thing, banks were prone
to lend to these countries that were growing very rapidly
during the late 1960s and early 1970s and, in fact,
during the first half of the decade, although they were
accumulating increased inflationary pressures. It is
easy to state, with the benefit of hindsight, that those
rates of borrowing were excessive. It was much more
difficult to anticipate at the time the coming of real
positive interest rates and, in fact, nobody did. Once
we take account of the fact that the future was unknown
by the mid-1970s, it must be recognized that it was
neither politically feasible nor economically efficient
to abstain from borrowing at real interest rates that,
even assuming domestic discipline, were very low by
historical standards.

The Contraction Process

Business cycle theorists were particularly eager
to show how a process of inflationary expansion brought
about by monetary disequilibrium carried with it the
seeds of a cumulative process of recession. Overindebtedness and depression phenomena were seen as having
their origins in previous overinvestment and inflationary
expansion, the gravity of the recession being related to
the magnitude of the causal inflationary disequilibrium.
Several forces are set in motion by the process of
growing monetary disequilibrium, which act by arresting
the inflationary growth of real output that accompanies
the expansionary movement. There is a learning process
by which savers anticipate better the effects of credit
expansion on the purchasing power of their earnings so
that they are less willing to hold their savings on
financial assets with very negative rates of interest
in successive steps of the expansionary process. When
inflationary expectations are very high relative to the
nominal rate of interest, not only do savers tend to
part with holdings of financial assets but producers also
use up idle balances and reserves whose opportunity cost
is very high when real interest rates are negative.
Thus, as inflationary expectations become embedded in
wealth holders, it is increasingly more difficult for
banks to extend credit at rates below expected inflation,
and the relationship between nominal interest rates and
prices tends to approach the long-term trend.
A second force at work in checking the growth of
real output accompanying a process of inflationary income

expansion relates to the risk component in the rate of
interest. At any moment the market for loanable funds
will be clearing by a structure of interest rates reflecting the different risk segments of the market.
Successively greater loans to the same borrower are not
the same commodity, but different ones each carrying
marginally greater risk. Even assuming an infinitely
elastic supply of international credit for a certain
period, a given borrower will not face a constant
interest rate for increased amounts of loans. Regardless
of what may happen to the internationally determined
interest rates, individual borrowers will generally be
faced with a gradually more inelastic supply of loans,
depending on the growth of their outstanding debt. The
transition from a risk-elastic to a risk-inelastic supply
schedule of credit may or may not be a smooth one, but
sooner or later heavy borrowers will face substantial
increases in average interest rates, as a reflection of
an increase in the risk component. On the other hand,
banks will not merely attempt to earn greater interest
rates for their loans but will also lower credit
expansion in order to restore the loanable assets-to-
capital ratio that deteriorated during the overlending
period. In so doing, they will attempt to reduce to an
even greater extent the riskiest assets corresponding to
the most heavily indebted borrower.

The structure of production will move so as to
conform with the new conditions in the money market. The
restoration of natural long-term rates of interest
places a heavy burden on those sectors in need of capital
whose increased rate of growth was contingent on the
continuance of monetary disequilibria and corresponding
cheap and abundant credit. Some investment projects
must be liquidated and others slowed down. Other sectors
and activities that, while not excessively indebted,
were dependent upon the overborrowing and growth of the
former sectors are also undergoing a serious squeeze
on their profitability resulting from the decreased
demand for their products. A substantial part of the
enlargement in real output built up during the upswing
will thereby be destroyed in the course of the ensuing
depression. It is not only that many investments are
liquidated in an intermediate stage, but that a share of
installed capacity is no longer profitable at all since
its marginal product does not cover costs inclusive of
external debt service.

A secondary depression might take place if the
feedback effects of adjustments in the real sector on
the monetary side of the economy are of sufficient
intensity. Since the expansion in many sectors was
financed to a large extent by debt contraction rather
than by savings of producers, shares, or long-term loans,
there is a risk that debtors might fail to fulfill their
obligations, especially if the transition from negative

to positive real interest rates has been too abrupt, and real interest rates have overshot. There is the possibility of an explosive debt cycle. Real debts increase with real interest rates, and their growth tends to induce a further contraction of credit by banks, which in turn will put additional pressures on the debtors to service their obligations.[5]

With the exception of the process of secondary depression, recent developments in the world economy have been in broad accord with the foregoing highly simplified theoretical pattern. However, over the period there were noncyclic events that should be put into the picture to explain more adequately the severity of the external debt crisis. Above all, it must be pointed out that current real interest rates are as far from equilibrium as the negative rates prevailing during the 1970s. As already mentioned, current real interest rates are the result of a distorted policy mix in the United States. The cyclic forces operating to arrest inflationary growth and negative real interest rates have been magnified by the size and expectations on the U.S. public-sector deficit. The U.S. economy, the richest in the world, is importing capital from other countries, many of them developing ones, through sizable current account deficits to finance a large proportion of its public-sector deficit. The United States is receiving considerable capital inflows not only directly from the rest of the world but also indirectly through the crowding-out effect in international and U.S. banking in favor of U.S. assets and securities and against assets in developing countries. This latter effect has been reinforced by financial deregulation and innovation in the U.S. capital market which have tended to reduce the degree of financial international intermediation through Eurocurrency markets. Thus, the process of contraction and the appearance of problems of servicing external debt have been accelerated and aggravated by those developments superimposed on cyclical factors.

The gravity of the situation calls for action on an international basis in order to prevent the onset of a secondary depression and eventual breakdown of the international monetary mechanism. The following section considers the scope for action by international monetary institutions to deal with the strains threatening the cohesiveness of the world economic fabric.

THE SCOPE FOR ACTION BY INTERNATIONAL
FINANCIAL INSTITUTIONS

In the short run, there is not much that international financial institutions can do without appropriate policies in the largest industrial countries. A necessary condition for the global recovery of the world economy

and a satisfactory solution to the external debt problem
is obviously the sustainability of the recent pickup in
the U.S. economy. There seems to be general agreement
that for this to happen a change in the current stance
of the policy mix, correcting the trend toward greater
budgetary disequilibrium, is needed. A vigorous and
stable economic recovery will require steadily growing
flows of private capital formation, which in turn call
for expectations of moderate and reasonably stable
prices for the services of capital. A U.S. economy that
is growing in the context of potential interest rates
closer to long-run values will exert a powerful and
beneficial influence on development countries and current
external debt strains. A restoration of world monetary
equilibrium and long-term normal real interest rates will
ease the pressures to serve the volume of outstanding
external debt that, for the most part, was contracted at
floating interest rates. Even though spreads over the
prime rate of international lending would continue to be
very high for debt-ridden countries, the impact of declining real interest rates and accompanying developments
in the real sector will substantially improve the economic
climate and entrepreneurial expectations in such countries.

Whereas the sustained recovery of the U.S. economy
is certainly a necessary condition for the stability of
the financial system, it is by no means a sufficient
one. Even if the recovery consolidates and a strong
noninflationary growth can be sustained, it will render
its effects on developing countries only after a certain
lag. Whatever the length of this lag may be, it should
be kept in mind that the capacity to adjust in many
developing countries is rapidly reaching unsurpassable
limits. Moreover, the deteriorated state of confidence
in economic prospects throughout the world is not going
to improve overnight, even if definite symptoms that the
depression is over become apparent. Therefore, the vital
role to be played by the international financial institutions in general, and by the IMF in particular, over
the period ahead can hardly be overestimated. The
following paragraphs review some possible actions by
international financial institutions in relation to the
adjustment process and international liquidity creation
in the short run. Their limitations and shortcomings
in coping with the present world economic crisis are
considered in the next section.

Adjustment Processes and Their Financing

One of the critical aspects of the adjustment
process is the viability of the economic programs that
many debt-burdened countries are currently implementing.
The achievement of stable equilibrium conditions in the

world economy may well depend on the success of these
programs in attaining sustainable balance of payments
structures. As analyzed in the section "The International
Business Cycle and the External Debt Crisis," these
countries absorbed the largest impact of world monetary
disequilibrium and are suffering the gravest consequences
of monetary adjustment in the largest industrial countries. They are now forced to transfer a significant
proportion of the external resources they received during
the expansionary process of the world economy. If, however, they are required to transfer an unbearable amount--
the total transfer of financial resources being measured
by the difference between nominal rates of interest
attached to outstanding debt and the proportion accounted
for by new lending over a corresponding period[6]--the world
economy could go into the secondary depression phenomenon
analyzed in the previous section.

The International Monetary Fund is monitoring and
cofinancing many of these adjustment processes. IMF
lending to finance adjustment programs is similar to
discount policy by central banks in that it provides a
certain amount of credit conditional upon the observance
of certain ratios related to the financial performance of
the borrower. Contrary to what happens in the case of a
central bank, however, the amount of lending the IMF can
extend is not significant in relation to the dimensions
of the balance-of-payments problems of these countries;
neither are the functional characteristics of the institution suited to allow it to perform a similar role in
conditions of worldwide economic disturbances that are
not of a mild, temporary nature. The Fund has not the
capacity to act as a lender of last resort to central
banks of the world, rapidly facilitating bridge financing
until either adjustment or negotiated liquidity provides
the needed external resources. This is a role that has
been played by the Bank for International Settlements
to some extent. The rationale for the Fund in these
circumstances depends on its capacity to channel international liquidity from the world banking system to the
countries carrying out severe adjustment processes. In
this respect, the role of the Fund in cutting the tendency
toward self-defeating economic behavior on the part of
the banks through the full exercise of its powers of
moral suasion and its pivotal position in coordinating
central-bank actions has certainly proved to be essential.
The Fund has been able to induce much greater flows of
international credit toward economies making substantial
adjustment efforts than voluntary lending would have
allowed. Having said this, there are some questions to
be raised in connection with the role of the Fund in the
adjustment process.

For instance, it is questionable whether the present
mix of adjustment and financing in many of these countries
is adequate enough to achieve balance-of-payments

equilibrium without inflicting considerable damage on the growth capacity or the social fabric of the countries concerned. Another fundamental and related question to be addressed is whether the response of the international financial system monitored by the Fund to the first stage of the external debt crisis could be repeated, should the timing of the recovery process in the largest industrial countries fail to make viable the sort of process toward external equilibrium assumed by current adjustment programs. The only degree of freedom left to the Fund in dealing with the problems involved in these questions is, as mentioned, to assist in the adjustment of those countries in need of its resources and of the pyramid of private credit that may be based on them. The room for maneuver of the Fund in this area, in turn, will depend on its capacity to extend adequate amounts of resources to all countries implementing appropriate adjustment policies. Private banks will not easily increase or maintain their exposure in developing countries if the IMF itself does not do the same. The continuous presence of the IMF in those countries could require changes in certain deeply rooted traditions like the revolving nature of Fund resources and the reluctance to resort to external sources of finance other than governments and central banks.

Problem of the IMF Resources

The IMF quota subscriptions, on which its lending capacity has traditionally been based, were increased by 47.5 percent from SDR61 billion to SDR90 billion (from about US$67 billion to US$98.5 billion) when the Eighth General Quota Review came into effect at the beginning of 1984. Most countries represented at the Executive Board of the IMF are concerned that these resources may prove inadequate to deal with the problems posed by current financial strains. These fears have been reinforced by the events associated with the difficulties of some countries in servicing the external debt and by the sizable increase in the demand for the Fund's resources.[7] Additionally, the potential impact of increased quotas on the Fund's contribution to the adjustment process has been somewhat eroded by the conclusions reached by the Interim Committee of the Board of Governors of the International Monetary System at the meeting held on September 25, 1983. At this meeting the decision was made to reduce the multiplier coefficient applied to the quota of members to determine the maximum amount of Fund loans and break the level of access into two tranches.

The extent to which this decision could offset the increased lending powers of the Fund involved in the augmentation of quotas will depend on the interpretation of the two-tier system of access to the resources

established in the decision. Even if the scheme is
applied with flexibility, the Fund could experience an
excess demand for its resources, since many countries
not hitherto involved with it may request financial
assistance in the period ahead, as the pulse of the
recovery does not seem to be firm enough. It will then
be necessary to resort to external sources of finance
other than quotas. Borrowing by the Fund from governments
and official institutions is a time-consuming process,
and apparently it is unable to cover the financial needs
of the institution in present circumstances of the world
economy. Therefore, the Fund should borrow from private
financial markets in amounts and with the maturity
dictated by the evolving world economic situation. The
Fund's borrowing from private capital markets is liable
to cause a crowding out of internal assets that are not
now available for developing countries. This is a more
desirable development in the present juncture of international capital markets, characterized by a considerable
decline in the desired external asset-to-capital ratios.
The Fund should make an attempt to seek the widest
possible spread of maturities and to cover most segments
of the international capital markets. Ideally, it should
borrow either in SDRs or in the currencies that compose
its basket.

The presence of the Fund in private capital markets
is fully justified on the grounds of short-run considerations and longer-term prospects. The uncertainties
surrounding the process of transition toward viable
external debt structures may give rise to a sudden need
for the Fund to have substantial resources at its
disposal, should a major unexpected development arise
either on the part of the banks or of the heavily indebted borrowing countries. From a longer-term perspective, the widespread presence of the Fund and the SDRs
in the markets could contribute to the march of the
institution into a central bank along lines considered
in the next section.

The SDR Allocations

Another area in which there is scope for further
action by the Fund is the issuance of internationally
controlled liquidity through SDR allocations. The
Fourth Basic Period (each basic period being the time
unit during which creation of SDRs is considered) started
in 1982 without any provision for allocation. As a
result of the voting structure of the Fund, proposals
for an SDR allocation have not yet obtained the necessary
majority.[8] All the requirements for an SDR allocation
considered in the Articles of Agreement of the Fund would
appear to indicate continuous allocation of SDRs over
time so as to convert this into the centerpiece of the

international monetary system. From the inception of the
SDR scheme it was clear that allocation of SDRs should
be considered as an instrument that would allow the share
of international reserves accounted for by SDRs to grow
over time. The development of international banking and
the growth of international liquidity over the period led
to questions about the viability of the SDR project.
Although not officially and openly recognized, the sort
of international monetary system centered on the SDR,
which commanded support by the majority of Fund members
in the past, is no more the longer-term objective into
which international monetary arrangements should converge.

Even though it is clear that the overall commitment
to promote the SDR as a principal reserve asset of the
international monetary system does not command the widespread majority that it once did, it is paradoxical that
the scheme has been questioned when it is most needed
from the standpoint of its short-run potentialities.
As analyzed in the previous section, the mechanism for
the generation of international liquidity is subject to
erratic fluctuations whereby a period of overexpansion
is followed by a phase of excessive contraction. The
fall in, or the absence of, importance of the SDR has
prevented it from playing any significant role in checking the expansion or contraction of liquidity. As for the
contractionary phase currently going on, although the
range of allocations contemplated in various meetings of
the interim committee would not have corrected the
situation of international liquidity in any fundamental
sense, given the negligible proportion of international
reserves accounted for by SDRs, it would have afforded
some relief and strengthened confidence in the existence
of a valve through which the IMF could exert the role of
lender of last resort to the international financial
system. Therefore, allocation of SDRs should be resumed
in the short run, although in the longer run the attitude
of some national authorities to the relevant sections of
the Articles of Agreement of the IMF, in accordance with
which the SDR would be made the principal reserve asset
in the system, must be clarified.

One of the problems related to the creation of SDRs
is that the allocation procedure tends to put more SDRs
in the hands of those that need them less. The distribution of unconditional liquidity in the form of SDRs
is not related to the relative reserve asset needs of
countries, at least not in the first impact, but to their
relative quota in the IMF. It would, therefore, be
convenient to conceive schemes so as to redirect
created reserves through SDR allocations to the countries
in relatively greater need of international liquidity,
which in any case would receive some relief by the SDRs
directly allocated to them. One possibility would be to
reach a compromise for a loan to the Fund on the part of
those countries that would receive the larger share in

SDR allocations. By this means, SDRs would be transferred to the General Resources Account of the Fund and would be available to increase the financing to countries carrying out adjustment processes.[9]

As can be inferred from the foregoing considerations, the room for maneuver of international monetary institutions in dealing with the current monetary crisis is rather narrow. In the next section, some possible explanations are given of the reasons behind this limited capacity of these institutions that are supposed to be the guardians of the international monetary system in preventing and coping with the external debt crisis.

SHORTCOMINGS AND LIMITATIONS OF INTERNATIONAL FINANCIAL INSTITUTIONS

The fundamental axiom upon which the Bretton Woods system was built was the continuous existence of conditions of approximate equilibrium in the world. The IMF, in particular, was designed to operate within the context of a world moving along an equilibrium path. It was conceived to support a world economic system in equilibrium, the foundations of which were to be established by means and actions beyond the scope of the Fund. The major postwar economies were brought into the equilibrium zone by direct grants and loans from the United States to the European countries that, by then, were the main capital importers in the world. Once these actions outside the Fund were implemented and took effect, that agency was considered responsible for providing the necessary guidance and international liquidity to correct minor deviations arising in the economic performance of a few countries and that of the rest of the world following an equilibrium path. It was believed that the commitment to full employment in the largest industrialized countries along with fine tuning policies would guarantee the achievement of adequate and stable rates of growth for the world economy as a whole. This view was fully embodied in the design of the functional features and general purposes of the IMF.

In a world in which overall depression or inflation was ruled out, instances of disequilibrium were contemplated as disparities between the levels of costs, incomes, and prices between one country and the rest of the world. According to the rules and regulations of the IMF, that country could finance its external disequilibrium by drawing from the institution if the factors leading to the imbalance were of a temporary and self-correcting nature. If the disequilibrium was judged to be "fundamental," the only precise definition for this being to consider it non-self-reversing within a relatively short period of time, the country was asked to devalue and implement a financial package as a prerequisite

to draw from the Fund. A non-self-reversing fundamental
equilibrium was thought to be amenable to short-run
treatment. The mix of expenditure-cut and expenditure-
switching policies of the Fund's programs would bring the
country back in line with international equilibrium conditions in a short period of time, allowing the prompt
repayment of the temporary credit extended by the Fund.
The financial resources of this institution were thus
seen as a revolving fund, drawings from which were to be
repaid after the relatively short period needed to
correct minor disequilibria.

It is important to realize that in the presence of
a worldwide cyclic depression of a certain length and a
given nature and degree of world economic interdependence,
this scheme breaks down completely. In the face of a
worldwide recession originating in one or more large
industrial countries, simultaneous efforts by other countries to correct external imbalances through domestic
deflation and devaluation could lead to further falls in
their export proceeds, thereby aggravating the situation
and placing the whole burden of adjustment on the income
mechanism operating through the import side. More
importantly, if worldwide depressions are caused by
inflationary overexpansion, what is needed then is to
curb excessive monetary growth in the largest industrialized countries. The IMF not only lacks the means
to achieve this end, but it also requires a completely
different conceptual apparatus. The built-in contradictions of the Bretton Woods system that ultimately led to
its breakdown are well known, and there is no need to
dwell upon them further. What is less frequently taken
into account, however, is the bearing that the assumption
of a world economy smoothly evolving around an equilibrium
path has on the effective functioning of the international
monetary system. From the beginning of the Bretton Woods
negotiations there were two distinct views as regards the
institutional structure needed to support the international monetary system: the Keynesian view of a world
central bank and the U.S. view of a stabilization fund.
If the world economy was supposed to move along a path
of stable equilibrium, there was obviously no need for a
world central bank using whatever assets it might have to
prevent major departures from equilibrium. All that was
needed was the sort of stabilization fund actually
brought into being. However, worldwide cyclic major
disequilibria call for an international agency endowed
with the powers and means to stabilize the world credit
cycle. Only if the IMF were redesigned around the image
of a central bank could it be in a position to carry out
one job of ensuring a path of stable growth for the
world economy.

These shortcomings and limitations of the Bretton
Woods institutional net did not pass unnoticed when the
system was initiated and, indeed, originated some

proposals for alternative international financial
arrangements. For instance, in Jacob Viner[10] there can
be found no less than five essays, dated 1945-1947, con-
taining his proposal for a countercyclic international
lending agency aimed at stabilizing employment throughout
the world. The central theme of this proposal was the
need for a set of international agencies that embodied the
responsibility of the largest industrialized countries
for stable world economic growth, including that in the
backward regions of the world. The main long-run operational principle was the apparently simple idea of
collecting funds at times of business expansion and lending them at times of economic pressures. For short-run
disequilibria stemming from a distorted world distribution of payment imbalances, compulsory arrangements were
envisaged by which external credit was to be extended
from surplus countries with reserve currencies to those
others whose shortages of international reserves and
liquidity were related to the formers' surplus. Similar
schemes were put forward by two United Nations reports,
National and International Measures for Full Employment
(1949) and Measures for International Economic Stability
(1951). It is interesting to note that the latter report
deemed it necessary to carry out far-reaching changes in
existing international arrangements along those lines
even though the world economy followed an equilibrium
path. It was believed by the authors of the report that
the cyclic instability of the U.S. economy, even if not
departing significantly from the equilibrium path, might
give rise to excessively distortive repercussions for
developing countries.

It must be accepted that any serious project of
international monetary reform must come to terms with the
problem of stabilizing the world credit cycle and avoiding major disruptions of an essentially monetary origin.
International monetary policy is the task of international monetary agencies. In a way, it would not be an
exaggeration to say that the severity of the current
crisis of the world economy is partly due to the persistence of the institutional tissue, with broadly the
same operational features, of the Bretton Woods system
even though the basic assumptions that made that system
viable no longer exist. A crucial opportunity to fundamentally correct the system and adopt it to the changed
structure and behavioral features of the world economy
was missed during the discussions on world monetary
reform during the early 1970s. For a number of reasons
those attempts were frustrated. First, there was the
reluctance of countries to accept constraints on the
conduct of their monetary policies in the short run that
are implicit in any serious project of a reformed
monetary system, and, second, the belief in the insulating
properties of a system of flexible exchange rates. The
nonreform of the international monetary system has

certainly not been without cost for the world economy.
As J. Williamson has put it, "And so the world ended by
getting exactly what is implied by those attitudes--a non-
system with no coherent mechanism for monetary coordina-
tion but relying instead on markets to reconcile the un-
coordinated. We are still learning how high a price in
terms of economic efficiency has been paid for the triumph
of monetary nationalism."[11]

THE WORLD MONETARY SYSTEM AND THE INTERNATIONAL
BUSINESS CYCLE: A LONGER VIEW

The view that the profit motive, if working alone,
cannot lead to an optimal structure of the money markets
has long been shared by most economists. Theoretical
considerations as well as historical experiences suggest
that if left unchecked competition in these markets will
tend to break down any monetary standard. Thus, a role
for government in monetary and banking arrangements has
been accepted by economists of all schools. Either a
commodity standard or a fiduciary standard, if left to
private initiative, would be inherently unstable and
eventually break down. The maintenance of a commodity
standard in a growing economy with price stability requires a considerable amount of real resources to produce
the desired accretions to the stock of the monetary
commodity. The use of a relatively substantial volume of
real resources devoted to this purpose, together with the
great difficulty had by producers of the monetary
commodity to match the demand for it, establishes strong
incentives to find cheaper ways of providing the exchange
medium. Fiduciary elements are thus introduced into the
monetary system.
If the government does not intervene at this stage,
many individual issuers will be encouraged to issue
additional amounts of fiduciary currency as long as its
cost of production is lower than its purchasing power,
whereby there will be a tendency to drive the monetary
commodity out of circulation. Additionally, it would be
difficult to prevent overissue of the fiduciary commodity
by individual producers, and eventually a failure of some
producer to fulfill its promises to pay will take place.
Because of the pervasive and ethereal nature of money,
there is a risk for a chain reaction associated with the
failure of individual producers. Even if the consequences of eventual failures on the part of individual
producers did not lead to the breakdown of the system,
the issuance of the fiduciary medium would be subject to
costly erratic oscillations. The government has,
therefore, a role to fulfill in the control and expansion
of monetary and banking arrangements setting boundaries
to the oscillation of fiduciary media induced by the
working of the profit motive.[12]

The question arises as to whether this reasoning is also applicable to the argument in favor of a supernational central bank supervising national banking and monetary arrangements. Caution should be exercised in drawing too straightforward a parallel between national and world monetary arrangements. It is difficult, however, not to think that the international monetary system has over time been subject to a dynamic instability of a nature essentially identical to that ruling in purely private monetary systems. The so-called gold standard, which was of course a mixed commodity--fiat money system, broke down because of the inability of governments to control the ratio of gold to internationally accepted fiduciary media despite the calls, on the part of many economists, for a world central bank-like institution to manage that ratio.[13] The gold exchange standard of the Bretton Woods system ceased to exist because of overissue of the international fiduciary money. The fiduciary dollar standard has certainly been subject to episodes of overissue by the main producers of the international medium of exchange, with costly consequences for the world economy. It is true that the existence of central banks at the national level would seem to be sufficient to prevent a widespread failure and eventual breakdown of the world monetary system. In any event, the consequences of overissue could still be very damaging for the world economy and particularly for those countries with a lower share of the wealth of the world. There is no mechanism in the dollar or multiple-reserve international standard to prevent processes of cumulative monetary disequilibrium from happening along with the accompanying phenomena of overindebtedness, overinvestment, and malinvestment and the ensuing overkilling adjustment efforts.

Assuming that the short-term problem of attaining monetary equilibrium in the United States and the world can be solved, the long-run question of what should be done to prevent these experiences from happening again must be addressed. The only efficient corrective to deal with deficiencies in monetary arrangements arising from the tendency of individual entities, be they commercial banks in a national monetary system or reserve currency countries in a world financial system, to overissue from time to time is to ensure the imposition of ceilings and floors on the credit cycle by a superior authority.

Certainly the fact that political interdependence and cooperation have not kept pace with the growth of economic interdependence must be reckoned with. After all, the Bretton Woods institutions we now have were conceived and made possible as a result of World War II. It could then be that there is no scope for effective international monetary schemes, unless some major disruptions of the economic fabric of the world take place. The possibility may arise, therefore, that optimal monetary arrangements for the world are not politically feasible yet. This, however, is not for the economist to decide. If suboptimal projects are put forward with a view to the political constraints, the final outcome of their discussion would be a more in-adequate system than would otherwise be produced. With these considerations in mind, it might not be altogether useless to review some elements of the theory of a world central bank.

One of the most articulated theoretical approaches to a world central bank can be found in the second volume of J. M. Keynes's A Treatise on Money. Writing within the context of the interwar restored gold standard, Keynes proposed a scheme to ensure the viability of the international gold standard and make it compatible with stability of prices and incomes throughout the world. It may be useful to look into these proposals with some detail once again since, although they were formulated with the international gold standard in mind, they are no less valid for an international fiduciary standard.[14]

At the time of writing the Treatise, Keynes placed heavy emphasis on the role of monetary factors behind the trade cycle and the importance and effectiveness of monetary policy in stabilizing it. For the very open British economy it was not possible, however, to control the growth of the domestic stock of money if the external sources of its viability were not likewise controlled. This led Keynes to tackle the issue of needed monetary management at the supranational level. Speculating on the desirable and feasible monetary arrangements for the world economy, Keynes came to the conclusion that the creation of a supranational central bank was needed to carry out an international monetary policy aimed at stabilizing the long-run value of gold and minimizing short-run fluctuations.

> I am disposed to conclude, therefore, that if the various difficulties in the way of an inter-nationally managed gold standard could be over-come within a reasonable period of time, then the best practical objective might be the management of the value of gold by a Super-national Authority, with a number of national monetary system clustering around it, each with a discretion to vary the value of its local money in terms of gold within a range of, say, 2 percent. . . .[15] The ultimate problem before us is, therefore, the evolution of a means of managing the value of gold itself through the agency of some kind of supranational institu-tion.[16]

Having established the need for a "supranational" institution responsible for the management of international

monetary policy, he then set out to analyze the ends and
means of international monetary management. In Keynes's
view, international monetary policy should be so managed
as to stabilize the long-period trend of the value of
gold in terms of an index of wholesale products internationally traded, which Keynes called the international
tabular standard.[17]

Some of the properties Keynes associated with this
standard are particularly relevant for today's international monetary disease. Since prices of commodities
and wholesale products are likely to fall relative to
the price of services with the pace of technological
advance, stability of the value of national moneys in
terms of the tabular or wholesale standard will imply a
downward tendency of the purchasing power of national
moneys in terms of consumption or retail goods. National
structures of prices evolving along such a long-term
path were considered by Keynes to be most efficient.
According to him, such an upward trend in the cost of
living induced by the stability of the tabular standard
would fit in with the exogenously given tendency of
nominal incomes to rise, thereby preventing the short-run
disequilibrium stemming from increases in nominal earnings unmatched by corresponding movements in prices of
final goods.

In assessing this view, the circumstances that
surrounded the appearance of Keynes's A Treatise on Money
in 1930 should be taken into consideration. Keynes had
in mind a process of deflation that had a particularly
damaging impact on those individuals and enterprises
that had contracted debt obligations at a fixed interest
rate and were facing a growing burden to service the
debt. These obligations eventually proved to be unbearable. As he said,

> I think it is desirable that obligations arising
> out of past borrowing, of which National Debts
> are the most important, should, as time goes on,
> gradually command less and less of human effort
> and of the results of human effort; that progress
> should loosen the grip of the dead hand; that the
> dead hand should not be allowed to grasp the
> fruits of improvements made long after the live
> body which once directed it has passed away.[18]

A second property of this international monetary
system would be, in Keynes's opinion, its stabilizing
effects on short-term business fluctuations. Business
cycles were seen by Keynes as essentially the result of
erratic behavior of credit leading to investment disequilibria that reflected rapidly on the wholesale index
(note that this was also written before his 1935 General
Theory). Therefore, the pursuit of a stable tabular

standard, with its need to concentrate on the behavior of
wholesale prices and their determinants, involved close
attention to investment phenomena by the national and
supernational authorities.

As for the methods and control procedures of international monetary policy, Keynes advocated the regulation
of the amount of gold put in active circulation in the
national systems--depending on the relative scarcity or
abundance of the metal--and the management of an international fiduciary asset created through the operations of
the supernational central bank with the central banks of
the world. The liabilities of this institution would
consist of deposits by central banks--supernational bank
money (SBM) in Keynes's terminology--fully convertible
into gold or national moneys at fixed rates allowing for
a difference of 2 percent between the buying and the
selling price. Ideally, national moneys should only be
cashable in terms of SBM, thereby moving toward a full
gold-SBM international standard. The supernational
central bank should be allowed to extend loans to
national central banks at a managed discount rate, the
maximum amount of the loan (the discount quota) being a
factor of the bank's deposits in the supernational bank.
The supernational central bank should also be endowed so
as to effect open-market operations in markets for different national securities. As mentioned earlier, the main
aims of this supernational bank would be to stabilize
the long-term value of gold or SBM in terms of a tabular
standard while avoiding worldwide economic disturbances
in the short run. To this end, the bank would be endowed
with the powers to implement discount rate, discount
quota, and open-market policies.

There are certainly many questionable aspects within
this scheme. One instance is the monetary role of
gold. Gold is not, however, a vital piece of the Keynes
international tabular standard. The presence of gold in
the Keynes scheme is due to his effort to advance a
proposal of international monetary management to save the
gold standard and to prevent the disequilibrating effects
of the breakdown of any standard. There is a trade-off,
though it may be relatively short-lived, between gold and
a world central bank. In the Bretton Woods system gold
still had the very positive role of imposing a discipline
on the issuance of fiduciary money by the countries
whose currencies were used as international reserve assets.
Indeed, the Bretton Woods system broke down as soon as
excessive creation of fiduciary money, either by monetary
policy in the United States or by passive assistance by
U.S. monetary policies to monetary demands originated
abroad, took place. If there existed an international
monetary institution endowed with the powers of a central
bank and embodied with a commitment to long-run price
stability there would be no need for any monetary
commodity to check excessive growth of fiat money. That

could be done by such an institution.

Another questionable point is that a stable tabular standard as advocated by Keynes could have undesirable distributional effects on developing countries or could fail to stabilize national price levels. Once it is accepted that international monetary policy should be concerned with stabilizing an index of tradable goods, there is the possibility of choosing a basket that could have desirable distributional consequences. Additionally, the basket could be subject to minor modifications from time to time to assure its effectiveness.

Another possible shortcoming of the scheme is its reliance on the effectiveness of monetary policy at the international level. In any scheme involving a supernational central bank the monetary liabilities of such an institution will be largely created by monetary developments in the largest industrial countries accounting for the greatest share of international securities markets. It is arguable, therefore, as to whether international monetary policy could do what national monetary policy cannot do, that is to say, a monetary policy aimed at stabilizing the long-run purchasing power of a basket of tradable goods will not necessarily cushion short-run fluctuations around trend. As it happens at the national level, it would not be easy for international monetary authorities to distinguish between temporary developments consistent with and necessary for money market equilibrium and the onset of an inflationary process. As is the case with national economies, it would be difficult to interpret monetary data and follow up the movements of the demand for money. Moreover, any program for international monetary policy would be subject to the same objections as those against national monetary policies that point to the difficulties of choosing the optimal monetary aggregate for intermediate variables whose behavior is linked to that of prices and the control variable through which the intermediate monetary aggregates should be monitored.

In response to these objections it must be recalled that the main objective of an international world central bank is to prevent major disequilibria in the world economy from happening. Short-run fine tuning may certainly not be effective and perhaps should not be sought. As already stated, there is not much disagreement among economists as to the need for a national central bank. There is no agreement at all on the optimal degree of monetary activism. Still it would be possible to design long-run monetary rules that would ensure the prevention of worldwide depression and major inflationary processes.

In spite of the possible drawbacks that stand in the way of an international world bank, it would seem that the advantages are still greater and that profitable action cannot go unexploited for very long. It should be noted that it took more than two centuries to introduce central banking institutions in national economies. The world economy took a major step in that direction with the inception of the SDR scheme in 1969. The principles embodied in that scheme are still valid and the conversion of the Fund into a central bank along the lines envisaged in it should be accelerated. Perhaps the major short-coming of the SDR was the belief that the functions of money are separable and that an international money can be created in stages. The SDR was thus created as an international reserve asset without practical scope for its being used as an international means of payment and effectively fulfilling the accompanying function of standard of value. This proved to be incorrect, and the role played by the SDR as an international reserve asset has been negligible if not nil. This has been due partly to the reduced magnitude of allocations. But allocations are, in turn, constrained by the limited use of the SDR. A more effective reform of the Fund in terms of a central bank should turn the SDR into a monetary asset, thus securing its full convertibility into other monetary assets by either public or private agents and encouraging its presence into effective monetary circulation.[19]

SUMMARY AND CONCLUSIONS

One of the main themes of this chapter is that given the nature of world interdependence and existing mechanisms for the generation and world distribution of international liquidity, the international economy is again subject to cyclic oscillations of considerable amplitude and eventually of an explosive character. The evolution of the developing countries will be particularly affected by these erratic fluctuations. As in the past, movements of industrial prices will be accompanied by much wider movements of primary-product prices in the same direction, whereby the terms of trade will work to magnify the business cycle of primary-producing countries. Moreover, the procyclic behavior of protectionist barriers, grants and official aid, flows of concessional finance, and private investment will also contribute to intensify the cyclic swing in developing countries. More importantly, given the behavioral pattern of international capital markets consolidated over the past ten years, excessive inter-national credit will tend to be moved into developing countries in times of expansionary monetary policies in the largest industrial countries and out of them in phases of monetary contraction. Monetary disequilibria will induce maladjustments in the real sector and set in motion self-reversing forces whereby a period of world monetary overexpansion and overindebtedness will be followed by world monetary contraction and will impose

a highly exacting transfer effort on developing countries. Given the nature and degree of world economic
interdependence, external debt crisis and worldwide
depression may well prove to be a recurrent event
following phases of excessive monetary growth.
The current external debt crisis and world depression, therefore, must be seen as a result of the
process of excessive world monetary expansion that took
place during different intervals of the 1970s. Those
who blame some developing countries for their overindebtedness and encourage too strong adjustment efforts
for these countries as a sort of purgative process,
neglect the fact that this problem was caused by monetary
overexpansion in the U.S. economy and other financial
centers of the world.
The world economy is still in a trial period as it
makes its way toward the attainment of sustainable and
stable growth. Even if this situation is achieved without further setbacks, the adjustment costs of this process
for the world have already been very high. The productive
capacity of most countries has been heavily damaged and,
in the best of scenarios, it will take time to cure the
ills of the world economic organism. There is no safeguard at all in present international monetary arrangements to prevent that from happening again. Present
international monetary institutions were conceived for a
world economy not departing significantly from conditions
of equilibrium. They are not equipped for preventing the
onset of a cumulative inflationary process or recession
and secondary depression phenomena like those experienced
by the world during the nineteenth century and the inter-
war period. Business cycles of a certain amplitude are
inherent and needed for the effective working of markets.
Fluctuations that run the risk of setting in motion a
process of cumulative disequilibrium are neither necessary
nor unavoidable. Economists have devoted special
attention to these matters for a long time and developed
theoretical and practical principles to deal with cyclic
phenomena. The appropriate mechanism to cope with these
aspects for improving the functioning of the economic
system over time is a central bank. This is as applicable
to national economic systems as to the world economy.
Discussions on the reform of the international monetary
system are again being launched. Any scheme for international monetary arrangements must come to terms with
the need to stabilize the world business cycle. It is
difficult to see how this could be done without a central
bank-like international institution.

NOTES

1. Business cycle literature went out of fashion
with the Keynesian revolution and further development of

Keynesian economics and is now coming back with the rational-expectations approach to macroeconomics, though in a rather narrow form. As it happened with Keynesian economics, a distinction should be made between the assumptions used and the policy implications drawn by authors of the rational-expectations school and the useful insights into cyclic phenomena some of these theoretical constructs may provide. This distinction is made explicit in Lucas (1977). Perhaps the main message of this literature is the need to recover the use of a business cycle, a complete oscillation, as the reference unit of macroeconomic analysis. For bibliographical sources of monetary theories of the business cycle, see Note 4.

2. There would be some repercussive effects of the U.S. monetary restraint that, operating through the market for tradable goods, could affect somewhat the initial upsurge in U.S. interest rates. The interest-rate impact of the U.S. liquidity squeeze would decrease world income and U.S. exports, whereby U.S. income would be affected by an order of magnitude given by the relevant Keynesian multiplier. Additionally, if higher interest rates in the United States are accompanied by an appreciation of the real exchange rate of the dollar, these effects could be reinforced by a reduction of tradable goods shares in output. The fall in income, in turn, would induce a lower demand for real balances and corresponding downward pressures on interest rates.

3. There are other factors, deriving from the pervasive presence of the U.S. dollar in the world monetary scene, that help to nullify the insulating properties of exchange rates. For instance, the fact that a large share of the external debt of countries is denominated in U.S. dollars and is not forward covered means that an appreciation of the U.S. dollar vis-à-vis the currency of the country concerned will generate wealth effects of a depressive impact on domestic producers. Similar effects stem from the increase in the local currency value of oil and other U.S. dollar-denominated and highly inelastic imports associated with an appreciation of the U.S. currency. On these questions, see Dornbusch (1983).

4. The standard reference to these and other theories of the business cycle is still Haberler (1939). The main works from which the views put forward in this section are drawn are Keynes (1930); Hawtrey (1928, 1932); Hayek (1933); and Fisher (1933).

5. A debt-deflation theory of great depressions is put forward by Fisher (1933). Fisher attributed a central role to overindebtedness in inducing secondary recessions and deflation, which ultimately led to a great depression: "The very effort of individuals to lessen their burden of debts increases it, because of the mass effect of the stampede to liquidate in swelling each

dollar owed. . . . [This] is the secret of most, if not
all, great depressions: the more debtors pay, the more
they owe. The more the economic boat tips, the more it
tends to tip. It is not tending to right itself, but is
capsizing." Fisher (1933, 344).

6. This is the relationship embodied in Domar's
formula (Domar, 1950). In this respect, it should be
noted that the rate of growth of new lending to nonoil
LDCs was of the order of 7 percent in 1982, whereas the
average annual interest rate was of about 14.1 percent
(LIBOR plus 1 percent) for that year. For 1983, net new
lending was estimated to be of the order of 5 percent,
whereas average interest rates were not expected to fall
significantly. The order of magnitude of the transfer of
resources implied by those figures may well prove to be
unsustainable, especially if account is taken that the
transfer effort is not uniformly distributed among LDCs.

7. On the same date that the increase in quotas
corresponding to the Eighth General Review was agreed
(January 18, 1983), the Group of Ten (G-10) leading
countries and Switzerland agreed to increase their commitments to supply lines of credit through the General
Agreement to Borrow from SDR6.4 billion to SDR17 billion
(from about US$6.7 billion to US$16.2 billion). GAB
resources would potentially be available for the IMF to
lend to all its members (not only--as hitherto--to the
G-10 countries) if certain conditions were met. These
commitments, like the quota increase to augment resources
available for the Fund, had to obtain parliamentary
approval before being made available at the beginning
of 1984.

8. According to current regulations governing the
issuance of SDRs, a decision to allocate SDRs cannot be
taken without the positive vote of the United States.

9. The potential role of the other financial institutions in the short run has been somewhat downplayed by
events in relation to that of the Fund. From a medium-
term perspective, there is no question that a large and
effective world bank is essential if the needs of
developing countries for long-term capital are to be met.
An area of expansion for the institution would be its
lending lines on terms that cover the cost of its financial
resources raised in private markets. In the near future
it will be convenient to raise larger amounts of funds
in these markets in order to expand the lending flows to
developing countries. There is a multiplier effect
associated with this increased lending through the policy
of inducing private banks to provide cofinancing of
World Bank projects. This increased lending activity of
the World Bank would have a stabilizing effect on the
supply of long-term capital to developing countries.
From the standpoint of the poorer region in the international community, an issue that deserves serious and
urgent consideration is the replenishment of the

International Development Association, the soft long-term
window of the World Bank. The importance of this agency
in financing projects aimed at creating the potential to
cover the basic needs of poorer countries cannot be
emphasized enough.
    10. Viner (1951).
    11. Williamson (1982).
    12. This is the classic argument for a government-
controlled central bank as developed in Friedman (1959).
    13. See, in this respect, Cassel (1936) and Keynes
(1930).
    14. Indeed, Keynes's plan to the Bretton Woods
Conference was fully based on the theoretical under-
pinnings elaborated in the treatise.
    15. Keynes (1930, 338).
    16. Keynes (1930, 388).
    17. Characteristically, Keynes chose to include
those goods for which adequate statistical information was
available. Thus, Keynes's tabular standard comprised
the sixty-two commodities included in the production
index calculated by the Economic and Financial Section
of the League of Nations. See Keynes (1930, 391).
    18. Keynes (1930, 393).
    19. Initial steps to reform the Fund along these
lines have been advocated by, among others, Polak (1974).

BIBLIOGRAPHY

Brunner, K., and Meltzer, A., eds. Stabilization of the
    Domestic and International Economy, vol. 5 of
    Carnegie-Rochester Series on Public Policy.
    North-Holland, 1977.
Cassel, Gustav. The Downfall of the Gold Standard.
    London, 1936.
Domar, Evsey D. "Foreign Investments and the Balance of
    Payments." American Economic Review. December 1950.
Dornbusch, R. "Flexible Exchange Rates and Inter-
    dependence." IMF Staff Papers, vol. 30, no. 1 (1983).
Fisher, Irving. Booms and Depressions. London, 1933.
____. "The Debt-Deflation Theory of Great Depressions."
    Econometrica, vol. 1, no. 4 (1933).
Friedman, Milton. A Program for Monetary Stability.
    New York, 1959.
Haberler, Gottfried. Prosperity and Depression.
    Cambridge, Mass., 1939.
Hawtrey, R. G. Currency and Credit. London, 1928.
____. The Art of Central Banking. London, 1932.
Hayek, F. A. von. Monetary Theory and the Trade Cycle.
    London, 1933.
Keynes, J. M. A Treatise on Money, vol. 2. London, 1930.

Lucas, R. "Understanding Business Cycles." In
Stabilization of the Domestic and International
Economy, edited by K. Brunner and A. Meltzer.
North-Holland, 1977.
Polak, J. J. Thoughts on an International Monetary Fund
Based Fully on the SDR. Pamphlet Series no. 28,
1974.
United Nations. National and International Measures for
Full Employment. 1949.
____. Measures for International Economic Stability. 1954.
Viner, Jacob. International Economics: Studies.
Glencoe, Ill., 1951.
Williamson, J. The Lending Policies of the International
Monetary Fund. Washington, D.C., 1982.

Part 2

Case Studies

9
Argentina's Foreign Debt: Its Origin and Consequences

Marcelo Diamond
Daniel Naszewski

INTRODUCTION

On February 2, 1981, less than two months prior to General Roberto Viola's takeover from his predecessor, General Jorge Videla, a 10 percent devaluation of the peso occurred that was to initiate a dramatic change in Argentina's economic situation.

The effect of this apparently insignificant devaluation was similar to that of a crack in a retaining wall: In the two months that followed, interest rates rose sharply, reaching unusually high real levels, even for Argentina; financial panic ensued as foreign short-term credit agreements were not renewed and the flight of private capital increased. Owing to this situation, the new economic team, led by Lorenzo Sigaut, was forced to undertake another devaluation of 30 percent with which the retaining wall gave way once and for all.

A minidevaluation policy, which until February 4 of the same year had been undertaken in accordance with a table announcing the monthly rise in the price of the dollar at decreasing rates systematically lower than the monthly real rate of inflation actually registered, gave rise to several consecutive maxidevaluations. Thus, although during the twelve months prior to this the peso had been devalued 22.6 percent, in the course of the following year--when the crisis occurred--the price of the dollar rose 390 percent (4.9 times). Inflation, which in January 1981 had fallen to a rate of 84 percent per annum, rose sharply again reaching 146 percent during the following twelve months.

Interest rates that had already been positive in real terms for a number of years (although not to the extent that they were to register later) rose sharply in nominal as well as real terms. All activity suddenly slowed down, and in a period of a few weeks, one of the deepest recessions of the century occurred. Thus, the gross domestic product along with domestic consumption fell sharply, as can be seen from the data in Table 9.1.

Table 9.1 Argentina: GDP and Consumption (millions of pesos
at 1970 market prices)

Quarterly Development	GDP	Consumption
1980		
III	114.376	90.180
IV	115.689	93.086
1981		
I	109.638	98.977
II	109.711	89.229
III	102.215	79.971
IV	100.649	79.070
1982		
I	101.919	85.096
II	98.220	76.297
III	98.491	75.851
IV	99.794	76.605

Source: Banco Central de la República Argentina.

Having slowly recuperated from the loss of earning
power of 1976 and 1977, real wages fell sharply, and the
basic wage decreased 14 percent in real terms in four
months. A slight recovery occurred in the following
months but wages fell even farther with the ensuing change
in government and the rise of General Leopoldo Galtieri
to power at the end of 1981. Thus, by June 1982, the
agreed basic wage had fallen 21 percent in real terms in
relation to January 1981, which coincides with the fall
in consumption shown in Table 9.1. Already weakened by
the policy of economic openness introduced in the previous
administration and by the size of the debts the private
enterprises were obliged to assume together with the high
real interest rates they had to pay, businesses suffered
another serious setback as a result of the recession and
the consequent fall in the demand and profitability
margins.

For the educated middle class, the days of "easy
money"[1] were over. For example, the airlines that in
previous months had transported hundreds of thousands of
Argentine tourists abroad and whose aircraft would return
loaded to the brim with purchases, were obliged to suspend services on a large scale due to the reduction in
the number of passengers.

As far as the situation in the foreign sector was
concerned, international reserves dropped considerably,
and without previous notice, Argentina slowly lapsed into
a partial suspension of payments of its foreign debt.
Finally, as time went by, it became known by word of mouth
that during the period from 1976 to 1982 the country's
foreign debt had risen to US$30 billion, a figure
equivalent to five years' exports. Very slowly the

country became aware of the burden that this mortgage, which in interest alone would absorb nearly 50 percent of Argentina's annual revenue from exports, meant for the economic future of the country.

At the same time there was added concern as to the reasons for this indebtedness and its eventual outcome. It was logical to suppose that the growth in the foreign debt, which was incurred basically as from 1978, would have been accompanied by a parallel increase in productive investment and the country's economic activity. This, however, was not the case. Instead of growing, the economy shrank, as can be observed in the figures in Table 9.2 for the gross domestic product, which in 1982 remained at the same level it had reached in 1973 and 1974.

In describing this situation, the Argentine economist Aldo Ferrer pointed out at the end of 1982 that "from 1976 to 1982, the increase in the foreign debt to more than US$30 billion has been accompanied by the destruction of domestic capital by more than US$60 billion. This estimate does not include losses in human resources as a consequence of the brain drain."[2]

Table 9.2 Argentina: Gross Domestic Product (millions of pesos at 1970 market prices)

1970	86.970
1971	91.221
1972	92.882
1973	96.198
1974	102.136
1975	101.287
1976	100.815
1977	107.310
1978	103.610
1979	110.979
1980	112.194
1981	105.553
1982	99.581

Source: Banco Central de la República Argentina.

The purpose of this chapter is to analyze the complex subject of Argentina's foreign debt and to provide an answer to a number of queries concerning it. For example: What were the causes of the indebtedness? Why did it have a destructive effect on national productive capacity? In what way was foreign indebtedness related to worsening inflation, the fall in real wages, and recession? How were the attempts to renegotiate the foreign debt with the IMF and the private international banks conducted as from 1982? Is Argentina faced with a qualitative change in its typically oscillatory cycle characterized by periodic crises in its balance of payments? Or, on the other hand, are we

234

dealing with a new phase of the same cycle, perhaps
drastically accentuated for various reasons, such as the
international financial situation that has prevailed since
the oil crisis? How should Argentina face its indebtedness? And lastly: What will be the consequences for the
economic future of the country?

In order to answer these queries we will first
attempt to bring to light the reasons why Argentina (and
other countries in a similar position) are faced with a
crisis that cannot be classified in our opinion as a
momentary lack of liquidity but rather as a case of
structural insolvency in its foreign sector. Later, we
will analyze the process that fed foreign indebtedness
from 1976 onward and accentuated it as from 1978, at the
same time provoking the unprecedented destruction of
Argentina's economic system. Third, we will examine the
comings and goings of the country's economic policies
applied since the beginning of 1981, when the present
global national economic crisis began to develop. In
this context, an explanation will be given of the way in
which negotiations to refinance the foreign debt were
undertaken as from the latter months of 1982.

Thus, we will show that despite the unprecedented
severity of the situation, indebtedness, inflation, the
fall in real wages, and recession are typical of a balance-
of-payments crisis of the kind periodically suffered by
Argentina (and the majority of the countries that
export primary products and that are undergoing the
process of industrialization) and indeed are an integral
part of the oscillatory movement that has affected the
country's political and economic life during the last few
decades. At the same time, however, we will attempt to
show that the unprecedented magnitude of the crisis in
the external sector of Argentina's economy invalidates
past extrapolations that predicted an automatic recuperation and that the severity of the phenomenon in itself
leads one to believe that this time it will be much more
difficult to overcome.

ARGENTINA'S STRUCTURAL TENDENCY TOWARD
DISEQUILIBRIUM IN THE EXTERNAL SECTOR

Concern due to the magnitude of worldwide foreign
indebtedness, and the indebtedness of countries at an
intermediate stage of their industrialization process
(like Argentina, for example), would tend to make the
phenomenon of external debt seem like a new and unheard-
of occurrence produced as a result of the international
economic crisis that began with the oil crisis or with
the recent change in direction of the U.S. economic policy
toward a more orthodox monetary one. However, the growth
in the foreign debt of these countries has been a continuous process during the last few decades. In fact,

it can be seen from the data in Table 9.3 that, in the
case of Argentina, the foreign debt had been undergoing
sustained growth (although not at the rate of recent
years) since well before the 1970s. The same may be said
of the foreign debt of other countries with similar
productive structures.

Why did this foreign indebtedness occur in Argentina?
The problem has its origins in the peculiar characteristics of its economic system. Argentina belongs to a
group of countries that are at an intermediate stage in
their industrialization process and that export primary
products. All of these countries possess a fundamental
characteristic that the textbooks always fail to mention:
the presence of two basically distinct sectors. One is
the primary sector (in Argentina's case it is farming;
in Venezuela, the petroleum industry; in Brazil, coffee;
and so on), and the other is the industrial sector. The
primary sector is highly productive or "efficient,"
thanks to bountiful natural resources such as rich
mineral deposits, a benevolent climate, or, in Argentina's
case, the fertile land of the "pampa." A different
situation is present in the industrial sector where productivity does not depend on natural resources but is a
direct function of the level of development and maturity
of the industrial system.

Countries at the beginning of the industrialization
process generally have a highly productive primary sector
and an industrial sector whose relative productivity
stays behind. Under these conditions the industrial
sector cannot compete internationally with the industries
of the more developed countries. However, this non-
competitiveness is not due to insufficient industrial
productivity, measured in absolute terms, but rather to
its relatively low productivity in relation to the
primary sector.

Industrial prices expressed in dollars will always
depend on domestic prices and the country's current
exchange rates, which in turn translate the domestic
prices into international terms. However, this exchange
rate is set precisely on a scale necessary to place the
prices of what is produced in the country on an international level. No matter how inefficient a country may
be (as were Taiwan and Korea when they started out), they
can always be internationally competitive if the appropriate exchange rate is applied. Their low overall
efficiency will be the reason behind a low standard of
living but will never prevent them from competing on the
world market. This adaptation mechanism for the exchange
rate ceases to function in primary exporting countries in
the process of industrialization, because their exchange
rate is not set on the basis of the parity of the industrial sector, but rather on that of the primary
sector, which has traditionally been the one to export.
Thus, in Argentina the exchange rate is set at a level

Table 9.3   Argentina: Growth of Foreign Debt (millions of
current U.S. dollars)

	Foreign Debt	Foreign Debt[a]
1958[b]	1,000	1,848
1963	3,390	6,278
1964	2,916	5,390
1965	2,650	4,801
1966	2,663	4,664
1967	2,644	4,622
1968	2,805	4,787
1969	3,231	5,305
1970	3,876	6,143
1971	4,356	6,681
1972	5,900	8,664
1973	6,400	8,312
1974	8,100	8,852
1975	7,875	7,875
1976	8,900	8,509
1977	9,678	8,719
1978	12,500	10,443
1979	19,034	14,131
1980	27,162	17,684
1981	35,671	21,296 ·
1982	38,736	22,639

Note: Disagreement exists in the data provided by the Banco
Central de la República Argentina (BCRA) depending on the period
in question, because on some occasions the short-term debt is
taken into account, and on others it is not.   Therefore, the figures
shown in this table should be considered as an approximate estimate
only.

[a]Deflated by the U.S. wholesale price index, basis 1975=100

[b]Estimate based on data provided by the BCRA

Source: BCRA, Series estadísticos sobre compromisos financieros
externos y balances de pagos de la República Argentina; other
reports; and personal research.

that allows wheat and meat to be exported comfortably.
In other words, Argentina has a "pampan" dollar that is
inadequate for the level of industrial productivity
attained.[3]
    Therefore, for prices to be competitive on the
international market, industry in the developing countries needs a protective tariff barrier.   It was behind
this protective wall that industrialization began in
Argentina and in all the other primary exporting countries mentioned earlier.   If we go back to the last
century, we can see that industrialization in the United
States and Germany and the introduction of these two
countries into a world market dominated by Great Britain

also began in this way. It is important to point out
that this protective tariff is in no way indicative of
industrial "inefficiency." What these tariffs do, in
fact, is to create a system of multiple exchange rates at
a parity appropriate to the industrial productivity
attained by a country at a given stage of development.
     Through industrialization, takeoff is achieved,
along with a greater utilization of labor. But at the
same time, a persistent deficit in the foreign sector
arises. The problem stems from the peculiarities of the
productive structure that has emerged, characterized by
an industrial sector that works at higher than international prices and a primary sector working at international prices. In what is referred to as an imbalanced
productive structure, because its prices are higher,
industry does not export unless there is an adequate
system of compensatory incentives.
     Furthermore, as industry grows it will require an
ever-increasing amount of foreign exchange for importing
raw materials, intermediate products, and capital goods.
By not exporting, industry leaves the generation of
foreign exchange to the primary sector, whose growth is
much slower than that of industry. At the initiation of
industrialization, import substitution economizes on
foreign exchange. However, the substitution process
becomes more and more sluggish, and at some stage the
savings made on foreign exchange are insufficient to
cope with industry's growing need for the same.
     Therefore, a mixed productive structure emerges
composed of two sectors. The industrial sector creates
jobs and grows rapidly. As it grows it requires more
and more foreign exchange to supply its raw materials and
capital goods. The other is the primary sector that,
because of its slower rate of growth, finds it more and
more difficult to supply the foreign currency needed by
the industrial sector. Sooner or later the reserves of
foreign exchange are exhausted, and the country is unable
to pay its foreign debt and to acquire the raw materials
and the intermediate and capital goods it needs to continue its economic activity.
     To avoid the paralysis of production, the government
resorts to foreign capital and credit. Contrary to what
is assumed, these funds are sought not to complement
national savings but to avoid a crisis in the balance of
payments, in the sense that they enter the country as
foreign exchange. However, as foreign indebtedness is
mainly incurred to finance expenditure in foreign
currency, we are dealing with a palliative measure that
merely prolongs the problem and at the same time worsens
it as the foreign debt and the interest services increase.
Thus, the need arises for even larger contributions in
order to maintain an equilibrium. The resulting accumulative foreign indebtedness always ends in a new crisis
in the balance of payments even more serious than the

one it was hoped to avoid.

This is the fundamental problem of all unbalanced productive structures, not only in Argentina but also in Chile, Colombia, Brazil, and so on: development in a situation where two different sectors exist, a primary sector working with international prices and an industrial sector working with higher than international prices; the impossibility of exporting on the part of the industrial sector; a higher rate of growth in this sector than in the primary one; the consequent disparity between the consumption of foreign exchange and the ability to produce it, and a recurrent tendency to disequilibrium on the part of the external sector. The tendency to palliate this imbalance in Argentina by means of foreign loans has, in the last two decades, led to an accumulative and permanent growth in the foreign debt and periodic crises in the balance of payments. From the time these crises have occurred, there have been many other upsets, such as huge devaluations, increased struggles for higher income, hyperinflation, and oscillating political changes.[4]

Orthodox Stabilization Programs: Phase One

In Argentina, the usual way of confronting crises in the balance of payments, and one that has traditionally been approved of both at the domestic level and internationally, coincides with the stabilization plans recommended by the IMF. The initial measure is always a devaluation of considerable proportions that, it is supposed, will be an incentive to export and to carry out import substitution in domestic production. However, considering that in Argentina the high prices of manufactures prevent the industrial sector from exporting (except in cases where there are special incentives) and that in general imports are indispensable products essential for continued productive activity, the main stimulating effect of a devaluation lies in its ability to motivate farming production and exports. However, as this effect takes some time even in the most favorable cases, it becomes necessary to resort to a balancing mechanism in the external sector. This mechanism is provided by the recession and induced by the devaluation itself.

To begin with, the devaluation raises the prices of exportable farming products and imported products, together with other costs and prices. In this way real wages are depreciated and revenue is transferred from the city to the countryside and from the industrial salaried sector to the rural landowners, thus reducing the buying power of the working class and lowering overall demand.

Furthermore, the government deliberately restricts money issue and the availability of credit, thus creating monetary illiquidity. As a result, there is a rise in

interest rates and once more the demand falls. In this
way, recession, which has already been induced by the
devaluation, is reinforced even more. Factories come to
a standstill, the need for the importation of raw
materials and capital goods is reduced, and the external
sector tends toward a low-level equilibrium as a result
of the overall reduction in the level of economic activity
and income.

This recession has also a second objective: to
assure continued incentives for farming production. For
these incentives to be maintained and to bear fruit, it
is necessary that the farming sector retain the relative
price advantages obtained as a result of the devaluation.
At the same time, for this to occur, real wages must not
be allowed to recuperate to their previous level. And
to keep real wages low, the recession must necessarily
continue.

Finally, the third objective of monetary restraint
and the consequent rise in domestic interest rates is the
creation of incentives for the massive entry of foreign
capital.

In conclusion, the balancing effect of stabilization
plans on the external sector occurs in the short run
through the reduction in imports and the flow of capital
from abroad and in the long run through the stimulation
of the farming sector by changes in relative prices in
favor of the same. The common denominator of these
three factors is that they all depend on the continuing
recessive domestic conditions.

The recessive nature of stabilization plans is the
cause of the difficulties that these same plans face.
Owing to social pressure, on one hand, and the technical
difficulties of maintaining the necessary monetary
restraint, on the other, the government--either voluntarily or involuntarily--ends up taking a number of
reactivating measures. Salaried workers begin to apply
pressure in an attempt to restore their level of income.
The same occurs in the industrial sector. The spiral of
costs and prices initiated by the devaluation is thus
complete. The balancing effect of the stabilizing plan
for the external sector disappears. To restore it the
government is forced to devaluate again, unleashing
another inflationary spiral. In this way, highly
virulent outbreaks of a special type of inflation occur
that are typical of Argentina and other primary exporting countries in the process of industrialization that
one of the authors (Diamond) called elsewhere exchange
rate inflation.[5]

Generally speaking, the inflation in Argentina has
been attributable to different causes and, at different
stages in its history, has had different driving forces.
However, the most virulent outbreaks have been derived
precisely from the attempts to solve the problem of the
external sector by means of heavy devaluations and the

consequent transfer of income to the farming sector. As resistance is met from the other sectors, this procedure leads to long periods of struggle for higher income, giving rise to rather violent inflationary phenomena that are very difficult to suppress. The most virulent inflation experienced in Argentina took place in 1959, 1962, 1971-72, 1975, and 1981, after very heavy devaluations that had been provoked by crises in the balance of payments. In each case, this was related to the aforementioned exchange-rate inflation.

In order to contain this type of spiral, the government is finally forced to delay the rate of the devaluation in relation to domestic prices, thus allowing a slow recuperation of income in the salaried industrial sector and allowing reactivation to be established. However, as the economy becomes reactivated, there is an increase in imports. Moreover, as the exchange rate is held back once more, the farming sector begins to lose its price advantage obtained through the initial devaluation. The only balancing mechanism that remains in the external sector, in principle, is the entry of capital and loans from abroad. Thus, sooner or later, these stabilization plans move from the first highly recessive stage to a second less recessive--or even extensive--stage, based on foreign indebtedness.

Stabilization Programs: Phase Two

To obtain the foreign loans needed by the country, the government usually resorts to inducing public and private companies to become indebted in foreign currency by means of attractive incentives. In the first phase of the stabilization programs, this maneuver is achieved by increasing the domestic rates of interest, which renders foreign credits more advantageous. However, this procedure is incompatible with the economic reactivation that is hoped to be achieved in the second phase of the plans, for if the interest rates are high in real terms, the recession will continue.

The solution to the dilemma lies in holding back devaluation in relation to domestic costs toward the end of the first stage of the stabilization programs. The consequent delay in the adjustment of the exchange rate has a highly stimulating effect on the entry of foreign capital. Normally it is thought that incentives directed toward foreign indebtedness are achieved by high real interest rates, taken as the difference between nominal rates and inflation. But this is not quite true: What are important are the nominal domestic rates, on one hand, and the interest rate for dollars abroad plus the devaluation rate, on the other. It is sufficient that there be a permanent holding back of devaluation in relation to domestic inflation for foreign borrowing to increase considerably, even where real interest rates are low or even negative.

It would therefore seem that a continued delay in adjusting the exchange rate would be the ideal remedy for external disequilibrium, that is, the ability to attract credit from abroad with no, or relatively few, recessive consequences. In order to continue benefiting from this effect, once the postponement of the adjustment of the exchange rate has begun during the transition from phase one to phase two, the government often tends to perpetuate it. In other words, a rate of devaluation that is slower than that of inflation is adopted. This technique encourages, in fact, the entry of foreign capital without the need for recession. But at the same time, it initiates a vicious circle of indebtedness that will inevitably lead to the final fall.

First, as time goes by, the initial structural external deficit grows, and with it the indebtedness necessary to compensate it. Then, there is the interest that increases the original deficit, making it necessary to incur even greater loans in order to service the debt. Second, the postponement in the adjustment to the exchange rate inhibits exports even further and encourages imports, thus increasingly deteriorating the trade balance and aggravating the initial external deficit.

Once initiated, this process of accumulative indebtedness is very hard to curb. The longer it goes on the greater the accumulated disequilibrium in the external sector and the need for new loans. The greater the need for these loans the more urgent it is to acquire compensatory capital and therefore to hold back the exchange rate adjustment in order to maintain the incentives that encourage the entry of such capital.

On the other hand, according to the traditional orthodox ideas that inspire these plans, the main cause of the whole problem of the countries like Argentina is their excessive protectionism and the development of presumably inefficient industries. Thus, while being momentarily in possession of an abundant supply of foreign exchange due to the entry of capital, the country is faced with considerable pressure to open up its economy. As a result, the degree of protection is reduced along with the occasional differential incentives for industrial exports. Although these measures are designed to increase industrial efficiency, in fact they have the opposite effect. They increase imports even more and exports decrease, which reinforces the effects achieved by the postponement of the exchange rate adjustments. The degree of industrial integration falls, whole sectors of activity disappear, and the productive apparatus is impaired. In general, the current account balance of payments becomes more and more unstable, and the foreign indebtedness required to compensate this is greater than what would have been needed had the policy of economic openness not been employed.

Lastly, in the advanced stages of this phase of orthodox stabilization plans, the situation worsens as a result of the growing number of people who begin transferring their savings abroad to protect themselves against an inevitable devaluation. As this flight of capital must also be compensated, the country must become more indebted. Thus, pressure is exerted mainly on the companies in the public sector to obtain foreign currency by becoming indebted. Finally, the whole process explodes, the chain of indebtedness is broken, and the magnitude of the accumulated external deficit becomes apparent, reflected in the total indebtedness, unleashing an even more serious crisis in the balance of payments than the one that initiated the stabilizing policy to begin with.

Occasionally events occur differently. When the recovery of exchange reserves during the first phase coincides with a favorable change in the terms of trade and with the coming into power of a populist party, conditions are created that favor an expansive phase that lasts only as long as the international reserves last.

On the other hand, it must be added that during this whole process, statistics show that there are two factors that are normally classified as decisive in the deterioration process of the external sector in countries like Argentina, but that do not appear to be significantly relevant. First, the well-known secular deterioration in the terms of trade cannot be proved with any certainty (at least in the case of Argentina), although what can in fact be observed is that, on a number of occasions, the terms of trade have been favorable for the country, as in 1979-80, for example. However, due to a lack of awareness of the foreign limitations described, the governments have never taken advantage of these situations to compensate for future deterioration. Second, remittances for royalties, dividends, and technology payments taken out by transnational companies for their head offices are not of a sufficiently significant magnitude to explain the recurrent crisis in the balance of payments faced by Argentina and all in all appear to be a lesser contributing factor.

THE ERA OF MARTINEZ DE HOZ

What has occurred in Argentina since 1976 coincides exactly with the outline described. Although Argentina's current foreign debt would appear to be partly due to the accumulative indebtedness of three decades, the greater part was incurred under Minister of Finance José Martinez de Hoz, who held that post between April 2, 1976, and March 29, 1981. More precisely, 64.4 percent of the foreign debt by the end of 1980 (three months before Martinez de Hoz left his job) was incurred from 1978 to 1980 (see Table 9.3). Apart from this, the subsequent increase in indebtedness is also attributable to his administration, because Martinez de Hoz's successors had no alternative but to postpone payments and allow the debt to increase even if this was only through the capitalization of interest that was impossible to pay.

Two clearly differentiated stages can be identified within the Martinez de Hoz management of Argentine finances. The first extended until the middle of 1978, which more or less corresponds to the description of phase one of the stabilization plans. The second, completed with his departure from the government in March 1981, evolved according to the indications for the usual second phase of these plans corresponding to the policy of accumulated indebtedness. It was within this period that the rapid growth in the foreign debt occurred.

The first phase of the stabilizing plan arose in response to the grave balance-of-payments crisis of 1975. Its equilibrating effect was very rapid, and by 1976 a marked recovery could already be observed in the balance-of-payments current account. From then on, until 1978, a growing current account surplus was registered. The foreign debt rose to US$4.6 billion during this period, if the whole of 1978 is included in this estimate, and to US$1.8 billion if 1976 and 1977 only are taken into account. This is a small figure if considered in the light of later events. Furthermore, this increase in the debt was compensated by a simultaneous rise in international reserves of nearly US$3.4 billion, to the extent that the Martinez de Hoz administration began 1978 with a surplus in the external sector.

The economic costs of this recovery were considerable. First of all, there was the usual recessionary effect. Therefore, apart from a brief period of economic expansion in the first half of 1977, during the first three years of the period there was virtual stagnation in the gross domestic product. There was also a slow drop in the contribution of industry to the GDP, which fell from 28.2 percent in 1974 to 25.3 percent in 1978 and continued to fall until it reached 22.4 percent in 1982.[6] Another significant occurrence was the growth in the participation of the services sector in the GDP, as a result of the expansion in the finance subsector.

The second adverse consequence was that the elimination of the disequilibrium in the external sector took place at the cost of a dramatic fall in real wages. Thus, the salaried sector's participation in income fell from 45 percent in 1975 to about 35 percent in the following three years. The decrease in real wages in 1976 may be estimated at about 40 percent.[7]

The third adverse consequence of this policy was the continued high rate of inflation that remained at around 170 percent per annum during 1977 and 1978. However, it did not reach the unprecedented 433 percent registered in 1976 as a result of the typically inflationary spiral that occurred after the great devaluations, in which the different sectors struggled to recuperate their share of income.

In order to curb this inflationary process, the government resorted to a number of measures without success. In 1976, during the first phase, wage freezes were imposed. But as the economy became reactivated, wage controls were exceeded in what were euphemistically called wage slides. In 1979, price controls were implemented but were also overrun. Finally, in the second half of 1977, the government applied even heavier monetary restraints, causing a spectacular rise in interest rates on short-term loans, which remained at a positive monthly real rate of about 4 to 6 percent for several months. This produced a fall in the GDP of no less than 11.6 percent from the third quarter of 1977 to the first quarter of 1978.

The 1978 Change in Course

After two years of the Martinez de Hoz administration, the government's economic team was in serious trouble. Its objective to balance the external sector had been achieved, but at the cost of an acute problem characteristic of recessive stabilization programs. Several years of very impoverished real wages ensued, together with overall economic stagnation, marked conflicts between the different economic sectors in the struggle for higher incomes and the consequent inflation of 170 percent per annum. The consecutive restraint measures applied to the distinct sectors to curb the inflationary spiral--wage and price controls and heavy recession--had exhausted their effect.

In the first half of 1978, as a result of this situation and of political pressure to increase real wages and reactivate the economy, the Martinez de Hoz administration underwent a substantial change. A preparatory measure that had been undertaken in phase one, consisting of an overall reduction in import tariffs, had been intended to be a gradual reform but in actual fact turned out to be rather hasty. This was brought about for two reasons. First, the reform consisted of a particularly exaggerated diagnosis of Argentina's ills, contemplated in terms of industrial inefficiency, which could be remedied through international competition. Second, it was intended that this foreign competition be used to fight inflation.

In mid-1978, the government made the crucial decision to hold back devaluation and tax increases in the public sector in relation to domestic costs, and thus began what we have called phase two of the stabilization plans. Toward the end of 1978, the plan was modified with the addition of a schedule, or rather an explicit program, according to which the government promised to undertake future devaluations at predetermined and decreasing rates. This was justified by the need to increasingly support international competition and involved a double balance-of-payments objective from the monetary point of view: to intensify the presumed efficiency measure of tariff reduction, on one hand, and to curb the rise in domestic prices, on the other, thus provoking a slow descent in the rate of inflation until the programmed decreased rate of inflation was reached.

Unfortunately, the plan had been inspired by a particularly simplistic view of the Argentine economy. To begin with, even with the reduction in tariffs, only a small part of the economy was exposed to foreign competition. Neither services, the liberal professions, nor the construction and foodstuffs industries were exposed to commercial and financial intermediation. About half of the industrial sector was left unexposed due to the existence of certain inherently protective privileges: high transport costs, difficulties in packaging, the perishable nature of certain goods, restrictive administrative and health regulations, and the need for supplies in close proximity in order to produce custom orders, to produce parts and spare parts for certain domestic industrial models, and to carry out maintenance. Lastly, traditional farming activities, although in principle exposed to foreign competition, were faced with a marked rise in international prices, which neutralized any curbing effect that the post-ponement of the exchange-rate adjustment might have had on domestic prices.

All in all, foreign competition affected only the exposed part of industry, whereas the prices in the non-exposed sector continued to rise at a much faster rate than that of the devaluation as there was nothing to curb them. As this sector exerted pressure on the labor market, it also brought about wage increases far greater than the rate of devaluation. Meanwhile, the exposed sector, whose prices were restricted to the rate of devaluation, was under pressure because of the increased costs of inputs bought from the unexposed sector: services and labor.

The result was a rate of inflation several points above that of devaluation. This rate was not uniform because the increases in the unexposed sector were very much higher than the average rate of inflation, and the increases in the exposed sector were very much lower.

The expected convergence did not occur and the adjustment of exchange rate continued to be postponed. The consequences of this accumulated lack of protection were very serious. In 1978, no productive activity worked with profit margins wide enough to resist two years of increases of costs of several points per month that could not be transferred on to prices. Consequently, the profits of activities directly exposed to inflation dropped until they were eventually converted into losses. The final stage of the process was massive decapitalization. Many production lines were abandoned, and manufacturing plants closed down or even went bankrupt. The shutdown process has not extended even more because of the extremely high cost and irreversible nature of closing down a manufacturing plant. This has led many businesses to opt to continue accumulating their losses rather than paying off employees, in the hopes that the situation would improve.

The counterpart of the sectorial deterioration described was to be seen at a more general level in the growing deficit in the balance of payments on current account, due to the continued increase in imports, tourist spending abroad, the massive flight of capital toward the end of the period, and a relatively lower rate of growth in exports.

This deficit was compensated for by short-term loans, the indebtedness of public and private businesses, and the entry of foreign funds for deposit in Argentine currency in the domestic banking system. The incentive was provided by a combination of moderately positive real rates of interest and the unrealistic rates of exchange. Thus, the invisibles in the balance of payments--noncompensatory capital entry--began to grow. In this way the balance of payments maintained its equilibrium from the point of view of the growing national reserves and the large amounts of foreign currency available for imports, trips abroad, and other transactions. The rapid growth of the foreign debt went unnoticed at that time because of the delay in the elaboration and publication of the corresponding statistics and the inefficient method used by the Banco Central to carry out that job.

The study undertaken by Antonio Lopez,[8] based on the official figures supplied by the Banco Central, reflects the course of the balance of payments from 1976 to 1981 through the disaggregation of data. This permits identification of the negative results of the combination of tariff and exchange-rate policies followed after the change of course in 1978. If one follows the path of the foreign debt as it appears in Table 9.4, one can see that in the triennium of 1976-1978, there was an increase in the debt of only US$1.438 billion as opposed to the US$18.594 billion that accumulated during the triennium of 1979-1981.[9] Because during most of the second triennium the international prices for products exported

Table 9.4 Argentina: Balance of Payments for the 1976-1981 Period (in millions of current U.S. dollars)

| | Triennium | | Total |
	1976/1978	1979/1981	1976/1981
1. Trade balance	4,939.2	-1,706.8	3,232.4
2. Tourism: travel and expenses (net)	-314.0	-4,152.7	-4,466.7
3. Royalties	-191.4	-593.4	-784.8
4. Services (net)	992.9	2,548.9	3,541.8
5. Profits and dividends	-511.6	-1,746.5	-2,258.1
6. Interest (net)	-1,240.2	-4,404.6	-5,644.8
7. Unilateral transfers	98.2	35.5	133.7
8. Non-disaggregated capital outflow (net)	-405.9	-9,245.4	-9,651.3
9. Adjustments due to changes in parity of the dollar or other currency	158.9	-444.3	-285.4
10. Statistical errors and omissions	-74.1	-298.4	-372.5
11. Accumulated result for the balance of payments	3,452.0	-20,007.7	-16,555.7
12. Export financing	527.3	-746.9	-219.6
13. Accumulated increase in the foreign debt	1,438.0	18,594.4	20,032.4
14. Accumulated variation in international reserves	5,417.3	-2,160.2	3,257.1

Note: (1) through (13): The positive figures refer to foreign currency inflow, the negative to outflow.
(14): The positive figures refer to increases in reserves; the negative indicate decreases.

Source: Antonio López, based on Banco Central de la República Argentina figures.

by Argentina, mainly meat and grain, remained at high
real levels, the deterioration in the trade balance over
this period was not worse.

The presence of a negative balance despite the high
prices of Argentine exports can be explained by several
concurrent developments. First, there was the sharp
increase in imports, which tripled from 1978 to 1980 (an
increase of 175 percent in current dollars). This was
due mainly to the importation of unnecessary or luxury
consumptive goods. Thus, for example, consumer goods,
almost all of which face a competitive national market
in the case of Argentina, went from 2.2 percent of total
exports in 1976 to 17.6 percent in 1980. A similar
phenomenon occurred in intermediate and capital-goods
sectors, where the increase was accounted for by products
that had replaced local production. Second, expenditure
on tourism abroad was unprecedented, going from US$314
million in the 1976-1978 triennium to US$4.2 billion
during 1978-1981. Third, there was a sharp increase in
the area of "nonindividual capital outflow," which
accounted for the total sum of US$9.2 billion in invest-
ments and financial remittances abroad, made possible by
the absolutely free exchange that prevailed up until the
last few months of 1981.

The increase in exports was much less than the increase in the expenditure of foreign exchange. The
positive effect of the high international prices obtained
for traditional exports was counteracted by the delays
in the adjustment of the rate of exchange. As regards
nontraditional exports, owing to this delay and the reduction in a number of incentives for the sake of
"efficiency," both industrial and agro-industrial
exports slowly came to a standstill.

The flow of short-term credit to private and state
businesses, whose foreign indebtedness was encouraged
to cover the growing foreign deficit on current account,
was responsible for the high increase in interest payments of US$1.2 billion in the first triennium of the
political administration to US$4.4 billion in the second.

The figures for the uses of foreign exchange are
even more dramatic if one considers that the total
foreign debt, considered correct by the Banco Central
and based upon its surveys on the final stocks of the
debt, is US$7.7 billion higher than the previous figures
based on the balance-of-payments registers. This means
that the outflow of foreign currency over this period,
shown in the accounts of the balance of payments, is also
underestimated by US$7.7 billion. If this figure is
compared with estimates based on the observation of
reality, one may assume that this additional outflow was
partly due to increased outflow of capital, partly to
increased spending on the part of tourists going abroad,
and partly to higher interest rates.

To sum up, Argentina's indebtedness arose as a result of increased imports, increased tourism, the flight of capital, and interest service. In a number of other countries (such as Brazil, for example), most of the indebtedness was produced by the deterioration in the terms of trade resulting from the rise in oil prices. In Argentina, however, a country that imports virtually no oil and enjoyed high prices for its farming products during the Martinez de Hoz period just analyzed, the terms of trade were rather favorable.

For this reason, Argentina's foreign debt is less attributable to the adverse international situation than is that of other countries. This is so only in the sense that the deterioration in the terms of trade in the years following the demise of the Martinez de Hoz administration was felt with the fall in nontraditional exports, which was not attributable to the reduction in domestic incentives, but rather to the closure of markets and increased protectionism on a world scale. Also, the rise in world real interest rates caused an increase in the cost of servicing the debt as from 1980.

Neither can it be argued that Argentina became indebted in order to grow or to increase its productive efficiency. On the contrary, Argentina became indebted to finance with foreign currency a policy of economic openness that resulted in the massive destruction of its productive capacity and the disintegration of its industrial production, a huge technological step backward owing to the closing down of industrial laboratories, design departments, and so on; a massive desubstitution of imports; and the loss of foreign markets for its exports. In short, this policy on the whole led to a general economic crisis and an unprecedented setback in production and the living standards.

The main effect of the international situation on the Argentine crisis was more indirect. On one hand, the almost unlimited availability of credit from international banks made it easier to become indebted and encouraged irresponsible behavior on the part of the local authorities. On the other hand, the worldwide spread of orthodox doctrines in general, particularly the financial approach to the balance-of-payments problems, had a drastic impact on South America. It permitted the international banks to rationalize and justify the massive recycling of funds at their disposal, thus offering international respectability to the promoters of Argentine domestic orthodoxy.

The End of a Dream

By 1980 it began to be obvious that the Martinez de Hoz administration was leading the economy into a

blind alley. If the rate of devaluation were to increase
in order to set the Argentine currency at a level that
would counteract the deterioration in the balance of
payments, it would immediately curb the inflow of short-
term foreign capital, provoke its massive exodus, and
make the crisis in the external sector even more marked.
If the currency were to be devalued sharply, it would
provoke the transfer of income to the agro-exporting
sector, an effect typical of stabilization plans that,
to work, must be accompanied by a policy of monetary
restraint and renewed recession. If the exchange-rate
adjustment delay were to continue, capital would continue
to flow into the country but at the expense of a growing
deterioration in the different sectors in the country,
due to competition from imported products and the increased difficulty in exporting. This, in turn, would
accentuate even more the disequilibrium in the balance of
payments on current account.

Furthermore, as the domestic interest rates were
linked to the expected future movements in the rate of
exchange, the adverse expectations caused by the postponement in the adjustments to the rate of exchange caused
the interest rates to remain very high. Thus, the unsustainable financial costs incurred by the country's
productive sector were accentuated. In short, the
economic policy moved toward a deadend and therefore
posed a dilemma in which every alternative would be
disastrous.

Toward the middle of 1980, one of the authors wrote,

from a general point of view, the situation
still remains unsolved. The triple dilemma
caused by the need to put an end to the postponement of the exchange rate adjustment, to
continue to encourage foreign investment and
maintain a reasonable level of activity is
still evident. Any two of these three
objectives may be easily achieved. But to
achieve all three at the same time would be
extremely difficult, particularly within the
framework of the self-restraint measures imposed
by the present government.

A chain is only as strong as its weakest
link. The postponement of the adjustment in
the exchange rate will have to be stopped
eventually, the incentives for foreign investment must be maintained, and therefore the
only adjustable variable that remains is the
level of activity. Sooner or later the process
will lead inevitably to renewed recession, the
severity of which will depend on the flexibility
of the economic measures to be employed from
now on.[10]

Unfortunately, the flexible use of economic measures did not occur. The only defense mechanism available in the face of the balance-of-payments problem was the monetary policy to be applied to the situation in the external sector. So, in the light of the ever-increasing skepticism as to the continuing of the current process, the demand for funds (necessary to settle foreign debts) in the local financial market grew more and more, causing the real interest rates paid and collected by the finance system to increase continually. In December 1980, three months prior to the change in the Ministry of Finance administration, the current interest was at a monthly rate of 7 percent. Taking into account a monthly rate of inflation of nearly 4 percent, that rate was equivalent in real terms to 3 percent per month accumulative, or 42 percent per annum. Given the low rate of devaluation at that time, this interest rate meant about 5 percent interest per month for the dollar--in other words, about 80 percent profit for investments made in dollars.

In February 1981, the monthly current interest rate rose to a nominal 9 percent. In a desperate attempt to find a way out, Martinez de Hoz devalued the peso 10 percent just two months prior to the end of his term. This turned out to be a disastrous measure, for although the magnitude of the devaluation was insufficient to calm apprehension, the mere fact that there had been a devaluation that had violated the commitments assumed with the devaluations schedule published earlier implied a death blow to the house of cards on which the Martinez de Hoz policy was built. During the last two months of his financial administration, the tension in the money market grew more and more, and current rates of interest rose to around 16 percent per month for the leading companies.

THE NEW CRISIS IN THE BALANCE OF PAYMENTS

The rise to power of Lorenzo Sigaut occurred in the midst of a violent slide in the exchange rate. This apparently conjunctural movement reflected a serious crisis in the balance of payments, a disintegrated financial system, and a stagnant, partly destroyed system of production. Added to this critical domestic inheritance there was the aggravation of the international situation: the worldwide rise in real interest rates, the worsening international recession, and the fall in the prices for Argentine exports. Lastly, the ease with which international credit had been made available (since the oil crisis) also began to diminish as the international banking system began to realize that the debts of the developing countries were far greater than their capacity to pay. In other words, the increased difficulty

in obtaining credit when it was most needed was added to
the other problems the new minister of finance had to
face.

The first measure undertaken by the Ministry of
Finance under the new head was a devaluation of 30 percent. After this inevitable devaluation, there were two
possible courses to follow. The first was to introduce
once more an orthodox stabilization program, this time
even more severe than the one in 1976 and assuming the
consequences of the recession as well as the drop in real
wages that it implied. The other alternative was to
attempt to solve the external-sector deficit by avoiding,
or at least attenuating as much as possible, these
recessive and regressive effects. However, the election
of this second course of action implied renouncing the
balancing effect of the recession on the external sector
and made it essential to substitute for this other
equivalent measures capable of stimulating in a more
direct way the generation and saving of foreign exchange.
In actual fact, as we will see, it became necessary to
become highly selective in import substitution, and the
ministry, in giving its active support, had to provide
definite incentives to encourage the exportation of
industrial goods, establish marginal incentives to
increase farming production, and, finally, establish
some sort of control over the exchange-rate system or at
least a dual rate of exchange, one for financial
transactions and one for trade.

The new financial administration took a very in-
coherent course. While following the orthodox policy,
not only did it avoid taking any direct action in the
external sector, but at the height of the crisis and
following the steps of the Martinez de Hoz administration, it also proceeded to implement efficiency measures.
Thus, the devaluation was accompanied by a reduction in
import tariffs and tax refunds for exports, which partly
counteracted the effect of the measure. This, along with
the tremendous inertia that existed in traditional exports and imports (in the latter case because of the
large number of binding contracts taken out by importers
through irrevocable letters of credit), prevented
exports from increasing with any celerity and failed to
inhibit imports, thus maintaining the disequilibrium in
the balance of trade. However, in contrast to the
government's orthodox treatment of the exchange and
taxation measures, it adopted a lenient attitude toward
wage increases and liquidity, which counteracted the re-
distributive and recessive effects of the devaluation.
Consequently, a galloping "exchange-rate inflation" such
as that described earlier was unleashed at a rate almost
double that of the inflation that had existed prior to
March 1981.

The rapid rise in domestic costs and prices in
response to the devaluations foretold the need for

further devaluations. Pessimistic expectations regarding future exchange-rate stability sustained the heavy demand for foreign currency for settling loans, thus contributing to the flight of capital. In response to the continued foreign-exchange disequilibirum, in May 1981 the current interest rates remained at 12 percent per month (approximately 4 percent in real terms).

At the beginning of June, another devaluation of 30 percent was inevitable and provided new impetus to exchange-rate-induced inflation. At the end of June, the demand coming from the financial sector made another devaluation of 30 percent necessary. All in all, in the first six months of the crisis, the accumulated devaluation of the peso against the commercial dollar reached 125 percent, and the devaluation in the case of the financial dollar was about 228 percent. During that same half of the year, inflation reached 60 percent compared to the rate of 35 percent for the previous six-month period.

Inflation was not as high as it might have been, because with the third devaluation the government finally authorized a double parity of the exchange market and established a financial dollar that fluctuated freely and a commercial dollar set at a lower rate that required periodic adjustment depending on the rate of inflation. The aim of this measure, which would have helped to control the crisis if it had been applied from the start, was to dissociate as far as possible domestic costs and prices and the devaluations produced by the financial imbalance.

It is important to keep in mind that the great demand in the financial exchange market was due to the fact that only part of the accumulated short-term foreign debt was payable on demand. In fact, one of the most important measures adopted was that of heavily subsidized exchange insurance for those with debts in dollars, on the condition that loans be renewed for a period of no less than a year. As a result of this measure, the government managed to postpone a short-term debt of about US$5 billion until the second half of 1982.

When Sigaut was replaced by Roberto Alemann with General Galtieri's takeover from President Viola, a change took place: A much more coherent orthodox and recessive stabilization plan was adopted. Thus, the exchange market was united once more, which implied a devaluation of 30 percent in the commercial rate of exchange. At the same time, a new "efficiency" reduction in the nontraditional export incentives, in keeping with this orthodox approach, was undertaken. There was an increase in value-added taxes; the nontaxable income floor was frozen; and the money circulation (M_1) was reduced by 20.8 percent in nominal terms from January to March 1982. Wages were frozen in the public sector, along with retirement funds and pensions, and wage increases in the

private sector were discouraged. The recession worsened
and domestic consumption fell 10.6 percent between the
first and second quarter of 1982. The real wages of the
private sector, which in December 1981 were 20 percent
below the average for 1970-1975, were reduced a further
15 percent in the first quarter of 1982, while the
remunerations in the public sector fell about 22 percent
in real terms.[11]

Despite the fact that exports decreased as a result
of the fall in international prices for farm products,
the situation in the external sector improved as a result
of a considerable decrease in imports. The recession
caused these to drop during the first quarter of the year
to almost half that of the same period of 1981. The
entry of new capital also contributed to this situation,
reaching a positive balance of US$450 million in the first
quarter of 1982.[12] However, the improvement gained at
the expense of the recession by no means implied that it
would be possible to pay the foreign public debt that,
with amortizations and interest to be paid that year,
reached the sum of US$12 to 15 billion. With this it
was clear that it was absolutely essential for talks to
be commenced regarding the refinancing of the debt.

However, on April 2, 1982, the armed conflict with
Great Britain arose and had serious repercussions on the
crisis in the external sector. To begin with, it led to
the suspension of payments to British banks. This
measure, taken in reprisal for the blocking of Argentine
funds in the United Kingdom, also reduced the short-term
inflow of foreign capital to zero. In the face of the
emergency, control of the rate of exchange was introduced. Considerable delays in the settlement of Argentina's debts that had arisen from imports were produced.
Unpaid letters of credit began to accumulate. Importers
began to have more and more difficulty in obtaining
foreign credit.

During this period the information available concerning Argentina's position on its foreign debt was very
confused and sometimes even contradictory. According to
foreign newspapers at that time, the country failed to
pay part of its foreign obligations in order to cover
the interests alone, which it also paid late. Nevertheless, the syndicated debts due to British banks continued
to be paid, although perhaps with some delay and only
partially. The policy was that the amounts to be paid
to these banks be deposited in the New York branch of the
Banco de la Nación Argentina, the non-British banks being
paid according to the percentage of their participation
in these syndicated credits. Apparently the aim was to
show the international banks that it was Argentina's
intention to pay its debts at all cost and that it did in
fact have the money to pay the British banks. The blocking of payments to Great Britain caused an initial conflict between Argentina and foreign banks because the

latter, through an agreement to share losses and gains
with the British banks, also shared the payments by
Argentina, and it was their intention that these funds be
refunded.

On May 18, 1982, an article in the New York Times
published declarations made by new Minister of Finance
Roberto Alemann to the effect that Argentina intended to
substitute a medium-term debt for its short-term maturity
debts of US$3.5 billion. The article gave the impression
that these debts were in fact refinanced. During the
same period, Alemann made public the assurances made by
the U.S. bankers that they would continue to refinance
Argentina with short-term credit until the end of the war
in the South Atlantic. Lastly, in Wall Street Journal,
on June 21, 1982, the opinion was that "technically
Argentina has suspended payments."

The political crisis that arose as a result of the
military defeat that culminated in the fall of Galtieri
put an end to the management of the Ministry of Finance
by Alemann. At that moment, in the second quarter of
1982, the country's GDP stood as low as that of 1973, and
the GDP per capita was 12 percent lower than that in
1973. The situation was characterized by very low wages,
high unemployment, the largest foreign debt in the
country's history, a negative balance on current account
despite the heavy recession, and huge private business
indebtedness.

An Attempt to Change Course

During the first few days of July 1982, José María
Dagnino Pastore became the new minister of finance, and
the young economist Domingo Cavallo took control of the
Banco Central. In the following months, the latter was
to wield almost as much power as the minister himself.
On the initiative of Cavallo, the first attempt to undertake a drastic change in the course of the economic policy
was made. The priorities were to reactivate the productive capacity and to refinance and settle the high
business liabilities that were impossible to pay and that
accumulated during the progressive indebtedness incurred
by the private sector during the crisis.

To achieve the reactivation of the economy and the
settlement of debts, a financial reform was introduced
that included a considerable reduction in the interest
rates paid on short-term deposits by the banks (to
negative real levels). It also included granting a
certain amount of preferential credit to the private
sector at these lowered interest rates. At the same
time, the refinancing of business liabilities was undertaken also at these preferential rates, in pesos as well
as in foreign currency.

These measures were accompanied by a number of steps designed to alleviate the situation in the external sector and allow the intended economic expansion. The measures introduced included another change in the dual exchange rate: a devaluation of nearly 30 percent in the commercial exchange rate, tempered by some retentions of foreign exchange entering for traditional exports, together with the establishing of a floating financial and services exchange-rate market. At the same time, to relieve the burden of the heavy demand on the financial market, the Banco Central reestablished exchange insurance for credit that was to be renewed for more than one year and also authorized "swaps." The settlement of overdue foreign debts through governmental foreign-exchange bonds provided for this purpose by the Banco Central at a subsidized exchange rate was also authorized. Lastly, the disposal on the financial market of part of the foreign currency obtained as payment for industrial exports was approved.

As regards the domestic market, the reduction in the rates of interest was responsible for some savings being used in the acquisition of goods. This effectively reactivated the economy. Unfortunately, it also channeled a considerable part of the funds into the exchange market, either directly or indirectly.

The immediate impact was manifested by the rapidly broadening gap between the financial dollar and the commercial dollar, to the extent that in a very short time the difference between the two was 75 percent. Meanwhile, the devaluation of the commercial dollar, along with the rise in the financial and services dollar (due to its impact on transport, interest payments, and so on), produced severe inflation that rose to around 15 percent per month. Owing to the progressive reduction in liquidity due to inflation and to the progressive shrinkage in the preferential credit, the initial re-activating effect was slowly lost.

As far as the other objective is concerned--the settlement of the private-sector debt--this was achieved by a heavy transfer of revenue to the indebted sector at negative real interest rates. Without going into an analysis of the costs and benefits of this transfer to the economy as a whole, it undoubtedly made possible the survival of a great number of enterprises that, under the previous conditions, had been destined to disappear.

The Dagnino Pastore-Cavallo experiment was cut short by the resignation of Dagnino Pastore and the elimination of both officials just a few days before the annual assembly of the IMF and the World Bank, which took place in Toronto in September 1982.

REFINANCING

Dagnino Pastore was replaced by Jorge Wehbe, who assumed office in the midst of total political debilitation of the armed forces and a strong fight of many civilian sectors for participation in the severely diminished income resulting from the continual recessive policies implemented to stabilize the external sector and curb inflation. Wehbe also faced the task of initiating formal renegotiation of the foreign debt. Up until that moment, the dramatic problem of the debt had never really been confronted. The country's reaction was limited, on one hand, to the encouragement of all possible means of postponing payments or to measures that would attract more short-term capital, almost without heed to its cost. Thus, the Argentine government, which for the sake of presumed increased efficiency scrimped on tax resources for years when in fact moderate state support through the right channels would have been sufficient to obtain foreign exchange at reasonable terms, was forced to incur monstrous expenditure merely to postpone maturities. On the other hand, in many instances Argentina simply suspended payments on its debts without going into any formal renegotiation.

This proverbial attitude of hiding one's head in the sand to avoid facing a problem was due to the politically delicate nature of everything related to the foreign debt. First, the fact that the debt had been acquired to finance destructive efficiency policies, along with the squandering of foreign currency, created strong resistance to any official discussion related to payments, for to admit publicly that debt payments were overdue would have been considered a confirmation of the inadequacy of the policy that had led to the indebtedness.

Second, the inexact account of the foreign debt on the part of the Banco Central, and the fact that the figures taken from surveys did not coincide with the balance-of-payments registers, created doubts as to the real magnitude of the debt and also the legitimacy of the figures supposed to be owed by the private sector.

The third political obstacle took the form of resistance to the intervention of the International Monetary Fund in the renegotiations, a condition that is usually insisted upon by foreign banks. Through Argentina's repeated experience in agreements with the Fund (nine standby agreements have been subscribed to in the course of the country's history), there was ample knowledge of the recessive conditions brought about the the same, which fostered the strong political resistance to any commitments being made with that institution.

The last political obstacle was the armed dispute with the United Kingdom. While the conflict continued it made all open talks regarding the debt impossible.

Even when it was over, it made discussion difficult because the private international banking institutions,
as a prerequisite for any negotiation, insisted that
there be a formal declaration on the cessation of hostilities and the lifting of economic sanctions against
British business--once again a very delicate political
issue.
However, the delay in payments continued, and as
more debts matured, formal negotiation became inevitable.
So Wehbe decided to take advantage of his visit to the
Toronto IMF annual meeting to begin the first explicit
talks with the international banks and the IMF concerning
the renegotiations.
The first step taken by the Argentine government was
to fulfill the banking institutions' prerequisite regarding the termination of hostilities with Great Britain.
Nevertheless, due to the reasons already mentioned, the
political atmosphere as regards the problem of the debt
continued to be highly explosive. It is for this reason
that all negotiations from September 1982 onward have
been undertaken in a highly reserved manner. The terms,
amount, and conditions of the renovations; the talks with
the IMF; the alternatives; and so on have been surrounded
by an aura of mystery. Information has been fragmentary,
and in order to reconstruct the whole picture, it is
often necessary to resort to information provided by the
international press and to work with a number of con-
jectures. The following is an attempt to explain the outcome of the reconstruction of that stage of negotiations.

The Negotiations

    In general, four different courses of action can be
differentiated in the talks. The first was the negotiation of a standby credit with the Fund, granted not so
much because of the magnitude of the debt but rather
because it meant the green light--a kind of good conduct
certificate for the country--that opened up the way to
refinancing by the private banks. The second aspect
concerned relatively small auxiliary credit from private
banks, destined to finance interest payments while
negotiations regarding the principal of the debt continued. The third aspect was the negotiation of the debt
of the companies of the public sector with the international banks. The fourth aspect was the renewed
postponement of payments on all short-term revolving
credit of the private sector obtained through "swaps"
or as a result of successive postponements obtained
since 1981 with exchange insurance.
The talks with the Fund were undertaken in accordance with the established norms and with the utmost
discretion up to the point at which the Memorandum of
Agreement made with the Fund (signed on January 7, 1983)

was published on March 11, 1983, by La Prensa, a daily
newspaper in Buenos Aires, along with an article entitled
"Objectives and Strategy for Economic Recovery." The
conditions set by this agreement were of three kinds.
The first referred to the targets of the external sector.
Definite limits were established for the deficit in the
balance of payments measured in terms of changes in net
international reserves, which up until 1984 were not to
fall more than US$5 billion. The acceptable delays
in foreign payments were defined and the settlements were
to be made before June 30, 1983.

The second type of conditions covered the measures
introduced to reduce overall demand. In this case, the
public-sector deficit and monetary expansion were strictly
limited, if annual inflation was not to exceed 160 percent. Based on this assumption and using restrictive
criteria, the permitted monetary expansion was calculated.

Lastly, the third kind of conditions referred to the
elimination of limiting measures related to the external
sector. Thus, Argentina agreed to impose no new
restrictions on imports and to progressively do away
with the existing ones. Essentially it was agreed to
rescind the decision that prevented payments to be made
for imports before 180 days. Another agreement involved
new steps toward a liberalization and unification of the
exchange system, which would reverse the dual parity of
the exchange rate and the restrictions established during
the Dagnino Pastore-Cavallo term. Also, without assuming
any other commitment in this case, Argentina agreed to
review its system of export incentives. A final rather
decorative ingredient, related to the substantive
measures proposed, was the manifested intention to attain
a 5 percent growth in the gross domestic product
during 1983.

The first fruit of the negotiation with the Fund was
an agreement by which a standby loan of US$2.15 billion,
to be spread over a given period, was granted as compensation for diminished exports. The loan was to be
delivered in full by March 1984, the latest date set for
the newly elected government to assume power.

From partial information that exists concerning
these loans, it can be deduced that by September 1983
US$560 million in IMF loans for diminished exports and
two standby tranches of approximately US$318 million
each entered the country. Apart from this, the progress
made in the negotiations with the Fund opened the doors
to auxiliary credit from the international banks, which
was to be used for the payment of interest and to service
the outstanding debt that had been pending since April
1982.

For this purpose a bridge loan of US$1.1 billion,
signed on December 30, 1982, was obtained, and the first
two installments were made with no problem. According
to the newspaper Clarín of September 13, 1983,

"originally the loan was not to be refinanced or postponed, and its gradual amortization was directly tied to
the payment of funds from the above-mentioned IMF standby credit." At the same time, it was agreed that, in
principle, a medium-term loan of US$1.5 billion would be
granted in three installments, the objective being also
to aid the payment of interest and outstanding amortizations.

However, trouble arose with the payment of the last
installment of the bridge credit and the whole of the
medium-term credit. To begin with, after March 1982
Argentina had fallen behind in the payment of some
interest. The lending banks demanded that these payments
be brought up to date before they would disburse the last
installment of the bridge credit, thus creating a vicious
circle: Argentina had insufficient funds to pay the
interest, and the new funds were withheld until these
interests were paid. Finally, according to the July 1,
1983, edition of the New York Times, it was to have been
agreed that Argentina would not receive US$300 million
of the last bridge credit installment, diverting it
directly to the payment of the interest owed in May. It
was added that the operation was part of a new agreement
concerning the medium-term credit of US$1.5 billion that
had been agreed upon beforehand but had not been disbursed. In fact, by September this loan had still not
been handed over. This time the problem arose because
the lending banks insisted on a modification to Argentine
law that placed foreign lenders on an equal standing with
the local lenders. This modification in the legislation
finally came through. But even this was not enough to
overcome all the obstacles, for the banks insisted that
renegotiation be completed previously with Aerolineas
Argentinas and other state enterprises.

As was said before, one of the largest portions of
Argentina's foreign debt is that of state enterprises,
whose maturities in 1982 and 1983 totaled approximately
US$7 billion. It would therefore seem reasonable that
the lending banks should demand the renegotiation of the
capital debt before disbursing further credit. However,
it is sufficient to take into account the conditions set
by the lending banks for renegotiation for this
impression of their reasonableness to be erased. These
conditions included such abusive demands as interest
rates set 2.125 points above LIBOR; a commission at over
1.125 percent; very high additional moratory interest in
the case of default; the global guarantee that the term
default apply to all state enterprises, or the state itself, when any one of them falls behind in its payments;
an explicit renunciation of all efforts on the part of
the state or its enterprises to defend itself from any
embargo whatsoever; the obligation to provide detailed
information to the lenders regarding the economic performance of the state and its enterprises; and other

similar conditions applied to a country manifesting a genuine intention to pay its debts. The cut of the remainder of the credit already agreed upon to a lesser amount, credit which was vital to a country on the verge of a suspension of payments, and the taking advantage of the needs of that country in order to obtain a signed contract reinforce the impression of abuse.

Lastly, this impression is confirmed when the restrictions imposed on the country through the agreement are examined: To fail to provide the information agreed upon implied the suspension of payments; to question or argue about any of the clauses of the agreement in the future implied the suspension of payments; the withdrawal of IMF support also implied suspension of payments. In other words, to adopt an economic policy approved by the IMF implied that the repayment of the debt might be demanded immediately, along with the payment of moratory interest.

Despite the strong opposition from the state enter-prises, reluctant to sign such an agreement, the govern-ment backed down and approved a general agreement for state enterprises in accordance with the lenders' demands. The first concrete agreement was signed with Aerolineas Argentinas.

However, the troubles were still not over. The publication of this agreement caused a strong generalized public reaction that called for the intervention of federal judge Pinto Kramer. Kramer's basic objection was to the submission to the jurisdiction of the New York courts, as convened in the signed agreement (which paradoxically was probably the least serious of the conditions). First he ordered the government not to proceed with the renewal of other pending contracts; later he nullified the agreement already signed with Aerolineas Argentinas; finally he detained the president of the Banco Central, Jorge Gonzalez del Solar, on charges of having apparently failed to fulfill his official obligations in this respect.

On hearing this news the lending banks not only decided to suspend the first installment of the medium-term credit once more but also to suspend the whole credit operation with Argentina. The International Monetary Fund, which had suspended the payment of the third installment because of its inconformity with the fulfillment of the clauses of the standby credit, main-tained the suspension. While the government appealed the orders of the judge, the Banco Central suspended the delivery of new import permits and the delivery of foreign currency to travelers. Financial panic ensued. This was the situation at the beginning of October 1983 at the time of this writing.

Furthermore, even though this conflict were to be solved, there is another problem that must not be ignored, about which there is very little information. This is the exchange insurance and "swap" operations, which totaled US$7 billion. These debts were assumed by the state and postponed unilaterally until 1985 or 1986, the corresponding promissory notes being handed over to the foreign lenders. However, rumor has it that there is dis- agreement as to the conditions of the rollover established by the Argentine government.

An attempt to estimate Argentina's overall commit- ments shows about US$2.8 billion that must be paid in interest and amortizations on loans that matured in 1982; US$7 billion in outstanding private debts or debts due to be paid in 1982 for exchange insurance and "swaps"; nearly US$7 billion in capital debts by public enter- prises due in 1983; and interest that must be paid on debts maturing after 1983, on debts that were refinanced in 1983, and on outstanding debts. All in all, accord- ing to different national and foreign publications, this amounts to a total of about US$21 billion.

This commitment made it necessary to obtain re- financing with foreign resources to the sum of US$17.65 billion, to be divided into the US$3.65 billion that Wehbe hoped to obtain from the IMF and the private inter- national banking institutions, on one hand, and US$14 billion to refinance "swaps," exchange insurance, and the debts of public enterprises. Lastly, it was hoped that approximately US$3.35 billion more would be obtained to pay the remainder, most of which was interest on debts that were either due, outstanding, or refinanced. With this, the above-mentioned US$21 billion would be covered. The US$3.35 billion would be obtained from the expected trade balance surplus and possibly through an additional loan for a much lesser amount, as the agreement with the Fund included restrictions regarding the taking out of further foreign loans. As funds were also needed almost immediately to cover needs until the arrival of the US$3.65 billion, it became necessary to resort to the aforementioned bridge loan of US$1.1 billion and to funds from the BIS estimated at US$650 million.

However, as has been shown, the refinancing plan for the debts was only partially fulfilled due to the increasing difficulties that arose. In Table 9.5, the very small contribution registered so far during Wehbe's term can be seen as regards the obtaining of US$5.4 billion of the aforementioned foreign funds.

To sum up, after two and a half years of crisis, the situation in the fall of 1983 continued unstable. Maturities were not being paid on time, and the problem was being handled on the basis of last-minute decisions made under pressure, amid an atmosphere of conflict and considerable uncertainty and anxiety.

Table 9.5   Argentina: Estimate of Loans Applied for and Received
During 1983 (millions of U.S. dollars)

Item	Amount Requested	Entry[a]
Bridge loan from private banks for 1 year	1,100	1,100 in July 1983
IMF: Compensation for diminished exports	560	560 beginning of 1983
IMF: Standby credit, 5 tranches	1,590	636 end of September 1983
BIS: Short-term	650	
Medium-term loan from private banks	1,500	
Total credit granted for outstanding payments and settlement of debts of 1983	5,400	2,946

[a]The loans were agreed upon although in some cases the sums were
not delivered to the country but were sent directly to settle
accumulated outstanding debts.

Source: Estimates based on information released by Coyuntura y
Desarrollo, no. 57; Informe Industrial, no. 67, Clarín newspaper,
several different dates; La Nación newspaper, several different
dates (all of these published in Buenos Aires); Wall Street Journal,
Financial Times, and other foreign publications issued between
September 1982 and June 1983.

The Term of Finance Minister Wehbe

As far as Wehbe's influence on internal order is
concerned, his economic team began its term with a renewed and progressive unification of the exchange rate,
which was completed by November 1982 with the usual
recessive and inflationary consequences. As regards
the rate of inflation, the proposed 160 percent was
overtaken by a considerable amount. The desperate
struggle on the part of the wage earners to recuperate
their share of income, generalized strikes, the prevailing preelectoral atmosphere, and the progressive loss of
authority on the part of the government gave way to
massive wage increases that in turn caused an acceleration in the progressive devaluation of the official
market rate. At the same time, the sharp rise of the
"parallel" dollar market originated by the uncertainty
of the situation also had a considerable inflationary
effect. As a result, in September 1983 the rate of
inflation reached 550 percent per annum.

The guidelines related to the fiscal deficit were breached for several reasons. First, there was unforeseen state expenditure due to floods in the northeastern part of the country to an extent never before experienced in the history of Argentina. Second, phenomena commonly found in all stabilization plans appeared: On one hand, the recessive conditions adversely affected the taxpayers' capacity; on the other, the rise in the rate of inflation led to considerable delay in tax collection. Thus, to a great extent the budget deficit arose as a result of the inflation, which was in turn fed by the struggle for higher income that at least seemed to generate a certain recovery in real wages.

Lastly, as regards monetary liquidity, the expansionary limits agreed to with the Fund--based on an assumed 160 percent inflation--were in fact too low in relation to the accelerated growth of the prices and led to drastic illiquidity. The total credit available at the rate regulated by the Banco Central was completely inadequate in the light of the demands of the economic system. Meanwhile, in September, interest rates rose to 35 percent monthly in the parallel open credit market. In short, even for the Argentines accustomed to tremendous distortion and uncertainty in the economic system, the situation in October 1983 bordered on science fiction.

CONDITIONS FOR A WAY OUT

By the process just described, Argentina found itself in an extremely difficult position. As we have seen, the interest alone on the foreign debt accounted for half the country's exports. The inflow of foreign exchange was never sufficient to sustain even moderate economic growth, so by the fall of 1983 Argentina had at its disposal no more than half the foreign currency amount needed to support its productive structure with imports. Under these conditions, not even the severe recession is sufficient to free the necessary foreign funds to pay the interest on the debt. In other words, to achieve the relatively modest aim of freezing the capital debt and paying the interest alone, an even deeper recession will be necessary.

What are the prospects for a way out? Traditional financial sectors with orthodox tendencies are awaiting a solution in the form of international recovery and a greater demand for Argentine exportable products. However, the basic disequilibrium in the international payments system that led to the present situation still prevails. So, permanent worldwide recovery seems very unlikely. Moreover, even if this reactivation were achieved, this situation might improve but could never solve the problem, because of the magnitude of the foreign debt.

As opposed to the orthodox point of view, political parties place emphasis on the need to renegotiate and to postpone interest payments and payments on the debt principal. The experience of Argentina and other countries has shown that although renegotiation is not difficult, problems arise from the conditions the lenders attempt to impose. Those causing most concern are the typical recessive conditions set by the International Monetary Fund, whose intervention is always insisted upon by the foreign banking institutions. If these are accepted, they render expansion and growth virtually impossible. The question here is whether these recessive conditions are inalterable or whether it is possible to postpone debt service without accepting them.

Let us first consider the reason why the Fund establishes these recessive demands. The main concern of the IMF in approving renegotiation is to ensure that the indebted country takes advantage of the respite granted to it to generate the capacity to service the debt. However, as regards practical free-exchange measures of restraint on which the Fund has imposed its own philosophy, the only effective method remaining that would enable a country like Argentina to attain the surplus in its current balance-of-payments account needed to pay its debts is an overall drop in the level of activity. Thus, the insistence on recessive measures.

Although recession is by no means desirable, the external balancing effect that is sought is essential, even from the point of view of the indebted country. If the necessary funds for the payment of the debt are not generated, the only thing the country would achieve by postponing the maturities would be a brief respite, but it would find itself faced with the same problem two or three years later, aggravated in the interim by the burden of additional accumulated interest and an even greater basic external disequilibrium due to the disparity between imports and exports, which tends to restrict both recovery and growth.

The correct approach to the problem is to reject the recessive orthodoxy of the Fund and to advocate responsible heterodoxy. That is to say, it is not enough to merely reject orthodox procedures; they must be replaced by other measures that will make the repayment of the debt feasible. Specifically, while demanding a nonrecessive renegotiation, the country must design and establish an alternative foreign economic policy capable of providing the surplus of foreign exchange necessary to pay its debts, without the need for recession.

A lasting solution to the present situation in Argentina therefore requires a policy compatible with domestic expansion and equilibrium in the external sector. We are convinced that a policy of this kind is feasible in Argentina, which has a particularly high exporting and substitutive capacity untapped owing to the lack of the appropriate economic tools.

The Basic Concepts Behind a Compatible Policy

In view of limitations of space, we will simply mention the main conceptual changes that are implied when compared with customary policies.

First, there is the problem of diagnosis. For many years Argentina has alternated between two theoretical models derived from conflicting economic policies. The first is neoclassical, based on orthodox policy. As the past experiences largely demonstrated, it leads to recession, stagnation, and accumulative foreign indebtedness. These consequences are a result of the model's complete inadequacy to cope with reality. But in actual fact, this model is based on the presumed optimum utilization of productive capacity, and the conclusions and priorities derived from it are being applied to a country whose main problem is precisely the subutilization of this capacity.

The alternative model that provides the inspiration for the more acceptable policies and alternates with the orthodox model in the pre-Alfonsín government policies is of Keynesian origin. It would appear that this model is appropriate for Argentina as it is based specifically on assumed reduction in the productive capacity. However, this is an erroneous conclusion: The Keynesian model is applicable to cases in which unemployment is due to spontaneous insufficiency in domestic demand, that is, a fall in demand that occurs where acute contraction of the external sector does not exist; yet the recession in Argentina and countries in a similar position is derived precisely from such a deterioration. The insufficiency in demand that can be observed is not spontaneous, but is deliberately provoked by the Banco Central in order to bring balance to the external sector. It can be overcome with expansionist Keynesian policies once the foreign restraint motivating the insufficiency is overcome.

Therefore, the first step toward a change in economic policy is <u>to adopt a different theory</u> as distinct from the classical and Keynesian theories as these two are from each other, <u>taking as its point of departure the existence of external constraint and the priority of overcoming it</u>.[13]

The second conceptual change concerns the need to accept unbalanced productive structure as part of reality. Argentina has systematically confused the need for protectionist barriers for its industry with industrial inefficiency, attributing the latter to the incompetence or indolence of its entrepreneurs. This ideological prejudice is behind the numerous destructive episodes of "efficiency" and has impeded the design not only of a

stable coherent import-substitution policy but also of
a policy for industrial exports. Therefore, it is of
prime importance to understand that the gap between
international and Argentine industrial prices is not the
result of industrial inefficiency, measured in absolute
terms, but rather results from the relative disadvantage
of industry as opposed to the primary sector, which is
characteristic of the initial and intermediate stages of
development. For this reason, in the case of unbalanced
productive structures based on the coexistence of a
highly productive primary sector and a less productive
industrial sector, protectionist tariffs on imported
goods are not a sign of inefficiency. Rather they
constitute an indirect way of generating multiple rates
of exchange on imports suited to the industrial parity.

A clear understanding of this concept will pave the
way for intense import substitution, which is at present
impeded by the notion that relates any increase in
industrial prices over and above the international level
to inefficiency. Of course, this does not imply substitution at any cost. A rational attitude toward industrialization in Argentina requires that there be a higher
rate for the industrial dollar than for the farming
dollar, but within reason. An appropriate analytic frame
of reference of the kind just mentioned would allow the
wealth-generating power of each additional dollar in an
economy that has been strangled by an inefficient foreign-
exchange system to be compared with the eventual sacrifice in efficiency that goes hand in hand with the
assignation of funds for import substitution at a higher
than international cost. On the basis of this comparison,
the maximum cost of substitution allowable in each
different stage of development may be calculated, and
incentives for import substitution established within
these limits.

The mobilization of industrial exports, which is
the third concept to be examined here, is also facilitated
by the clarification of the problem of efficiency. We
have seen that the main reason for Argentine balance-of-
payments problems has been the disparity between exports
and imports, due to the impossibility (or at best the
difficulty) of exporting industrial products. This
difficulty in turn is attributable to the gap between
Argentine industrial prices and those of the international market. We stated that the cause of this gap
was a relatively lower industrial activity in relation
to that of farming activities, as well as the fact that
the rate of exchange was based on the productivity of
the latter.

As far as import substitution is concerned, this
inadequacy in the rate of exchange, when applied to
industrial productivity, was gradually overcome through
import tariffs applied from the time the industrialization process commenced. But when dealing with exports,

for decades the same rate of exchange was maintained for industry as for traditional farming. It is here that the basic incoherence in Argentina's industrial process lies. On one hand, it was accepted that there was a need for differential rates of exchange when industry worked for the domestic market, but when it was a question of exporting industrial goods, this criterion was not applied.

In order to eliminate constraints in the foreign sector and remove the obstacles to Argentina's growth, this incoherence must be rectified once and for all. To do this it is necessary to modify the underlying philosophy. Instead of insisting on greater industrial efficiency as a condition for exporting, it must be realized that achievement of greater efficiency is one of the goals of the process of industrial development and cannot be considered a prerequisite for the same. Therefore, the degree of industrial productivity attained at any given moment must be accepted as a fact, at least in the medium run. From this can be derived the need to eliminate constraints in the foreign sector. One of the main ways of achieving this is to develop a system of differential incentives for industrial exports.

There are a number of techniques available that could achieve this objective. One is the utilization of a system of tax refunds similar to that used for tariffs. Another is to set the nominal rate of exchange closer to the industrial parity and to readjust the traditional farming industry's rate of exchange through adequate export taxes. The truth is that both procedures have been followed in the last twenty years and are still being utilized in Argentina today. But their application has been so indecisive and inconsistent that they have been quite ineffective. The aim would be to convert these measures, which up until now have merely been used as conjunctural palliatives or as a reluctant concession to industrial inefficiency, into key elements of sector policy and the country's development.

The fourth option involves the encouragement of exportable farming products. The problem here is that a rise in production implies either the cultivation of new land that at present is lying fallow or more intense farming of cultivated land using more technology and investing more capital. Both procedures imply a relatively higher cost for the additional production required (for example, the second tonne of wheat per hectare would cost more than the first). Orthodox policies attempt to encourage increased farming production by means of heavy devaluations and consequent price increase that would compensate for this increased cost. However, these higher prices, apart from being applied to the new production, are also applied to the previous one, the costs of which remain the same. Thus, massive transfers of income are made in favor of the farming sector. These transfers are unsustainable for the rest of the society and constitute the main provocation of the struggle for increased income and the severe inflationary phenomena in Argentina.

The answer to the problem is to design and establish incentives that would have a marginal effect and be applicable specifically to increases in production without provoking unnecessary transfers of income in favor of production already undertaken. This can be achieved through an appropriate combination of moderate increases in farming prices along with appropriate fixed land tax. Another means is to use state subsidies or to lower taxes on technological input or strategic capital goods necessary to increse the productivity of the land.

The fifth and last technique involves the exchange regime and domestic financial system. In this respect, policies in Argentina move between two extremes. The orthodox policies are always characterized by free exchange and a domestic financial system designed to attract short-term foreign capital. This means either high domestic positive real interest rates or not so positive real rates, combined with postponement of adjustments to the exchange rate. The first variable is heavily recessive. The second, even though it may be expansive, leads to a much more accelerated accumulative foreign indebtedness that in a very short time would lead to a renewed balance-of-payments crisis.

At the other extreme there are the more populist policies that are characterized by interest rates heavily negative in real terms, combined with exchange controls aimed at isolating the domestic financial circuit from the foreign. However, the moment the difference between foreign interest rates and real domestic rates becomes pronounced, the control of the exchange rate is over- ridden, and there is a heavy flight of capital via the "parallel" foreign-currency market. There is no perfect solution here. The most that can be achieved is a reasonable compromise between the conflicting external and domestic objectives. Such a compromise can only be achieved by:

1. maintaining the exchange control with a basic rate of exchange that retains its real level, that is, that evolves in real terms according to domestic inflation less international inflation

2. establishing the short-term passive bank interest rates at levels that are only slightly negative and the active rates at neutral levels

3. maintaining sufficient monetary efficiency to allow short-term active nonbank rates to establish them- selves at a slightly higher positive level than that of the international market

4. providing measures to encourage long-term domestic saving at rates similar to those of the

international market.

If the economic policy is restructured according to
these outlines, Argentina may effectively reconcile its
economic expansion with the creation of the surplus
necessary to service its debt. It is true that from a
more traditional point of view, some of the proposed
measures may seem costly in terms of the efficient allocation of resources or fiscal expenditure. But, if seen
from the point of view of a theoretical model worked out
on the basis of the dominant characteristic, that is,
constraints in the external sector, these costs become
less important in the light of the economic benefits
obtained through the recovery and growth that the proposed measures would allow.[14]

Renegotiation of the Debt

Any measure designed to modify the productive
structure will take time to bear fruit, even assuming
that the external economic policy adopted were very
effective, since it would be impossible to eliminate
constraints in the external sector immediately. Therefore, the renegotiation of capital debts and part of the
interest would have to continue. Nevertheless, the need
for recessive conditions would be avoided, because in
adopting a nonrecessive program for achieving equilibrium
in the external sector--a program based on differential
rates of exchange for importers and exporters, greater
marginal incentives for farming, and a flexible exchange
and finance policy--it would again be possible to show
the creditors that Argentina was capable of generating
the capacity necessary to settle its debts and to achieve
economic expansion.
The problem that arises in this case is that this
nonrecessive program would clash with the second condition usually demanded by the International Monetary Fund
as regards the withdrawal of protectionist measures, the
unification of the rate of exchange, the elimination of
differential incentives for nontraditional exports, and
other "efficiency" measures. The Fund usually insists
on the removal of the measures that Argentina and other
countries in a similar position need in order to reconcile economic expansion with equilibrium in the external
sector. This paradox is due to the Fund's double
objective. Apart from assuming the task of making sure
that the economic policies of the indebted countries are
compatible with their capacity to settle their debts,
because of its traditional ideology the Fund feel that
its second task is to safeguard free international trade.
No one with any common sense could fail to see the
obvious contradiction between these objectives. The more
that differential protectionist measures and those

designed to stimulate exports are eliminated in countries
like Argentina, the greater will be the tendency for
imports to grow and for industrial exports to diminish.
The tendency toward disequilibrium in the external sector
will increase, the recession needed to counteract it
will have to be greater, and it will be more difficult to
implement the IMF program.

From the point of view of doctrine, this contradiction is always denied by the Fund on the basis of neoclassical rationale advocating automatic equilibrium in
the foreign sector through free-market activity. Market
freedom is insisted upon as an automatic cure for all
ills. Nevertheless, in the light of their practical
experience, the Fund's officials realize that the procedures proposed by this institution for countries like
Argentina for external adjustment do not work according
to theory. For this reason although the Fund never
proposes heterodox plans for adjustment in the external
sector on its own initiative, it may accept them when
proposed by the indebted country. The main condition is
that the program be theoretically sound. In other words,
the International Monetary Fund will ultimately tolerate
heterodoxy if and when it is technically reliable.

In Argentina the problem has always been that with
the usual oscillation in economic policies, reliable
heterodoxy has never occurred. The local orthodox trend
has usually tended to be even more rigidly free-exchange-
oriented than the Fund itself. In fact, in order to overcome domestic objections to the policies being imposed,
the Fund's point of view has often been used as an
argument, thus making it appear even more villainous and
its negotiable suggestions are presented as categoric
impositions impossible to be resisted.

Moreover, up until now the popular opinion has
usually repudiated orthodox policies without tackling
the basic problem, that is, without proposing coherent
concrete alternatives for adjustments in the external
sector that would be compatible with expansion. The
country's greatest challenge is to get out of this
oscillatory movement.

There is still one more aspect of the negotiation
to be considered, and that is cost. When payment is
postponed the IMF usually applies heavy risk surcharges
to the rollover credit, plus rollover commissions and
additional surcharges for delayed payment or default.
These lack any reasonable justification. In private
commercial activity, when a mistake is made and credit
is granted to a company that later appears before a
creditors' meeting, it is considered satisfactory if
the amount lent is recuperated along with the normal
accrued interest and without punitive measures. It is
highly unlikely that additional gains from the postponement would even be considered.

In the renegotiations between the international banking institutions and indebted countries, the opposite occurs. Here, the postponement of payments has become a considerable additional source of profits for the banks. Furthermore, as can be seen in the agreement with Aerolineas Argentinas, the government tends to agree to legal clauses that are extremely difficult to fulfill. These clauses may totally inhibit freedom of action, impose excessive penalties for even the slightest default, and imply the application of penalties. In short, rather than ensuring payment of the debt, these renegotiation contracts reflect the creditor's intention of taking maximum advantage of the situation and gradually securing the dependence of the debtors.

Why does Argentina allow itself to be subject to these conditions? In this case it is not a question of any real disadvantage in the bargaining situation, but rather the inability of the country to determine its own position adequately. Between Argentina and its creditors there clearly exists a situation of mutual dependence. Argentina cannot run the risk of a suspension of payments for it would mean delinkage from the rest of the world. On the other hand, due to the size of Argentina's debt and the legal implications for the banks of an explicit suspension of payments, the creditors cannot take the risk of this occurring either. In view of this, conditions do exist that would allow very equilibratory negotiations.

The attitude of the Argentine government is not derived from any true balance of power but rather from the lack of any local political cohesion, the habit of always resorting to last-minute negotiations when a suspension of payments is imminent, and the strong ideological, social, and cultural pressure exerted on the country's ruling elites by the international banking institutions. Moreover, the representatives of the leading parties tend to ignore the real severity of the financial conditions and to overestimate the country's negotiating capacity. Hard-line tactics insisted on in the talks in practice are very difficult to sustain. Once more the familiar attitude that oscillates between imagined omnipotence and excessive submission becomes apparent. What is needed is a more serious, more realistic, and less improvisational attitude toward the negotiating process.

THE FUTURE

Is Argentina capable of emerging from the present crisis by adopting a rational attitude and establishing coherent economic policies? Or will the habitual cycle of expansion and recession continue? Certain objective circumstances would appear to indicate that, for better

or for worse, we are on the verge of a great qualitative
change.

After many years of military government, elections
will be held in Argentina shortly to choose a constitutional government. Drawing a rather loose parallel
with the United States, the military government in
Argentina could be compared to the Republican administration with its recessive orthodox and economic "recovery"
policies. The constitutional government could be compared
to the Democrats' expansive Keynesian policies. However,
up until now, either as an effect of a recent recession
or as a result of a favorable situation in the world
market, the representative governments have always been
in power in situations where abundant international
reserves have made domestic economic expansion possible.
On each occasion, this expansion has lasted only as long
as the international reserves. This will be the first
time that a constitutional government assumes power in
the absence of reserves, with the country on the verge of
a suspension of payments and with a foreign debt on
which the interest alone accounts for half the revenue
from exports. Therefore, the government will lack its
usual margin of maneuverability in the external sector
needed to achieve the reactivation of the domestic market.

On the other hand, the prospects for an eventual
swing toward orthodoxy would not be advantageous either.
With these turnabouts, after the accustomed "atonement
for sins" of the first recessive phase, there was always
the prospect of a "reward," typical of phase two and
provided by economic expansion on the basis of foreign
credit. Such a reward always lasted only as long as the
country's debt-servicing capacity. But today the international financial crisis makes further indebtedness
on the part of Argentina impossible and will continue to
do so for a long time, so that this door to a solution
is closed.

Therefore the usual oscillation between expansion
and recession would appear to have ended. In the light
of the present situation, there are two possible courses
to take. If the economic policies followed up until now
are not modified, the only alternative will be a prolonged recession, intense enough to allow the payment of
interest on the foreign debt. With the present debt
magnitude an even deeper recession than the present one
is necessary. But with the social, political, and
economic tension and national frustration that has
accumulated, this alternative is unsustainable and would
have unforeseen political consequences.

The second alternative is the adoption of a rational
economic policy adapted to the needs of the country.
There are two points in favor of this proposal. The
first is the growing awareness on the political scene
that the days of improvisation are over and that drastic
solutions are necessary. The second is the maturing

technical knowledge of the two major democratic parties,
one of which will shortly assume power. Today these
parties are much more qualified than before to free themselves from the yoke of deep-rooted ideas and to adopt a
creative approach in keeping with reality.

The Overall Nature of the Problem

The analysis of Argentina's indebtedness that has
been done up until now is incomplete. The present disequilibrium in the balance of payments of the different
Latin American countries is not due solely to individual
structural problems or to errors in the individual economic policies of each country. Independently of these,
the disequilibrium stems also from an overall disequilibrium in the worldwide payments system that arose
in part as a result of the oil crisis.

In fact, the major consequence of this crisis was
that for almost ten years the oil-importing countries
accumulated an overall balance-of-payments deficit on
current account in relation to the oil-exporting countries. A number of oil-importing countries were forced
to maintain this deficit because, while the worldwide
disequilibrium continued, it was not mathematically
possible for all countries to maintain an equilibrium in
their balance of payments. Finally, mainly as a result
of world recession, the overall oil deficit tended to
recede. But the surpluses that the oil-exporting countries had accumulated in the interim, which had been
recycled via the world banking institutions to the
importing countries, continued to generate interest.
Thus, the overall deficit in the current account per-
sisted--not, strictly speaking, as a result of the oil
crisis but rather of the disequilibrium generated through
the servicing of debts that had accumulated as a result.
These services have become particularly heavy with the
rise in real world interest rates over the last few years.

In this situation, it continues to be impossible for
all countries to achieve an equilibrium in their balance
of payments on current account, and it is even less
likely that they can accumulate the surpluses necessary
to settle their debts.[15] It is possible that this
objective might be reached by Argentina alone, but if
this were the case, it would mean the aggravation of the
deficit of some other country or group of countries.
Presumably, that country would try to defend itself by
restricting imports or encouraging exports, which would
then make Argentina's aim to achieve equilibrium even
more difficult to attain. The hoped-for recovery of the
industrial countries will not solve the problem either,
because its immediate effect might be to increase oil
prices, which would then aggravate the overall imbalance
even more.

A definitive solution applicable to all countries simultaneously can only be found by the combination of policies adapted to the needs of each individual country and by an overall solution for the payments problem. This would imply a heavy reduction in world interest rates and, until the overall disequilibrium has receded, an adequate recycling system established with the intervention of some kind of intergovernmental security network. Above all, it would imply the need for governments and banking institutions to realize that they are not merely facing a simple aggregate of problems arising from countries unable to balance their foreign accounts, but rather the consequences of an overall disequilibrium in the system that must be treated as such. This subject, however, goes beyond the scope of this chapter.

NOTES

1. This is the title of an Argentine film reflecting that particular situation.
2. Aldo Ferrer, "La Deuda Externa Argentina: Problemas y Perspectivas," paper presented at conference held at the University of New York (published in *Informe Ganadero*, Buenos Aires, 1982).
3. An analysis of this exchange effect can be found in Marcelo Diamond, *Doctrinas Económicas, Desarrollo e Independencia*, Buenos Aires, 1973. Also in Marcelo Diamond, "La Estructura Productiva Desequilibrada y el Tipo de Cambio," *Desarrollo Económico* (Buenos Aires), April-June 1972.
4. A detailed description of the economic model of imbalanced productive structures and their characteristics can be found in Diamond, *Doctrinas Económicas*.
5. This type of inflation is analyzed in ibid.; Marcelo Diamond, "Towards a Change in the Economic Paradigm Through the Experience of Developing Countries," *Journal of Development Economics* 5:19-53; and Marcelo Diamond, "Los Cuatro Tipos de Inflación Argentina," *Competencia* (Buenos Aires), April 1971.
6. Calculated on the basis of data from the Banco Central.
7. Guido Di Tella, *Perón-Perón 1973-76*, Buenos Aires, 1983.
8. Antonio Lopez, "La Deuda Externa en Cifras," unpublished (synthesis in the newspaper *Clarín*, Buenos Aires, July 1983).
9. As shown later, the figures for the foreign debt obtained from the Banco Central survey differ from those obtained from the analysis of the balance of payments for 1976 to 1981. Thus, according to the survey, the foreign debt increased during this period by US$27.79 billion, whereas the balance of payments indicates an increase of US$20.0344 billion. This means

a difference of US$7.764 billion.
    10. Diamond, Doctrinas Económicas.
    11. Calculated according to data from IFED,
Coyuntura y Desarrollo, several issues and statistical
appendices, Buenos Aires, 1982.
    12. IFED, Coyuntura y Desarrollo, no. 50, Buenos
Aires, April 1982.
    13. Diamond, Doctrinas Económicas.
    14. Marcelo Diamond, "Hacia una Política del Sector
Externo," paper presented at the seminar La Construcción
de la Democracia en Argentina, Buenos Aires, August 1983.
    15. Diamond, "Towards a Change in the Economic
Paradigm."

10
Rescheduling Brazil's Foreign Debt: Recent Developments and Prospects

Paulo Nogueira Batista, Jr.

INTRODUCTION

Since the final months of 1982, Brazil has been involved in the laborious process of rescheduling its
external debt.[1] Renegotiating a debt as large as Brazil's
is of course a most difficult task. According to
official data, in March 1983 Brazil's foreign debt (including short-term obligations) was in the range of
US$86 billion[2] of which US$57 billion had been provided
by foreign private banks operating within the Bank for
International Settlements' reporting area.[3] Given the
structure of the debt, two-thirds of which is owed to
foreign commercial banks, and the fact that several
hundred individual credit institutions from the United
States, Europe, Japan, and other countries are involved,
the problem of coordinating and keeping in balance all
these interests transforms the whole renegotiation process
into a veritable administrative nightmare.

In this context, it is difficult to evaluate
adequately the recent restructuring and refinancing
of Brazil's debt service as implemented by the Brazilian
economic authorities with the support of the International
Monetary Fund and a group of large U.S. commercial
banks. Nevertheless, because of the importance of this
issue for the short- and long-term prospects of both
Brazil and international financial markets, it is
essential to examine how negotiations between Brazil
and its foreign creditors are being conducted.

This essay attempts to describe how Brazil's
external financial relations have evolved recently,
highlighting the major drawbacks in present rescheduling
procedures. The first section comments briefly on the
origins of the current balance-of-payments crisis and the
impact it has had on Brazil's international reserves.
The second section discusses the reasons for the early
failure of the first phase of debt renegotiations from
December 1982 to mid-1983. The third section deals with
the general outline of the financing and rescheduling

277

agreement for 1984, now under negotiation. In the final
section, the main problems involved in the present
approach to Brazil's debt-servicing difficulties are
underlined and an attempt is made to sketch some aspects
of a new debt-restructuring strategy. My view is that,
unless Brazil's policymakers radically change their
attitude toward the foreign debt problem, they will find
it difficult to avoid a further deterioration of the
country's already serious economic situation.

THE BRAZILIAN FOREIGN-EXCHANGE CRISIS

The immediate cause of the recent foreign-exchange
crisis was the sudden, unexpected interruption in the
flow of foreign bank credit. This interruption came
about in the third quarter of 1982 in the wake of the
confidence crisis generated by the Mexican moratorium.
However, Brazil's balance-of-payments problems evidently
started much earlier, and the drastic reduction in the
inflow of external credit has only brought into the open
the latent liquidity crisis that had existed since 1980,
as can be seen from figures for foreign-exchange reserves
presented later in this section.
    In fact, Brazil's balance-of-payments situation,
already precarious since the first oil crisis of 1973-74,[4]
became considerably more serious after 1979 as a result
of the second oil shock, the dramatic increase in international interest rates, the world recession of 1980-1982,
the contraction in international trade, and the fall in
the prices of several of Brazil's major exports. The
impact of these external shocks was magnified by the
Brazilian economic authorities' failure to evaluate
correctly the evolution of the international situation.
In fact, economic policy during this period was extremely
erratic and totally lacking in a clear definition of
main objectives.[5]
    Consequently, Brazil's foreign-exchange position at
the start of 1982 was already quite unfavorable. After
the Mexican payments suspension and its effect on international bank credit, it became increasingly difficult
to admit that Brazil's foreign liabilities could continue
to be refinanced or "recycled" through normal market
mechanisms. In 1982, a series of unfavorable circumstances (a fall in exports, an unexpected increase in
interest payments, a reduced inflow of medium- and long-
term foreign funds, and the problems involved in refinancing the short-term commercial debt and the
liabilities of foreign branches and subsidiaries of
Brazilian banks) wore down Brazil's resistance (see
Table 10.1).
    In November 1982, the Brazilian government made
public its intention to seek maximum access to IMF funds.
In December, after being assured direct support from the

Table 10.1 Brazil: Balance of Payments (main items), 1968-1982 (in billions of U.S. dollars)

Item	1968-73ᵃ	1974-78ᵃ	1979	1980	1981	1982ᵇ
(A) Trade balance	0.0	-2.3	-2.8	-2.8	1.2	0.8
Exports (FOB)	3.3	10.3	15.2	20.1	23.3	20.2
Imports (FOB)	3.3	12.6	18.1	23.0	22.1	19.4
(B) Services	-1.0	-3.7	-7.2	-9.6	-12.2	-15.5
Interest (net)ᶜ	-0.3	-1.8	-4.2	-6.3	-9.2	-11.4
Other servicesᶜ	-0.7	-1.9	-3.0	-3.3	-3.0	-4.1
(C) Current transactions (A+B)	-1.0	-6.0	-10.0	-12.4	-11.0	-14.8
(D) Capital	1.9	7.1	6.9	9.3	12.0	6.3
Direct Investmentsᵈ (net)	0.3	0.9	1.5	1.1	1.6	1.0
Currency Loans & Financing (medium- and long-term)	2.3	8.6	11.2	10.6	15.6	12.5
Amortizations (medium- & long-term)	-0.9	-3.3	-6.4	-5.0	-6.2	-7.0
Other	0.2	0.9	0.6	2.6	1.1	-0.3
(E) Errors & omissions	0.2	-0.3	-0.1	-0.3	-0.4	-0.4
(F) Surplus or deficit (C+D+E)	1.0	0.9	-3.2	-3.5	0.6	-8.9

Note: In some cases numbers may not add because of rounding.

ᵃAnnual average

ᵇPreliminary data

ᶜExcludes reinvested profits and includes unilateral transfers

ᵈExcludes reinvestment

Source: Banco Central do Brasil.

Fund, Brazil presented its major private creditors with
a global financial scheme for 1983 and decided to
partially suspend amortization payments. In spite of the
bridge loans provided by a group of large private international banks, the U.S. Treasury, the Bank for International Settlements, and the first tranche of the
compensatory financing facility from the IMF, Brazil's
international reserves were considerably lower at the
end of 1982, falling from US$7.5 billion in December 1981
to only US$4 billion by December 1982.

Furthermore, it must be noted that these official
figures, which refer to the "international liquidity of
the monetary authorities," provide only a partial indication of the real situation. In fact, these figures
should not be considered as correct indicators of the
effective international liquidity of the monetary
authorities. First, because there is some uncertainty as
to the real convertibility of the assets registered as
international reserves by the central bank. Although the
exact composition of the reserves is unknown, there are
indications that foreign-exchange crises in several of
Brazil's trading partners, such as Poland and Mexico,
to which substantial amounts of export finance credit had
been extended, have led to a reduction in the value and
effective liquidity of some assets included in Brazil's
official reserves statistics. Second, since these
figures correspond to gross assets (see Table 10.2), the
monetary authorities (and other government agencies) can
artificially maintain official liquidity levels by taking
out short-term credits or through accounting operations
with branches of Brazilian banks abroad. This is exactly
what seems to have been happening in Brazil over the past
three years. As can be seen from the data in Table 10.3,
the monetary authorities' short-term liabilities increased significantly during 1980 and were consistently
above US$3 billion in 1981. In the early months of 1982,
they increased considerably again. The reduction in net
reserves was much greater than the reduction in gross
reserves in this period, and the former have almost
always stood at less than the value of two months' imports
since mid-1980.

More recent data for September 1982 were included
in the Technical Memorandum annexed to the Letter of
Intent sent to the IMF on January 6, 1983 (see Table
10.4). On September 30, 1982, the gross reserves of the
monetary authorities came to a total of US$4.3521 billion
and short-term liabilities to US$3.3037 billion. Thus,
net international reserves amounted to only US$1.0484
billion, equivalent to less than twenty days' imports.

By the end of 1982, net international reserves of
the Brazilian monetary authorities, as defined in the
Technical Memorandum of Understanding, were already
negative by several billion dollars. In December 1982
the total of short-term foreign liabilities of both the

Table 10.2 Brazil: Gross International Reserves of the Monetary
Authorities (Banco Central and Banco do Brasil), 1976-1982
(in millions of U.S. dollars)

Period	Special Drawing Rights (A)	Reserve Position in IMF[a] (B)	Foreign Exchange[b] (C)	Gold[c] (D)	Gross Reserves of Monetary Authorities (E=A+B+C+D)
1976: December	199	188	6,101	56	6,544
1977: December	210	195	6,787	64	7,256
1978: December	239	181	11,406	68	11,894
1979: December	383	241	8,342	722	9,688
1980					
March	468	262	6,185	1,036	7,951
June	508	288	4,825	953	6,574
September	504	271	4,534	1,179	6,488
December	384	344	5,042	1,143	6,913
1981					
March	456	301	4,749	971	6,477
June	447	258	4,496	948	6,149
September	444	255	4,759	887	6,345
December	452	264	5,888	905	7,509
1982					
March	439	260	5,594	789	7,082
June	425	274	5,428	814	6,941
September	189	282	4,714	871	5,056
December	0	287	3,641	65	3,993

[a]Unconditional IMF related reserve assets

[b]Claims against foreigners in the form of bank deposits, treasury
bills, and other documents that may be used to cover balance-of-
payments deficits, including nonnegotiable credit bills obtained
through agreements between central banks or governments

[c]Since October 1979 gold has been assessed on the basis of the
daily average closing quotations in London during the preceding
two months.

Source: International Monetary Fund.

Banco Central and the Banco do Brasil, plus the liabilities incurred by making use of IMF funds, exceeded the
value of their foreign assets by approximately US$3.0
billion.[6]

DEBT RENEGOTIATION: THE FIRST ROUND

On December 20, 1982, the Brazilian economic
authorities presented the country's major bank creditors
with a comprehensive financial program for 1983, sub-
divided into the following four projects:

Table 10.3 Brazil: Net International Reserves of the Monetary Authorities, 1976-1982 (in millions of U.S. dollars)

Period	Gross Reserves of Monetary Authorities (1)	Short-Term Liabilities of Monetary Authorities (2)	Net Reserves of Monetary Authorities (3=1-2)	Imports[a] (FOB) (4)	Reserves/ Imports Ratio (%) (5=3/4)
1976: December	6,544	887	5,657	13,196	42.9
1977: December	7,256	1,040	6,216	11,934	52.1
1978: December	11,894	1,613	10,281	14,465	71.1
1979: December	9,688	1,763	7,925	21,950	36.1
1980					
March	7,951	2,883	5,068	21,931	23.1
June	6,574	3,147	3,427	22,999	14.9
September	6,488	3,329	3,159	24,174	13.1
December	6,913	3,413	3,500	22,717	15.4
1981					
March	6,477	3,578	2,899	22,423	12.9
June	6,149	3,403	2,746	22,261	12.3
September	6,345	3,258	3,087	22,441	13.8
December	7,509	3,237	4,272	21,238	20.1
1982					
January	7,284	3,808	3,476	21,036	16.5
February	7,080	4,769	2,311	19,738	11.7
March	7,082	4,577	2,505	19,216	13.0

[a]Imports of preceding three months at annual rate

Source: Banco Central do Brasil and International Monetary Fund.

Table 10.4 Brazil: Net International Reserves of the Monetary
Authorities (Banco Central and Banco do Brazil), September 30, 1982
(in millions of U.S. dollars)

(A) Assets	4,352.1
Spot Assets	1,386.1
Short-Term Assets	2,617.4
Medium- and Long-Term Assets	348.6
(B) Liabilities	3,303.7
Spot Liabilities	--
Short-Term Liabilities	3,303.7
Medium-Term Liabilities (IMF)[a]	--
(C) Net International Reserves (A-B)	1,048.4

[a]Includes all repurchase obligations arising from the use of Fund
resources in the first credit tranche, under the extended agreement, the compensatory financing facility, and the buffer stock
financing facility

Source: Technical Memorandum of Understanding (annexed to Letter
of Intent of January 6, 1983).

1. a "jumbo loan" of US$4.4 billion to be provided
    by foreign commercial banks in proportion to
    their outstanding credits to Brazil
2. the rescheduling of amortizations due to
    foreign banks in 1983 (total value estimated
    to exceed US$4.0 billion)
3. the renewal of short-term commercial credit
    lines
4. the restoration of total interbank lines for
    foreign branches and subsidiaries of Brazilian
    banks to the level observed in mid-1982.[7]

The volume of funds requested depended of course on
the forecasts for the current and capital accounts of the
balance of payments, including the estimates concerning
short-term foreign debt and interbank debts of the subsidiaries and foreign branches of Brazilian banks. The
central aspect of the projections was Brazil's commitment
to generate an unprecedented surplus of US$6.0 billion
in its trade balance and to ensure an also unprecedented
reduction of over 50 percent in its current account
deficit in 1983. It was hoped that the resources provided by these four projects along with loans from
official credit sources, suppliers' credits, and direct
investment would create a capital account surplus
sufficient to cover the deficit on current account and to
finance an increase of approximately US$1.0 billion in
gross international reserves.

It must be stressed first of all that even if the
financial program for 1983 had been successful in all its
basic points, it would not have been able to assure a

smooth administration of Brazil's foreign accounts. When one considers that Brazil started 1983 with negative net reserves, and gross reserves totaling less than three months' imports, it is obvious that an increase of barely US$1.0 billion in reserves would not have brought about any significant change in the country's foreign-exchange situation. Despite the adjustment effort implicit in a reduction of over 50 percent in the current account deficit, Brazil's external vulnerability would still have been extremely high by the end of 1983.

In fact, most of the new resources provided by the foreign commercial banks and the IMF in 1983 were already committed to the settlement of bridge loans disbursed during the final quarter of the previous year. More than 60 percent of the resources to be provided by the IMF in 1983 were to be primarily destined to settle short-term debts owed to the U.S. Treasury and to the BIS; more than 50 percent of the US$4.4 billion jumbo loan was to be used in the settlement of bridge loans advanced by commercial banks. More important, however, is the fact that the program proposed to the foreign banks was based on a series of rather controversial hypotheses regarding the behavior of Brazil's foreign accounts in the short term. In fact, the four-project package proposed in December 1982 did not contain enough medium- and long-term financial resources and therefore became excessively dependent on short-term credit lines.

After a few months, it became apparent that the plan for adjustment and foreign financing designed by the Brazilian government for 1983 could not be fulfilled as initially formulated. Brazil was then obliged, even before the end of the first semester of 1983, to seek a way of broadening the scope of the financing program presented to the private international banks in December 1982. It had become absolutely clear that one of the basic assumptions of the program was unrealistic, namely, the assumption that foreign banks would voluntarily maintain or even increase their short-term exposure with Brazil or foreign branches of Brazilian banks. The partial failure of the third project (short-term commercial liabilities) and, in particular, of the fourth project (reestablishment of interbank lines for foreign branches of Brazilian banks) seems to have largely contributed to the deterioration of the situation. The obstinate resistance of a substantial part of the international banking community prevented Brazil from reaching the expected levels of short-term financing. This resistance can be attributed to a number of factors, the most obvious being a general dissatisfaction with the way in which negotiations were carried out, the incompatibility of the fourth project with the normal functioning of the interbank market, a general lack of confidence in Latin American borrowers, growing doubts concerning Brazil's trustworthiness, and, finally,

discontentment among various banking sectors in face of
the preeminence of New York banks during the negotiations
on the four Brazilian projects.[8]
Furthermore, as has already been stated, the four-
project program was based on a series of controversial
hypotheses regarding the behavior of Brazil's foreign
accounts in 1983. From monthly data issued by the government, one could see that the balance-of-trade surplus
would probably equal, or even exceed, the target of
US$6.0 billion. Nevertheless, on the whole the foreign
accounts did not adjust to the government's forecasts for
1983, and there was a considerable deterioration in the
global balance-of-payments position. The discrepancies
between targets and actual results seem to have been
partly due to a larger than expected deficit in the
interest and other services accounts. More important,
however, were the deviations observed in capital account
of the balance of payments. As a result of the failure
of the fourth project, of a substantial fall in foreign
direct investment, and of delays in the disbursement of
loans, net reserves became increasing negative while the
volume of payment arrears expanded. Under these circumstances, Brazil was unable to respect the quarterly
ceilings for the global balance-of-payments deficit
agreed upon with the IMF.
In fact, the inevitable redefinition of the debt-
renegotiation process suffered considerably from the premature failure of the first and second versions of the
internal adjustment program negotiated between Brazil and
the Fund. The four-project program was merely a financial
compensation for a severe adjustment program approved by
the IMF Executive Board in February 1983. The disbursement of resources for the first project was linked
contractually with the release of IMF funds, which in
turn depended on the quarterly monitoring of the adjustment program and the previously established performance
criteria.
In mid-April 1983, the president of the Banco Central
announced the IMF's decision to suspend the disbursement
of the second tranche of its loan to Brazil until the
reasons for the nonfulfillment of some of the performance
criteria were clarified. Brazil had greatly exceeded
the targets fixed for the public sectors' borrowing
requirements as well as for the net domestic assets of
the monetary authorities and for the global balance-of-
payments deficit.[9] Thus, in less than two months it had
become public that the agreement signed in January and
revised in February had become obsolete. The targets
were so unrealistic that the quantitative criteria
stipulated in the Letter of Intent prepared at the end of
February proved impossible to achieve only one month
later.
In fact, the shortcomings of the adjustment program,
as well as the speed with which this first phase of

negotiations between the Brazilian authorities and the
IMF had been concluded, did show, on one hand, a negli-
gent attitude on the part of Brazil and, on the other,
a lack of understanding of the peculiarities of the
Brazilian economy by the IMF technical staff. As a
result, the disbursement of credits that had already been
agreed upon was called to a halt, and there was a growing
erosion of the domestic and foreign credibility of
Brazilian policymakers.[10]

The combination of these problems exerted unprecedented pressure on Brazil's foreign accounts. Since its
international reserves were exhausted and it was impossible to continue raising short-term compensatory
loans, Brazil had no alternative but to allow arrears
to accumulate. Brazil's net international reserves,
already negative by several billion dollars at the end of
1982, were even further reduced in the first semester of
1983. At the end of June, the short-term and medium-term
(IMF) liabilities of the monetary authorities exceeded
the value of their foreign assets by some US$4.5 billion
(see Table 10.5). The total sum of payment arrears
amounted to almost US$1.0 billion at the end of March[11]
and exceeded US$2.5 billion at the end of August.[12]

DEBT RENEGOTIATION: THE SECOND ROUND

Given the failure of the first financing and adjustment program negotiated with the foreign commercial banks
and the IMF, the Brazilian government was forced to
initiate a second round of negotiations halfway through
1983. However, the delay in arriving at a new agreement
with the IMF resulted in the slowing down of negotiations
with foreign commercial banks and other sources of credit.
Although negotiations had not been concluded at the time
of this writing, the new version for the program had
already been outlined, permitting a preliminary evaluation.

The new foreign financing program has been designed
to meet the credit requirements for 1984 and to cover the
shortfalls of the 1983 program. The most important
change is perhaps the decision to apply to the Paris Club,
that is, to reschedule the amortizations and interest
due on loans from foreign governments or guaranteed by
foreign governments. During the previous round of
negotiations, only medium- and long-term amortizations
due to foreign banks (and Brazilian banks abroad) were
rescheduled. There has also been a slight reduction in
the spread (and other costs) and an extension of the
grace period and the final maturity applied in the first
project (US$6.5 billion in "new money") and the second
project (rescheduling of amortizations due to banks in
1984). Finally, there are signs that the governments
of industrialized countries will be willing to step up,

Table 10.5 Brazil: Net International Reserves of the Monetary
Authorities (Banco Central and Banco do Brasil), June 30, 1983
(in millions of U.S. dollars)

(A) Assets	2,940.8
Spot Assets	677.8
Short-Term Assets	1,739.7
Medium- and Long-Term Assets	523.3
(B) Liabilities	7,434.8
Spot Liabilities	--
Short-Term Liabilities	5,978.3
Medium-Term Liabilities (IMF)[a]	1,456.5
(C) Net International Reserves (A-B)	-4,494.0

[a]Includes all repurchase obligations arising from the use of Fund
resources in the first credit tranche, under the extended arrangement, the compensatory financing, and the buffer stock financing
facility

Source: Technical Memorandum of Understanding (annexed to Letter
of Intent of September 15, 1983).

although only marginally, their level of involvement in
financing the country's imports.
      Despite these improvements it cannot be said that
there has been a basic change in the manner of approaching the issue of debt renegotiation. Given that the debt
owed to foreign governments (or guaranteed by government
agencies) amounts to a relatively small fraction of total
debt, applying to the Paris Club does not imply any significant increase in the liabilities subject to rescheduling. As far as the cost of bank credit is concerned, the
new program will not improve conditions significantly:
The .125 percent reduction in spread should lead to a
reduction of only about US$15.0 million in interest
payments in 1984 and the extension of the final maturity
(from 8 to 9 years) will have no significant effect on
the debt's time structure. However, the increase of the
grace period from 2½ to 5 years will help avoid a major
concentration of payments in the mid-1980s.
      It ought to be emphasized, however, that all these
changes and amendments are part of a program that at
present is still under negotiation. It must also be
stressed that these changes are clearly only of secondary
importance. In fact, the program resulting from this
second round of negotiations retains all the major
characteristics of the first one. The adjustment program
outlined in the third version of the Letter of Intent is
as harsh as or even harsher in its approach than the
previous documents.[13] The new agreement with the IMF
continues to demand a substantial reduction in the current
account deficit and in the public-sector's borrowing
requirements without providing adequate foreign financing
in compensation. In fact, this new program will probably

not allow an appreciable increase of international reserves in 1984. The main problem appears to be that
Brazil is supposed to continue paying nearly all interest
payments. To highlight the inadequacy of the present
program, one only has to compare the volume of new loans
put at Brazil's disposal for 1984 with estimates referring
to the interest account. Approximately US$4.0 billion of
the new US$6.5 billion jumbo loan was in fact to be used
to cover additional credit requirements in 1983, meaning
that liquid funds available from this loan in 1984 will
cover less than one-third of the estimated US$9.0 billion
of interest payments due to foreign commercial banks in
the same year. Excessively ambitious targets for the
trade balance and the consequent adoption of policies
that increase inflationary pressures and/or reduce the
level of economic activity are thus made inevitable.

In these circumstances one cannot exclude the
possibility of a third round of negotiations in the not
too distant future. In all probability, new talks would
involve a redefinition not only of the foreign financing
program but also of the terms of adjustment imposed by the
IMF. Nonetheless, one should not forget that this never-
ending process of negotiation and renegotiation aggravates
domestic instability and makes the task of finding a
suitable solution to the problems posed by Brazil's
foreign debt even more difficult. Alternative debt-
restructuring strategies, which by now appear to be
essential, will be dealt with in the following section.

MAIN PROBLEMS INVOLVED IN THE PRESENT APPROACH AND AN
OUTLINE FOR AN ALTERNATIVE DEBT-RESTRUCTURING STRATEGY

The attitude adopted by the Brazilian government
since the opening of formal debt renegotiations in late
1982 has been far too cautious and hesitant. The initial
attempt (by now totally discredited) was to differentiate
Brazil from the rest of Latin America. Brazil even went
so far as to try to project an image of itself as the
victim of the effects of a confidence crisis generated
by events in Mexico and Argentina. Instead of presenting
an explicit policy program and a coherent debt-renegotia-
tion scheme, Brazil engaged in a series of dubious delaying maneuvers that have primarily resulted in a continuous
decline in the possibility of serious negotiations with
the IMF and bank creditors.

But the basic problem with the economic policies
supported by the IMF and the international banks is that
the degree of adjustment demanded from Brazil is clearly
excessive, threatening to surpass the limits deemed
tolerable from both political and social points of view.
From 1983 on, Brazil will be obliged to effect a premature transfer of real resources abroad. For the first
time in many years, aggregate expenditure on investment

and consumption will be considerably lower than the
gross domestic product. The difference will be transferred abroad in the form of a positive balance in the
trade and nonfactor services accounts. In 1983 this
outward transfer was to amount to about US$3.0 billion.

From the new Letter of Intent sent to the IMF on
September 15, 1983, it can be deduced that this trend
would continue during 1984. If official targets are
fulfilled, there will be a negative "resource gap" of
about US$6 billion in 1984, that is, an outward transfer
twice as large as the one observed in 1983. In fact,
if the balance between adjustment and financing is not
changed, this premature transfer of resources will be a
great burden to Brazil throughout the 1980s and could
substantially reduce its capacity for economic growth.[14]

The increase in the next external debt reflects
essentially the difference between the current account
deficit and the net inflow of direct investment. Ignoring other factor services, unilateral transfers, and net
lending to other countries, the rate of growth of the
net stock of debt is determined by the resource gap, the
average international interest rate, and the net foreign-
exchange contribution of equity capital:

$$\frac{\Delta ED}{ED_{t-1}} = \frac{RG}{ED_{t-1}} + \frac{I}{ED_{t-1}} + \frac{DI-PD}{ED_{t-1}}$$

where ED = net external debt, RG = resource gap, I =
interest payments (net), DI = direct investment (net),
and PD = profits and dividends (net).

Assuming that the remittance of profits and
dividends is more or less compensated for by the inflow
of direct investment, the resource gap can be seen as
reflecting the difference between the rate of growth of
the debt and the average international interest rate:

$$\frac{RG}{ED_{t-1}} = \frac{\Delta ED}{ED_{t-1}} - \frac{I}{ED_{t-1}}$$

Under present circumstances, international banks,
the major source of credit for Brazil, are apparently
refusing to agree to an increase of their exposure above
7 or 8 percent annually.[15] Unless there is an increase
in official and multilateral credits, and if the average
annual interest rate remains at the present level of
about 13 percent, Brazil will have to generate during the
next few years net exports of goods and nonfactor
services equivalent to 6 or 7 percent of outstanding
debt. We therefore face a hitherto unknown situation
in which a low-income country such as Brazil is having to
transform itself overnight into an exporter of real
resources, as a result of a large and unexpected reduction

in foreign loans.[16]

Instead of accepting commitments of this nature and programs that require a substantial transfer of real resources abroad, Brazil should make it clear that it is not prepared to bear the full burden of a balance-of-payments crisis that was partially caused by external factors, such as the rise in the price of oil, unresolved contradictions in U.S. economic policy, a dramatic increase in international interest rates, and world recession, coupled with an abrupt and unexpected contraction in the inflow of foreign bank loans since mid-1982. A sharing of the adjustment burden is unavoidable given the critical situation in which Brazil finds itself as a result of policy mistakes and also of a protracted international crisis.

International banks, which in the past have benefited substantially from making loans to Brazil, will have to prepare themselves to accept emergency solutions and to absorb losses. They must now recognize that Brazil is not in a position to cover interest payments with an increasing trade surplus and a continuously growing transfer of real resources abroad. On the other hand, it must also be recognized that the banks themselves are facing serious restrictions and going through a crisis on a scale unknown since the 1930s. The simultaneous non-fulfillment of obligations on the part of major debtors such as Brazil, Mexico, Argentina, Poland, and Venezuela will probably have a lasting negative effect on the growth rate of international bank credit. Recent estimates show that Brazil's total interest payments will reach approximately US$35.0 billion in 1984-1986.[17] Since these payments will not be financed with additional credit flows, it seems inevitable that the interest on the debt be rescheduled. If not, Brazil and other debtor countries will be forced to generate massive outward transfers of real resources.

There are clear advantages in capitalization of interest payments as compared with the present system for partial financing of interest by jumbo loans organized in a semicompulsory manner and based on a combination of political pressure on the banks and very high spreads. First, rescheduling interest payments could lead to a change in the balance between adjustment and financing, avoiding (or at the very least minimizing) the outward transfer of resources. Second, automatic protection would be provided against an unexpected rise in international interest rates. Third, it would allow Brazil to negotiate a significant reduction in spreads and also extend maturities, since it would no longer be necessary to attract the banks' participation in jumbo loans by enticing them with extortionate financial conditions. In fact, given support from bank supervisory authorities and changes in bank regulations in certain countries, rescheduling interest repayments could be a more favorable solution even for the banks themselves. Contrary to the financing of interest payments via new loans, the capitalization of interest would automatically guarantee the balanced and equitable involvement of the several hundred individual creditors in financing the additional requirements of Brazil. In these circumstances, the exposure of each bank in Brazil would increase proportionately to loans outstanding.

A realistic debt restructuring adjusted to Brazil's effective repayments possibilities should include the following basic points: (1) rescheduling of all, or almost all, medium- and long-term amortizations; (2) rescheduling or capitalization of interest payments; (3) conversion of short-term financial debt into medium- or long-term debt; (4) lengthening of maturities and considerable reduction in spreads and other charges and commissions imposed by the banks in recent deals; and (5) extension of the consolidation period (the period in which payments to be rescheduled fall due) from one to three or five years. A realistic restructuring of the debt service due over the next few years would avoid (or at least reduce) outward resource transfers and enable Brazil to defend the level of domestic employment, rebuild international reserves, and bring under control inflationary pressures caused by external constraints. If Brazil fails to win the understanding and support of its creditors, it will probably be obliged to adopt a very inflexible approach in the future and impose conditions on a unilateral basis. In Brazil, it is becoming increasingly clear that a radical change of attitude is essential if the country is to restore a minimum level of economic growth and bring inflation under control over the next few years.

NOTES

1. This chapter was written on the basis of information available in October 1983. Part of this study was carried out with financial support from the Instituto de Planejamento Econômico e Social Aplicado (IPEA).

2. Banco Central do Brasil, Informativo Mensal, September 1983, p. 11.

3. Data reported by banks in the Group of Ten countries; by Luxembourg, Switzerland, Austria, Denmark, Ireland, and by branches of U.S. banks in the Bahamas, the Cayman Islands, Panama, Hong Kong, and Singapore. Bank for International Settlements, International Banking Developments--Second Quarter 1983, Monetary and Economic Department, Basle, October 1983, p. 1 and table 5.

4. For an analysis of the effects of external shocks and Brazil's economic policy response in the years 1974-1978, see Antonio Carlos Lemgruber, Paulo Nogueira

Batista, Jr., and Roberto Fendt, Jr., Choques Externos e
Respostas de Política Econômica no Brasil: O Primeiro
Choque do Petroleo, Estudos Especiais IBRE, no. 3, Rio de
Janeiro, 1981.

5. For a recent evaluation of the Brazilian economy
and its place in the world economy, see Edmar L. Bacha
and Pedro S. Malan, "Brazil's Debt: From the Miracle to
the Fund," paper presented at the conference on Democrati-
zing Brazil? Yale University, March 1983; and Pedro S.
Malan and Regis Bonelli, "Crescimento Economico,
Industrializacão e Balanco de Pagamentos: O Brasil dos
Anos 70 aos Anos 80" (IPEA/INPES, Texto para Discussao
Interna no. 60, October 1983, mimeo).

6. According to preliminary information included in
a report prepared by the technical staff of the IMF, the
net reserves of the monetary authorities were negative
by US$1.5 billion on December 31, 1982 (see the appendix
to the speech given by the finance minister, Ernane
Galveas, "A Crise Mundial e a Estratégia Brasileira de
Ajustamento do Balanço de Pagamentos," in the federal
Senate on March 23, 1983). Since the estimated balance-
of-payments deficit for 1983 was later increased by
US$1.4 billion, net international reserves must have
been negative by almost US$3.0 billion at the end of 1982.

7. Carlos Geraldo Langoni, "A Estratégia do Brasil
na Crise Financeira Atual," speech given in New York on
December 20, 1982, at a meeting of Brazil's major bank
creditors (published by the Brazilian press on December
24, 1982).

8. For a good journalistic description of some of
the problems of this first round of debt negotiations,
see "The War Among Brazil's Bankers," Fortune, July 11,
1983, pp. 50-55.

9. According to a document prepared by the Western
Hemisphere Department of the IMF, released unofficially
by the Brazilian press on July 8 and 9, and also in
accordance with the Letter of Intent sent to the Fund on
September 15.

10. For an account of recent negotiations between
Brazil and the IMF, see Maria Silvia Bastos Marques and
Paulo Nogueira Batista, Jr., "A Terceira Versão do
Acordo Brasil-FMI" (Fundação Getulio Vargas, IBRE/CEMEI,
October 1983, mimeo.), pp. 3-7. For an analysis and
critical observations on the theoretical model used by
the IMF, see, for example, Edmar L. Bacha, "The IMF
Threat: The Prospects for Maladjustment in Brazil"
(Pontifícia Universidade Catolica de Rio de Janeiro,
May 1983, mimeo.); Maria Silvia Bastos Marques, "O
Conceito de Ativos Domésticos Líquidos e Sua Aplicação
ao Brasil" (Fundação Getulio Vargas, June 1983, mimeo.);
Paulo Nogueira Batista, Jr., "Em Defesa de Critérios de
Desempenho Indexados" (Fundação Getulio Vargas, IBRE/
CEMEI, June 1983, mimeo.); Edmar L. Bacha, "Do Brasil
para o FMI: Prólogo para a Terceira Carta" (Pontifícia

293

Universidade Catolica de Rio de Janeiro, June 1983,
mimeo.); Rogério L. F. Werneck, "A Armadilha Financeira
do Setor Público e as Empresas Estatais" (Pontifícia
Universidade Catolica de Rio de Janeiro, June 1983,
mimeo.).
    11. Preliminary data released by the Bano Central
in April 1983 to the foreign banks participating in the
liaison committee. Later these figures were also made
available to the Brazilian press, indicating that at the
end of March the central bank's cash position was negative
by US$999 million.
    12. See para. 8 of the Technical Memorandum annexed
to the Letter of Intent of September 15, 1983.
    13. For a recent analysis of the third version of
the agreement between Brazil and the IMF, see Bastos
Marques and Batista, "A Terceira Versão," pp. 8-34.
    14. Since Brazil's net exports of goods and "non-
factor" services only cover a part of factor payments
to nonresidents, total domestic expenditure is greater
than the GNP. Despite the fact that domestic expenditure
is now lower than GDP, there is still a fairly large
deficit on current account that basically corresponds to
the difference between net factor payments and the surplus
in the trade and "nonfactor" services accounts. The
excess of GDP over aggregate domestic expenditure
"finances" part of the income transferred in the form
of interest payments, profits and dividends, and so on.
    15. The US$4.4 billion "jumbo loan" of 1983
represents a 7.5 percent increase in bank exposure to
Brazil, as estimated by Banco Central, Informativo
Mensal, January 1983, p. 8.
    16. Paulo H. Pereira Lira, "A Crise Internacional
da Dívida Externa--Um Tratamento Orientado para o
Crescimento," paper presented at conference on the
International Debt Crisis held in London, sponsored by
the International Banking and Finance Centre, The City
University, October 5, 1983.
    17. Pedro Sampaio Malan and Paulo Nogueira
Batista, Jr., "Estimativa das Necessidades de
Financiamento Externo do Brasil até 1986" (July 1983,
mimeo.), table 1.

11
The Mexican External Debt: The Last Decade

Ernesto Zedillo Ponce de León

Until a decade ago the history of Mexico's foreign debt had comprised four clearly distinguishable periods. First, the period from 1824 to 1888. These two dates mark the year that the country obtained its first significant foreign loan and the year the original English debt of 1824 and 1825 was finally settled after many bitter incidents involving defaults, moratoriums, and the like. The second period was from 1888 to 1911, which essentially corresponds to the Porfiriato era. During the period, thanks to the image of political stability and improved management of public finances, Mexico enjoyed ready access to foreign financing. As a consequence, the country's foreign debt grew more than eightfold. Third was the period ranging from the start of the Mexican Revolution to the signing of the Suárez-Lamont Agreement in 1942. During these difficult years, the Mexican government was repeatedly unable to fulfill its foreign-debt obligations or to reach a rescheduling agreement with its creditors. The episode was finally closed with the signing of a rather advantageous agreement for Mexico, as had happened in 1888. The fourth period was from World War II until the early 1970s. During those years, in which the country regained its access to international capital markets, foreign financing was mostly obtained from official sources and was kept in a modest proportion with respect to most macroeconomics aggregates. If not quite unimportant, the role of foreign financing was strictly limited to supplementing other policy instruments.[1]

1973 was a real turning point. Between 1954 and 1972, the net flow of the foreign public debt averaged US$218.7 million a year. It increased to something more than US$1.6 billion in 1973 alone and kept growing in subsequent years. As a consequence, the stock of the foreign public debt, which amounted to US$6.8 billion at the end of 1972, increased to almost US$21 billion by the time the Echeverría administration was over (1976) and to US$58.1 billion when President López Portillo left office (1982). Considering the foreign debt of commercial banks and of private-sector firms, the country's total external debt had reached US$27.5 billion in late 1976 and US$84.1 billion six years later. Not surprisingly, the last two financial crises experienced by Mexico (1976 and 1982) have been closely linked to the external-debt problem.

It is the purpose of this chapter to review--albeit briefly and rather informally--the evolution of Mexico's foreign debt since 1973. For reasons of relevance and opportunity, emphasis will be given to the latest events.

THE ECHEVERRÍA EPOCH (1971-1976)

As far as the growth of the external debt is concerned, the first two years of President Echeverría's term were not different from the Stabilizing Development period,[2] yet the active pursuit of financial stability that still commanded a great deal of importance in 1971 started to taper off in 1972. For one thing, GDP growth in 1971 had been the smallest in eighteen years. On the other hand, there was a mounting current of opinion at the highest government level that felt the economic policy model in effect since the mid-1950s had been "exhausted," and therefore a change in priorities and in courses of action was long overdue. Consequently, public expenditure began to expand.

Notwithstanding that the new strategy had an immediate negative impact on the public sector's deficit and on monetary expansion, it seemed to work properly in many other important respects: GDP growth surged to 8.5 percent, inflation was a bit more than 5 percent, and the current account deficit was not very different from the levels registered in the two previous years-- around US$1 billion (see Table 11.1). These results reaffirmed the stance of those advocating a more active government involvement in the solution of social and economic problems through the expansion of public expenditure.

The "new medicine" was applied vigorously in 1973: Public expenditure as a proportion of GDP, which had averaged 21 percent during 1966-1970, reached 27 percent, whereas the overall public sector's deficit relative to GDP (historically less than 2.5 percent) soared to 6.9 percent. This time, however, the "magic of 1972" worked rather imperfectly. Inflation climbed to a double-digit figure for the first time in almost two decades, and the current account deficit jumped to US$1.5 billion. Yet GDP growth was sustained at the highly respectable rate of 8.4 percent, and furthermore, financing of the en- larged external disequilibrium did not pose an important problem. As stated before, the net flow of the foreign public debt was easily increased many times over its

Table 11.1 Mexico: Some Basic Indicators of the Echeverría Term

Year	Real GDP Growth[a] (%)	Inflation[b] (%)	Public-Sector Deficit[c] (%)	Public Expenditure[d] (%)	Public Income[d] (%)	Current Account Deficit (millions of U.S. dollars)
1966-1970[e]	6.9	3.5	2.5	21.1	19.0	750.5
1971	4.2	5.3	2.5	20.9	18.2	928.9
1972	8.5	5.0	4.9	23.6	18.5	1,005.7
1973	8.4	12.0	6.9	27.0	19.8	1,528.8
1974	6.1	23.7	7.2	28.3	20.9	3,226.0
1975	5.6	15.1	10.0	33.2	23.0	4,442.6
1976	4.2	15.8	9.9	33.6	23.5	3,683.3

[a]Mexico's National Accounts were revised in 1980; as a consequence, GDP growth figures from 1970 onward have been adjusted upward.

[b]For 1966-1970 the average annual percentage increase in the workers' cost of living was used. For 1971 onward the average annual percentage increase in the consumer price index was taken.

[c]The overall financial deficit as a percentage of GDP

[d]As a percentage of GDP

[e]Average for the period

Source: Nacional Financiera, La Economía Mexicana en Cifras (México, D.F., 1981); Banco de México, Indicadores Económicos, Subdirección de Investigación Económica, several issues; Banco de México, Indices de Precios, Subdirección de Investigación Económica, several issues; Secretaría de Hacienda y Crédito Público, Estadísticas Hacendarias del Sector Público, Dirección General de Evaluación Hacendaria, 1983.

trend value.
      In spite of the significant acceleration of infla-
tion and the financial and current account disequilibria
of 1973 and of the following year, economic policy was
kept on the same track until the end of the administration. The early warning signals did little to induce a
change of course. Undoubtedly, there was a marked change
in the priorities of policymakers during those years,
partly provoked by the past accumulation of social and
political demands and partly the result of the very
peculiar way in which President Echeverría exercised his
governmental authority. Yet the main justification for
the economic policy that prevailed at the time came from
conditions abroad. Thus, inflation was explained not as
a phenomenon caused by internal factors, but rather as a
consequence of the worldwide rise in inflation. This was
a most powerful argument for neglecting the urgency of
pursuing an antiinflationary policy. In turn, the
recession in the industrial countries served as an
argument for increasing domestic expenditure to compensate for the fall in external demand. The latter, because of its impact on Mexican exports, was also blamed
for worsening the current account disequilibrium.
      If the above external factors were used to justify
the economic policy, it was quite another external
phenomenon that made such a policy sustainable over
several years: the ample availability of foreign
financing. Table 11.2 shows the evolution of the stock
and flows of the foreign public debt during the period
1970-1976.[3] The fast growth in the nominal value of the
stock of the foreign public debt starting in 1973 has
already been mentioned. The sheer size of the debt says
little, if not measured in real terms or--preferably--
against other economic variables, especially against a
measure of the national wealth. Unfortunately, such a
measure does not exist for Mexico, and one has to settle
for the use of some proxies. This is done in Table 11.2,
where the net flow of the debt is assessed against
several macroeconomic aggregates. Of course, comparing
debt figures--which are measured in dollars--with
variables that are calculated in domestic currency has
to be done with some care. The usual procedure is to
convert peso-denominated figures into dollars by means of
the observed exchange rate. This method yields a very
distorted picture when the period of analysis has been
characterized by high inflation rates and an insufficiently
adjusted exchange rate. A major distortion in such
comparisons may also arise for periods following a
significant devaluation in the exchange rate. In order
to smooth out--if not avoid altogether--these difficulties, all ratios of Table 11.2 involving a peso-
denominated variable have been calculated with an
"equilibrium" exchange rate, derived from a purchasing
power parity method, as explained in the Appendix to

Table 11.2 Mexico: Evolution of the Foreign Public Debt During the Echeverría Term

| Year | Stock[a] | Net Flow[a] | Interest[a] Payments | Net Flow as Percentage of | | | | | Interest Payments/ |
				GDP	Fixed Investment	Current Account Income	Total Public Expenditure	Public Sector's Deficit	Current Account Income
1970	6,255.5	443.4	290.3	1.4	7.2	13.6	6.3	37.8	8.9
1971	6,666.7	411.2	306.2	1.2	6.7	11.6	5.8	48.8	8.7
1972	6,820.9	154.2	321.4	0.4	2.0	3.6	1.6	7.7	7.5
1973	8,448.8	1,627.9	442.1	3.2	16.8	30.1	12.0	47.3	8.2
1974	11,373.8	2,925.0	707.1	4.6	23.1	42.8	16.2	63.5	10.3
1975	15,705.1	4,331.3	1,031.5	5.5	25.8	60.7	16.7	55.2	14.5
1976	20,846.4	5,141.3	1,318.7	6.1	29.2	62.1	18.2	62.0	15.9

Note: All comparisons between a dollar and a peso variable were made by means of an "equilibrium" exchange rate calculated as described in the Appendix to Chapter 11.

[a] Millions of U.S. dollars

Source: Secretaría de Hacienda y Crédito Público, Estadísticas Hacendarias del Sector Público, Dirección General de Informática y Evolución Hacendarias, 1983; Ernesto Zedillo, "External Public Indebtedness in Mexico: Recent History and Future Oil Bounded Optimal Growth," Ph.D. dissertation, Yale University, 1981.

this chapter.
What is suggested by the nominal figures is amply
confirmed by all the relative measures. During 1970-1972,
the net flow of the foreign public debt averaged only 1
percent of GDP. That proportion more than tripled in
1973 and averaged 5.4 percent in 1974-1976. Equally
dramatic was the increase in the ratio of net flow to
current account income--a proxy closer to depicting the
growth of the debt with respect to the economy's capacity
to serve it. That ratio--11.6 percent in the first year
of the administration--rose to more than 60 percent in
the final year of the period. It can also be seen that
the increase in the foreign public debt went far beyond
the increase in public expenditure and fiscal deficits
during those years. Thus, the ratio of the net flow to
public expenditure, which was normally around 6 percent--
look at the figures for 1970-1971 in Table 11.2--doubled
in 1973 and tripled in 1976. As a proportion of the
public sector's deficit, the aggregate averaged 60 percent in the second half of the administration; it had
averaged less than 40 percent during the first half. In
short, the relative measures in Table 11.2 confirm that,
starting in 1973, public external borrowing took on increasing importance for the Mexican economy. This
importance was not reversed during the rest of the
Echeverría administration.
The impressive growth of the foreign debt from 1973
onward was accompanied by significant changes in several
debt-management aspects that seem worth mentioning.[4]
Let us look at the sources of credit. During the 1950s
and early 1960s, credits granted by official entities--
bilateral or multilateral organizations--were the main
source of foreign public borrowing. This predominance
of official lending started to decline rather rapidly in
the mid-1960s, so much so that by 1967 private financial
flows were the main source of public external financing.
This trend accelerated with the expansion of Mexican
borrowing. Thus, by 1973, 55 percent of the total stock
of foreign public debt was owed to private financial
institutions; three years later the proportion had increased to 75 percent. Also during the same period,
loans raised through syndicates in the Eurocurrency
market became the most popular instrument to tap
financial markets. Previously, direct bank loans had
constituted the usual instrument. In turn, the greater
reliance on syndicated Eurocredits allowed Mexico's
foreign public debt to become much more diversified with
respect to the number and nationalities of lending
institutions. It also permitted a modest degree of
diversification in the currencies in which the debt was
denominated.
Relying on external financing was doubtless further
encouraged by the relatively low cost of foreign savings.
The nominal implicit interest rate paid on the foreign

public debt averaged somewhat less than 9 percent during 1973-1976. However, when international inflation is accounted for, the real rate proves to be negative (around -2.0 percent) for the same period. This helps to explain why, in spite of the manyfold increases in borrowing, the ratio of interest payments to total current account income did not rise very much until 1975-1976, as shown in the last column of Table 11.2. Of course, as the debt mushroomed, lending conditions began to harden. Thus, whereas the typical Mexican Eurocurrency credit carried a total maturity of over ten years and a spread above LIBOR of only .625 in 1973, such terms became five years and 1.5, respectively, by 1976.

The seemingly smooth workings of the "new" model did not last very long. In 1974, the rate of inflation-- 12 percent in 1973--almost doubled, whereas GDP growth-- though still high--fell by more than two percentage points with respect to the rate registered the previous year. Economic growth further decreased in 1975 and 1976. At the same time, public finances continued to deteriorate and other economic policy instruments, such as the exchange rate and domestic interest rates, con- tinued to be handled inflexibly. A process of financial disintermediation resulted that, together with the effective crowding out induced by public expenditure and other factors, produced stagnation in private investment. The explosive combination of phenomena--mounting fiscal deficits, high rates of inflation, a fixed exchange rate, negative real rates of interest, and bitter exchanges between the public and the private sectors about each other's role in the economic and political life of the country--was bound to provoke capital flight.

The situation became openly worrisome by late 1975, yet only minor adjustments were made. After all, 1976 was an election year, and foreign financing, if more expensive, was still available. However, during July and August capital outflows became unbearable and on the eve of the last presidential address--on August 31--the crash occurred. The twenty-two-year-long era of fixed parity was terminated, and the peso was allowed to float against the dollar. By then, foreign sources of credit had shrunk, and it became only a matter of days before a standby agreement had to be signed with the IMF as a precondition to avoid a complete exhaustion of external financing. In short, another chapter of Mexico's history as foreign debtor had been closed--albeit temporarily--by the final months of 1976. Perhaps the epitaph for the period was provided by The Economist in 1977 when it stated rather cynically, "Mexico used to be the darling of international bankers. Not any more."

Why the debt cycle had become so pronounced, short, and explosive--not only for Mexico but also for many other developing countries--became a focal point of

conferences and articles. The early attempts at probing
into the general causes of the higher indebtedness unan-
imously pointed to the 1973-1974 oil shock and the subsequent world depression as the main causes of the
spectacular increase in the LDCs' foreign public debt.
In other words, external shocks were to be blamed for
what happened. This point of view also prevailed among
Mexican officials and was taken as an excuse to avoid,
or at least delay, significant changes in the conduct of
economic policy. This view as applied to Mexico, however,
was wrong.

If the external-shocks hypothesis was correct for
countries such as Brazil, it had only a minor content of
truth with respect to Mexico. In previous works guided
by Balassa's 1979 pioneer study, "Policy Responses to
External Shocks in Developing Countries," I analyzed the
influence of external disturbances on the growth of the
foreign public debt during the period of concern.[5] The
methodology used consisted of decomposing increases in
the debt over and above its trend value during several
years. Some were strictly identifiable as caused by
external shocks; the rest were attributable to policy
responses to external shocks and/or to internal shocks
themselves.

Within this framework, two types of external shocks
were carefully defined and accounted for: the balance-
of-payments effects of reduced world demand for Mexican
exports and the balance-of-payments effects of adverse
terms-of-trade changes. The results of this research
could not be more striking: During the period 1973-1976,
the foreign public debt grew US$10.1 billion beyond what
was warranted for past trends. Yet, of this additional
growth, only 22 percent can be accounted for by external
shocks. Actually, external conditions proved to have a
favorable impact on the country's balance of payments in
1973, regarding the expansion in foreign demand as well
as the improvement in the terms of trade. During the
1974-1976 period, these external phenomena were truly
debt inducing--especially the worsening of terms of
trade, but their overall impact falls very short of
explaining the tremendous growth in Mexico's debt.

Consequently, one has to look at internal factors in
order to explain the growth of the debt. Results of the
study showed that increased import demand was the most
important factor underlying the surge in the debt level
during the 1973-1975 period, whereas private capital
flight--by a wide margin--became the main debt-inducing
phenomenon in 1976.

Put in a nutshell, the greater external disequilibrium
of the Mexican economy during the Echeverría administration was provoked not by external shocks but rather by
internal ones. The adoption of a broader range of
economic and social objectives on the part of the government was not accompanied by more and better policy

instruments.[6] A sharply increased aggregate demand
implied not only more demand for imports but also a
reduced availability of surpluses to be exported. Such
effects were further reinforced by the acceleration of
domestic inflation vis-à-vis external rates. The latter
phenomenon, interacting with a rather inflexible interest-
rates policy, implied a significant reduction in real
yields of liabilities offered by domestic financial
intermediaries. As a consequence, the rate of real growth
of financial savings started to decline very rapidly,
becoming only one-sixth of what it had been during the
period 1965-1970. As inflation continued--thus over-
valuing the real exchange rate--and the external disequilibrium persisted, expectations about a peso
devaluation sharply increased. This led to an avalanche
of capital flight that was resisted only by means of
contracting more foreign loans and draining off foreign-
exchange reserves.

In short, the Echeverría government, sincerely or
not, tried to achieve more political and economic
objectives than the administrations that preceded it in
the previous forty years. Such efforts, however, demanded much more than an unbridled expansion of public
expenditure and external borrowing. The final result
could be nothing less than a financial crisis, in the
midst of which the López Portillo administration took
over in December 1976.

FROM BOOM TO BUST: THE LÓPEZ PORTILLO
ADMINISTRATION (1977-1982)

Mexico's economic outlook was extremely gloomy in
early 1977. The country's postwar record of fast
economic growth had begun to look like a phenomenon of
the past with little chance it could be repeated in the
near future. Very few observers doubted that the
stabilization program signed with the IMF in November
1976 marked the start of a long period in which slow
economic growth would be the price to pay if the country's precarious financial situation was to be improved.
In spite of the IMF standby agreement and the firmness
with which it began to be applied in early 1977, there
were widespread fears about the country's ability to
continue borrowing in international capital markets.

In many--but not all--respects, the country's
economic performance lived up to those expectations during
1977 (see Table 11.3). Adjustment, if not dramatic, was
truly drastic. Total real investment decreased almost
7 percent in 1977. The public sector's deficit as a percentage of GDP fell by more than three percentage points.
The average exchange rate for 1977 was 80 percent higher
than the rate that was kept fixed during more than two
decades. The current account deficit fell by almost 60

Table 11.3 Mexico: Basic Economic Indicators During the López Portillo Term

	GDP Real Growth	Inflation December to December	Inflation Average	Public Investment (1)	Public Investment (2)	Private Investment (1)	Private Investment (2)	Total Investment (1)	Total Investment (2)	Current Account Deficit (millions of U.S. dollars)	Exchange Rate Nominal[a] (pesos per U.S. dollar)	Exchange Rate Real[b] (Index)	Oil Reserves[c]	Oil Production[d]
1977	3.4	27.4	27.2	-6.0	8.9	-7.3	10.7	-6.7	19.6	1,596.4	22.7	102.5	16,001.6	981.1
1978	8.2	16.2	17.5	20.9	10.0	10.5	11.1	15.2	21.1	2,693.0	22.7	99.1	40,194.0	1,212.6
1979	9.2	20.0	18.2	17.8	11.0	22.4	12.4	20.2	23.4	4,870.5	22.8	93.9	45,803.6	1,471.0
1980	8.3	29.8	26.3	12.4	11.0	17.1	13.2	14.9	24.2	7,223.3	23.3	83.9	60,126.3	1,936.0
1981	7.9	28.7	28.0	--	--	--	--	14.7	25.7	12,544.3	26.2	77.4	72,008.4	2,313.0
1982	-.5	98.9	58.9	--	--	--	--	-15.9	22.7	2,684.5	122.5	146.9	72,008.4[e]	2,748.2

(1) Percentage change in real investment
(2) Investment as percentage of GDP

[a] Nominal exchange rate at the closing of December of each year (for 1982 it is the average of the free and controlled rates)
[b] Real exchange rate index calculated as described in the Appendix to Chapter 11 (value at the closing of December of each year)
[c] In millions of barrels (includes oil and natural gas)
[d] Daily production in thousands of barrels
[e] According to the source, the 1982 figures are the same as 1981 because the major oil fields are currently being studied for a better evaluation of total reserves.

Source: Banco de México, Indicadores Económicos, Subdirección de Investigación Económica, several issues; Banco de México, Indices de Precios, Subdirección de Investigación Económica, several issues; Secretaría de Programación y Presupuesto, Sistema de Cuentas Nacionales de México, several issues; Petróleos Mexicanos, El Sector Petrolero Mexicano, 1979-1982. Estadísticos Seleccionadas, Gerencia de Análisis y Evaluación del Mercado Internacional, Coordinación de Comercio Internacional, 1983.

percent, and GDP growth registered its lowest rate in more than two decades.

Contrary to what had been expected earlier about the availability of external financing, the public sector was able to raise the targeted amounts in international capital markets. Ex post, this achievement was not surprising. A deus ex machina had begun to appear. Shortly after taking office, the new government changed the policy of handling almost secretly the figures on the country's oil reserves and revealed that figures were much higher than previously thought. Thus, proven hydrocarbon reserves of 6.4 billion barrels by the end of 1975 increased to 11.2 billion by the end of 1976 and to 16 billion by late 1977. These figures, as well as the decisiveness shown by the new government in taking advantage of the country's oil potential, made international bankers once again enthusiastic about Mexico.

The "nightmare of 1976" was over soon. By late 1977, expectations about Mexico's economic prospects were very different from what they had been only a year before. Although other factors--such as the conciliatory tone of the new administration and the early successes of its economic adjustment program--played an important role, there should be no doubt that the announcements about oil reserves and the plans to exploit them were the main factor behind the renewed vigor in aggregate expenditure that led to the "earlier-than-expected" recovery of the economy in 1978.

Actually, the public-expenditure-led growth model was revived with as much vigor as it had been during the peak Echeverría years. In 1978, public investment grew more than 20 percent, and overall public expenditure started to increase again as a proportion of GDP (see Table 11.3). In spite of the fact that the traumatic events of the mid-1970s were too recent to be forgotten, nobody seemed to panic, for it was claimed that the revival of the failed model was being implemented on bases quite different from the ones observed before. First, it was said, the resources to finance the development of Mexico in a noninflationary fashion were going to be provided by the new oil wealth. Furthermore, taking advantage of such wealth required the expansion of public investment at any event.

Second, it was also affirmed that the government was going to more actively use other policy instruments left practically untouched before. In this respect, there were some encouraging symptoms at the beginning. A financial reform was undertaken by which the banking system was restructured and the instruments of monetary control were modernized. Interest-rate policy became much more flexible and attentive to real yields and to developments in foreign financial markets, and Treasury Certificates (CETES) were introduced as a more rational way to finance the public sector's deficit. On the

fiscal side, an in-depth reform was announced with the
introduction of the value-added tax. With respect to
industrial and commercial policy, there were some early
attempts to rationalize the whole structure of relative
prices through the elimination of quantitative restrictions on imports and the simplification of fiscal incentives for industrial activities. Third, this time the
public sector was not going to be alone in enhancing the
country's stock of capital. Private investment was to be
encouraged so that a more balanced pattern of growth
evolved.

The model, as supported by this rationality, seemed
to perform satisfactorily--some would say, terrifically--
for a few years. It led to the highest GDP growth--a
rate of 8.4 percent on average during the 1978-1981
period--ever experienced by the Mexican economy. As
predicted, not only public investment soared but also
private investment. Consequently, total fixed investment,
which had been less than 20 percent of GDP in 1977,
reached a proportion of 25 percent in 1981. Although
Mexican labor statistics are rather unreliable, it is
indisputable that employment grew significantly, so much
so that legal minimum wages stopped having much of a
significance. The labor market became, indeed, a
suppliers' market.

The bet on oil was a winning one, at least for a
while. Proven reserves continued growing every year,
and their exploitation evolved rapidly. Oil exports,
which had been only .2 million barrels a day in 1977,
surpassed the one-million-barrel-a-day mark by late 1980.
The timing to tap the new oil wealth seemed even more
striking: Crude prices increased two and a half times
between the date the first optimistic news on oil reserves
was known (late 1976) and 1980.

On the external-debt front, some developments were
also very positive up to 1980. The stock of foreign
public debt grew rather conservatively during the period
1977-1980. The net flow of the aggregate averaged only
US$3.2 billion during that period--far less than the
average flow of more than US$4 billion registered in the
last three years of the Echeverria term. Other components
of the country's external debt grew more dynamically.
Thus, the private sector's foreign debt--of firms and
banks--that had amounted to US$6.8 billion at the end of
1977 reached almost US$17 billion by late 1980. Yet,
the total external debt, when measured against the
size of economy, consistently decreased through 1980.
As shown by the figures of Table 11.4, the ratio of total
debt to GDP fell from 35.8 percent in 1977 to 31.3 percent in 1980.[7] However, when the net flow of the total
external debt is assessed against total fixed investment
and current account income, its importance started to
climb right after 1978, as shown in Table 11.5.

Table 11.4 Mexico: The Evolution of the Total External Debt During the López Portillo Term

	Stock of Foreign Debt (millions of U.S. dollars)				Stock of Foreign Public Debt[a]	Stock of Total Foreign Debt[a]
	Public	Private	Commercial Banks	Total		
1977	23,834	5,000	1,800	30,634	27.8	35.8
1978	26,422	5,200	2,000	33,622	25.7	32.7
1979	29,757	7,900	2,600	40,257	23.2	31.4
1980	33,873	11,800	5,100	50,773	20.9	31.3
1981	52,156	14,900	7,000	74,056	27.6	39.1
1982	58,146	18,000	8,000	84,146	29.8	43.1

Note: All comparisons between a dollar and a peso variable were made by means of an "equilibrium" exchange rate calculated as described in the Appendix to Chapter 11.

[a]As percentage of GDP

Source: Banco de México, Indicadores Económicos, Subdirección de Investigación Económica, several issues; Secretaría de Hacienda y Crédito Público, México: Economic and Financial Statistics, December 1983.

Table 11.5 Mexico: The Flows of the External Debt During the López Portillo Term

	Net Flow (millions of U.S. dollars)		Interest Payments (millions of U.S. dollars)		Net Flow of Total External Debt as Percentage of		Net Flow of Foreign Debt as a Percentage of			Interest Payments of External Debt as a Total Percentage of
	Total External Debt	Foreign Public Debt	Total External Debt	Foreign Public Debt	Total Fixed Investment	Current Account Income	GDP	Public Expenditure	Public Sector Deficit	Current Account Income
1977	3,287.3	2,987.3	1,973.9	1,542.3	19.5	35.8	3.5	11.3	51.8	21.5
1978	2,988.8	2,588.8	2,571.6	2,023.1	13.8	25.6	2.5	7.8	37.8	22.1
1979	6,634.7	3,334.7	3,709.3	2,888.4	22.1	40.8	2.6	7.8	35.3	22.8
1980	10,515.5	4,115.5	5,476.7	3,957.6	26.9	42.2	2.5	7.1	32.3	22.0
1981	23,283.3	18,283.3	8,383.2	5,476.0	48.0	75.6	9.7	22.8	66.0	27.2
1982	10,089.6	5,989.6	10,879.4	7,791.3	23.2	32.8	3.1	6.4	17.4	35.4

Note: All comparisons between a dollar and a peso variable were made by means of an "equilibrium" exchange rate calculated as described in the Appendix to Chapter 11.

Source: Banco de México, Indicadores Económicos, Subdirección de Investigación Económica, several issues; Secretaría de Programación y Presupuesto, Sistema de Cuentas Nacionales de México, several issues.

In any case, the public foreign debt, which had been the bankers' headache in 1976, evolved very reasonably through 1980. Its net flow, with respect to several relevant macroeconomic aggregates after the initial adjustment of 1977, was kept in rather modest proportions during two-thirds of the López Portillo administration. Thus--with respect to GDP, public expenditure, and the public-sector deficit--the net flow averaged 2.5 percent, 7.5 percent, and 35.1 percent, respectively, during 1978-1980.

The relative adjustment in the size of the foreign public debt during that period, together with the expectations created by the new oil wealth, should help to explain the tremendous upgrading Mexico's credit experienced in international capital markets. Fierce competition among foreign lenders to grant new loans to the Mexican government and to public enterprises was an everyday event during the booming years. In a matter of hours and days, important credit lines could be arranged. Putting together Eurocredit syndicates was not a difficult task by any means; there was always an excess demand to subscribe them. It is interesting to notice that 35 percent of the gross borrowings undertaken by public agencies in 1979 was made through close syndicates; the participation in such deals had been nil in 1977. Undoubtedly, the frustration of many foreign lenders in placing new loans in the public sector was not unrelated to the ease with which the Mexican private sector was able to finance itself abroad during the same period.

Needless to say, Mexican negotiators took full advantage of the bullishness of the market to improve on the maturity profile and cost of the country's debt.[8] Whereas the maturity of credits obtained by Mexican public agencies in the Eurocurrency market was, on average, a bit less than five years during 1975 and 1976, such average maturity became longer than eight years by 1978 and 1979. Equally important was the improvement in the spreads over LIBOR charged in Eurocurrency credits. The typical Mexican long-term credit carried an average spread of around 1.625 percentage points during the 1975-1977 period. For the same customers the spread fluctuated between .625 and .875 percentage points in 1978 and 1979. In fact, what had been a very expensive debt, with maturities heavily concentrated in the medium term in 1976, two years later had become a nicely scheduled one carrying very low spreads only comparable to those paid by prime customers in Western industrialized countries. Needless to say, the national oil company Petróleos Mexicanos was of paramount importance in improving on the cost and profile of the debt. Its "financial glamor" was fully utilized for such purposes. The state oil monopoly's participation in gross borrowing by the Mexican public sector increased from 14.5 percent in 1977 to almost 40 percent by 1979.

Table 11.6 Mexico: Current Account During the López Portillo Term (in billions of U.S. dollars)

	1977	Percentage Change (1976-1977)	1978	Percentage Change (1977-1978)	1979	Percentage Change (1978-1979)	1980	Percentage Change (1979-1980)	1981	Percentage Change (1980-1981)	1982	Percentage Change (1981-1982)
Expenses	10.8	-9.9	11.7	8.2	21.1	81.4	32.2	52.2	43.4	34.8	33.4	-23.0
Imports (CIF)	6.0	-9.8	8.3	38.4	12.6	51.0	19.8	57.1	25.2	27.2	15.0	-40.2
Interest & Profits	2.2	4.5	2.8	28.8	4.1	45.9	5.9	45.6	8.9	50.9	11.4	27.7
Services & Others	2.5	-20.6	3.2	26.5	4.5	38.9	6.5	44.4	9.3	43.3	7.0	-24.9
Income	9.2	10.9	11.7	27.0	16.3	39.6	24.9	53.4	30.8	23.5	30.7	-0.3
Oil exports[a]	1.0	19.3	1.9	80.7	3.9	107.6	9.9	154.5	14.6	47.5	16.5	13.1
Nonoil exports	3.6	12.7	4.2	16.0	4.9	17.7	5.3	6.4	4.8	-7.8	4.5	-6.5
Interests abroad	0.2	32.0	0.4	75.1	0.7	72.4	1.0	47.2	1.4	35.6	1.2	-10.0
Services & others	4.3	-3.4	5.2	20.7	6.8	30.2	8.8	30.2	10.0	13.8	8.5	-15.4
Current Account Deficit	1.6	-56.7	2.7	68.7	4.9	80.1	7.2	48.3	12.5	73.7	2.7	-78.6

Note: The percentage changes were calculated with figures in millions of U.S. dollars.

[a] Includes oil, gas, derivatives, and petrochemicals

Source: Banco de México, Indicadores Económicos, Subdirección de Investigación Económica, several issues.

310

Unfortunately, booms are not forever. While the idyll between international bankers and Mexico was reaching its most intense stages (1980-1981), some fundamental disequilibria in the domestic economy had taken on renewed force and reached tremendous proportions. At the same time, the outside world had also changed.

Table 11.6 shows in gross terms what happened in the external sector. The early adjustment in the current account deficit of 1977-1978 had frankly subsided by 1979, when the deficit reached US$4.9 billion in spite of the fact that the value of oil exports had increased almost four times in just a couple of years and nonoil exports had also been growing very dynamically. By 1979, the Mexican economy was importing US$12.6 billion (CIF) worth of merchandise--a pretty high figure if assessed against any macroeconomic variable. Yet, imports further increased to almost US$20.0 billion the next year. As a consequence, and notwithstanding the fact that oil exports had almost reached the US$10.0 billion level, the current account deficit exceeded US$7.2 billion. This seemed inconceivable for an oil-endowed developing country. Even if due account is taken of international inflation and its impact on import prices and interest rates, the fact that the current account deficit could reach such a level in a year in which oil revenues increased two and one-half times should have caused observers of the Mexican economy to raise their eyebrows. To the international bankers' comfort, Mexico became the "champion of absorption"--not only of its own oil revenues, but of others as well.

The external disequilibrium was just the tip of the iceberg. It was purely a consequence of many other disarrays in the Mexican economy--most notably, the unchecked expansion in aggregate demand led by the growth in public expenditure. Table 11.7 tells the story of the public finances during the López Portillo years. As was shown in Table 11.7, public expenditure as a proportion of GDP had peaked at 33.6 percent during the previous administration. In spite of the early rhetoric, this proportion was reached again in 1979 and was surpassed by two percentage points in 1980. It was not caused only by the need for increasing PEMEX investment; non-PEMEX public expenditure as a share of GDP was consistently augmented from 1977 on. Of course, within the context of short-run macroeconomic policy, a mushrooming public expenditure is not so much of a problem in itself. It becomes so, however, when politicians of any ideological stance forget about the financing side of it. Although the public income derived from the oil sector almost doubled as a proportion of GDP between 1977 and 1980, the overall deficit could never be reduced to the levels contemplated at the beginning of the administration. What happened was just the opposite, worsening after 1978. The macroeconomic impact of the

Table 11.7 Mexico: Public Finance During the López Portillo Term (as percentage of GDP)

	Total Public Expenditure	Public Expenditure Without PEMEX	PEMEX Expenditure	Public Expenditure Without Interest Payments[a]	Total Public Income	Income Oil Sector	Income Nonoil Sector	Financial Deficit	Financial Deficit Internal	Financial Deficit External
1977	30.9	27.2	3.7	29.0	24.2	4.3	19.8	6.7	3.1	3.7
1978	32.2	27.5	4.7	30.2	25.5	5.0	20.4	6.7	4.0	2.7
1979	33.6	28.3	5.3	31.4	26.2	6.1	20.1	7.4	4.5	2.9
1980	35.6	30.4	5.2	33.5	27.8	8.0	19.7	7.9	4.9	2.9
1981	42.4	35.0	7.5	40.0	27.7	8.0	19.7	14.7	6.2	8.5
1982	48.9	41.3	7.6	40.8	31.0	12.4	18.6	17.9	14.1	3.8

[a]Paid by the public sector on its internal and foreign debts

Source: Secretaría de Hacienda y Crédito Público, Estadísticas Hacendarias del Sector Público, Dirección General de Informática y Evaluación Hacendaria, 1983.

public sector's financial disequilibrium is better
assessed by looking at a concept that in Mexican public
finances is called the internal deficit.[9] As shown in
Table 11.7, the deterioration of this factor was more
acute than that registered by the overall financial
deficit. The government's retreat from early intentions
of increasing the relative size of fiscal and public-
enterprise revenues explains this disequilibrium as much
as the overflow of all categories of public expenditure.

The impact of the fiscal deficit on the domestic
market's disequilibrium was reinforced by the rapid
expansion of private demand, both in consumption and
investment. In spite of the rather precipitate and un-
planned opening of the economy to foreign imports, the
strong demand pull was bound to have a significant effect
on domestic inflation. As shown by the figures of
Table 11.3, inflation could not be lowered even to the
levels of 1975-1976, and it started to accelerate again
in 1979. Yet, during more than four years and well into
1981, the exchange rate was kept practically fixed.
Obviously, this situation had to lead to a consistent
overvaluation of the Mexican peso, as proven by the index
of the real exchange rate of Table 11.3. Considering
the overheating of the economy and the exchange-rate
policy followed at the time, it is not surprising at all
that the external-sector disequilibrium worsened to the
degree it did despite increased oil revenues.

The economic balance of 1980 should have sufficed to
alert policymakers of the risks ahead. At that point,
far less than an overall adjustment was needed. A clean-
up of public finances to stop the worsening trend of the
fiscal deficit, plus some adjustments--especially in
exchange-rate policy with possibly a more active crawl--
would have done the trick. Admittedly, the budget
approved for fiscal year 1981 explicitly incorporated
the objective of not allowing the overall deficit to become further increased in nominal terms. Unfortunately,
this was just a formality. In practice, even a timid
gradualistic approach on fiscal matters and exchange-rate
policy sounded like heresy--even an insult--to the
rationale of the time. The most popular members of the
cabinet were those who produced the grandest projects and
programs, overriding the budget approved by the congress.
(In contrast, the head of the central bank was no longer
summoned to the economic cabinet meetings by early 1980.)
Just as had happened in the Echeverría years, the
president himself authorized the ampliaciones pre-
supuestales (out-of-budget items) that were needed.

The inertia of the public-expenditure-led growth
model proved to be overwhelming. The warning voices of
the more prudent members of the cabinet were completely
ineffective to provoke a change of course. It is not an
exaggeration to say that the majority of the pessimistic
economic forecasts made then found their way, not to the

cabinet meetings, but to the wastebasket. This explains why the 1981 budget overlooked not only internal bottle-necks but also conditions abroad. Perhaps the most dramatic example of this miscalculation is provided by the projections on the value of crude exports for 1981. The budget makers assumed that Mexico could export a volume 75 percent higher at a price 10 percent above what was registered in 1980, when oil prices were already above thirty U.S. dollars a barrel and the world economy had started to enter into a deep recession.

The official scenario still had some credibility during the first half of 1981. The beginning of the debacle took place in June when it became clear that PEMEX had to lower sale prices in order to continue placing orders of crude abroad. This was too hard to swallow. Instead of facing the signals of the market--as naturally as had been done two years before, when oil prices started their upward swing--the Ministry of National Properties and Industrial Development (SEPAFIN) designed a "new" marketing strategy by which those buyers unwilling to pay the Mexican prices would be erased from PEMEX's customer list.[10] Forgetting about the "small country" assumption--perhaps for being too neoclassical?--a good percentage of Mexican oil exports was left out of the international crude market over the space of several weeks. Although holders of wealth had started to read the basic economic statistics in a less complacent way, the possibility of an exchange-rate devaluation still looked somewhat academic just before the "oil price affair." Such a possibility became an open threat by mid-June, however, leading to a tremendous capital flight and to "dollarization" of deposits in the Mexican banking system.

The seriousness of the situation demanded bold actions that again were not taken or were postponed. Even though there was official admission that the peso was under heavy attack, little was done beyond rhetoric to face what had started to be a financial crisis. The exchange rate continued to be depreciated daily at an annual rate of only 9 percent. An across-the-board cut of 4 percent in public expenditure was decreed, but with respect to the already higher than budgeted level. And, as it turned out, not even this timid adjustment was made. By late July, the targeted overall deficit had been revised upward to 540 billion pesos (from less than 415 billion pesos in the original budget). Yet, when the year was over, the deficit reached 865 billion pesos. This outcome was not caused by a relative fall in public income, since the same proportion of GDP was kept. Actually, the underlying factor was the tremendous in-crease in public expenditure. The latter aggregate evolved from 35.6 percent of GDP in 1980 to 42.4 percent in 1981 (Table 11.7). As a consequence, the overall deficit reached almost 15 percent of GDP (it had been 10

percent in the "worst" Echeverría year). One does not
have to be a monetarist to realize that such an imbalance
has to produce a profound disequilibrium in the money
market that sooner or later has to be settled either via
prices, the balance of payments, or a combination of both.
The balance-of-payments effect was the dominant one
in the Mexican economy during 1981. The current account
deficit soared to US$12.5 billion. It can be said that
an impressive imports bill (US$25.1 billion) and a sharp
worsening in the traditionally favorable services account
was what led to such a result. Although oil exports did
not reach the level officially forecast, they did reach a
value of US$14.6 billion--47.5 percent more than during
the previous year. Equally impressive was the drain via
capital account. There is no foolproof way of estimating
capital flight. An idea can be gained, however, from the
fact that the official balance-of-payments statistics of
1981 reported an increase of Mexican financial assets
abroad of US$2.5 billion, as well as a negative errors
and omissions item for US$8.4 billion. Most probably,
the latter figure contains other phenomena such as
smuggling, but at any rate a total estimate for capital
flight between US$8 and 9 billion does not seem un-
reasonable.[11]

The question is why right after the oil problem the
Mexican economy, far from sinking into a financial crisis
that would have forced an immediate adjustment, was able
to continue growing at the expense of enlarging its
fundamental disequilibria. The answer to this riddle
can be found in the availability of foreign financing.
As shown in Table 11.4, Mexico's total external debt grew
more than US$23 billion in 1981 alone. Of course, most
of the new debt was contracted by the public sector. The
net flow of the foreign public debt was US$18.3 billion.
Yet, all of the increase in the commercial banks' external
debt of that year (around US$2.0 billion) was also relent
to the public sector. Undoubtedly, in 1981 foreign
financing became the slack variable that served to avoid
the adjustment that otherwise would have been warranted.

Needless to say, resorting to external borrowing in
such a way had to bring about profound and adverse
consequences. Immediately, there was a sharp deterioration in lending conditions to Mexico. At the close of
1980, the short-term foreign public debt was only
US$1.5 billion. A year later, the same aggregate jumped
to US$10.8 billion, not counting the amounts obtained
through Mexican commercial banks. The enviable spreads
of a few months earlier had also started to vanish and
were replaced by new ones that were considerably higher.[12]

It will take the talent of a top specialist on highly
competitive but imperfect markets to understand why
international bankers did not stop lending to Mexico
before they did. One possible yet unexplored explanation is that they did not individually realize what they

were doing as a whole. Some of them might have believed
the official story that Mexico was just experiencing a
temporary cash-flow problem and had fallen into the temptation of recycling (short-term and profitably) the then
abundant petrodollars. Others, traditionally involved in
Mexico, just followed the inertia of past years. What
seems to be clear, however, is that very few knew that
Mexico's debt was growing so fast during the second half
of 1981. It is highly suggestive that the balance-of-
payments statistics released in February 1982 still
reported a net increase in the foreign public debt of
US$14.5 billion for 1981--almost US$4 billion less than
the actual figure.[13]

Despite some final resistance, it was announced that
the peso was being devalued on the night of February 17--
initially by 40 percent; some days later an overall
stabilization package of rather orthodox making was
announced. For a few days, it seemed possible that the
Mexican economy could pass from a booming situation to an
orderly adjustment. This was far from true; the initial
adjustment program was soon overridden by measures that
were clearly inconsistent with it. Although the program
was never officially repudiated--and was even formalized
as a presidential decree--it was not put into real
practice either. Thus, for example, the program called
for a maximum emergency wage increase of 10 percent.
Instead, and just a few weeks after the devaluation,
wage raises of up to 30 percent were decreed by the
government. The program also called for immediate increases in the prices charged for services and goods
produced by public enterprises; several months had to
pass, however, before the first significant raise was
announced. Rather, an "emergency" plan to support
productive firms was implemented. By providing fiscal
relief and granting outright subsidies, this plan constituted another clear signal that it would take a while
before public finances could indeed be improved.
Pressures to finish projects already started made it
very difficult to control the nominal expansion in public
expenditure.

Meanwhile, the clashes between the government and the
private-sector spokesmen--quite reminiscent of the ones
that had occurred six years previously--became more
frequent and fiery. Not surprisingly, as soon as mid-
March 1982 there were signs that capital flight had
started again. Another major devaluation was avoided
for several months, but only at the expense of exhausting
foreign-exchange reserves and using the last "voluntary"
foreign credit available to Mexico. Renewing short-term
credits that had been obtained during 1981 became increasingly difficult. Renewal periods became shorter and
shorter while spreads climbed higher and higher.

In order to alleviate an impressive piling up of
short-term credits inherited from 1981, three important

medium-term syndicates were arranged during the first
semester of 1982. The first, placed by PEMEX in February,
raised US$2.0 billion. A state development bank
(Nacional Financiera--NAFINSA) was the borrowing agency
in the second, which took place in March. It provided
US$1.2 billion. The last syndication consisted of a
"jumbo" of US$2.5 billion with the Mexican federal
government as debtor and was arranged during May and June.
In many ways, this credit was a turning point. As the
facility was being put together, it became clear that
market perception concerning Mexico's creditworthiness
was completely deteriorating. Even though the pricing of
the loan to lenders was very attractive compared to
previous deals, it took an enormous effort on the part
of Mexican negotiators to gather the necessary commitments.[14] To their dismay, only 75 banks out of 650
accepted the invitation to subscribe the facility.
Considering the enormous difficulties that had to be
faced before signing the loan on June 30, it became clear
that the only debt-management expedient left was to
continue rolling over short-term credits--at any price and
at any maturity. This, of course, could not last.

The peso continued to be under heavy speculation
during July 1982. Too late, it was decided to implement
some of the measures included in the Economic Adjustment
Program that had not been put into effect. Accordingly,
at the beginning of August, it was announced that the
prices of some basic products were being raised. After
this announcement was made, pressure on the central bank's
reserves became unbearable. On August 6, 1982, a new
two-tier foreign-exchange system was set up. Still
speculation continued, and just one week later, dollar-
denominated deposits in the Mexican banking system were
made payable only in domestic currency. Banks were also
ordered to temporarily suspend foreign-exchange transactions. In the face of those events, it became evident
that foreign creditors had been totally scared away and
that the resumption of any kind of normal credit conditions could not be expected for a long time.

At that moment, the financial authorities could
either wait for foreign creditors to make public the
country's insolvency or confront the facts and declare
unilaterally that the country was not able to keep up
with payments of principal. Wisely, the second approach
was followed. On August 20, the secretary of finance,
Jesús Silva-Herzog, met with representatives of a large
number of creditor banks and requested a three-month
moratorium on payments of principal as well as the
formation of an advisory group of creditors to negotiate
the restructuring of the foreign public debt. A few days
earlier, the Mexican government had obtained important
financial backing from its U.S. counterpart in the form
of credits from the Commodity Credit Corporation and the
Treasury Department. Negotiations with the Bank for

International Settlements to obtain a US$1.5 billion credit from several of its members were initiated in the last days of August. Early that month, formal talks about a standby agreement had been started with an IMF mission.

The realism of August comforted Mexico's creditors for only a few days. On September 1, President López Portillo announced that private banks were being nationalized and that overall foreign-exchange controls were being instituted. The international banking community must have panicked at the idea that such a radical stance could also spread to the management of the foreign-debt problem--a possibility that, indeed, was very feasible for a few weeks. To everybody's luck, it did not happen.

EPILOGUE, OR HOW TO ATTEMPT MENDING A COUNTRY'S INTERNATIONAL CREDIT

When President López Portillo left office on December 1, 1982, the Mexican economy was experiencing a crisis even more profound than the one registered six years earlier--something inconceivable for a country that had earned US$47 billion in oil revenues and had gone through a rapid process of capital formation during the previous five years. Thus, by the end of 1982, real GDP had fallen by .5 percent; inflation had reached almost 100 percent (consumer price index growth, December to December); the monetary authorities had completely lost control of the foreign-exchange market, so much so that the black-market rate was more than double the average official rates;[15] capital flight continued practically unchecked, in spite of the supposedly overall foreign-exchange controls; the public sector's financial deficit had reached 17.9 percent of GDP during the year; the domestic financial system was shrinking; and, for practical purposes, the country was in a moratorium with respect of its foreign-debt obligations.

In fact, during the last four months of 1982, the country complied only with payments of interest and a minor percentage of payments on principal of the foreign public debt. All payments corresponding to the private foreign debt had been suspended. The country's overall external debt picture was dismal. The public sector had arrears of US$8.1 billion in payments of principal already; furthermore, US$14.3 billion would have come due in 1984 and 1985. Relatively speaking, the private sector's situation was worse. It owed US$18.0 billion to foreign financial institutions, two-thirds of which had repayment periods that went no farther than 1984. It also declared US$4.0 billion in liabilities outstanding with foreign suppliers when a registry at the Secretariat of Commerce was opened.

On general economic policy, the new administration opted for a drastic adjustment--it actually had no other alternative. Not surprisingly, the core of the Economic Adjustment Program was to correct the public finance disequilibrium. The target was to reduce the deficit to 8.5 percent of GDP in 1983. As a consequence, in addition to important across-the-board real cuts in public expenditure, stiff actions on the income side were taken at once. They included significant increases both in the value-added tax and in income-tax rates for upper brackets, as well as major revisions in the prices charged by public enterprises (gasoline, electricity, and so on). At the same time, important rectifications were made on the exchange-rate and financial policies. The overall system of exchange controls was replaced by a rather standard dual system consisting of a controlled market (including all merchandise exports, the majority of merchandise imports, and all foreign-debt-related flows) and a free market (for the rest of transactions). The initial level in the exchange rate for the free market was placed close to the rate prevailing on the black market, thus leading to a significant reduction in the latter's volume of transactions. In the controlled market, an opening rate that overshot the value considered to be equilibrium from a PPP criterion was dictated. A daily "crawl" in this rate also followed. In the financial sphere, domestic interest rates were increased, and a strict monetary targeting consistent with the pursued adjustment in public finances was implemented.

A number of the above measures were contained in the letter of intention submitted to the IMF Board of Directors in November 1982 and were ratified as soon as the new administration took over. The agreement reached with the technical mission of the IMF called for a net flow of foreign lending to the public sector provided by private banks of US$5.0 billion in 1983. To the creditors' surprise, the IMF managing director let everybody know that he would "not recommend the approval of the IMF Agreement to the Executive Board of the IMF without assurances from both official sources and commercial banks that adequate external financing was in place for the success of the Mexican Adjustment Program and the IMF Agreement, and the principles of a realistic restructuring scheme of the Mexican debt would be favorably considered by the community."[16] The telex from which the foregoing quote was taken contained the principles of the strategy followed by the Mexican government to deal with both the borrowing of net resources and the restructuring of the foreign public debt in 1983.

The essence of the approach to obtain the additional financing required for 1983 was to organize an unprecedented number of banks to subscribe a "mammoth" loan (US$5.0 billion). Each creditor's relative participation in the deal was defined on the basis of the exposure of

each in the country as of August 1982. It implied that
every bank with assets in Mexico was requested--and some-
how subtly forced--to underwrite the facility. This
element of "fairness" explains, to a great extent, the
enthusiastic support received from the largest banks to
raise the needed resources. The attractive pricing also
helped to close the deal. Creditors were offered, at
their own option, a spread of 2.5 over LIBOR or 2.125
over prime. The maturity requested did not punish lenders
either; it consisted of only six years, including a three-
year grace period. Attractive commitment and facility
fees were offered as well. With the assistance of the
advisory group and of top officials from the IMF and
several central banks, including the Federal Reserve,
the credit was granted practically on time, an impressive
total of 526 banks having participated in this syndication.
     Regarding the restructuring of the foreign public
debt, the target was to reschedule all payments to fall
due between August 23, 1982, and December 31, 1984, with
the exception of payments to be due on "excluded" debt.
The latter comprised, besides other minor categories,
credits granted or guaranteed by official entities--
either government or multilateral. Consequently, the
rescheduling was basically applied to the debt owed to
private financial institutions. Mexican negotiators
asked for a principal repayment period of eight years,
including a four-year grace period. In exchange,
creditors were to be paid at their own election a rate
of LIBOR plus 1.875 or prime plus 1.75. They were also
offered a 1 percent restructure fee. The reschedule
undertaking was also quite successful. Only a year after
the original request was made, the first set of restructuring contracts was signed. By the end of 1983,
twenty-seven, restructure agreements between Mexican
public-sector entities and their foreign creditors had
been concluded, representing liabilities of US$23 billion.
     The problem of the private sector's foreign debt
proved to be as challenging as the public sector's.
Arrears in interest that had accrued during the last four
months of 1982 and early 1983 (almost US$.9 billion)
were the first problem to solve. Debtor firms were asked
to constitute, through a peso payment and at the controlled rate of exchange, dollar-denominated deposits in
favor of their foreign creditors. These deposits earned
a commercial rate (typically LIBOR plus 1.0) and were
transferred by the central bank through several installments for complete liquidation by the end of 1983.
     It was clear, however, that the simultaneous
occurrence of the halt in the automatic rolling over of
the debt, the balance-of-payments crisis, and the abrupt
deterioration of domestic business conditions inevitably
had to lead to an overall renegotiation of the private
sector's debt. From the start, two important decisions
were taken by the Mexican financial authorities: First,

the government was not going to assume the private
sector's debt--that is, foreign lenders would have to
retain the commercial risk involved in their credits,
with debt renegotiation having to take place individually
between lenders and borrowers; second, debtors would
receive no subsidy to settle their foreign obligations.[17]

In order to encourage the restructuring process, it
was decided to offer exchange risk coverage of principal
and interest for debts that could be rescheduled according to the guidelines issued by the financial authorities.
Plainly speaking, firms were able to substitute their
peso-denominated liabilities for their dollar obligations,
as long as the latter could be restructured at long term.
Accordingly, firms were able to transfer the foreign-
exchange risk of their liabilities to the public sector.
This mechanism was also successful, and by the time the
deadline rolled around (late October 1983), private
liabilities for almost US$12 billion had been covered
by the facility. Almost 100 percent of that amount
corresponded to obligations renegotiated to mature at
eight or more years, including a four-year grace period.
Nearly three hundred different financial institutions
agreed to the mechanism in addition to two hundred foreign
suppliers.

As this chapter was being written, the private foreign
debt that did not enter under the program was being
settled or restructured through other mechanisms. Debt
owed to foreign suppliers was repaid through two other
programs, which were made public by the central bank on
February 28 and August 3, 1983. Basically, these programs
allowed firms--through a peso payment--to constitute
dollar-denominated deposits whose ownership could be
transferred in payment to foreign suppliers. In addition,
up to 100 percent of income from exports of debtor firms
was permitted to be used to pay off the same type of
debt. Another segment of private foreign debt--involving
some US$2 billion--was already long-term and covered for
exchange risks by virtue of another system of foreign-
currency swaps offered by Banco de México since 1977.
Loans guaranteed by agencies of foreign governments are
to be settled through bilateral agreements that are in
the process of negotiation. The remainder was largely
that of firms in excellent financial condition whose
liabilities had been restructured and whose prospects
were good for exporting, thus automatically granting them
coverage against fluctuations in the exchange rate.

The process of restructuring the country's foreign
debt was greatly favored by the way in which the economy
adjusted itself during 1983. To the astonishment of many
people, the target was achieved of reducing the public
sector's overall financial deficit to 8.5 percent of GDP.
But even more striking was the adjustment in the balance
of payments: The trade surplus amounted to US$13.7
billion, and that of the current account was US$5.6 billion.

In spite of the pronounced devaluation and the short-run impact of increased prices on many products produced by the public sector, inflation (December to December) was reduced by one-fifth with respect to the rate registered during 1982.

The economic adjustment paid off in terms of improved creditworthiness. In December 1983, a general agreement was reached with the advisory group, defining the conditions for the new money to be lent to the Mexican government during 1984. According to the agreement, the package would comprise US$3.8 billion. Lending banks were again asked to participate on the basis of their pro rata exposure to Mexico in August 1982. This time, however, conditions were softened significantly, with creditors being offered 1.5 percent over LIBOR or 1.125 over prime, at their own election. Instead of the six-year maturity obtained in the previous deal, the new credit would carry a ten-year term, including a five-year grace period. Commitment and facility fees were also reduced, and even though the amount requested was not fully committed as of early February 1984, it was expected that eventually the deal would come through as expected.

In short, one could say that the debt crisis of 1982 was overcome. Fears that Mexico would provoke an international financial hecatomb began to fade as problems of other debtor countries came into focus. It is too soon to say whether at any moment in the near or not-so-near future this respite will give way to another disastrous episode in the country's history as foreign debtor. Much will depend on whether the Economic Adjustment Program proves to be successful--not only for correcting the basic macroeconomic disequilibria but for leading to a new stage of fast economic growth.

Growth of the same quality as in recent decades could only be sustainable for a few years at most. In order to avoid a new crisis, much more than controlling inflation or resuming growth will be needed. It is not an exaggeration to say that it will require deep structural changes in Mexico's economic and political life-- changes that have yet to be conceived and undertaken and whose analysis goes beyond the scope of this chapter. A critical factor also would be that the international environment--both economic and institutional--not be any worse than the one now prevailing.

APPENDIX

As studied by Artus[18] and many other authors, all procedures to calculate an "equilibrium" exchange rate have several shortcomings. More for simplicity in its calculation and interpretation than for its theoretical appeal, a purchasing power parity (PPP) method was chosen here to estimate such an equilibrium rate. Using the formulation suggested by Lipschitz,[19] an index of the real exchange rate was computed with the following formula:

$$IRR = \prod_{i=1}^{n} (e_i\ P_i/P)^{W_i}$$

where e_i is an index of the domestic currency price of foreign currency; P_i, an index of the price level in country i; P, an index of the domestic price level; and w_i, the weight of country i in the index

$$(\ \sum_{i=1}^{n}\ w_i = 1.0).$$

The wholesale price index of each country was used; n=21; w_i was determined according to each country's participation in Mexico's total merchandise trade; the base year is 1978 and was chosen for several--albeit arbitrary--reasons. First, it was a year of high economic growth. Second, merchandise imports--excluding those by the oil sector--grew 15 percent in real terms, not a very high income elasticity. Third, nonoil merchandise exports grew 8 percent in real terms; other exports such as tourism also grew very dynamically. And fourth, the errors and omissions item of the balance of payments was negligible, a fact that suggests that capital flight and smuggling were insignificant. In short, even though 1978 was a year of rapid growth, the external sector was very much in equilibrium. The fact that it is a rather recent year is convenient, too.[20] All relevant data were obtained from the International Financial Statistics of the IMF.

According to the above methodology, during the period 1972-1982 the equilibrium exchange rate (pesos per U.S. dollar; average value for the year) was as follows:

1972	-	13.845
1973	-	13.788
1974	-	14.152
1975	-	14.049
1976	-	16.356
1977	-	21.592
1978	-	22.753
1979	-	23.963
1980	-	26.383
1981	-	32.758
1982	-	50.566

NOTES

The opinions in this chapter are mine and should not be attributed to my employer. I thank Norman Glass for his helpful suggestions in regard to my use of English.

1. Good sources on the history of Mexico's foreign debt are Turlington (1930); Bazant (1968); and Green (1976).

2. Term used by a former minister of finance to describe the economic policies followed during the second half of the 1950s and the 1960s; this was a period of rapid growth and price stability.

3. Data on the external private debt are rather unreliable for this period; therefore, the analysis of this section focuses on the foreign public debt.

4. These facts on debt management are more extensively studied in Zedillo (1981a), pp. 58-89.

5. Zedillo (1980) and Zedillo (1981a, chap. 4).

6. For an interesting analysis of the period see Solís (1981).

7. These comparisons are also made by means of an "equilibrium" exchange rate.

8. See Zedillo (1981a) pp. 58-89.

9. Equals total financial deficit minus the "external deficit." The latter is defined as the difference between public sector's income in foreign exchange (e.g., oil revenues) minus expenditures abroad (e.g., imports and payments of interests).

10. New York Times (1981).

11. Foreign-exchange reserves still had a modest gain during the year.

12. See Castro (1983).

13. See Banco de México (1982).

14. See Castro (1983).

15. At the time there were two official rates (50 and 70 pesos per dollar); the black-market rate fluctuated around 140 pesos.

16. Quoted from p. 4 of a telex sent by the minister of finance of Mexico to the international banking community on December 8, 1982.

17. A description of this mechanism is given in Zedillo (1983).

18. Artus (1978).

19. Lipschitz (1979).

20. Further justification of this index can be found in Zedillo (1981b). I thank Miguel Durán of Banco de México for gathering the data and computing the index.

BIBLIOGRAPHY

Artus, J. R. 1978. "Methods of Assessing the Long-run Equilibrium Value of an Exchange Rate." Journal of International Economics 8:277-299.

Balassa, Beli. 1979. "Policy Responses to External Shocks in Developing Countries: Implications for International Trade and Long-Time Growth." Washington, D.C. Mimeo.

324

Banco de México. 1982. Informe Anual 1981. México, D.F.

Bazant, Jan. 1968. Historia de la Deuda Exterior de México (1823-1946). México, D.F.

Castro, E. 1983. "Algunas Consideraciones Sobre el Financiamiento Externo de México en los Años de 1980-1982." México, D.F. Mimeo.

Green, Roserio. 1976. El Endeudamiento Público Externo de México 1940-1973. México, D.F.

Lipschitz, L. 1979. "Exchange Rate Policy for a Small Developing Country, and the Selection of an Appropriate Standard." IMF Staff Papers 26: 423-449.

"Mexico, in Switch, Will Lift Oil Price." 1981. New York Times (June 17).

Solís, Leopoldo. 1981. Economic Policy Reform in Mexico: A Case Study for Developing Countries. New York.

"Mexican Headache for International Banks." 1977. The Economist (January 22):99.

Turlington, Edgar. 1930. Mexico and Her Foreign Debtors. New York.

Zedillo, Ernesto. 1980. "The Balance of Payments Effects of External Shocks in Non-OPEC Developing Countries. The Case of Mexico." Paris.

___. 1981a. "External Public Indebtedness in Mexico. Recent History and Future Oil Bounded Optimal Growth." Ph.D. dissertation, Yale University.

___. 1981b. "Algunas Consideraciones Sobre el Tipo de Cambio del Peso." Subdirección de Investigación Económica, Banco de México. Mimeo.

___. 1983. "The Program for Coverage of Exchange Risks. A General Description and Financial Aspects." México, D.F. Mimeo.

12
The Renegotiation of Venezuela's Foreign Debt During 1982 and 1983

Eduardo Mayobre

PROBLEMS IN RENEGOTIATING

By the end of 1982, Venezuela's foreign debt had reached approximately US$33 billion. Although this is a high figure, it is low when compared to that of other Latin American countries. In terms of foreign earnings, the Venezuelan debt is equal to 151 percent of the country's exports of goods and services. By way of contrast, the corresponding figure for Argentina's debt is 388 percent, for Brazil 354 percent, Chile 287 percent, and for Mexico, Peru, and Equador 264 percent, 260 percent, and 230 percent, respectively.

However, in the renegotiation processes that became general practice throughout the continent during 1982 and 1983, it has been Venezuela that has found it most difficult to reach an agreement with its creditors. Since March 1983, when the need for renegotiation was officially recognized, the Venezuelan government has had to recur on two occasions (in April and July) to a ninety-day deferments of payments on its debt, and at the end of the second of these periods it barely managed to obtain a third deferment of thirty days. In addition, there was very little probability that an agreement would be reached before the end of the year as regards a re-scheduling of the debt, and it was thought that it would only be possible for meaningful negotiations to be initiated when the new government came to power in February 1984.

This development is surprising, for until recently Venezuela enjoyed a privileged place in the international finance markets; due to the characteristics of its debt and the size of its reserves, the rescheduling of maturities seemed, at first glance, an easy objective to attain. However, what seemed an easily manageable situation has become more and more complex, with serious repercussions on the country's domestic economy as well as its international position. On first examination, several facts appear that explain the changes mentioned.

1. The structure of the debt is very vulnerable, as 45 percent of Venezuela's foreign indebtedness is short-term. This means that although the total debt is not excessive, the maturities due in 1983 and 1984 exceeded the country's repayment capacity during this period. The portion subject to renegotiation, which includes long-term debt amortization due during the same two years, is US$18 billion without taking account of the private-sector debt whose share of short-term maturities is higher than that of the public sector. If one makes comparisons with other countries in Latin America, one finds that their short-term debt accounts for 19 percent of the total debt in Brazil, Argentina, and Chile and 20 percent, 29 percent, and 30 percent in Ecuador, Peru, and Mexico, respectively.

2. The drop in earnings from oil sales that began in 1982 should be pointed out. These earnings, which account for more than 90 percent of Venezuela's exports, fell by 20 percent in 1982, and a similar decline was expected in 1983. This fall in foreign revenue is due to a reduction in crude export prices and to a considerable contraction in export volume as a result of the production quotas agreed upon by OPEC in response to the depressing conditions in the international oil market. Initially, since the Venezuelan authorities thought that this would be a minor temporary reduction, no appropriate preventive action was considered.

3. The emergence of difficulties in serving the debt in other countries in Latin America, and the Mexican crisis of 1982 in particular, led the international banks to act with more caution with regard to their Latin American debtors and to reexamine the risks they had assumed in the region. This general attitude proved detrimental to Venezuela when it became obvious that the country was experiencing difficulties in meeting its foreign commitments as well. Although the need to refinance the short-term debt had already been recognized, to the extent that in August 1981 the Venezuelan Congress had passed a law authorizing the undertaking of appropriate commitments, the executive branch refrained from taking action for administrative reasons and because it misunderstood what was occurring in the market. Thus, when the Latin American situation began to be viewed as a world crisis, only small amounts of credit had been renegotiated by Venezuela.

4. The fact that Venezuela had ample international reserves at the beginning of 1982 made the authorities believe that they would receive special treatment from the international banks. At the beginning of 1982, its official international reserves totaled US$8.6 billion. Added to these were the financial reserves of the oil industry and Venezuela's Investment Fund, giving a total of approximately US$19 billion. There was also the possibility of revaluing the gold reserves still valued

at the official price of US$42 per ounce. When problems
in the foreign-trade sector and difficulties in the
renegotiating process started to become apparent, the
authorities decided that centralizing the international
reserves in the Central Bank and revaluing the gold
reserves would demonstrate the country's financial strength
and thus facilitate the negotiations. This, however,
turned out to be self-defeating, since it gave the
impression that this was the government's last recourse
and one that could adversely affect the oil industry.
    5. The domestic economic situation and the monetary
policies that were adopted brought about a flight of
capital that began in 1981 and became more acute throughout 1982. From 1979 onward, policies were adopted that
were designed to restrict economic activity. These led
to a 50 percent reduction in real terms in private investment between 1978 and 1981. A great deal of the surplus
capital that had previously been invested internally
was withdrawn from the country. In addition, in mid-1981,
domestic interest rates fell while foreign rates remained
at a much higher level and had a tendency to rise. This
meant a differential of more than four points in favor
of foreign interest rates within the framework of a free-
exchange system, which encouraged the flight of capital.
    This flight of capital was condoned by the monetary
authorities as part of a very strange policy termed
"deliberate leaks," which was designed to reduce the cash
flow in the domestic economy. Toward the end of the
year, when domestic interest rates were allowed to float
and tended to rise to international levels, the outflow
of capital continued due to a growing lack of confidence
in the future of the domestic economy. Later, the drop
in earnings from oil sales, the centralization of the oil
industry's financial reserves, the executive's intervention in the largest bank in the country--Banco de los
Trabajadores de Venezuela, and the growing conviction
that a devaluation was imminent undermined confidence
even further and accelerated the flight of capital.
In the months preceding the introduction by decree of
exchange controls and differential exchange rates in
February 1983, there was a net weekly capital outflow
of US$400 million. This meant that while in a normal
year, such as 1978, the short-term capital outflow was
US$1.3 billion, this figure reached US$5.5 billion in
1981, US$7 billion in 1982, and over US$2 billion in the
first two months of 1983.
    6. The fact that the currency had remained stable
for twenty years, with the exception of two minor
readjustments at the beginning of the 1970s and only one
devaluation since 1941, meant that a change in the
exchange rate would prove economically and politically
traumatic. This led the authorities to delay and
attempt to avoid the devaluation of the bolivar. When
the devaluation became inevitable in February 1983, it

was disguised under an extremely complex system of
exchange rates.

The Venezuelan currency has usually been overvalued
since its par value is determined relative to the oil
sector and not to the rest of the economy. But, even
without taking this fact into account, it is easy to see
that from 1978 onward the bolivar underwent considerable
real appreciation in value, as a consequence of inflation
rates in Venezuela higher than those of its trading
partners and of the strengthening of the dollar against
the European currencies (the bolivar maintained a fixed
par value in relation to the dollar).

Calculations show that in the four years preceding
the exchange measures of February 1983, the currency
became overvalued by approximately 35 percent in relation
to that of the industrial countries. The exaggerated
value of the bolivar led to an increase in imports and
foreign travel and made it practically impossible to
increment nontraditional exports. Subsequently, when it
became obvious that the exchange rate could not be sustained, capital flight increased. The government's
reluctance to implement exchange measures allowed these
effects to reach an extreme.

7. The difficulties in arranging the refinancing
of the debt can be explained by the fact that after having
maintained an average annual growth rate of 5.5 percent
over the twenty years from 1958 to 1978, the country's
economy underwent four consecutive years of stagnation.
During this last period the authorities were unwilling
to take the measures necessary to deal with the situation
that they faced for fear of the social and political
repercussions these could have. On the contrary, although
there were some reductions in central government spending, state enterprises and public financial institutions
became more heavily indebted. Both groups resorted to
foreign credit in order to compensate for their operating
deficits, the reduction in funds assigned by the central
government, and the lack of liquidity in the internal
market.

8. The political situation tended to make the
government postpone any measure that might have proved
unpopular, and consequently it became evasive in its
negotiations with its creditors. Almost from the outset,
the government's popularity was damaged by the stagnation
in the economy, unemployment, and rising inflation that
far outstripped levels customary in Venezuela. When
the financial and fiscal crisis became evident in mid-
1982, the selection of the presidential candidates to
stand in the December 1983 elections had just begun.
During the period of negotiations with the foreign
creditors, the electoral campaign was in full swing,
and polls were showing a clear disadvantage for the
government party candidate. In these circumstances the
authorities avoided taking any action or making any

commitment that would undermine their popularity. For
example, as will be seen later, attempts were made to
avoid reaching an agreement with the International
Monetary Fund and strong objections were even made to the
measures recommended by that institution. As a result,
no serious negotiations with the Fund came about. In
addition, there was an absence of unified criteria on
the part of the fiscal and monetary authorities, which
reached the extreme of a public dispute between the
minister of the Treasury and the director of the Central
Bank.

9. The central government's lack of control over
the indebtedness of both the state enterprises and other
decentralized government bodies made it virtually
impossible to arrive at a clear idea of the total of
the public-sector debt. The absence of hard data in
turn hindered the negotiations, as it created a discrepancy
between the parties involved as to the amount that was to
be negotiated. There were also delays in the interest
payments of the state institutions, and difficulties arose
over the recognition of loans contracted without
attention to the pertinent legal procedures. Moreover,
there was the problem of private foreign debt, for which
there were neither records nor control, making it
impossible to determine the nature or the total of the
same with any precision. Since the exchange control law
stipulates that foreign currency will only be provided
for certain types of private debts, for which refinancing
has already been arranged, the foreign debt of the
private sector is considered together with that of the
public sector in the negotiations with the creditors.

10. As a result of several of the aforementioned
points, not only was there no reduction in public spending during the period in which the crisis was developing,
but it actually expanded considerably between 1980 and
1981 as a result of increases in oil earnings, and
remained virtually stable over the following two years.

These facts can be more clearly understood once the
reader is acquainted with the negotiating process that
took place during 1982 and 1983.

THE RENEGOTIATION PROCESS

In August 1981, the National Congress passed a
Refinancing Law for a sum of 61 billion bolivars. This
law, which authorized the executive to assume, consoli-
date, and restructure the short-term debt of the public
sector, was discussed in the Sixth National Plan. The
plan's investment program entailed public borrowing for
several projects and contained a number of legal
initiatives designed to facilitate their financing.
A plan for the refinancing of short-term debts contracted
prior to June 1982 was also included in the national plan,

so that total public borrowing could be taken into account. A significant proportion of this borrowing had been undertaken by state enterprises without the authorization of the executive and in some cases without complying with all the relevant legal requirements. In order to prevent these practices from continuing, the Refinancing Law was passed, and modifications were made to the Public Credit Law that introduced controls and sanctions to be applied to whoever assumed obligations for the state without authorization. One of the requirements established for refinancing was the approval by the Finance Commission of the legislative chamber of a detailed list of the debts involved.

Despite the authorization that had been given by Congress, the executive delayed in starting refinancing negotiations and in approaching the international finance markets. First it attended to administrative problems in gathering the information required by Congress, and then it decided that the market conditions were not suitable. Negotiations initiated with the international banks on several occasions in 1982 in most cases did not lead to any agreement, as the Venezuelan authorities considered that the terms they were offered were not in keeping with the country's financial position.

The decline of the oil markets and the application of production quotas agreed upon by OPEC during the summer of that year made the government believe that Venezuela would create a false impression before the international banks of being weak, for they thought that the oil demand would increase during the second half of the year and the estimates of foreign earnings would therefore be much more favorable. On the basis of these assumptions, the Venezuelan government considered that it would not be wise to accept the interest rates it was being offered, which were approximately an eighth of a percent higher than those it had obtained previously, since this could create a precedent and undermine the country's position in the international finance markets.

For these reasons, the Venezuelan government decided to postpone the refinancing negotiations until midyear and to renew short-term loans as they matured. As part of this strategy, credit for the vast sum of US$2 billion was being arranged and was to be ready by June or July. Meanwhile, the Falklands crisis occurred in which Venezuela supported the Argentine position actively and with determination. The resulting rumors and opinions adversely affected relations with the British financial community. Some of the funds from the Venezuelan oil industry were withdrawn from British banks when it was rumored that they might be frozen, and a number of the United Kingdom's banks abandoned the talks regarding the giant credit.

At the same time, Mexico was already involved in negotiations for credit for an amount similar to that

requested by Venezuela and had decided to accept higher
interest rates in order to obtain resources. This influenced the terms offered to Venezuela, which were
rejected. The government objected to the combined use
of the U.S. preferential rate and the London interbanking
rate, which had been used on previous occasions, and
considered that, in its view of the market, the money
was overpriced. Events that followed were to show that
to reject the terms that had been offered was a great
mistake.

Later, the Mexican crisis and the difficulties faced
by other countries in the region led the international
banks to adopt a more inflexible position toward Latin
America. This, coupled with the deterioration in the
internal situation in Venezuela and the fact that several
state enterprises were behind in their payments, resulted
in some short-term credit not being renewed. In the face
of this situation, which was also compounded by the
reduction in reserves due to the flight of capital, the
authorities decided to centralize the reserves of the
state enterprises and to set a new par value for gold in
order to show that "dollar for dollar" the country's
foreign liabilities were matched by its international
reserves. This measure particularly affected the
nationalized oil industry, which until then had maintained
a position of absolute financial independence, thus allowing it to finance its own current account operations and
maintain enough foreign currency to finance its expansion
program. By the end of 1981, the net short-term international assets of Petróleos de Venezuela (the Venezuelan
oil company) totaled US$7.66 billion. The new gold par
value, which rose from US$42.22 to US$300 per ounce,
meant a US$3 billion dollar increase in international
reserves. These measures did not overly impress the
international banks, which had long been aware of the
different types of reserves held by Venezuela.

In the light of these new market circumstances,
toward the end of September a new refinancing plan was
presented by the government that was designed to reschedule US$8.7 billion of the current account debt.
Under this new plan the government was willing to pay
much higher interest rates (of between 1 percent and
1.625 percent above LIBOR) than those it had rejected
a few months previously and abandoned the idea of
obtaining giant loans. Under these conditions, it
managed to refinance approximately US$1 billion by the
end of 1982.

The aggravation of the crisis in Mexico, Brazil, and
Argentina, fear of a reduction in oil prices, and the
collapse of the domestic economy (involving intervention
in the Banco de los Trabajadores de Venezuela) impaired
the success of the above-mentioned plan. A report by
the Financial Times at the beginning of January 1983
commented in this regard that the "Euromarket responded

332

enthusiastically to the announcement in October of the
refinancing plan, particularly as conditions were offered
that were considered exceptionally generous by the banks
which had been used to bargaining with Venezuela over
the price of its foreign credit." It added that the
"enthusiasm due to these refinancing plans is beginning
to wane." By this time, the imminent reduction in oil
prices and the flight of capital had seriously eroded
confidence in the Venezuelan economy. It was not
difficult to foresee that a currency crisis was probable.
     During 1982, efforts had been made to deal with the
problem of the short-term debt. These were unsuccessful,
as the Venezuelan authorities had failed to perceive the
deterioration of conditions in the international finance
markets. They considered that the extent of their
international reserves gave them a financial stability
that deserved preferential treatment, and they remained
under the illusion that an upturn in the oil markets
would increase their foreign earnings. None of these
hopes came to fruition, and the domestic economic situation meanwhile continued to worsen.

THE SITUATION IN 1983

     By 1983 the situation had become even more difficult.
There was the need not only to renew short-term credit
but also to pay the amortizations on the medium- and long-
term loans contracted in previous years that were heavily
concentrated in 1983 and 1984. The unsuccessful negotiations undertaken in 1982 had undermined the country's
international credibility, and the foreign drain on
reserves had become more acute, as a result of a loss
of confidence within the nation and of rumors of a
devaluation.
     Furthermore, during the first four months of 1983
the oil market had deteriorated even further, and there
was fear that a price war could begin between the exporting countries. The production quotas agreed upon by OPEC
in the summer of 1982 were no longer applicable in the
second half of the year, and the production increases by
countries like Nigeria, Venezuela, Iran, and Indonesia
were causing friction within the organization. Furthermore, the OPEC countries were accusing one another of
granting discounts that violated the price schemes agreed
upon. The OPEC countries' loss of a considerable share
of the market to new exporters was making the situation
even more difficult. Under these circumstances, the free
convertibility of the bolivar was suspended on February
18, 1983, and after several days of discussion and disagreement between members of the government a new exchange
scheme was established.
     This consisted of the introduction of three exchange
rates. The exchange rate of 4.30 bolivars to the dollar

was maintained for public-sector transactions, including debt servicing and the importation of essential goods. A rate of 6 bolivars per dollar was set for the remainder of trade transactions, which would be subject to a system of exchange control. Lastly, a free floating rate was established for financial operations, traveling expenses, and other international transactions.

It was established that for the payment of the private-sector foreign debt, dollars would be made available at the preferential rate of 4.30 bolivars for the total debt amount, provided that the latter had been refinanced by the creditors allowing at least a one-year grace period and a three-year period of maturity. This was one of the points that caused most controversy among members of the government and that still has not been completely worked out, owing to the difficulty of defining the total debt amount and the fact that one of the conditions, that of refinancing, is beyond the control of the debtors.

In order to administer this exchange plan the Office for the System of Differential Exchange Rates (RECADI) was set up under the control of the Treasury, as a result of the differences in opinion between it and the Central Bank of Venezuela. The establishment of RECADI led to administrative difficulties that caused a permanent delay in furnishing foreign currency at the preferential rates of 4.30 and 6 bolivars per dollar. This office was practically created from nothing, and it spent the greater part of its time establishing the legitimacy of requests for preferential rates of currency. Later, the Central Bank of Venezuela refused to recognize some of the authorizations given by RECADI, particularly those relating to the private foreign debt, thus prolonging an atmosphere of uncertainty that still continues to be felt.

As a complement to the exchange measures, a decree was passed freezing prices for two months. This was later replaced by an "administrated prices system" that stipulated that any price increases must be authorized by the Ministry for Development. Under this system the authorities had three months in which to consider proposed price rise. In actual fact prices were frozen for nearly six months.

Under the exchange system that had been adopted, the government decided not to intervene in the free market. Initially, the bolivar sold at around 8 to the dollar, but then rapidly started to rise due to a shortage of foreign currency. A peculiarity of the Venezuelan economy is that 90 percent of its foreign-currency earnings are generated by the public sector; thus the action the monetary authorities either do or do not take determines the market. Faced with this rise in the price of the dollar, the Central Bank decided to intervene in the Stock Exchange, but its intervention gave rise to exceedingly easy speculative practices and destabilized the market. In the light of these circumstances, the Central Bank withdrew from the market and started to provide the commercial banks with foreign currency at a fixed rate of 9.95 bolivars per dollar, while the Stock Exchange withdrew from the foreign-currency market. The amount sold by the Central Bank (US$120 million per month) was greatly inferior to the demand and led to the emergence of alternative markets. One of these operates through the money-exchange offices, providing limited quantities to purchasers; the other, with higher rates, has no restrictions as regards quantity, its transactions being carried out directly between vendor and purchaser.

Having remained stable at between 8 and 9 bolivars for a few weeks, the free dollar rose continuously to reach 12 bolivars, when the Central Bank withdrew. By mid-July it reached 17 bolivars, only to fall to a rate of between 13 and 14 bolivars per dollar during August and September. As a result of all these factors, in October 1983 there were five different exchange rates: two preferential rates of 4.30 and 6 bolivars, the bank rate of 9.95, the money-exchange-office rate of 13 bolivars, and the free rate of 14. To these can be added several special intermediate rates. As can be observed, there is more than a 300 percent variation among the different exchange rates, which not only makes for complete uncertainty (since access to the different rates is not clearly defined) but also encourages irregular transactions to be made.

It is easy to imagine that as a result of this exchange disorder, the consequent uncertainty, and the administrative difficulties in obtaining foreign currency at preferential rates, there has been a tendency for production to fall dramatically on one hand and for unemployment to rise steeply on the other. This can be clearly observed in the monetary indicators: Despite a notable increase in domestic liquidity as a result of exchange control, the demand for credit has remained stagnant.

In addition, the lack of foreign currency at preferential rates has led to a fall in input supplies to the production centers. Faced with difficulties in obtaining foreign currency at such rates, manufacturers have only used the free market in extreme cases, leading to a reduction in imports and a shortage of raw materials and making it necessary for manufacturers to reduce production levels. There have been no serious shortages, since it was customary for the country to maintain high levels of inventories, and with an impending devaluation, extra supplies were in many cases purchased in advance. Thus the shortage of foreign currency has resulted in lower levels of inventories rather than chronic shortages. In any case, reliable estimates show that imports have fallen by more than 40 percent so far in 1983, a decrease that can only be explained by a marked reduction in inventories.

RELATIONS WITH THE IMF

The renegotiation process has been accompanied by the paralysis of the economy and the retention of an unsustainable exchange-rate system. When the exchange control was introduced in February 1983, the authorities made a final attempt to refinance the short-term debt following the outlines it had been proposing since October 1982. These negotiations failed and, by the second half of March, gave way to negotiations to obtain a three-month moratorium on capital payments, the idea being that during this period conditions could arise that would ensure the country's medium-term payment capacity. The moratorium was obtained without major difficulties, and the same interest rates were maintained for the debts outstanding. However, the total sum to be refinanced rose from US$8.7 billion, which was the originally suggested figure, to US$18 billion, accounted for by the loans due to mature in 1983 and 1984.

For the purpose of these new negotiations, the Venezuelan authorities adopted the attitude that Venezuela's case was different from that of other Latin American countries in that its total debt was relatively smaller; the country still had about US$9 billion in reserves and did not require new credit to satisfy its foreign requirements. For these reasons the government hoped to reach an agreement that would not involve the International Monetary Fund or, at least, that would not imply the kind of conditions a credit agreement with that institution normally implies.

In the meantime, in mid-March 1983 OPEC decided to considerably reduce its official oil prices and to reintroduce production quotas for its members. Although this decision meant an additional reduction in Venezuela's foreign earnings, it introduced an element of stability into the oil market that allowed better planning of the action to be taken in the home sphere and dissipated a series of fears concerning the oil market that had become widespread during the previous months.

Under these circumstances, an advisory committee of creditor banks was set up, headed by the Chase Manhattan Bank, to serve as the counterpart to the Venezuelan authorities in the negotiations. The committee demanded first that the total of Venezuela's debt be made clear. This requirement turned out to be more of a problem than was at first thought, because the debts of the state enterprises and institutes were often neither controlled nor registered. The committee also demanded that some

of these institutions that had not been included in
previous refinancing schemes (in particular the Banco
Industrial de Venezuela) bring their delayed payments
up to date. This requirement was not carried out to the
full because of a lack of organization and for domestic
legal reasons. The delay in outstanding interest payments was to become a permanent source of irritation
throughout the whole negotiating process between the
Venezuelan government and its creditors, particularly
because promises to solve the problem were made several
times without these commitments being honored. The third
condition stipulated by the creditors was that talks
should be initiated with the International Monetary Fund.
At first the nature of these talks was not clear, since
it was not propounded that Venezuela needed to reach a
credit agreement with the Fund.

The initial talks with the International Monetary
Fund were consultative. However, the government hinted
that it might request a credit agreement and even went so
far as to ask to be informed of the basic conditions
demanded by the Fund. As part of the Fund's routine
procedures in the supervision of exchange systems, a
consultation had been proposed for 1983 to examine the
case of Venezuela. The government requested that this
meeting be brought forward, this being the official
reason for the exchange of missions. At the time of
their second visit to the country, the Fund representatives, who were expecting to commence negotiations for a
credit agreement, found that the Venezuelan authorities
were not prepared to discuss their exchange system. The
talks were limited to establishing the veracity of the
official figure for the fiscal deficit.

Meanwhile the Venezuelan authorities had been
discussing how they could solve the problem of obtaining
the Fund's approval for their policies without having to
constrain themselves to the conditions of the standby
credit agreements of that institution. The government
expected the Fund to be sympathetic toward its concerns,
since Venezuela had made significant contributions to
the Fund during the years of its oil bonanza. As a
result of these contributions, the country had a net
credit with the Fund of US$1.2 billion. This amount,
considered part of its international reserves, could be
used automatically but was not an endorsement for the
world monetary authority of the way the Venezuelan
government would manage the economy.

The apparently obvious solution to the problem of
obtaining the support of the International Monetary Fund
without having to meet its conditions lay in the
compensatory credit facility. This service is provided
for countries that have suffered a temporary setback in
export earnings, provided that the cause of their shortfall in income be beyond the control of the authorities.
Usually, this reduction in earnings is due to fluctuations

in the raw-material markets in countries whose exports
depend on these products. This was the case in
Venezuela, where oil exports had fallen by almost 20
percent in two consecutive years.

However, the compensatory credit facility had never
been applied to an oil-exporting country for the simple
reason that none of these had ever needed it. Given the
important role that the OPEC countries had played in the
financial upheavals that occurred following the increases
in oil prices between 1974 and 1979, it was a politically
delicate matter to consider allowing the oil exporters to
use the IMF compensatory facility.

In order to oppose the oil countries' access to the
compensatory credit facility, it was argued that the
price of crude oil was not outside the control of the
authorities in the OPEC countries, since it is fixed by
a cartel of producers. A more technical argument held
that there was no certainty that this shortage of
resources was reversible and therefore temporary, since
oil prices are not subject to the cycles affecting other
raw materials.

On the basis of these facts, the managing director
of the IMF addressed himself to the general problem of
whether the oil-exporting countries could have access to
the compensatory credit facility. During consideration
of the matter, it was concluded that no impediment
existed in this respect, but that requests by the oil-
exporting countries should be studied on a case-by-case
basis. The main argument in support of this conclusion
was that OPEC does not act as a cartel, since the fixed
prices established by it do not determine market conditions but rather respond to them. This line of
thought is important in the light of propaganda that
circulated in previous years, which held that price
fixing by OPEC had been the cause of most international
economic ills. However, the Fund, whose arguments tend
to suit its own convenience, could not admit discrimination against a group of countries without contradicting
its principle of equal treatment for all members.

The Venezuelan authorities considered the IMF
Executive Board's decision a victory. They thought that
it would make an agreement possible, which in turn
would facilitate a refinancing arrangement. They forgot,
however, that a further requirement for access to be
had to the compensatory facility is that "the authorities
cooperate with the Fund in solving their balance of
payments problems." Since they had not taken any measures
that could be interpreted as doing so, access to the
facility proved practically impossible.

Meanwhile, the Venezuelan government made the grave
mistake of announcing to its creditors that in principle
it had reached an agreement with the IMF, although such
an agreement did not exist. Denial of this by the Fund
authorities damaged the credibility of the Venezuelan

authorities, as was to be expected.

In the consultation on Venezuela that took place in the Executive Board of the Fund, the general impression regarding the measures taken by the government and its intentions for future action was negative. The report by the IMF authorities declared, for example, that "the recent action by the Venezuelan authorities is insufficient to deal with the country's economic difficulties and the measures they have taken are not the appropriate ones." It explained that the measures "ran the risk of rapidly depleting international reserves, seriously increasing inflation and distorting the allocation of resources." By way of conclusion, it said that "the country's serious problems can only be solved through adjustment measures" in the most diverse areas of the economy.

In the talks with the Venezuelan authorities, the Fund missions had recommended the following measures:

1. modification of the exchange system, preferably by means of a devaluation aimed at unifying the exchange rates
2. raising the domestic price of crude oil to international levels
3. reduction in public spending
4. increase in the prices of public services and of goods produced by state enterprises
5. increased income tax and the introduction of a sales tax
6. reduction of net internal credit and allowing interest rates to continue to float
7. lifting the recently decreed restrictions on imports
8. freeing prices and freezing wages

These recommendations were never seriously discussed, since at no time did the talks on a possible credit agreement between Venezuela and the Fund go beyond the preliminary stages. In their report, the authorities of the Fund recorded that although the Venezuelan authorities expressed agreement with some of the recommendations, they considered "that it was not possible to contemplate immediate action in these areas, due mainly to the impending December 1983 elections."

In these circumstances the Venezuelan government publicly rejected the Fund's recommendations, alleging that they were impossible to accept because of their high social cost. This practically closed the doors to an agreement. It should be noted that the aforementioned measures were recommendations made during the consultation process and not conditions for a credit agreement, since there exists, in principle, a limit to the conditions that can be set in such agreements. As the possibility of a contingency credit was never seriously considered, the Fund did not modify its initial recommendations.

The consultation in the Executive Board of the IMF took place at the beginning of July 1983, and it was supposed that it would form the basis for the negotiations. By that date the Venezuelan government had requested and obtained a second moratorium for its amortization payments. As a condition for granting it, the creditors had insisted that talks with the Fund continue with the object of reaching an agreement within the three-month period of payments deferred. They had also insisted that the outstanding interest payments be met and that a solution be found to the problem of the private debt.

At the end of July a new mission from the Fund visited Venezuela. This proved to be fruitless, for in a televised message to the nation the minister of treasury stated that there would be no changes in the policies adopted up until then--in the exchange system in particular--and that any settlement with the Fund would have to be made following the December 1983 elections. Shortly after, at the beginning of September, the foreign banks' advisory committee agreed that it would make no formal proposal to the government of Venezuela for the rescheduling of its debt, since it considered it essential that Venezuela reach a parallel agreement with the International Monetary Fund and meet its outstanding payments. This reference to a "parallel" agreement can easily be interpreted as a demand for a contingent credit agreement, since this arrangement is the only one that could be carried out simultaneously, as it is subject to a quarterly review.

An additional problem was the public dispute between the minister of treasury and the president of the Central Bank concerning the handling of the private foreign debt. The Central Bank invoked legal reasons for refusing to provide currency already approved by RECADI for the debt payments of a number of private companies. The matter was important since one of the creditor banks had threatened legal action if the outstanding payments were not made. The Venezuelan company concerned was willing to meet its obligations but could not obtain the foreign currency it had been authorized. After several days of public discussion, a bill was passed on September 27 by which dollars could be granted at the preferential rate up until December 31 for the payment of the private sector's debt, provided that the difference between the preferential and the bank rate for the dollar was put up as surety and that the debt was recognized by a commission created especially for this purpose. Although this bill dispelled the uncertainty of the moment, it did not solve the question of the private trade debt and the treatment that the private sector would receive from January 1984 onward.

Subsequently, on the day on which the second
moratorium ended, the creditor banks granted a third
deferment of payments of only one month and at a higher
rate of interest. This limit was designed to observe
Venezuela's behavior in relation to meeting its outstanding interest payments. If this situation was rectified,
the moratorium would be extended for another three months
until January 31, 1984, four days before the takeover
of the new government. It can therefore be concluded that
the refinancing process initiated in 1981 and the renegotiation of the debt attempted during 1983 were
unsuccessful and that the rescheduling of Venezuela's
foreign commitments could not be achieved before mid-1984
at the earliest.

ACHIEVING ECONOMIC STABILIZATION

All the facts related so far explain why the 1983
negotiations to reschedule the debt have failed and why
Venezuela, in spite of being in a more favorable position
than other countries in the region, has become one of the
most difficult cases. It would, however, seem pertinent
to make a few additional comments.
Venezuela is not only in the position of having to
solve a delicate foreign-debt problem, but is also faced
with the dilemma of having to adopt a program of economic
stabilization after four years of economic stagnation.
Normally, a disequilibrium in the balance of payments is
caused by the excessive utilization of resources in the
domestic economy, producing rates of growth that are unsustainable in the medium term. Thus, the International
Monetary Fund's customary prescription consists of
reducing the level of internal economic activity, which
then leads to a fall in the demand for imports and
generates exportable surpluses. In the case of
Venezuela, however, four years of recession came between
the period of accelerated growth and the time when
balance-of-payments problems arose. This peculiar
situation is due to the recession coinciding with a
marked increase in foreign-currency resources.
The 1979 increases in oil prices meant that between
1978 and 1981 export earnings went up from US$9.2
billion to US$20.2 billion. Despite this, the gross
national product dropped during these years at an average
annual rate of .2 percent. In 1982 it rose by .6 percent,
and estimates suggested that it would drop again in 1983
by at least 3 percent. Thus, at the time of the balance-
of-payments problems, unemployment had reached an all-time
high, and the utilization of installed capacity was
particularly low.
Under these circumstances, it would be counterproductive to follow traditional remedies. Greater
deflation could lead to the destruction of the production

capacity, increase the already existing distrust,
inhibit investment, raise unemployment to socially
unacceptable levels, and discourage the return of capital
previously taken out of the country. The social tension
that would be caused by higher unemployment deserves
special attention as good labor relations have been one
of the most positive features of the Venezuelan economy
in the last twenty-five years, despite the existence of
strong trade unions. It should also be underlined that
the financial situation of the manufacturing companies
could prove impossible to sustain if there were a further
drop in demand. In short, in Venezuela at the present
moment there is not the social tolerance to a deflationary
policy that might possibly exist in countries whose
balance-of-payments problems emerged immediately following periods of accelerated growth.

Furthermore, the existence of considerable idle
capacity leads one to believe that it would be possible
to adopt policies to reactivate the economy without un-
necessarily aggravating the balance-of-payments and
inflation problems. The overvaluation of the currency
has meant that the Venezuelan economy is extraordinarily
open and that there are, therefore, ample opportunities
for import substitution, even of finished consumer goods.
The reactivation of the economy, moreover, would serve to
encourage the return of capital from abroad that has not
yet been invested in other economies, since it would
create new investment opportunities in the domestic
sector.

The devaluation could have become an incentive to
reactivate the economy since, in itself, it implied increased protection. But the adoption of an essentially
unstable exchange system inhibited investment, creating
uncertainty as regards the financial situation of enterprises. Moreover, the repeated announcement of a refinancing agreement that never actually materialized
maintained the suspense as to the future of the economy,
which brought production to a standstill.

In order for production to return to normal,
therefore, it is essential that an exchange policy be
defined. But this is just one aspect of a wider
stabilization program whose aim should be to achieve a
return to reasonable rates of growth. The designing of
such a program would facilitate negotiations with the
creditors. But, by the same token, no program of any
kind will be accomplished if the negotiations are unsuccessful.

Now, the course the 1983 negotiations have taken
leads one to conclude that, if the debt is to be rescheduled, it is practically inevitable that an agreement be made with the International Monetary Fund.
However, an agreement with the Fund can only be made if
the need to reactivate the economy is recognized. The
Venezuelan government should, therefore, be clever

enough to formulate a reactivation program that would reestablish a basic equilibrium in the balance of payments and in the fiscal situation. As far as the Fund is concerned, it needs to be flexible and realistic enough to recognize that this equilibrium will only be achieved if a climate of confidence can be created and a domestic demand capable of setting the production apparatus in motion can be maintained. If this does not occur, the only remaining alternative will be a settlement with the creditors that would not involve the Fund or a moratorium that would have negative effects for both Venezuela and the international financial community.

A stabilization and reactivation program will require as much discipline as that demanded by traditional Fund strategy, except that the discipline would be of a different kind. Whatever the approach adopted it is essential that public finances be put in order, which could serve as common ground between the orthodox recommendations and a strategy more in keeping with the needs of the country. Theoretically, such ordering is easy to achieve, since there is a wide margin of wastage and disorderly utilization of resources for public spending. Furthermore, since taxes are excessively low in Venezuela, their increase is feasible. Thus one sees that the Fund's recommendations concerning fiscal austerity, increases in the domestic price of oil, and the introduction of new taxes form an acceptable and even necessary part of any stabilization program.

The differences mentioned might arise in other areas, such as the role to be played by the public sector. In Venezuela the state has for many years been the driving force behind the economy. The fact that it generates more than 40 percent of the gross national product makes this practically inevitable. Therefore, although one might accept that the weight of reactivation should lie with the private sector and that it is essential that resources be freed to allow private industry to recover, it is also true that the private sector will only increase its level of activity if the public sector maintains an adequate level of demand. In this sense, the adoption of doctrinaire points of view concerning the relative importance of one or other sector is totally misplaced. In the Venezuelan economy the public sector plays a role that cannot be modified in the short term, and if this sector is paralyzed, the rest of the economy will also come to a standstill.

The second area in which differences should be reduced is trade policy. While in the medium and long term Venezuela needs to increase its nontraditional exports, the short-term possibilities for diversifying exports are quite slim, even taking into account the incentives created by the devaluation. In the field of imports, on the other hand, there is a wide margin for reducing foreign-currency needs, since income levels in

previous years and the overvaluation of the bolivar
created consumer patterns that encouraged imports. This
resulted, for example, in imports representing more than
27 percent of the gross national product in 1982. There
is therefore a wide margin for import substitution. As
previously mentioned, the production capacity standing
idle could achieve this goal in the short term. This
would constitute one of the key elements for reactivation and cannot, therefore, be subordinated to theoretical
positions regarding trade liberalization.

A third area in which an understanding of the
Venezuelan situation is required in order to design an
economics program is prices and wages policy. For many
years, Venezuela has been a country in which prices have
been stable. Between 1958 and 1978 the average annual
increase in the cost of living was 4 percent. In the
past four years this average has risen to 15 percent.
However, wage increases have not kept pace with inflation.
Wage negotiations are still carried out on the basis of
nominal consumer prices and, with only two exceptions in
the last ten years, no general wage increases have been
granted. This situation has prevailed despite the fact
that the country has strong trade union organizations
and enjoys freedom of contract and civil rights.

In the past, real increases in income generated by
economic activity and the low rate of inflation allowed
an income-price spiral to be avoided. But after three
years of real decreases in income, any increase in
prices that is not at least partially compensated by
wage increases is quite likely to produce changes in the
attitudes of the workers. The risk of a wage increase
causing a conflict cannot be taken, as it would destroy
the peaceful labor relations that have formed one of the
most positive features of Venezuela's economy and
democracy and could cause an inflationary spiral that
would undermine the equilibrium of the economic and
social fabric.

For this reason, any economic stabilization program
in Venezuela should remain flexible in the treatment of
wages and prices. The possibility should not be pre-
cluded of adopting wage policies that would incorporate
control mechanisms applicable to both wages and prices.
This is particularly pertinent in the present situation,
since the effect of the devaluation and the checking of
inflationary pressures brought about as a result of the
price freeze (which lasted more than six months) could
create an unmanageable situation in the absence of
suitable control mechanisms.

The problems concerning price increases and their
effects on incomes must be taken into account in determining the exchange rate. It is clear that the present
exchange system cannot be maintained. It is necessary for
it to be simplified and for the number of differential
exchange rates and the difference between the official

and the free rates to be reduced. Here the reactivation policy can be reconciled with orthodox policy without any major problem. But the extreme must not be reached where determining an equilibrium exchange rate could provoke uncontrollable instability in wages and prices. For this reason it is necessary to either limit the extent of the devaluation or make available suitable tools for adjustment and control.

It would seem possible to design a reactivation and stabilization program that would ensure Venezuela's medium-term payment capacity and that could consequently lead to an agreement with its creditors concerning the rescheduling of the debt. The International Monetary Fund's support for a program of this kind is important in that it would facilitate the negotiations and maintain the ritual of international financial relations. But it would be lamentable if maintaining this ritual prevented reaching a solution to the problem of Venzuela's debt-- one of the easiest to solve, since it is the most artificial in what has come to be termed the international foreign-debt crisis.

APPENDIX

For many years Venezuela has been a country with a small foreign debt. Following the blockade imposed in 1902 by Great Britain, Germany, and Italy in retaliation for the delay in paying outstanding debts, the governments of Venezuela have avoided becoming indebted to foreign countries, and public opinion has remained particularly sensitive and averse to international finance commitments. The dictatorship of General Vicente Gómez, who ruled the country between 1908 and 1936, set itself the task of eliminating the foreign debt. In 1930, on the occasion of the centenary of the death of Simón Bolívar, the general gave the following address to the country: "I believe that the best, most pleasing and enduring gift we can offer to his memory is to totally eliminate the foreign debt, for by this uncommon action the nation will achieve new glory and respect." Funds were mobilized for this purpose, and from then until 1957 officially Venezuela had no foreign debt. This was made possible by the discovery and exploitation of the country's oil wealth and the resultant increase in its foreign reserves.

However, during the 1950s the decentralized public-sector enterprises had begun to acquire debts without registering them. As a result, by January 1958 this debt had reached the figure of 3 billion bolivars, twice that of the nation's official debt.

During the year in which the present period of Venezuelan democracy began, the debts were consolidated. But at the same time the flight of capital brought about by political instability and a fall in oil prices led to a decrease in international reserves. In the light of these circumstances a loan for US$2 billion was agreed upon in 1960 with a consortium of foreign banks. This operation signified Venezuela's return to the international finance markets. Following that date, "the country began a policy of complementing its public savings with foreign resources to cover both its day-to-day and development needs, a process which was encouraged by Venezuela's permanent solvency resulting from its balance of payments situation."[1] This process meant a moderate increase in indebtedness up until 1973. In 1957 Venezuela's total foreign public debt was US$236 million. In 1960 it was US$294 million; in 1963, 161 million; in 1968, 437 million; and in 1973, US$1.212 billion (these data are from the Banco Central de Venezuela).

After 1974 and the increase in oil prices, the situation changed radically. The new foreign earnings were too large to be absorbed by the economy, and mechanisms such as the Venezuelan Investment Fund were created to take money out of circulation in order to assign it at a later date to profitable investment. The increase in aggregate demand made it necessary, however, to increase imports. The economy had acquired new dimensions and very rigorous investment projects were drawn up to absorb additional resources. What held most sway at this time was the conviction, confirmed by the forecasts of the international organizations, that the real price of oil was to increase steadily. From 1975 onward investment grew in real terms at an interannual rate of more than 20 percent. By 1978, total investment represented 40 percent of the gross national product.

From 1974 onward, however, oil earnings fell, and the government thought it wise to maintain high levels of reserves, particularly following the nationalization of the oil industry in 1976. Thus, it turned to foreign credit in order to finance its large investment projects, many of which implied undividable expenditures. By this time, the multilateral finance agencies, such as the World Bank, had suspended credit to the oil-exporting countries; therefore the latter turned almost exclusively to the private international banks. The tendency to use the private banks rather than the international organizations had existed for several years. Thus, while three-quarters of the debt contracted in 1965 was granted by public finance institutions, in 1973 this percentage had dropped to 30 percent.

The attraction of the oil countries for the international banks also meant that Venezuela was offered the most advantageous credit conditions for almost any purpose. The central government's difficulties in controlling the debts of the state enterprises and agencies, which had been growing in previous years, increased to the extent that by 1978 approximately 30 percent of the debt consisted of short-term loans taken out by these institutions. These were not registered as part of the public debt, so total public debt figures for the period 1974-1982 (as well as those already cited for 1957-1973) are underestimated. The 1974-1982 figures on Venezuela's total foreign public debt (also from the Banco Central de Venezuela) are: 1974, US$1.095 billion; 1976, 3.290 billion; 1978, 7.253 billion; 1980, 9.655 billion; and 1982, 12.101 billion.

The increase in the debt between 1974 and 1978 can be traced to the Law for the Nationalization of the Oil Industry by which bonds for the public debt were issued to the value of US$918 million; the Law for Investment in the Basic Sectors of Production, which represented a debt of approximately US$5.4 billion; and the Refinancing Law designed to improve the short-term position of the state institutions.

Fifty-two percent of the registered debt for 1974-1982 matured in the five years between 1979 and 1983. To this should be added the short-term debt for which reliable figures are not available and whose total has been the subject of controversy. Estimates reveal its total to be at least 23 billion bolivars but do not give a breakdown for the foreign and the internal debt. If the same percentage is used for the foreign debt as for the registered debt, this gives a short-term foreign debt of US$3.7 billion, to which can be added a similar sum for liabilities outside the public-finance sector.

By the close of 1982, according to Venezuelan calculations made for the renegotiation talks, the total foreign debt was running at US$26.690 billion. This total, which included debt of state enterprises and finance bodies, was made up of US$13.992 billion in registered medium- and long-term debt and US$12.698 billion in short-term debt and foreign liabilities of the public-finance sector. This is in marked contrast to the previous figure of US$12.101 billion in registered debt for 1982. The unusual increase in the indebtedness of the public sector's finance institutions was due to the use of short-term foreign credit to bridge operating deficits and to finance long-term investment. To the short-term debt of state agencies should be added the private sector's foreign debt. According to RECADI, that total lies somewhere between US$8 and 9 billion and mainly consists of short-term debt.

NOTES

1.   Venezuelan Investment Fund, Evolution of the Public Debt in Venezuela, Caracas, 1979.

13
The External Debt, Financial Liberalization, and Crisis in Chile

Ricardo Ffrench-Davis

Most Latin American countries are facing a dramatic problem of external indebtedness. The sharp deterioration in international markets registered since 1981 has affected the developing nations with unusual severity; the drop in export prices and difficulties of access to the markets of industrialized countries, the rise in interest rates, and the sharp reduction in the new inflow of capital have all joined together to give rise to the biggest external shock in the last half century.

Although generalized, the effects of the external shock on the economies of the debtor nations display considerable variety, which is due to the diverse bargaining powers of the countries, the different speeds and magnitudes of each country's indebtedness process, and the development and indebtedness strategies adopted by them. The latter was also a determining factor in the level of development that each country had reached when it was hit by the external crisis. In other words, there are nations whose economies stagnated or even contracted during the last decade, yet there are others that grew vigorously by using for this purpose the abundant external credit available to them on international markets.

During the last decade the Chilean economy has undergone changes of overwhelming importance. After the 1973 coup d'état, an orthodox monetarist economic model was imposed that progressively liberated various markets, transferred public enterprises to private hands, and systematically did away with the capacity of the state to regulate economic activity. In the area of international economic relations, an import liberalization process was carried out that suppressed selectivity in trade policy, eliminated paratariff restrictions, and established a uniform tariff of 10 percent for almost all imports. This opening-up process in trade was accompanied by a similarly unrestricted opening-up process vis-à-vis foreign investment and by the reduction of restrictions on the purchase and sale of foreign currency and capital movements.

Within the context of the innumerable changes that have taken place in recent years, it is difficult to single out the effects of a particular area of economic policy. This study concentrates, however, on the external debt of Chile. Because of the intimate relation this had with the operation of the domestic capital market and the balance-of-payments policy, the main features and results registered in these two areas will be set forth here, too.

As has been shown in other studies, the Chilean economy registered a very unsatisfactory performance during the period 1973-1982.[1] At the same time, a spectacular process of concentration of income and wealth took place.[2] The total failure of the experiment carried out in these years is associated to a significant extent, albeit not exclusively, with the trade and financing policies imposed in the period in question. The way these policies were applied made it possible for the external debt to grow very rapidly in the most recent years. At the same time, instead of supporting domestic capital formation, this increase in debt discouraged it. This resulted from five important causes: the rapid and indiscriminate liberalization of imports (especially of consumer goods), the lag in adjustment of the nominal exchange rate, the persistence of high real interest rates on the domestic market, the absolute freedom given to the market forces to decide on the use made of funds of both domestic and external origin, and the difficulty in identifying the market comparative advantages or finding attractive opportunities for productive investment in the context of the market conditions determined by the application of an orthodox monetarist model.

Finally, a high level of vulnerability of the national economy was generated. Thus, in view of the passive and neutral domestic policies pursued, the economy had no weapons to deal with changes originating in the exterior. Furthermore, the rapid indebtedness and the magnitude of the deficit on current account could obviously not be maintained in the medium term, even if the international financial crisis had not occurred. Consequently, the external sector was placed on a course that would inevitably call for a traumatic adjustment process. The seriousness of this situation was accentuated, of course, by the fact that during this ten-year period the national production base and capacity for adjustment were actually weakened rather than developed. Thus, for example, the value added by Chilean manufacturing in 1982 was 16 percent less than in 1973: a flagrant contrast with the developing countries as a whole, which raised their production over the same period by 50 percent.

The first section of this chapter sets forth the main features of the financial opening-up process and gives brief details of the official conceptual framework,

the policies adopted, and the evolution of capital movements and the external debt; special attention is given
to bank loans and the behavior of the capital flows
received by private debtors. In the second section,
the macroeconomic impact of the external indebtedness is
examined (especially the way in which it affected monetary
and exchange-rate policies), the global adjustment
processes to which it gave rise are analyzed, and the
evolution of interest rates--especially the persistent
gap between domestic and external interest rates--is
studied. An examination is made in the third section of
the various sources of external vulnerability to which
Chile has been exposed as a result of the financial
openness. I argue in contradiction to the orthodox
monetarist approach that the problems that arose were
concentrated in the private-sector segment of the debt,
and I attempt to explain why the massive inflow of
financial capital, as well as being accompanied by a
reduction in national saving, was associated with a
decline in the rate of capital formation. The section
ends with a brief description of the main features of
the external financial situation and the renegotiation
process faced by Chile in 1983. Finally, the last
section contains a brief recapitulation of the lessons
provided by the orthodox monetarist experiment in the
field of financial relations and foreign debt.

FINANCIAL OPENNESS AND EXTERNAL INDEBTEDNESS

The official policy postulated an unrestricted
opening up to capital movements and the indiscriminate
liberalization of the domestic financial market. In
this section I set forth the conceptual framework on
which the financial opening up was based, then examine
the way in which the principles in question were applied
and finally analyze the quantitative details of the
volume and composition of capital movements and external
indebtedness.

The Conceptual Framework of the Experiment

There are of course some very sophisticated orthodox
monetarist versions of how the liberalization of capital
markets should work and of its effects as compared with
those of the so-called financial represssion. The
essential aspects of the official version can be
conveyed by a very simple scheme, however.
The liberalization of the domestic financial market
and the opening up to capital movements sought to increase saving from both domestic and external sources
and to improve the allocation of credit resources. In
response, it was expected that there would be an increase

351

in the volume of investment and in its efficiency that
would provide the basis for vigorous economic growth.
     In simple terms, the conceptual framework may be
described with the aid of Figure 13.1. Curves O and D
show the supply of and demand for lendable funds prevailing in the market, identified with saving and
investment, respectively. To begin with, there had
prevailed what is called in the jargon of monetarism a
situation of financial repression, in the sense that
there were restrictions regarding the organization of new
banks and the operations they could carry out. Against
this background, the authorities fixed an interest rate
(rc) lower than the equilibrium rate for a closed
economy (re) and also less than that of an open economy
(rf<re). This gives a volume of savings Vc, and demand
is rationed to the same level (for the sake of simplicity
it is assumed that initially there was no net inflow of
foreign capital). The volume of saving and investment
(Vc) is less than that in a closed market situation with
a free rate, which would be Ve; at the same time, some
unprofitable investments are made, since the rationing
means that not all of the most efficient investments are
made. Thus, some investments would be made that even had
returns equal to rc, whereas others with a higher yield
would remain without financing (inevitably, in some the
return would be greater than re, since the total investment would not exceed Vc).

Figure 13.1 Conventional Conceptual Framework of the
Liberalization of Capital Markets

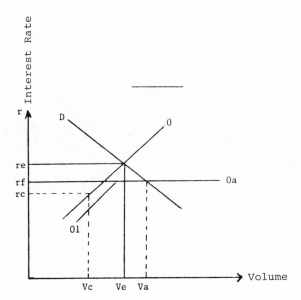

The domestic financial reform would permit r to rise
to its equilibrium level and would give savers more
alternatives for investing their funds. Thanks to the
greater variety of alternative options, there would be a
greater supply ($\underline{O}$l, located to the right of $\underline{O}$), which
would displace in particular "investment" in "non-
productive" assets. At the same time, the opening up of
finance to the exterior would permit the entry of foreign
capital to supplement the funds available for investment.
With the free movement of capital, a volume of invest-
ment $\underline{Va}>\underline{Ve}$ would be reached, and the domestic interest
rate $\overline{would}$ become equal to $\underline{rf}$.

The exchange-rate policy adopted is a determining
factor in the results obtained. In order for interest
rates to be equal, there must be no expectations of
variation in the real rate of exchange (deflated by net
inflation). First of all, this was sought through a
policy of minidevaluations. Subsequently, an attempt
was made with a fixed exchange rate. Official policy
assumed that, in a free trade regime such as was already
in operation in 1979, with a fiscal budget that registered a surplus and an exchange rate close to the
"equilibrium level," freezing of the nominal exchange
rate would rapidly prevent domestic inflation from
exceeding external inflation. Thus, the exchange rate
would become the main instrument for stabilizing the level
of domestic prices.[3] The authorities thus formally
adopted the most extreme type of monetarism: that is to
say, the monetary approach to the balance of payments,
with its corollary of a fixed exchange rate and neutral
monetary policy.

The discrepancies between official thinking and
reality were very marked. The volumes of national saving
and capital formation were less than $\underline{Vc}$: That is to say,
instead of growing, they went down markedly. The domestic
interest rate stood at unexpectedly high levels and was
spectacularly higher than the external rate. Fixing of
the nominal exchange rate led to a significant loss of
purchasing power. Private indebtedness grew out of all
proportion, encouraged by borrowers' assumption that its
real cost would remain low and that there would continue
to be easy access to credit in the future. Finally, the
excessive indebtedness, with the correspondingly higher
service costs, weakened the system of production and the
payments capacity instead of proportionately strengthening them. The intensity of these discrepancies contributed to the general failure of the model imposed during
the 1970s in Chile.

The New Institutional Framework

In the period under consideration,[4] three sub-
periods may be distinguished as regards the application

of these financial policies. The first ran from 1973 to
1975. During that period there were no substantial
changes in the domestic financial system. Various
measures taken to encourage foreign investment and
external credits had little effect, in the sense that
the net flows were not significant. The second period
began in 1975, with the drastic reform of the domestic
financial system and the transfer of most of the commercial banks to private ownership. The application of
the principles in question as regards external financing
was gradual, however. The evolution that took place in
this aspect was in contrast to the speedy opening up
to the exterior as regards trade, an opening that was
still expanding. In the following years, however, there
was a heavy inflow of capital, which grew rapidly between
1976 and 1981. The determining factors of this flow were
the abundance of funds available on the international
market, the low initial bank debt, the "image of creditworthiness" that Chile managed to project, and the
absence of domestic and external restrictions regarding
the use of the funds. In the last part of the period,
from the end of 1981 onward, even though the liberalization of capital inflows was intensified still further,
the net flows shrank drastically, both as a result of the
emergence of the international financial crisis and of
the tardy recognition by the international banking system
of the overindebtedness incurred by Chile.

The main reason for the limitations on the size and
periods of the capital movements is to be found in the
aim of ensuring control over the money supply, which for
several years played the principal role in the anti-
inflation policy. It was considered that, in view of
the big differences that had existed between the domestic
and external interest rates, "a drastic liberalization
of the capital account would attract credit in such
volume that this would hold up the stabilization program.
For this reason, a gradual liberalization process was
preferred."[5] The official declarations always insisted
on the temporary nature of the restrictions imposed,
however. Indeed, with the passage of time, the movement
of capital was liberalized through increases in the
maximum amounts of indebtedness and the elimination of
restrictions or their replacement with more flexible
controls.

In 1981, the year in which the net use of foreign
capital came to 21 percent of the GDP, the entry of
financial credits (under Article 14 of the law on international exchange operations) was subject to a minimum
stay in the country of twenty-four months and the
compulsory deposit of a percentage of the credit (10
or 15 percent, depending on the term) in the case of
operations for less than sixty-six months. There were no
special restrictions on the volume of credit that the
banks could procure abroad and grant in the form of

foreign-currency loans in Chile, but there was still a
limit on the security that could be provided. During
1982, in the midst of the internal crisis of the Chilean
economy, the minimum term of twenty-four months for
credits was eliminated and the compulsory deposit was
set at 5 percent of the external loan, which was a rate
similar to the reserves demanded in respect of domestic
bank deposits.

The capital movements have been influenced by the
conditions in which the financial institutions have
operated. At the end of 1973, the commercial banks were
mostly in the hands of the state, as a result of the
process of nationalization of the banking system promoted by the previous government. During 1975, most of
the banks were offered for sale and returned to the private
sector. Together with the freeing of interest rates in
April of that year, wide facilities were also given for
the setting of readjustment conditions (monetary corrections) in respect of operations for more than ninety days
and for the payment of interest on short-term deposits.
Furthermore, the regulations regarding control of the
amount of credit in national currency, which had mainly
been aimed at channeling credit to production rather
than consumption, were eliminated, and both the authorized
operations and their conditions were made the same for the
different types of financial institutions.

Changes in the regulation of foreign banks were also
included within this trend toward uniform treatment. The
activities of foreign banks had been restricted during
the governments of Presidents Frei and Allende, and they
did not begin to return to the market until December
1974, when the restrictions prohibiting their operation
in the country were lifted.

Financial Capital Movements and Indebtedness, Volume,
Origin, and Destination

Capital movements grew rapidly from 1977 onward.
Even though after that date the Chilean external sector
registered a large and growing current account deficit,
the net inflow of capital was sufficient to permit significant accumulation of international reserves until
1981. The larger flow took place against the background
of big expansion of the external sector, especially of
imports of nonessential consumer goods. The capital
movements were overwhelmingly concentrated in credits to
the private sector without any state guarantee, less than
20 percent of the inflow being accounted for by direct
foreign investment and loans to the public sector.

Table 13.1 shows the evolution of various indicators
of annual capital movements. The flows, expressed in money
of constant purchasing power, increased very markedly in
the second half of the 1970s (columns 1 and 2). They

Table 13.1 Chile: Annual Deficit on Current Account and Capital Movements (millions of 1977 U.S. dollars)

Year	Balance on Current Account (1)	Cross Inflow of Credits (2)	External Financing of Investments (%) (3)	External Financing of Domestic Expenditure (%) (4)	Export Deficit (%) (5)	Debt-Servicing Coefficient (%) (6)
1970	-166	941	6.8	1.4	6.5	27.0
1971	-367	772	15.5	2.8	16.9	38.4
1972	-690	1,302	36.4	5.4	40.0	27.9
1973	-441	1,106	24.7	3.6	20.7	25.4
1974	-256	1,064	12.0	2.1	8.9	35.1
1975	-534	1,109	32.5	5.0	29.3	55.6
1976	160	1,086	-11.4	-1.4	-6.5	52.7
1977	-551	1,390	34.1	4.6	22.5	52.8
1978	-965	2,559	50.9	7.4	38.5	58.3
1979	-933	2,691	42.2	6.6	27.3	50.8
1980	-1,382	3,270	51.2	9.0	36.8	47.7
1981	-3,348	4,640	108.1	20.7	103.2	70.8
1982	-1,693	2,238	87.2	12.2	53.4	88.5

Note: All the nominal figures in U.S. dollars were deflated by the External Price Index (R. Ffrench-Davis, "Indice de Precios Externos para Calcular el Valor Real del Comercio Internacional de Chile, 1952-80," Notas Técnicas no. 32 [Santiago: CIEPLAN, 1981]) in order to convert them into figures at 1977 prices. Column (3) measures the percentage relationship between the deficit on current account and gross fixed capital formation; column (4) indicates the relationship between the deficit on current account and the gross domestic product; column (5) is the relation between the deficit on current account and exports of nonfinancial goods and services; column (6) is the quotient of the gross outflow plus net interest payments and total exports of nonfinancial goods and services. For the conversion into U.S. dollars of the figures for GDP and investment, which were originally given in 1977 pesos, the average real exchange rate for the three-year period 1976-1978 was used, expressed in 1977 pesos per U.S. dollar of the same year.

Source: Calculated on the basis of Banco Central de Chile, Balanza de Pagos, Deuda Externa de Chile, and Cuentas Nacionales Nuevas.

also grew as a proportion of various domestic variables.
Thus columns 3 and 4 show that the capital movements
markedly increased as a proportion of gross domestic
investment and of the GDP. This was partly a result of
the relative stagnation of the latter two variables during the 1970s. External savings (deficit on current
account) and the servicing of capital also grew, with
some ups and downs, in relation to exports (columns 5 and
6), in spite of the dynamic growth of the latter in the
early years of the orthodox monetarist experiment. The
total debt servicing amounted in 1981 to 71 percent of
exports of goods and services, and in 1982 it rose to
88 percent: that is to say, three times the servicing
coefficient of the years 1970-1974. In short, various
quantitative data show that from 1977 onward, capital
movements assumed a rapidly growing relative weight in
the Chilean economy. The coefficients reflecting their
incidence show a debt-servicing burden substantially
greater than for Latin America as a whole in the 1970s.[6]
     Debt-related transactions (as reflected by the
volume of gross transactions and amortization payments)
increased faster than the net capital flows, since the
terms of the external credits grew shorter. This was a
direct consequence of the increased share accounted for
by debts with private creditor banks (see Table 13.2),
which operate with shorter maturities. The magnitude
reached by capital movements is reflected by the fact
that in the two-year period 1980-1981, the gross inflow
of credits was equivalent to 25 percent of the GDP.
     During the period under analysis, significant
changes took place as regards the agents (creditors and
debtors) participating in movements of capital. In
regard to creditors, in 1981 over 80 percent of the
external debt was with banks and financial institutions,
which had accounted for only 19 percent of it at the end
of 1974 (Table 13.2). This increased participation by
private lenders in the origin of funds was reflected in
a decline in the nominal amount of the debt with
official bodies. This reassignment of borrowing was
partly the result of greater use of an external supply
of bank funds, which had previously been relatively
little used by Chile as compared with other semiindustrialized countries. Before 1977, Chile had had less
recourse than the rest of the Latin American countries
to the international banking system. From then on,
however, it rapidly caught up and (according to the
Bank for International Settlements data) became one of
the principal debtors with the private international
capital market among the non-oil-exporting developing
countries, moving up from eleventh place in 1976 to fifth
place in 1981. Within the Latin American context,
Chile's per capita bank debt in 1982 came to over
US$1,000, compared with a regional average of US$600
and only about US$500 in the case of Brazil.[7]

Table 13.2   Chile: Total External Debt and Debt with Private
Financial Institutions

Year	Total Debt (millions of US$)	Financial Institutions (millions of US$)	Share in total (%)
1974	4,776	923	19.3
1975	5,453	1,352	24.8
1976	5,392	1,506	27.9
1977	5,763	2,144	37.2
1978	7,153	3,723	52.0
1979	8,790	5,885	67.0
1980	11,331	8,579	75.7
1981	15,706	13,169	83.8
1982	17,263	14,986	86.8

Source: Banco Central, Deuda Externa de Chile, 1982, tables 1, 3,
and 11; R. Ffrench-Davis and J. P. Arellano, "Apertura Financiera
Externa: La Experiencia Chilena en 1973-80," Colección Estudios
CIEPLAN 5, 1981, table 7.   The total debt refers to the current
disbursed balance.   In addition to the traditional debt, it
includes national currency liabilities, liabilities with the IMF,
and short-term international liabilities of the monetary system.
From 1975 onward, it includes short-term debts contracted by
sectors other than the monetary system, with the exception of
direct foreign-trade operations.

Furthermore, Chile's bank debt grew at the rate of 57
percent per year between 1977 and 1981, compared with an
average of 28 percent for the developing countries as a
whole.
      As regards debtors, the inflow of credits for the
private sector showed marked growth; in the public sector
debt-amortization payments predominated.   Thus, after
1975 the growing net inflow of capital was received
mostly by the private sector.   This situation was in
line with a deliberate policy of the government, as part
of its program of reducing state participation.   This was
facilitated by the change that took place in international markets: the loss of weight on the part of
official finance institutions, which operated mostly
with government bodies, and the vigorous emergence of the
private international capital markets, which offer
access to both public and private debtors.
      This evolution, described so far in terms of annual
flows of resources, is also reflected in the external
debt balances.   Table 13.3 shows the composition of the
gross and net debt (gross debt less reserves), by primary
borrowers.   It will be seen that the private sector
(including the commercial banking system) increased its
share as gross debtor from 19 percent in 1973 to 73 percent in 1982.
      In addition, the level of the international reserves
rose steadily up to 1981.   This has implications for the

Table 13.3   Chile: External Debt, by Borrowers (millions of U.S. dollars)

Year	Gross Debt Public Sector (1)	Gross Debt Private Sector (2)	Net Debt Public Sector (3)	Net Debt Private Sector (4)	Private-Sector Share in Net Debt (%) (5)
1973	3,276	786	3,063	716	18.9
1974	3,897	879	3,709	773	17.2
1975	4,426	1,027	4,252	931	18.0
1976	4,252	1,140	3,718	1,016	21.5
1977	4,319	1,444	3,763	1,339	26.2
1978	4,858	2,295	3,648	2,147	37.0
1979	5,018	3,772	2,882	3,053	54.9
1980	4,905	6,426	1,569	5,986	79.2
1981	5,145	10,561	1,878	9,761	83.9
1982	5,892	11,371	3,866	10,586	73.2

Note: Column (1) excludes state-guaranteed private debt and external debt contracted by the Banco del Estado de Chile; column (2) includes state-guaranteed private debt and debt contracted by the Banco del Estado de Chile; columns (3) and (4) represent the gross debt less the international reserves of the Banco Central and of the financial system, respectively. For the purpose of measuring reserves, holdings of gold were valued at the constant real price of US$42.222 per ounce of fine gold, base 1977.

Source: International Monetary Fund, International Financial Statistics Yearbook, 1982, and May 1983; Banco Central, Boletín Mensual (May 1983), Deuda Externa de Chile (1979 and 1982), and Indicadores Económicos y Sociales (1960-1982); DIPRES, Exposición Sobre el Estado de la Hacienda Pública, October 1982.

effects caused by the external indebtedness of domestic purchasing power. When foreign credit has as its counterpart a bigger current account deficit (corresponding, for example, to a similar increase in imports), the recipient of the credit increases purchasing power without a direct impact on the rest of the economy. When the external credit ultimately involves an increase in the reserves, however, the debtor's purchasing power is increased at the expense of the Central Bank emission corresponding to the excess foreign currency on the exchange market that the Central Bank is obliged to acquire. The final incidence on the purchasing power of the public and private sector will therefore depend on the reaction of the government to the accumulation of reserves, which may be expressed through such measures as raising the exchange rate, further liberalizing imports, reducing domestic credit, or reducing public expenditure.

An estimate of the impact or initial effect of the movement of capital is shown in columns 3 and 4 of Table 13.3, which show the total debt less the reserves of the respective sectors. As the accumulation of assets was concentrated in the public sector (Central Bank), up to 1981 this was reflected in a substantial reduction in its net liabilities (accumulated balance of current loans less reserves of the sector). In the case of the private sector, in contrast, the net indebtedness grew very rapidly, increasing by a factor of fifteen between 1973 and 1983. These data show clearly that the inflow of external capital helped to accentuate the process of greater private participation in expenditure in the Chilean economy.

It should be noted that the majority of the private debt was contracted without state guarantee. Thus, in 1981 almost two-thirds of Chile's total debt lacked official guarantee, and the figure was still over 60 percent toward the end of 1982. The presence of a non-guaranteed debt of over US$10.5 billion undoubtedly constitutes a decisive factor in the process of re-negotiation of the external debt.

In regard to the intermediaries dealing with the external capital, up to 1977 the private sector obtained a significant part of the credits directly, because of the quantitative restrictions faced by the banks in these operations. This statement calls for two qualifications, however. On the one hand, the section of the nonfinancial private sector with most access to external credit was that with the closest connections with national and foreign banking institutions. On the other hand, a substantial proportion of these loans had bank guarantees. From 1978 onward, the domestic financial sector assumed greater importance in the direct intermediation of external private financing. Table 13.4 gives details of the credits that entered the country under the terms of Article 14. This table shows that between 1978 and 1981, the public sector virtually disappeared as a user of this source of external funds while the banking institutions achieved marked predominance as intermediaries, operating with them directly or indirectly (i.e., as guarantors).

During the first years of the process, in spite of the expansion of external indebtedness and the increase in the deficit on current account, the government did not show much concern in this respect. On the contrary, it maintained that what was important was the way in which the real net debt evolved, the rate of interest paid, and the sectors contracting indebtedness.

The official figures for the real net debt showed a reduction over the five-year period 1976-1980: According to them, it went down from US$5.3 billion in 1975 to US$4.3 billion in 1980 (in 1977 dollars). Two external factors explained this reduction in contrast with the high annual rate of indebtedness. The first factor in terms of its importance was the rate of international inflation, which eroded the real value of the debt balance; the second factor was that the debt also went

Table 13.4   Chile: Article 14--Gross Annual Flows of
Credit, by Debtors

Year	Total Flow of Credit (millions of US$) (1)	Public Sector (2)	Percentage Breakdown		Financial Institutions (5)
			Private Nonfinancial Sector (3) and (4)		
1976	262.6	13.3	86.3		0.4
1977	336.4	13.2	80.1		6.7
			Nonguaranteed (3)	Guaranteed (4)	
1978	780.2	4.2	31.0	26.0	38.8
1979	1,245.2	1.8	34.7	21.6	41.9
1980	2,503.7	3.1	14.5	17.6	64.8
1981	4,516.7	1.9	20.6	4.6	72.9
1982	1,770.8	24.4	24.7	6.1	44.8

Note: Column (1) shows the gross annual flow of disbursed credits,
less compulsory deposits. The breakdown over columns (2) to (5) was
estimated on the basis of that for Santiago.

Source: Prepared on the basis of Banco Central, "Créditos
Liquidados Artículo 14" (December 1980), and Boletín Mensual,
no. 662 (April 1983).

down in response to the rise in the value of that portion
of the reserves maintained in gold. Between them, these
two factors explained a reduction of US$2.7 billion in
real net indebtedness in the five-year period in
question.[8] Thus, instead of having gone down in real
terms by 18 percent, the debt would have grown by one-
third if it had not been for these two factors and would
have shown a sharp acceleration toward the end of the
period in question. It was therefore clear that the
rapid growth of external indebtedness permitted was
dangerous, and also prejudicial to national development,
as is shown later. Nevertheless, the government insisted right up to the end that entering into debt was
good business because the real interest rate was very low
or actually negative; furthermore, the debtors were in
the private sector, which was subject to "free" market
laws so that, in official opinion, there could be no
doubt that it was efficient.

INDEBTEDNESS AND MACROECONOMIC ADJUSTMENT

A massive process of external indebtedness such as
the one that took place between 1977 and 1981 has significant effects in many areas of the national economy.
This was demonstrated with great intensity in Chile.
The process profoundly affected total demand and its
composition, contributed to the spectacular concentration

of wealth, considerably altered the functioning of the
process of saving and investment, and conditioned to a
decisive extent the handling of monetary and foreign-
exchange policies.

The initial impact of the external indebtedness
involved an increase in the availability of foreign
exchange. This increase gives rise to two possibilities
that are its counterpart. One is an increase in the
international reserves, usually accompanied by an increase in monetary issue; the other consists of the
expansion of the current account deficit. In practice,
up to 1981, the growing indebtedness manifested itself in
both ways simultaneously, since the net inflow of capital
was greater than the capacity of the national economy to
absorb the resources provided by external credits. The
current account deficit steadily increased by considerable amounts (see Table 13.1, columns 1 and 4): In 1980,
net use of foreign capital was close to the equivalent
of 9 percent of the gross domestic product, in contrast
with 5 percent for Latin America as a whole. In spite
of this, the inflow of capital through private debtors
grew still more quickly. The corresponding surplus (the
difference between the volume of funds received and those
used) gave rise to the increase in international reserves
registered up to 1980; in that year the total Central
Bank reserves represented 68 percent of annual imports
of goods.

The rapid accumulation of reserves had substantial
effects on the handling of monetary and foreign-exchange
policies. Furthermore, the big capital movements--both
those used to finance greater spending on imports and
those that went to swell the international reserves--
meant that a very high proportion of the total credit
available in the national economy originated from foreign
funds, and its cost was associated with the evolution
of the exchange rate. This section is devoted to these
three topics, ending with a summary of the principal
distortions--with their effects as regards assignment and
distribution--caused by the greater financial openness
to the exterior.

Monetary Policy and the Crowding Out of Domestic Credit

From 1975 onward, exchange operations (net purchases
of foreign exchange by the Central Bank) constituted the
main source of expansion of money issue.[9] As time went
on this phenomenon was further intensified, and in the
three-year period 1978-1980 these operations represented
over 100 percent of the total money issue. As already
noted, the overwhelming proportion of net purchases of
foreign exchange by the Central Bank came from the private
sector. Indeed, in some years exchange operations with
the public sector even had a contractive effect. As

regards the credit operations of the Central Bank,
those carried out with the public sector showed a negative
balance from the year 1975 onward, whereas those with the
private sector showed modest expansion throughout the
period. This situation continued until 1981, when the
serious macroeconomic disadjustments that had been buildup in the Chilean economy began to emerge into the open,
and the loss of international reserves began. Correspondingly, the monetary effect of exchange operations became
markedly restrictive.

As indicated in the first section, during certain
periods direct restrictions were used with regard to the
inflow of capital, as an instrument of monetary programming. One of these restrictions was particularly
directed toward controlling the monetary effect of the
inflow of capital, by limiting the amount of resources
that could be changed in the Central Bank each month.
This limitation was enforced--with successive modifications in the maximum amounts of exchange operations
authorized--from September 1977 to April 1980. These
restrictions were not sufficient to keep the inflow of
loans to the private sector down to a volume compatible
with the monetary expansion desired by the economic
authorities, however. Consequently, the latter took
action regarding the other sources of money issue and
regarding the exchange rate. In both cases, there was a
crowding out of the domestic economy by the economy
associated with the exterior. Domestic credit was
restricted in the face of the increase in money issue
through net foreign-exchange purchase operations. The
exchange rate, for its part, was revalued or lagged
behind the actual situation (see the next section) in
response to the accumulation of reserves, thus crowding
domestic producers of tradable goods out of the market.

The goals in regard to the expansion of liquidity
remained in force as long as the closed-economy monetary
approach predominated. Subsequently, in 1979, the open-
economy monetary approach was adopted. Under this, the
nominal exchange rate was frozen, a "neutral" monetary
policy was explicitly adopted, and it was hoped that a
process of automatic adjustment of the money supply would
enter into force. Thus, the variations in the international reserves were to be the determining factors of
the degree of liquidity of the national economy, against
the background of a balanced fiscal budget and stable
bank reserve rates.

This monetary approach to the balance of payments
prevailed to the full for three years, from mid-1979 to
mid-1982, with a "neutral" monetary policy based on the
dollar standard. During the last year in which it was in
force, a contractive "automatic adjustment" began to
operate, with disastrous effects on employment and
national production.[10]

Exchange Policy: Instability and Lag

Exchange policy assumed varied forms during the
period under analysis.   Up to June 1976, the exchange
rate was changed between one and four times per month.
From then on, after a sudden revaluation at that date and
another in March 1977, it was devalued daily according
to a scale fixed every month in advance.   This arrangement was kept up until February 1978, when a table of
daily exchange-rate adjustments was fixed for the rest
of the year.   The same scheme was announced for 1979,
but in June of that year it was interrupted when the
exchange rate was devalued to the nominal level that it
had been programmed to reach at the end of the year
(thirty-nine Chilean pesos per U.S. dollar).   It was kept
at this level until 1982, when there was an 18 percent
devaluation.   This was followed by the announcement of a
table of minidevaluations, soon replaced by a free rate;
this lasted only a short time and was then replaced by
various forms of minidevaluations according to domestic
or net inflation.   The effect of these minidevaluations
on the real exchange rate is shown in Table 13.5.
    I have analyzed the exchange policies applied in
Chile in detail in other studies.[11]   Here, I shall limit
myself to stressing a very important feature of exchange
policy that consists of the notable discrepancies between
the real situation and the monetary approach to the
balance of payments.   It has been demonstrated in practice
that through their policies the authorities can bring
about notable variations in the level of the real exchange
rate.   In other words, the single-exchange-rate law,
even in an economy whose external trade is as liberalized
as in the case of Chile since 1979, has very limited
validity.   In particular, the exchange rate lags can be
so large that they involve adjustments diverging from
equilibrium for the space of several years, thus
generating erroneous signals, faulty assignment of
resources, and a low rate of utilization of production
capacity.
    These tendencies were manifested very forcibly in
Chile, especially during the period when the fixed
nominal exchange rate was thirty-nine pesos per dollar.
During the three-year period when the exchange rate was
frozen, its real level deteriorated by close to one-
third.   Domestic inflation went down significantly,
from over 30 percent per year to less than 10 percent,
but during the transition between these two levels an
imbalance of the size mentioned was accumulated between
domestic and external prices.   Consequently, in order to
return to the initial level of the real exchange rate,
which was apparently considered by the government and
its advisers as being close to equilibrium,[12] it would
be necessary for inflation in Chile to be over thirty
percentage points lower than the international level.

Table 13.5 Chile: Real Exchange Rate and Wages
(Chilean pesos per 1977 U.S. dollars)

| | Real Exchange Rate | |
Year	Deflated by Corrected Consumer Price Index	Deflated by Index of Wages and Salaries of National Statistical Institute
1974	23.40	27.90
1975	32.14	39.44
1976	25.89	29.89
1977	21.54	21.54
1978	23.81	21.48
1979	23.16	19.31
1980	20.09	15.41
1981	16.93	11.92
1982	19.63	13.86

Note: The annual average nominal exchange rate was inflated by the external price index.

Source: Central Bank, Boletín Mensual, various issues; National Statistical Institute, Indice de Sueldos y Salarios; R. Cortazar and J. Marshall, "Indice de Precios al Consumidor en Chile: 1970-78," Colección Estudias CIEPLAN 4, 1980; and R. Ffrench-Davis, "Indice de Precios Externos para Calcular el Valor Real del Comercio Internacional de Chile, 1952-80," Notas Técnicas no. 32 (Santiago: CIEPLAN, 1981).

During the last months of 1981 and the first half of 1982 there was a slight adjustment of relative prices in this direction.[13] At the same time, however, there was a violent increase in open unemployment and a rapid drop in manufacturing production.[14] It may be noted that the segment of the economy with debts expressed in pesos (nonreadjustable) would have had to suffer an increase in its real liabilities if there had indeed been an intensive deflationary process. As domestic indebtedness was generalized, the perturbing effects on the debtor enterprises would have been substantial.

The plain truth is that, after some months of automatic adjustment, with a slight movement in the direction of the required readjustment of relative prices, the economic results were disastrous. The economic team did not succeed in achieving the imposition of the suggested plan to accelerate the adjustment through a reduction by decree of nominal wages. Instead, the abrupt devaluation of June 1982 took place.

Throughout the ten-year period, the effect of exchange-rate variations on capital flows practically did not figure among the objectives taken into account in determining exchange policy. The inflow of external financial resources, however, was crucial in order to permit the handling of the exchange rate in the light of objectives other than those of the efficient assignment

of resources without (up to 1981) bringing about a
deterioration in the overall balance of payments. The
use of the exchange rate to guide expectations (in
1976-1979) and/or to set a limit on domestic price rises
(1979-1982) did indeed result in smaller inflation. The
net inflation persistently went down more slowly than the
exchange rate, however: The latter acted as a variable
tending to repress inflation, but devalued itself during
the process. This, together with the liberalization of
imports and the recovery in economic activity registered
between 1977 and 1981, led to a significant current
account deficit that amounted in 1981 to 21 percent of
the GDP.[15] At the same time, the gradual deterioration
in the real exchange rate reduced the cost of external
indebtedness, so that in 1979 and 1980 this cost was
negative. Consequently, the flows were affected by the
variations in the real exchange rate, accentuating the
problem of the composition of the balance of payments:[16]
the growing deterioration in the current account deficit
and a likewise growing surplus on the capital account.

Interest-Rate Differentials

The official approach expected both a sharp tendency
toward a reduction in financial intermediation spreads
and the leveling of domestic and foreign interest rates,
in response to the overall liberalization of the
financial system. However, throughout the period large
differentials persisted between the rates of interest
for loans and deposits on the domestic financial market,
while the level of both rates was notably high. Furthermore, in spite of the big inflows of capital registered,
especially from 1979 onward, domestic rates were
considerably higher than international rates, as shown
by Table 13.6. The domestic rate refers to the predominant segment of the market, covering transactions
for terms of thirty to eighty-nine days, and the
international interest rate is that paid for bank
credits obtained under Article 14, plus the cost in
respect of compulsory deposits and the financial intermediation margin, all converted into their peso
equivalents.

It may be noted that the ex post gap between the
domestic and external rates for loans never dropped
below an annual rate of eighteen percentage points. In
this respect, the traditional explanations that the
differential is due to expectations of a bigger devaluation than the effective evolution of the official
exchange rate do not seem to be valid. For example,
between 1977 and 1982 the parallel or black-market rate
was very similar to the official rate.[17] The easy
access to the exchange market that existed at that time
and the cash nature of the parallel rate do not make

Table 13.6   Chile: Domestic and External Real Interest Rates
Reflecting Their Level with the Conversion of External Transactions
into Pesos (annual percentages)

	Domestic (1)	External (2)	Differential (3)
1975 (second half)	121.0	--	--
1976	51.2	-21.1	72.3
1977	39.4	0.2	39.2
1978	35.1	3.8	31.3
1979	16.9	-0.9	17.8
1980	12.2	-8.0	20.2
1981	38.8	12.4	26.4
1982	35.2	45.0	-9.8

Source: Prepared on the basis of data from the Banco Central;
Instituto Nacional de Estadisticos; J. P. Arellano, "De la
Liberalización a la Intervención: El Mercado de Capitales en
Chile, 1974-83," Colección CIEPLAN 11, December 1983; R. Cortazar
and J. Marshall, "Indice de Precios al Consumidor en Chile:
1970-78," Colección Estudios CIEPLAN 4, 1980; and R. Ffrench-Davis
and J. P. Arellano, "Apertura Financiera Externa: La Experiencia
Chilena en 1973-80," Colección Estudios CIEPLAN 5, 1981. In 1982,
the "preferential" exchange rate fixed by the government for
existing debtors was used in calculating the external interest rate.

it a precise indicator as regards expectations of devaluation over twenty-four months, which is the minimum
term for the entry of capital under Article 14, but they
do reflect the prevailing atmosphere of a quiet market
in which there was continual sale of foreign exchange by
the public over bank counters.

It is possible, however, that despite the quietness
displayed by the market, debtors with the exterior did
not foresee the lag repeatedly suffered by the real
exchange rate. Likewise, it seems quite possible that
the market was not very aware of the need to make an
adjustment for external inflation when measuring the
real exchange rate. It is therefore probable that the
expected "external interest rate," comparable on the
"market" with the real domestic rate, would be closer to
its nominal level in dollars than to the ex post rate
given in column 2 of Table 13.6. This nominal rate
fluctuated between 14 percent and 23 percent between
1976 and 1982. Consequently, even using this hypothesis,
there would still be a substantial gap with the rate
for domestic credit.

In addition to the domestic/external gap, there were
substantial differentials between the domestic rates for
deposits and for loans. There were various reasons for
these high spreads, and their significance was changing
over the course of the period. This topic has been
dealt with elsewhere.[18] I shall therefore limit myself
here to mentioning some of the aspects that have the

greatest implications for the central analysis, that is
to say, the subject of the external debt and capital
movements.

Traditional explanations put forward are as follows:
(1) the requirement to maintain bank reserves is adduced
as a determining factor in the gap between domestic
interest rates on deposits and loans (the financial
intermediation spread), (2) the fiscal deficit and the
inelastic demand for credit by public enterprises are
indicated as being responsible for the high interest
rates on loans, and (3) the restrictions on movements of
capital are said to be responsible for the differential
between rf and re (Figure 13.1). None of these possible causes
was of significant importance during the whole period,
however. The first of them was of some importance only
in 1975-1976, because of the high requirements for non-
interest-bearing bank reserves and high inflation (over
300 percent per year). Nevertheless, very high levels
of financial intermediation spread, net of the costs
of maintaining these reserves, persisted during most of
the period from 1975 to 1982. Moreover, the fiscal
deficit went down rapidly and substantially (to less
than 3 percent of the GDP in 1975) and became a surplus
in 1979. Finally, in spite of the persistence of
restrictions on movements of capital, such movements
reached very high levels, as was shown in the first
section. Consequently, the orthodox analysis is not
capable of explaining why, with net capital inflows
equivalent to an average of 7.7 percent of the GDP in
1978-1980, the gap between domestic and external interest
rates stood at an average of twenty-three percentage
points per year (see Table 13.6). In this period, as
noted, it was clear that there were as yet no expectations of a massive devaluation.

It must therefore have been other factors that
carried greater weight in explaining the behavior of
interest rates and of the financial intermediation spread.
Various items of information suggest that the banking
system has been inefficient and that its operating costs
rose after the reform.

1. One of the reasons for this up to 1977 was the underutilization of the installed capacity. Furthermore,
the fact that the system has operated with such short
terms for both deposits and loans has constituted another
cause of increased costs. This would seem to explain
why in 1978 the cost level of the system was of the
order of 8 percent of total loans, a very high figure by
comparative international standards. Nevertheless,
even after discounting the operating costs, the
financial intermediation spread still remains very high.
The persistence of these high costs and projects has
been associated with the structure of the financial
market and the degree and form of competition among the
institutions in the sector.

2. The short term of the operations facilitated the prevalence of high rates.[19] Applicants who had no access to external credit had to face a severe recession in domestic demand simultaneously with the freeing of interest rates. Against a background of heavy propaganda to the effect that the recession would only be brief, many business people resorted to expensive short-term credit instead of closing down their operations, expecting a rapid reactivation of demand. In these circumstances, debtors did not view themselves as taking out a loan at a real interest rate of 40 percent per year, but rather as borrowing for thirty days at 3 percent, with the probability of renewing the loan for a few months.

Effective demand, however, remained generally depressed (and lagging behind aggregate demand), and interest rates continued to be high and unstable. In the face of the continuing delay in the hoped-for reactivation, business people engaged in successive renewals of their bank debts, with the increased risk that this involved. This phenomenon was further strengthened by the demand for credit by activities that were adversely affected by the tariff liberalization. In spite of business expectations that it would be abandoned, this liberalization process was maintained and even--unexpectedly, on a number of occasions--further intensified until it culminated in a uniform tariff of 10 percent in 1979.

3. Certain opportunities for highly profitable "investments" arose. Numerous public enterprises were disposed of at prices significantly below normal market levels. Similar opportunities were offered by "investments" in real estate and movable assets, whose prices rose notably in real terms: The securities index increased fivefold in constant values between 1975 and 1979. The elimination of regulations on the use of credit made possible its rapid redistribution toward these uses, which were good investments from the private point of view, although not from that of the country as a whole.

4. In recent years there has been a noteworthy increase in consumer credit, especially for imported consumer durables. Here, too, the suppression of the previous restrictions on bank credit for consumers facilitated the change in the composition of expenditure. Furthermore, the liberalization of imports also promoted the expansion of demand for credit to be used in the marketing or purchase of imported consumer goods. Thus, the savings of some nationals filtered through, by way of the financial system, to the consumption of imported goods. This is one explanation for the drop observed in the rate of national saving. In the three-year period 1978-1980, which was the period of alleged great success of the economic model, the rate of national saving, measured as the gross fixed-capital formation rate less the rate of utilization of foreign capital, came to

barely 8 percent.

5. The gradual recovery in domestic economic
activity and wages from the very depressed levels reached
in 1975, together with the massive official publicity
within the prevailing authoritarian framework, helped to
create an image of a dynamic and rapidly growing economy.
And as the recovery on the basis of the utilization of
existing installed capacity began to come to an end,
the aggregate demand was fed with the very big external
credits that propped up the semblance of a boom period
until far into 1981. The atmosphere of success created,
together with the consequent expectations of growing
income, induced consumers and businesses to continue increasing their indebtedness while it prompted the banks
to renew and rapidly expand their lines of credit. Within this context, the banking institutions competed with
each other, partly by reducing the cost of their services
(the financial intermediation spread) but also by reducing
the security demanded from their borrowers.

6. A significant proportion of the funds involved
were assigned by the banks to businesses linked to them
as regards their ownership. Thus, for example, in 1982
the main bank of the biggest economic group in the
country had 44 percent of its portfolio loaned to firms
that were openly and directly related to that same group.
Consequently, financial transactions became mere internal
group operations, weakening appraisal criteria and
procedures for recovering debts.

7. In the context already described the high cost
of loans on the domestic capital market helped to
increase the demand for them rather than to reduce it.
Thus, the factors described in paragraphs 2 through 6
tended to make the demand for credit more inelastic,
while at the same time the high financial costs caused
an increase in the demand for funds in order to pay
interest commitments, with this effect predominating over
the pure price effect. The fact that credit, viewed as
just another product, was traded and used in the same
unit as products proper, in contrast with transactions
of nonfinancial goods and services in a monetary
economy, gave rise to this different behavior of demand
referred to. The magnitude of the financial cost effect
is illustrated by the fact that between 1976 and 1982 an
average debtor paid excess interest, over and above a
real "normal" rate of 8 percent per year, amounting to
the equivalent of 300 percent of the initial loan. In
other words, a borrower who effectively paid the 8 percent to the creditor each year, renewed the principal,
and capitalized the interest commitments in excess of 8
percent would be liable by the end of 1982 for a debt
over four times the original amount, in money of constant
purchasing power.[20] It should be noted, in contrast,
that a debtor with the exterior on similar terms would
be liable in 1982, just before the devaluation, for a

real debt 44 percent below that contracted in 1976.
Consequently, even after a massive real devaluation of
80 percent the debtor would have ended up with a debt
equal only to the original amount (and equivalent to only
a quarter of the liabilities of a person having a debt
expressed in pesos). This calculation is, of course,
sensitive to the period taken for the starting time. Thus,
for example, "tardy" debtors who took out credits in
foreign currency only in 1981 or in the first half of
1982 suffered a serious loss, taking into account the
real devaluations registered in the remainder of 1982.
This is in sharp contrast with the case of "early" debtors.

8. Credit of external origin played a different role
from the one that it had traditionally assumed. It is
usually supposed that such funds entered an integrated
market characterized by great substitutability between
resources of domestic and external origin, so that both
types of interest rates would therefore tend to equalize.
It is probably true that the external credit did help
to relieve the demand for funds on the domestic market.
Nevertheless, the effects of the factors mentioned earlier
were stronger, and they therefore pushed up the domestic
rate of interest on loans. This was because of the persistent segmentation displayed by the market. In effect,
only some of the debtors could enter into indebtedness
directly with the exterior or gain access to credit
through the intermediation of local banking institutions.
As a result, the difference between the domestic and
external interest rates reached notably high levels,
fluctuating in the period 1977-1981 between eighteen
and forty percentage points per year (see Table 13.6).
As already noted, the explanation for this does not lie
in the expectations of devaluation, since until far into
1981 these were of no significance, but it is to be found
rather in the marked segmentation that prevailed in the
financial market. Of course this segmentation was not
absolute. In a considerable part of the market there
were borrowers who had simultaneous access to both
domestic and external sources of funds, in proportions
that varied according to their banking connections.[21]

Credit of external origin was available on a very
large scale, representing as much as some 40 percent
of the total loanable funds of the financial system.
The differentials in interest rates therefore had substantial effects, from the point of view of both assignment and distribution. Small- and medium-sized producers
were mostly relegated to the segment where high interest
rates prevailed. In contrast, entities having links
with the management of the financial institutions and
the main economic groups had easy access to external
credit, either directly or through the intermediation of
national banks. This noteworthy and prolonged segmentation of the market helps to explain the spectacular
concentration of income and wealth in these years.

EXTERNAL VULNERABILITY AND THE DYNAMICS OF INDEBTEDNESS

The conditions prevailing in the world economy and on the domestic market promoted a process of growing indebtedness that gave rise to great vulnerability of the Chilean external sector. Moreover, the form assumed by the transfer of external resources and the incentives given by the economic model caused the external indebtedness to be accompanied by a decline in domestic investment and saving (see Table 13.1, column 3) and the crowding out of national production.

As shown in the second section, for several years the real external debt did not appear to be growing strongly, in spite of the growing deficit on current account. The behavior of real net indebtedness, the ease with which new credits could be obtained, and the low real rates of interest on international markets led many countries to take a complacent attitude during the 1970s and the early 1980s. This was backed up by the opinion prevailing in domestic official circles that, since the indebtedness was predominantly of a private nature, the use made of it would naturally be efficient.[22]

The growing indebtedness made possible a gradual appreciation in the exchange rate. This, in turn, made it still more attractive to resort to external loans; thanks to this appreciation, the real cost of foreign-currency credit was negative during almost the whole period of financial liberalization. The process was thus self-encouraging, accelerating the inflow of capital, which increased aggregate demand and permitted the continuation and intensification of the process of exchange-rate appreciation. This led to growing accommodation of the national economy to a massive inflow of financial capital.

In the production system, however, what was taking place was the opposite to what was maintained by the official version. Both components of the saving investment process showed unsatisfactory behavior, with rates of savings investment manifestly below the levels reached in the 1960s. An increasing proportion of the resources was directed toward the consumption of imported goods, crowding out spending on national products and domestic saving. There was discouragement of investment, especially in the production of tradable goods. The clearest "comparative advantages" were in the purchase of assets on the domestic market from deeply indebted business people at depreciated prices. Except for some sectors making intensive use of natural resources, such as fruit production and fisheries (which did indeed expand) and luxury construction, investment ran into the difficulty of identifying comparative advantages: The lag or instability of the exchange rate, the behavior of interest rates, the deliberate running down of public production-support activities, the reduction of public

investment, the indiscriminate liberalization of imports,
the noteworthy deterioration in income distribution--all
combined to provide a discouraging environment for
productive investment. Paradoxically, in spite of the
prevailing climate of euphoric success and the close
communication between the government and the economic
groups, the accumulation process languished. This was
because of the intrinsic nature of the model, the
financial bias given to the national economy, and the
difficulty of identifying opportunities for productive
investment in a context subject to such drastic changes
and with no provision for the state to play an active
role in its function of guiding national development.

Quite apart from the unsatisfactory performance of
the system of production, it was obvious that the impetus
imparted to the external sector could not be kept for
long, even if there were no change in the external situation. Nevertheless the official view was that the process
would regulate itself automatically. It was maintained
that since there was no fiscal deficit, since money
issue was less than the value of the international
reserves,[23] and since the monetary policy was "neutral,"
it was impossible for an exchange crisis to arise. It
was confidently believed that imports of consumer goods
would rapidly reach saturation level and that the adjustment capacity of the economy had been strengthened by the
policy imposed since 1973. In contrast with these
beliefs, however, when the international financial
problems emerged in 1981, the trade deficit amounted
to 11 percent of the GDP, and the current account deficit
stood at 21 percent. The deterioration in the financial
and foreign-trade situation thus coincided with the
inescapable need to reduce the size of the external-sector
imbalance and the exchange-rate lag.

The difficulties experienced by Chile in procuring
external credits coincided with a domestic situation in
which there was a pressing need for fresh resources and
in which the government had done away with economic
regulation mechanisms and relied on the automatic
corrections implicit in the dollar standard. At the
same time the system of production was weakened and deep
in debt. Thus, the external shock was multiplied at the
level of the domestic economy and was reflected in a
decline of 14 percent in the GDP in 1982, concentrated
in the manufacturing and construction sectors (which
declined together by 23 percent).

In short, the external shock found Chile in a highly
vulnerable position, and this multiplied its negative
effects on the national economy. At the same time,
Chile's production base was seriously weakened. As
already demonstrated,[24] if the value added in financial
activities and in the trading of imported goods is
deducted, the per capita national product in 1981, before
the effects of the shock, stood only at a level similar

to 1974. This is an unmistakable sign of stagnation
compared with the growth of the rest of the world. Consequently, the violent deterioration observed in 1982
came on top of a situation in which the economy was
already functioning badly.

Chile's access to financial markets was becoming
increasingly difficult, while its international reserves,
although still high, were going down rapidly. After
repeated announcements that it was not necessary to
renegotiate the country's external debt, the Chilean
government initiated a long process, the final stage of
which--the signing of contracts between debtors and
creditors--has still not been completed.

The renegotiation was carried out by the government
of Chile, in spite of the fact that most of the debt
corresponded to the private sector and did not enjoy
state guarantees. This is not in the least surprising,
of course, but it is in sharp contradiction with the
arguments put forward by the economic authorities right
up to 1982 regarding the "efficiency" of private indebtedness. The renegotiation covered the amortization payments
due between February 1983 and the end of 1984 on the
bank debt of public and private entities domiciled in
Chile. It covered about two-thirds of the total liabilities falling due in the period in respect of medium-
and long-term debt.

As in the case of most of the renegotiation operations carried out in the last two years, this was preceded by an agreement with the IMF. The terms regarding
payment schedules and interest rates agreed upon with the
committee representing the hundreds of creditor banks were
similar to those reached in other cases, such as those of
Argentina, Brazil, and Mexico. At first sight, there
would not appear to be any substantial differences in
result obtained by Chile. Without wishing to enter
here into an examination of the rules established regarding the principle of immunity from jurisdiction and
execution and the undertakings entered into on domestic
economic policy, however, I would like to emphasize two
decisive differences observed in the case of Chile.
These concern the agreement with the IMF and the absence
of any prior public guarantee in respect of most of the
debt with the banks.

The agreement with the IMF is particularly
restrictive, the provision with the most serious consequences being that connected with the fiscal deficit.
This was fixed at 1.7 percent for 1983, but after only
a short time it was necessary to raise it to 2.3 percent.
This level meant that, despite the 14 percent drop in the
GDP in the preceding year, the decline in production
continued in 1983. This drop in the GDP was the
determining factor in the 1983 trade surplus of close to
5 percent. The cost in terms of the loss of production,
employment, and economic potential has been extremely

high. There has been an "adjustment," it is true, but
it seems to be clearly inefficient.[25]

As regards the terms agreed upon with the committee
of banks, the similarity between the financing terms
obtained in the different national cases does not take
due account of the fact that in Chile the debt was predominantly without state guarantee. This feature should
have represented a factor of great weight in any renegotiation process, especially when the private sector
in debt to the exterior is not in a position to pay off
its liabilities in the period covered by the renegotiation. The fact is that the Chilean government gave its
guarantee in respect of the debt of national financial
entities that had previously not enjoyed such backing,
but did not, in spite of this, manage to obtain noticeably
more favorable conditions than other countries.

The level of overindebtedness of the Chilean economy
is so serious that in spite of the renegotiation process,
payments of interest and capital in 1983 were equivalent
to almost 12 percent of the 1983 product. There is also
a tendency for the problem to get worse, since the
scheduled amortization payments are due to increase
enormously in 1985. In the two-year period 1985-1986
they are due to exceed the amortization payments prior
to the 1983-1984 renegotiation process by 50 percent.
This increase is due mainly to the maturity of liabilities
in respect of the credits used between 1979 and 1981.
Clearly, the mid-1983 renegotiation only tackled part of
the problem generated by the present economic policy.
Together with the deterioration that has taken place in
international financial markets, this leaves outstanding
a volume of debt-servicing liabilities that will keep the
national economy, year after year, sunk in uncertainty
and obliged to give priority to financial aspects at the
expense of the urgent and serious social and production
problems the country is suffering.

SOME LESSONS OF THIS EXPERIENCE

In this recapitulation I want to emphasize four
lessons deriving from the financial opening-up process.
They refer to the distortions caused by indiscriminate
opening up in regard to concentration and inefficiency
in the allocation of resources; the alternative ways in
which the domestic and external financial markets could
be interrelated; criteria regarding the regulation of
volumes of capital movements; and the channeling of funds
to investment.

The financial opening-up process is not neutral
concerning the allocation of resources, especially during
the transition from a closed economy to an open economy,
because of the pressures it generates on aspects such as
the composition of money issue, the level of the exchange

rate or tariff protection, and public investment. During
the transition it is necessary to adapt the structure of
aggregate supply and demand, as well as to establish a
bigger gap between expenditure and domestic production.
The key questions in this respect concern the optimum
path to be followed by the adjustment and the question
of whether the access to external funds and their cost
will be stable in the future. The financial market
operates with very narrow horizons and does not take
due account of the repercussions on national productive
activity. Consequently, it is essential that the opening-
up process should be regulated in a programmed manner.

As regards the repercussions in the financial sphere
itself, access to external credit is not homogeneous,
not only because of domestic regulations but also because
of the nature of the international financial markets.
In practice, this type of credit has been available mainly to certain segments of the national economy such as
big import and export enterprises and firms associated
with foreign financial institutions. In the case of
credit for importers, for example, the differences in
cost already analyzed meant that the opening-up process
constituted yet another form of removal of protection
from those engaged in import substitution. The differences observed between different applicants regarding
access to and cost of external credit affect not only
the efficiency of resource allocation but also the
distribution of income and wealth. In particular,
the opening up of the capital account in Chile provided
substantial profits for those who were able to obtain
external credits. There can be no doubt, however, that
the effects and their distribution will depend on the
forms of regulation and channels of intermediation
used. Thus, for example, the effects on income distribution and the level of investment can be varied depending on whether the intermediation is carried out by
enterprises, by commercial banks, or through the Central
Bank or a public body responsible for promoting productive investment (such as the Development Corporation--
CORFO).

From another point of view, the change from public
to private entities as the destination of flows of funds
and the concentration observed in the access to those
funds have had very noteworthy consequences in the
political sphere. First, they contributed to the
spectacular concentration of economic power observed in
recent years. Second, they generated powerful antidevaluation forces that, together with the prevailing
economic ideology, helped to keep the exchange rate
frozen for three years (from mid-1979 to mid-1982), while
its real value displayed a pronounced deterioration;
in this connection the antidevaluation pressures of the
importers were reinforced by those of the economic groups
that had taken out debts in foreign currency.

A second lesson that emerges very clearly from the
experience of Chile and other countries in the Southern
Cone is that indiscriminate liberalization is not a
suitable condition for bringing about the integration
into a single market of funds of domestic and external
origin. Indeed, in reality the opposite took place. If
an objective is to promote an alternative option leading
to an integrated market, functionally beneficial for
national development, important conditions are seen to
be: (1) channeling external funds, except for external
trade and compensatory credit, into a common pool with
domestic resources; (2) eliminating the exchange risk
borne by debtors with the exterior by expressing in
national currency the external resources transferred to
the domestic market; (3) explicitly pushing the market
toward a maturity structure compatible with productive
investment, which calls for long maturities; and (4) regulating real interest rates with the objective of avoiding
both negative rates and excessively high rates, since
both extremes are prejudicial to the efficiency of
investment.

A third lesson is connected with the destabilizing
nature of capital movements. In small countries and those
where the domestic markets are not fluid and integrated,
this instability can be very disturbing to economic
activity. It is not just a question of the conditions
that the free movement of capital imposes on monetary,
fiscal, and/or exchange policies. Another feature of
great practical significance is that the international
financial markets suffer from fluctuations that are
promptly transmitted to the domestic markets unless there
is some form of regulation. In addition to this overall
feature of markets, the supply of new funds available
to each country in particular is subject to abrupt changes
in response to variations in the lenders' perception of
those countries' creditworthiness or in connection with
the using up of the amounts of credit lenders are willing
to make available to each country--amounts that are related more to the total amount of the debt than to the
volume of the net flows in each period. For the debtor
countries, however, it is the net flow and the corresponding current account financing that is the most pertinent
variable for their short-term policy.

In the macroeconomic literature, emphasis is
usually placed on regulations on capital movements that
operate exclusively on relative prices; among these is a
tax on interest designed to compensate for certain
"externalities." It is quite true that this mechanism
may make it possible to tackle the particular problem of
a country that has a stable supply of loans with a
positive trend. Likewise, certain kinds of taxes can
reduce short-term speculative movements by making them
more expensive compared with longer-term movements. The
existence of external instability in the supply of funds,

however, must be tackled with mechanisms acting directly
on the volumes of credits. In other words, it is necessary
to establish machinery to regulate the total volume of
indebtedness registered in each period. Within this
context, there may be room, in a complementary capacity,
for instruments acting on prices, such as taxes and
compulsory deposits. It must be understood, however,
that these will carry out a fundamentally distributive
function, taxing the differentials between interest rates.
When, some day in the future, an abundant but probably
unstable supply of financial credit again becomes available, we should not forget the lesson provided by recent
years regarding the evils of excessive and disturbing
external indebtedness.

A fourth lesson is that, except in the case of flows
of a compensatory nature, the regulation of capital
movements should provide for their channeling toward
the process of savings/investment. Insofar as these
funds are directed toward the domestic financial market
without any clear guidelines as regards their destination,
they can easily filter through to consumption. The
experience of various developing countries suggests that
the final use of funds is determined to a significant
extent by the way in which the inflow of capital is
regulated and channeled.[26]

NOTES

This chapter presents a study that is part of the
CIEPLAN (Corporation for Economic Research for Latin
America) research program on Economics and International
Relations, which is receiving the support of the Ford
Foundation. A study of the financial opening-up process
in the period 1973-1980 is made in R. Ffrench-Davis and
J. P. Arellano, "Apertura Financiera Externa," 1981.
Grateful acknowledgment is made to J. P. Arellano for
his authorization to use in the present study part of the
material contained in that publication. I wish to
express my gratitude for the comments by CIEPLAN
researchers J. Estévez and C. Massad and the collaboration of J. A. Ruiz.
1. See A. Foxley and R. Ffrench-Davis, "Latin
American Experiments in Neo-Conservative Economics,"
Colección Estudios CIEPLAN 7, March 1982, special
issue, and University of California Press, 1982.
2. R. Cortazar, "Chile: Resultados Distributivos,
1973-82," Notas Técnicas No. 57, CIEPLAN, Santiago, 1983.
3. R. McKinnon, "Foreign Exchange Policy and
Economic Liberalization in LDCs," in Alternativas de
Políticas Financieras en Economías Pequeñas y Abiertas
al Exterior, Estudios Monetarios 7, Santiago, 1981.
4. More detailed information on the regulations
that have governed the movement of capital is given in an

378

annex published in Colección Estudios CIEPLAN 5, July
1981, and in J. A. Ruiz, "Regulaciones del Movimiento de
Capital Financiero: Chile, 1974-82" (CIEPLAN, 1983,
mimeo.).

5. S. De la Cuadra, paper presented at the seminar
organized by the Fundación de la Facultad de Ciencias
Económicas de la Universidad Católica, in Banco Central
de Chile, Boletín Mensual, no. 627, May 1980.

6. Inter-American Development Bank (IDB), Progreso
Económico y Social en América Latina: El Sector Externo,
Informe 1982, Washington, D.C., 1982. E. Bacha and C.
Díaz-Alejandro, "Mercados Financieros: Una Visión Desde
la Semiperiferia," and A. Fishlow, "La Deuda Externa
Latinoamericana: Problema o Solución," both in R. Ffrench-
Davis, ed., Relaciones Financieras Externas y Desarrollo
Nacional en América Latina, Mexico City, 1983c.

7. R. Ffrench-Davis, ed., "Una Estrategia de
Apertura Externa Selectiva," Reconstrucción Económica
para la Democracia, Santiago, 1983a.

8. R. Ffrench-Davis, "Indice de Precios Externos
para Calcular el Valor Real del Comercio Internacional
de Chile, 1952-80," Notas Técnicas no. 32, CIEPLAN,
Santiago, June 1981.

9. R. Ffrench-Davis and J. P. Arellano, "Apertura
Financiera Externa: La Experiencia Chilena en 1973-80,"
Colección Estudios CIEPLAN 5, Santiago, July 1981,
table 13.

10. J. P. Arellano and R. Cortazar, "Del Milagro a
la Crisis," Colección Estudios CIEPLAN 8, Santiago,
July 1982.

11. A brief summary is given in Ffrench-Davis and
Arellano, "Apertura Financiera Externa," pp. 333-336;
and a detailed analysis is made in R. Ffrench-Davis,
"Exchange Rate Policies in Chile: The Experience with
Crawling Peg," Colección Estudios CIEPLAN 2, December
1979 (and in J. Williamson, Exchange Rate Rules,
London, 1981).

12. R. Ffrench-Davis, "Exchange Rate Policies in
Chile."

13. The wholesale price index actually went down by
8 percent, mainly as regards agricultural goods, between
May 1981 and May 1982, whereas the consumer price index
went down by 1 percent between February and May 1982.
By May 1982 the external price index had gone down by
2 percent in twelve months.

14. Open unemployment in Santiago rose from 11 percent to 23 percent between September 1981 and June 1982.
Manufacturing production went down by 22 percent in 1982.

15. The increase in the deficit was associated with
the increase in imports and in the volume of indebtedness,
the decline in nontraditional exports, the rise in
interest rates, and the deterioration in the price of
copper. With regard to this latter item, it may be
noted that the smaller fiscal income in 1981 from this

source compared with the average for 1960-1970 was equivalent to US$109 million (US$266 million if only the period 1965-1970 is considered) at 1977 prices, that is to say, .7 percent (1.6 percent) of the 1981 GDP. The figures (at current values) for the contribution made to fiscal income by the large-scale copper-mining industry were provided by the Comisión Chilena del Cobre; here they have been deflated by the external price index. The deterioration in the price of copper was offset by the improvement in the price of molybdenum and the procurement for Chile of the economic rent of the copper deposits through the process of nationalization of these activities.

16. Some of the quantitative restrictions used to control the inflow of capital helped to make movements of private capital independent of short-term fluctuations in the exchange rate. Mention should be made in particular of the minimum limit of two years for indebtedness and the compulsory deposits, which went down in proportion to the term of the loan.

17. P. Meller and A. Solimano, "Inestabilidad Financiera, Burbujas Espectaculativas y Tasa de Interés Real: Chile, 1975-83" (CIEPLAN, Santiago, 1983, mimeo.).

18. J. P. Arellano, "De la Liberalización a la Intervención: El Mercado de Capitales en Chile, 1974-83," Colección Estudios CIEPLAN 11, Santiago, December 1983. Ffrench-Davis and Arellano, "Apertura Financiera Externa."

19. A more traditional factor, which was of some importance on several occasions, was the downward trend in the rate of inflation and the lag in the adjustment of nominal interest rates.

20. These calculations were made using the corrected consumer price index. If the official consumer price index had been used, then the total amount of the "real" debt would be 5.3 times greater. The accumulated "error" in the calculation of the official consumer price index in the three-year period 1976-1978 was close to 30 percent. See R. Cortazar and J. Marshall, "Indice de Precios al Consumidor en Chile: 1970-78," Colección Estudios CIEPLAN 4, Santiago, November 1980.

21. There was also significant dispersion within the domestic market itself. For example, the average publicly offered nominal interest rates for loans exceeded the weighted average rate calculated by the Central Bank by five and ten percentage points in 1979 and 1980 respectively.

22. W. Robichek, "Some Reflections About External Public Debt Management," in Alternativas de Políticas Financieras en Economías Pequeñas y Abiertas al Exterior, Estudios Monetarios 7, Santiago, 1981, pp. 171-172.

23. At the end of 1980, the Central Bank reserves amounted to US$4.072 billion. The bank had liabilities not taken into account in the definition of "reserves"

380

for a total of US$945 million, however, while the banking system had net liabilities equivalent to US$3.260 billion.
   24. R. Ffrench-Davis, "The Monetarist Experiment in Chile: A Survey," Colección Estudios CIEPLAN 9, Santiago, December 1982 (and in World Development, Oxford, November 1983).
   25. For an alternative approach, see my article "Una Estrategia de Apertura Externa Selectiva."
   26. Ibid.

BIBLIOGRAPHY

Arellano, J. P. "Macroeconomic Stability and the
     Optimal Degree of Capital Mobility." Journal of
     Development Economics, June 1982.
___. "De la Liberalización a la Intervención: El
     Mercado de Capitales en Chile, 1974-83." Colección
     Estudios CIEPLAN 11. Santiago, December 1983.
Arellano, J. P., and R. Cortazar. "Del Milagro a la
     Crisis." Colección Estudios CIEPLAN 8. Santiago,
     July 1982.
Bacha, E., and C. Diaz-Alejandro. "Mercados Financieros:
     Una Visión Desde la Semiperiferia." Relaciones
     Financieras Externas y Desarrollo Nacional en América
     Latina, edited by R. Ffrench-Davis. Mexico City,
     1983.
Bank for International Settlements (BIS). Annual Report.
     Basle, various years.
Banco Central De Chile. Balanza de Pagos. Santiago,
     annual publication.
___. Deuda Externa. Santiago, annual publication.
___. Estudios Monetarios, nos. 4-7.
Center for Planning Research and Studies (CIEPLAN).
     Reconstrucción Económica para la Democracia.
     Santiago, 1983.
Cortazar, R. "Chile: Resultados Distributivos,
     1973-82." Notas Técnicas No. 57. Santiago,
     June 1983.
Cortazar, R., and J. Marshall. "Indice de Precios al
     Consumidor en Chile: 1970-78." Colección Estudios
     CIEPLAN 4. Santiago, November 1980.
De la Cuadra, S. Paper presented at the seminar
     organized by the Fundación de la Facultad de
     Ciencias Económicas de la Universidad Católica.
     In Banco Central de Chile, Boletin Mensual, no. 627,
     May 1980.
Devlin, R. "Renegotiation of Latin America's Debt:
     An Analysis of the Monopoly Power of Private Banks."
     CEPAL Review, no. 20 (Santiago, August 1983).
DIPRES. Somos Realmente Independientes Gracias al
     Esfuerzo de Todos los Chilenos. Santiago, 1978.

Ffrench-Davis, R. Economía Internacional: Teorías y Políticas para el Desarrollo. Mexico City, 1979a.

___. "Exchange Rate Policies in Chile: The Experience with Crawling Peg." Colección Estudios CIEPLAN 2, Santiago, December 1979b (and in J. Williamson. Exchange Rate Rules. London, 1981.

___. "Indice de Precios Externos para Calcular el Valor Real del Comercio Internacional de Chile, 1952-80." Notas Técnicas no. 32, Santiago: CIEPLAN, June 1981.

___. "The Monetarist Experiment in Chile: A Survey." Colección Estudios CIEPLAN 9, Santiago, December 1982 (and in World Development [Oxford], November 1983).

Ffrench-Davis, R. (ed.). "Una Estrategia de Apertura Externa Selectiva." Reconstrucción Económica para la Democracia. Santiago, 1983a.

___. "El Problema de la Deuda Externa en América Latina: Tendencias y Perspectivas en 1983." Integración Latinoamericana. Buenos Aires, 1983b (and in Inter-American Development Bank [IDB]. Progreso Económico y Social en América Latina: El Sector Externo, Informe 1982. Washington, D.C., 1982).

___. Reláciones Financieras Externas y Desarrollo Nacional en América Latina. Mexico City, 1983c.

Ffrench-Davis, R., and J. P. Arellano. "Apertura Financiera Externa: La Experiencia Chilena en 1973-80." Colección Estudios CIEPLAN 5, Santiago, July 1981 (and in Relaciones Financieras Externas y Desarrollo Nacional en América Latina, edited by R. Ffrench-Davis. Mexico City, 1983.

Fishlow, A. "La Deuda Externa Latinoamericana: Problema o Solución." In Relaciones Financieras Externas y Desarrollo Nacional en América Latina, edited by R. Ffrench-Davis. Mexico City, 1983.

Foxley, A., and R. Ffrench-Davis. "Latin American Experiments in Neo-Conservative Economics." Colección Estudios CIEPLAN 7, Santiago, March 1982, special issue (and University of California Press, 1982).

Griffith-Jones, S. "The Evolution of External Finance, Economic Policy and Development in Chile, 1973-78." Institute of Development Studies (IDS), Sussex University, England. Mimeo. 1980.

Guardia, A., J. E. Herrera, A. Martinez, C. Ominami, and C. Rojas. "Una Renegociación Global para una Nueva Política de la Deuda Externa Chilena 1974-1982." Informe de Coyuntura Económica. Santiago, March-April 1983.

Gutierrez, M. "Reflexiones Sobre Apertura Financiera: El Caso Chileno." Estudios Económicos No. 14. Santiago, 1982.

382

Herrera, J. E., and J. Morales. "La Inversión Financiera
Externa: El Caso de Chile, 1974-78." Colección
Estudios CIEPLAN 1. Santiago, July 1979.
Massad, C. "The External Debt and the Financial Problems
of Latin America," CEPAL Review No. 20, Santiago,
August 1983.
McKinnon, R. "La Intermediación Financiera y el Control
Monetario en Chile." Cuadernos de Economía No. 43
(Santiago), December 1977.
___. "Represión Financiera y el Problema de la
Liberalización Dentro de los Países Menos
Desarrollados." Cuadernos de Economía No. 47
(Santiago), 1979.
___. "Foreign Exchange Policy and Economic Liberalization
in LDCs," in Alternativas de Políticas Financieras
en Economías Pequeñas y Abiertas al Exterior.
Estudios Monetarios 7. Santiago, 1981.
Meller, P., and A. Solimano. "Inestabilidad Financiera,
Burbujas Espectaculativas y Tasa de Interés Real:
Chile, 1975-83." CIEPLAN. Santiago. 1983. Mimeo.
Ministerio de Hacienda. Exposición Sobre el Estado de la
Hacienda Pública. Annual publication.
Ominami, C. "Del Colapso de la Economía de Endeudamiento
Internacional, a la Necesidad de una Estrategia de
Independencia Nacional." Academia de Humanismo
Cristiano, CERC. Santiago. November 1983. Mimeo.
Robichek, W. "Some Reflections About External Public
Debt Management." In Alternativas de Políticas
Financieras en Economías Pequeñas y Abiertas al
Exterior. Estudios Monetarios 7. Santiago, 1981.
Ruíz, J. A. "Regulaciones del Movimiento de Capital
Financiero: Chile, 1974-82." CIEPLAN. Santiago.
1983. Mimeo.
Sanfuentes, A. "Antecedentes Sobre la Deuda Externa
Chilena." Estudios Monetarios 4. Santiago, 1978.
Sjaastad, L., and H. Cortéz. "El Enfoque Monetario de
la Balanza de Pagos y las Tasas de Interés en
Chile." Estudios de Economía No. 11, Universidad
de Chile, First semester 1978.
Tapia, D. "Apertura al Mercado Financiero Internacional."
Institucionalidad Económica e Integración Financiera
con el Exterior. Santiago, 1979.
Zahler, R. "Repercusiones Monetarias y Reales de la
Apertura Financiera al Exterior: El Caso Chileno,
1975-78." Revista de la CEPAL, April 1980.

14
Peru and Its Private Bankers: Scenes from an Unhappy Marriage

Robert Devlin
Enrique de la Piedra

INTRODUCTION

In the postwar period, Peru was one of the first countries in Latin America to develop an articulation with private commercial banks that went beyond short-term trade credits. Its relationship with private banks has not always been a happy one, however, and in the last twenty years it has had the distinction of going through three complete borrowing cycles with these institutions, each with its boom period followed by a severe crash. This chapter will attempt to tell, in a synthetic way, the story of Peru's experience with private banks and then to explore what lessons might be drawn from it.

Peru is not unlike other developing economies; its underdeveloped economic and social structure brings forth a chronic shortfall of internal savings vis-à-vis investment possibilities. In other words, there is a valid and real need for capital imports and external savings. Since the mid-1960s, an ever-growing portion of these external savings has had its source in private-bank loans (see Table 14.1). This factor alone was enough to increase the external vulnerability of the country since management of interface with banks is considerably more challenging than that involving more traditional sources of finance: Interest rates are commercial and subject to great variability; amortization periods are relatively short, thereby boosting refinancing requirements; and bankers' private perception of risk induces a sharply procyclic lending behavior on their part.[1]

Whatever the vulnerability associated with a dominant role for private banks in the financing of development, it was exacerbated in the case of Peru by what might be termed "overborrowing." This refers to a situation--characteristic of the 1970s--in which the supply of credit is extremely abundant and demand adjusts itself to available supply rather than to a real savings gap per se. In other words, demand for finance becomes delinked from the savings/investment mechanism; indeed,

383

Table 14.1   Peru: Distribution of External Public Debt by
Source of Finance (percentage)

	Private				Official		
	Suppliers	Banks	Bonds	Others	Multi-lateral	Bi-lateral	Total[a]
1965-1966							
Peru	41	11	5	-	23	21	100
Latin America	20	11	8	1	23	37	100
1975-1976							
Peru	14	42	-	-	9	35	100
Latin America	10	45	4	2	19	21	100
1979-1980							
Peru	14	37	-	-	11	38	100
Latin America	7	56	7	-	17	13	100

Note: The dash indicates an amount that is nil or negligible.

[a]May not sum to 100 because of rounding.

Source: Inter-American Development Bank, External Debt of the
Latin American Countries (Washington, D.C., 1982).

any nominal gap in savings becomes inflated, or
artificially overstated, as easy finance gives rise to
relaxation of the internal discipline needed to minimize
the effects of the basic economic disequilibria that
a developing country is expected to face in a variable
and uncertain external economic environment.

Peru's actual shortfall of internal savings has its
origins in two intractable financing gaps: the government budget and the balance of payments.   Even if Peru
has been most imaginative and aggressive in tackling the
gaps when foreign finance was restricted, the advent of
abundant credit on easy terms usually caused this
discipline to unravel and debt to build up to unsustainable proportions.   Because finance came largely from the
procyclically inclined private banks, the debt buildup
was extremely rapid and the later restriction very severe,
with unusually adverse consequences for the country's
development.

With regard to the government budget, since the
early 1960s Peru has confronted an asymmetry between
rapidly growing demands on the state to perform economic,
welfare, and defense functions and--not withstanding
the real obstacles to expanding the tax base of a
developing country--a perennial political reluctance to
give it the financial wherewithal to carry out this
mandate.[2]   Consequently, public current expenditures and
investment programs have been oversized, tax pressure
has tended to lag, state enterprises have had to operate

on a less than commercial basis, and the defense establishment has become disproportional to the level of development of the country. This situation has been possible,
in part, because authorities could all too frequently
substitute foreign finance for the hard political
decisions needed to give the state the degree of financial
autonomy it needed. This arrangement would, of course,
be satisfactory if continued and exponentially growing
foreign finance could be counted on, but the very policies
that gave rise to a need for foreign finance also gradually
undermined the creditworthiness of the state that was
needed to sustain the credit flows.

   As for the external accounts, they have suffered
from a long-term stagnation in the export sector,
coupled with a high propensity to import. The export
sector's volume has been variously handicapped by factors
such as uncertain policies regarding the role of foreign
investment in Peru's all important mineral subsector,
uncompetitive exchange rates, and ecological disasters
(such as those affecting fishing). On the other hand,
Peru's proclivity to import has been enhanced by overvalued exchange rates and direct subsidies, unrealized
expectations regarding exportable petroleum reserves in
the Amazon jungle, massive arms purchases, overscaled
investment projects with high import content, stagnant
local food production, and--more recently--attempts to
follow the example of Southern Cone neighbors to open up
the economy. Foreign finance, rather than filling the
commercial gap, has often encouraged it to grow by under-
pinning policies that inflated external disequilibria.
Once again, if finance were eternally available in
exponentially growing amounts, this situation would be
perfectly satisfactory. Unfortunately, the rise to
dominance of procyclic commercial-bank finance brought
an ever more sensitive link between trends on the current
account of the balance of payments and the behavior of
capital flows, making the economy even more vulnerable
to crisis and upheaval.

   These themes will recur throughout the paper. As
to its organization, the next three sections treat Peru's
three modern borrowing cycles with private banks, each
with its credit boom and subsequent crash: 1965-1971,
1972-1978, and 1979-1984. The 1972-1978 cycle is of
special importance because it gave rise to the impressive
external debt that plagues Peru and its creditors until
this very day. The last section will provide a more
conceptual, or theoretical, explanation of Peru's problems
with its bankers, focusing on a flawed bargaining strategy
both with regard to the country's contraction of new debt
and the rescheduling of old debt.

386

THE FIRST ROUND OF INDEBTEDNESS: 1965-1971

As has been mentioned, Peru was one of the first
countries in Latin America to establish a significant
articulation with private banks based on medium-term
lending. Although both the magnitude of the indebtedness
and the qualitative relations with the creditors were very
different from what would follow in the 1970s and 1980s,
it is worthwhile to provide a brief overview of events
in this period.

Peru's newly elected civilian administration, under
the leadership of Fernando Belaúnde Terry, assumed power
in mid-1963.[3] It was activist and reformist in spirit,
representing a sharp inversion of the passive role
traditionally attributed to the state in an economy
molded by liberal principles.[4] Public-sector activity
expanded relatively fast as reflected by the fact that
expenditure (excluding amortization of the debt) more
than doubled over the period 1963-1965, and growth--even
in real terms--remained substantial at more than 50 percent.[5]

The government encountered almost immediate difficulties in the financial area. While expenditures were
pushed upward by an ambitious public program, revenues
lagged due to a narrow and relatively inelastic tax base
and an extremely recalcitrant congress that refused to
support the government's proposed tax reforms. The consequence was a considerable expansion of the fiscal
deficit; the accounts went from being roughly in balance
in 1962-1963 to a deficit of nearly 5 percent of GDP by
1965. This, of course, contributed to price instability
as the rate of inflation reached 16 percent in 1965,
compared to the average rate of 7 percent for 1961-1964.
On the external side, imports grew rapidly on account of
the government investment program and the overvaluation
of the sol, while export performance slumped--after the
relative boom of the early 1960s--as both volume and unit
prices slackened. Consequently, the trade account,
which had tended toward equilibrium at the beginning of
the decade, registered a deficit equivalent to 12 percent of export earnings in 1965-1966; meanwhile the
current account deficit rose from .7 percent of GDP in
the 1960-1964 period to nearly 4 percent by 1965-1966.

The government made considerable use of foreign
finance. By 1967 the public external debt as a percentage
of product had nearly doubled its average of 1960-1964,
rising from 6.5 percent to 12.2 percent. Peru took
relatively heavy recourse to finance from foreign
suppliers as reflected in the fact that the participation of these creditors in the public external debt was
41 percent, compared to a Latin American average of 20
percent (see again Table 14.1). Official government and
multilateral lenders held another 44 percent of the public
debt. Private banks' participation was relatively small

at 11 percent, but played a very important role at the margin of events.

During the period 1964-1968 private banks provided continuous budgetary support to the government. In the midst of precarious fiscal and balance-of-payments situations, bankers came forth with many short-term bridge loans (the exact amount of which is difficult to determine) and medium-term credits to the tune of roughly US$30 million annually. The terms of lending were relatively stiff: 1.50 to 1.75 percent over the U.S. prime rate for loans with a five-year maturity and grace periods of one or two years. Most of the lending was concentrated in a handful of large, internationally experienced U.S. banks.[6] Although lending by U.S. banks to LDCs was not yet in vogue, these institutions were attracted to Peru by familiarity (there was a long and large presence of U.S. transnational corporations--TNCs-- in the country), the government's still relatively liberal economic regime, and the very attractive price the authorities were willing to pay for the loans. At the same time the banks were quite cautious lenders: They usually insisted on the establishment of escrow accounts for loans to semiautonomous government agencies.

The continued buildup of economic difficulties, coupled with the reverse repayment flow stemming from the relatively hard lending terms of foreign suppliers and banks, soon culminated in serious problems in 1967 and open financial crisis in 1968.

The banks, now somewhat committed to Peru because of earlier outstanding loans, continued to provide support to the government during the crisis. Short-term bridge loans were awarded, and bankers restructured their debt via the technique of refinancing. Interestingly, the banks also agreed to provide a new "standby credit": US$65 million from U.S. banks and US$25 million from European institutions. However, the loans (never actually drawn upon), in addition to bearing the stiff terms noted earlier, also carried some rather rugged conditionality. The money was directly linked to the fulfillment of the tough IMF standby agreements signed by the government, and banks imposed restrictions on public-sector foreign borrowing that were similar to the terms laid down by the IMF itself. The IMF put a virtual halt on borrowing for maturities of between 180 days and 10 years and placed strict limits on loans with a maturity of between 10 and 15 years.

An emergency economic law introduced in June 1968 (which included new tax measures) came too late to save the government, which was suffering from an increasing lack of popularity due to its economic problems and to the controversy over the handling of a long-lasting dispute with an Exxon subsidiary. In October, the government fell victim to a military coup headed by General Juan Velasco Alvarado.

The new government had an interesting objective:
It sought what it termed to be "a third way" to development that would bridge the gap between capitalism and
socialism. There was a declared goal of reducing foreign
dependence, reforming agriculture, and industrializing
via exports with emphasis on internal savings for investment. The government also showed interest in pursuing
the stabilization effort initiated in the last days of
the previous government.[7]

Peru's bankers took a cautious, if not hostile,
attitude toward the new government. After all, it was
very interventionist and was engaged in vigorous disputes
with subsidiaries of U.S. enterprises as well as with the
Nixon administration, which attempted to defend their
interests. Major commercial lenders awarded practically
no new loans to Peru in the period 1969-1971, thereby
tacitly, if not explicitly, cooperating with the foreign
financial blockade organized by the U.S. administration.
Bankers did agree to refinance their past loans, if for
no other reason than fear that the new, more radical
government might default on its debts. However, they did
so on very onerous terms: Spreads were 1.75 to 2.25 percent over base interest rates, maturities only 5 years,
and grace periods a Spartan-like .5 to 1.5 years.

The private bankers, did, however, alter their view
of the need for the protection of the IMF. The new
military government refused to renew the IMF standby
agreement signed by the Belaúnde administration and set
to expire in mid-1969. Fears of default, coupled with
signs of successful stabilization, encouraged New York
bankers to accede to Peru's wishes. However, they
advanced conditionality of their own. Essentially this
consisted of extremely strict limits on debt contraction
through the first half of the 1970s, thereby hamstringing
the financing of the government's ambitious investment
program.

The military authorities, facing the Nixon administration's pressure on official lenders (which also
adversely affected guarantees for suppliers' credits)
and restrictions by private bankers, found themselves
in a financial straitjacket. Interestingly, however, its
stabilization efforts in this hostile external environment were relatively successful, restoring a degree of
balance to the fiscal and external accounts, all while
achieving respectable growth rates.[8]

THE SECOND ROUND OF INDEBTEDNESS: 1972-1978

During the period 1972-1978, Peru's total foreign
debt increased two and a half times with practically all
this growth being attributable to borrowing by the public
sector. Total debt as a percentage of product over the
period started out at 69 percent, dipped to a low of 54

percent, and ended up at 69 percent once again. There was, however, a dramatic boost of the public sector's share, as its debt as a percentage of product rose from 19 percent in 1971 to 44 percent in 1978 (see Table 14.2).

The heavy borrowing by the state reflected events on both edges of the Marshallian scissors. On the demand side, the government as early as 1971 had initiated an ambitious and now inward-oriented development strategy that implied a strong increase in investment, largely based on public projects, many of which were now targeted in productive sectors.[9] Also to play an important part in the demand for foreign finance was a vigorous military arms purchase program.[10]

On the supply side, there developed a major turn-around in Peru's fortunes with foreign creditors. After 1970, private banks, subject to very liquid balances in the Eurocurrency market and virtually no restrictions on lending from this platform, began to expand their horizons to developing areas. In reality, LDCs--and Latin America in particular--became the last frontier in an extremely hectic international expansion of finance capital that had been under way throughout the postwar period. In this expansion many of the large, traditionally international banks that had controlled lending found their market shares being challenged by other large- and medium-sized institutions that formerly had only been interested in their domestic markets. This global expansion, coupled with severe competition for new markets, worked to Peru's favor.

The Initial Years

In 1972 Peru began to be the center of a competitive struggle among the banks. On the one hand, petroleum deposits had been found in the Amazon region, which gave rise to rumors about Peru becoming one of the largest oil producers in the world. On the other hand, the Velasco regime enjoyed a large measure of political power and had managed to implement successful stabiliza-tion efforts.

As noted earlier, prior to 1972 Peru's access to bank credit depended on the disposition of a few large U.S. banks that were not very forthcoming with the new regime. However, some newcomers to international lending--U.S. regional, European, and Japanese institutions--were seeking out markets not cornered by the big established banks and began to lend to Peru. A major actor in this regard was Wells Fargo of California, which interestingly had a former public servant of the Belaúnde government as a high-level executive in the office of international lending.

The initial loans were quite lucrative for the new, more aggressive lenders: 2.25 percent over LIBOR for

Table 14.2 Peru: Total External Debt (millions of U.S. dollars)

	1970	1971	1972	1973	1974	1975	1976	1977	1978	1979	1980	1981	1982	1983[a]
Total external debt	3,681	3,692	3,832	4,132	5,237	6,257	7,384	8,567	9,324	9,334	9,594	9,638	11,097	12,418
Medium- and long-term	2,190	2,242	2,370	2,709	3,441	4,352	5,250	6,263	7,226	7,941	8,125	8,172	9,279	10,927
Public[b]	986	1,031	1,188	1,508	2,182	3,066	3,939	4,937	5,886	6,633	6,753	6,665	7,615	9,324
Private	1,204	1,211	1,182	1,201	1,259	1,286	1,311	1,326	1,340	1,308	1,372	1,507	1,664	1,603
Short-term	1,491	1,450	1,462	1,423	1,796	1,905	2,134	2,304	2,098	1,393	1,469	1,466	1,818	1,491
Memorandum Items (percentages)														
Total debt/GDP	74.2	69.1	63.1	54.5	62.1	64.1	68.9	72.5	69.2	57.4	51.2	51.3	58.6	70.8
Public debt/GDP	19.9	19.3	19.6	19.8	25.9	31.4	36.8	41.8	43.7	40.8	36.1	35.4	40.2	62.4
Total debt service/ Exports	25.1	40.8	35.6	46.0	40.8	51.8	56.5	51.4	54.0	35.1	46.2	72.7	69.7	49.5[c]
Public debt service/ Exports[d]	16.2	24.0	23.2	38.9	30.3	35.6	36.2	36.0	35.6	22.4	33.8	54.0	48.6	26.3[c]
Public debt service[d] (millions of U.S. dollars)	167	213	219	433	456	474	485	622	702	825	1,323	1,756	1,491	1,257

[a] Preliminary data

[b] Includes Banco Central de Reserva del Perú

[c] Excludes renegotiated service payments

[d] Medium- and long-term; excludes Banco Central de Reserva del Perú

Source: Banco Central de Reserva del Perú, El Proceso de Renegociación de la Deuda Externa Peruana: 1978-1983 (Lima, 1984).

maturities between 4½ and 6½ years. These terms were considerably higher than those that could be contracted with more coveted Latin American borrowers where competition was stiff; Brazil, for example, could regularly attract loans at 1.5 percent over LIBOR for 10-year maturities. However, as more lenders became attracted to Peru, terms were enhanced for the country; price cutters such as Wells Fargo and Dresdner Bank were instrumental in driving down the cost of borrowing in the early 1970s (see Table 14.3).

Table 14.3 Peru: Index of the Cost of Bank Borrowing, 1971-1976 (1975=100)

1971	1972	1973	1974	1975	1976
131	99	57	36	100	146

Note: Based on consideration of the margin over LIBOR, the maturity, and commissions using the following formula:

$$\frac{[(C_1/A_1) + M_1]/A_1}{[(C_o/A_o) + M_o]/A_o} - 1$$

where $\underline{C}$ represents average flat fees, $\underline{A}$ equals the amortization period, and $\underline{M}$ the average margin over LIBOR, all weighted by the face value of the loans.

Source: Based on data in Robert Devlin, Los Bancos Transnacionales y el Financiamiento Externo de América Latina (Santiago, 1980).

The euphoria in banking circles was such that a former pariah became the darling of international banks, eventually ranking sixth among non-oil-exporting developing-country clients. The number of commercial lenders had risen from just twenty-seven in the late 1960s to nearly two hundred in the first half of the 1970s. Net lending expanded dramatically from slightly negative flows in 1970-71 to an average of US$236 million in 1972-1974. Moreover, terms had shifted strongly in Peru's favor: By 1974 the country could negotiate margins near 1 percent over LIBOR for maturities of ten years, conditions only slightly less favorable than those offered to prime developing-country clients like Brazil and Mexico (see Figure 14.1).

Another advantage of the competitive struggle around Peru was that it broke the grips of the aforementioned financial blockade. With all the new lending coming from the banks, the Nixon administration's effort to financially strangle Peru became increasingly fruitless. The Peruvian government used new loans from the upstart banks to prepay the old loans granted by the big U.S. money center banks that contained conditionality with respect to new indebtedness and hence handicapped the

Figure 14.1   Comparison of Margins and Maturities on
Bank Credits for Peru, Brazil, Mexico, and Bolivia,
1973-1979[a]

Margin over LIBOR

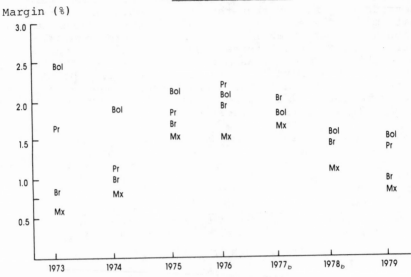

Amortization Period

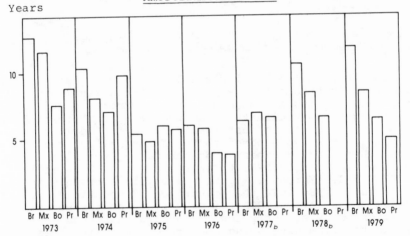

[a]Average for public-sector borrowing weighted by values.
[b]Peru did not obtain loans in these years.

Key to abbreviations: Bolivia (Bo), Brazil (Br),
Mexico (Mx), Peru (Pr)

Source: Mexico and Brazil: World Bank, Borrowing
in International Capital Markets, Washington, D.C.
(various numbers); Peru and Bolivia: Robert Devlin
and Michael Mortimore, Los Bancos Transnacionales,
el Estado, y el Endendamiento en Bolivia, Santiago, 1983.

investment program. Moreover, the volume of bank lending
became so large as to dilute the effect of any restriction
placed on official government and multilateral lenders.
Finally, one by one, the big U.S. money center banks,
some more rapidly than others, began to renew lending
to Peru; they did not like to see an eroding share of
the market in a country with a stable military government
and with prospects of major oil exports. Also, the U.S.
government, now sensing Peru's strategic importance as a
potential oil exporter, sought and achieved a settlement--
on the whole favorable to Peru--concerning the investment
disputes with the Velasco regime.[11]

The relationship with the private banks began to sour
in mid-1975. In essence, what happened was that the
deterioration of basic economic indicators that had been
hidden and in some respects facilitated by abundant
finance now became more evident. This, coupled with
false expectations with regard to the extent of petroleum
reserves, broke the bankers' confidence in Peru, and new
lending was stopped.

Not surprisingly, the country was in crisis again.
On the fiscal front, the government let tax pressure
slide, in part because of exemptions provided to the
private sector in attempts to win its confidence and
induce investment. The incentives, which could not overcome the ideological contradictions between the interventionist regime and private business, help to explain
why tax revenue as a percent of product slipped below
the 16 percent of GDP achieved in 1970 as a result of
the stabilization effort then in force (see Table 14.4).
Meanwhile, central-government expenditure, pushed upward
by heavy investment, military expenditure, and subsidies
on food and fuels, increased from 17.5 percent of product
in 1970 to 21.4 percent in 1975. The consequence of
course was a considerably expanded deficit, from 1.4
percent to 5.6 percent of product over the period
1970-1975. (For the consolidated public sector the
deficit rose to 9.7 percent.) The relaxed fiscal situation contributed to the acceleration of the average yearly
rate of price increases, from the relatively modest pace
of 5 percent at the turn of the decade to one of 24 percent by 1975.

The country's external position also eroded during
the period of massive indebtedness. On the one hand,
the value of imports showed remarkable growth, reaching
an equivalent of 23 percent of product in 1975, compared
to 16 percent in 1970 (see Table 14.4). This growth was due
primarily to an oversized public-investment program:[12] the
stagnation of local food production, subsidies on
essential consumer items, the fixing of the exchange
rate for seven years (1968-1974), tariff rebates on
capital imports, and military outlays, which some
estimates have put as high as the equivalent of 30 percent of export earnings in the period 1973-1975.[13]

The proclivity to import was contrasted by a remarkably deteriorated export performance. Exports as a percentage of product declined from an average of 20 percent in 1970 to 13 percent by 1975; indeed the coefficient registered in this latter year was two-fifths less than the average recorded in 1960-1964 (see Table 14.4). Several factors were behind this weak performance.

First, the long gestation period of the government's mineral projects, coupled with uncertainty surrounding policies vis-à-vis foreign private investment, was a factor. At the end of the 1950s there were important investments in the mining sector, and their coming on stream in the early 1960s contributed to an export boom. But the impetus was not sustained. During the 1960s all the perspectives for new foreign investment were adversely affected by government commissions examining charges of excess profits in foreign mining firms and by plans to revise the liberal 1950 Mining Code. Consequently, as Thorp and Bertram have put it, an investment strike in the Gran Minería took place.[14] Just when uncertainties were beginning to diminish and investment prospects improved, the 1968 coup took place and brought with it a very nationalistic policy on the subject of foreign participation in the economy, further stifling investment in this vital sector. In spite of the agreement that the Velasco government eventually reached with the U.S.-owned Southern Peru Copper Corporation to develop a major deposit and two projects developed by state-owned mining companies, Peru was left with a "window of vulnerability" in its export sector until the late 1970s because of the very long gestation period of these ventures.

A second major factor in the poor export performance was the already mentioned severely exaggerated expectations about petroleum. The government prematurely implemented a giant US$1 billion trans-Andean oil pipeline only to find out that available petroleum could barely reach one-half of planned throughput. With petroleum failing to materialize in expected volumes, a gaping hole was left in the export structure.

A third feature underlying sluggish exports was a less than vigorous dedication to export promotion. Neither the fixing of the exchange rate nor high tariff walls encouraged exports, and prevailing subsidy schemes were less than adequate to provide a counter-balancing stimulus.

Finally, Peru also suffered from a certain degree of ecological bad luck in the disappearance of the anchovy, a very important foreign-exchange earner. It is to be noted, however, that some measure of overfishing took place in 1970-1971.

Added to the deteriorating trade performance was a buildup of payments for factor services. Peru's heavy recourse to bank debt brought with it the relatively higher interest rates and shorter maturities that

Table 14.4 Peru: Selected Expenditure as a Percentage of GDP

	External Sector					Domestic Sector		Central Government			Public-Sector Deficit
	Exports		Imports		Current Account	Consumption	Fixed Investment	Expenditure	Income	Deficit	
	Current	Real	Current	Real							
1960-1964	22.3	...	20.9	...	-0.7	76.5	14.1	15.7	14.2	-1.5	...
1970	19.7	19.7	15.7	15.7	2.3	83.0	12.4	17.5	16.1	-1.4	-0.8
1973	14.8	14.2	15.3	15.1	-2.1	84.9	12.7	18.7	14.8	-3.9	-4.6
1974	16.1	12.5	21.5	18.7	-7.0	86.5	15.2	18.3	15.2	-3.1	-6.9
1975	12.9	12.1	22.7	20.8	-11.2	90.1	17.4	21.4	15.8	-5.6	-9.7
1976	12.4	11.0	18.1	15.6	-7.8	87.8	16.6	20.7	14.4	-6.3	-10.0
1977	16.7	13.0	20.3	14.5	-6.3	88.5	14.6	22.1	14.6	-7.5	-9.8
1978	22.4	15.6	19.2	11.2	-1.5	82.2	14.0	20.9	15.8	-5.1	-6.2
1979	30.5	19.3	17.9	11.3	6.9	72.9	14.3	18.5	17.9	-0.6	-1.1
1980	27.0	17.4	23.2	16.0	-0.6	78.3	17.2	23.5	20.6	-2.9	-4.7
1981	20.3	16.1	24.3	17.0	-8.3	82.0	20.2	23.0	18.1	-4.9	-8.4
1982	20.6	17.1	24.5	15.6	-8.3	82.6	20.3	22.0	18.1	-3.9	-8.7
1983	...	...	...	...	-5.5[a]	...	...	...	...	-7.5[b]	-10.3[b]

Note: The dots indicate data that are not available or not separately reported.

[a]Unpublished Central Bank data cited in the Andean Report, February 1984

[b]Unpublished Central Bank data cited in the Andean Report, January 1984

Source: Based on data in the Memoria of the Banco Central de Reserva del Perú (various numbers).

accompany commercial indebtedness. This was reflected
in the fact that the outflow of debt payments nearly
tripled between 1970 and 1974; as a percentage of exports,
public debt service rose from 16 percent to 30 percent
(see Table 14.2). Given the harsher terms of indebtedness, the new government had to seek an exponentially
growing amount of new credit just to facilitate payment
of old debt and avoid a net outflow of financial resources.

The asymmetry between import and export trends,
coupled with growing debt-service obligations, had its
counterpart in a ballooning current account deficit,
which went from an average of practically zero between
1968 and 1970 to 11 percent of GDP by 1975. This
situation was made possible only by massive lending from
the banks during the period, which masked the underlying
deterioration in the balance of payments. Moreover, the
lending was sufficiently voluminous not only to cover the
deficit but to amass nearly US$1 billion of gross inter-
national reserves by 1974. This, coupled with the
relatively high growth rates of product (see Table 14.5),
provided a sense of security and well-being concerning
the direction of economic policy. Indeed, in the midst
of the oil crisis that rocked most non-oil-exporting
LDCs, government authorities in early 1976 expressed
satisfaction that the world crisis had not set foot into
Peru.

The 1975-1976 Crisis

Had Peru been able to sustain the massive lending
from private banks, a policy best described as one of
simultaneous pursuit of guns and butter would have been
perfectly feasible. However, with the arrival of private
commercial banks as the overwhelmingly dominant source of
external finance, a new sensitivity developed between
events on the current and capital accounts. In other
words, private banks are procyclic lenders; once the
initial momentum of the euphoric expansion winds down,
a country can be left vulnerable to a massive retreat by
creditors if economic parameters have moved way out of
line and undermined the delicate confidence of private
bankers.

What perhaps detonated Peru's latent crisis was the
failure of Bank Herstatt of Germany in mid-1974, which
set off a semipanic in international banking circles.
Even though the bankruptcy was due to poor foreign-
exchange management and unrelated to LDC loans, nervous
bankers restricted credit, and the terms of lending
underwent severe deterioration both with respect to
volume and conditions. This in turn made more transparent
the financial veil that had been draped over the internal
and external structural weaknesses of the Peruvian economy.
The world credit crisis, together with the now evident

Table 14.5   Peru: Growth Rates of Selected Economic Indicators (billions of U.S. dollars)

	GDP[a]	Consumption[a]	Investment[a]	Exports[a]	Imports[a]	Inflation[a]	Terms of Trade[b]
1973	6.2	10.4	17.2	-18.3	9.7	9.5	21.9
1974	6.9	9.0	30.4	-5.8	31.9	16.9	42.6
1975	3.3	4.8	10.0	0.4	15.3	23.6	-23.4
1976	3.0	1.6	-11.2	-6.7	-22.8	33.5	4.2
1977	-1.2	-0.3	-22.4	16.7	-7.9	38.0	-6.3
1978	-1.8	-6.7	-12.8	18.1	-24.5	57.8	-15.1
1979	3.8	-1.9	12.1	28.6	5.3	67.7	35.1
1980	3.0	6.8	30.4	-7.0	44.9	59.2	11.5
1981	3.1	1.5	25.2	-4.9	10.0	75.4	-18.4
1982	0.7[c]	0.0	-8.3	6.8	-7.7	64.5[d]	-12.8
1983	-12.0[c]	...	...	...	...	111.1	3.2

Note: Dots indicate data that are not available or not reported separately.

[a]1970 prices

[b]1970=100; goods fob/fob

[c]Banco Central data cited in the Andean Report, January 1984

[d]Based on Banco Central data cited in the Andean Report, February 1984

Source: Banco Central de Reserva del Perú, Memoria 1982; Economic Commission for Latin America, Division of Statistics and Quantitative Analysis.

overestimation of the prospects for petroleum in the
Amazon and the depressive effects of a world recession,
induced the banking system as a whole to perceive that
there was a problem in Peru and brought with it special
attempts to restrict exposure in the country, serving to
deepen the crisis.

Peru had to confront its problems in the context of
an extreme dependency on its private banks, an ironic
situation given that one of the government's major
objectives--and a factor behind the severe investment
disputes--was a search for autonomy from "foreign capital."
One angle of this dependency is presented in Table 14.6.
It can be seen that by 1975 the net transfer of foreign
financial resources was equivalent to more than 60 percent of the country's "indigenous" foreign-exchange
earning capacity as represented by exports; in other
words, a very high percentage of the country's import
capacity depended on the tricky business of securing and
maintaining net flows from foreign creditors. A second
indicator of dependency is seen in Table 14.7: By 1975
the gap between internal savings efforts and investment
rose to an amazing twelve points, six times greater than
that prevailing in 1973. But more importantly, it should
be noticed that the gap was aggravated by a considerable
substitution of foreign for domestic savings as indicated
by the marked decline in the internal savings coefficient
through 1975.

What this implies is that the Peruvian economy was
in a poor state to weather the storm once creditors
replaced their enthusiasm with caution. It can be seen
from the data in Table 14.8 that after 1974 private banks--
by now Peru's most important creditor--began a progressive
and seriously debilitating reduction of lending to the
government. This necessitated an adjustment on Peru's
part that, however, was slow in coming and quite dis-
organized.

In August 1975 the crisis contributed to a political
change as General Francisco Morales Bermúdez replaced
General Velasco as head of state. With this, the
"revolution" began to take on a more conservative tone.[15]
Late in the year, a new team consistent with the new
orientation took control of the economy and attempted
adjustment in face of a massive US$1.5 billion current
account deficit and the loss of half of the country's
gross international reserves (from US$1 billion at the
end of 1974 to less than US$500 million at the end of
1975). One of its first measures was to devalue the sol
by 16 percent after seven years at a fixed rate.

The crisis worsened in 1976. At the beginning
of the year some additional adjustment measures were
introduced. The government toyed with the possibility
of an IMF stabilization program, but after informal
contacts with Fund officials in Washington, authorities
decided that the Fund's requirements were harsh and

Table 14.6 Peru: Net Capital Inflows and Transfer of Financial Resources (millions of U.S. dollars)

	Effective Inflow of Capital^a (1)	Unregistered Transactions (2)	Balance on Capital Account (3)	Net Payment of Profits and Interest			Transfer of Resources I (1)-(4) (5)	Transfer of Resources II (3)-(4) (6)	Exports of Goods and Services (7)	Ratio (5)/(7) (8)	Ratio (6)/(7) (9)
				Profit	Interest	Total (4)					
1970	137.0	-35.0	102.0	(73.0)	(60.0)	133.0	4.0	-31.0	1,224.0	0.3	-2.5
1971	3.1	16.0	19.1	(50.1)	(75.2)	125.3	-122.1	-106.2	1,067.2	-11.5	-10.0
1972	160.7	-90.1	70.6	(46.7)	(73.9)	120.6	40.1	-50.0	1,153.0	3.5	-4.3
1973	435.1	-41.7	393.4	(79.9)	(83.5)	163.4	271.7	230.0	1,343.5	20.2	17.1
1974	1,219.5	-72.2	1,147.3	(42.1)	(129.9)	172.0	1,047.5	975.3	1,841.2	56.9	53.0
1975	1,268.8	-190.6	1,078.2	(14.6)	(227.0)	241.6	1,027.2	836.6	1,688.9	60.8	49.5
1976	1,262.6	-326.5	936.1	(43.8)	(326.5)	370.3	892.3	565.8	1,744.2	51.2	32.4
1977	1,155.1	-112.7	1,042.4	(53.7)	(368.4)	422.1	733.0	620.3	2,131.0	34.4	29.1
1978	215.2	52.9	268.1	(84.1)	(494.8)	578.9	-363.7	-310.8	2,400.6	-15.2	-13.0
1979	449.6	-36.0	413.6	(392.5)	(545.1)	937.6	-488.0	-524.0	4,101.1	-11.9	-12.8
1980	911.2	-185.7	725.5	(291.7)	(542.0)	833.7	77.5	-108.2	4,649.7	1.7	-2.3
1981	686.7	451.0	1,137.7	(252.4)	(767.8)	1,020.2	-333.5	117.5	4,054.8	-8.2	2.9
1982	1,901.1	-147.9	1,753.2	(160.1)	(894.2)	1,054.3	846.8	698.9	4,060.5	20.9	17.2
1983	...	...	1,370.0	(...)	(...)	1,200.0	...	170.0	3,680.0	...	4.6

Note: Dots indicate data that are not available or are not separately reported.

^a Equivalent to the capital account before considering the effect of unregistered transactions

^b Errors and omissions of the balance of payments

Source: Based on data supplied by Economic Commission for Latin America, Division of Statistics and Quantitative Analysis.

Table 14.7 Peru: Savings/Investment Coefficients

	INTERNAL SAVINGS GDP (1)	INVESTMENT GDP (2)	DIFFERENCE (1)-(2)
1970	15.9	12.9	3.0
1973	13.9	16.0	-2.1
1974	12.3	19.5	-7.2
1975	8.5	20.8	-12.3
1976	10.1	17.9	-7.8
1977	8.2	14.1	-5.8
1978	11.2	12.5	-1.3
1979	19.9	13.5	6.4
1980	16.5	17.1	-0.6
1981	12.9	20.7	-7.8
1982	11.5	18.9	-7.4

Source: Banco Central de Reserva del Perú, Memoria 1982.

politically risky for the new and somewhat uncertain regime.[16] Hence, the authorities approached their major U.S. bank creditors in a meeting in New York organized by Manufacturers Hanover Trust and attended by staff members from Bank of America, Citicorp, Wells Fargo, Chase Manhattan, and Morgan Guaranty Trust. In the meeting the Peruvians made a novel proposal: They sought a US$350-400 million refinance credit (termed a balance-of-payments loan) and proposed a stabilization program that would be implemented without the IMF.

The banks at first were reluctant to accede to the request. On the one hand, other LDC borrowers were also confronting difficulties, and extension of financing without the presence of the IMF would establish an uncomfortable precedent. Moreover, there was concern about how the banks might monitor the program. But some institutions such as Citicorp felt that they could handle this monitoring process; there also was concern that unless they supported the new regime, the Velasco forces might regain control of the government and/or authorities would enter into default. Several institutions resisted the proposal, but in the end the Citibank coalition prevailed.

Having won the support of all U.S. banks in July, the government was then in a position to gain the support of European, Canadian, and Japanese institutions. A banking committee was formed with representative institutions from each regional bloc. Total finance was to be US$386 million under the very severe terms of 2.25 percent over LIBOR, for five-year maturities with flat fees of 1.5 percent.

The banks approached the monitoring problem in the following way. The large banks in the committee were largely responsible for evaluating the progress of the

Table 14.8 Peru: Net Flows of Medium- and Long-Term Loan Capital by Type of Creditor
(millions of U.S. dollars)

	Private Banks	Suppliers	Western Governments	International Organizations	Socialist Countries	Total
1970	-11	39	26	15	-	69
1971	-4	-8	20	20	-	28
1972	57	-16	48	19	14	122
1973	244	-20	62	7	27	320
1974	407	-8	177	24	97	697
1975	376	22	253	17	125	793
1976	203	31	165	23	92	514
1977	-120	137	206	63	379	665
1978	-36	109	202	36	105	416
1979	266	198	118	73	-12	643
1980	18	87	56	147	69	377
1981	247	78	-50	102	12	389
1982	498	249	48	199	1	995
1983[a]	354	384	259	160	148	1,305

Note: Dash indicates an amount that is nil or negligible.

[a]Preliminary data that do not include adjustment for exchange-rate variations

Source: Banco Central de Reserva del Perú, El Proceso de Renegociación de la Deuda Externa Peruana:
1978-1983 (Lima, 1984).

government's program. An arrangement was made whereby
the government would voluntarily provide the necessary
reports and data for the evaluation of the stabilization
effort. A sense of conditionality was given to the
agreement by providing for a two-tranche disbursement.
The first tranche would be disbursed upon signing and the
second in January 1977, with the latter being contingent
upon approval of 75 percent of the creditors, weighted by
the amounts authorized.

For Peru, the agreement--although expensive--allowed
it to avoid the IMF. Its stabilization plan[17] had all the
trappings of an IMF program--it included a 44 percent
devaluation, budget cuts, price adjustments, and so on--
and was presented to the banks as being a fair equivalent.
But in fact it was a good deal softer than any such
program. At least implicitly the bank loans also were
conditioned by the requirement that the government settle
recent investment disputes with two U.S. firms, but the
new government was disposed to a settlement in any event
and the bank conditionality merely accelerated the
process.[18]

As for the private banks, they did a 360-degree turn.
During the credit boom of the early 1970s, conditionality
on private-bank loans had all but disappeared. Its
appearance in 1976 marked a return to practices of the
1960s. Nor was the decision to extend conditional credit
without the IMF a new one: As noted in the section on
1965-1971, from 1969 to 1971 banks provided conditional
finance to Peru on their own. What was novel was that
bankers took it upon themselves to monitor the whole
economy and not just a few parameters like external debt.

Although some large banks had the ability to monitor
the economy, and as a group banks objectively enjoyed
considerable leverage over government policy, the foray
into IMF territory failed. Outside criticism of the
venture was strong and arose from concern about having
private profit-making institutions monitoring the
affairs of a sovereign government. The possibility for
conflicts of interest obviously loomed large. Also,
given the magnitude of the disequilibrium upheld by the
previously abundant finance, as well as the lingering
populism in the political structure, authorities were
unable to muster the political cohesion necessary to make
the hard economic decisions that bankers wanted so that
foreign exchange could be made available for the payment
of debt.

With the stabilization effort falling short of its
targets, and the criticism about the role of the
commercial banks in the economy mounting, these institutions withdrew their support for the government. Thus
the Morales Bermúdez regime entered into a second phase
whereby the banks returned to more familiar terrain and
insisted that Peru arrange a standby credit program with
the IMF as a condition for the refinancing of the

private debt.

1977-1978:   The Crisis Deepens

Once the banks insisted on an IMF "green light," the government passed down a long, circuitous, and often highly conflictive road to an agreement. In 1977 the foreign-exchange crisis deepened; by the second quarter gross international reserves had fallen to only about one month of import cover, and large upcoming payments were due to creditors. Reaching an accord with the IMF proved exceedingly difficult. In mid-1977 new austerity measures were introduced; they met with strong public resistance, however, and this brought the rapid fall of a recently installed finance minister. In late 1977 a new economic team--under severe pressure from bankers, who refused all credit except for last-minute short-term rollovers to avoid a technical default--reached an agreement with the IMF implying adjustments that were extremely ambitious. Following the agreement, banks consented to the extension of new refinance credits.

However, as many expected, the IMF program targets were not met, and in early 1978 both the IMF and the banks withdrew their financial support again. Faced with embarrassment over the IMF fiasco, continuous strikes and demonstrations over austerity measures, and an ex-treme scarcity of foreign exchange (the country was now taking recourse to part of its gold reserves[19]), there was another change of the economic team in May 1978. With the introduction of new austerity measures, street riots broke out in Lima. In order to stem the drawdown of gold reserves, the new economic minister quickly arranged US$260 million in "swaps" from friendly Latin American central banks.[20] After midyear, broader inter-national support was obtained. A compensatory finance agreement and a more realistic standby accord provided US$311 million of resources from the IMF, and the private banks agreed to roll over for 180 days US$186 million in debt-service payments.[21] Toward the end of the year the economic team, now enjoying a degree of credibility with respect to its economic program, arranged a Paris Club meeting that resulted in the rescheduling of 90 percent of the payments of principal owed to OECD governments for 1979 and 1980 (US$211 million and US$248 million, respectively). Debts of US$154 million due to the socialist countries in 1978-1980 and US$35 million due to Venezuela in 1979 were restructured as well.[22] Finally a refinancing accord was reached with the private banks for maturities falling due in 1979 and 1980, for a total of US$722 million (see Table 14.9).

By the end of 1978 Peru was well on its way to ordering its financial affairs. However, the country had paid a very high price. Moreover, Daly has shown

Table 14.9 Peru: 1978 Restructuring of Commercial Bank Debt

Coverage	Amount (millions of U.S. dollars)	Maturity (years)	Grace Period (years)	Interest Rate (% over LIBOR)	Commissions[a]
90% of maturities falling due in 1979 and 1980	363 (1979)	7	3	1.875	0.5
	359 (1980)	6	3	[b]	[b]
50% of US$186 million rolled over in June 1978 and due January 1979	...	1	–	1.75	...

Note: Dots indicate data that are not available or not separately reported. Dash indicates that the amount is nil or negligible.

[a] Flat fee payed on face value of the credit

[b] Were to be negotiated in 1980. Subsequently Peru renegotiated the entire package for 1980 maturities: US$340 million were refinanced over six years (four years' grace) at 1.25 percent over LIBOR and .375 percent in flat commissions.

Source: International Monetary Fund, Recent Multilateral Debt Reschedulings with Official and Bank Creditors (Washington, D.C., 1983); Banco Central de Reserva del Peru, Desarrollo de la Deuda Externa Peruana, 1968-1979 (Lima, 1981) and El Proceso de Renegociación de la Deuda Externa Peruana: 1978-1983 (Lima, 1984).

that the adjustment over 1975-1978 was rather perverse and achieved to a large extent by exogenous factors.[23] Peru's balance-of-payments situation was greatly aided by the fall in aggregate demand brought by falling real wages, cutbacks in investment and imports, and negative growth of product (see Table 14.5). Although there also was an enhancement of export performance, this rested to a large degree on the coming on stream of investment projects in the copper and petroleum sectors initiated well before the adjustment effort. Meanwhile, net negative transfers of financial resources were received from private banks during the heat of the crisis (see Table 14.8), an event that undoubtedly contributed to the forced and disorderly nature of the adjustment process.

It may be noticed from the data in Table 14.8 that the sharp inversion of bank finance in 1977-1978 was to some degree offset by new suppliers' credits and government loans. However, these loans did not provide much relief inasmuch as they were largely for the purchase of arms abroad; indeed in 1977-1978 these purchases were as large as in the previous four-year period. In 1977 they more than doubled with respect to 1976 due to the acquisition of Soviet warplanes. Even though such purchases fell in 1978 along with other imports, they remained approximaely 40 percent above their 1976 level and had increased their participation in imports from 13 percent to 23 percent.

THE THIRD ROUND OF INDEBTEDNESS: 1979-1984

Peru's fortunes turned around dramatically in 1979. Although erratic and negative in character, the economy did achieve an adjustment over the period 1976-1978. Moreover, as mentioned earlier, output from mining investments was now on stream, and petroleum from the Amazon, although well below expectations, was now being produced at a rate of about 135,000 barrels a day, allowing Peru to become a net exporter to the tune of approximately 60,000 barrels a day.[24] When OPEC prices underwent their second major adjustment of the decade in 1979, Peru experienced a large windfall profit. The petroleum bonanza, coupled with better prices for almost all major mineral exports, contributed to a 35 percent rise in the terms of trade in 1979 after a fall of 20 percent in the two preceding years (see Table 14.5). The improvement of the purchasing power of exports (which incorporates the effect of volume as well as prices) rose even more dramatically: 54 percent.

The sudden and unexpected burst of foreign-exchange earnings, coupled with the stemming of dollar outflows via the earlier debt renegotiations, produced an extremely liquid balance of payments: The current account ran its first surplus since 1970 (US$953 million) and the overall

balance of payments had a surplus of US$1.6 billion.
The export boom also had a strong positive effect on
public savings as nonfinancial public-sector revenues
rose by 25 percent in real terms. (As a proportion of
GDP they increased from 42 percent in 1978 to 47 percent
in 1979.) This occurred simultaneously with the stagnation of private consumption, causing internal savings
to swell to 20 percent of GDP (more than double the level
of 1977), giving rise to a considerable excess of savings
over investment for the first time in several years
(see Table 14.7).

With the new influx of liquidity Peru could once
again increase imports (their volume rose by 5 percent),
and the economy grew by 4 percent (see Table 14.5).
Despite what had been an extremely conflictive relationship with private bankers during the 1976-1978 crisis,
these institutions, sensing the turnaround, now once
again began to actively court Peru as a client. US$463
million of new publicized Eurocurrency credits were
organized for the government.[25] Typical conditions were
1.375 percent over LIBOR for maturities of five years.

Peru's liquidity situation was such that authorities
took some bold initiatives on the debt. First, they
waived the renegotiation of 1980 maturities with the Paris
Club. Then they prepaid in January 1980 the US$363
million loan related to the bank refinancing of 1979
maturities; at the same time, practically all short-term
foreign Central Bank debt was paid (US$304 million).
Furthermore, a new agreement was reached with private
bankers to the terms of the refinancing of 1980 maturities
(see footnote b of Table 14.9). The strategy was related
to two objectives. First, the prepayment of the 1979
loan allowed the government to get rid of a relatively
costly credit; the renegotiation of the terms of the 1980
refinancing represented Peru's use of its improved bargaining position to gain better conditions. Second, it was
reported in journalistic circles that the authorities
wanted to reduce external liquidity at a time when
apparently there were pressures from the military to
pursue more arms purchases.

In July 1980, after twelve years of military rule,
a new civilian government, headed again by Fernando
Belaúnde Terry, assumed office. This brought with it an
economic policy that built on and intensified the market
(and the apertura or liberalization) orientation that began to take hold during the Morales Bermúdez regime.
The fundamental short-term objectives were the curbing
of inflation (a problem that was never overcome in the
Morales Bermúdez period), incentives for renewed
dynamism and leadership on the part of the private
sector, and liberalization of imports as a way to improve
the competitiveness and efficiency of Peruvian industry.

The new government also had another interesting
objective: pursuit of a more cautious borrowing strategy,

suggesting that countries do learn from bad experiences. Authorities seemed to recognize the disorderly and counterproductive nature of foreign indebtedness in the 1970s, hence the raising of internal savings, the ex ante programming of debt contraction, the seeking out of longer maturities and softer conditions, especially via more active use of official and multilateral sources of debt, and a general reduction of the weight of the debt in the economy were guidelines for policy.[26] In the face of the considerable external liquidity of 1979-1980 (gross reserves were nearly US$2 billion by mid-1980), authorities--in contrast to the 1970s--pursued an anti-cyclic stance and contracted only US$18 million of net bank debt, while short-term obligations showed very modest growth (see Tables 14.2 and 14.8). Moreover, in April 1981, the government--aiming to reduce the cost of external debt, to improve the structure of amortiza-tion, and to enhance Peru's financial image--decided to prepay US$359 million corresponding to the refinanced 1980 maturities with the banks and replaced them with credits on better terms from Morgan Guaranty (US$150 million), Wells Fargo (US$120 million), and Manufacturers Hanover (US$120 million). Concomitant with this strategy was an effort to mobilize loans from official and multi-lateral lenders that culminated in a July 1981 World Bank Consultative Group meeting in Paris for support of the 1981-1985 public investment program comprising US$4.5 billion in external financing.

This behavior was not only consistent with the more prudent borrowing strategy, but it also was concordant with the anti-inflationary struggle that had a high priority in economic policy. There could as well have been the additional motive of discouraging arms purchases. In any event, the strategy backfired somewhat as the buoyant external situation began to fade. On the one hand, prices for major export products slumped (the terms of trade fell by 18 percent in 1981) and the liberalization program, coupled with a sharp deteriora-tion of the real effective exchange rate,[27] provided more pressure to import (value rose by 23 percent and volume by 10 percent). On the other hand, world interest rates began their unprecedented escalation (LIBOR rose to 5 percent in real terms), and net interest payments in-creased 42 percent, absorbing fully 19 percent of the nation's export earnings.[28] Meanwhile, new loans from international agencies--earmarked for projects--encounter-ed delays, inducing balance-of-payments deficits; by the third quarter of 1981 gross reserves had fallen by half to just US$1 billion, less than three months' import cover.

The advent of less buoyant external conditions exposed the somewhat cosmetic nature of the adjustment program of previous years; exogenous and temporary factors had weighed heavily in the turnaround of the economy, and

when these favorable conditions dissipated, the same old structural problems in the Peruvian economy reappeared.

Just when the government's investment program was gearing up (consolidated public-sector investment rose from 6 percent to 10 percent of GDP between 1979 and 1981), revenues growth became sluggish; the overall public-sector deficit ballooned from 1 percent of GDP in 1979 to more than 8 percent in 1981. Likewise, internal savings slumped, and the savings/investment gap widened to magnitudes not unsimilar to those of the Velasco period.[29] Finally, as mentioned earlier, the real effective exchange rate accelerated its move in an uncompetitive direction, having deteriorated by 24 percent with respect to its level of 1978.[30] These events were accompanied by a major turnaround in the foreign borrowing strategy: In the last quarter of the year the government intensified borrowing and contracted new loans of US$734 million (compared to a total of US$1.154 billion in the previous three quarters), 75 percent of which came from private banks.[31]

The difficult year of 1982 proved to be the beginning of the worst economic crisis in the postwar period. The persistent internal structural disequilibria in the Peruvian economy were aggravated by a deepening of the recession in the OECD area (the terms of trade declined by another 13 percent), the persistence of very high real rates of interest in the Eurocurrency market, and the outbreak of a generalized financial crisis in Latin America that adversely affected access to bank credit.

In 1982 the government's attention shifted from the control of inflation to balancing the external accounts. Early in the year, authorities approached the IMF about the possibility of a standby agreement; it was felt that an IMF program, although politically costly, would facilitate the access to bank credit that was needed to close the now large current account deficit. Also the exchange rate, which had been adjusted cautiously but continuously, began to be devalued at a noticeably accelerated pace.[32] At the same time a very restrictive monetary policy was introduced, causing the sol share of the money supply to fall by 9 percent in real terms.[33] However, there was no success in reducing the current account deficit, in part because imports were resistant to compression on account of public-sector investment (now 11 percent of GDP) and in part because of purchases of military equipment.

With the Mexican financial crisis of August 1982, private banks became reluctant to lend to Latin America generally, detonating unmanageable payments problems in most countries that had any degree of reliance on private credit. Mexico's initiation of a debt rescheduling with its private bankers was followed by a wave of petitions from other Latin American borrowers, overwhelmed as they

were by the combination of record debt-service payments,
and by a near halt in new net lending, which destroyed
the rollover mechanism that had facilitated payment
throughout the 1970s.

Peru tried to isolate itself from the rest of the
troubled borrowers in Latin America. It was the second
of what was to become sixteen Latin American countries
(excluding Jamaica) to agree to submit to an IMF adjustment program,[34] providing bankers with the security of
Fund conditionality and a symbol of Peru's seriousness
with regard to adjustment. Then, in the midst of all the
petitions to reschedule Latin American debt, the Peruvian
economic team attempted to distance the country from the
phenomena by declaring on numerous occasions that it would
honor its obligations punctually and would not follow the
example of other countries that were seeking to restructure
obligations. Undoubtedly the economic authorities--
several of whom had very close ties to Wall Street--
also thought that their professional connections in world
financial circles might help instill confidence in
foreign bankers and permit Peru to distinguish itself
from the pack of sinking debtor countries in the region.

Ironically, in the face of its deteriorating external
accounts and a widespread state of internal disequilibrium,
the only way Peru could, in fact, honor its debts was by
contracting new loans from the banks to pay its old debt.
This strategy became increasingly fruitless as the
country could not avoid the generalized financial
depression facing Latin America from mid-1982 onward.[35]
However, for 1982 as a whole, a considerable amount of net
borrowing was successfully undertaken with the banks
(Table 14.8), and a sizable net transfer of foreign
financial resources was achieved (Table 14.6). But this
was done at the expense of a severe aggravation of Peru's
ongoing debt problem, as loans could be secured only on
increasingly onerous terms. For instance, in January
1982 Peru was charged LIBOR plus .75 percent for a
seven-year US$308 million loan led by Morgan Guaranty
Trust. At the end of May 1982 a US$320 million loan
organized by Wells Fargo carried an average 1.375 percent
spread for six-year maturities. By the end of December,
however, Peru was paying 2 to 2.25 percent over LIBOR for
five-year maturities. Moreover, medium-term credit was
increasingly difficult to secure, necessitating a buildup of short-term debt (see Table 14.2), a lethal event
for a country trying to avoid a rescheduling since this
accelerates the reverse flow of debt payments.

By early 1983, Peruvian authorities were fully
drawn into the Latin American crisis. Small U.S. banks
and Japanese institutions were now closing down short-
term lines of credit as their confidence in the country
waned and they perceived Peru "as just another one of the
half-collapsed economies of Latin America."[36] Interestingly, Peruvian economic authorities resisted rescheduling

to the end and it was Citicorp and Chase Manhattan Bank, Peru's two largest commercial creditors, that forced the government's hand. In effect, these institutions worried that the Japanese and smaller banks--with less of a commitment to international lending--would withdraw from Peru and transfer the risks of the country's situation to the big banks in whose portfolio Peruvian obligations carried relatively more weight.

In fact the two banks "counseled" authorities to declare a unilateral moratorium on debt payments so that retreating institutions would be "locked into" the country's fate. The plan called for a forced refinancing of short-term debt: Starting on March 7, 1983, all amortization payments were deferred. Short-term trade-related debt falling due between March 7 and May 31 (around US$500 million) was deferred for 90 days beyond the original date of maturity; public-enterprise working-capital debt (US$1.2 billion) and private-bank short-term debt (US$300 million) falling due between March 7, 1983, and March 7, 1984, were deferred for 360 days. The conditions of the operation were 1.5 percent over LIBOR and flat commissions of .375 percent, plus 1.5 percent for commercial credit lines.

At the same time Peru rescheduled US$408 million of medium-term debt payments falling due between March 7, 1983, and March 6, 1984. Additionally, the banking committee--led by Citicorp and including Chase Manhattan, Manufacturers Hanover Trust, Banco Central (Spain), Bank of Nova Scotia, Bank of Tokyo, Credit Lyonnais, Crocker National Bank, and National Westminster Bank--were to organize new loans of US$450 million. The cost of these operations was 2.25 percent over LIBOR for eight-year maturities (three years' grace) and flat commissions of 1.25 percent (an undisclosed agent's fee was also paid).

The terms of the agreement were extremely stiff: equal to the most onerous borrowing conditions recorded through the three aforementioned borrowing cycles. However, the agreement fell within the general framework of the rescue packages arranged by the banks for other Latin American countries, which were characterized by a marked rise in the cost of debt upon rescheduling obligations. A comparison of the conditions of medium-term syndicated bank credits in 1980-81 with those of the 1983 rescheduling suggests a deterioration of the "negotiated cost" of borrowing of 97 percent for Peru, which, although lower than that experienced by several other borrowers in Latin America, was nevertheless very dramatic (see Table 14.10). Assuming a LIBOR of 5 percent in real terms, the deterioration over the same period with respect to real financial cost was a hefty 19 percent (see footnote d of Table 10).

Notwithstanding the rescue package from the banks, a US$1 billion Paris Club rescheduling later in the year,

Table 14.10 Latin America: Provisional Data on Terms of Debt Rescheduling: 1982-1983

Country	Margin over LIBOR (percentage)			Amortization Period (number of years)			Grace Period (number of years)			Commissions[a]			Deterioration of Terms (percentage) (2):(1)[b]	Cost of Credit in Real Terms (increase)[c]
	1980-1981 (1)	R (2)	AC	1980-1981 (1)	R (2)	AC	1980-1981 (1)	R (2)	AC	1980-1981 (1)	R (2)	AC		
Argentina	0.67	2.13	2.50	7.5	7.0	5.0	...	3.0	3.0	1.09	...	1.25	...	...
Brazil	1.62	2.50	2.13	8.5	8.0	8.0	...	2.5	2.5	2.01	1.50	1.50	44	9.3
Chile	0.91	2.13	2.25	7.6	8.0	7.0	...	4.0	4.0	0.81	1.25	1.25	125	21.6
Costa Rica	1.13	2.25	-	6.0	8.5	-	...	3.0[d]	-	1.23	...	-	...	...
Cuba	1.00	2.25	-	5.0	8.0	-	...	3.2	-	0.88	1.25	-	28	19.9
Ecuador	0.74	2.25	-	8.0	9.0	-	...	2.0	-	0.97	1.25	-	146	26.1
Mexico	0.65	1.88	2.25	7.6	8.0	6.0	...	4.0	3.0	0.70	1.0	1.25	181	23.5
Peru	1.12	2.25	2.25	8.2	8.0	8.0	...	3.0	3.0	1.07	1.25	1.25	97	18.6
Uruguay	0.98	2.25	2.25	9.1	6.0	6.0	...	2.0	2.0	...	...	...	...	...

Note: Dots indicate data that are not available or not separately reported. Dashes indicate that amounts are nil or negligible. The information in the table is provisional and subject to revision. Columns headed 1980-1981 show average credit terms in 1980 and the first half of 1981. Columns headed R relate to rescheduled maturities. Columns headed AC relate to terms for additional credits.

[a] Calculated as percentages of the face value of the loans and represent a flat payment at the time of signing the loan contracts

[b] Based on the index of the cost components of credit that are subject to negotiation, as shown in the note to Table 14.3

[c] Assumes a LIBOR in real terms of 5 percent for 1980-1981 and for the rescheduled debt/new loans of 1982-1983 and adds the effect of commissions and margins by the formula C/P + M where C = commissions, P = amortization period, and M = margin. Averages are weighted by values. For Peru one finds a financial cost of 6.25 percent for 1980-1981 and 7.41 percent for the 1983 rescue package.

[d] Weighted average

Source: Robert Devlin, "Renegotiation of Latin America's Debt: An Analysis of the Monopoly Power of Private Banks," CEPAL Review, no. 20, August 1983.

and the support of the IMF, Peru's economy went into a
tailspin. Interest payments alone represented more than
31 percent of 1983 export earnings, and although the
banks effectively refinanced part of these payments with
the so-called new loans, Peru had to generate a trade
surplus to help finance the balance of these payments.
The surplus (estimated at US$130 million)[37] had to be
effected in an environment of depressive world trade and
severe natural disasters in Peru (floods in the north
coast, droughts in the Altiplano), and the weight of
adjustment fell on imports: Estimates have it that
volume declined by 27 percent in 1983. It is not surprising that per capita income fell by an amazing 14 percent (to the level recorded in 1962[38]), underemployment
exceeded 50 percent of the work force, and--in the face
of an average rate of inflation of 111 percent--real
wages fell sharply. Also, the government was unable to
comply with the IMF program targets; at the end of 1983
it had to begin negotiations for a new agreement. Peru
entered 1984 facing severe social unrest of both a
political and an economic nature. Furthermore, in the
midst of these difficulties there were reports manifesting another of Peru's perennial problems: The military
was seeking to purchase fighter planes worth US$700
million.

Finally, in February 1984 Peru reached a tentative
settlement with its 280 private banks for payments falling due that year. Peru's advisory committee had
apparently agreed to restructure US$1.56 billion. This
involved US$950 million of short-term working-capital
obligations that were to be converted into medium-term
debt and another US$610 million of maturities falling due
in the period March 1984--July 1985. The terms would
be nine years of amortization including five years'
grace, at 1.75 percent over LIBOR (information is not
available on commissions). At the same time, trade-
related short-term credit lines were to be rolled over
until November 1985.[39] These conditions, for reasons
to be explained in the next section, are much softer than
those in effect in the first round of reschedulings.

PERU AND THE BANKS: SOME THEORETICAL
AND PRACTICAL ISSUES

This section will briefly address some of the
conceptual issues behind Peru's debt problems. The first
part will outline what is felt to have been an erroneous
borrowing strategy by the Velasco regime that was
responsible for the initial debt buildup that has under-
lain much of Peru's current difficulties. The second
part will suggest that Peru (as well as other Latin
American countries) perhaps misinterpreted the proper
theoretical framework for undertaking the rescheduling

exercises.

Supply-Led Indebtedness

In dealing with private banks, borrowers must remember that commercial lenders are very exposure conscious.[40] Thus banks are especially attracted to what might be termed "virgin borrowers," countries that meet some minimum standard of creditworthiness but have little or no exposure with the lending institution. For a bank, a decision to lend under these circumstances is an extremely easy one: Portfolio diversification means the cost of running the risk of a new loan is nominal, whereas the profitability of the loan can be considerable since new borrowers often must pay stiff premiums on their loans (as did Peru in 1972) until their recognition factor is higher and competition among the banks flattens out the price structure of credit. But as the borrower's participation in the portfolio of the bank rises, the lender can become more conscious of exposure considerations, and enthusiasm for new loans shifts into greater degrees of reticence. In these circumstances bargaining power slowly shifts to the lender: As the eagerness to lend becomes relatively less pronounced, the eagerness to borrow is on the rise, if for no other reason than to roll over the exponentially growing debt-service payments to the banks. These exposure considerations--and the consequent erosion of the bargaining power of the borrower--can be offset only by an improved image of creditworthiness, an expanded supply of deposits in international financial markets, new entrants to international lending that intensify competition, or new premiums on the price of the loan. But even here there is a limit to the granting of credit given any capital and reserve structure of the lending institution.

This evolution of bargaining power is illustrated in Figure 14.2. The figure represents two potential points in the borrowing cycle, labeled $\underline{a}$ and $\underline{b}$. It is assumed that the number of lenders, the level of international liquidity, and the perceptions of creditworthiness remain unchanged throughout the cycle.

On the horizontal axes there is borrowing $\underline{B}$ by a country and lending $\underline{L}$ awarded to it by the banks in period $\underline{t}$ (obviously, $\underline{B}_{\underline{t}} = \underline{L}_{\underline{t}}$); on the vertical axes are the borrowing requirements and loan availability for the country in the subsequent period $\underline{t} + 1$. On the basis of the amount borrowed and lent in period $\underline{t}$, a certain price for credit is established; at this given price future borrowing and lending become a function of the previous period's borrowing and lending. The second derivative of the borrowing function is positive, reflecting the fact that there is an increasing

Figure 14.2 The Evolution of Bargaining Power In
the Borrowing Cycle

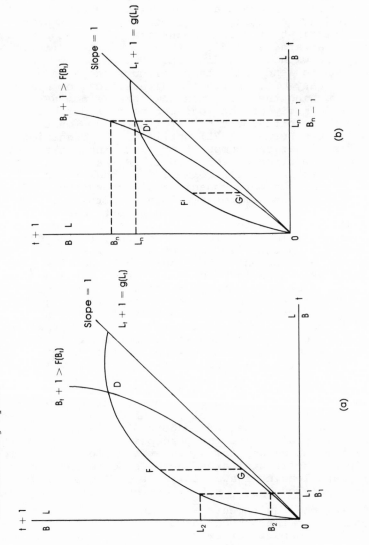

(a)

(b)

L=Lending
B=Borrowing

propensity to borrow as a result of expanding absorptive
capacity in the country and the growing requirements for
the refinancing of old debt. For the banks, however,
the second derivative is negative, reflecting exposure
and risk considerations as the country's position in the
banks' loan portfolio rises.

Segment (a) of Figure 14.2 depicts an early phase
in the borrowing cycle. In period t the country has
borrowed $\underline{B}_1$, and the banks have lent an identical amount
$\underline{L}_1$, the transaction being cleared at a given market price.
For reasons of the asymmetry of scale between the banking
system and an individual borrowing country at this given
price, what the banks are able to lend in period $t + 1$
$(\underline{L}_2)$ is considerably more than what the country is able
to effectively demand $(\underline{B}_2)$. This is not a stable situat-
tion. In effect, private commercial banks are very
concerned about their market position vis-à-vis competing
institutions; banks will therefore seek to gain a footing
in the demand-constrained credit flow. Thus, in the
initial periods of borrowing where $\underline{L}_{t+1} > \underline{B}_{t+1}$ the
country can affect the terms of credit (both the price
and nonprice components). In other words, the country's
bargaining position is potentially very strong. To the
extent that there are new entrants to international
lending (as was the case in the 1970s[41]) the bargaining
power of the borrower is further enhanced.

Ceteris paribus, the country's situation can
deteriorate as the demand for credit rises. Segment (b)
of Figure 14.2 displays a potential position in an
advanced stage of the borrowing cycle. Here the demand
for credit has been pushed beyond point $\underline{D}'$, and negotiating power has decisively shifted in favor of the lenders
as future borrowing needs exceed available loans. The
terms of credit (both price and nonprice) can now
severely deteriorate for the borrower simultaneously with
a restriction in supply.

In view of the foregoing, an advantageous strategy
for the borrower during the course of a credit cycle is
to locate itself in or around the area $\underline{F}'\underline{G}'$--the maximum
divergence between demand and available supply of credit
and hence the strongest bargaining position--and still
maintain an adequate growth of the flow of credit for
investment and finance needs. One possible strategy is
to assuage the growth of the demand for foreign credit
via increased domestic savings, thus shifting the
curve $\underline{ODB}_{t+1}$ downward and to the right and enhancing
overall bargaining power. But there also is a "dividend"
to this strategy: Raising domestic savings will probably
improve the image of creditworthiness and shift the curve
$\underline{ODL}_{t+1}$ upward and to the left, as would any policy that
improves that image. The net effect, then, is a broadening of the opportunity for new borrowing under favorable

terms.

What we posit here is what might be termed an active and "defensive" borrowing strategy vis-à-vis the banks. In the face of a rapidly expanding supply of bank loans, a country should attempt to keep the banks "on the hook" by minimizing the share of foreign commercial resources in the financing of development. This is done through the raising of domestic savings, the promotion of exports, the efficient minimizing of foreign content in projects, the establishment of extremely controlled interface with commercial creditors, and so on. Essentially what is being exploited here is the principle that private banks are most eager to lend to borrowers that do not need the resources.

Peru, during the Velasco regime, pursued policies that were not in accordance with such principles, and in the absence of some precise countervailing strategy the country eventually put itself into the deteriorating bargaining position pictured to the right of point D in Figure 14.2. The regime correctly viewed the bank loans as a new and timely instrument to support its objectives, yet it did not realize that the instrument cuts two ways and that when employed carelessly, it could actually run counter to objectives and undermine an entire political program directed at reducing foreign dependency. Instead of establishing a carefully planned defensive relationship with the banks, the public authorities, in moments of objective bargaining strength, became engulfed by the forces of the market, thereby letting enthusiastic bankers dictate the volume of credit.

In fact, once authorities received favorable signals from the commercial banks, they did not establish a reserved borrowing posture, but rather readily accepted all the credit available to them regardless of whether it could be deployed efficiently or not. Moreover, the situation was aggravated by the fact that private banks evidently do not seriously evaluate government-guaranteed projects and that they displayed an amazing willingness to extend free disposition credits during the Velasco period (see Table 14.11),[42] all of which essentially allowed borrowing to be delinked from effective absorptive capacity.[43] As a consequence, overborrowing took place, that is, borrowing in excess of absorptive capacity (productive use of resources). When overborrowing occurs, foreign capital does not necessarily translate itself into a larger economic surplus, but rather can encourage a misallocation and wastage of resources through increased consumption and imports, speculation and inflation, as well as capital flight. It also can culminate in loss of creditworthiness and economic crisis.

In effect, a massive influx of loans that exceeds productive possibilities can convert itself into an opiate that provides a false sense of security and hides the need for adjustment in economic policy. Just prior

417

Table 14.11 Peru: Distribution of Commercial Bank Loans
According to Purpose, 1971-1976

Capital Goods Imports	Other Imports	Refinance Credits	Free Disposition Credits	Projects	Nationalizations	Other	Total
2.0	0.1	48.6	27.8	14.7	6.1	0.7	100.0

Note: Excludes loans with export credit guarantees

Source: Robert Devlin, Los Bancos Transnacionales y el
Financiamiento Externo de América Latina: La Experiencia del Perú,
1965-1976 (Santiago, 1980), p. 86.

to gaining access to credit from international banks the
Velasco regime displayed a credible performance in
stabilizing the internal and external accounts. However,
this effort slackened considerably once authorities
confronted a seemingly endless flow of bank loans.
Consumption went on the rise; export coefficients declined
dramatically in the face of expanding import coefficients;
tax pressure stagnated or fell while public-sector deficits
reached highly inflationary levels and exchange-rate
parities encountered marked deterioration. All this was
sustainable as long as flows of commercial bank loans
and international commodity prices were high. However,
the latter are notoriously transitory, and the volume of
bank loans is itself very sensitive--albeit with a
deceptive lag--to the level of these prices and current
account deficits more generally. The current account,
of course, is in turn adversely affected by the relaxation of monetary, fiscal, and exchange-rate discipline
that the bank loans themselves facilitated. In sum,
authorities failed to realize the contradiction between
maintenance of the growth of bank loans and deterioration
of basic economic parameters. Eventually the contradiction between eroding creditworthiness and growing
exposure led the banks to react, and only then did the
latent economic crisis come into full focus.

    Of course the second Belaúnde administration attempted
to correct this situation. But the mountain of debt had
already been accumulated, making the task a difficult
long-term venture. Moreover, attempts to rectify the
situation were based to a large extent on very favorable
external factors that were unlikely to persist, and the
advent of a prolonged world recession and restrictions
on access to new credit quickly put Peru back in the so-
called debt trap with its consequent political and socioeconomic costs.

418

The Cost of Rescheduling: A Case of Monopoly Rents

It is common practice[44] for private banks to sharply
raise the price of credit when forced refinancing/re-
scheduling exercises are undertaken.[45]   This happened to
Peru in 1969-1971, 1976, 1978, and 1983. The bankers
have given various market-oriented arguments to justify
the practice, among them: (1) the market perceives more
risk in the country and therefore demands a higher price
for the right to reschedule; (2) competition had driven
the price of credit too low, therefore necessitating an
adjustment by the banks during the relief exercise;
(3) the payment of a higher price for credit is viewed as
the best way to induce the banks to reschedule and to
grant future credit flows, and (4) the banks must be re-
imbursed for the time and money spent on a rescheduling
exercise.

Peru and most countries in Latin America have
traditionally accepted these arguments and when faced
with a rescheduling, they have acted as if they were in
a market situation where the price of credit has risen
simply as a result of an upward shift in the supply curve.
This would appear, however, to be a misconception that
has serious ramifications for policy during a rescheduling
exercise.

It must be remembered that private banks develop
loan portfolios under assumptions of risk. Risk is
evaluated and taken into account in two ways: portfolio
diversification and risk premiums. Thus, when a bank
lends it incorporates a risk premium into the price of
the credit based on its evaluation of the risk involved.
Theoretically, should a borrower be unable to pay, an
efficient bank would have incorporated the risk into its
portfolio and would be in a position to draw on the
premiums if and when the risk materializes. Moreover, in
a competitive market situation, banks would have to
accept the losses involved with having clients unable to
pay, and banks that had inefficiently evaluated risk
would go bankrupt because the premiums collected (and
diversification) would not be adequate to absorb the
materialized risk.

This is what happened in the 1930s. When developing-
country borrowers were unable to liquidate their bond
obligations, creditors took heavy losses and some went
bankrupt. Today, however, bankers can do something that
dispersed and anonymous bondholders could not do at that
time: coordinate their action vis-à-vis a borrower
through the so-called banking advisory committee. Moreover, there is a strong incentive for cooperation among
the banks given the binding nature of the cross-default
clauses present in practically all loan agreements.
In other words, the banks can group together in a bloc
and effect a rescheduling of the debtor's obligations to
avoid a default and losses. Seen from this angle, a

rescheduling, rather than being the curse that bankers often imply as they justify the high price of such an exercise, is a great "historical privilege" that allows banks to elude the losses that a competitive market would impose on them.

The same perspective allows one to better understand the banks' strategy: The increase of the price of credit upon rescheduling is an effective ex post adjustment of terms that passes the cost of an erroneous evaluation of risk onto the borrower. This, of course, could not be done in a competitive market environment. Furthermore, countries like Peru could have explored ways to avoid this higher cost because the extra charges on a rescheduling are a monopoly rent that in theory and practice can be reduced.

In rescheduling a loan there is no real credit transaction with a supply price since the operation simply consists in the administration of a loan already granted and not immediately recoverable. Nor does rescheduling imply additional risks or costs for the banks since the alternative is a stoppage of payments and liquidation of part of the portfolio; indeed, the banks gain additional security and lower risk in the form of IMF agreements and state guarantees on private debt. In practice, then, rescheduling effectively reduces the risk of default and therefore of major losses. As for the outlays on telex, cables, travel, and so on connected with the negotiation of a rescheduling operation, these are expenses that should already have been incorporated in the risk premium paid for by the country when it originally contracted the debt. Thus, any increase in the margin over the base interest rate and payment of commissions on the amount of rescheduled debt signifies rent; that is, it constitutes an income in excess of economic costs, which is generated by virtue of the bargaining power of the few large banks that control access to credit for a country of questionable credit-worthiness. In other words, the bank charges extra for an administrative operation (the rescheduling of debt service) necessary in any event to avoid large losses; therefore, the additional income it receives on re-programming the debt is an "excess profit."

The so-called new credits offered to Peru in the 1982-83 round of reschedulings in Latin America must be viewed in the same perspective. The new credits were extended to effectively refinance about 60 percent of the interest payments to the banks that otherwise would be in arrears. In other words, the new loans are an integral part of the administration of old debt: They are a disguised rescheduling of interest payments that permits the country to keep current its interest payments on past debt and thereby permits the banks to avoid having their assets classified as nonperforming by their local banking supervisors. In sum, these loans too are nonmarket

transactions.

What one faces in a rescheduling exercise is really a bilateral monopoly; the country on one part and the banks on the other negotiate to determine how losses on a weak portfolio will be shared. The price of credit is not a market-determined price but rather a negotiated price that is indeterminate and depends on the cat-and-mouse game of a bilateral monopoly. Nevertheless, the practice that the banks have of sharply boosting the cost of credit upon rescheduling involves rents, and Peru could have attempted to capture some of these.

What are the limits of tolerance of bankers? This is hard to say, but the bankers' evident reluctance to declare a default on borrowers even in the face of a large accumulation of arrears suggests that their fear of the precedent of default and accounting losses could have been better exploited. It must be remembered that the banks' marginal cost of funds is the LIBOR and any interest rate above this enters into the terrain of profits. In other words, a bank could very well reschedule at, for example, 1 percent over LIBOR for fifteen-year maturities and still be much better off than if it had to declare a default on the borrower.[46] The bank benefits because it avoids accounting losses; indeed its books will show a profit, albeit profits much reduced from those achieved in the first round of rescheduling and probably even with respect to those on the originally contracted debt. The country also benefits because it gains a rescheduling that has terms more consonant with a positive adjustment process, that is, one that facilitates development and growth and minimizes costs--economic, social, and political. Moreover, since the banks avoid accounting losses--even while making real sacrifices--the country in all likelihood will find a renewed access to autonomous credit flows from the banks once its economic situation improves (the likelihood of which is enhanced by a more equitable rescheduling exercise).

In all fairness to Peruvian authorities, however, the financial crisis of 1982 erupted suddenly, and the precedent of the higher cost of debt upon rescheduling was on the side of the banks. This, coupled with the tremendous power wielded by the banking committee and the fact that Peruvian authorities (along with the rest of their Latin American counterparts) acted--erroneously--as if they were competitors with other countries for bank credit, helps to explain the high cost of the 1983 rescheduling. Fortunately, Peruvian authorities were clever in rescheduling only one year of maturities instead of the two years sought by many other countries: The margins and commissions invariably charged by the banks on rescheduled 1982-83 debt in Latin America were equivalent to the highest ever imposed on a commercial transaction[47]; thus there was very little chance of the cost rising in 1984 and a good probability that it would

fall. Indeed, consternation in influential circles of the North and South about the excessive cost of the 1982-83 reschedulings in Latin America induced a willingness on the part of the banks to lower the cost of rescheduling-refinance exercises in 1984, an event that, as mentioned earlier, Peru itself apparently is taking advantage of. It also is interesting to note in closing that the softened terms in 1984 have occurred at a time when most of the countries benefited are deeper in crisis and many have accumulated substantial arrears; this is good empirical evidence of the rents captured by the banks in the first round of reschedulings in Peru and Latin America more generally.

NOTES

The views expressed in this chapter are those of the authors and not necessarily those of ECLA.
1. See Devlin (1983b); and Ffrench-Davis (1983).
2. See Fitzgerald (1979, chap. 7); and Thorp and Bertram (1978, chap. 14).
3. For a most interesting "insider's" account of economic policy of the Belaúnde administration, see Kuczynski (1977). Also see Devlin (1980).
4. However, authorities remained within the limits of the traditional liberal state, restricting activities to infrastructure and the like, leaving commercially productive activities to the private sector.
5. Calculated on the basis of fiscal data in Kuczynski (1977), deflated by the consumer price index.
6. In total there were only twenty-seven commercial banks lending to Peru. The most important medium-term lenders were Manufacturers Hanover Trust, Bankers Trust, Bank of America, Chase Manhattan, Citibank, and Continental Illinois, institutions that provided 72 percent of all medium-term loans.
7. For the analysis of economic policy in this period see Pinto and Assael (1981); and Schydlowsky and Wicht (1983).
8. The results of the 1969-1971 stabilization effort are reviewed in Cabrera (1978).
9. The plan called for a rise in the global investment coefficient from 13 percent in 1970 to 21 percent by 1975; the participation of the public sector in total investment was to rise from 36 percent to 58 percent over the same period.
10. A detailed analysis of Peruvian military expenditures is to be found in Encinas del Pando (1983).
11. The negotiations were initiated in mid-1973 by a delegation headed by James Greene, a former vice-president of Manufacturers Hanover Trust. The end result was a US$150 million payment from the Peruvian government to its U.S. counterpart to be distributed by the latter as

it saw fit among the affected enterprises. Much of the payment was financed by a US$76 million syndicated loan--on terms very favorable to Peru--organized by Morgan Guaranty Trust.

12. See Fitzgerald (1976, 89).
13. See Encinas del Pando (1983, 85).
14. See Thorp and Bertram (1978, chap. 11).
15. See Stallings (1983).
16. See Stallings (1979).
17. The entire plan is republished in Devlin (1980, annex 5).
18. The details on the disputes are found in Devlin (1980, 171-172).
19. Banco Central de Reserva del Perú (1981, 11).
20. See Silva Ruete (1981).
21. Banco Central de Reserva del Perú (1981, 11).
22. Banco Central de Reserva del Perú (1984).
23. See Daly (1983, chap. 4).
24. Total output from all sources in 1979 was 190,000 barrels a day, and local consumption was 130,000 barrels a day. See Pontoni (1981, 21).
25. See World Bank (3d and 4th quarters 1979). Interestingly, there is evidence once again of a "Peruvian connection" in the renewed interest of the banks. One of the earlier loans to Peru came from LIBRA Bank where a former public servant held a high executive post. However, Peru's good reception apparently was not uniform: Ugarteche (1983) argues that although U.S. and Canadian banks were quite disposed to lend to Peru, European and Japanese institutions were relatively more restrictive.
26. See Banco Central de Reserva del Perú (1981) and Banco Central de Reserva del Perú, Memoria, 1982.
27. See Economic Commission for Latin America, Economic Survey for Latin America, 1982, table 42.
28. A coefficient of 20 percent is considered a sign of trouble by bankers.
29. See Banco Central de Reserva del Perú, Memoria, 1982; and De la Piedra (1983).
30. See Economic Commission for Latin America, Economic Survey for Latin America, 1982.
31. See Banco Central de Reserva del Perú, Reseña Económica, March 1982.
32. Inflation in 1980-1982 was roughly 70 percent annually on a December to December basis; on the same basis the exchange rate was adjusted 37 percent in 1980, 48 percent in 1981, and 95 percent in 1982. See Banco Central de Reserva del Perú, Nota Semanal, no. 33, 1983; and Economic Commission for Latin America, Economic Survey for Latin America, 1982.
33. At the same time, however, the dollar share of the money supply grew by 31 percent, speeding up the so-called dollarization process of the economy. Hence, the participation of soles in the domestic money supply

dipped from 72 percent of the total at the end of 1981 to only 65 percent at the end of 1982. See Banco Central de Reserva del Perú, Nota Semanal, no. 33, 1983.

34. In June 1983 Peru signed an SDR735 million Extended Fund Facility credit and a compensatory financing agreement for SDR225 million. For data on Peru and other Latin American countries, see Economic Commission for Latin America, Economic Survey for Latin America, 1982, table 46; and Ground (1984).

35. See Chapter 4 by Iglesias in this book.

36. See the Andean Report, April 1983, p. 57.

37. See Chapter 4 by Iglesias in this book.

38. According to data furnished by ECLA's Division of Statistics and Quantitative Analysis, National Accounts Section.

39. See Perú Económico, February 1984.

40. A more elaborate analysis of the following points can be found in Devlin (1983a).

41. Estimates have placed this at sixty new banks per year. See Bank for International Settlements, Press Review, November 2, 1983, no. 214, pp. 1-6.

42. In terms of the lack of seriousness in evaluation of projects, this was most evident in the loans to the petroleum sector. It also should be mentioned that refinance loans can have an effect similar to free disposition credits inasmuch as they free resources that otherwise would be destined for debt-service payments.

43. It should be noted that freely disposable resources are clearly a blessing for a country with adequate absorptive capacity and a coherent program of adjustment, but in the absence of these two conditions they can become a vice as resources find their way into activities of questionable merit. Precisely because of this latter problem, Peru's dependency on the foreign banks became extreme, and the regime paid a high political and social cost when the banks lost confidence in the economic program and decided to restrict their exposure in the country.

44. This is elaborated on in greater detail in Devlin (1983c); and Economic Commission for Latin America (1984).

45. The difference between a forced refinancing and a rescheduling is only a cosmetic one.

46. Peru also should attempt to use its bargaining power to achieve a 90 percent refinancing of interest payments.

47. For information on the terms and conditions of the first and second round of rescheduling, see Economic Commission for Latin America (1984).

424

BIBLIOGRAPHY

American Express Bank. Amex Review. London. Monthly
    publication.
The Andean Report. Lima. Monthly publication.
Banco Central de Reserva del Perú. Nota Semanal. Lima.
    Weekly publication.
___. Memoria. Lima. Annual publication.
___. Reseña Económica. Lima. Quarterly publication.
___. 1981. Desarrollo de la Deuda Externa Peruana,
    1968-1979. Research Document no. 1. Lima.
___. 1984. El Proceso de Renegociación de la Deuda
    Externa Peruana: 1978-1983. Lima.
Cabrera, Cesar Humberto. 1978. "Perú: La Crisis y la
    Política de Estabilización." Serie Materiales de
    Trabajo no. 17. Lima.
Daly, Jorge. 1983. The Political Economy of Devalua-
    tion: The Case Study of Peru, 1975-1978. Boulder,
    Colo.
De la Piedra, Enrique. 1983. "Peru: Debt and Crisis,
    1977-1983." Santiago, United Nations ECLA, Economic
    Development Division. Mimeo.
Devlin, Robert. 1978. "External Finance and Commercial
    Banks: Their Role in Latin America's Capacity to
    Import Between 1951 and 1975." CEPAL Review, no. 5
    (Santiago). First semester.
___. 1980. Los Bancos Transnacionales y el
    Financiamiento Externo de América Latina: La
    Experiencia del Perú, 1965-1976. Santiago.
___. 1983a. "Banca Privada, Deuda y Capacidad
    Negociadora de la Periferia: Teoria y Práctica."
    Notas Técnicas, no. 60. Santiago, November.
___. 1983b. "La Banca Privada Internacional y el
    Endeudamiento de América Latina." Comercio
    Exterior, vol. 33, no. 7 (Mexico). July, pp. 641-643.
___. 1983c. "Renegotiation of Latin America's Debt:
    An Analysis of the Monopoly Power of Private Banks."
    CEPAL Review, no. 20 (Santiago). August.
Devlin, Robert, and Michael Mortimore. 1983. Los Bancos
    Transnacionales, el Estado, y el Endeudamiento en
    Bolivia. Estudios e Informes no. 26. Santiago.
Economic Commission for Latin America. Economic Survey
    for Latin America. Santiago. Annual publication.
___. 1984. Policies on Adjustment and Renegotiation of
    the External Debt. E/CEPAL/SES.20/G.17. Santiago.
Encinas del Pando, Jose. 1983. "The Role of Military
    Expenditure in the Development Process: Peru,
    a Case Study, 1950-1980." Ibero-Americana, Nordic
    Journal of Latin American Studies, vol. 12, nos.
    1-2.
Ffrench-Davis, Ricardo. 1983. "El Problema de la Deuda
    Externa en América Latina: Tendencias y Perspectivas
    en 1983." Integración Latinoamericana, no. 83.
    September.

Fitzgerald, E.V.K. 1976. The State and Economic
    Development: Peru Since 1968. Cambridge.
___. 1979. The Political Economy of Peru 1956-1978:
    Economic Development and the Restructuring of Capital.
    Cambridge.
Ground, Richard Lynn. 1984. "Los Programas Ortodoxos de
    Ajuste en América Latina: Un Examen y una Crítica de
    las Políticas del Fondo Monetario Internacional."
    Santiago. United Nations ECLA, Economic Development
    Division. Mimeo.
Iglesias, Enrique. 1983. "Reflections on the Latin
    American Economy in 1892." CEPAL Review, no. 19,
    April.
___. "External Debt Problems of Latin America," Chapter
    4 in this book.
Inter-American Development Bank. 1982. External Debt
    of the Latin American Countries. Washington, D.C.
International Monetary Fund. 1983. Recent Multilateral
    Debt Reschedulings with Official and Bank Creditors.
    Occasional Paper no. 25. Washington, D.C.
Kuczynski, Pedro-Pablo. 1977. Peruvian Democracy Under
    Economic Stress. Princeton, N.J.
Perú Económico. Lima. Monthly publication.
Pinto, Anibal, and Hector Assael. 1981. Peru 1968-1978:
    La Política Ecónomica en un Proceso de Cambio
    Global. Estudios e Informes no. 2. Santiago.
Pontoni, Alberto. 1981. Transnacionales y Petróleo en
    el Perú. Lima.
Schydlowsky, Daniel, and Juan Wicht. 1983. "The Anatomy
    of Economic Failure." In The Peruvian Experiment
    Reconsidered, edited by Cynthia McClintock and
    Abraham F. Lowenthal. Princeton, N.J. (Abridged
    from the Spanish version Anatomía de un Fracaso
    Económico: Peru 1968-1978. Lima, 1979.)
Silva Ruete, Javier. 1981. Yo Asumí el Activo y el
    Pasivo de la Revolución. Lima.
Stallings, Barbara. 1979. "Peru and the U.S. Banks:
    The Privatization of Financial Relations." In
    State and Capitalism in U.S.-Latin American Rela-
    tions, edited by Richard Fagen. Stanford, Calif.
___. 1983. "International Capitalism and the Peruvian
    Military Government." In The Peruvian Experiment
    Reconsidered, edited by Cynthia McClintock and
    Abraham F. Lowenthal. Princeton, N.J.
Thorp, Rosemary, and Geoffrey Bertram. 1978. Peru
    1890-1977: Growth and Policy in an Open Economy.
    New York.
Ugarteche, Oscar. 1980b. La Banca Transnacional, la
    Deuda Externa, y el Estado: Perú 1968-1978. Lima.
___. 1980a. Teoría y Práctica de la Deuda Externa en
    el Perú. Lima.
___. 1983. "Concentración del Crédito y Fragilidad
    Financiera." Actualidad Económica. Lima. August.

World Bank. Borrowing in International Capital Markets.
Washington, D.C. Periodic publication.

15
The Role of External Debt Problems in Central America

Jorge González del Valle

INTRODUCTION

The five Central American countries (Costa Rica, El Salvador, Guatemala, Honduras, and Nicaragua) have traditionally been rather cautious and conservative as far as foreign borrowing is concerned. This is probably a result of the long-lasting unfavorable experiences arising from the failure to service external debts arranged in the first three decades of this century. Some of those countries (Guatemala and El Salvador) had to pay dearly for the refinancing of such debts, and Nicaragua actually suffered foreign military intervention prompted by the excuse of financial default.

Another important reason for the limited reliance of the Central American countries on external financing appears to be a generally conservative attitude of governments and central banks as regards fiscal policy, foreign-exchange management, and domestic credit regulation. It is well known that in the Latin American context the Central American countries have for a long time been able to maintain stable exchange rates, positive net international reserves, and low rates of inflation. Thus capital formation has been financed primarily with domestic savings and whatever long-term foreign investment is attracted by economic growth and stability in the region.

Still another factor that explains the limited role of external debt in Central America's economic performance is the strong influence of official development financing based on rather liberal terms in the last twenty years. It may be recalled that the Central American integration program, which began in 1961, was particularly attractive to the novel concessional lending of the Alliance for Progress agencies and the social progress fund of the Inter-American Development Bank. Moreover, the Central American countries in 1961 established their own regional development bank (the Central American Bank for Economic Integration) with the

427

specific purpose of mobilizing long-term, low-interest
foreign borrowing to finance both public and private
priority projects.

In fact it is only in recent years that the external
debt burden and refinancing have become important in
Central America's economic policy. Even so, except in the
case of Costa Rica, such problems have not exerted a
decisive influence on the direction of the adjustment
policies adopted by all countries to minimize the adverse
effects of the economic recession. This is probably due
to the relatively successful combination of exchange
controls, trade restrictions, and reserve utilization in
the context of a depressed economic performance that
has discouraged new investment and reduced import demand.
In short, the external dependence of the Central American
economy is more a problem of international markets for
primary goods than a problem of foreign financing for
capital formation.

FOREIGN DEBT STRUCTURE AND TRENDS

It was estimated that by the end of 1983 the overall
external debt of the five Central American countries would
amount to some US$10 billion, only about 3 percent of the
Latin American total. This is slightly higher than the
2.5 percent that the five countries' combined GDP
represented within Latin America in 1981 and therefore
closely corresponds to their economic importance in the
subcontinent. On the other hand, there are significant
differences as compared with other Latin American countries regarding the pattern of debt accumulation, the
sources of external financing, average cost burden, and
apparent ability to pay.

The Trend of Debt Accumulation

For the Central American region as a whole, foreign
indebtedness doubled between 1980 and 1983, reflecting
a marked and progressive deterioration of the external
sector as a result of the world economic recession. It
must be recalled that in spite of important achievements
in the industrialization process during the last ten to
fifteen years, the five countries still depend heavily
(perhaps up to 70 percent) on the exportation of a few
primary products that are subject to pronounced recession-
induced shortfalls in international markets, such as
coffee, bananas, cotton, sugar, and fresh meat.

The pace of debt accumulation was relatively more
accelerated in Guatemala, El Salvador, and Honduras,
whose aggregate external debt accounted for less than 37
percent of the region's total in 1977 but increased to
more than 50 percent in 1983. Moreover, the average

ratio of external debt to GDP of the three countries was
31 percent at the end of 1983, as compared with only 12
percent in 1977. On the other hand, the external debt
of both Costa Rica and Nicaragua increased in a rather
normal fashion during the six-year period (see Table 15.1).

Table 15.1 Central America: External Debt Outstanding
(millions of U.S. dollars)

	1977	1979	1981	1983[a]
Costa Rica[b]	1,160	1,750	2,240	2,640
El Salvador	360	610	860	1,400
Guatemala	270	590	1,300	1,960
Honduras[b]	590	880	1,330	1,670
Nicaragua[b]	870	1,110	1,980	2,380
Total	3,250	4,940	8,710	10,050
As percent of GDP	21.6	27.4	41.5	43.7

[a]Estimated

[b]Long-term debt only

Source: World Bank and International Monetary Fund.

To illustrate the severe impact of the world
recession on the external position of the Central
American countries it may be appropriate to point out a
few key macroeconomic indicators. First, whereas the
annual growth of the region's real GDP averaged 2.9 percent in the period 1977-1979, the average annual shortfall reached the depression level of -7.9 percent in the
period 1981-1983. Second, net aggregate international
assets (in U.S. dollars) fell from 1,090 million in 1978
to -570 million in 1981 and further to -1,040 million in
1983. Third, the region's deficit on current account
increased from 28 percent of exports in 1978 to 49 percent in 1981 and then fell to 36 percent in 1983 only
because imports were reduced by 18 percent in the two-
year period.

It is evident therefore then the accumulation of
external debt in Central American has been quite abnormal
since 1979 and is directly related to the region's
overall economic deterioration. This in turn was
precipitated by the world recession, but there is little
doubt that the political events in both Nicaragua and
El Salvador also played an important role. In Nicaragua,
for instance, real GDP fell by 26 percent in 1979, the
year in which a violent change in government took place;
in El Salvador real GDP fell by 19 percent in 1979 and
1980 as the civil war took an initial, destructive
impulse.

The Maturity and Interest-Rate Terms

The predominant reliance on borrowing from international financial institutions has helped the Central American countries to avoid the complicated accumulation of service payments at difficult times that many Latin American countries have faced in the last two years. Borrowing from such institutions is normally linked to the financing of long-term development projects and to interest charges somewhat lower than those of the financial markets.

In connection with the maturity profile, the average long-term external debt to official creditors increased up to 70 percent of the total debt outstanding by the end of 1983 from about 54 percent in 1981. This improvement was particularly marked in El Salvador, Honduras, and Nicaragua, whose bilateral debt to foreign governments almost trebled after 1980. On the other hand, Guatemala substantially increased its borrowing from private creditors, which was virtually nonexistent in 1980 (see Table 15.2).

Table 15.2 Central America: Long-Term External Debt to Official Creditors (percent of total outstanding)

	1977	1979	1981	1983[a]
Costa Rica	40.8	40.2	37.6	45.1
El Salvador	80.7	76.5	88.4	90.2
Guatemala	96.3	99.5	66.3	52.0
Honduras	76.9	76.3	76.4	81.9
Nicaragua	51.8	62.3	61.2	75.8
Average	60.1	62.1	53.9	70.0

[a]Estimated

Source: World Bank and International Monetary Fund.

The role of bilateral external debt has probably been enhanced in El Salvador and Nicaragua as a result of the special aid granted those countries by different governments to finance economic reconstruction associated with the internal military activity. In Nicaragua external financing from private sources virtually ceased in 1980, shortly after the revolutionary government took over, and bilateral borrowing became the main factor in the external debt structure. In the case of El Salvador a similar trend in debt accumulation began in 1981, so that bilateral borrowing now represents 41 percent of the total debt outstanding, as compared with 24 percent in 1980.

As far as the cost of external debt is concerned, the Central American countries have been unable to avoid the impact of high international interest rates during

the world recession. On the average, however, the ratio
of payments abroad on account of interest and other
charges to total debt outstanding has been moderate by
Latin American standards. This appears to be primarily
due to the substantial increase of low-interest bilateral
loans received by El Salvador between 1981 and 1983, as
well as to the doubling of Guatemala's debt to international financial institutions in the same period, including the use of IMF credit for the first time in many
years (see Table 15.3).

Table 15.3 Central America: Apparent Overall Cost of External
Debt[a] (percent per annum)

	1977	1979	1981	1983[b]
Costa Rica	5.9	8.0	13.7[c]	20.6[c]
El Salvador	8.8	11.8	7.4[d]	4.5[d]
Guatemala	11.8	7.8	8.4	6.6
Honduras	7.1	8.2	9.5	10.7
Nicaragua	5.7	5.6	6.1	10.8
Average	6.9	8.0	7.3	10.8

[a] Investment income payments abroad (except on direct foreign
investment) as percent of total external debt outstanding at
the end of year

[b] Estimated

[c] Probably overstated because of interest payments on short-term
debt for which no data are available

[d] Mainly bilateral official credits on concessional terms

Source: International Monetary Fund.

    The exceptional case of abnormal increases in
external debt costs in Costa Rica since 1980 requires
some explanation. In the first place, Costa Rica is the
only country in the region whose reliance on private
international financing has exceeded 50 percent of total
debt outstanding, which means a substantial vulnerability
vis-à-vis the evolution of market interest rates. In
the second place, the ratio of external-debt interest
payments to debt outstanding is probably overstated
in the case of Costa Rica because of the impact of
interest charges on an undetermined (but perhaps considerable) amount of direct private foreign debt. Finally,
there are indications that as a result of the complex
combination of exchange-rate devaluation and exchange
controls adopted in 1981, payments abroad on account of
external debt outstanding include unspecified refinancing
and/or default charges.

The Repayment Capacity Position

In the absence of comprehensively reliable data on the repayment schedules of the Central American external debt, estimates on the evolution of their ability to pay are restricted to interest charges. From this standpoint it is evident that the region's ratio of interest payments to exports has deteriorated markedly since 1980, but is still far below the Latin American overall level, which is estimated at 40-50 percent. There are, however, significant discrepancies among the five countries that correspond to the varied characteristics of each country's external debt profile (see Table 15.4).

Table 15.4 Central America: Apparent External Debt Burden on Interest Account (percent of merchandise exports)

	1977	1979	1981	1983[a]
Costa Rica	8.2	14.9	29.9	50.2
El Salvador	3.3	6.4	8.1	8.3
Guatemala	2.8	3.8	9.1	11.0
Honduras	7.9	9.5	16.2	22.9
Nicaragua	7.8	11.5	24.2	34.0
Average	5.4	8.6	16.5	25.3

[a]Estimated

Source: International Monetary Fund.

On the one hand, the interest-payments burden of Costa Rica appears to approach a critical point, the main reason being a threefold increase of debt-related payments abroad from 1980 to 1983, since the value of exports actually recorded an 8 percent growth in the period. This in turn is a result of the excessive reliance on both public and private borrowing from commercial banks and import suppliers, which reflects the abnormal increases in market interest rates. On the other hand, El Salvador's interest-payments burden has stabilized at a very favorable low level despite a crushing 29 percent shortfall in the value of exports from 1980 to 1983. The obvious reason behind this performance is the overwhelming incidence of both institutional and bilateral borrowing from official creditors within the debt structure. In particular, it is presumed that the fast-growing importance of foreign aid in the form of bilateral loans also carries an interest-subsidy element. The unfavorable trend of the interest-payments burden in Guatemala, Honduras, and Nicaragua is the result of a combination of increased debt charges and weak export performance. Whereas Guatemala and Honduras suffered export value shortfalls of 24 percent and 8 percent from 1980 to 1983 respectively Nicaragua enjoyed an 11 percent

increase. However, in the same period payments abroad
related to the external debt increased by 79 percent in
Honduras, 39 percent in Guatemala, and 13 percent in
Nicaragua.

DEBT-RESCHEDULING EFFORTS

Efforts by the Central American countries to
restructure their external debt have been going on since
1980, when the adverse effects of both the world economic
recession and the internal political disturbances began
to seriously weaken their external sector. Such efforts,
however, have not followed any uniform pattern in the
region and are conducted instead in a pragmatic fashion
by the national authorities according to their own needs
and possibilities. The most publicized cases of debt
rescheduling and refinancing are those of Nicaragua in
1980-81 and Costa Rica in 1982-83, but both Honduras and
El Salvador have also undertaken similar efforts involving small portions of their external debt to private
creditors.

The debt-rescheduling package of Nicaragua is notable
on three accounts: (1) it took place at a time when the
external-debt problem had not reached any critical
proportions in the Latin American context; (2) it involved
a comprehensive revision of maturity, amortization, and
interest-rate conditions of both public and private debt;
and (3) it was based on joint negotiations with the
private creditors with a view to standardizing the rescheduling terms. The negotiations lasted almost two
years, involved about 65 percent of Nicaragua's external
debt outstanding at the end of 1979, and were arranged in
four different stages in accordance with the type of
borrower.

It is no secret that Nicaragua's successful external-
debt renegotiation was helped by the private creditors'
realization that the new revolutionary government had the
option to simply disregard foreign obligations for which
it had no responsibility, particularly in view of the
abundant accusations of corruption and immorality that
befell the former dictatorship. Moreover, the nationalization of banks, financial entities, and large
agricultural and industrial holdings after the devaluation clearly left the foreign creditors in a weak
bargaining position.

In the end, the Nicaraguan government was able to
refinance a substantial part of the overall debt to
private international lenders on the basis of a ten-and-
more years' maturity, average five-year grace period, and
a 7 percent fixed interest rate. However, the direct
obligations of former private banks and private enterprises were refinanced at variable maturities and interest
rates, depending on the original loan conditions and the

expectation of further financing from the international creditors. As a rule, the new debt schedules were linked to the projected payment capacity of the government and the nationalized borrowers.

Costa Rica's external-debt renegotiation took place in a radically different environment as regards both the international financial conditions and the bargaining position of the borrower. Among other things, by the time negotiations started, Costa Rica had substantially devalued the national currency, exhausted international reserves and short-term foreign credits, established a complex exchange-control system, and incurred considerable debt-service arrears. Moreover, because of the change in government, negotiations had to be delayed until the second half of 1982, precisely the period when international lending was drying up, interest rates were rising to record levels, and fears of a world debt muddle were spreading. Negotiations were also conducted by stages and on the basis of joint agreements with the creditors. The Paris Club rescheduling was completed in early 1983 and had the conventional outcome: the postponement of amortization payments falling due in the short run without a full restructuring of official bilateral obligations. Nevertheless, it represented about 10 percent of the overall external debt outstanding at the end of 1982. On the other hand, it must be noted that both official and private creditors insisted that negotiations were linked to Costa Rica's performance under a standby arrangement with the IMF, which in turn would release fresh balance-of-payments financing.

Costa Rica's negotiations with private international banks took longer, were difficult most of the time, and were not completed until the end of 1983. Rescheduling of external debt held by such banks involved about 45 percent of the total debt outstanding at the end of 1982 and was intended to link service payments to the projected capacity to pay of the Costa Rica government in the medium term. Amortization payments may be postponed by up to three years and involve some refinancing of overdue interest payments. However, the cost of rescheduling is higher than originally expected due to the uniform application of the higher market interest rates, plus refinancing fees and commissions.

The debt-rescheduling operations of Honduras, El Salvador, and Guatemala are rather insignificant by comparison with the previous two cases. Honduras undertook a limited rescheduling of government-guaranteed debt in 1983 due to certain specific problems of the official finance corporation that might affect adversely to government's fiscal position. This operation was related to a small group of private international banks and in no case would represent more than 13 percent of the total external debt outstanding at the end of 1982. The details of the agreement reached with the banks have not

been publicized.

Finally, neither in Guatemala nor in El Salvador does the external debt problem appear to have reached the point at which an overall rescheduling policy is required. The still modest importance of external debt to private creditors (5 percent in El Salvador, 8 percent in Guatemala) is the main reason, and whenever there is a need to avoid an unfavorable concentration of service payments the national authorities apparently favor a case-by-case approach based on direct and informal arrangements with their creditors. However, the possibility of rescheduling policies might become greater if the external position of both countries does not improve in 1984.

THE PROBLEM OF INTRAREGIONAL DEBT

Since 1961 the Central American countries have settled all payments arising from intraregional trade through a clearing house. Until 1980 this mechanism operated normally, but as soon as global balance-of-payments difficulties began to appear debtor countries were unable to honor their obligations. In order to avoid an unmanageable accumulation of such balances, the five governments agreed to establish a new regional financial entity (the Central American Common Market Fund--CACMF) specifically designed to raise medium-term foreign loans that refinance intraregional official debts. Unfortunately the CACMF was unable to borrow more than US$50 million in 1981, which proved quite insufficient as outstanding balances continued to accumulate rapidly in 1982.

As of the end of 1983 unsettled intraregional debts amounted to some US$300 million, of which about 84 percent corresponded to Nicaragua's share of unpaid obligations (equivalent to about 10 percent of Nicaragua's total external debt). On the other hand, the aggregate claims of Costa Rica and Guatemala accounted for 94 percent of total intraregional debts; about one-third of such claims has not been scheduled, and negotiations on possible repayment programs are still going on (see Table 15.5).

Given the practical impossibility of further foreign borrowing by the CACMF to refinance outstanding intraregional debts, an agreement to reschedule existing obligations in accordance with the projected payments capacity of debtors was reached in January 1984 by the Central American Monetary Council, which coordinates the central bank policies of the five countries. This renegotiation involved some US$235 million, and the standard arrangement was based on a new seven-year maturity including a two-year grace period.

From a broader point of view, the Central American countries are determined to reactivate intraregional

Table 15.5   Central America: Intraregional Debt Positions,
End 1983 (millions of U.S. dollars)

	Scheduled Debt	Unscheduled Debt	Total Outstanding
Costa Rica	92.6	63.8	156.4
El Salvador	-36.6	-10.5	-47.1
Guatemala	102.1	23.4	125.5
Honduras	15.6	2.1	17.7
Nicaragua	-217.1	-35.4	-252.5
Total	-43.4	43.4	(299.6)

Source: Central American Monetary Council.

trade and therefore to avoid the inconvenience of debt
accumulation in the context of the clearing system. With
this objective in mind, a joint program of action that
includes foreign borrowing by the CACMF has been agreed
upon with the support of the Inter-American Development
Bank. Such borrowing, however, would be limited to the
financing of a modest portion (perhaps up to one-third)
of new unsettled balances within the clearing system.
It has been understood that both the creditor and the
debtor countries would finance the remainder in equal
parts.

16
Where Do We Go from Here?

Miguel S. Wionczek

> The prospects of a major [debt]
> default is just like a nuclear war:
> No one wants to talk about what would
> happen if the bomb went off.
> --<u>Philip Wellons</u>, Harvard Business School[1]

THE OUTLOOK IN 1977

The quote with which this concluding chapter starts did not originate with just any Harvard Business School professor. It comes from an academic expert on the LDC external indebtedness who published in 1976 under the OECD official auspices an almost six-hundred-pages-long study on borrowing by developing countries on the Eurocurrency market in the mid-1970s.[2]

In contrast, I plead guilty to having organized in October 1977, under the auspices of El Colegio de México in Mexico City, a closed international seminar on LDC external debt and the world economy, with participation of some thirty experts and practitioners in the field of North-South financial relations from all over the world. The meeting was attended by people from international agencies (World Bank, OECD, OPEC, and UNCTAD) and from central banks of creditor and borrowing countries, as well as by executives of large private banks from both sides of the Atlantic and academic economists from the United States, Canada, Mexico, Brazil, and Chile, all participating in their individual capacity. The fact that six years later, in 1983, one of the participants of that seminar occupied the post of a vice president of the World Bank, two were finance ministers, one a deputy foreign minister, and one a key adviser at the Commonwealth Secretariat would suggest that the gathering was not exactly a random social get-together of a bunch of radical friends with an amateurish knowledge of the subject.

Careful reading in the winter of 1983-84 of the final report of the 1977 seminar was sort of depressing. Although the correct and detailed diagnosis of where the

437

LDCs were inexorably heading in a not too distant future
and a set of concrete proposals for preventive action as
well emerged from that meeting, practically nothing
happened during the following six years that might have
slowed down, or alleviated at least, the gestation of the
full-fledged crisis of global proportions both in respect
to the state of the world economy and the LDC indebtedness.

As I might be accused of bias, let two quotations
from a report that emerged at the meeting speak for
themselves. The first deals with the diagnosis of the
LDC debt situation:

> . . . the views seemed to coincide in a number
> of important points including:
> a) the LDC external debt problem must be handled
>   within a larger framework which recognizes
>   global interdependence and covers balance-of-
>   payments adjustments, LDC development needs,
>   official development assistance, "stag-
>   flation" in the LDCs, international trade
>   and world economic recovery;
> b) finding solutions to the debt problem is the
>   joint responsibility of the LDC borrowers
>   and the DC lenders;
> c) the LDC's external indebtedness is only one
>   face of the general problem of ensuring
>   "acceptable" growth rates in the LDCs;
> d) up till now, the problem of the debt and
>   declining net financial flows to the LDCs
>   has been treated in a piecemeal and hap-
>   hazard ex-post way;
> e) the LDC debt built up in 1974-1976 cannot
>   be repeated--not so much because of its
>   aggregate size but because of its structure
>   [italics added];
> f) linking short-term stabilization and adjust-
>   ment with long-term economic growth and
>   development finance would make it possible
>   to combine the generalized and the case-by-
>   case approach;
> g) the combination of the generalized and the
>   case-by-case approach must take into
>   consideration the different situations of
>   the poor and the middle-income LDCs;
> h) the balance-of-payments adjustment facilities
>   available to the LDCs need to be strengthened
>   and expanded; exclusive emphasis on short-
>   term finance for adjustment purposes is not
>   enough;
> i) in addition to expanded adjustment facilities,
>   the poorest LDCs need a continuous increase
>   in long-term official concessionary
>   assistance;

j)   the debt of the middle-income LDCs might be
handled by increased official lending at
non-concessionary terms and by international
private capital markets, but only if there
is a speedy recovery in the world economy;

k)   it would be much easier to solve the middle-
income LDC debt problem if new mechanisms
were devised to recycle more OPEC surpluses
into capital formation, through--inter alia--
more OPEC investments in middle-income LDCs;

l)   even if adjustment facilities were strengthened
and development financing increased, the
trade policies of the developed countries,
particularly on nontraditional (manufactured)
LDC exports, would have to be liberalized;
and

m)   a satisfactory solution to the problem of
LDC indebtedness and development financing
depends heavily upon the pace of world
economic recovery.[3]

Recalling the guidelines elaborated already in 1975
in Geneva by the ad hoc UNCTAD Group of Governmental
Experts on Debt Problems of Developing Countries, even
more applicable to the 1983-84 conditions than to those
prevailing in 1977, the second quote from the same report
suggested that:

a)   Debt re-organization should take into account
the development prospects of the debtor country, to enable it to continue debt servicing
payments and restore its credit-worthiness.

b)   Re-organization should be conducted within
the customary multilateral framework with the
aim of concluding an agreement as speedily
as possible to avoid prolonged uncertainty
regarding the availability of foreign exchange.

c)   The terms of debt relief, such as consolidation, repayment, grace periods and interest
rates, should take into account both the
anticipated long-term debt servicing capacity
of the debtor country and the legitimate
interests of the creditors.

d)   Debt re-organization arrangements should
provide for flexibility to review the situation at the end of the consolidation period
in the light of unforeseen circumstances.
They should also provide for accelerated
repayments in an agreed upon manner if the
debtor's economic situation improves more
rapidly than anticipated.[4]

Moreover, the report stressed, again reflecting consensus, that the developed lender countries must keep in mind that the problem of LDC indebtedness can be managed in the long run only if LDCs are assured a constant flow of development finance on terms and conditions that are in accordance with the goal of "acceptable" growth rates and that take into account their repayment capacity. The LDCs' repayment capacity will depend not only on these terms and conditions but also on world trade that, in turn, will depend to a great extent upon the growth rate of the advanced economies. Quelle sagesse--Voltaire's Candide would have said in 1983--quelle sagesse!

THE OUTLOOK IN 1984

The absolute lack of such elementary sagesse among all actors of the international indebtedness game, which brought most debtors countries, some creditor countries, and the whole fabric of the international financial system to the brink of disaster by 1982-83, has been convincingly documented in this book by fifteen experts of many nationalities with varied experiences at global, regional, and national levels. In spite of large differences between individual contributors' approaches, the content of the volume makes even more depressing reading than the results of the 1977 Mexico City exercise, independently of whether the present authors have a background in international financial agencies, have been or are actually involved in central and private banking activities, or are competent academics from the social sciences.

If any sort of consensus emerges from this book it can perhaps be summarized in four points. First, the prospects for the world economy and the LDCs of getting out of the present mess, which is more serious than is generally thought, are uncertain. Second, although the debt-service burden of all LDCs but the poorest ones continues to increase even in the few cases of "successful" debt renegotiations, the inflow of new net public and private capital resources to the whole developing world has practically been brought to a standstill, forcing the LDC debtors into a reverse transfer of their savings abroad to pay just a part of the interest accrued on the accumulated external debt. Third, all the major actors (international agencies; national governments of the creditors and the debtor countries; actual lenders and borrowers, whether public or private; and private financial intermediaries) share responsibility for the debt crisis. Fourth, at international operational levels, all these major actors continue business as usual under the most optimistic assumptions about the prospects for worldwide economic recovery, the subsequent expansion of

international trade, and the orderly functioning of the
international financial system in spite of the impressive
growth of competent literature questioning convincingly
all these assumptions. Although it is not the purpose of
this concluding chapter to treat with detail these four
key characteristics of the present situation, some additional evidence supporting them may be in order.

THE CONTINUING DEBT CRISIS

     With 1984 being an election year in the United
States, much has been made of the recovery of the U.S.
economy following three years of Reaganomics. Official
forecasts made public at the beginning of 1984 put real
GNP growth for the whole year at close to 5 percent with
price increases of only about 4.5 percent and a considerable decline in unemployment. Alongside a rather strong
consensus in U.S. financial circles and among business
economists that the administration's economic performance
targets for 1984 are attainable, there is, paradoxically,
a sizable number of nonpartisan observers who express
most serious doubts about the duration of the U.S. recent
strong recovery beyond 1984. As a prestigious and
widely read monthly, the Morgan Guaranty Survey, put it
in late 1983:

>   Against the background of major surprises in
>   1983, continued advance in the economy--while
>   the most likely expectation--cannot be taken
>   for granted. One obvious source of concern is
>   the fragile debt condition of developing coun-
>   tries. Another is the policy drift in Washington
>   on ways to narrow massive budget deficits. A
>   further uncertainty is the still unsettled state
>   of Federal Reserve policy.[5]

Any careful and constant reader of U.S. financial journals
and magazines in early 1984 discovered that the minority
concern about the possibility of a new cyclic downturn
of the U.S. economy in 1985 was increasing steadily
instead of diminishing. In a survey of the current
thinking about the U.S. economic prospects a very
reliable source noted that a growing minority of analysts
believes that the optimistic majority consensus has no
solid and convincing base and "some are even predicting
a new recession before the year is out."[6]
     But regardless of who will prove to be right in the
present controversy about the duration of the U.S.
recovery, the OECD made it clear in late December 1983
that even strong recoveries in 1984 in the United States
(and Japan) will not be sufficient to bring an equivalent
resurgence in West European countries whose economies,
in marked contrast, will grow very little if at all, one

more year and where unemployment will continue to rise.
The weak West European performance means that the recovery in the whole nonsocialist industrial world will
remain disappointingly slow. The OECD warned, as it has
done regularly in past few forecasts, that the large
U.S. budget deficits, together with the high interest
rates and the strong dollar they cause, remain a threat
to the economic recovery of the United States and to the
upturn in the rest of the OECD region.[7]

One may add, not for the purpose of spreading more
gloom but in the way of supporting evidence for this
point, that a number of private research centers in Japan
and the key Western countries released forecasts for 1984
and beyond that are considerably more pessimistic than
even the OECD latest figures. In Japan, the economic
research department of one of the largest banks forecast
for the next three years (1984-1986) an average annual
growth rate of 2.8 percent in real terms as against the
OECD's 4 percent.[8] The National Institute of Statistics
and Economic Studies in Paris has predicted that the
French economy could remain sluggish--at close to a zero
growth rate--for another five years.[9] Moreover, reports
from West Germany stressed that despite some positive
signals

> . . . a peculiar sense of fragility hangs over
> the recovery. Real interest rates, pushed up
> by central banks seeking to stem capital out-
> flows to the United States, remained uncomfortably
> high, crimping investments. Export orders,
> despite the 1983 autumn upswing, remained roughly
> at 1982's depressed levels. And tough wage
> negotiations were approaching, with the threat
> of higher production costs and reduced profits.[10]

In the face of all this evidence it takes heroism or
wishful thinking to assert that the recovery of Western
industrial economies is in the cards for the mid-1980s,
thus becoming the engine of growth for the LDCs through
the expansion of international trade. What must be kept
in mind is that under the renegotiation arrangements
signed in 1982 and 1983 and those (the majority) that
are still pending, the LDC debt-ridden economies will have
to increase by 1985-1986 the repayment not only of
accumulated interest charges but also of sizable portions
of the principal of their external debt. Nobody seems to
know how these ambitious targets that were the base of all
renegotiations arrangements in process through 1984 will
be reached.

In 1982, the "bad boys" who were unable or unwill-
ing--according to different schools of thought in the
creditor countries--to pay their external obligations
on time were Latin Americans and a few socialist economies
like Poland and Yugoslavia. In 1983 the "debtors crowd

on the brink" expanded to all latitudes by the addition
to the list, among the others, of the Philippines and
potentially South Korea in Asia; Nigeria, Ivory Coast,
Morocco, and Sudan, without counting the hopeless case
of Zaire, in Africa; Portugal in Western Europe; and
Israel, whose external per capita debt happens to be the
highest in the world. The little-known fact that France's
external debt is estimated at about US$50 billion
suggests that the list of "bad boys" may grow even more
in the years to come. Asking himself in the fall of 1983
how serious was the international debt crisis, the chief
economic commentator of the New York Times said "The
short answer is 'Very'."[11]

The chapters in this book by such contributors as
Dragoslav Avramovič, senior adviser to the UNCTAD
Secretary General; Albert Fishlow from the University of
California at Berkeley; Enrique Iglesias E., secretary
general of the UN Economic Commission for Latin America;
and Pedro-Pablo Kuczynski, the former minister of energy
of Peru and president of First Boston International,
together with the seven Latin American case studies,
provide almost excessive detailed factual evidence that
the debt crisis is not only very serious but very, very
serious indeed. Since the crisis does not limit itself
only to Latin America, even such conservative sources as
the Wall Street Journal complain about the fact that
within less than a year after the beginning of the present
debt crisis in August 1982

> . . . the crisis atmosphere has faded and a
> routine has set in. Banks work out complicated
> plans to postpone debt repayments and lend new
> money. Countries borrow from the International
> Monetary Fund, too, agreeing in return to change
> their economic policies. International bankers
> assure everyone that everything is under con-
> trol. . . . The result is that a second debt
> crisis, or "second wave" is beginning and is
> likely to become more pronounced soon. The
> second wave is simply defined as what happens
> when the initial rescue packages fall apart.[12]

THE LATIN AMERICAN SCENE

Against the voices that claim that in Latin America
things are getting slowly under control, the latest
developments suggest that the progress in the region
presents not only a very complicated and difficult picture
but on the debt-rescheduling front is extremely limited
in spite of high economic and social costs. Argentina's
external debt at the beginning of 1984 was officially
estimated at US$43.6 billion as compared with US$387
million available in foreign-exchange reserves. Because

of the lack of long overdue data on some debts contracted
outside the country and the fact that about US$1 billion
of the private and state agencies' debt had not been
properly registered with central-bank authorities, it is
quite probable that the Argentine total debt is of the
order of US$45 billion rather than the 40 billion used
as a reference figure throughout 1983. Since Argentina's
arrears in its external-debt repayments amount to close
to US$3 billion, the new president of Banco Central,
Enrique García Vázquez (given this post by the Alfonsin
government, the first civilian government since 1976),
announced that Argentina would not be able to renegotiate
its foreign debt or to pay interest on it until mid-1984
but would seek a new agreement with the IMF for an
immediate loan of US$900 million. The delay of rene-
gotiations is explained by the fact that the new government needed time to determine which borrowings by the
former military regimes were legitimate. In the meantime, the new economy minister, Bernardo Grinspun, held
periodic talks in Washington, D.C., with the president
of the World Bank, A. W. Clausen; the managing director
of IMF, Jacques de Larossière; and high U.S. Treasury
officials and told the U.S. commercial bankers in New
York that Argentina would need a considerable amount of
short-term trade credit to meet pressing import requirements if it was expected to raise foreign exchange to pay
interest on the outstanding external debt. Although the
international private banking community does not foresee
Argentina's formal declaration of unilateral moratorium
on debt payments, European banks are presumably very wary
of extending the country additional short-term trade
finance, and the discussions on this relatively minor but
important point may last quite a time.
     Following three and a half months of traveling the
world over to persuade private creditor banks to participate in Brazil's financing program for 1984, the country's minister of planning, Delfim Netto; minister of
finance, Ernane Galveas; and president of Banco Central
do Brasil, Alfonso Celso Pastore, at the end of January
1984 in New York signed another four-part package agreement with more than 550 commercial banks that included the
rescheduling of about US$5 billion of loans that mature
in 1984, the maintenance of US$10.3 billion of short-
term trade financing, US$6 billion of interbank credit
lines, and a US$6.5 billion "jumbo-loan" of "fresh money."
A US$5.4 billion loan program from the IMF was expected
to follow the agreement with private banks. Since some
150 U.S., Spanish, Latin American, and Middle East banks
with relatively small exposure opted out of the "jumbo
loan" operations, it took the Brazilian negotiating team
supported by high IMF officials almost two months to
raise the US$500 million needed to reach the "jumbo loan"
target. For the loan to be adequate to meet foreign-
exchange needs in 1984, Brazil committed itself to follow

an adjustment program even tougher than in the previous
year, including a US$9 billion trade surplus. A drastic
reduction in imports was crucial in Brazil's ability to
run a US$6 billion trade surplus in 1983.

In the fall of 1983 Bolivia defaulted on the US$30
million debt-interest payment agreed on previously as a
precondition for a further rescheduling of US$450 million
in foreign debt falling due in 1984 and 1985. The country's
total foreign debt is of the order of US$3 billion, but
its extreme shortage of foreign exchange continues to be
exacerbated by the inability of Argentina to pay for
Bolivian exports of natural gas. Bolivia has been negotiating a US$350 million extended fund facility with the IMF,
a first step toward rescheduling its commercial loan obligations, which have been technically in default since
September 1982. Private foreign banks demand that the
country repay all the interest due before any serious discussions of debt restructuring take place.

Chile in early 1984 was in the midst of protracted
negotiations with the IMF, which was not showing any willingness to accept the country's request to raise the public-
sector deficit from 2.3 percent to 5 percent of GDP. The
delays in the IMF approval of reflationary policies in the
country, whose GDP dropped by 14 percent in 1982 and an
additional 5 percent in 1983, cast serious doubts about
Chile's access to "new money" from abroad. Its central-
bank estimates in that respect amounted to about US$1
billion. In 1984 Chile is due to pay US$1.8 billion in
interest on its foreign public debt of US$18 billion.

Ecuador, whose external debt stands at US$6.6 billion
(US$4.7 billion public and 1.6 billion private), has been
reported to have accepted the interest rate set at 2.25
points above LIBOR or 2.125 points over U.S. bank prime
rate. However, the actual agreement with foreign banks
signed at the end of January 1984 covered only US$300
million falling due in the first half of the year. Short-
term trade credits totaling some US$700 million were
extended through individual agreements between the Ecua-
dorian government and private creditor banks that reserved
to themselves the right to change the recipients of these
credits. About half of the private-sector debt is being
converted into obligations of the central bank.

Peru, with its external debt estimated at US$12.8
billion at the end of 1983, expected to sign a stabilization agreement with the IMF in the spring of 1984.
The agreement would presumably pave the way for refinancing and rolling over of about US$3 billion of short- and
long-term debt and for disbursement of some US$250-300
million of "fresh money" from the foreign commercial
banks. The country's net international foreign-exchange
reserves dropped in early 1984 to US$500 million, suf-
ficient only for two months' imports. The draft letter
of intent, presumably agreed to in principle by Peru and
the IMF, provided, among other things, for the reduction

of the public-sector deficit from 10.3 percent of GDP in 1983 to 4 percent in 1984 and the cutting of the inflation rate from over 100 percent to 70 percent. The country's GDP declined in real terms by 11 percent in 1983, the sharpest drop in Latin America, and the government's failure to meet the targets of its US$700 million extended facility program with the IMF led to the delay in about US$500 million of credit, including US$200 million from the World Bank for specific investment projects.

Finally, in the expectation of the change of government in Venezuela in early February 1984, negotiations on the debt issue were suspended for many months. After having taken office, the new president of Venezuela, Jaime Lusinchi, declared immediately that his country would repay the debt, estimated conservatively at US$33 billion, "to the last cent." The Venezuelan debt renegotiations will be complicated, as will be those in other countries, by some three-quarters (US$18.4 billion) of the public-sector debt falling due in 1983 and 1984, neither interest nor principal having been paid recently on the private debt of some US$8 billion, and Venezuelan oil-exports value having declined from the peak reached in 1981 of US$20 billion to US$14 billion in 1983. Advisers to the new government intimated that Venezuela will seek extension of debt repayment over eight to ten years with a three- to four-year grace period on the repayment of principal. For a number of reasons the process of investigating the size of the private debt and settling it is expected to take as long as one year.

The only Latin American country doing better than all others seemed to be Mexico. This results partly from such facts as that its debt crisis came after four years of a very rapid oil-fed economic growth, it was the first to recognize the seriousness of the situation, and its financial negotiators proved to be experts of the first order. Last but not least, the country's size and its closeness to the United States forced its powerful neighbor--at the same time its largest creditor--into a more conciliatory stance than is the case of the rest of the subcontinent. But even in Mexico nobody really knows what may happen if all the optimistic external assumptions go awry in 1985 and 1986 unless a broad longer-time rescheduling of the debt payments due between 1985 and 1988 goes through.

A NEED FOR WORLDWIDE SOLUTIONS

At the international level the present routine is of a negative kind. Although on the one hand after several years of the predominance of international private intermediaries in the financial flows to LDCs, the International Monetary Fund recovered its leadership role in setting the conditions of access to external dwindling

private resources,[13] the toughness of the IMF adjustment
programs, on the other hand, has not been accompanied
by the adequate expansion of the IMF lendable resources.

In the aftermath of the difficulties that arose in
the U.S. Congress in 1983 in respect to the increase of
its IMF quota by US$8.4 billion as a part of a general
round of the expansion of the member countries' contributions to the IMF (difficulties that took several months
to overcome), the IMF Executive Board formally approved
in early January 1984 a limitation in the amount of loans
that needy countries may obtain. Under the previous
policy, a member country could borrow up to 150 percent
of its IMF quota with a ceiling of 450 percent over three
years. The new rule reduces these ceilings to between
102 and 125 percent a year, or 375 percent over three
years, depending on how stringent an austerity program
a country adopts "to put its economy in order." Furthermore, a new limit has been put on the amount the member
countries may borrow from the IMF compensatory financing
fund, designed to help debtor countries offset the impact
of falling commodity prices, to 83 percent of their
quotas rather than 100 percent as was the case before.
And the borrowing limit on a companion buffer stock fund
was reduced to 45 percent of a quota from 50 percent.
Finally, the IMF agreed to increase gradually the interest
it pays countries whose money it uses for loans to debtor
countries. Present rates, which stand at 85 percent
of prevailing market rates, amount to 7.39 percent
annually. They will be increased between 1984 and 1987
by at least 3.3 percentage points a year until the rate
is just below market rates by 1987 or shortly later.

Even though the latest restrictions on the IMF
lending seem to be relatively small, they send several
disquieting signals: the expectation that the number of
the countries that will come to the IMF to negotiate
stabilization agreements will increase very considerably
in the near future, the concern at the IMF in respect to
the possible rapid exhaustion of its loanable resources
in spite of the most recent overall increase in the IMF
quotas, and the awareness of the fact that the next round
of general quota increases will be very difficult and
will take a long time unless there is a sustained
recovery of the industrial countries' economy accompanied
by the unlikely disappearance of their national budgetary
difficulties. In the past, under much easier international
conditions, it used to take about five years from the
initial proposal to raise IMF quotas to the actual
ratification of their increase by all member countries.
Presently, the prospects for initiating a new round of
increases are very dim both on political and economic
grounds. Bringing the IMF lending interest level to
prevailing market rates, expressly asked for by the U.S.
Congress as one of the conditions of the approval of the
increase in the U.S. quota, eliminates any concessional

element from the IMF stabilization agreements and may increase the debt-service burden—albeit slightly—if international interest rates continue as high as they are now. Here again no good news for the debtors can be expected either from the United States or Western Europe.

It is of common knowledge that during 1982-83 all debt-rescheduling negotiations with international private banks were accompanied by an increase in the total cost of debt servicing through augmented spreads over LIBOR or the U.S. bank prime rate and through additional charges and commissions known in the international banking parlance as front-loading or up-front fees, imposed by creditors on the debtor countries. Although no global estimates of these additional costs exist because private banks generally do not disclose how much they earn from loan rescheduling, the available scant information strongly suggests that the total amounts are substantial.

Debtor countries argue correctly but without success that spreads should fall instead of rising, because refinancing arrangements improve the quality of the portfolios of loans and the signing of a rescheduling agreement does not involve any additional risks for the private banks. Consequently, renegotiators from the debtor countries in Latin America and elsewhere express with growing frequency (at least privately) opinions that by taking undue advantage of the weak negotiating position of debt-burdened countries, international private banks work in the long run against their own interests. The extra costs of debt service might become in some cases a burden that debtor countries will not be able to bear. But since business is business, private creditors as in the past care only about fattening their immediate profits.

Thus, for example, Albert Fishlow, one of the contributors to this volume, estimates that the nine largest U.S. banks together earned between US$70 million and US$130 million extra in 1983 thanks to stiffer terms and up-front fees on debt-rescheduling operations with seven Latin American countries including Argentina, Brazil, and Mexico. These windfall profits contributed between 14 and 26 percent of the 1983 profit gain of the same banks, which at the same time were able to cut their exposure to developing countries (including seven Latin American debtors) by about US$500 million in the first half of 1983.[14] Moreover the same trends can be observed on the global scale. At the very end of 1983 OECD reported that the non-OECD borrowing (both bank loans and bond issues) on the international capital market amounted to slightly over US$25 billion in that year.[15] Once the OPEC members' borrowing of US$9 billion is excluded from this total, some US$16 billion only corresponds to the non-OPEC LDCs and the socialist bloc, with the largest part representing several "jumbo loans"

to major Latin American debtors. In other words, with
few exceptions, the outflow of new capital resources from
the industrialized countries was brought to an abrupt
stop in 1983.

These two parallel developments--first, increases in
interest rates on rescheduled debt, which often includes
not only the principal but the overdue original interest
rates cost, and second, declines in "new" lending--add
greatly to the net reverse financial transfers from LDCs
to the creditor countries that started taking place in
1982. If unchecked, these "perverse" capital movements
may become--perhaps long before the end of the present
decade--the proverbial straw that will break the camel's
back. The nature of the global problem of the LDC
resources gap that urgently needs to be filled, if only
to cover now the present interest payments on the accrued
LDC debt and within a couple of years to start repaying
the rescheduled principal, is finally becoming recognized
in some international banking circles as suggested by
Figure 16.1 that originated with Morgan Guaranty Trust.

Figure 16.1

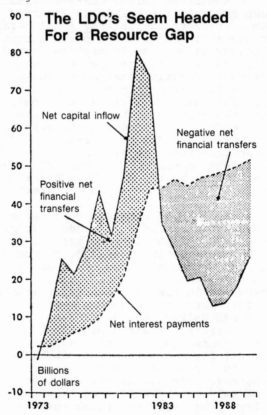

Even in the face of the potential magnitude of this problem, the low-key discussion in international agencies and private financial centers of the issues involved limits itself as yet to suggestions of a possible interest-rate relief for "needed countries" if, of course, they behave. Speaking lately before international finance audiences in the United States and Western Europe, both the president of the World Bank, A. W. Clausen, and the managing director of the IMF, Jacques de Larossière, called for "reasonable terms" on credits to heavily indebted countries. Clausen noted that although in 1981 private capital sources in the developed market-economy countries had made a net transfer of US$16 billion in medium- and long-term lending to the LDCs, the negative transfer of some US$7 billion from LDCs to the creditor countries took place in 1982 and increased to over US$21 billion in 1983. In the World Bank president's words "Productive investment yields a return and foreign investors should get back more than they invest. But it is premature for developing countries, as a group, to be transferring resources to the high income countries on this scale."[16]

Senior economist of Morgan Guaranty Trust Rimmer de Vries went one step farther in an interview granted in mid-December 1983 to the International Herald Tribune in Paris by suggesting that large private banks from industrial countries may see themselves forced to "reduce substantially," by two to three percentage points, interest rates to countries like Argentina and Brazil if these countries "are ever to become credit worthy." Rate relief--added the same New York banker--would be applied discriminately to countries that have no other way out of the debt trap and that have the domestic policies needed--those aimed at increasing exports and at soliciting foreign direct investment--already in place.[17]

These signs of concern about the LDC "debt trap," an expression coined in the mid-1970s by radical economists and accepted by now by at least some bankers, are accompanied by a growing number of calls from the LDCs for a world financial and monetary conference. Such a conference would include in its agenda four closely interrelated topics: debt reorganization, reconstruction of the international monetary system, reform of development finance, and reorganization of international financial institutions.

All these LDC initiatives and exhortations, however, fall on the deaf ears of the powerful Group of Ten consisting of the United States, Canada, Japan, and major West European nations. Their deputies met in Paris in mid-November 1983 for just one day, agreeing only to seek in the next few months new contributions by the IMF, BIS, and OECD to further analysis of international monetary problems. The agenda for the next Group of Ten meeting to be held in the spring of 1984, once again at the deputy level, was to cover three points: possible

steps to stabilize currency values, ways to help the IMF
tighten discipline over the economic policies of the member countries, and ways to maintain sufficient worldwide
liquidity to continue financing the emerging economic
recovery. Press reports from the Paris meeting made it
clear that it concentrated on conflicts between Western
Europe and the United States with regard to the U.S.
budgetary and fiscal policies and did not dedicate any
attention to the LDC debt problems and their international economic implications. Within this political
framework, what 1984 could bring to the LDC creditors,
if anything, was some "interest-rate relief."

It is obvious that whatever interest-rate relief is
finally granted by international private creditors to LDC
debtors, it will again be equivalent to treating a very
serious and protracted disease with aspirin. As the
content of this volume amply demonstrates both at global
and national levels, because of their short-term approach
the "rescue packages" of 1982 and the subsequent debt-
rescheduling operations are not linked in any way with a
much wider range of worldwide economic, financial, and
monetary issues whose adequate solutions cannot be postponed indefinitely. As a U.S. banker quoted in the
opening chapter by Dragoslav Avramovič put it bluntly
in the spring of 1983,

> The flaw in the current strategy is that there
> is not enough direct [italics in the text]
> emphasis on the LDC growth. We are all talking
> about growth, but there is too much risk that
> current policies won't be sufficient. Without
> faster growth, we are buying not only economic
> and financial chaos, in my view, but de facto
> defaults on the order not yet seen.[18]

Facing such prospects, it is not enough to ask the
question, How much austerity can Latin America take?
and to answer it with another question to the effect that
"rescue, in the form of economic growth, could come as
the world economy slowly recovers, but will it come soon
enough?"[19] Neither is it of great help to arrive at the
conclusion that the crisis is clearly going to last a
long time, and that because the situation will be gloomy,
"it is conceivable that . . . people will become resigned
to low growth as the only available option, and refinancing negotiations will become institutionalized,
so that a new normalcy will appear."[20]

Under the demographic, political, and social conditions prevailing in most of Latin America, analyzed in
this volume by Víctor L. Urquidi, chances for a "new
normalcy" of this sort in the medium and long run seem to
be close to nil. In the 1930s under the impact of the
Great Depression, all the subcontinent, except Mexico,
fell into the hands of military dictatorships. Fifty

years later, in the mid-1980s, the contrary political
wave is taking place judging by the recent developments
in Argentina, Nicaragua, and Brazil and the growing
challenge to the authoritarian regimes in Chile, Uruguay,
and Central America.

In the final analysis, supported by the contents of
this volume, what is at stake is not whether the private
and not so private creditors of Latin America and of
other LDC regions as well will recover or to what extent
their financial investments will be repaid through
technically ingenious monetary bailout operations,
revolving debt-rescheduling agreements and interest-rate
relief measures, supported by stringent IMF stabilization programs. From the Latin American viewpoint the
issues involved form a key part of the dilemma of how to
reconcile the stiff austerity programs required by the
IMF and international private creditors in spite of the
worldwide economic crisis with the rising popular and
far from radical demands in the region for relief from
negative economic growth and widespread distress. No
satisfactory solution for this dilemma has been found any
place as yet, if only because in the industrial North--
and not only in Latin America and elsewhere in the
South--all rules of economic, fiscal, and financial
rational behavior have been violated many times over
during the past ten years to the detriment of all parties
involved.

Without expanding further on this last subject,
which would merit at least another volume, it may be
worthwhile to recall only that world military expenditures
in 1983 surpassed the whole LDC external outstanding
debt. Although in many quarters the debate continues as
to whether the LDC debt issue is that of temporary
illiquidity or of more basic long-run insolvency, I may
as well close this concluding chapter with the quotation
offered at its beginning from the 1977 diagnosis of the
world economy ills and the LDC indebtedness: "The LDC
external debt problem must be handled within a larger
framework which recognizes global interdependence and
covers balance-of-payments adjustments, LDC development
needs, official development assistance, 'stagflation'
in the LDCs, international trade and world economic
recovery."[21] As long as this general proposition is not
translated into meaningful policy at international,
regional, and national levels, one can expect only the
worst for the not so distant future in Latin America and
elsewhere.

As far as Latin America is concerned, a first--
albeit limited--step in the right direction might have
been the implementation of a common strategy--not to be
confused with a "debtor cartel"--proposed in September
1983 jointly by ECLA and SELA (Latin American Economic
System), a consultative body formed by the governments
of the region. Starting with the warning that the IMF,

the World Bank, and the Inter-American Development Bank resources would not be sufficient to meet the demands made on them in the near future by the LDC borrowers, the proposal suggested a new Latin American strategy composed of six major points: (1) the creation of a new tranche of Special Drawing Rights by the IMF to be assigned to developing countries; (2) an institutionalized procedure for the restructuring of the debt in the form of a joint effort by the IMF and the World Bank; (3) rescheduling, which would effectively transform some countries' short-term and medium-term debt into long-term obligations; (4) the provision of additional resources to allow countries to service their accumulated debt and at the same time to continue their normal international trade; (5) relief from the present high costs of refinancing; and (6) access to additional public credit to stimulate economic development.[22]

The fact that most of the substance of these proposals was diluted beyond recognition at the Latin American Economic Conference held in Quito in early 1984 strongly suggests that not only international agencies and creditor countries but Latin American debtors as well still give preference to business as usual on the debt front in spite of all its obvious longer-term risks. Quelle sagesse!--Voltaire's Candide would say again, this time ironically--quelle sagesse!

POSTSCRIPT--LATE 1984

The main body of this final chapter was written in early 1984 when the LDC indebtedness looked particularly grave as witnessed by the detailed global and regional analysis and the seven Latin American case studies contained in the book. In the fall of 1984 when this volume goes to press the indebtedness situation of a few major Latin American debtor countries looks somewhat less bleak in short and medium terms, especially from the creditors' viewpoint. The limited but painful debt renegotiation progress achieved by Mexico and Brazil does not warrant, however, the wave of optimism in the lending countries that accompanied the agreement in principle on the rescheduling in early September of about half of the Mexican public debt and the agreement reached at about the same time (also in principle) on the content of the Brazilian letter of intent deposited at the IMF.

Although some of the rules of the debt-rescheduling game underwent certain adjustments, the general approach toward the indebtedness problem continues without major change, and the parameters of the global economy perhaps look even worse than a year ago. What seems assured if other conditions are fulfilled (the world-wide reasonably strong economic recovery, the compression

of the U.S. domestic budget deficit, and the overall
decline of interest rates, among others) is that the
private creditors of Latin America will be paid--over
one decade or so--interest on the outstanding debt,
interest slightly lower than that in force during the
debt crisis years of 1982-1984. And since international
banks live from profits and not from the debt repayments, they may feel quite relieved by the disappearance
of the sudden moratorium threat hanging over their heads
and of its pyramiding consequences for the whole international financial system.

Looking with more detachment at the agreements
already reached in principle with Mexico and Brazil or
emerging from the current discussions with Argentina
and Venezuela, one comes to two inescapable conclusions.
The first is that the price paid by creditors for all
these deals is rather low. Second, the new arrangements
amount only to once again buying more time by both
creditors and debtors.

No serious attempt to adopt the more stable approach
to the underlying nonviability of international economic,
financial, and trade relations between the industrialized
and the underdeveloped worlds can be detected in the
1984 rescheduling exercises. In other terms, while
Pedro-Pablo Kuczynski's explicit predictions in
Chapter 6 to the effect that the "second act" of debt
negotiations in Latin America would be accompanied by
great difficulties proved correct, the "third act"
(postponed for a while) will be--one can predict safely--
even more complicated than the second one. Even before
the second act ended, the questions being asked raised
some serious doubts about its successful conclusion.
Three such questions were asked by The Economist in
early September 1984, a few days after Brazil agreed on
a new letter of intent with the IMF and a few days
before the terms of the longer-term rescheduling agreement with private creditors were made public by Mexico
and before Venezuela disclosed its renegotiation proposals. If the negotiations are to end successfully,
certain questions have as yet to be answered, according
to this influential British source speaking for Latin
America's creditors from all over the world. How much
new money will the private banks put up? What to do
with short-term loans made to the banks of the debtors'
countries, loans known in technical jargon as interbank credits? Who will monitor the debtor countries'
economies after Mexico's IMF agreement expires in
December 1985 and Brazil's in February 1986 and while
Venezuela insists on renegotiating its debt without
IMF intermediation?

These three questions of political and technical
character are of very tall order. Their clumsy handling
by both the private creditor community and the public
debtors may break the deals made "in principle." There

are reasons to assume that the debtors' negotiators believe that from the creditors' viewpoint the costs of "no deal" would be very much higher than those of coming closer to the position of the countries in debt. Brinkmanship and suspense will not be absent from the rest of the second act negotiations, particularly as it seems quite obvious that the lessons of the series of regional consultations started with the Cartagena meeting of June 1984 will be put to the best use by Latin Americans.

The not yet answered questions of The Economist deal with the short-term horizon. An impressive list of longer-term issues and problems appears in the most recent overview of the situation, written by William R. Cline of the Institute for International Economics (established in early 1982 in Washington, D.C., to study world economic and financial problems with emphasis on international debt). In his latest contribution on the prospects of LDC indebtedness, Cline is far from optimistic by stating that in spite of the "impressive cases of recovery in Mexico and Brazil" the 1980s will amount to the "lost decade" in terms of Third World growth and development.[23]

The same highly regarded author puts the responsibility for such present and future developments in the LDCs on the doorsteps of the Reagan administration. In his opinion the present U.S. fiscal and budgetary policy will most probably lead to the further increase of domestic and international interest rates that, in turn, may cancel all recent growth rate improvements in LDCs and in most of them may bring again pressures-- impossible to contain--in favor of a moratorium of payments on account of external debt. According to Cline, if one demands from political leaders of developing countries the application of highly unpopular measures of economic adjustment, it is impossible not to demand from leaders of advanced nations the correction of budgetary disequilibria and of other economic errors whose elimination would offer the only road to international sustained and balanced economic growth. With this admonition, I may as well end this volume.

NOTES

1. Quoted in Art Pine, "Theodore Roosevelt Knew How To Collect on Defaulted Loans--He Would Send the Marines to Protect U.S. Bankers from 'Deadbeat' Nations," Wall Street Journal, January 12, 1984.
2. P. A. Wellons, Borrowing by Developing Countries on the Eurocurrency Market, Paris, 1976, p. 585.
3. Miguel S. Wionczek (ed.), LDC External Debt and the World Economy, Mexico City, 1978, pp. 445-446.

456

4. Ibid., p. 457.

5. Morgan Guaranty Trust, Morgan Guaranty Survey (New York), November 1983.

6. Alfred L. Malabre, Jr., "Gloomy Minority--More Analysts Doubt Consensus Prediction of Brisk 1984 Growth," Wall Street Journal, January 19, 1984.

7. Organization for Economic Cooperation and Development (OECD), Economic Outlook (semiannual survey), Paris, December 1983.

8. DKB Economic Report, vol. 13, no. 1 (Tokyo, Dai-Ichi Kangyo Bank, January 1984).

9. "French Study Says Economy May Stay Sluggish for 5 Years" (dispatch from Paris), Wall Street Journal, January 17, 1984.

10. John Tagliabue, "Recovery Cautious for West Germany" (dispatch from Bonn), New York Times, January 26, 1984.

11. Leonard Silk, "Economic Scene--Debtors Crowd on the Brink," New York Times, October 5, 1983.

12. S. Karene Witcher and Lawrence Rout, "The Second Wave--New Crisis Has Begun in International Debt, Banking Experts Warn," Wall Street Journal, June 8, 1983.

13. According to Financial Times Washington, D.C., correspondent, "No detail of an adjustment programme with even the smallest member, be it Fiji or Haiti, can be agreed without the Larossière's personal imprimatur." Anatole Kaletzky, "Where the World's Credit Is Rated," Financial Times, September 23, 1983.

14. Federal Financial Institutions Examining Body, A Survey of the U.S. Banks Exposure, January-June 1983, Washington, D.C., December 1983.

15. "International Loans Fell by 19% in '83, OECD Analysts Say," Wall Street Journal, December 30, 1983.

16. As quoted in Jonathan Carr, "World Bank Chief Seeks End to 'Negative Transfers,'" Financial Times, January 27, 1984.

17. Carl Gewirtz, "Bankers May Cut Rates on Latin Loans," International Herald Tribune, December 12, 1983.

18. Jeffrey E. Gasten from Lehman Brothers Kuhn Loeb Inc., New York, "Sovereign Debt: Next Step," International Monetary Conference, Brussels, May 18, 1983.

19. "How Much Austerity Can Latin America Take?" The Economist, July 16, 1983.

20. Thomas O. Enders and Richard P. Mattione, Latin America: The Crisis of Debt and Growth, Brookings Discussion Papers no. 9, Washington, D.C., December 1983, p. 78.

21. See Note 3.

22. Economic Commission for Latin America/Latin American Economic System (ECLA/SELA), Bases for Latin American Reply to the International Economic Crisis (Caracas, August 1983, mimeo.).

23. William R. Cline, International Debt: Systemic
Risk, and Policy Response (Washington, D.C., 1984).

SELECTED BIBLIOGRAPHY

Abbott, George C. International Indebtedness and the
    Developing Countries. London, 1979.
Adler, John E. (ed.). Capital Movements and Economic
    Development. New York, 1967.
Avramovič, Dragoslav. Debt Servicing Capacity and
    Postwar Growth in International Indebtedness.
    Baltimore, 1958.
Avramovič, Dragoslav, et al. Economic Growth and External
    Debt. Baltimore, 1964.
Bell, Geoffrey. The Euro-Dollar Market and the Inter-
    national Financial System. New York and Toronto,
    1973.
Bindert, Christine. "Debt: Beyond the Quick Fix."
    Third World Quarterly (London), vol. 5, no. 4
    (October 1983).
Bitterman, Henry J. The Refunding of International Debt.
    Durham, N.C., 1973.
Bolin, William H., and Jorge del Canto. "LDC Debt:
    Beyond Crisis Management." Foreign Affairs
    (New York), vol. 61, no. 5 (Summer 1983).
Cline, William R. International Debt and the Stability
    of the World Economy. Washington, D.C., September
    1983.
Cleveland, Harold, and W. H. Bruce Brittain. "Are the
    LDCs in over Their Heads?" Foreign Affairs, vol.
    55, no. 4 (July 1977), pp. 732-750.
Collyns, Charles. Alternatives to the Central Bank
    in the Developing World. Occasional Paper no. 20.
    Washington, D.C., July 1983.
Cuddy, John. "Third World Liquidity Needs, 1984-86."
    Third World Quarterly (London), vol. 5, no. 4
    (October 1983).
Dale, Richard S., and Richard P. Mattione. Managing
    Global Debt. Washington, D.C., 1983.
Dhonte, Pierre. "Describing External Debt Situations:
    A Roll-over Approach." International Monetary Fund
    Staff Papers, vol. 22, no. 1, March 1975,
    pp. 159-186.
Enders, Thomas O., and Richard P. Mattione. Latin
    America: The Crisis of Debt and Growth. Brookings
    Discussion Papers in International Economics,
    no. 9. Washington, D.C., December 1983.
Ferreira, Luís Pinto. Capitaís Estrageíros e Dívida
    Externa do Brasil. São Paulo, 1965.
Ffrench-Davis, R. "El Problema de la Deuda Externa en
    América Latina: Tendencias y Perspectivas in 1983."
    Integración Latinoamericana (INTAL, Buenos Aires),
    año 8, no. 83 (September 1983).

458

Friedman, Irving S. The Emerging Role of Private Banks
     in the Developing World. New York, 1977.
Group of Thirty (Consultative Group on International
     Economic and Monetary Affairs). Annual Report.
     New York, 1983.
Helleiner, G. K. (chairman). Towards a New Bretton
     Woods: Challenges for the World Financial and
     Trading System. Report by a Commonwealth Study
     Group. London, 1983.
Kuczynski, Pedro-Pablo. "Latin American Debt." Foreign
     Affairs, vol. 61, no. 2 (Winter 1982-1983).
Lieftinck, Pieter. External Debt and Debt-Bearing
     Capacity of Developing Countries. Princeton,
     N.J., 1966.
Naciones Unidas, Consejo Económico y Social. Balance
     Preliminar de la Economía Latinoamericana Durante
     1983, CEPAL, Comisión Económica para América
     Latina, Documento Informativo, December 16, 1983.
Nogueira Batista, Jr., Paulo. Mito e Realidade na
     Divida Externa Brasileira. Rio de Janeiro, 1983.
Payer, Cheryl. The Debt Trap: The International
     Monetary Fund and the Third World. New York and
     London, 1974.
Saddy, Fehmy. "OPEC Capital-Surplus Funds and Third
     World Indebtedness: The Recycling Strategy
     Reconsidered." Third World Quarterly (London),
     vol. 4, no. 4 (October 1982).
Sargen, N. P. "Commercial Bank Lending to Developing
     Countries." Federal Reserve Bank of San Francisco
     Economic Review, Spring 1976.
Solomon, Robert. "A Perspective on the Debt of
     Developing Countries." Brookings Papers on Economic
     Activity 2 (1977).
UN Conference on Trade and Development (UNCTAD). "The
     Current World Economic Crisis." Trade and Develop-
     ment Report, 1983. Report by the Secretariat of
     the United Nations Conference on Trade and
     Development, Geneva, September 7, 1983 (UNCTAD/
     TDR/3).
_____. Debt Problems in the Context of Development.
     Report by UNCTAD Secretariat, New York, 1974
     (United Nations publication TD/B/C.3/109/Rev.1).
_____. Multilateral Debt Renegotiations--Experience of
     Fund Members, 1971-1974. Study prepared by the
     staff of the International Monetary Fund, note by
     the UNCTAD Secretariat, Trade and Development Board,
     Committee on Invisibles and Financing Related to
     Trade, Ad Hoc Group of Governmental Experts on
     the Debt Problems of Developing Countries, 2d
     sess., Geneva, December 11, 1974 (TD/B/C.3/AC.8/R.2).
_____. Trade Prospects and Capital Needs of Developing
     Countries, 1976-1980. Report by the UNCTAD
     Secretariat, Trade and Development Board, and
     Committee on Invisibles and Financing Related to

Trade, April 15, 1976 (TD/B/C.3/134).

Watson, Paul M. Debts and the Developing Countries:
New Problems and New Actors. Overseas Development
Council Development Paper no. 26, NIEO Series.
Washington, D.C., April 1978.

Wellons, P. A. Borrowing by Developing Countries on the
Eurocurrency Market. Paris, 1976.

Williams, Richard, et al. International Capital Markets,
Developments and Prospects, 1983. Occasional Paper
no. 23. Washington, D.C., July 1983.

Wionczek, Miguel S. "La Deuda Externa de los Países de
Menor Desarrollo y los Euromercados: Un Pasado
Impresionante, un Futuro Incierto." Comercio
Exterior (Mexico), vol. 27, no. 11 (November 1977).

____. "External Indebtedness of Less Developed Countries."
In The Year Book of World Affairs 1981. London,
1981.

Wionczek, Miguel S. (ed.). International Indebtedness
and World Economic Stagnation. London, 1981.

____. LDC External Debt and the World Economy. Mexico
City, 1978.

Acronyms

ASEAN	Association of Southeast Asian Nations
BCRA	Banco Central de la República Argentina
BIS	Bank for International Settlements
CACMF	Central American Common Market Fund
CEPAL	Comisión Económica Para América Latina
CETES	Treasury Certificates
CIEPLAN	Corporation of Economic Research for Latin America
CORFO	Development Corporation
DRI	Data Resources, Inc.
ECLA	UN Economic Commission for Latin America
EEC	European Economic Community
GAB	General Agreement to Borrow
GATT	General Agreement on Tariffs and Trade
GDP	gross domestic product
GNP	gross national product
G-10	Group of Ten
IDB	Inter-American Development Bank
IDS	Institute of Development Studies, Sussex University, England
IISS	International Institute of Strategic Studies
IMF	International Monetary Fund
LAFTA	Latin American Free Trade Association
LAIA	Latin American Integration Association
LDC	less developed country
LIBOR	London Inter-Bank Offer Rate
NAFINSA	Nacional Financiera
NIC	newly industrializing country
OECD	Organization for Economic Cooperation and Development
OPEC	Organization of Petroleum Exporting Countries
PEMEX	Petróleos Mexicanos
RECADI	Office for the System of Differential Exchange Rates
RIAL	Program for Joint Studies on Latin American International Relations

SBM	supernational bank money
SDR	Special Drawing Right
SELA	Latin American Economic System
SEPAFIN	Ministry of National Properties and Industrial Development
TNC	transnational corporation
UNCTAD	UN Conference on Trade and Development
UNESCO	UN Educational, Scientific, and Cultural Organization

About the Contributors

Dragoslav Avramović is a former official of the World Bank, former director of the Secretariat of the Independent Commission on International Development Issues (the Brandt Commission), and senior adviser to the UNCTAD Secretary General. He is the author of <u>Debt Servicing Capacity and Postwar Growth in International Indebtedness</u> (1958) and <u>Economic Growth and External Debt</u> (1964).

Ariel Buira served as an executive director of the International Monetary Fund from 1978-1982 and is currently deputy director of the Bank of Mexico in charge of international organizations and agreements. His recent publications include "IMF Financial Program and Conditionality," <u>Journal of Development Economics</u>, vol. 12, no. 1/2 (February-April 1983); <u>The Mexican Exchange Crisis and Adjustment Program</u>, Institute for International Economics, Washington, D.C., 1983; and <u>On the Nature and Direction of International Monetary Reform</u>, Group of Twenty-Four, 1983.

Enrique de la Piedra has been working since 1980 in the United Nations Economic Commission for Latin America (ECLA), first as an expert in the United Nations Development Program/ECLA project on critical poverty and afterward as economic affairs officer in the Economic Development Division. He has drafted several papers on the subject of poverty and is responsible for the preparation of the survey on Peru for ECLA's annual economic survey of Latin America.

Robert Devlin is economic affairs officer of the Economic Development Division of the United Nations Economic Commission for Latin America. He has worked for a number of years on the subject of foreign debt and private banks and has written books on the experiences of Peru and Bolivia (the latter with Michael Mortimore), as well as a number of articles on the subject.

Marcelo Diamond is an Argentine industrialist and economist. He is the author of <u>Doctrinas Económicas,</u> <u>Desarrollo e Independencia</u> (1973) and "La Estructura Productiva Desequilibrada y el Tipo de Cambio," <u>Desarrollo Económico</u> (1972).

José Luis Feito is alternate executive director of the International Monetary Fund. He has been director of the International Economic Studies Department of the Ministry of Economy, Finance, and Trade of Spain and has served as financial analyst to several Spanish private agencies.

Ricardo M. Ffrench-Davis is director of the Corporation of Economic Research for Latin America (CIEPLAN). Professor of economics at the University of Chile until 1973, he has been a visiting fellow at Oxford and Boston universities. He is the author of <u>Economía</u> <u>Internacional: Teorías y Políticas para el Desarrollo</u> (1979), <u>Políticas Económicas en Chile, 1952-70</u> (1973), and numerous articles on development, economic policies, trade, and international finance.

Albert Fishlow is professor of international economics at the University of California-Berkeley, the author of many books and articles on the U.S. economic history and Latin American development problems, including <u>American Railroads and the Transformation of the Ante-</u> <u>Bellum Economy</u> (1965) and <u>Rich and Poor Natives in the</u> <u>World Economy</u> (1978).

Jorge González del Valle is an economist at Universidad de San Carlos, Guatemala, Columbia University, Yale University. He was the director of the Center of Monetary Studies for Latin America (CEMLA) and from 1968 to 1978 executive secretary of the Monetary Council for Central America. From April to December 1983 he was president of the Banco de Guatemala.

Enrique V. Iglesias was chairman of the Central Bank of Uruguay and is currently secretary general of the United Nations Economic Commission for Latin America. He is a member of the Third World Foundation, the Society for International Development (SID), the North-South Round Table, and other developmental institutions.

Pedro-Pablo Kuczynski is president of First Boston International and a managing director of the First Boston Corporation. From 1980 to 1982, he was Minister of Energy and Mines of Peru. Previously, he served at the World Bank, the International Monetary Fund, and the International Finance Corporation, and in the private sector has been a partner of Kuhn, Loeb & Co. International and the president of Halco Mining, Inc., in Pittsburgh. He is the author of <u>Peruvian Democracy</u> <u>under Economic Stress: An Account of the Belaunde</u> <u>Administration, 1963-68</u>.

Eduardo Mayobre is deputy minister of finance for Venezuela, formerly director general of the Ministry of Finance, adviser to the Council of National Economy, executive director of the International Monetary Fund, executive director of the World Bank, and director of economic research of the Ministry of Finance.

Daniel Naszewski is an Argentine economist.

Paulo Nogueira Batista, Jr., is professor of economics at Catholic University of Rio de Janeiro; a member of the research staff at the Center for Monetary Studies of the Getulio Vargas Foundation; and author of the book Mitoe Realidade na Dívida Externa Brasileira [Myth and Reality of the Brazilian External Debt], Rio de Janeiro, 1983.

Luciano Tomassini was formerly an adviser to the president of the Inter-American Development Bank (IDB). He is now a consultant for the United Nations Economic Commission for Latin America and coordinator of the Programme of Joint Studies on Latin American International Relations (RIAL), as well as the editor of the journal Estudios Internacionales. Among other works, he edited Relaciones Internacionales de la América Latina, Fondo de Cultura Económica, México, 1981.

Víctor L. Urquidi is president of El Colegio de México, former president of the International Economic Association, and a member of the Club of Rome. He is author and editor of a number of books on global and Latin American economic development problems.

Miguel S. Wionczek is a senior research fellow and director of the Energy Research Program at El Colegio de México. He is author and editor of many books on problems of development, including Some Key Issues for the World Periphery (1982) and World Hydrocarbon Markets: Current Status, Projected Prospects and Future Trends (1982).

Ernesto Zedillo Ponce de León is director of the Trust Fund for Coverage of Exchange Risks (FICORCA) of Banco de México, where previously he served as deputy manager of the economic research department. He teaches international economics at El Colegio de México.

Index

472

About the Book and Editor

Since 1981 Latin America has been in the midst of a protracted external debt crisis due, among other reasons, to emergency borrowing at record-high real interest rates and the decline in the region's export proceeds. Until now, most literature on the subject originated in industrial lender countries, whose primary concern is the impact of the debt crisis on their own profits and on the world financial system. This volume, written by Latin American experts, presents the Latin American debt experience and difficulties from the viewpoint of borrowers. The first part of the book analyzes links between the international financial crisis and the present external debt difficulties in the region. The second part contains case studies of Argentina, Brazil, Mexico, Venezuela, Chile, Peru, and Central America.

Dr. Miguel S. Wionczek is a senior fellow and the head of the long-term energy research program at El Colegio de México. He is co-editor of *Energy in the Transition from Rural Subsistence* (with Gerald Foley and Ariane van Buren; Westview, 1982) and *Mexico's Energy Resources: Toward a Policy of Diversification* (with Ragaei El Mallakh; Westview, 1985). Dr. Luciano Tomassini is director of the Program for Joint Studies on Latin American International Relations (RIAL) in Santiago, Chile.